HARRAP'S
ILLUSTRATED DICTIONARY OF
MUSIC & MUSICIANS

HARRAP'S
ILLUSTRATED DICTIONARY OF
MUSIC & MUSICIANS

HARRAP'S *REFERENCE*

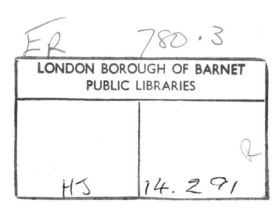

First published in Great Britain 1989
by Harrap Books Limited
Chelsea House
26 Market Square
Bromley, Kent BR1 1NA

New edition 1990

ISBN 0 245-60071-X

Copy preparation by Clark Robinson Limited,
London
Typeset by Communitype Communications
Limited, Leicester

CONSULTANT EDITOR

Bernard Keeffe, B.A. Cantab. Hon., F.T.C.L.

EDITOR

Elisabeth Ingles

CONTRIBUTORS AND CONSULTANTS

Ian Bartlett

Roger Clegg, G.R.S.M., A.R.C.M.

William Gould

Richard Langham Smith

Steve Stanton, B.A., D.Phil., A.R.C.M.

Roy Teed, F.R.A.M.

ACKNOWLEDGEMENTS

Clark Robinson Limited would like to acknowledge the help of all those who have contributed to the creation of this dictionary. In particular, we would like to thank Donald Binney, Alan Blackwood, Louise Bostock, Katy Guess, Stephen Luck, Roy Minton, Caroline Morrow Brown, Lawrence Norfolk, Victoria Ramsay and Mark Trewin for their editorial contributions, and Janet Tanner and Sheila Stanton for their illustrations.

Foreword

Harrap's Illustrated Dictionary of Music and Musicians was designed to satisfy the general music-lover who goes to concerts and opera, who listens to records and the radio, who wants to know more than the average programme note can reveal about a composer's life and works, without having to grapple with a comprehensive list of compositions or a full biography, both of which are available in special individual studies. You should be able to reach for this book and hold it comfortably in your hand without straining your eyes, and know that you will find information about a wide range of music and musicians, past and present, from the great masters to the brilliant young composer who has just won his or her first important commission for the BBC Proms; from the legendary prima donnas and virtuosos of the past years to the stars of today, the conductors, singers and instrumentalists who command a world stage through compact discs and video recording.

Every writer on music can learn from Bernard Shaw's promise, when he took up the trade of music critic, not to write about Bach in B flat; you can be thrilled by a symphony of Mozart or Mahler without knowing a crotchet from a cor anglais, but if such matters intrigue you, you will find here an explanation you can understand, unencumbered with the jargon of the musicologist or the empty phrases of the professional publicist.

Not only non-experts, but students too will find the basic information needed to broaden their knowledge and deepen their understanding, before going on to specialist studies. Every task of this character is inevitably a team effort, but I should specially like to thank Elisabeth Ingles, upon whose shoulders the main bulk of the work has fallen.

Preface

This dictionary aims to be concise and up to date, and to provide information in an easily accessible form on all aspects of art music as it is today. Readers may find it helpful to have an idea of its coverage, and an indication of the lexicographical principles on which it is compiled. The particular emphasis is on composers and performers, with extensive coverage of the present day. In the case of composers, most of the principal works have been given, and many recent works by current figures are included. For performers, a brief indication of their recorded range has been included where relevant. It was felt, however, that new young performers should not generally be included unless they have already become established in an international career.

While we have not attempted to cover the areas of jazz, pop or folk music, there are articles on the main genres and on certain composers of jazz and the stage musical whose works are now firmly woven into the perceptions of music-lovers; there are also entries on certain terms or instruments peculiar to national or ethnic music. A special feature is the treatment of Eastern music, above all that of India, the Arab world, China and Japan, which is now included in some school and college syllabuses. Instruments, modes of composition and technical terms are also covered, although we have tried to keep technicalities to a minimum for the sake of accessibility. Technical and theoretical terms are illustrated where this helps to clarify the point.

Certain principles have been adopted with regard to such matters as cross-references and translations. Cross-references, in **bold** type, are used freely; we have not, however, in general cross-referred to the 'first-division' composers, whose names come up constantly throughout the book and who have long individual articles. Thus there are few cross-references to such composers as Bach, Handel, Haydn, Mozart, Beethoven, Schubert, Chopin, Schumann, Berlioz, Wagner, Verdi, Tchaikovsky, Brahms, Debussy, Mahler, Bruckner, Strauss, and Stravinsky, unless the article cross-referred to would provide specific further illumination. For example, in the article on the Wagnerian soprano Kirsten Flagstad, Wagner is not cross-referred; but in the article on Bayreuth he is, because the Wagner article gives a little further background to the story of Bayreuth. An article may contain a cross-reference to one of those composers if it is about a contemporary with whom the composer worked or for whom he may have written a piece. All lesser composers and all performers are generally given cross-references, so that the reader knows they are to be found in the dictionary.

In general we have given the original titles of all works by French, German, Italian, and Spanish composers. Translations have been provided, where necessary or illuminating, in the long articles on 'first-division' composers; in shorter articles where a piece is best known by its English title (for example, Nicolai's opera is far better known in English as *The Merry Wives of Windsor* than as *Die lustige Weibe von Windsor*); and in articles on composers from Scandinavia, Russia and Eastern Europe (the original titles of Smetana's *The Bartered Bride* or Tchaikovsky's *The Queen of Spades* would mean little to most readers). It is worth mentioning that occasionally foreign composers have given their works English titles: Henze's opera *The English Cat* has an English libretto.

Capitalization has followed the system normal to the relevant language, as utilized by *The New Grove Dictionary of Music and Musicians*: in French, Italian and Spanish only *personal* proper names are generally capitalized (thus *La Cenerentola*, but *La bohème*), while German uses capitals for all nouns. Romantic/Romanticism is capitalized only where it refers specifically to the 19th-century French and German composers belonging to that movement, such as Schumann and Berlioz.

Alphabetization of entries runs through every part of the headword, whether one or more words, as far as any comma. Thus **musical glasses** comes before **musica reservata**; **Fischer, Johann** before **Fischer-Dieskau, Dietrich**; **Patterson, Paul** before **patter song**; **Bach, W.F.** before **Bach trumpet**. Names beginning Mc are treated as Mac.

Finally, I must express my appreciation of and gratitude to Bernard Keeffe, a kindly and patient guiding light. Thanks are also due to the contributors, and to all those performers and their agents or managers, too numerous to list, who were unfailingly helpful and courteous in responding to requests for information.

E. A. I.

A

A First note of the scale, one tone above G and one tone below B. The scale of A major has three sharps in the key-signature.

A   A major

aak (Korea) Court orchestral music of Chinese origin, mainly associated with Confucian ritual music. Literally, 'elegant music'. Two orchestras are used alternately – *tŭngga* (orchestra on the terrace) and *hŭn'ga* (orchestra on the ground) – distinguished by their repertory and instrumentation. Both, however, include stone-chimes, bell-chimes, a wooden clapper and scraper, bamboo flutes, a clay **ocarina** and barrel drums. See also **hyangak**; **tangak**.

abandonné (Fr.) Free or abandoned, indicating that a passage or piece should not be played too strictly; it applies mainly to **rhythm**.

Abbado, Claudio (1933-) Italian conductor, born in Milan, the son of the violinist and teacher Michelangelo and brother of the composer Marcello Abbado. He studied at the Milan Conservatoire and with Hans Swarowsky at the Vienna Academy of Music, 1956-8. After winning the Koussevitsky Competition (1958) and the Mitropoulos Prize (1963), he made his début at La Scala in 1967 (where he subsequently became principal conductor and, later, musical director) and at Covent Garden in 1968. He became principal conductor of the London Symphony Orchestra in 1979 and principal guest conductor of the Chicago Symphony Orchestra in 1982. In 1989 he was appointed music director of the Berlin Philharmonic Orchestra.

Although noted mainly for his performances of late 19th- and early 20th-century works, particularly the operas of Verdi, Abbado is also an enthusiastic exponent of the music of such contemporary composers as **Berio, Ligeti, Nono, Penderecki** and **Stockhausen**.

Claudio Abbado

abbandono (It.) Abandonment. See **abandonné**

abdämpfen (Ger.) Instruction to muffle or stop a sound. See **mute**

Abel, Carl Friedrich (1723-1787) German composer and viola da **gamba** player. He moved to England during the late 1750s and in 1763 established an association with **J.C. Bach**, performing in an annual series of public concerts which were to introduce many notable continental musicians to London. Although he won popular acclaim as a performer, Abel is chiefly remembered as a composer of lively and lighthearted instrumental music. His works include symphonies, overtures, numerous concerti for various instruments, and sonatas for the viola da gamba.

Abendlied (Ger.) Evening song; sometimes used by composers as a title for a song or instrumental piece.

Abendmusik (Ger.) Evening music; originally a type of concert held on Sundays in the Marienkirche, Lübeck, during the 17th and 18th centuries; it now refers to concerts held in any church. The Lübeck concerts probably began in the mid-17th century. They were financed by local businessmen and admission to the church was free. The earliest were organ recitals, organized by the organist at the Marienkirche, Franz **Tunder**. Later, vocal and instrumental soloists were included. Dietrich **Buxtehude**, Tunder's successor, added orchestra and chorus and composed **oratorios** for these concerts, some of which were in several parts, presumably to be performed on successive Sundays. In 1752 the practice of charging admission to the Friday dress rehearsals was introduced and these performances eventually assumed greater importance than the Sunday ones. Sunday performances were abolished in 1800 and Friday ones ceased in 1810 as a result of the Napoleonic wars.

abnehmend (Ger.) Taking away; it implies 'taking away' volume, and hence is the same as **diminuendo**.

Absil, Jean (1893-1974) Belgian composer who trained as an organist but went on to study composition with **Gilson**, winning national prizes with his Symphony No.1 and his **cantata**, *La guerre*. With other young Belgian composers he founded *La sirène*, a series of concerts to promote new music in Brussels and abroad. In 1937 he published his *Postulats de la musique contemporaine*, declaring that the distinction between consonance and dissonance is meaningless. Absil's own style began to evolve in his chamber music after 1934. He wrote polyphonically and with irregular metric divisions, often superimposing different metres, but used conventional and straightforward forms. After 1938 he tried to make his work more accessible, making use of folk material, and later he concentrated almost entirely on instrumental music.

absolute music Concept of music subject to many shades of interpretation. Broadly speaking, it denotes music that is understood purely on its own terms and without reference to external factors. This excludes music with words, which determine the musical structure to some extent, while the music in turn contributes to the sense of the words. It also excludes dramatic music and **programme music** (such as the symphonies and symphonic poems of Liszt and Berlioz). It has even been argued that music of a definite emotional character is not absolute music. On the other hand, it has also been argued that any music is absolute only insofar as it reveals the divine in nature; in this view, liturgical music is the purest of all.

The idea of absolute music appears in medieval writings, but aroused much interest in the 19th century, debated by philosophers, critics and composers such as Liszt and Wagner. Many of the compositional techniques of the 20th century are based on a concept of absolute music understandable purely through structure.

An alternative term for absolute music is abstract music.

absolute pitch Ability to recognize and name a sounded note, or to sing a named note. The facility for absolute pitch is quite rare, although some say it can be taught. An alternative term for it is perfect pitch.

abstract music Alternative term for **absolute music**.

Abt, Franz Wilhelm (1819-1885) German composer who studied theology and music in Leipzig, where he was a friend of **Mendelssohn** and **Schumann**.

From his post as *Kapellmeister* at Bernburg, Abt went to Zurich to embark upon an immensely successful career as a choral conductor. From 1855 until his retirement in 1882, he was *Kapellmeister* at the Court Theatre in Brunswick. During this time he conducted in many cities in Europe, and toured the United States (1872). He composed more than 3,000 works, mostly songs and part-songs in a popular and simple style, often close to folk-song. His work also included two operas and some piano pieces.

Academy of Ancient Music Name given to an 18th-century society of music and to a present-day orchestra.

In the 18th century, the Academy of Ancient Music was an influential London society of aristocratic amateur and eminent professional musicians. It was apparently a continuation of the Academy of Vocal Music, established in 1726 'in an attempt to restore ancient church music', changing its name after a schism in 1731. It met regularly at the Crown and Anchor tavern in the Strand until 1781, and thereafter at Freemasons Hall until its disbanding in 1792. Pepusch was its first director. **Handel** and **Geminiani** were among the musicians who played at its meetings.

The orchestra of this name was founded in 1973 by Christopher **Hogwood** and was one of the first English professional groups to perform **Baroque** music on period instruments or copies of them. Since its formation its repertory has extended into classical and Romantic music.

Academy of Music, New York New York theatre, opened in 1854; at the time it contained the largest stage in the world. Until the opening of the **Metropolitan Opera House** in 1883, it was the only theatre in the city devoted exclusively to concerts and opera.

Academy of St Martin-in-the-Fields English orchestra formed in 1959, which was originally a string ensemble directed by the leader. The orchestra's name derives from the church in Trafalgar Square, London, where its concerts were first given. Under its founder and principal conductor, Sir Neville **Marriner**, the orchestra established an international reputation in a wide range of music. The present director is Iona **Brown**.

a cappella (It.) 'In chapel'; term used for unaccompanied choral singing.

Accardo, Salvatore (1941-) Italian violinist and conductor. Accardo graduated from the Naples Conservatoire in 1956, although he had already won international competitions at Vercelli in 1955 and Geneva in 1956, and in 1958 won both the Italian Radio Spring Trophy and the **Paganini** International Prize at Genoa. Accardo is considered a fine interpreter of Paganini, although his repertory ranges from the music of Vivaldi to contemporary works.

accelerando (It.) Direction indicating that the music should get faster.

acciaccatura (It.) A crushed stroke. Indicated by a small note above or below the main note, often with a stroke through it. In the 18th century it meant that two adjacent notes on a keyboard were struck simultaneously, with the accessory note immediately released. Later, when used in music for voice or other instruments it came to mean a very short note, performed sometimes before, sometimes on the beat according to taste and fashion. In modern times it is used as the equivalent of the grace note.

accidental In Western musical notation, any symbol of **chromatic** alteration other than in the key-signature. Should a note during the course of a piece require such an alteration, the accidental is placed immediately before the note to be altered, on the same line or space. The five accidentals in common use are:

The sharp (♯), raising the natural note by a semitone.

The flat (♭), lowering the natural note by a semitone.

The natural (♮), restoring a note which has been altered by the key-signature, or by a previous accidental, to its natural pitch.

The double sharp (♯♯), raising the natural note by a tone.

The double flat (♭♭), lowering the natural note by a tone.

By convention, if a note has been altered by an accidental, the accidental holds for any subsequent repetition of that note within the same bar unless such a repetition is preceded by another accidental, although some 20th-century composers have adopted a system in which accidentals apply only to the notes they immediately precede. Any accidental is cancelled by a bar-line. To clarify any possible confusion arising from this, and also as an occasional reminder of an alteration required by the key-signature, cautionary accidentals are sometimes added before the relevant notes.

accompaniment Feature of any music that has a tune or musical line standing out from the other musical lines in interest or importance. These other musical lines are collectively known as the accompaniment. A song may have a piano or guitar accompaniment, for example, although a solo piano or guitar piece may equally have a 'tune' and an 'accompaniment' (both played by one and the same player on the same instrument). A player of separate accompaniments is called an accompanist.

accordion Portable instrument of the reed organ family consisting of large rectangular

Piano accordion

bellows to push air through two sets of **reeds** which sound on both inspiration and expiration. The tune is played on buttons or keys on the right side; buttons operated by the left hand provide accompanying chords.

On the simplest instruments (e.g. the **melodeon**), the right-hand control buttons give a **diatonic scale**, usually of D or C. Later models add one or two extra rows of buttons, each tuned a semitone higher than the preceding row so that all the notes of the **chromatic scale** may be obtained.

The piano accordion has a piano-style **keyboard** for the right hand, rather than buttons. This innovation was made by Bouton in 1852, and by the 1920s this model had superseded its predecessors.

In French-Canadian music the accordion may be heard at its most virtuosic, but it is also commonly used in most Western European folk-music. Tchaikovsky and others composed for it.

accoupler (Fr.) To couple. Instruction in organ music to join two **keyboards** together or one keyboard to the **pedal-board**, by using a **coupler**. This enables music played on one keyboard to be heard as if it were played on both.

Ackermann, Otto (1909-1960) Swiss conductor. He studied in Bucharest and Berlin; his first post was as *Kapellmeister* at

Düsseldorf Opera House. He subsequently held posts in theatres and opera houses at Brno, Berne, Zurich and Cologne, and gave guest performances in Vienna, Monaco and Italy. Ackermann gained international fame as an opera conductor, especially for his interpretations of Johann Strauss's operettas and Mozart's operas.

Ackté, Aïno (1876-1944) Finnish soprano. She studied with her mother and at the Paris Conservatoire and made her début at the Paris Opéra in 1897, singing Marguerite in Gounod's *Faust*. She went on to sing at the Metropolitan Opera in New York and at Covent Garden in London, taking the title-role in the first English performances of Strauss's *Salome* under Sir Thomas **Beecham**. Most of the later part of her career was spent in Finland, where she helped to found the Finnish Opera and was its director from 1938 to 1939.

acoustics The word is derived from the Greek word 'to hear'. It is the study of the paths that sound follows from its source to the ear. Although it must deal with the design, construction and material of instruments, and the consequences of instrumental or vocal techniques, it is commonly applied to the influence on sound of the shape and material of rooms, halls, theatres, churches, studios, or any building where speech or music is performed.

Sound travels direct to the ear or microphone only in a specially designed non-echoing room used for research. In all other places sound is reflected, diffused, or absorbed by the walls, the floor, the ceiling or roof, and other objects such as reflectors, beams, and even people. Direct reflection may create an echo, which is usually undesirable and very troublesome – an effect often found in large churches, and until recently in the Albert Hall, London. The amount of reflection or absorption is determined by the design and material of the surfaces – hard flat surfaces, such as stone, reflect; open windows, soft or perforated materials such as curtains, certain tiles, and people absorb sound.

When sound persists, it is said to reverberate for a specific period, which varies according to the pitch or frequency of the sound; low sounds usually reverberate longer than high ones but need a high ceiling. Since speech and music combine sounds of different frequencies, the hall or theatre must be designed to give optimum range of reverberation periods to suit its prime purpose. Speech requires a short period for clarity; a solo instrument or a small group sounds well with a slightly longer period; an orchestra requires a longer period for the middle and low frequencies, while a choir often sounds best in the long reverberation period of a church, where the vocal tones are blended and diffused by multiple reflections. The modern science of acoustics – when wrongly applied – has produced disasters: the Royal Festival Hall, London, was designed with too little low-frequency reverberation and produced a sound that tended to be over-brilliant or even hard, until it was corrected by electronic reverberation. The Philharmonic Hall in New York was so unsatisfactory that the interior was ripped out and replaced at great cost, met by the hi-fi magnate Avery Fisher on condition that it was renamed after him. However, acoustic scientists do have their successes: the Albert Hall's problem was cured by the suspension of saucer-shaped discs, which by impeding and diffusing the direct reflections from the concave roof removed the troublesome echo. Multi-purpose halls have been tried, but unless large-scale mechanical adjustments are available, they usually disappoint. A notable exception is the **IRCAM** studio in Paris, where elaborate mechanical adjustments can produce a variety of acoustic environments.

action 1. The mechanism which transmits the player's movement from the keys to the strings of a piano or harpsichord, or to the pipes of an organ: for example, the direct mechanical link between striking a piano key and the hammer striking the string. Actions are usually given trade names and are often patented, or they may be described under general categories such as the various organ actions: tracker action, pneumatic action, electric action, etc.

2. In the orchestral harp, a mechanism that alters the pitch of the strings when a pedal is depressed.

3. The distance between strings and fretboard on an instrument such as a guitar (the greater the distance, the 'higher' the action).

adagio, adagietto (It.) At ease. A slow movement or tempo, slightly faster than **largo**.

When a passage of **Baroque** music is marked *adagio* it does not necessarily mean a slowing down of tempo, but it does indicate some relaxation.

Adagietto signifies slightly faster than *adagio*.

Adam, Adolphe Charles (1803-1856) French composer. He studied at the Conservatoire in Paris, where he eventually became professor in 1849. He produced his first operetta, *Pierre et Cathérine*, at the Opéra-Comique in 1829 and his first opera, *Danilowa*, the following year. He was a prolific composer of operas but is probably best known for *Giselle* (1841), which has become one of the best loved of all ballets. Among his other compositions are choral and sacred music.

Adam, Theo (1926-) German bass-baritone. He studied in Dresden and Weimar before making his début at the Dresden Staatsoper in 1952. During the same year he played his first role at Bayreuth, where he was later to form his reputation as a Wagner singer. The role with which he is particularly associated is Wotan, but he has produced excellent portrayals of many roles in the works of Wagner and other composers.

Adami, Giuseppe (1878-1946) Italian librettist. He is best remembered for his libretti for operas by such composers as **Puccini**, Vittadini and **Zandonai**. For Puccini he provided the texts for *La rondine*, *Il tabarro* and (with R. Simoni) *Turandot*.

Adamis, Michael (1929-) Greek composer and musicologist who studied at Athens and Brandeis Universities. He taught neo-Byzantine music at the Holy Cross Theological Academy, Boston, Massachusetts, and was appointed head of the music department at Pierce College, Athens, in 1968. His career as a composer began in the late 1950s mainly with instrumental pieces. Later he began to work more particularly with electronic media, often turning to Byzantine chant for source material. Adamis is best known for employing new techniques within old forms, such as the *Byzantine Passion* (1971).

added sixth A **chord** formed by adding the **sixth** from the **root** to the major or minor **triad**. In classical **harmony** it usually occurs on the **subdominant** chord, resolving to the **dominant** or the **tonic**. In later music it was freely used for its colour, without any strict rules governing its **resolution**. It has been much used by jazz musicians, especially as the last chord of a piece.

Addinsell, Richard (1904-1977) English composer who studied at Oxford, the Royal College of Music, Berlin and Vienna. In 1941 he became composer and accompanist to Joyce Grenfell, writing music for her one-woman shows such as *I'm Going to See You Today*. His greatest success was a one-movement piano concerto in the style of **Rachmaninov** called the *Warsaw Concerto*, composed for the film *Dangerous Moonlight* (1941). He wrote many film scores, music revues and songs.

additional accompaniments Additional orchestral parts written for 17th- and 18th-century vocal works with orchestral accompaniment, to make them more suitable for performance in large 19th-century concert halls. Often they were written without any real understanding of the **Baroque** style. The works of Bach and Handel were commonly rearranged in this way.

The practice of writing additional accompaniments has now fallen out of favour. The study of performance practice in the second half of the 20th century has led to a growing understanding of Baroque music and a demand for authentic performances using the forces intended by the composer, and often on instruments of the period.

Adler, Kurt (1905-1988) American conductor and opera director. He was born in Austria and studied in Vienna, where he made his conducting début in 1925. He went on to conduct at opera houses throughout Europe, assisting **Toscanini** at Salzburg in 1936. In the same year he went to the United States, first to Chicago and then to San Francisco in 1943. He became director of the San Francisco Opera in 1956, where he introduced new repertory, engaged untried singers and implemented modern staging techniques. Adler has been honoured by the governments of Italy, Germany, Austria and the Soviet Union.

Adler, Larry (1914-) American virtuoso harmonica player now resident in Britain, the first to achieve recognition by classical musicians and to raise the status of the harmonica to that of a concert instrument. **Vaughan Williams**, **Milhaud**, Gordon **Jacob** and Malcolm **Arnold** are among those who have written works for him. He has toured extensively, broadcast in many countries and been much concerned with teaching the harmonica; he has also written a number of film scores, most notably for *Genevieve* (1953).

Adler, Peter (1899-) American conductor, born in Czechoslovakia. Having studied composition and conducting in Prague, he held conducting posts in Bremen and Kiev and gave guest performances throughout Europe. In 1939 he went to the United States, working alongside **Toscanini** in television opera from 1949 to 1959. He was musical director of the Baltimore Symphony Orchestra (1959-68) and director of the American Opera Center at the Juilliard School (1973-81). Adler was a pioneer director of television opera in the United States, for which he commissioned many new productions.

ad lib Direction in written music allowing the player the freedom to improvise with the written notes, for example to vary the tempo or to include a **cadenza** of his or her own invention.

Aeolian harp Instrument comprising a long narrow box, with six or more gut strings stretched inside it over two bridges. The strings are of various thicknesses and hence have different tensions although they are tuned in unison. Named after Aeolos, the Greek god of the winds, the strings 'sing' when the harp is placed in a free current of air, producing a variety of **harmonics**, all with the same **fundamental**. First known in ancient China and India and then in Europe during the Middle Ages, the Aeolian harp underwent a surge of popularity in the Romantic period, when Berlioz composed a piece with this title (in *Lelio*). See also **acoustics**.

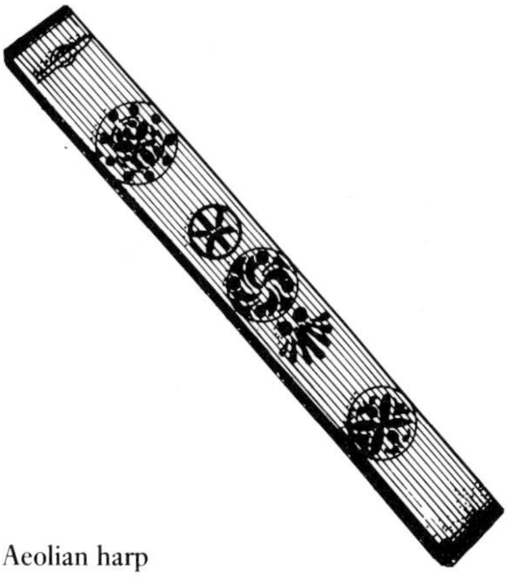

Aeolian harp

Aeolian mode One of the modes added in the 16th century to the 8th-century modal system used for **Gregorian chant**; it is now extensively employed in jazz improvisation and in modern compositions. The note structure of the mode can be obtained by playing the white notes on the piano from A to A, the note acting as a quasi-**tonic**. See also **mode.**

affettuoso (It.) Tenderly, with affection.

affrettando (It.) Hurrying. An indication to increase the tempo with an added sense of nervous energy.

Agazzari, Agostino (1578-1640) Italian composer and organist, chiefly remembered as the author of one of the first and most influential treatises on the basso **continuo**, first published in Siena in 1607. Its value lies in its lists of contemporary continuo instruments (which include harp, lute, guitar and violin), its description of their roles, and its introductions on how to play from an unfigured bass. Agazzari also published five volumes of madrigals and much sacred music, being one of the first composers to use the basso continuo in this idiom.

agitato (It.) Agitated or restless. Often used to qualify other terms, as in *allegro agitato*, it may also imply an increase in tempo.

Agnus Dei (Lat.) Fifth movement of a musical setting of the Roman Catholic Mass. When sung liturgically it accompanies the breaking and sharing of the bread. The text reads '*Agnus Dei qui tollis peccata mundi*' ('O Lamb of God that takest away the sins of the world'), with alternative endings '*miserere nobis*' ('have mercy upon us'), and, on the last repeat, '*dona nobis pacem*' ('grant us peace') or, as during the **Requiem** Mass, '*dona eis requiem*' ('grant them rest'). See also **Mass**; **plainsong**.

Agricola, Alexander (*c.*1446-1506) Franco-Netherlands composer. He composed eight complete Mass cycles, and other sacred music and secular music with French, Flemish and Italian texts. His large body of instrumental music is particularly important – often extremely intricate and of great rhythmical complexity. The wide-ranging parts suggest that these may be rare written examples of early virtuoso string music.

Ahle, Johann Rudolf (1625-1673) German composer, organist and poet. Born in Mühlhausen, he studied theology at the University of Erfurt, at the same time serving as cantor at the Andreaskirche. Returning from Erfurt to Mühlhausen in 1650, he held the post of organist at the Blasiuskirche from 1654 to 1673. Ahle composed much sacred music, including some popular chorales, among which were the hymns *Es ist genug* and *Liebster Jesu, wir sind hier*, both used in works by **J.S. Bach**. He also wrote a set of dances and a singing tutor for use in elementary schools. Active in local politics, he became burgomaster of Mühlhausen in 1673, shortly before his death.

air Term first used in 16th-century England and France to denote a simple song or melody. In England it was frequently known as an **ayre**, particularly to describe a song of a light nature. After the decline of the lute ayre in the 17th century, the word air was used in a much more general sense. In 16th-century France, air was used to describe many forms of lute songs, such as the *air de cour* and the *air à boire*. From the early part of the 17th century the word also regularly applied to instrumental pieces.

Alain, Jehan (1911-1940) French organist and composer. He wrote chamber music, songs and several pieces for organ and piano, although little of it was published during his lifetime. While drawing influences from **Satie**, **Debussy** and **Messiaen**, Alain's music is full of individual charm and picturesque imagery. A skilful organist and brilliant performer, he was killed in action during World War II.

Alain, Marie-Claire (1926-) French organist who studied harmony under Duruflé and organ with Dupré at the Paris Conservatoire, subsequently winning several prizes. She specializes in 17th- and 18th-century music, and is concerned with the recreation of historical authenticity in her performances. Also notable among her many recordings are the complete works of her brother Jehan **Alain**.

ālāp/ālāpana (India) Improvised prelude in various classical genres of northern Indian music in which the melodic features of a **rāga** are introduced. It is characterized by unmeasured rhythm, slow tempo and serene mood, and is one of the most expressive forms of Indian music, regarded by some musicians as a religious invocation.

Albéniz, Isaac (1860-1909) Spanish pianist and composer. He was a child prodigy, making his first public appearance at the age of four. He studied for a while at the Madrid Conservatoire and then, at the age of 12, stowed away on a ship to the United States, where he supported himself as a pianist. On returning to Europe he studied at the Leipzig Conservatoire, the Brussels Conservatoire (with **Liszt**) and in Paris (with **d'Indy** and **Dukas**). He was persuaded to set the opera librettos of the English banker Francis Burdett Money-Coutts, but although he worked on several of these, the only successful opera was *Pepita Jiménez* (1896). From 1893 he lived for some years in Paris, where he became well known as a composer. He was one of a number of late 19th-century composers to draw his inspiration from Spanish idioms in music – for example, in his orchestral works *Rapsodia española* and *Catalonia*. He is probably best known for his four sets of piano pieces, *Iberia*.

Albéniz, Mateo Pérez de (*c*.1755-1831) Spanish composer, active in San Sebastián. He wrote primarily for the Church (Masses, motets, etc.) but also composed some piano music and a theoretical work on ancient and modern music. An admirer of Haydn and Mozart, he was among the first to introduce their works into Spain.

Albert, Eugène (1816-1890) Belgian maker of woodwind instruments, whose high reputation was established by designing models for individual players. Specializing in clarinets, he was also influential in the development of bass and contrabass clarinets. His most notable contribution was the addition of an extra C♯′ on the clarinet, created around 1860, and now known as the Albert System. His business, established in 1846, was awarded the gold medal for clarinets and saxophones at the Paris Exhibition of 1889, and still continues in Brussels today.

Alberti bass Type of accompaniment to a melody that consists of a series of arpeggios and appears most often in keyboard music. It was named after Domenico Alberti (*c*.1710-40), an early composer of keyboard sonatas. The Alberti bass was frequently used by such composers as Haydn and Mozart. See also **figured bass**.

Albinoni, Tomaso Giovanni (1671-1751) Italian composer, violinist and singing teacher. Born the son of a Venetian paper merchant, he first came to light as a composer in 1694 with the staging of his first opera *Zenobia* and the publication of a set of 12 trio-sonatas. He had a brilliantly successful career as a composer for the stage, producing more than 70 operas, although few appear to have survived. Modern critics prize his instrumental works, notably his concertos for strings, his **concerti grossi** and his concertos for trumpet and for oboe. A contemporary of **Vivaldi**, he was one of the earliest composers to write concertos featuring wind instruments. **Bach** borrowed some of Albinoni's themes and used his bass parts for practice in **figured bass**. The popular Albinoni *Adagio* for organ and strings owes little to him; it was composed by the 20th-century Italian musicologist Remo

Giazotto, who used an authentic Albinoni bass line from an unidentifiable work as the foundation for his highly romanticized composition.

alborada (Sp.) Type of Spanish music, played on the dulzaina (rustic oboe) and tamboril (small drum), originally a morning song. **Ravel**'s *Alborada del gracioso* (1905) derives certain features from the Spanish alborada.

Albrechtsberger, Johann Georg (1736-1809) Austrian composer and organist. After a career in the provinces he was appointed court organist in Vienna in 1772, and eventually became *Kapellmeister* at St Stephen's Cathedral in 1793. A prolific composer – he wrote 284 church compositions (oratorios, cantatas, Masses and motets), 278 keyboard works (preludes and fugues) and 193 works for other instruments – he taught thorough-bass and harmony, and derived his strict **counterpoint** from the practice of 16th-century polyphonic composers, although he admired Mozart and Haydn (who reciprocated). He is best remembered as a teacher and theorist: Beethoven was numbered among his many pupils.

Albumblatt (Ger.) Album leaf. Originally, a composition written in the album of a friend or patron and usually dedicated to him or her. It came to be used as a convenient title for any such short, simple piece (later entitled simply *Blatt*). Collections were published under the title *Album*, sometimes by one composer (e.g. **Schumann**'s *Album für die Jugend*) or sometimes by several composers. Such pieces were usually for piano solo, although Beethoven wrote a song with accompaniment for piano duet, and Wagner wrote an *Albumblatt* for violin and piano.

Alcock, John (1715-1806) British organist and composer. He was born in London and served as a choirboy at St Paul's Cathedral. He went on to hold several positions as organist at churches throughout England. He was also organist at Lichfield Cathedral. Alcock is particularly noted as a composer of church music and of glees, popular choral part-songs written in a largely homophonic style. Alcock's son, also called John Alcock (1740-91), was likewise an organist and composer of church music.

Aldeburgh Festival Major annual festival of music and the arts founded by the composer Benjamin **Britten** and the singer Peter **Pears** in 1948 and centred upon the Suffolk fishing town of Aldeburgh and the surrounding district. The festival is held each June and features operas, concerts and some non-musical events. Several of Britten's works have been premièred at the festival, including his operas *A Midsummer Night's Dream* (1960) and *Death in Venice* (1973). Many concerts take place in the Maltings at nearby Snape, a purpose-built concert hall completed in 1970 to replace an earlier brick building that was part of an old barley-importing complex. The building, which had been converted and used as a concert venue by the festival since 1967, had burned down in 1969. Its rapid 'resurrection' moved Britten to celebrate the fact by writing a grand overture, *The Building of the House*, for the start of the 1970 festival. Following the deaths of Britten in 1976 and Pears in 1986, artistic direction of the festival was carried on by a group of Britten's friends, including the cellist Mstislav **Rostropovich** and the pianist Murray **Perahia**, and more recently Steuart Bedford and Oliver **Knussen**.

Aldrich, Henry (1647-1710) British writer on musical theory and composer of music for the Church. He was also a notable composer of **catches**. Born in London, Aldrich went on both to study and to teach at Oxford University, where he became dean of Christ Church and was twice elected vice-chancellor of the University. In addition to his numerous musical achievements, he was also a classical scholar, theologian, architect and expert on heraldry.

aleatory A technique by which the composer has deliberately withdrawn control of some parameter of its performance or composition. Commonly recognized aleatory techniques include (1) the use of random procedures in the composition of a work (e.g. *Music of Changes* by John **Cage**), (2) the choice of a number of performance alternatives as stipulated by the composer, and (3) the use of an abstract notation system (e.g. *Intersection and Projection* by Morton **Feldman**).

Alfano, Franco (1875-1954) Italian composer who began his career as a professional pianist but subsequently took on numerous teaching and administrative roles throughout Italy. He is known principally as the composer who, after **Puccini**'s death in 1924, completed the unfinished opera *Turandot* from the composer's autograph sketches. Alfano was, however, a prolific composer in his own right; his numerous operas include *Risurrezione*, written largely in the style of Puccini, and *La leggenda di Sakuntala*, which demonstrates a growing and less conformist, personal style. Among his other works are two symphonies, a piano concerto, several ballets and various chamber works.

Alfvén, Hugo (1872-1960) Swedish composer, violinist and choral and orchestral conductor. He studied at the Stockholm Conservatoire and spent some years as a violinist in the Royal Opera Orchestra, while studying composition. A state scholarship allowed him to train in Brussels under the violinist César Thomson (1857-1931). He wrote the first of his five symphonies in 1897. In 1904, after studying conducting in Dresden, he became director of the Siljan Choir, based at Dalecarlia, and held this post for 53 years. From 1910 to 1939 he served as music director of Uppsala University and also directed the Initiates of Orpheus choir, from 1910 to 1947. Apart from his symphonies, Alfvén is noted for his choral works, although few are known outside Sweden. He has also written much orchestral music, including film scores. He is probably best known for the first of his three *Swedish Rhapsodies*, which is subtitled 'Summer Vigil'.

Alison, Richard (1592-1606) English composer, mainly of sacred music. He composed metrical psalms for voices with chamber ensemble and published two such collections. He also wrote some solo pieces for **lute**.

Alkan, Valentin (C.H.V. Morhange) (1813-1888) French pianist and composer. He was a child prodigy, winning the *premier prix* for **solfège** at the Paris Conservatoire at the age of seven, and publishing his first piano piece at the age of 14. He was regarded as one of the leading virtuoso pianists of his day. He composed works for piano and pedal-piano, exploiting the technical resources of the fast-developing 19th-century instrument. He was a close friend of **Chopin**, and was greatly valued by **Liszt, Busoni** and others.

alla breve (It.) An indication, usually shown by the time signature ¢, that the metrical unit should be a degree faster than in 4/4 time, often indicated by C. This often meant 2/2, with two beats to a bar, although in the Credo of Bach's B minor Mass it means 4/2, with four beats to the bar. According to **Quantz**, the 18th-century theorist: 'In alla breve time: in the allegro each bar has one beat of the pulse; in the allegretto each half-bar one beat of the pulse; in the adagio for each crotchet one beat'. In modern times it has come to mean simply two beats in a bar.

Alla breve

allant (Fr.) Going. Direction for tempo, as in *plus allant*, to go faster. It may also mean going on, as in *allant grandissant*, continuing to grow.

allargando (It.) Broadening or spreading. Direction that the piece should slow down and be played more majestically.

Allegri, Gregorio (1582-1652) Italian singer and composer, whose most popular work is his setting of the *Miserere* (Psalm 51). This setting has traditionally been sung in the Sistine Chapel in Holy Week every year since its composition, and so closely did the choir guard it that for many years no copy of the music was allowed to leave the Chapel. This monopoly was supposedly broken only by the 14-year-old Mozart, who wrote it down from memory after only one hearing.

Allegri sang at the cathedrals of Fermo and Tivoli and became *maestro di cappella* at S. Spirito in Sassia, Rome. He published four Masses and many motets, chiefly in the old Roman style of **Palestrina.**

allegro, allegretto (It.) Lively or happy, often used at the head of a fast movement or piece, but not to be taken as fast as **presto.** *Allegretto* generally means a little slower and more light-hearted. Both are often qualified by other words, as in *allegro agitato.*

alleluia, hallelujah Praise Yahweh. A term that occurs in many Biblical texts, especially psalms, and is retained untranslated in many liturgies. The word therefore appears, often repeated many times for effect, in a great deal of sacred music of joyful character, in whatever language. In the Roman Catholic liturgy the third item of the Proper is the alleluia, which consists of a verse of scripture preceded and followed by the word 'alleluia'.

In the early Middle Ages extra texts and music (known as **tropes**) were added to the 'ia' syllable (known as the *jubilus*). Because this was the earliest type of free-composed music condoned by the Western Church, the *jubilus* is regarded as the birthplace of Western composition.

allemande (Fr.) German. Used to describe two types of dance, which both probably originated in Germany. One was a dignified dance of moderate tempo in quadruple or duple time that was used as the first or second movement of the classical suite. The other, still in use in Germany and Switzerland, is a rustic dance in triple time and has the character of a waltz or *Ländler.* Alternative spellings are allemand, almand, almain, almayn.

Allen, Thomas (1944-) English baritone. A graduate of the Royal College of Music (1964-8), he sang in the chorus of Glyndebourne Opera before joining the **Welsh National Opera**, where he made his début as Figaro in Rossini's opera *Il barbiere di Siviglia* in 1969. He joined Covent Garden in 1972, and while continuing to make frequent visits to Cardiff, he established an international reputation through extensive freelance engagements. By the mid-1980s he had become an established principal at most major opera houses, including the Metropolitan Opera House in New York.

In addition to his operatic repertory, Allen is admired as a recitalist and oratorio soloist. He has a wide and even-toned vocal range and possesses an impressive dramatic presence. He is equally at ease in the portrayal of tragedy, *bravura* or comedy.

Allende, Humberto (1885-1959) Chilean composer, ethnomusicologist and teacher. His studies in France and Spain (1910-11) are evident in his mature compositional style, which combines the techniques of French **impressionism** with the native rhythms and melodies of Chile. His output is varied and includes works written specifically for children, choral pieces, songs, chamber music and orchestral compositions such as his violin concerto (1942) and award-winning symphony (1910).

Alpenhorn (Ger.) Swiss peasant wind instrument, made of wood and varying in length up to 12 feet. It has a cup-shaped mouthpiece and can only produce notes of the **harmonic series**. The French equivalent term is *cor des Alpes*.

al rovescio (It.) Reversed; meaning the melody is to be played/sung either backwards or upside-down.

alto Second highest of the four categories into which the human voice is generally divided in Western music. This part is generally sung by women or boys, but by men in church music; before the 18th century it was almost always sung by men. This practice has been revived in recent years. Male altos are often referred to as **counter-tenors**, whereas the term **contralto** is now generally used to distinguish a female alto.

Alva, Luigi (1927-) Peruvian tenor who studied in Lima and at La Scala, Milan. He made his professional début in Lima and his European début in Milan in 1954, singing Alfredo in Verdi's *La traviata*. In 1955 he sang for the opening of La Piccola Scala in Milan. Since the 1960s Alva has performed at Covent Garden, London, and the Metropolitan Opera, New York, in addition to regular appearances in Milan. He is best known for his interpretations of Mozart and Rossini.

Alwyn, William (1905-1985) British composer, flautist and teacher who studied at the Royal Academy of Music in London. In 1926 he took a post at the Royal Academy of Music, teaching composition. His early works, including a piano concerto and an oratorio (*The Marriage of Heaven and Hell*, after William Blake), were highly successful but in 1939 he rejected all his early work and began to concentrate on technical perfection. His concern with both the nature of artistic experience and craftsmanship is shown in his long essay poem, *Daphne, or the Pursuit of Beauty* (1972).

Alwyn's artistic development is marked by constant self-assessment and the search for new creative stimuli. In several works (1955-62) he used a tonal form of **twelve-note** technique based on Indian music. He has written more than 60 film scores and was a founder-member of the Composers' Guild of Great Britain.

Alypius Greek musicologist who lived around the 3rd century AD. He is remembered for his treatise *Eisagoge mousike* (Introduction to Music), which gives information on Greek scales and **modes** and their system of transposition. It represents the most comprehensive and authoritative surviving survey of the musical notation of ancient Greece. Published in Italy in 1616, it proved highly significant for the studies of humanist scholars of music.

Amadeus Quartet English quartet founded in 1947. Its members were Norbert Brainin (violin), Siegmund Nissel (violin), Peter Schidlof (viola) and Martin Lovett (cello). One of the finest string ensembles of its time – the individual members received many honours – it made frequent tours all over the world and appeared at many of the major festivals. The quartet has recorded a wide classical repertory, in which the works of Mozart, naturally, and Schubert are predominant; they have also been successful with 20th-century works. The death of Peter Schidlof in 1987 meant the break-up of the ensemble, as the other members felt that he was irreplaceable after 40 years. Their range of fine recordings is a legacy of their superlative musicianship.

Amati family Family of violin-makers who worked in Cremona, Italy, during the 16th century. The most famous was Nicolo Amati (1569-1684), who taught both **Stradivari** and **Guarneri**, all of these names being associated with the finest violins in the world, still highly prized by today's virtuoso players.

Ambrosian chant A type of **plainsong** peculiar to the rite of the Milanese or Ambrosian Church. It is the only corpus of Western chant to have survived other than **Gregorian chant**, and like the latter has its origin in Eastern chants which may have reached Milan in the 5th-7th centuries.

In chants that derive from a common root, the Milanese is often the closest to the original, and is longer and more melismatic than the Gregorian version. The oldest surviving manuscript sources date from the 11th and 12th centuries.

Ameling, Elly (1934-) Dutch soprano. The most influential of her several teachers was Pierre **Bernac**, who encouraged her to study French song. Since the firm establishment of her reputation as a recitalist, she has become known for her highly personal interpretation of works from such diverse composers as Bach, Britten, Handel, Mozart, Ravel, Satie, Schubert and Stravinsky.

amoroso (It.) In an amorous or loving style.

Amy, Gilbert (1936-) French composer and conductor. **Milhaud** and **Messiaen** were among his teachers, but he was most influenced by Pierre **Boulez**. He took up conducting in 1962 and succeeded Boulez as conductor of the Domaine Musical concerts in 1967, retaining the post until the concerts were discontinued in 1973. Since then Amy has combined an international conducting career with the duties of music adviser to the French broadcasting organization ORTF. As a composer, he has progressed from an affinity with **Webern** to an increasingly experimental style. His works include: a piano sonata (1957-60); *Diaphonies* (1962) for two chamber orchestras; *D'un espace déployé* for orchestra and soprano (a work almost in the style of a *concerto grosso*); and *Sonata pian' e forte* (1974) for soprano, mezzo-soprano and 12 players. His later works, such as *Messe* (1982-3) for soloists, chorus and orchestra, with optional children's choir, have moved away from the strictures of **Boulez** to the mysticism of **Messiaen**.

ancora (It.) Again, still more.

Anda, Geza (1921-1976) Swiss pianist and conductor of Hungarian origin. He studied in Budapest under Ernst von **Dohnányi**, but moved to Switzerland when he was 22, quickly gaining international recognition for his deep understanding of the Bartók concertos. He was also valued for his interpretations of Mozart as well as Schumann and Brahms. His dynamic style was perhaps more suited to the Romantic than the classical repertory. He turned to conducting in later years, and made several recordings in which he directed piano concertos from the keyboard.

andante (It.) Walking. Indication of tempo (at a walking pace), generally interpreted as being a moderate speed, lying between **allegretto** and **adagio**. There is no real agreement among musicians as to whether it is a quick or slow category of tempo. Mozart used *più andante* to mean faster, whereas Tchaikovsky used the same phrase to mean slower.

andantino (It.) Diminutive of **andante**, usually used to define a piece of andante tempo or character. If used as a tempo mark it means a slight moderation of andante. Whether this modification should be faster or slower is a matter of debate, but the consensus among modern musicians is that it indicates a somewhat quicker tempo.

Anderson, Marian (1902-) American contralto who studied with Giuseppe Boghetti in New York, and went to Europe in 1930. She sang in England, Germany and Scandinavia, winning high praise from **Toscanini**. Her recital début was at Town Hall, New York, in 1935 and she made her opera début as Ulrica in Verdi's *Un ballo in maschera* at the Metropolitan Opera, being the first black soloist to appear there. Anderson was mainly known as a fine singer of **spirituals**, to which her large voice was admirably suited. She gave her last recital at Carnegie Hall in 1965.

André, Maurice (1933-) French trumpeter who, after studying with Sabarich at the Paris Conservatoire, quickly established himself as the leading trumpeter of his generation, achieving particular success through his use of a four-valve piccolo trumpet. He has recorded the complete trumpet repertory and has had compositions written for him by **Jolivet**, **Tomasi** and **Blacher**, among others.

Andriessen, Hendrik (1892-1981) Dutch composer, organist and teacher, brother of Willem **Andriessen**. He studied at the Amsterdam Conservatoire and held positions as organist in Haarlem and Utrecht between 1916 and 1938. In 1926 he combined his duties as organist with a teaching post at the Roman Catholic School for Church Music in Utrecht. He was director of the Utrecht Conservatoire from 1937 to 1949, and of the Royal Conservatoire in The Hague from 1949 to 1957. He was professor of music history at Nijmegen University from 1952 to 1962. He wrote several Masses with organ accompaniment and secular vocal and choral music. His orchestral works include five symphonies and the fine *Hymnus in Pentecostem*, written during his 84th year.

Andriessen, Juriaan (1925-) Son of Hendrik **Andriessen** and brother of Louis Andriessen, and composer of incidental and film music. More recently he has worked in television. Andriessen's music displays a skilful absorption of various styles rather than striking individuality.

Andriessen, Willem (1887-1964) Dutch composer and pianist, brother of Hendrik **Andriessen**. He studied at Amsterdam, and rose to be director of the Amsterdam Conservatoire from 1937 to 1953. He composed a variety of mainly choral and orchestral works.

Anerio, Felice (*c.*1560-1614) Italian church composer, brother of Giovanni **Anerio**. He succeeded **Palestrina** as composer to the Papal court at Rome and with Francesco Soriano (1549-1620) completed Palestrina's task of revising and modernizing the **plainsong** of the Gradual, Antiphonal and Psalter. The first edition of the new and revised plainsong melodies was published in 1614-15. He composed four Masses, spiritual madrigals and lively secular canzonettas.

Anerio, Giovanni (*c.*1567-1630) Italian composer and priest, brother of Felice **Anerio**. After holding major musical posts in Rome and Verona, he went to Warsaw in about 1624 as director of music to Sigismund III, King of Poland. After handing over this post in 1628 to his pupil Marco Scacchi, he decided to return to Italy. As a composer of sacred music, Anerio wrote very much in the old style epitomized by **Palestrina**. He made a four-part version of Palestrina's *Missa Pappae Marcelli*. But he also composed secular madrigals in which he embraced many aspects of the new style that was sweeping Italy at the beginning of the 17th century.

Anfossi, Pasquale (1727-1797) Italian composer who, after studying the violin in Naples and playing in a theatre orchestra, began to study composition with **Piccinni**. He worked in Rome and Venice, and between 1781 and 1783 was employed as the director of the King's Theatre, London, where among the numerous operas staged were several of his own compositions. Anfossi is chiefly remembered for his operatic works such as *L'incognita perseguitata* (1773), but in his later career he also wrote a large number of sacred pieces, on both Italian and Latin texts.

Angeles, Victoria de Los See **Los Angeles, Victoria de**

angklung (Indonesia) Tuned bamboo rattle instrument which consists of two or more tubes tuned an octave apart, suspended over a slotted resonator tube. The term is also used as the collective name for a group of the rattles tuned at different pitches, one for each pitch in the melody.

anglaise, anglois, angloise (Fr.) Loosely applied in the late **Baroque** era to any of the English dance types. More particularly it refers to a fast dance movement in an orchestral **suite**, typically in **duple time**; the *anglaise* is usually simple and heavily accented.

Anglican chant Method of choral singing of psalms and canticles evolved by the Anglican Church (and later adopted by other reformed churches). An Anglican chant consists of a short sequence of chords to which the words of each verse (in a single chant) or pair of verses (in a double chant) are fitted by means of a system of pointing (i.e. special punctuation marks in the text indicating the position of the bar-lines in the chant). There are several thousand chants in the Anglican repertory, the main period of their composition being the 19th century, although the origins of the system go back to **plainsong** and the Festal psalm settings of the Tudor composers. Psalms are generally chanted antiphonally, i.e. alternate verses are sung by alternate sides of the choir.

animato (It.) Animated, an indication to enliven or quicken the tempo.

Animuccia, Giovanni (*c.*1500-1571) Italian composer who, after an early training in Florence, worked in Rome, where he was later appointed head of the Cappella Giulia. He is now known principally for his association with the oratory of Filippo **Neri**, for which he wrote many *laudi*; these sacred compositions consist of vernacular texts with several voice parts set in a simple homophonic style, and are noted for the clarity of their word setting.

Ansermet, Ernest (1883-1969) Swiss conductor who studied with **Bloch**. He joined **Diaghilev**'s Ballets Russes in 1915 as conductor and toured extensively. In 1918 he founded l'Orchestre de la Suisse Romande. He was most famous for his interpretations of the works of such composers as Stravinsky and Debussy and conducted the première performance of **Britten**'s *The Rape of Lucretia* at Glyndebourne in 1946.

answer The music which answers the opening statement, in (usually) a fugal exposition. This is normally pitched a **fifth** higher or a **fourth** lower (that is, **dominant** answer to **tonic** statement) than the initial statement. Where the answer exactly reproduces the opening **theme**, it is called a real answer; if it is altered it is called a tonal answer. Alterations are usually made to ensure that the dominant note in the opening statement is answered by the tonic note in the answer, so that the sense of **key** is preserved. The term may also be applied to the second of any subsequent pair of entries that stand in a tonic-dominant relationship, or to the second of any pair of **phrases** that balance each other in a musical structure.

antarā (India) Second section of a composition, of which the first part is the *sthāyī*, set in a particular mode (**rāga**) and rhythm (**tāla**) and often used as a basis for subsequent improvisation.

Antheil, George (1900-1959) American composer who is best known for his contribution to the 1920s craze for 'machine music'. In the search for music that reflected the century of the aeroplane, composers constructed noise machines which imitated the sounds of factories and industry. In 1926 Antheil caused a sensation in Paris with his *Ballet mécanique* scored for eight pianos, eight xylophones, pianola, two electric doorbells and an aeroplane propeller.

anthem Until the Reformation this word was synonymous with **antiphon**. The new Anglican Church swept away the antiphon in praise of the Virgin Mary (which traditionally concluded Evensong) and replaced it with a more general choral work. The word is now used to denote any non-liturgical choral composition of a nature suitable for use in the Anglican and other Reformed Churches.

For the earliest composers of anthems in the 16th century there were two stylistic ideals. One was the *short* style, which heeded the church leaders' directive that 'for every syllable there should be a note' and which was generally used for everyday, simple anthems. The second was the broad, polyphonic **motet** style, differing from the works of the continental Catholic composers only in having English rather than Latin words. In fact, most early anthems used aspects of both these forms, and could be either full anthems, in which the whole choir sang throughout, or verse anthems, which included passages for soloist(s) accompanied by organ, viols or cornets and sackbuts. Early masters of the anthem include **Byrd, Gibbons** and **Tomkins**.

After the Restoration the verse anthem was developed further, with string accompaniment sometimes added by the composers to the Chapel Royal (**Purcell** and **Blow** among them) in response to King Charles II's tastes. Later Handel, with his orchestrated anthems, took the genre to its peak.

By the later 18th and the 19th centuries, the anthem's popularity had declined, following a general change of focus away from sacred music. Nevertheless some fine and enduring anthems were composed by **Boyce**, **Stanford**, **Parry** and **Wood** among others.

anticipation Unaccented note sounded before, and then tied over into, the **chord** to which it belongs. It is usually sounded on a weak beat. More than one note of a chord may be anticipated.

Antill, John (1904-) Australian composer who studied at the New South Wales Conservatorium and later carried out detailed research on the music of the Aborigines. One of the results of this work was his composition of the ballet *Corroboree* in 1947, as well as numerous other pieces which can be said to express distinctive Australian characteristics. He has also carried out research on other ethnic musical styles. He was for many years involved in work for the Australian Broadcasting Company, retiring in 1971. He has written music for the stage and choral and orchestral works; the operas *Endymion* and *The First Christmas* (1970, for television), the ballets *Black Opal* and *Paean to the Spirit of Man*; and *Cantate Domino*, 1970.

antiphon 1. A text sung in association with a psalm. In the Roman Catholic Office Hours the Proper antiphon precedes and follows each psalm. Antiphons also feature in the current form of the Proper of the Mass, although down the years the accompanying psalms have been reduced to only one verse, or omitted altogether. The Introit and Gradual retain the form antiphon – psalm verse – repeat of antiphon, while the Offertory and Communion retain only the antiphon.

2. A number of texts in praise of the Virgin Mary are collectively known as Votive or Marian Antiphons, and these have frequently been set to music. The four most common Votive antiphons are *Salve Regina, Alma Redemptoris Mater, Ave Regina Caelorum* and *Regina Caeli*.

3. A musical performance is said to be antiphonal if it involves two or more groups playing or singing alternately. This can refer either to the antiphonal performance of a pre-existing work (e.g. a **plainsong** psalm), or a work expressly composed to include antiphonal effects.

antique cymbal **Cymbals** invented in the early 19th century, so called because they were depicted in ancient wall paintings. They are considerably smaller than their modern counterparts, and are shaped differently, having an upward curve. This gives them a tinkling sound with a definite pitch which has been used in orchestral works for special effect by composers such as Berlioz (the first to use them) in the 'Queen Mab' scherzo of his *Roméo et Juliette* symphony, **Ravel** in *Daphnis et Chloé* and **Debussy** in *Prélude à l'après-midi d'un faune*.

anvil Small steel bar, struck with a hard wooden or metal beater, which has sometimes been used as a percussion instrument. The anvil is most frequently found in operatic works as stage props whose sound is integrated into the musical content, e.g. as in Verdi's *Il trovatore* and Wagner's *Das Rheingold*.

ApIvor, Denis (1916-) Composer of Welsh origin now resident in Ireland. After qualifying as a doctor he studied with Alan **Rawsthorne**, from whom he gained an understanding of **twelve-note** techniques, and Patrick **Hadley**; he was also influenced by the work of Constant **Lambert**, particularly in the area of ballet. He is noted for his opera and ballet scores but has also composed prolifically for the voice and for orchestra and individual instruments. His first opera was *She Stoops to Conquer* (completed in 1947); the ballet *A Mirror for Witches* (1951) was performed at Covent Garden (through Lambert). His ballet *Blood Wedding* (1953, after Lorca) was also performed at Covent Garden, and his opera *Yerma* produced by the BBC in 1959.

Apostel, Hans Erich (1901-1972) German composer who settled in Vienna. His work reflected his allegiance to the Second Viennese School of composers, passing through **expressionism** to a period of strict **serialism**.

appassionata (It.) Impassioned. The term is well known as the title of a piano sonata by **Beethoven** (Op. 57 in F minor, 1804). The name was not used by the composer but added by his publisher to describe the overall mood of the work.

appoggiatura (It.) An auxiliary note, indicated by a small note above or below, which is said to lean expressively on the main note. It usually takes half the value of the main note, except when the main note is dotted, when it takes two-thirds of its value. In some contexts it may replace the main note altogether. In early music, appoggiaturas were often improvised, especially in vocal music such as **recitative**, even though there might be no written indication.

Appoggiatura

arabesque (Fr.) Originally used to describe architectural decoration in the Arabian style. It is also a term for a pose in ballet.

In music, it is a florid, delicate composition, for example **Debussy**'s *Deux arabesques* for piano, which show an intertwining of phrase reminiscent of the term's decorative origin.

Aragall, Giacomo (1939-) Spanish tenor. He studied in Italy and specializes in the Italian repertory. He made his début at La Scala, Milan, in 1963. He has sung in London, Milan and New York in the big Verdi and Puccini roles (the Duke of Mantua in *Rigoletto*; Cavaradossi in *Tosca*).

Arbeau, Thoinot (anagrammatic pen-name of Jehan Taburot, 1520-1595) Canon of Langres, chiefly remembered for having written the most authentic and detailed surviving record of the 15th- and 16th-century social dances, the *Orchésographie* (published 1589). As well as giving descriptions and tunes for some 40 dances, he discusses style and instrumentation as well as giving sample drum beats. Themes from the collection were used by **Delibes** (in *Le roi s'amuse*) and **Warlock** (in *Capriol Suite*).

Arbós, Enrique Fernández (1863-1939) Spanish violinist, conductor and composer. He studied with **Vieuxtemps** and **Joachim**, with whom he later performed. For a time he was professor of violin at the Royal College of Music in London and later turned to conducting. He worked with the Madrid Symphony Orchestra and he was guest conductor with several United States orchestras, including the Boston Symphony. A champion of 20th-century music, Arbós gave the première of Stravinsky's *Rite of Spring* in Spain.

Arcadelt, Jacques (*c.*1505-1568) Flemish or northern French composer. In his middle years he lived and worked in Italy, where he applied Franco-Flemish polyphonic techniques to the new genre of the **madrigal**, of which he published six volumes between 1539 and 1544. His most often printed madrigal was *Il bianco e dolce cigno*. In 1551 he returned to France and turned to producing large numbers of **chansons**.

arco (It.) Bow. As a musical term (*arco* or *coll'arco*, with the bow) it is a direction to string players indicating that the bow is to be used. It usually follows and counteracts the direction *pizzicato* (plucked).

Arensky, Anton Stepanovich (1861-1906) Russian pianist, composer and conductor. He studied with **Rimsky-Korsakov** and later became a professor at the Moscow Conservatoire. He numbered **Rachmaninov** and **Scriabin** among his pupils. From 1895 to 1901 he was director of the Imperial Chapel in St Petersburg. His music reflects the work of his idols, Chopin and Tchaikovsky, and his variations on the latter's *Legend* (1894) remains one of his best-known pieces. He composed operas (*A Dream on the Volga*, 1891; *Nal and Damyanti*, 1903) and ballets (*Egyptian Nights*, 1900), for the Maryinsky Theatre; *The Fountain of Bakhchisarai*, 1899, is still performed by the Kirov Ballet, the Maryinsky's successor. He also wrote two symphonies, a piano concerto 1882), many other piano pieces, cantatas and songs.

Argento, Dominick (1927-) American composer and teacher. He has composed many stage works, both operas and incidental music, as well as orchestral music and songs. A founder of the Minnesota Opera, and a professor at the university there, he was winner of the Pulitzer Prize in 1975.

Argerich, Martha (1941-) Argentinian pianist renowned for her dynamism, technical brilliance and forceful tone. Numbering **Gulda**, Magaloff and **Michelangeli** among her teachers, she is best known for her performances of the Romantic repertory, as well as for her performances of **Prokofiev** and **Bartók**.

Martha Argerich

aria Set piece for solo voice with instrumental accompaniment, mainly associated with opera, but also a feature of oratorio and cantata. In the 16th century, the term described a **strophic** setting of a poem, as opposed to a **madrigal**, which was **through-composed**. It did not necessarily imply music for solo voice, but the form was important in the early development of **monody**. The aria around 1600 is well represented in Giulio **Caccini**'s collection *Le nuove musiche* (1602). All are strophic and set for solo voice with **continuo** accompaniment.

In the first half of the 17th century, composers tended to vary the settings of each strophe, often over an **ostinato** bass. It was not until towards the end of the 17th century that the aria showed more of the emphasis on **melody** that we now expect. Another development in the latter half of the 17th century was the use of the **ritornello**, a recurring instrumental passage between the strophes.

The **da capo** aria was the dominant form for about 100 years after 1650. The highly accomplished operatic librettos by the poet Pietro Metastasio were so successful that they were used by composers throughout the 18th century, thus perpetuating the poetic form of the aria. In the late 18th century many composers, notably **Gluck** in his 'reform' operas, rejected the *da capo* aria as being essentially non-dramatic.

The rise of comic opera alongside Metastasian **opera seria** gave composers the opportunity to experiment with freer and more varied forms.

The 20th century has been eclectic in its use of the aria. Stravinsky, for example, used the form in his neo-classical opera *The Rake's Progress*, while other composers have used song-like arias in an openly undramatic way.

The term aria may also refer to a short instrumental piece used as the basis for a set of variations, as in **Bach**'s *Goldberg Variations*. See also **arietta; arioso**.

arietta (It.) Piece in an opera, shorter than a fully developed **aria**, and usually in binary form. The term came into use only after the aria form had attained some degree of sophistication. It is also used in instrumental music (notably Beethoven's last piano sonata, Op.111).

arioso (It.) In the style of an **aria**. A style of singing that is halfway between declamation and **melody**; an *arioso* passage often occurs at the beginning or the end of a **recitative**. It has been used to mean a flowing melodic style, a short aria, or an instrumental piece in a semi-**recitative** style.

Ariosti, Attilio (1666-*c*.1729) Italian musician and composer whose work has attracted considerable scholarly interest but is rarely performed. He played many instruments and held court and church posts throughout Europe. As a composer, Ariosti was prodigious, writing operas, Italian cantatas, oratorios and some instrumental music. He is particularly remembered for his imaginative use of instruments.

arja (Bali) Popular operatic form with plots taken from the 14th-century Javanese *Panji* romance. *Alus* (distinguished or elegant characters) sing and speak in Kawi, an ancient Javanese language, which is then translated into modern Balinese for the benefit of the audience by *penasar* or clowns during comedy interludes. It is commonly performed by youths and young girls, although leading parts in the comedy sections may be taken by older men. There are usually 12 dancer/actors involved.

The performance is accompanied by a small **gamelan** consisting of two small flutes or **suling**, drums, cymbals, a guntang (single-string bamboo tube zither), and a small gong.

Armstrong, Sheila (1942-) English soprano who studied at the Royal Academy of Music, winning the Kathleen Ferrier Memorial Scholarship in 1965. In the same year she made her operatic début at Sadler's Wells as Despina, singing the role of Belinda (*Dido and Aeneas*) the following year at Glyndebourne. Her Covent Garden début was as Marzelline in Beethoven's *Fidelio* in 1973. Her bright, pleasing voice and warm stage presence are well suited to a wide variety of roles.

Arne, Michael (*c.*1740-1786) English composer, son of the more celebrated Thomas **Arne**. He was also famous as a keyboard player, performing works by his father and by Handel. As a conductor he introduced the latter's *Messiah* to Germany. Arne's compositions, mainly for the theatre and pleasure gardens, are now largely forgotten.

Arne, Thomas (1710-1778) English composer and violinist. His first stage work, the masque *Dido and Aeneas*, was performed in 1734, and from then until his death he worked almost continuously, producing music for the London stage. He was one of those responsible for bringing the Italian *coloratura* style to London, notably in his oratorio *Judith*, but was also noted for the tunefulness of his songs, the most famous being *Rule, Britannia* from the masque *Alfred* (1740). Also among his 88 stage works are *Comus* (1738), *Artaxerxes* (1762) and *Thomas and Sally* (1760). He also composed secular cantatas and some sacred music, and his instrumental works include *VIII Sonatas or Lessons* for keyboard (1756).

Arnell, Richard (1917-) English composer. A pupil of John **Ireland**, he became a professor at Trinity College of Music, London, and later in the United States, where he has spent much of his time. His reputation was established with the *Sinfonia quasi variazioni* in 1942. His ballet *Punch and the Child* (1947) was composed for the New York City Ballet; another ballet, *Harlequin in April* (1951), was performed in London by Sadler's Wells Ballet. He has also written the symphonic poem *Lord Byron*, five symphonies, a piano and a violin concerto, cantatas (*Ode to the West Wind*, 1949) and film scores.

Arnold, Malcolm (1921-) English composer who studied with Gordon Jacob at the Royal College of Music (1938-40). He then earned his living as a trumpeter (he was first trumpeter with the London Philharmonic Orchestra, 1942) before turning to composition in 1948. He has been influenced by Sibelius and Berlioz; he is a fine orchestrator whose output is attractive and accessible. As well as nine symphonies and concertos for a variety of instruments (flute, clarinet, harmonica, horn, and guitar) he has produced two operas and five ballets. His popular *English Dances* and *Four Scottish Dances* were combined into the ballet *Solitaire* for Sadler's Wells in 1957. Other orchestral pieces include the *Tam O' Shanter* overture; the *Fantasy on a Theme of John Field* (1975) for piano and orchestra; cantatas and chamber works. He is well known for his film scores, such as that for *The Bridge over the River Kwai*. He was made a CBE in 1970.

Arnold, Samuel (1740-1802) English composer and keyboard player. In sacred music he was active in the Chapel Royal, for which he wrote oratorios. In the theatre he was for a time chief keyboard player at Covent Garden, but later acquired, with his wife's money, the pleasure gardens at Marylebone. Later he moved on to the Little Theatre in the Haymarket, and in his church affiliations became organist at Westminster Abbey. His output was prolific but of variable quality.

arpeggio (It.) From *arpeggiare*, to play the harp. 1. The notes of a chord played in succession, ascending or descending, either on or before the beat. Many notations have been used to denote an arpeggiated chord, the most common being a wavy vertical line preceding the chord to be arpeggiated. In the keyboard music of the 17th and 18th centuries the word *arpeggiando* was sometimes used to indicate that a whole passage of chords was to be arpeggiated at the will of a player.

2. The method of playing successive notes of a chord over the range of an instrument for practice purposes.

arpeggione Fretted six-stringed instrument similar to a cello, and played with a bow. It was tuned in the same way as the modern guitar. **Schubert**'s *Arpeggione* sonata was composed for this now obsolete instrument, and is its main claim to fame, although the sonata is now played mainly on the cello.

arrangement 1. An adaptation or transcription of a musical composition for performance by forces other than those for which it was originally written.

2. The addition of harmonized accompaniment to an existing melody.

3. A composition that uses as its basis themes and other salient features of another piece of music.

Arrau, Claudio (1903-) Chilean pianist who studied with Martin Krause in Germany. He made his international début before he was 20, and undertook many long and successful tours throughout his career. Although his early reputation was partly based on his Bach playing, it is with the Romantic repertory that he has made his most lasting impression, along with his interpretations of the works of Mozart and Beethoven. His recorded repertory is extensive. His playing reflects a profound understanding of the music rather than a dazzling virtuosity.

Arriaga, Juan Crisóstomo (1806-1826) Spanish composer and violinist. His prodigious talent, especially in instrumental music, was displayed during his teens. His untimely death deprived the Spanish repertory of a major talent. It is now largely in Spain that Arriaga is remembered.

Arroyo, Martina (1936-) American operatic soprano, best known for her interpretation of principal roles in Italian opera. She gave her first Covent Garden performance as Aïda, and has sung at most major opera houses in the world. Her voice is rich but flexible.

ars antiqua (Lat.) Ancient art. This term was used in French theoretical writings of the early 14th century to describe notational systems employed before the technical advances of the **ars nova**. The rhythmic notation was much stricter than in the latter, when it became more broken up. Forms used during the *ars antiqua* period include **organa**, **conductus**, **hockets**, **motets** and **cantilenas** (only motets and cantilenas being continued into the *ars nova* period). The term is often used to describe all **polyphonic** music of the 12th and 13th centuries, especially that of the Notre Dame School as exemplified by Léonin and Pérotin.

ars nova (Lat.) New art. The term first appeared about 1322 in a treatise by Philippe de **Vitry**, which gave an account of the new notational techniques used by the French in the 14th century. *Ars nova* is generally used to describe all French music from the *Roman de Fauvel* manuscript (1320) up to the death of **Machaut** (1377). A new system of notation also grew up in Italy at that time, but with a less dramatic change, and by the end of the 14th century composers were using a combination of the two systems to achieve a much greater range of expression and rhythmic variety than before.

Art of Fugue, The (*Die Kunst der Fuge*) Collection of 20 fugues and canons by **J.S. Bach**, written at Leipzig in the mid- to late 1740s and published incomplete by his sons after his death. All but the last of the pieces are based on one subject, starting with simple fugues and working through more complex ones, employing the full range of contrapuntal devices: **inversion**, **stretto**, **augmentation**, **diminution**, **canon**, double fugues, and finishing with a triple fugue, the third of whose themes is based on the notes B-A-C-H (see

counterpoint). This, and the fact that Bach does not state what instruments are to be employed (although a keyboard instrument seems most likely), caused *The Art of Fugue* to be regarded primarily as a series of teaching pieces; it was not until the work was revived in performance in Leipzig in 1927 that it was also recognized as a magnificent piece of music.

Chamber and orchestral arrangements have been made of *The Art of Fugue*, and attempts have been made by Donald **Tovey**, among others, to complete the unfinished final fugue.

Asafiev, Boris (1884-1949) Russian composer, teacher and writer on music. After studying with **Rimsky-Korsakov**, Asafiev first worked in Leningrad as a professor of composition and music history. He moved to Moscow in 1943 and is mainly known for his writings on Russian music, although he was also a prolific composer, especially of ballets.

āsāvari (India) One of the ten parent scales (**thāt**) in Hindustani music, corresponding to C, D, E♭, F, G, A♭, B♭, C′. An alternative transliteration is *asawari.*

ASCAP Acronym for (The) American Society of Composers, Authors and Publishers. ASCAP was founded in 1914 as a non-profit-making copyright collection agency. Its function is to establish licensing rates and to distribute fees to its members for any public performances of their works. Any writer or publisher of music with at least one regularly performed work may join ASCAP.

Ashkenazy, Vladimir (1937-) Soviet pianist and conductor who settled in Iceland in 1968. In 1962 he was joint winner (with John **Ogdon**) of the first prize in the Tchaikovsky competition. He has recorded widely, mainly classical and Romantic works, and is considered one of the leading exponents of this repertory. Ashkenazy is also to be seen directing concertos from the keyboard, and more recently has turned to conducting: he is music director of the **Royal Philharmonic Orchestra**, which he took on a triumphant tour to the Soviet Union in 1989 (his first visit for 23 years).

Vladimir Ashkenazy

Ashley, Robert (1930 -) American composer and performer of electronic music. Influenced by John **Cage**, Ashley has spent much of his composing career promoting live electronic music with touring companies such as the American-based Sonic Arts Union. He often collaborates with other musicians and visual artists on large-scale electronic music-theatre works such as *The Trial of Anne Opie Wehrer and Unknown Accomplices for Crimes Against Humanity* (1968). In 1969, Ashley became co-director of the Centre for Contemporary Music at Mills College, Oakland, California.

astāī (India) See **sthāyī**

Aston, Hugh (*c.*1485-1558) English composer who graduated from Oxford after eight years' study in 1510. His *Hornepype* is the earliest surviving piece in the idiomatic keyboard style of the English virginalists.

Atherton, David (1944-) British conductor who studied at Cambridge

University and the Royal Academy of Music. He founded the **London Sinfonietta** in 1967 and served as its first musical director until 1973. In 1968 he became the youngest conductor ever to appear at a Henry Wood Promenade concert, and in the same year made his début at the Royal Opera House, Covent Garden. He was principal conductor with the **Royal Liverpool Philharmonic Orchestra** (1980-3) and musical director of the San Diego Symphony Orchestra (1980-7). In 1985 he became principal guest conductor of the BBC Symphony Orchestra. Atherton has edited the complete instrumental music of Arnold **Schoenberg** and Roberto **Gerhard**.

atonal Any piece of music that rejects the traditional **tonal** system, although often used to describe, rather inappropriately, music whose harmonic and melodic structure seems unfamiliar to the listener. The 'breakdown' of tonality is usually seen as occurring towards the end of the 19th century, especially in the works of **Wagner** (such as *Tristan und Isolde*) and **Liszt**. Increasing use of **chromaticism** and transposition at this time inevitably led to a complete reappraisal of the tonal system that eventually saw a systemization of atonality in the form of **twelve-note** or **serial** music.

attacca (It.) Attack, or attach, an indication to begin the next movement or section immediately, without a break.

Attaignant, Pierre (*c*.1494-*c*.1551) Parisian music publisher. He invented the system of music printing in which each note had its own portion of the stave on the same block; this brought printed music within the price-range of large numbers of people for the first time. His publications date from the mid-1520s, and include some of the most important music of his time, notably the **chansons** of Claudin de Sermisy and Clément **Janequin**, and seven volumes of dance music, some of which he may have arranged himself.

Atterberg, Kurt (1887-1974) Swedish composer and writer. An active figure in Swedish musical life, Atterberg held many influential posts in the academic and professional world. Like many Nordic composers, much of his output is descriptive or programmatic in conception, and he has written a great deal of ballet music. His nine symphonies are rarely heard but a few shorter pieces have found a modest place in the repertory. In 1928 he won the Gramophone Company's Schubert Prize with his Symphony No. 6, which was recorded by both **Toscanini** and **Beecham**.

Attwood, Thomas (1765-1838) English composer and organist. After serving as a chorister in the Chapel Royal, Attwood travelled extensively abroad, receiving lessons from **Mozart** while in Vienna. This experience influenced his musical style profoundly. He held appointments as organist at St Paul's Cathedral and later at the Chapel Royal, and was in addition a founder professor of the Royal Academy of Music. In 1792 he made a successful début as a theatrical composer with *The Prisoner* and wrote music for about 30 different productions during the next decade. Thereafter he turned increasingly to sacred music, and is particularly remembered for his coronation anthems.

aubade (Fr.) Early morning music (from *aube*, dawn). Aubades were played in 17th- and 18th-century courts in honour of royalty. The Spanish equivalent is **alborada**. Composers have used both terms as titles for instrumental music, for example **Lalo**'s *Aubade* for five wind and five string instruments.

Auber, Daniel-François-Esprit (1782-1871) French composer, influential in the rise of **opéra-comique** during the early 19th century. His early attempts attracted the attention of **Cherubini**, under whom he subsequently studied, and from 1820 onwards he achieved lasting successes in collaboration with the librettist Scribe with such works as *La muette de Portici*, *Fra*

Diavolo and *Le domino noir*. With 42 operas to his credit, he is best remembered for his vivacious yet melodious style, somewhat influenced by **Rossini**. During his lifetime he received many public honours and in 1842 was appointed director of the Paris Conservatoire in succession to Cherubini.

Aubert, Jacques (1689-1753) French composer and violinist whose early career was largely spent in the service of the court, where he absorbed stylistic influences from the Italianate repertory he played. He wrote much music for the theatre as well as a number of sonatas and concertos for his own instrument, the violin. The concertos are among the earliest to be composed in France.

His ballets and stage entertainments include the *Fête royale* in honour of Louis XV and *Le ballet de 24 heures* for his master the Duke of Bourbon. He also wrote comic operas (*La reine des péris*).

Aubert, Louis (1720-after 1783) French violinist and son of Jacques **Aubert**, therefore often referred to as *le jeune*. As a young child he played in the orchestra of the Paris Opéra, eventually becoming first violinist and one of the Opéra's principal conductors. Aubert was also a composer of dance music and of *simphonies*.

auditorium Area in a theatre or concert hall in which the audience is seated.

Audran, Edmond (1840-1901) French composer of some 30 operettas, written during the last quarter of the 19th century. His best-known works include *Les noces d'Olivette* and *La mascotte*. *La poupée*, written towards the end of his career in 1896, is regarded as his masterpiece. His popular style made him a successful rival of Lecocq, and he enjoyed widespread fame throughout Europe.

Auger, Arleen (1939-) American operatic soprano. Born in California, she studied in the United States and made her professional début in Vienna, where she sang with the Staatsoper for seven years (till 1974). An international career followed, with performances at the Metropolitan, New York; Covent Garden, London; Glyndebourne, and various German houses. She is possessed of a rich, warm voice and an agility which is well suited to Mozartian and Baroque roles. She also has an exciting stage presence and interpretative ability.

augmentation Increasing (usually doubling) the note-values of a **theme**. It is a common device in fugues, canons and other contrapuntal works. It was also used frequently by Renaissance composers for the **cantus firmus** in Masses and motets.

augmented interval Perfect or major **interval** that has been increased by a semitone. Augmented intervals occurring naturally in the scale are the augmented 4th (between the 4th and 7th degrees of the major or harmonic minor scale, e.g. F-B in the scale of C) and the augmented 2nd (between the 6th and 7th degrees of the harmonic minor scale, e.g. A♭-B♭ in C minor).

augmented sixth **Interval** of a major sixth increased by a semitone or, more usually, a **chord** containing such an interval. The three commonly used forms of the augmented sixth chord are: the French sixth, which contains a major third and an augmented fourth above the root; the Italian sixth, which contains the major third above the root (in four-part writing this is doubled); and the German sixth, which contains the major third and a doubly augmented fourth (resolving upwards) or a perfect fifth (resolving downwards) above the root. The German sixth is useful for

modulation because it sounds like a dominant seventh chord, and can be resolved as one.

aulos Most important instrument of ancient Greece, a slender pipe with a double reed having a thumb-hole and three to five finger-holes. It was played in pairs, both reeds in the mouth and a pipe held in each hand. Although we know nothing of the performance practice and how the two pipes functioned together, the instrument is depicted in use at all kinds of social occasions as a solo instrument and in the accompaniment of solo or choral singing.

Auric, Georges (1899-1983) French composer who was a member of the group of composers known as Les **Six**, along with Cocteau, **Poulenc** and others. His large output included several ballets, songs, piano pieces and scores for films by René Clair and Cocteau. He was also a music critic and director of the Paris Opéra (1962-8).

Austin, Frederic (1872-1952) English baritone and composer. As a singer he began his career as Gunther in the *Ring* cycle at Covent Garden in 1908. He joined the Beecham Company (founded in 1915) and was one of its leading singers. The company folded in 1920 but he became artistic director of its successor, the British National Opera Company, in 1924. He presented a version of Gay's *The Beggar's Opera* in London in 1920, in which he sang Peachum. His compositions include incidental music for theatrical productions, and a choral work, *Pervigilium veneris* (1931).

Austin, Larry (1930-) American composer who studied at North Texas State University under Andrew **Imbrie** and Darius **Milhaud** and held teaching posts in California, Florida and New York. He was editor of the avant-garde music journal *Source* from 1966 to 1971. Many of his compositions attempt to contain group improvisation (often by jazz soloists) within a controlling framework. He has also experimented with electronic and theatrical media.

authenticity Broadly, the performance of music of a particular period using only the instruments or quantity of instruments current in that period.

For the last 20 years or so there has been a great revival of interest in hearing the sounds of **Baroque** and classical music as the composer might have heard them. This applies to both solo instrumental and orchestral music. Domenico **Scarlatti's** sonatas are now mainly performed on the harpsichord, for which they were composed, instead of on the piano as many world-class players such as Horowitz have played them in the past. The composition of an orchestra, as well as the construction of the actual instruments, has also changed considerably since Bach's or even Beethoven's day, and certain ensembles, notably in Britain, Germany and Austria, have been dedicated to recreating the authentic period sound. They include the **Academy of Ancient Music** under Christopher **Hogwood**; the London Baroque and London Classical Players under Roger **Norrington**; the English Baroque Soloists under John Eliot **Gardiner**; the English Concert under Trevor **Pinnock**; the Vienna Concentus Musicus and the Schola Cantorum Basiliensis. Music from the Middle Ages and the Renaissance has been recreated as nearly as possible by such groups as David **Munrow's** Early Music Consort, but here the authenticity of sound is slightly less certain, since the manner of playing and the actual instruments are less fully documented.

The movement for authentic performance embraces not only instrumentation but also techniques of playing, notation, and so on. It grew out of the musical scholarship of the 19th century and the discoveries of such musicologists as Arnold **Dolmetsch**. The ensembles mentioned and their directors have fostered a great interest in the authentic performance of works by composers as far apart as Praetorius and Schumann, and their concerts and recordings are widely admired.

auxiliary note Unaccented note forming part of the prevailing harmony, which it decorates. It lies a step above (upper auxiliary) or below (lower or under auxiliary) the main note, from which it is approached and to which it returns. More than one auxiliary note may be sounded at once. In American usage it is known as a neighbour note.

Ave Maria (Lat.) Hail Mary, used as the opening words of various sacred texts set to music. Most are based on the Roman Catholic prayer *Ave Maria, gratia plena, dominus tecum...* (Hail Mary, full of grace, the Lord is with thee...). Particularly well-known settings include those of Robert Parsons (*d.*1570) and **Gounod**, whose version comprises a vocal line added to **J.S. Bach**'s Prelude No.1 from *The Well-Tempered Clavier*. Schubert also included, in his settings of poems by Walter Scott, the *Ave Maria* which Ellen sings.

Avidom, Menahem (1908-) Israeli composer of Russian birth. His compositions span many styles, from a modal **impressionism** using folk-music to purely **serial** works. His symphonies fall somewhere between these two styles, using an eclectic style based on tonal centres rather than on tonality. Avidom has been a formative influence in Israeli musical life.

Avison, Charles (1709-1770) English composer, conductor and writer on music, who lived all his life in Newcastle upon Tyne. His most important compositions are his *concerti grossi*, trio-sonatas and other chamber music, which shows the influence of **Rameau**. His *Essay on Musical Expression* (1752) caused a stir on its first publication.

Avni, Tzvi (1927-) Israeli composer born in Germany, who studied with **Copland**. Among his better-known works are *Meditations on a Drama*, an orchestral work; *Summer Strings*, for string quartet; and *Collage*, for voice, percussion, flute and electric guitar.

Avshalomov, Aaron (1894-1965) Russo-American composer. He studied in Zurich and lived for a time in China, where he studied the native idiom which he integrated into his own compositions. Among his works are two operas, *Kuan Yin* and *The Great Wall*; a symphonic sketch, *Peiping Huntings*; and a ballet, four symphonies and two concertos.

Axman, Emil (1887-1949) Czech composer, a pupil of **Novák**. His work was much influenced by the music of his native Moravia and he is well known for his choral compositions, most of which are for male voice choir.

ayre When the word is used with this spelling (rather than **air**), it almost invariably refers to a particular type of English song, generally scored for solo voice and lute, which flourished in the 1600s. Other voices and/or viols or other instruments could often be added *ad libitum*. John **Dowland**'s *First Book of Ayres* inaugurated the form in 1597; other composers include Thomas **Campion** and John Danyel.

B

B Second note of the scale, one tone above A and one semitone below C. The scale of B major has five sharps in the key-signature. In German terminology B signifies the note B♭; the letter H is given to the English B♮.

B B major

Babbitt, Milton (1916-) American composer who developed and extended the **twelve-note** techniques of the Second Viennese School. He studied both music and mathematics, and his music reflects his training in the mathematical discipline. He was a player in various jazz groups as a young man, and was drawn to the music of Schoenberg and Webern. He studied with Roger **Sessions** and later taught both music and mathematics at Princeton University. His association with Princeton culminated in the organization of the Columbia-Princeton Electronic Music Centre. He has also taught at the Juilliard School and elsewhere, and has lectured extensively.

His earliest works, *Three Compositions for Piano* (1947), *Composition for Four Instruments* and *Composition for Twelve Instruments* (1948), reveal his involvement with serial techniques. He is also a leading practitioner of the synthesis of music through electronic means, and was the first composer to work with the RCA synthesizer. The *Composition for Synthesizer* (1961) was one of the first results of his work with this new musical resource, which stimulated his interest by offering endless possibilities for changing and blending textures and colours. He has also combined synthesized music with live performance, as in *Philomel* (1964, with voice); *Images* (1979, with instruments). His music, while not readily accessible, offers great intellectual challenge.

Babell, William (*c.*1690-1723) English composer and harpsichord player. His works included chamber music, concertos and harpsichord pieces. His arrangements of popular operatic arias with imitations of the elaborate ornamentation added by singers of his time give a valuable guide to this style.

bacchetta (It.) 1. A **baton**.

2. The stick of the **bow** used with string instruments.

3. A **drumstick**, *bacchetta di legno* being a wooden one and *bacchetta di spugna* a sponge-headed stick.

Bacewicz, Grazyna (1909-1969) Polish violinist and composer. She studied violin with Carl Flesch and composition with Nadia **Boulanger**. Her works include four symphonies, a cello concerto, seven violin concertos and seven string quartets.

BACH In German notation, these letters form a theme first used by J.S. Bach in the final, unfinished fugue of *The Art of Fugue.*

It has since been used by many other composers including Schumann, Liszt, **Rimsky-Korsakov**, **Busoni**, **d'Indy**, **Reger**, and **Schoenberg**.

Bach, Carl Philipp Emanuel (1714-1788) German composer and harpsichord player, third son of **J.S. Bach** and his first wife, Maria Barbara. He was employed by **Frederick the Great** as a harpsichordist, and later appointed music director of five churches in Hamburg (1767). He is best remembered for his keyboard music and his early use of **sonata form**. His works, nearly 700 in total, emphasize **homophony** over **counterpoint** and include large-scale choral works (e.g. *Die Israeliten in der Wüste*, *Die Auferstehung und Himmelfahrt Jesu*), keyboard concertos, 19 symphonies, two Passions, cantatas, motets, psalms and solo vocal music. C.P.E. Bach also wrote a treatise on keyboard playing, which provides an invaluable guide to contemporary practice. He was regarded as the finest keyboard player of his time.

Bach, Johann Christian (1735-1782) German composer, eleventh and youngest son of **J.S. Bach** and his second wife Anna Magdalena. After studying music with his father and his brother Carl Philipp Emanuel, J.C. Bach studied in Italy with **Martini** before moving to England in 1762. He produced his first opera in London (*Orione*, 1763) and in the same year was appointed music tutor to Queen Charlotte. He befriended the young **Mozart** on his visit to London and has often been said to have provided him with one of his earliest sources of inspiration. With C.F. **Abel** he founded a series of subscription concerts, which were staged annually between 1764 and 1781. Despite visits to Mannheim (1772) and Paris (1778), Johann Christian maintained his strong ties with England, where he died; he is known as the 'London Bach'. Among his works were many operas, concertos, keyboard sonatas, symphonies and chamber works.

Bach, Johann Christoph Friedrich (1732-1795) German organist and composer; ninth son of **J.S. Bach** and Anna Magdalena. He studied music with his father and law at Leipzig University. He gained employment at the court of Bückeburg in 1750 as a chamber musician to Count Wilhelm of Schaumburg-Lippe. He has gained the informal title of the 'Bückeburger Bach' from his permanent links with the court where he was to remain for the rest of his life. His compositions include oratorios composed on words by Johann Gottfried Herder, 14 symphonies, keyboard concertos, chamber music (including keyboard sonatas) and an opera (now lost).

Bach, Johann Sebastian (1685-1750) German composer and keyboard player. The most significant member of the Bach family, Johann Sebastian was best known during his lifetime as an organist; he became widely known as a composer only after the revival of his works by **Mendelssohn** and others in the early part of the 19th century.

Bach was born in Eisenach and first studied music within his highly musical family. Among his teachers were (probably) his father Johann Ambrosius (who was employed at court as a string player and in Lüneburg) and his brother Johann Christoph, who gave him his first keyboard tuition.

Several years as a chorister at Lüneburg were followed by appointments in Arnstadt (1704-7) and Mühlhausen, where he married his first wife, his cousin Maria Barbara (1684-1720). In 1708 Johann Sebastian was appointed court organist in Weimar, and this is where he composed most of his works for organ. In 1717 he moved as *Kapellmeister* to Cöthen, where he wrote a large part of his orchestral, keyboard and chamber music and, after the death of Maria Barbara, married Anna Magdalena Wilcke (1721).

In 1723 Bach became cantor at St Thomas's Church in Leipzig. It was there that he composed most of his sacred music;

Johann Sebastian Bach

he was to live there until his death. From his two marriages Bach fathered 20 children, many of whom were to become eminent composers and performers in their own right.

His church music includes settings of the Passions, *St John* (1724) and *St Matthew* (1729), his perfectly constructed Mass in B minor (1733-8) and more than 200 cantatas. Bach's impressive settings of chorales, the hymn-tunes of the Lutheran Church, are to be found throughout his choral works. His best-loved instrumental compositions are probably the six *Brandenburg Concertos* (1721), his violin sonatas, concertos and suites for unaccompanied cello.

Bach's organ music includes more than 140 **chorale preludes** (a form in which he excelled), **toccatas** and **fugues**, **preludes** and fugues, **fantasias**, **sonatas** and **trios**. His other keyboard music includes the collection *The Well-Tempered Clavier* (1722-42), the *Goldberg Variations* (1742) and *The Art of Fugue*.

His compositions have been catalogued with the BWV (*Bach Werke-Verzeichnis*) numbering system devised in 1950 by Wolfgang Schmieder.

Bach's intellectual power, evident throughout his work in the use of fugue and counterpoint, was never to obscure the joy and vitality present in his compositions. His many hundreds of works contain some of the best-known and best-loved compositions of all time and demonstrate his complete mastery of every genre he employed. He used contrapuntal writing in a natural and unstilted way and exploited fully every possibility this form offered.

The study of Bach's work remains an essential part of every music student's education and his methods and thematic material have been frequently reassessed, re-interpreted and analysed over the years. His compositions are a constant source of inspiration to scholar and composer alike.

Bach, Wilhelm Friedemann (1710-1784) German organist and composer, the eldest son of **J.S. Bach** and his first wife, Maria Barbara, and a fine keyboard player.

After studying music with his father (who wrote the *Klavier-Büchlein* for use in his education, 1720) he was engaged as organist of St Sophia in Dresden (1723) and later for St Mary, Halle (1746). In 1764 he resigned in order to pursue a career as a teacher. His various compositions include keyboard works (concertos, **fantasias**, **sonatas**, etc.), nine symphonies, 21 **cantatas**, a Mass, **chorale preludes**, and **fugues** for organ.

Bach trumpet Term loosely applied to the natural trumpet for which **J.S. Bach** wrote, because his was for a time the only music in which it was heard. The players then used the instrument's high harmonics, because only in that register was there a complete scale.

The term has also been applied to an instrument with valves invented in the 19th century. A similar instrument is used today by the Royal Military School of Music for ceremonial fanfares.

Bäck, Sven-Erik (1919-) Swedish composer who studied in Rome with Petrassi. His works include a symphony for strings, *Sinfonia Sacra* for chorus and orchestra, a sonata for solo flute, three string quartets, an opera, *Crane Feathers* (1956), five ballets, including *Ikaros* (1963) and *Movements* (1965; a concert version of this work was prepared the following year), and two violin concertos. In recent years he has collaborated with artists in other fields to produce works such as *Favola*, in which sculpture, poetry and music are combined; he has also written music to accompany the murals of B.E. Evensen. Latterly he has turned to electronic compositions.

Backhaus, Wilhelm (1884-1969) German pianist, trained in Leipzig and held to be the last great exponent of the Leipzig tradition. He is known for letting the music speak for itself rather than for dazzling virtuosity. Backhaus's recordings of the classical and Romantic repertory show careful analysis of the works as a whole and give a sense of their architecture; he was particularly noted for his interpretations of Beethoven, recording all the sonatas late in his career.

Badings, Henk (1907-) Dutch composer who was originally trained in geology, which he taught at Delft University from around 1931. He studied composition with Willem **Pijper** from 1930, and composed his Symphony No.1 in that year. He has held teaching posts at Rotterdam, The Hague, Utrecht and Stuttgart, and lectured in Australia, South Africa and the United States.

Badings's works demonstrate a concern with problems of **tonality**, a fondness for **counterpoint** and attention to formal coherence. From the early 1950s, he developed an interest in electronic music, and produced some operas and ballets for radio and television. His works include 14 symphonies, concertos and double concertos, choral works, songs, chamber music and solo instrumental music.

Badura-Skoda, Paul (1927-) Austrian pianist and musicologist. A pupil of Edwin **Fischer**, he has concentrated on the works of the Viennese classics, often using his own collection of late 18th- and early 19th-century pianos for recordings. His editions of Beethoven, Mozart, Schubert and Chopin are models of excellence, and his book on Mozart interpretation (written with his wife Eva) is a classic. His recordings reflect his specialist understanding of the classical style, and the tonal character of the period instrument.

bagatelle (Fr.) Short instrumental piece, usually for keyboard. François **Couperin** used the title for some of his *Pièces de clavecin*, and **Beethoven** wrote 26 piano bagatelles, of which *Für Elise* is one.

bagpipe Generic term for a wind instrument which appears throughout Europe and in a variety of guises. Invariable elements are a reed pipe and a bag which acts as a reservoir of air between the air source and the pipe. Typical variations may occur: the air may be provided either by a mouth pipe, or by bellows held under the arm and pressed against the body; the reed pipe or chanter, holed to give a variety of pitches, may be complemented by one or more single-tone reed pipes or drones tuned to the tonic and sometimes the dominant; the reed in the chanter may be single or double; the chanter and drone pipes may be cylindrical or conical; and the number of drone pipes may vary.

Bagpipe

baguette (Fr.) 1. A baton.
2. A drumstick; *baguette de bois* - a wooden stick; *baguette d'éponge* - a stick with a sponge head.

Bailey, Norman (1933-) English operatic baritone. He studied in Rhodesia and Vienna and pursued his early career largely in Austria and Germany. In 1968 he sang his first Wagnerian role, Hans Sachs in *Die Meistersinger von Nürnberg*, in the famous Sadler's Wells production conducted by Reginald **Goodall;** this led to invitations to sing the same role in several other venues including Bayreuth. Other major Wagner roles followed: Wotan in the *Ring* cycle and Amfortas in *Parsifal*. He has been successful in Mozart (as Figaro), Prokofiev (in *War and Peace*) and other roles such as Balstrode in Britten's *Peter Grimes*. He was made a CBE in 1977.

Baillie, Dame Isobel (1895-1983) Scottish soprano noted for her high, pure tone. She studied in Manchester and Italy; her début was in 1923. She was renowned above all for her singing in Handel's *Messiah*, and her recording of *I Know That My Redeemer Liveth* is still frequently heard and much loved. She retired in the late 1950s and taught a great deal in the United States and Britain. She was made a DBE in 1978.

Baillot, Pierre (1771-1842) French violinist and composer of violin music. He is the last representative of the classical Paris school of violinists who favoured a clarity and neatness of style and a pure tone. His instructional textbook on the instrument, *L'art du violon* (1834), holds its place as a standard work, although his compositions are now almost entirely forgotten.

Baird, Tadeusz (1928-1981) Polish composer who studied in Warsaw with Kazimierz Sikorski. Although his first works are written in a conventional style, he began to use **serial** methods in 1951 and has emerged as one of the leaders of the Polish avant-garde. His works include three symphonies, an opera, *Erotica* (six songs for soprano and orchestra), *Variations Without a Theme* for orchestra, a piano concerto and music for film and theatre.

Baker, Dame Janet (1933-) English mezzo-soprano who studied under Hélène Isepp in London and began her career with the Leeds Philharmonic Choir. In 1956 she won the Kathleen Ferrier Competition and made her operatic début as Roza in Smetana's *The Secret* with Oxford University Opera Club. Other operatic roles include Dido in Purcell's *Dido and Aeneas*; Handel's *Tamerlano*; Dido in Berlioz's *Les troyens*; Dorabella in Mozart's *Così fan tutte*; Oktavian in *Der Rosenkavalier*; Charlotte in **Massenet**'s *Werther*; Kate in **Britten**'s *Owen Wingrave*. She was made CBE in 1970 and DBE in 1976. Janet Baker has had an outstanding international career in opera, concertos and recitals. Her recordings cover a wide range, and offer a comprehensive account of the artistry of one of the finest singers Britain has produced.

Balakirev, Mily Alexeyevich (1836/7-1910) Russian composer and guiding spirit of the group of 'nationalist' composers known as the Five or the **'Mighty Handful'** (*moguchaya kuchka*). Balakirev began learning the piano as a child and subsequently came to the notice of Aleksandr Uliybiychev, a wealthy musical amateur. With Uliybiychev, Balakirev visited St Petersburg in 1855; there he met and was encouraged by **Glinka**, who was much impressed by his already burgeoning nationalist aspirations.

Balakirev founded the Five in about 1861, drawing into his orbit the four young composers **Borodin**, **Cui**, **Mussorgsky** and **Rimsky-Korsakov**, propelling them on their nationalistic course by the force of his often irascible personality. In 1862 he founded a free music school, promoting the Five's music there, as well as works by **Lyadov** and **Glazunov**. He assiduously collected folk-songs and edited and produced the operas of Glinka. He suffered a nervous breakdown in 1871 and did not return to music until 1876. From 1883 to 1895 he was director of the Russian Imperial Choir, and devoted his last years to composition, completing or revising earlier pieces and producing a number of new ones, including his two symphonies.

Balakirev also wrote three overtures, based respectively on Spanish, Russian and Czech themes, and two symphonic poems. He is perhaps best known for his piano music, which includes the brilliant virtuoso piece *Islamey*, an Oriental fantasy, and for his songs. Balakirev's own music, however, is overshadowed by his strenuous championship of his country's indigenous talent, as represented by the Five and their friends.

balalaika Russian stringed instrument played like a guitar; it has a triangular body and usually three strings. It is played as a solo instrument and also in ensembles.

Balassa, Sandor (1935-) Hungarian composer who studied at Budapest Conservatoire with Szervansky. He then became a radio producer. His style is freely **serial**, using the **twelve-note** system. His works include *Iris* (1971); *Requiem for Lajos Kassak*; *Intermezzo* for flute and orchestra; *The Daydreamer's Diary*; *Lupercalia*; *Tabulae*; and a trio for violin, viola and harp. There is also some fine choral music (*Summer Night*; *Motet*).

Balfe, Michael William (1808-1870) Irish composer, singer and violinist. He began learning the violin and composing at an early age and, on the death of his father in 1823, was sent to London to study music. He studied composition and made his professional début as a singer in a performance of Weber's opera *Der Freischütz* in Norwich. He went to Paris, where after meeting Rossini he sang Figaro in *Il barbiere di Siviglia* (1827). After singing throughout Italy (including performances at La Scala, Milan), he played the role of Papageno in the first English production of Mozart's opera *Die Zauberflöte* (1838).

In addition to his highly successful career as a singer, he established his reputation as the foremost operatic composer in Britain. His compositions were all received well in London, but it was the production of his opera *The Bohemian Girl* in 1843 that brought critical recognition. This work, which was to be performed throughout Europe, demonstrates his synthesis of the continental operatic style and the contemporary British Victorian fashion for **ballad**.

Balfe's works include 29 operas, a ballet, choral works, songs, chamber music and three books of studies for singers.

ballabile (It.) Suitable for dancing. Sometimes used - for example by Verdi in *Aïda* - to describe balletic interludes in opera. The term also appears as the title of a piano piece by **Chabrier**.

ballad Word originating in dance terminology, but which lost its dance connotation as early as the 13th century, coming to mean a stylized form of solo song. It is the most characteristic of English folk-song types, consisting of a number of stanzas in which a story is told, the singer being a dispassionate narrator who takes no active part in the tale. Many have a **refrain**, although its presence does not define the ballad form. In non-literate societies the ballad serves to formalize and preserve historical tradition and mythological material, e.g. the *Oceanic Ballads*.

Much of the repertory of ballad singers in England was collected by Francis Child in the latter part of the 18th century and this collection has become the central body of songs used by today's performers.

ballad opera A popular form of opera developed in England in the 18th century, with spoken dialogue, and music often derived from folk-songs, or parodied from popular operatic arias. A notable example is John Gay's *The Beggar's Opera* (1728).

ballata (It.) Dance-song. Usually refers to an important poetic and musical form of the Italian *trecento*. The standard poetic form consists of a refrain (*ripresa*), two *piedi*, a *volta* and a repeat of the refrain. In music there are two sections: for the refrain and the first verse. The remainder of the text, usually aphoristic and concerned with courtly love, is fitted to these. The most celebrated composer of *ballate* is Francesco **Landini** (*c.*1325-97).

ballet Stylized and strictly disciplined form of dance which evolved from the danced interludes of plays and operas in Italy and France in the late 16th and the 17th centuries. The court of Louis XIV (1643-1715) nurtured the new art-form, with the king himself taking a prominent part (until 1670) in the performance of masques and plays, the music for which was generally supplied by **Lully**. Schools of dancing were founded in France (1661), and later in Russia (1738) following the reign of Peter the Great, whose admiration for French and Italian culture had profoundly affected the artistic development of his own country.

In the 18th century the severe formality of balletic performances was relaxed to some extent when costume became lighter and less restricting. La Camargo, the first famous ballerina, added leaping and jumping steps to the repertory, and Gaetano Vestris exhibited a virtuoso technique. Ballet progressed to a new level with Marie Taglioni (1804-84), who was the first dancer to exploit movement *en pointe*, and whose dancing was the embodiment of the ethereal Romantic style. *La Sylphide*, devised for her, was the first Romantic ballet; it is in the repertory of many companies today, including the Royal Danish Ballet and the Kirov, as is *Giselle*, the supreme ballet of the genre, created for Carlotta Grisi to music by Adolphe **Adam**.

The Russian tradition developed uninterrupted in St Petersburg and, from the 1770s, in Moscow, where the forerunner of the Bolshoi Ballet was founded. The French court style became gradually imbued with elements of folk-dancing; the resulting fusion was wonderfully vital and expressive, with full, sweeping movements and eloquent gestures. The French choreographer Marius Petipa (1822-1910) was responsible for maintaining the high standards of the Imperial School at the Maryinsky Theatre in St Petersburg (now the Kirov), as well as for the creation of three enduring classic works, all to music by Tchaikovsky: *Swan Lake*, *The Sleeping Beauty* and *The Nutcracker*.

In the early 20th century, faced with the traditionalists' unwillingness to embrace new ideas, the impresario Serge **Diaghilev** gathered a group of dancers, choreographers, composers and artists and in 1909 took this company, the Ballets Russes, to Paris and London. At the same time Anna Pavlova also took a company to the West. Each company scored a sensational success. Michel Fokine and others created such works as *The Firebird*, *The Rite of Spring*, *Petrushka*, *Les Sylphides* and *Schéhérazade*; the sets and costumes were designed by Benois, Bakst and Picasso among others, and the composers included **Stravinsky** and **Falla**. Diaghilev's company remained in France after the Russian Revolution and launched a new era in ballet history.

The first British company, the Vic-Wells, was founded in the 1930s by Ninette de Valois; it became the Sadler's Wells Company and then the Royal Ballet in Covent Garden. It fostered such talents as Alicia Markova, Anton Dolin, Margot Fonteyn, Michael Somes, and Frederick Ashton, who developed into one of the outstanding choreographers of the century (*Cinderella*, *Symphonic Variations*). In America the strictly classical form of ballet was expanded to embrace the modern dance ideas of Isadora Duncan, Martha Graham and Ruth St Denis. At the same time the Russian-born choreographer George Balanchine was creating an amalgam of American athleticism with Russian classical style at the New York City Ballet.

The Bolshoi Ballet of Moscow reached a peak of excellence in the 1950s and 1960s, when its most unforgettable production was Prokofiev's *Romeo and Juliet* with Galina Ulanova. The Kirov's style and technique are still regarded by many as unsurpassed, but there are exciting and superbly trained dancers in a wide range of fine companies all over the world. Both classical and modern ballet continue to grow in popularity and new creative talent is constantly coming to the fore in the world of ballet.

ballo (It.) Dance, a term used for centuries, in Italy and elsewhere, to denote a social dance or ball at any level of society. It has also been used, particularly in the 16th century, to denote a dance tune.

In the 15th century the word acquired a more specific, technical meaning, denoting a courtly dance choreographed by a dancing master; Domenico da Piacenzo, Antonio Cornazano and Gulielmo Ebreo da Pesaro each left descriptions of steps with music.

In the late 16th century the *ballo* often formed part of an *intermedio* or play. Fabrito Caroso and Cesareo Negri published steps and music for *balli* from this time, and **Monteverdi**'s *Ballo delle Ingrate* includes dance.

Baltsa, Agnes (1944-) Greek operatic mezzo-soprano. She studied in Athens, Munich, and then in Frankfurt, where she made her début in 1968 as Cherubino in Mozart's *Le nozze di Figaro*. She sang with several German companies, including the Deutsche Oper, Berlin, and made her London début in 1976. She has sung the leading mezzo roles in Vienna, Salzburg, London, and the United States. An exciting singer and performer with a flexible voice and at times steely timbre, she has been admired as Carmen and as Rosina in Rossini's *Il barbiere di Siviglia*.

balungan (Java) Skeleton-melody (*balung* means bone), the principal melody upon which the instruments of the **gamelan** orchestra elaborate, somewhat similar in concept to the Western **cantus firmus**. The *balungan* is the only notated melodic element in Javanese music. It is played in its exact form by the **saron** or **slentem** metallophone instruments, while other melodic instruments of the ensemble provide elaborated versions.

bamboo pipe Indigenous wind instruments of South-East Asia are commonly made of bamboo for ecological reasons, so the term has a wide application.

The most famous wind ensemble of South-East Asia consists of a group of **khaen**, the Thai or Laotian mouth-organ made of several bamboo pipes, related to the *sgeng* of ancient China and the *sho* of Japanese court orchestras.

The most famous legend concerning the origin of Chinese music recounts the tale of Ling Lun, sent to the western mountains to fetch bamboo pipes from which the fundamental pitches of Chinese music could be derived. The length of the imperial pitch pipes was traditionally calculated by court musicians and astrologers so that the tones resonated with the extra-musical forces of the universe. The first pipe produces the yellow bell tone, and from there the system is cyclic, working on overblown fifths.

Panpipes are also generally made of bamboo.

Banchieri, Adriano (1568-1634) Italian composer and theorist. He was one of the pioneers of basso **continuo**; his *Concerti Ecclesiastici* (1598) is one of the first publications to include a separate bass part for a continuo player, and his *L'organo suonarino* (Op.13, 1605) contains valuable instructions on realizing a bass part and provides bass lines for liturgical chants. He published 12 extant Masses and much sacred music, 12 volumes of secular music and three of instrumental. He was the founder of the Academia dei Floridi.

band Group of musicians who play together regularly. The ensemble may be of various combinations of instruments, but most commonly the word is associated with groups of brass or wind players and with military instruments, although its use has more recently come to be associated with traditional jazz line-ups (clarinet, trumpet, trombone, banjo, double-bass, drums) and pop groups using a standard format of drums, bass, one or two guitars and vocalist.

Bandora

bandora Large stringed instrument invented in England by John Rose in 1562 and used by such composers as **Ferrabosco** and **Morley**. The bandora was one of the six instruments necessary to form a **consort** of viols and was very important in music circles in England during the 16th and early 17th centuries. It was used as a **continuo** instrument (playing the **bass** line) and had 14 strings tuned in pairs. It is characterized by its scalloped and fluted decorative outline. An alternative spelling is pandora.

bandurría (Sp.) Twelve-stringed fretted instrument of Spanish origin used predominantly in folk-music. The strings are tuned in pairs so that each set of two strings plays identical notes. It is a hybrid of the **guitar** and **cittern** families and has a small body, short neck and very large peg-holder.

Banister, John (*c.*1625-1679) English violinist and composer, chiefly remembered for his promotion of the first series of concerts in London open to the public on payment of an admission fee (1662-9). He wrote incidental music for the theatre, played in the King's Musick and later led the Royal Band of 24 violins. His son, John Banister (*d.c.*1725), was also a violinist whose works include *The Compleat Tutor to the Violin* (1698).

banjo Afro-American stringed instrument of European derivation. It consists of a long neck and a body in the form of an open drum, spanned with parchment as a

Banjo

resonator. It usually has five strings; the highest of these is called the thumb-string and is shorter than the other four, starting at the fifth fret. It is most commonly used to accompany **blues** singing and in bluegrass and country music.

Banks, Donald (1923-1980) Australian composer who worked in London during the 1950s and 1960s, writing music for film and theatre and promoting concerts of contemporary music. He studied with Mátyás **Seiber** and **Dallapiccola** and was influenced by Milton **Babbitt**. His works include orchestral pieces, concertos for horn (1965) and violin (1968) and various chamber pieces for diverse ensembles, such as a string quartet (1975).

Bantock, Sir Granville (1868-1946) English composer who after training as a chemical engineer studied at the Royal Academy of Music in 1889. He began conducting with a touring theatre company, and later became music director of the New Brighton Tower Pleasure Gardens. He was appointed Principal of the Birmingham School of Music in 1900 and Professor at Birmingham University in 1908. A prolific composer of music in many forms, he was outstanding in his expert handling of large orchestras and choral music. His overture *Pierrot of the Minute* and his tone poem *Fifine at the Fair* are occasionally heard today. His part-songs and solo songs are favourites with amateur choirs and soloists, but his major choral works such as *Atalanta in Corydon* (1912) and the huge three-part setting of *Omar Khayyam* (1906-9) have fallen out of the repertory.

Barber, Samuel (1910-1981) American composer and musician. Best-known for his *Adagio for Strings*, extracted from his String Quartet of 1936, and for his setting of Matthew Arnold's *Dover Beach* for baritone and string quartet, he is firmly placed within a tradition that is both Romantic and European. A graduate of the Curtis Institute, Philadelphia, he won a Pulitzer scholarship in 1935 and the American Academy's Prix de Rome in 1936. His music early came to the attention of **Toscanini**, and premières of his orchestral works were given by such conductors as **Koussevitzky**, **Walter** and **Ormandy**. His opera *Vanessa* was given at the New York Metropolitan in 1958, and another opera, *Antony and Cleopatra*, opened the new Metropolitan at the Lincoln Center in 1966. In the post-war era Barber was regarded as a conservative and neglected, but since his death his music has been recognized for its warmth and rich melodic expression.

barber shop Form of part singing, either solo or choral, usually for male voices, which developed in the United States in the early years of the 20th century, and is now performed with great enthusiasm by amateur groups all over the world. There are usually four parts: the melodic line is in the second part, with the top line a form of descant above it. The style is sentimental, parodistic and theatrical.

Barbieri, Francisco (1823-1894) Spanish composer. After studying at the Madrid Conservatoire he devoted himself to the composition of theatrical music, and although a lover of Italian opera was more successful as a composer of **zarzuelas**. He wrote more than 60 pieces in this genre, many of which are still popular in Spain today. Barbieri also had a passionate interest in the history of Spanish music, acquiring a rich musical library during his lifetime and founding the periodical *La España musical*. He was the first musician to be received into the Royal Spanish Academy.

Barbirolli, Sir John (1899-1970) British conductor, born Giovanni Battista Barbirolli to Italian and French parents. He studied cello at the Trinity College of Music and the Royal Academy of Music in London. He made his début as a cello soloist at the age of 12 and joined the

Sir John Barbirolli

Queen's Hall orchestra five years later. After brief army service in World War I he took up a career as a freelance cellist and string quartet player. In 1924 he founded his own string orchestra and became its conductor. From 1926 to 1943 he held conducting posts with the British National Opera Company and the Covent Garden English Opera Company, the Scottish Orchestra (in Glasgow), and the New York Philharmonic Orchestra. In 1943 he was appointed conductor of the **Hallé Orchestra** in Manchester, retaining the post until his death. From 1961 to 1967 he was also principal conductor of the Houston Symphony Orchestra and performed with many internationally famous orchestras throughout the world. Barbirolli was particularly noted as an interpreter of Elgar and Vaughan Williams, Mahler, Sibelius and Puccini. In 1939 he married the oboist Evelyn **Rothwell**, his second wife.

barcarola (It.), **barcarolle** (Fr.) Song in 6/8 or 12/8 time, sung by Venetian gondoliers with an accompaniment suggesting the rocking of a boat. *Barcarole* are found in opera, for example Offenbach's *Les contes d'Hoffmann*, and also as instrumental pieces, such as in Mendelssohn's *Songs Without Words*.

Bardi, Giovanni de, Count of Vernio (1534-1612) Italian amateur composer and patron of the arts. He was host to the Florentine **Camerata**, a group of musicians, poets, playwrights, astronomers and noblemen, among whom the first experiments in dramatic **monody** and **recitative** took place. He helped in the creation of the Florentine *intermedii* of 1583, 1584 and 1586 and conceived the theme for the most lavish of them all, that of 1589, for which he composed the madrigal *Miseri habitator del ciel'averno*.

Barenboim, Daniel (1942-) Israeli conductor and pianist. He studied at the S. Cecilia Academy in Rome and with Edwin Fischer and Nadia **Boulanger**. He made his concert début as a pianist in Paris in 1955 and has since performed extensively, including several recital series of the complete Beethoven piano sonatas. In 1967 he married the English cellist Jacqueline **du Pré** and settled in England. He has worked as a conductor for many major orchestras, his début in this capacity being with the English Chamber Orchestra in 1966. He has also worked with the Berlin Philharmonic Orchestra (1969), the New York Philharmonic Orchestra (1970) and L'Orchestre de Paris (from 1975). His opera début was at the Edinburgh Festival (*Don Giovanni*, 1973). In 1989 he was appointed music director of the Chicago Symphony Orchestra.

baritone Male voice with a range lying between those of the **bass** and **tenor**. The usual **compass** is from A to F′. The term was used as early as the 15th century, but the baritone voice was not highly regarded until the late 18th century, when **Mozart** made prominent use of it in his operas *Don Giovanni* and *Le nozze di Figaro*.

Barnby, Sir Joseph (1838-1896) English church musician and an important figure in

Victorian church music. He held many posts as organist and choirmaster in London and York. Apart from his enthusiastic conducting of oratorios, Barnby gave the English première of **Wagner**'s *Parsifal*. His own music reflects the influence of **Gounod**, and several of his hymns and chants are still frequently performed.

barn dance Social gathering which centres on traditional country dances mostly of English or American origin. Most of the dances involve a 'set' of couples arranged either lengthways or in a square. Accompanied by a band of musicians, invariably including an accordionist and fiddler, the dancers go through steps as instructed by a caller who shouts or sings directions and figures.

Barnett, John (1802-1890) English singer and composer, mainly of theatre music. He was critically acclaimed in his day and learned much from his work at the English Opera House where he directed operas by foreign composers. Weber in particular influenced his style, and he mastered the art of supernatural and 'fairy' choral scenes in the style of Weber's *Oberon*. Some of his songs were popular in Victorian times.

Baroque Term borrowed from art and architecture, and applied to music displaying certain characteristics between the approximate dates of 1580 and 1750. In music, as in the other arts, the term refers to a 'style-period' whose features are an increased dramatic and emotional content, and a love of spectacular effects. The term implies 'bizarre' but there are formal as well as emotional effects in Baroque music.

Early Baroque music began with the experiments of the Florentine **Camerata** in setting poetry in a 'representative' way – making the voice contain, rather than describe, emotion with ejaculatory words such as *Ahi!* or *Ohimè* ('alas'). **Monteverdi** developed this style into opera, and also used the polychoral effects developed by the **Gabrielis** at St Mark's in Venice.

In France, **Lully** was a prolific writer of ballets and operas, and the French Baroque developed its own more classical style, based on set dance forms and overtures, and an elaborate but prescribed ornamentation, giving no scope for the emotional 'free' embellishments of the Italians.

England and Germany followed these models, adding some of their inherent traditions. The high Baroque, following in the wake of **Corelli**'s development of the **concerto**, fused the various national styles, with **J.S. Bach** and **Handel** in the forefront, absorbing and giving refined expression to every style in the Baroque idiom. Other important composers of the period were **Purcell**, **Vivaldi**, D. **Scarlatti**, **Rameau** and **Couperin**.

Barraqué, Jean (1928-1973) French composer who studied at the Paris Conservatoire with **Messiaen** and **Langlais**. His compositions include a piano sonata and *Sequence*, both of which are large-scale works using advanced **serialism**; *Song after Song* for six percussionists, voice and piano; a concerto for clarinet and vibraphone and six instrumental ensembles. In 1956 he started work on soundscapes on the novel *The Death of Virgil* by Hermann Broch but completed only three parts before his death. He also published articles and a book on Debussy (1962).

Barraud, Henry (1900-) French composer and critic. He studied with **Dukas** and Caussade at the Paris Conservatoire but was expelled from the institution after writing a string quartet (now lost), considered to be outrageously innovative. His works include three symphonies, a piano concerto, and vocal music including *Le testament de François Villon* and *La divine comédie*.

barré (Fr.) Barred; in lute and guitar playing, the stopping of all the strings at the same position with the forefinger. See **capo tasto**.

barrel organ Mechanical instrument based upon the principle of the barrel and pin mechanism. The barrel organ achieved popularity in England in the 18th century and was used by street musicians and in churches. It is a small organ connected with an arrangement of interchangeable barrels, each containing a number of popular tunes.

Barsanti, Francisco (1690-1772) Italian composer. He began as a scientist, but then played various orchestral instruments. He went to London in 1714, where he played in the orchestra of the opera, and then moved to Scotland, where he married. He returned to London in 1743, but was unable to regain his former success, although he was again employed in an orchestra.

In Scotland he arranged numerous Scottish songs, and composed a number of *concerti grossi* which are considered very fine, as well as some excellent recorder sonatas. On his return to London he composed a number of motets. His most creative and successful period was undoubtedly that spent in Scotland.

Barstow, Josephine (1940-) English soprano. She studied at Birmingham and at the London Opera Centre. Her début was at Sadler's Wells in 1967 as Cherubino in Mozart's *Le nozze di Figaro*. Her first leading role was in Tippett's *The Knot Garden* (1970). She specializes in strongly dramatic roles in which her acting ability and powerful, flexible voice are given full rein: Emilia Marty in Janáček's *The Makropoulos Case*; Violetta in Verdi's *La traviata*; Salome (Strauss) and Lady Macbeth (Verdi). She has sung regularly with the English National Opera and the Royal Opera House and has appeared at most of the major opera houses in the world. In 1986 she created the role of Benigna in **Penderecki**'s *Die schwarze Maske* at Salzburg. In 1989 she sang Amelia in **Karajan**'s last recording, Verdi's *Un ballo in maschera*.

Bartholomée, Pierre (1937-) Belgian composer and conductor who embarked on his musical career as a piano virtuoso. He began conducting when he founded the Groupe musiques nouvelles in Brussels in 1962, a group committed to promoting contemporary music in Belgium and elsewhere. His own compositions show a preoccupation with Baroque instrumentation and break new ground in the harmonic possibilities of Western music. Both of these concerns are explicit in his work *Tombeau de Main Morais* in which the octave is divided into 21 rather than the usual 12 divisions.

Bartók, Béla (1881-1945) Hungarian composer, pianist and collector of folk-music, arguably the greatest composer and musician of his nation. He studied in Bratislava and at the Royal Academy of Music, Budapest. Here he cultivated a growing nationalism along with a fondness for the music of Richard Strauss, Wagner, Liszt and even Brahms. His first major work, the tone poem *Kossuth* (1903), was a nationalistic piece inspired by the Hungarian hero of the 1848 Revolution.

Béla Bartók

Bartók toured abroad as a concert pianist of great virtuosity, but in 1905 he began a lifelong interest in Hungarian folk-music and started a systematic song collection, often collaborating with his friend Zoltán **Kodály**. Over the years, Bartók made many folk-song collecting tours in eastern Europe and in Turkey and Arabia.

In 1907, Bartók and Kodály joined the staff of the Royal Academy of Music in Budapest, Bartók as a piano teacher. Despite much opposition and hostility, the two set about revitalizing the musical life of Hungary. Bartók's own music was showing new influences, namely **Debussy** and **Stravinsky**. In 1909 the first of his six string quartets was written, and two years later he completed his opera *Duke Bluebeard's Castle*, a highly symbolic work in which he successfully married his music to the special phonetic needs of the Hungarian language. In 1917 a successful performance of his ballet *The Wooden Prince* (1914-17) led to the staging of *Duke Bluebeard's Castle* in 1918. It was followed by performances of his pantomime-ballet *The Miraculous Mandarin* (1918, subsequently censored) and his *Dance Suite* (1923). In the 1920s, Bartók resumed his interrupted career as a concert pianist. He reached maturity as a composer with the first two of his three piano concertos and his piano sonata of 1926, his six volumes of graded piano pieces, *Mikrokosmos* (1926; 1932-9), his sonata for two pianos and percussion (1937; orchestrated 1940), his impressionistic *Music for Strings, Percussion and Celesta* (1936), and his second violin concerto (1937-8). In 1934 he was commissioned by the Hungarian Academy of Sciences to prepare his folk-music collection for publication. His researches into melody variants proved invaluable and even influenced his own music.

In 1940, Bartók emigrated to the United States, where his talents as a composer and pianist went largely unrecognized. He completed only the ever-popular Concerto for Orchestra (1942-3; revised 1945) for the Koussevitzky Foundation and the Bachian sonata for unaccompanied violin, commissioned by Yehudi **Menuhin** (1944). His former pupil Tibor Sérly (1900-78) completed the finale of Bartók's third piano concerto and realized his viola concerto (commissioned by the British musician William **Primrose**) from Bartók's sketches. Bartók died of leukaemia in New York in 1945; in 1988 his body was reburied in Budapest.

Bartolozzi, Bruno (1911-1980) Italian composer who studied violin and composition at Florence and was a professional violinist from 1941 to 1965. He pioneered new techniques for woodwind instruments (described in his book *New Sounds for Woodwind*, 1967), and used these in works such as *Concertazioni* (1973). He has written orchestral, chamber, solo and accompanied vocal works, and a work for the stage, *Tutto cio che accade ti riguarda*.

baryton Brass instrument with six bowed strings popular (in varying degrees) in the 17th and 18th centuries. A number of extra strings (up to 20 or more) were placed beneath the fingerboard; some of these were exposed to allow their plucking from beneath by the player's left hand, while the others produced a drone-like effect. Its chief exponent was Joseph **Haydn**, who wrote some 175 works for his patron Prince Nicholas Esterházy, an enthusiastic amateur baryton player.

Baryton

basic set Original version of the note-row in a **serial** composition, before it is subjected to inversion, retrograde or retrograde inversion.

bass 1. The lowest category of the male human voice or instrument within a family.
2. In harmony, the lowest line of music, and the one which forms the basis of the harmonic structure. See also **Alberti bass**; **double-bass**; **figured bass**; **ground bass**.

basse (Fr.) **Bass**. *Basse de viole* means string bass (see **continuo**); *basse chiffrée* means **figured bass**.

basset clarinet Clarinet with a range extending to a major third below that of the conventional clarinet. It was invented by Anton Stadler. Mozart composed for it, and it is used for authentic performances of his Clarinet Concerto, K622, and the opera *La clemenza di Tito*.

basset-horn Clarinet in F, sounding a fourth below the standard B♭ clarinet, with a rich, even lugubrious tone. It came into use at the end of the 18th century, was used by Mozart in his *Requiem*, the operas *Die Zauberflöte* and *La clemenza di Tito*, and in certain of his pieces for wind ensemble; and by Mendelssohn in works for chamber ensemble and in his Scottish Symphony. Bernard Shaw used the name *Corno di Bassetto* as a pseudonym when he was writing music criticism at the end of the 19th century.

One form of basset-horn

bass fiddle Popular name for the string double-bass.

basso continuo See **continuo**

bassoon Large wind instrument with a conical bore, played with a double reed, which originally developed from the 16th-century dulcian. It plays the **tenor** and **bass** lines in the woodwind section of the orchestra. The 8-foot-long bore is folded in two, so that the instrument doubles back on itself. At one point there were five different sizes of bassoon in existence; now there are only two: the bassoon and the contrabassoon (which sounds an **octave** lower). Although the bassoon does have a small solo repertory, its main use has been in chamber music and in the orchestra.

Bassoon

Bate, Jennifer (1944-) English organist. She began her career in the 1960s, and has since acquired an extremely wide repertory. She has become a specialist in **Messiaen**'s works, having recorded the complete organ oeuvre in the 1980s. She gave the British première of the *Livre du Saint Sacrament*, and her 1986 prize-winning recording of it was the first. In 1985 she gave the world première of Peter **Dickinson**'s *Blue Rose Variations* in New York, a jazz/blues-based piece, and in 1990 the world première of William **Mathias**'s *Fenestra*. In the mid-1980s she designed a portable organ for the performance of Baroque music in small halls. In 1989 she won the *Personnalité de l'année* award, only the third British musician to do so.

Bateson, Thomas (*c.*1570-1630) English **madrigal** composer. His two books of madrigals follow in the tradition of **Wilbye** and **Weelkes**.

Bath Festival Annual series of concerts and other events held in the many historical and modern venues in the city of Bath. Founded in 1948, the Festival has had a number of distinguished artistic directors including Yehudi **Menuhin** (whose recordings with the Festival Chamber Orchestra achieved considerable acclaim) and Sir Michael **Tippett**, several of whose works have been premièred in Bath. Amelia Freedman became the director in 1986.

baton A short stick, usually made of wood, either plain or painted white, used for conducting. It is said to have been introduced by **Spohr** in about 1820, as a substitute for the violin bow, roll of paper or hand, which had been used hitherto. Conductors vary considerably in their choice of size and shape – some preferring cork handles, others plain wood. The skilled conductor develops a highly subtle and expressive baton technique by which he controls phrasing, accentuation and balance, as well as directing the rhythm and tempo.

Batten, Adrian (1591-1637) English composer of church music who worked at Westminster Abbey and St Paul's Cathedral as a vicar-choral, and composed services, full and voice anthems. Batten's music reflects the influence of his more famous contemporaries, Orlando **Gibbons** and Thomas **Tomkins**.

battery 1. The **percussion** section of an orchestra.

2. The act of strumming the strings of a guitar rather than plucking them.

3. The 18th-century term for an arpeggiated or **broken chord**.

4. A drum roll used as a military signal.

Battishill, Jonathan (1738-1801) English composer, organist and singer. Battishill was renowned for his extemporization and held posts at various London churches including the Chapel Royal. He was also involved in the theatre, and wrote one opera and some incidental music. As a member of the Gentlemen's Catch Club he also wrote glees and catches. His most famous anthem is *Call to Remembrance.*

Bauld, Alison (1944-) Australian composer, actress, singer and dancer, who is rapidly developing new forms and notations for music and dance. Her compositions are mostly theatrical and include *In a Dead Brown Land* for two mimes, two speakers, soprano, tenor, chorus and wind instruments, *On the Afternoon of the Pigsty* for female speaker, melodica, flutes and percussion, *One Pearl* and *I loved Miss Watson*.

Bax, Sir Arnold (1883-1953) English composer and novelist. Literary influences,

Sir Arnold Bax

especially the poetry of Yeats, were important in establishing Bax as the leading musical exponent of the so-called Celtic revival. Musical influences included Liszt, from whom he learned the art of thematic transformation, as well as the French **Impressionist** composers and English folk-song. He was an outstanding composer for the large romantic orchestra, in his seven symphonies, and in tone poems such as *Tintagel* and *The Garden of Fand*. His mastery of tone-colour and melody evoked a rich poetic atmosphere. His music for solo voice, chorus and piano has kept a small, but firm place in the repertory.

bāyān/bhāyān (India) Hemispherical metal drum. It is the larger, left-hand drum of the **tablā** pair.

Bayle, François (1932-) French composer who studied with **Stockhausen** and **Messiaen**. His early works are scored for conventional instruments but later he turned to the medium of tape, producing works either entirely created in the studio or for live musicians with tape. Examples of his work are *Espaces inhabitables*, a juxtaposition of natural and synthesized sounds, *Jeita*, a sequence of short pieces using sound recordings made in a Lebanese cave and *L'expérience acoustique*. The latter is a ten-hour projection intended to be a summary of the composer's ideas about sound and its effect on the listener.

Bayreuth Town in southern Germany, known principally for Richard **Wagner**'s Festival Theatre. Wagner chose the site himself for its central situation and peaceful surroundings. His attempts to raise money for the building were disappointing and he had to work on a much lower budget than he had anticipated. Nevertheless, the interior of the building was designed to satisfy the composer's theatrical ideals and was based on the classical Greek amphitheatre. A unique feature is the hood that surrounds the deep orchestra pit, which has the acoustical effect of throwing the sound on to the stage to blend with the vocal sound before being projected past the proscenium. The acoustics are so fine that the building, intended to be temporary, is now zealously preserved.

Regular Wagner festivals have been held at Bayreuth since 1876, when the *Ring* cycle was first performed in its entirety with the financial aid of Wagner's patron King Ludwig II of Bavaria. The annual festivals were staged by Wagner's descendants until 1973, when the Richard Wagner Foundation Bayreuth took over the administrative duties. Tickets are notoriously difficult to obtain and the Bayreuth Festival enjoys an almost cult-like popularity.

Bazzini, Antonio (1818-1897) Italian violinist, composer and teacher. His career as a professional violinist, encouraged by

Festspielhaus, Bayreuth

Paganini, proved highly successful. He worked in Germany, Denmark, Spain, the Netherlands and France, before finally settling in Brescia in Italy to devote himself to composition and teaching. Despite an attempt at writing an opera, Bazzini was most significant in Italy for his non-operatic compositions and is chiefly remembered for his chamber music. While working at the Milan Conservatoire, where he was appointed director in 1882, Bazzini taught **Catalani**, **Mascagni** and Puccini, among others.

BBC British Broadcasting Corporation (from 1927), originally the British Broadcasting Company.

The BBC was founded in 1922 and funded originally by the manufacturers of wireless receiving sets and later by licence fees from the public. From the first, music was a notable feature of its programmes, which brought high-quality performances to the ears of a large new audience. Solo recitals, chamber music and small orchestras were broadcast at first from studios in London, and later from regional centres. In 1923, a relay from Covent Garden Opera House was successfully broadcast, and with the advance of technology, performances were regularly relayed from concert halls and opera houses, in Britain and abroad.

Despite initial opposition from some sections of the music profession, public concerts were first sponsored in 1924. In 1927 the BBC took over the running of the Promenade Concerts, founded by Sir Henry **Wood** and still bearing his name. In 1930 the BBC Symphony Orchestra was founded under the direction of Adrian **Boult**. With some of the best players in the country, adequate rehearsal time and a secure financial basis, a new era of orchestral performance was inaugurated, with star guest conductors such as **Mengelberg**, **Walter** and **Toscanini**. Under the guidance of Edward Clark, the BBC led the world in the promotion of contemporary music, with many commissions of new works. Other orchestras were later established in Glasgow, Cardiff, Manchester, Birmingham, Belfast and Bristol. Opera, musical comedy and light music were catered for by the BBC Theatre Orchestra, for many years under the direction of Stanford Robinson. The BBC Military Band was directed by B. Walton O'Donnell, and the BBC Variety Orchestra provided music for many highly popular comedy shows. Choral music was given by the professional BBC Singers and chorus, and the amateur BBC Choral Society, all under the direction of Leslie Woodgate. In fulfilling its charter obligation to inform and educate as well as entertain, the BBC broadcast talks, interviews and discussions, and made music an important and influential part of schools programmes.

When television was inaugurated in 1936, the BBC soon introduced recitals, concerts and opera, though this fledgling service was closed down with the outbreak of the war in 1939. In wartime, the BBC maintained and extended its music broadcasts, with the Symphony Orchestra evacuated first to Bristol and later to Bedford. After the war, the most important development was the establishment of the Third Programme in 1946, which, for approximately six hours each evening, broadcast programmes of the highest quality, with a substantial proportion of music, although more popular concerts were still broadcast on the Home Service (later Radio 4) and the Light Programme (Radio 2). In 1965 the Music Programme, later Radio 3, extended specialist music broadcasting to about 12 hours a day, and under the direction of William **Glock** (1959-73) offered a brilliant, but often controversial, expansion of contemporary music, with many commissions of new works. Popular music is broadcast on Radios 1 and 2; Radio 4 concentrates on speech, broadcasting current affairs programmes, plays, serials and occasional music documentary programmes. BBC television gave a new dimension to music broadcasts, with studio concerts and operas, as well as relays from concert halls and opera houses. The music documentary, on film and in the studio, presented a new and highly influential aspect of television. The sale of BBC recordings on disc and videotape offers another aspect of its service to the public. Without question, the BBC was the single most powerful influence in the transformation of Britain from what was once described as 'the land without music' to what is now acknowledged as one of the most musically vital nations in the world.

Beach, Amy Marcy (1867-1944) American pianist and composer who studied the piano with Pedrabo and Baermann. She was largely self-taught in composition and her *Gaelic Symphony* was the first symphony to be composed by an American woman.

Beale, William (1784-1854) English organist and composer who began his musical career as a chorister at Westminster Abbey and was later the organist at Trinity College, Cambridge. His compositions are mainly madrigals and glees, the best known of which are *Awake Sweet Muse* and *Come Let us Join the Roundelay*.

beat 1. The basic pulse in a composition, and thus the temporal unit (see **tempo**). It also refers to the movements of a conductor's hand as he indicates this pulse. In fast tempos (say a fast 2/2 or 3/4) there may be only one beat to a bar; in slow tempos (say a slow 6/8) the beats may be subdivided into smaller units.

2. Used in 17th-century English music for a type of **ornament**: either a lower **appoggiatura** or an inverted **trill**.

beating-reed instruments Instruments in which the sound is produced by a fixed reed 'beating' (vibrating against) the main body of the instrument. The **clarinet**, **saxophone** and certain types of organ pipe are beating-reed instruments.

beats Acoustical phenomenon produced when two notes almost identical in **pitch** are sounded together. The interference of the sound waves causes the sound to vary slightly in volume at regular intervals. The number of the beats per second is the same as the difference in **frequency** (expressed in hertz) between the two notes. The beats disappear altogether when the notes are in perfect **unison**; they are thus useful for tuning instruments. Slow beats (2-4 per second) are not unpleasant to the ear and are deliberately used in certain organ stops (*voix céleste*, *unda maris*) by using two slightly out-of-tune pipes, to give an undulating effect.

Bebung (Ger.) **Vibrato** effect unique to the **clavichord**, obtained by alternately increasing and decreasing the pressure of the finger on the key. This technique was used in the 18th century and is notated by a **slur** and dots written above the note to which it is applied.

Bechstein, Karl (1826-1900) Founder of the firm of piano-makers whose instruments are considered to be among the finest in the world. His first instrument was produced in 1859, and the firm was established in 1863. After 1870 the firm adopted the Steiner model, with an iron frame and overstringing. Today the firm offers a wide selection of instruments, both upright and grand, still based on the original range produced when it was founded.

Beck, Conrad (1901-) Swiss composer who began as a mechanic before going to Zurich Conservatoire. He went to Paris to study, and stayed there nearly ten years (until 1932). He associated with **Roussel** and **Honegger**, and worked with Nadia **Boulanger**. In 1932 he moved to Basle, where he later became director of music for the radio. His music includes a choral work, *Oratorium* (1934); a play with music, *St Jacob an der Birs* (1944); a ballet, *The Great Bear* (1936); five symphonies, four string quartets, a piano and two violin concertos, fantasies, and chamber works.

Beck, Franz (1734-1809) German violinist and composer. In 1777 he moved to Paris and then to Bordeaux, becoming a concertmaster there in 1780. Among his works are 24 symphonies, a number of string quartets and piano sonatas, various church music and three operas.

Becker, John Joseph (1886-1961) American composer who was one of a group of avant-garde musicians calling themselves the American Five. The other composers involved were **Ives, Ruggles, Cowell** and **Riegger**. Becker's compositional style is characterized by clear orchestration and his use of **atonal** counterpoint and polyrhythmic patterns; while other composers were turning to **neo-classicism** and folk sources, Becker searched for new resources and techniques. Among his works are *Abongo* (1933) for large percussion ensemble; *Soundpieces*, chamber pieces for diverse instrumental ensembles, and a number of stage works in which he attempted to fuse mediums of mime, dance, stage design and music (for example, *A Marriage with Space*, 1935).

Beckwith, John (1927-) Canadian composer whose work explores the possibilities of collage treatment of text, music and theatre, drawing on the folk idioms of his environment (southern Ontario). His compositions include poetic documentaries using spoken and sung words and instrumental sound patterns - for example, *Twelve Letters to a Small Town* (1961), *Jonah*, a large choral work, and *Circle with Tangents* (1967) for harpsichord and solo strings.

Bedford, David (1937-) British composer and teacher. He studied at the Royal Academy of Music and also with Luigi **Nono**. A former member of the pop group The Whole World, Bedford makes much use in his work of electric guitar, amplified piano, and other electronic instruments. His compositions range from music theatre for schools, such as his Norse trilogy *Indiof's Saga*, *The Death of Baldur* and *The Ragnarök* (1979-82), to unaccompanied choruses, such as his setting of Dowson's *The Golden Wine is Drunk*. Many are scored for unusual instrumental combinations with and without voices and carry whimsical titles. Examples include *Star Clusters, Nebulae and Places in Devon* (1971), for chorus and orchestra; *Maple Syrup and Bacon and the TV Weatherman* (1973), for brass quintet; and *SPN/M Birthday Piece* (1983), for string quartet.

Bedford, Herbert (1867-1945) English composer. His music explored the resources of unaccompanied song and of the military band as media for serious musical composition. He wrote a great deal of vocal music, both with and without accompaniment, orchestral works and compositions for **brass band**, examples of his work being *Three Roundels*, *Over the Hill* and *Kit Marlowe* (1897), an opera.

Beecham, Sir Thomas (1879-1961) British conductor who played a major part in the development of musical life in Britain for much of the 20th century. He made his début at the age of 20, conducting a concert in his native town of St Helens, financed by his father Sir Joseph Beecham, who made a fortune in

Sir Thomas Beecham

selling pills. Beecham's first intention was to become a composer, but his great talent as a conductor soon determined the course of his career. With the help of his family's wealth he established his own orchestra in London, and, an entirely new idea, a large wind orchestra with which he toured the country. He soon turned to opera and in 1910 mounted a season at Covent Garden, including the first British performance of Strauss's *Elektra*. This was the first of many ventures into opera, where he spent and lost considerable sums of his father's or his own money.

In 1915 he was knighted for his services to music, although he also inherited his father's baronetcy. In 1932 he founded the **London Philharmonic Orchestra,** giving concerts and making recordings of a very high standard. During World War II, he spent much of his time in the United States, where he became music director of the Seattle Symphony Orchestra. In 1947 he founded the **Royal Philharmonic Orchestra,** and added to his enormous corpus of recordings with outstanding performances of the music that he favoured: Mozart, Haydn, Richard Strauss, **Bizet, Delius** and a number of composers from whom he took his famous 'lollipops' – encore pieces of great charm by **Massenet, Gounod**, or Tchaikovsky.

The secret of his poetic and engaging style was in the meticulous preparation of the orchestral parts, which he marked in great detail. This approach transformed the music of Delius, which might have fallen into oblivion without his magic touch. His conducting technique was original and often diverting to watch, but worked musical miracles. Less interested in structure or the profundities of the German symphony after Haydn, he once complained of the length of the *Eroica Symphony* of Beethoven, and caused great offence early in his career by cutting 20 minutes from Elgar's Symphony No.1. His wit was legendary and Beecham stories are still related in the profession. His numerous recordings fortunately preserve the inimitable style of this remarkable conductor.

Beeson, Jack Hamilton (1921-)
American composer whose main preoccupation is with opera, his librettos shaped from United States life and literature. After attending the Eastman School of Music he studied composition with Bartók. Examples of his operatic works are *Jonah* (1950), *Hello Out There* (1957), *New York City Opera* (1965) and *Kansas City* (1975). He also wrote for the orchestra (*Transformations*), for instrumental ensembles and for voices.

Beethoven, Ludwig van (1770-1827)
German composer who bridged the gap between classical and Romantic styles in the early 19th century, transforming every musical genre in which he worked and extending the technical and expressive powers of music beyond measure.

Born in Bonn, he moved to Vienna in 1792, where he studied for a time with Haydn. This was not a success: although the two respected each other there was no real understanding between them. Beethoven was soon able to establish a brilliant career as a pianist, and was much in demand for performances at the houses of wealthy and aristocratic patrons. He was also turning out numerous compositions in all genres during this period: between 1795 and about 1802 he produced the first three of his five piano concertos, the first two symphonies, piano trios, string quartets and the majority of his 32 piano sonatas, including the *Moonlight* (Op.27 No.2) and the *Pathétique* (Op.13): all of this in a continuation of the style of Haydn and Mozart.

By 1802 it became obvious to Beethoven that he was facing the onset of deafness. For a composer of his already proven stature this was not an insurmountable problem – he was able to compose his music in his head and simply 'copy' it from there. For the virtuoso pianist, however, it could not have been worse. He foresaw the end of his career and income, and a severe depression settled on him. From this time dates the Heiligenstadt Testament, a kind of farewell letter, explaining his state of mind.

Ludwig van Beethoven

His strength of character, however, and possibly the realization that greater things were yet to come, enabled him to overcome his depression, and his new determination was given expression in the works he now produced: between 1802 and 1812, the middle or 'heroic' period, there were five symphonies, a group of piano sonatas, the Violin Concerto, the Razumovsky string quartets, and the first version of his only opera. The symphonies reveal an astonishing development in form, with the *Eroica*, No.3, revolutionary in its scope and dimension. It was first intended to be dedicated to Napoleon, but Beethoven angrily ripped off the dedication when he heard that Napoleon had made himself Emperor. Other symphonies such as

Symphony No.5, with its 'Fate knocking' motif in the first movement and joyful, triumphant conclusion, and the programmatic *Pastoral*, No.6, a work of great lyricism which expresses the composer's deep love of the countryside, also carry symphonic form to a new stage. The piano sonatas include the brilliant *Waldstein* (Op.53), the *Appassionata* (Op.57), aptly named, and the elegiac Op.81a, *Les adieux*. The opera, *Fidelio*, also has a noble theme: the heroine, Leonore, rescues her beloved husband from certain death at great risk to herself. It was poorly received at its first performance in 1805, and Beethoven revised it twice, writing a new overture each time (the *Leonora* overtures Nos.1, 2 and 3). Eventually it scored a deserved triumph in 1814. The subtitle, 'Wifely Love', expresses something of the composer's forlorn wish for domestic happiness; although he fell in love several times, he was never to marry. He was a difficult man, gruff and blunt, and his deafness was a great social affliction.

By the time he reached his mid-thirties Beethoven had become more financially secure, thanks to some very supportive patrons; however, following the death of his brother, he attempted to gain legal custody of his nephew, Karl, and the long legal battles took their toll. Beethoven's output diminished for a time, but once again he found fresh strength from his troubles, and the last period of his life gave rise to his greatest achievements. His last symphony, the *Choral*, No.9, set the precedent for the combination of vocal and instrumental forces in symphonic compositions; its final movement, a setting of Schiller's *Ode to Joy*, has become the anthem of the European Community. The monumental *Missa Solemnis* gave a new character to religious music; the late piano sonatas (among them the *Hammerklavier*, Op.106) and above all the late string quartets (Opp.127, 130-3, 135, dating from 1825-6) reach an unparalleled level of development which was beyond the audiences of the time. The six quartets remain among the most challenging, emotionally intense and yet intellectually satisfying chamber works ever composed.

By his own life and career, Beethoven established a precedent for a new kind of composer – no longer the servant of rich men, but an artist in his own right, able to take his place in society on his own terms. Although contemporary response to his music was cautious, his genius was always recognized and at his death thousands mourned him.

Behrens, Hildegard (1937-) German operatic soprano. She studied at Freiburg, and first performed there and in Düsseldorf and Frankfurt, where she sang Fiordiligi in Mozart's *Così fan tutte* and Marie in Berg's *Wozzeck*. She first appeared in London (in *Fidelio*) and New York in the same year (1976). In 1983 she sang Brünnhilde in the *Ring* cycle at Bayreuth, and was warmly admired; she has since sung this and other Wagnerian roles in New York. She has also sung the title-role of Strauss's *Salome*. She is an expressive singer noted for the dramatic intensity of her performances.

bel canto (It.) Beautiful singing. A term loosely used to describe a style based on beauty of tone and line. It is also used equally loosely to describe the period in the 17th and 18th centuries, when the **castrato** male soprano developed extraordinary technical skill.

Bellini, Vincenzo (1801-1835) Italian composer. A municipal scholarship enabled him to study at the Naples Conservatoire (1819-22), where among his teachers was Niccolò **Zingarelli**. Bellini achieved recognition as a significant operatic composer with his third opera, *Il pirata* (1827). His next opera, *La straniera* (1829), was even more successful, but before the triumph of *I Capuletti ed i Montecchi* (1830), his *Zaira* proved a failure. Bellini's music over the years has been successful when singers of the calibre of Rosa **Ponselle**, Maria **Callas** and Joan **Sutherland** are available to perform it. His finest operas, *La sonnambula* and *Norma* (both 1831), have now secured a place in the repertory, the aria *Casta diva* from *Norma* being one of the great showpieces for sopranos in recitals and concert performances. *I Puritani* has also been revived recently, but others are rarely heard. He also composed instrumental and sacred vocal works.

bells A great variety of bells of all shapes and sizes has existed throughout history: they fall into two main types, the open or cup and the closed or hollow sphere. They are sounded by a clapper inside or outside the open type, or by loose weights inside the spherical type. Bells of all types have been used in religious ceremonies, as a summons or warning, and as musical instruments.

The **carillon**, found in churches, town halls and other buildings, provides a complete scale of bells upon which melodies are played from a keyboard by mechanical or electrical connections.

In the orchestra, bells of exact pitch are usually **tubular**, though Wagner, in *Parsifal*, and Puccini, who was obsessed with their sound, specified cup bells. **Cowbells**, of indeterminate pitch, were used by Mahler in his Symphony No.6 and by Richard Strauss in his *Alpine Symphony*.

In American orchestral usage, bells means **glockenspiel**, the term chimes being used for tubular bells.

Belyayev, Mitrofan Petrovich (1836-1904) Russian music publisher. He studied the violin and piano, and on hearing the music of **Glazunov**, conceived the idea of forming a business to publish it and other works. Because the copyright laws were not applicable in Russia, he set up his publishing house in Leipzig in 1885, and published the works of most of the important Russian composers of the time (Tchaikovsky excepted). He also organized several series of concerts of Russian music in Paris and St Petersburg. The firm continued to function after his death, but has now been taken over by Peters Edition, Frankfurt.

bémol (Fr.), **bemolle** (It.) The flat sign (♭).

Benda, Jiři Antonín (1722-1795) The most celebrated composer of a large family of Bohemian musicians. In 1725 he was appointed *Kapellmeister* to Duke Friedrich III of Saxe-Gotha and this period of his life was spent composing cantatas and instrumental music, operas being banned by Church edict. This was eventually revoked and in 1765 Benda's first opera was produced. In the same year he visited Italy, becoming acquainted with Italian opera. After this, Benda composed many works for the stage (*Ariadne auf Naxos*, *Walder*), while continuing to write sacred and instrumental music.

Benedetti Michelangeli, Arturo See **Michelangeli, Arturo Benedetti**

Benedict, Sir Julius (1804-1885) English composer and conductor of German birth. He studied with **Weber** in Dresden and his musical career started in Vienna. After a period in Naples he moved to London in 1835, where he conducted opera at various venues. He conducted the Norwich Festivals for over 30 years, and was conductor of the Liverpool Philharmonic Orchestra. His opera *The Lily of Killarney* (1862) is still occasionally performed; he also composed oratorios. His biography of Weber is an important first-hand source drawn upon by most later writers.

Benevoli, Orazio (1605-1672) Italian composer who received his early musical training in Rome, where he was a chorister between 1617 and 1623. He was engaged as *maestro di cappella* of the church of S. Maria in Trastevere, Rome, when he was only 18 and he remained there until 1630. He held similar posts throughout his career and was also a teacher. His compositions, which consist entirely of sacred vocal works, are noted for the use of clearly defined major/minor tonality and his approach to form, in the tradition of **Palestrina**. His works are often polychoral; he favoured homophony over complex polyphony and his works contain few solo lines.

Benguerel, Xavier (1931-) Spanish composer who studied in Barcelona with Christobál Taltabull. His early works are influenced by Debussy, Bartók and Schoenberg; later his compositional style was characterized by his use of contrapuntal lines and **serialism**. Among his works are *Dos Polifonias* for orchestra, *Music for Three Percussion* and *Musica riservata*.

Ben Haim, Paul (1897-) Israeli composer of German origin. His studies included piano and conducting, and he was a conductor in Germany before the rise of the Nazi regime. In 1933 he settled in Israel, and developed into its foremost composer. His work shows some Middle-Eastern characteristics, although it remains recognizably Western, of the Romantic school. An early work was his *Concerto Grosso* (1931); other works include *The Sweet Psalmist of Israel* (1953); *A Hymn to the Desert* (1963); *Six Sephardic Songs* (1971); two symphonies which reflect the emotional experiences of World War II; a violin concerto; a string quartet; a sonata for violin which was dedicated to Yehudi **Menuhin**; choral and other vocal music of great lyricism (*Three Psalms*, 1962).

Benjamin, Arthur (1893-1960) Australian-English composer and pianist who studied composition with **Stanford** at the Royal Academy of Music. He was mainly influenced by the popular dance idiom of Latin American music. His works are mostly light and accessible: examples are *Jamaican Rumba* (1938) for two pianos, *The Devil Take Her* (1951), and film music for *An Ideal Husband*; some of his later works, however, are in a less cheerful style. He composed some operas as well, the most important is *The Prima Donna*.

Benjamin, George (1960-) English composer and pianist who began writing music at the age of nine. He studied with **Messiaen** at the Paris Conservatoire and with **Goehr** at Cambridge. In 1980 his *Ringed by the Flat Horizon* was performed at the BBC Promenade concerts; he is the youngest composer ever to achieve this. Other important works are *A Mind of Winter* (1981) and, commissioned for the **London Sinfonietta**, *At First Light* (1982). He was commissioned by **IRCAM** in Paris to compose *Antara* (1987); it was broadcast on BBC television. *Cascade*, the first movement of an unfinished piece, was given its première in 1990 by the London Philharmonic Orchestra. In addition to composing he teaches at the Royal College of Music, conducts, plays the piano and lectures.

Bennet, John (*c.*1575-*c.*1614) English madrigal composer who also wrote songs accompanied by **viols**, for example, *Eliza, Her Name Gives Honour*. Another of his works, *O God of Gods: To the Almighty Trinity*, a verse anthem for soloists with viol accompaniment, weaves contrapuntal lines between the voices and instruments. Most of his madrigals are contained in the volume he published in 1599.

Bennett, Richard Rodney (1936-) British composer and pianist, resident in New York since 1977. He received his first music lessons from his mother, a former pupil of Gustav Holst. Bennett attended the Royal Academy of Music (1953-6), where his teachers included Lennox **Berkeley**, and then studied with Pierre **Boulez** from 1956 to 1959. He was professor of composition at the Royal Academy of Music from 1963 to 1965. A prolific composer, he shows easy mastery of a variety of styles, embracing jazz, **twelve-note** music and traditional harmony and forms. His works, in a wide range of genres, include the ballets *Jazz Calendar* (1963-4) and *Isadora* (1981); the operas *The Mines of Sulphur* (1963-5) and *Victory* (1968-9); a number of orchestral works and concertos; and scores for more than 35 films, including *Far from the*

Madding Crowd, *Murder on the Orient Express* and *Equus*.

Bennett, Robert Russell (1894-1981) American orchestrator, conductor and composer who studied with Nadia **Boulanger**. He worked in New York from 1919 orchestrating theatrical songs. He was the leading orchestrator of Broadway musicals from 1922 until the 1960s, and worked in Hollywood film studios from 1930.

Bennett arranged and orchestrated some 300 musicals, including Jerome **Kern**'s *Showboat* (1957), Richard **Rodgers**'s *The Sound of Music* (1959), and works by Rudolf **Friml**, George **Gershwin**, Cole **Porter**, Irving **Berlin** and Frederick **Loewe**. He wrote many concert pieces, sometimes based on popular material by other American composers such as Stephen **Foster** and Jerome Kern. His book on orchestration, *Instrumentally Speaking*, was published in 1975.

Bennett, Sir William Sterndale (1816-1875) English composer who, although his works are now largely forgotten, ranked as one of the most distinguished of the English Romantic School. He began his musical career as a chorister at King's College, Cambridge, and entered the Royal Academy of Music at the age of ten. Between the ages of 17 and 23 he studied in Leipzig, where he made close friends of both Mendelssohn and Schumann, and it was during this period that most of his works were written. Among his orchestral writings are five symphonies, four piano concertos and a number of concert overtures and **fantasias**. He also wrote for chamber ensembles and for solo piano. In addition, he was a conductor of note - for example, of the Philharmonic Society (1835); a distinguished teacher; and the founder of the Bach Society in London (1854).

Benoit, Peter (1834-1901) Belgian composer, conductor and teacher, the initiator of the Flemish music movement which brought the country's music to the attention of the rest of Europe. He was a teacher of great reputation and in 1867 founded the Flemish School of Music in Antwerp. Benoit's compositional style is firmly rooted in 19th-century Romantic nationalism, using melodies and rhythmic gestures from traditional Flemish folk styles. Much of his work is vocal, including three operas, three oratorios, a choral symphony (*The Mowers*), two Masses and a number of songs.

Bentzon, Jørgen (1897-1951) Danish composer and pianist. His first interest was in jazz, and he worked with Leo Mathiesen and then with Jeppesen at the Copenhagen Conservatoire. Among his works are 12 symphonies, a concerto for piano and orchestra, three string quartets, an opera (*Faust*), choral works and solo piano pieces.

Bentzon, Niels Viggo (1919-) Danish composer, teacher, pianist and critic. An early interest in jazz was cultivated by studying with Leo Mathiesen; he later studied piano, organ and theory at the Copenhagen Conservatoire. He is one of Denmark's best-known and most prolific composers since **Nielsen**, his compositional style being dissonant, but tonal in concept with a free, almost improvisatory character. Despite his book *Twelve-Tone Theory* his own work has never fully embraced **serialism**. Many of his works allow room for **improvisation**, some using graphic scores and **aleatory** techniques (*Variable Music*) or the modern jazz milieu (*Third Stream Music*). He has written two operas, many orchestral works including 18 symphonies, chamber music and solo piano pieces.

berceuse (Fr.) Lullaby or cradle-song, normally in 6/8 time with a rocking accompaniment. *Berceuses* occur as songs and short instrumental pieces, often for piano, such as those by Chopin, Schumann in *Kinderszenen* and Fauré in the *Dolly Suite*.

Berezovsky, Nikolai (1900-1953) American composer, violinist and conductor of Russian birth. After studying music in the Imperial Chapel in St Petersburg and working professionally as a violinist and conductor throughout Russia, he emigrated to the United States (1920).

Berezovsky studied composition at the Juilliard School, played the violin with the New York Philharmonic Orchestra and the Coolidge quartet, and worked as a conductor. His compositions include an oratorio, four symphonies, a children's opera based on the stories of Babar the Elephant (1953), chamber music, and numerous orchestral compositions for ensembles of various sizes. Berezovsky also played the viola and gave the first performance of his own Viola Concerto in 1941.

Berg, Alban (1885-1935) Austrian composer who, with **Schoenberg** and **Webern**, constituted the Second Viennese School, which ushered in the use of **atonality** and the **twelve-note** system and profoundly influenced the music of the 20th century. Berg's music adheres much less closely to the twelve-note system and the principles of atonality than does that of his colleagues. A meticulous and slow worker (he completed only 22 mature works), he was a master of structure and form, but his works are much more accessible than those of Schoenberg and Webern.

He was born in Vienna and, with no formal training in composition, began writing romantic songs at the age of 15. In 1904 he met Schoenberg, who took him on as a pupil; he eventually gave up his civil service job to devote himself to music. Along with his friend and fellow pupil Webern, Berg now entered the Viennese avant-garde circle of artists and writers: Loos, Klimt, Kokoschka, and Zweig among them. Berg's early music - some songs and a set of piano variations - was performed in Vienna over the next few years. In 1911 he married. Two years later the presentation of two of his five

Alban Berg

Altenberglieder at a concert of contemporary Viennese music led to a riot, and a disagreement with Schoenberg.

During World War I, in which he served as a soldier, Berg began work on his first opera, *Wozzeck*, based on a play by Büchner. The story, of a downtrodden, lower-class soldier who stabs his mistress when he realizes that she has been unfaithful, and is hanged for the crime, is at once harrowing and touching; the music portrays graphically the breakdown of a human being. It was first performed in Berlin in 1925 and enjoyed some success; not, as Berg himself said, because of the inventiveness of its musical structure, but because of its illumination of a difficult theme.

His other opera, *Lulu*, was begun in 1929. Based on two plays by Frank Wedekind, the theme was a powerful challenge to Berg, who despised the hypocrisy of the bourgeoisie in matters of sexual morality. The story is of a woman's rise and fall, from a wealthy marriage to prostitution, and her murder by Jack the Ripper. Berg was unable to finish it before his death; his widow refused to allow the sketches of the last act to be published, and a performing version was released only in 1979.

The two operas are the most important and memorable works of Berg's limited output; other notable pieces are the *Chamber Concerto* (1925); the *Lyric Suite* (1926) for string quartet; a concert aria, *Der Wein*; and a violin concerto in memory of Alma Mahler's daughter.

bergamasca (It.) Originally used to describe peasant dances and songs from the district around Bergamo in northern Italy. By the late 16th century the dance had a fixed harmonic pattern, which was used into the 17th century, particularly for guitar pieces. Bergamo is associated with the *commedia dell'arte*, and the title appeared frequently in the 18th and late 19th centuries in France, whenever there was an interest in the Harlequin figure. **Debussy** wrote a *Suite bergamasque* for piano, and **Fauré** wrote an orchestral suite entitled *Masques et bergamasques*.

Berganza, Teresa (1935-) Spanish mezzo-soprano. After training as a pianist at the Madrid Conservatoire she began her vocal studies with a former pupil of Elisabeth **Schumann**, Lola Rodriguez Aragon. She made her stage début at Aix-en-Provence, France, as Dorabella in Mozart's *Così fan tutte* and quickly established an international career. Among her early engagements was the role of Neris in Cherubini's opera *Medea*, which she sang alongside Maria Callas. Although her reputation is centred on her interpretations of Mozart and Rossini, her highly flexible and even-toned voice is equally suited to the performance of Purcell, Monteverdi, Cesti or the songs of her native Spain.

Berger, Arthur (1912-) American composer, teacher, music critic and journalist. He studied under Walter **Piston**, Nadia **Boulanger** and **Milhaud**. After various teaching positions he was appointed professor of music at Brandeis University in 1962. He has written orchestral, vocal and chamber music, and several works for piano, and while his early works are neo-classical in style, compositions from the late 1950s use serial techniques. His literary works include a book on Aaron **Copland**.

Berger, Jean (1909-) German composer who studied at the universities of Heidelberg and Vienna. After a long residence in France he moved to the United States and was eventually naturalized. His compositions include the choral work *Vision of Peace* and *The Pied Piper*, a play with music.

Berger, Theodor (1905-) Austrian composer who studied under Franz **Schmidt** at the Vienna Academy. He has written a variety of choral and orchestral works which are romantic in style, and several scores for films, radio and television.

Bergman, Erik (1911-) Finnish composer who studied at the Helsinki Conservatoire (now the Sibelius Academy) and Helsinki University from 1931 to 1938, later acquiring a grounding in **twelve-note** techniques from Vladimir Vogel in Switzerland (1949-50). After World War II, he took up a career as a music critic and choral trainer, while composing music that placed him at the forefront of Finland's musical avant-garde. Appointed professor of composition at the Sibelius Academy in 1963, Bergman continued his musical development beyond serialism into **aleatory** methods. His compositions, mainly choral, include a setting of the *Rubaiyat of Omar Khayyam* (1953), for male chorus and orchestra, *Aubade* (1958), for orchestra, *Noa* (1976), for baritone, voices and orchestra, and a violin concerto (1983-4).

Bergonzi, Carlo (1924-) Italian tenor. After studying as a baritone with Grandini in Parma he entered the Boito Conservatoire. His early professional career was interrupted by World War II, during which he was imprisoned by the

Carlo Bergonzi

Germans as a result of his anti-Nazi activities. Bergonzi finally made his professional début in Lecce in 1948 as Figaro in Rossini's opera *Il barbiere di Siviglia*. Further studies led to a second début, this time as a tenor, when he performed in Giordano's *Andrea Chenier* in Bari (1951). Bergonzi quickly established an international reputation for his interpretation of the tenor roles of Verdi's operas. His musicianship, competent acting skills and fine voice have led to great popularity with opera audiences throughout the world.

Bergsma, William (1921-) American composer and teacher, who studied at Stanford University with **Hanson** and **Rogers** and went on to teach composition at the Juilliard School where he instigated curricular reforms, bringing the syllabus up to date. Later he became professor and director of the School of Music at Washington University. His compositional style is essentially tonal, lyrical and conventionally orchestrated although his later works embrace many of the movements of the avant-garde. His works include two ballets, two operas, a number of orchestral pieces, vocal works and four string quartets.

Beringer, Oscar (1844-1922) English pianist, composer and teacher, born in Berlin. Beringer's family moved to London in 1849, where he gave his first public performance in 1859. Later he studied in Leipzig and Berlin. From 1869 to 1871 he taught in Berlin, but then returned to a performing career in England and ran a highly successful Academy for the Higher Development of Pianoforte Playing (1873-97). He gave the first English performance of Brahms's Piano Concerto No.2, in 1882. His compositions include songs, pieces for piano and an *Andante and Allegro* for piano and orchestra, but Beringer is probably best remembered for his piano tutors and technical manuals, and for his editions of piano classics.

Berio, Luciano (1925-) Italian composer who studied under **Ghedini** at the Milan Academy and with **Dallapiccola**. He has taught at several major American music schools, including Harvard University and the Juilliard School. He founded the Milan Electronic Studio in 1955. He has experimented with **serialism**, electronic music and 'collage' techniques (for example, his *Sinfonia* quotes several other composers including Mahler's Symphony No.2). He is a prolific composer and has written for many instrumental and vocal configurations and for the theatre. His electronic music includes *Mutations* (1954), *Theme* (1958) and *Chants parallèles* (1974). He was often associated in his work with his former wife, the mezzo-soprano Cathy Berberian (1925-83), for whom he wrote several works, including *Recital I (for Cathy)* (1972).

Bériot, Charles Auguste de (1802-1870) Belgian violinist and composer, whose instrumental technique combined the brilliance and showmanship of **Paganini** with the elegance and clarity of the Paris style (as exemplified by **Kreutzer**), establishing a more romantic approach and modernizing the French school of playing. His compositions are technically ingenious and aim for effect rather than depth. He wrote ten violin concertos, 12 airs and other shorter pieces for solo violin as well as violin duets and chamber music works.

Berkeley, Sir Lennox (1903-1989) English composer. Berkeley's music has always betrayed a French influence, perhaps because of his partly French ancestry, and because of his studies with Nadia **Boulanger**. His operas, *Ruth*, *Nelson*, *The Dinner Engagement* and *The Castaway*, combine elegance, wit and charm with an engaging melodic style. He composed four symphonies, a violin concerto for Yehudi **Menuhin**, and the delightful *Serenade for Strings*. His choral music was largely for the Catholic Church and includes two settings of the Mass and a number of Latin **motets**. His chamber music includes sonatinas for guitar, for oboe, and for violin; a wind and piano quintet, and a string quartet in memory of **Stravinsky**.

Berkeley, Michael (1948-) British composer, son of Sir Lennox **Berkeley**. He attended the Westminster Cathedral Choir School and the Royal Academy of Music, studying also with his father and with Richard Rodney **Bennett**. From 1976 to 1979 he was a full-time BBC Radio 3 continuity announcer and still broadcasts from time to time, chiefly on television. His works cover a wide variety of genres and include the anti-war oratorio *Or Shall We Die?* (1982), a symphony entitled *Uprising* (1980), a chamber symphony (1980), a number of pieces for vocal/instrumental ensembles, chamber music, and organ works.

Berlin, Irving (1888-1989) American composer, born in Russia. He achieved immense popular success as a Tin Pan Alley songwriter, composing innumerable hit songs, Broadway musicals and films. He never learned to write music properly. His first hit was *Alexander's Ragtime Band*, a simplified popular **rag**. His best-known song is probably *White Christmas*, made famous by Bing Crosby. Among the most memorable of his films and musicals are *Top Hat* (1935), *Annie Get Your Gun* (1946) and *Call Me Madam* (1950).

Irving Berlin

Berlin Philharmonic Orchestra One of the world's finest orchestras, founded in 1882. Its music directors have included **Joachim**, von **Bülow**, **Nikisch**, **Furtwängler** and **Celibidache**. From 1954 until his death in 1989 Herbert von **Karajan** maintained the orchestra's traditional precision and warmth of tone in the string section, matched by players of the highest standards in all other sections. His successor is Claudio **Abbado**. The orchestra has made numerous recordings of most of the classical and Romantic orchestral repertory. Several smaller ensembles have also been formed from within it.

Berlioz, Hector (1803-1869) French composer, the son of a doctor, who hoped the boy would take up his profession. A brief experience of the dissecting room in Paris determined him on a musical career. He managed to be accepted at the Conservatoire and soon proved a gifted if troublesome student, powerfully influenced by the music of Gluck and Beethoven, and the works of Virgil and Shakespeare. In 1830 he won the Prix de Rome at the third attempt; the same year he completed his *Symphonie fantastique*, inspired by his temporary disappointment in love with the Irish actress Harriet Smithson, who later became his wife. The symphony and its companion *Lélio* (1831) and the concert overture *Le Corsaire* (1831) displayed a wholly new orchestral style, demanding the utmost virtuosity.

Short of money, in 1834 Berlioz took up journalism, and proved himself as brilliant a master of prose as of the orchestra. By now a leading if controversial figure in Parisian musical life, he was commissioned by **Paganini** to write *Harold en Italie* with a part for solo viola, and by the government to compose a Requiem Mass (1837). In this huge work Berlioz asked for an orchestra of over 200 players and a chorus to match. In that same year he completed his opera *Benvenuto Cellini*; despite considerable critical support, it succumbed to hostile intrigues and was withdrawn after four performances. His financial difficulties were relieved by a gift from Paganini of 20,000 francs, which enabled him to give up journalism for a while, and work on his dramatic symphony *Roméo et Juliette* for soloists, chorus and orchestra, given with great success at the Conservatoire in 1839. In that year he was made Chevalier of the Legion of Honour, and was later commissioned by the government to compose the *Symphonie funèbre et triomphale* in honour of the patriots killed in the revolution of 1830; this huge work, designed for open-air performance, required over a hundred wind players with optional strings and chorus. Berlioz's marriage by now was in ruins, and he was glad to accept invitations to conduct his music outside France – he could be regarded as the first example of the modern virtuoso conductor, with triumphant tours in Germany and Russia, while also making a great impression on his visits to London.

In 1845 he began work on *La damnation de Faust*, which he mounted in 1846 with little success and ruinous expense. He now looked to England as a source of income, having been engaged in 1847 as a conductor for operas and concerts at Drury Lane; after a year, however, he returned to Paris. He was again in London in 1852 and 1855, conducting with great success concerts mounted by the New Philharmonic Society, including a triumphant account of Beethoven's Symphony No.9. In 1858 he completed his greatest work, the opera *Les troyens* (The Trojans), based on episodes from Virgil's *Aeneid*, but it was not produced until 1863. In the meantime he turned once more to his beloved Shakespeare, and composed the delightful comedy *Béatrice et Bénédict*, based on the play *Much Ado About Nothing* (1862). While his music was now being performed all over Germany, he still could not command the same respect in Paris, where the Opéra continued to ignore *Les troyens*; finally another smaller theatre agreed to perform only the second part, which led to 22 successful performances.

Berlioz's music provokes love and contempt in equal measure – for many he is an incomparable genius, while others find his music crude and amateurish. His fellow countrymen have never taken him to their hearts, and remain somewhat bemused by the passionate enthusiasm displayed by British, Russian and German audiences. The glory of *Les troyens* was revealed by productions in Germany, Scotland and London long before it was mounted in Paris. All are agreed, however, on the quality of his writings, especially his pioneering treatise on orchestration, and his delightful memoirs which offer an incomparable insight into the agony and ecstasy of a remarkable creative life.

Bernac, Pierre (1899-1979) French baritone, outstanding interpreter, especially of the songs of Francis **Poulenc**, who wrote many of them especially for him, and accompanied him in recitals and many fine recordings. Later in his career, Bernac taught and gave master-classes, sometimes on television. He left a valuable book on the interpretation of French song.

Berners, Lord (Gerald Hugh Tyrwhitt-Wilson) (1883-1950) English composer, writer and painter. He is often considered a mere eccentric, obscuring the fact that in his early years he was judged an important and avant-garde figure, much admired by Stravinsky. Berners is perhaps best remembered for his ballets *The Triumph of Neptune* (1926) and *A Wedding Bouquet* (1936) but there is also a corpus of piano music and songs. His novels were also well received and his film scores for *Champagne Charlie* and *Nicholas Nickleby* are considered classics of their kind.

Bernstein, Leonard (1918-) American composer, pianist and conductor, who studied at Harvard University (1935-9), the Curtis Institute, Philadelphia (1939-41) and under Koussevitzky at the Tanglewood summer schools (1940-3).

Bernstein made a highly successful début in 1943, substituting for Bruno **Walter** at a New York Philharmonic concert. Following an international career as a conductor he became music director of the orchestra (1958-68), and remains one of the outstanding conductors of his day. As a composer, his greatest success has been the musical *West Side Story* (1957); he has also composed other successful stage works, such as the ballet *Fancy Free*, the musical *On the Town*, the operetta *Candide* and an opera to his own libretto, *Trouble in Tahiti*.

In a completely different idiom are his three symphonies, the *Chichester Psalms* (commissioned for Chichester Cathedral, Sussex), the *Songfest*, written in 1977 to commemorate the Bicentennial of the United States the year before, and a variety of piano and other chamber music. His explorations of religious themes, exemplified in the *Kaddish* Symphony, No.3, and his theatrical idiom come together in the *Mass* of 1971, an enactment of the Roman Catholic rite.

Leonard Bernstein

Berwald, Franz (1796-1868) Swedish composer and violinist. His early compositions went unnoticed. In 1828 he won a scholarship to study in Berlin but again met disappointment. In the 1840s he twice visited Vienna and found some encouragement there. In 1846 Jenny Lind sang in his opera *Ein ländisches Verlobungfest in Schweden* (1847). But generally his music failed to impress. Returning to Sweden in 1849 he remained neglected and spent most of the rest of his life running a glass factory, composing in his spare time. Berwald is now acknowledged as Sweden's greatest 19th-century composer. Very much a Romantic in a Berliozian mould, he has left four symphonies, of which only No.1 (*Sérieuse*) was performed in his lifetime, several operas, including *The Queen of Golconda* (1864), a concerto each for violin and piano, three string quartets, two piano quintets, and a septet in B♭.

Best, William (1826-1897) English organist. Best was one of the most famous exponents of the 19th-century grand manner of organ playing, which exploited the full orchestral resources of large town-hall organs. He was for a long time organist to the Liverpool Philharmonic Society and it was he who inaugurated the organ at the Royal Albert Hall. Particularly celebrated for his arrangements of orchestral music as well as piano pieces, Best edited and arranged a large amount of music, some of which is still in use today.

Bevin, Elway (1554-1638) English composer, organist and theorist of Welsh extraction. He worked at Wells and Bristol and later at the Chapel Royal. He is mainly known for his Dorian or Short Service, and for an explanatory treatise *A Briefe and Short Instruction in the Art of Musicke* (1631).

bhairav (India) One of the ten parent scales (*thāt*) in Hindustani music, corresponding to C, D♭, E, F, G, A♭, B, C′.

bhairavī (India) One of the ten parent scales (*thāt*) in Hindustani music, corresponding to C, D♭, E♭, F, G, A♭, B♭, C′.

bhāyān (India) See **bāyān**

bian jing Stone chimes, used in the Chou court orchestras of China. The 12 tones (*lu*) of Chinese music are divided into two series of six so that the system is in line with the male-female *yin* and *yang* principles of Chinese metaphysics. The male and female chimes are arranged separately, running outward from the middle of the instrument rather than in ascending order.

Biber, Heinrich Ignaz Franz von (1644-1704) South German violinist and composer. He was described by many as the greatest violinist of his age. From the mid-1660s to 1670 he served in the chapel of Prince-Bishop Karl, Count Liechtenstein-Kastelkorn of Olomouc, in Kroměříž. His best-known works are those for solo violin, demanding an unprecedented level of virtuosity, and making use of several special effects, notably **scordatura**, especially in his *Mystery* (or *Rosary*) sonatas, and in the *Harmonia artificiosa-ariosa*.

In his other instrumental music and in his sacred vocal music he makes unusually extensive use of wind instruments, such as in his sonata *Sancti polycarpi* and the *Requiem* for choir, soloists, strings and trombones. His sonata for two violins and trombone demands as much virtuosity from the trombone as from the violins.

Biggs, E. Power (1906-1977) American organist of British origin. He studied at the Royal Academy of Music, and settled in the United States in 1930. There he became very well known for his regular radio broadcasts (1942-58), in which he did much to popularize organ music by his wide-ranging repertory and engaging style as a presenter. He gave many recitals all over the country, and also played with a variety of orchestras. His numerous recordings feature some famous old organs in Britain, Germany, and elsewhere; they include important series of Handel's and Bach's organ works, as well as 20th-century organ music.

bilāval (India) One of the ten parent scales (*thāt*) in Hindustani music, corresponding to the Western major scale C, D, E, F, G, A, B, C.

Billings, William (1746-*c.*1800) New England composer whose publication in 1770 of *The New-England Psalm-Singer* was the first American volume to consist entirely of works written by one composer. He wrote choral music, psalms, hymns, patriotic anthems and what he himself called *fuguing tunes*. His patriotic song *Chester* was one of the most popular anthems of the American revolution.

bīn/bīna (India) Northern Indian plucked stringed instrument which comprises two large gourd resonators fixed at each end of a tube zither. It has fixed frets and no sympathetic strings.

Binchois, Gilles (*c.*1400-1460) French or Flemish composer. After an episode in the service of William Pole, Earl of Suffolk, Binchois joined the chapel of the court at Burgundy some time in the late 1420s. Burgundy had the most lavish private musical establishment in Europe at the time, and Binchois was a major contributor to the then flourishing 'Burgundian style'. His chief output was secular songs concerned with various aspects of courtly love – 54 *rondeaux* and seven *ballades* survive in this genre. His song *Dueil angoisseus* was used as the basis for a Mass by John Bedyngham, and his *Filles à marier* became adapted as a popular court *basse danse*. Twenty-eight of his motets survive, as well as six magnificats, and several isolated Mass movements. *Déplorations* were composed by Dufay and Ockeghem on his death, and he was hailed by all contemporary music theorists as one of the greatest composers of his age.

Birmingham Symphony Orchestra See **City of Birmingham Symphony Orchestra.**

Birtwistle, Sir Harrison (1934-) English composer, sometimes referred to as belonging to the Manchester School, having been a pupil of Richard **Hall** alongside Peter **Maxwell Davies** and Alexander **Goehr**. He was notable for his interest in the music of the Second Viennese School and also for his allegiance to Stravinsky, **Varèse** and English medieval music, of which he has made some arrangements. His music-theatre pieces have also reflected an interest in English folk-music, especially the dramatic pastoral *Down by the Greenwood Side*.

There is often a streak of violence in Birtwistle's works (*Punch and Judy* is significant in this context), and his purely instrumental music has arrestingly clear timbres. Several pieces have associations with the classical world of Ancient Greece, in which the Greek use of chorus and refrain has been influential. His best-known orchestral piece is *The Triumph of Time*. Operas include *Yan Tan Tethera* (1986) and *The Mask of Orpheus*.

bis (Lat.) Again. See **encore**

bisbigliando (It.) Whispering; a virtuoso effect in orchestral harp-playing. It consists of rapidly repeated notes or chords played *pianissimo* in the upper or middle registers of the instrument, resulting in a soft tremolo. It is played on adjacent strings or sets of strings previously set to the same pitch with the pedals.

Bishop, Sir Henry (1786-1855) English composer, most famous for his song *Home, Sweet Home*. He worked at Covent Garden, Drury Lane and Vauxhall Gardens and had enormous success with his many stage works. He also wrote prolifically in other fields and his dance music and songs were favourites in Victorian times. Towards the end of his life his public deserted him, and few of his works are remembered today.

Bishop-Kovacevich, Stephen (1940-) American pianist of Yugoslav extraction, formerly known as Stephen Bishop. He studied with Myra **Hess** and has recorded and performed widely, mainly the standard repertory. He has shown a particular interest in Beethoven and Schubert, but has also played some 20th-century music. His performances are always considered and never brashly virtuosic.

bitonality Simultaneous use of two different keys in a musical composition. It has been used almost exclusively in the 20th century, although early examples exist (Hans Neusidler's *Der Juden Tantz*, Mozart's *Ein musikalischer Spass*, K522). One famous example is the use of C against F♯ in the fanfares in Stravinsky's *Petrushka*.

Bitonality was widely used in the first half of the 20th century by the group of French composers known as Les **Six**, especially by Darius **Milhaud**. It has also been much used in the piano repertory, often in teaching pieces intended for children (Prokofiev, *Sarcasmes*, Op.17 No.3, Bartók, *Mikrokosmos*). See also **polytonality**.

biwa (Japan) Japanese lute, originating from India and China and believed to be a direct descendant of the Chinese **p'ip'a**. Strings of gut or silk are attached to a scroll at the neck and stretched over high frets and secured to a tailpiece. The strings are pressed down either between or onto the frets, and plucked with a large plectrum of wood or bone.

The *biwa* may be found in a variety of forms, the most common of which are the

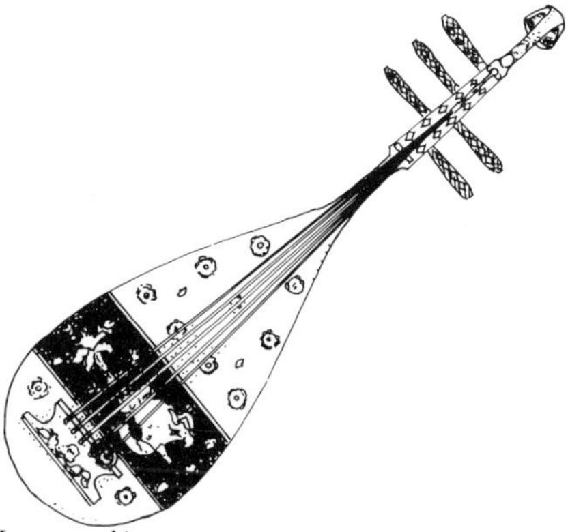

Japanese *biwa*

gaku-biwa, *Heike-biwa* and *Satsuma-biwa*. The *gaku-biwa*, used in the **gagaku** court orchestra, has four frets and four strings which are pressed down only onto the frets, resulting in a limited number of definite pitches. It plays short fixed motifs at regular intervals and its function may therefore be considered **colotomic**. The *Heike-biwa* is the middle-sized of the three main types, with five frets and four strings, and is used as an accompaniment to the narrative tradition associated with the epic concerning the wars of the Heike clan. There were two schools of lute players associated with the blind priest or *moso-biwa* tradition, the *Chikuzen* and *Satsuma*. Of these, the latter flourished and its *biwa* is relatively narrow, but has a larger scroll than other *biwas*, usually having four strings and four frets.

Bizet, Georges (1838-1875) French composer, whose father and uncle nurtured the boy's prodigious talent with such care that at the age of ten he was admitted to the Paris Conservatoire. He proved a precocious student, carrying off prizes for piano, organ and composition, culminating in the Prix de Rome at the age of 18. He had already composed two of his most delightful works, the prize-winning *Le docteur Miracle*, and the Symphony in C, which lay forgotten in the Conservatoire archives for 80 years. While in Rome he worked at an Italian comic opera, *Don Procopio*, and the five-act grand opera *Vasco de Gama*, neither of which were produced in his lifetime. His first mature opera was *Les pêcheurs de perles* (The Pearl-Fishers) (1863), a work of great lyric charm. This was followed by *La jolie fille de Perth* (The Fair Maid of Perth) (1866) to a libretto derived from Walter Scott; this showed a notable advance in dramatic effect, and won praise from audiences and critics alike at its production in 1867. Two years later Bizet married Geneviève Halévy, the daughter of one of his teachers at the Conservatoire.

After protracted negotiations with the Opéra-Comique, he was asked to work on three projects, only one of which, *Djamileh*, came to fruition, though it achieved little success. Bizet's next task was to provide music for a production of Daudet's play *L'arlésienne*, using a small orchestra of 26 players. It is a delightful, subtle score, strongly coloured by the sound of the saxophone. Neither the play nor his music won much praise until Bizet rescored four extracts for full orchestra to make the familiar first suite. In 1873, Colonne introduced Bizet's elegant orchestration of five movements from his set of piano duets, *Jeux d'enfants* (Children's Games).

Georges Bizet

Meanwhile Bizet had been working on another project for the Opéra-Comique, *Carmen*, based on a novel by Prosper Mérimée, despite considerable misgivings on the part of the management, who regarded the story as too sensational. Bizet was appointed Chevalier of the Legion of Honour on 3rd March 1875, the day of *Carmen*'s première, an honour he might not have enjoyed after the work's hostile reception by a scandalized public. The press described the story as obscene, and the music totally lacking in melody; one critic, unbelievably, said it was undramatic. Bizet was deeply wounded by the failure, and this hostility undoubtedly contributed to his untimely death later that year. If he had lived a few months longer he would have witnessed a complete reversal: its production in Vienna was a sensational success, and in the following years it swept across Europe. *Carmen* remains one of the most popular operas in the repertory.

Björling, Jussi (1911-1960) Swedish tenor. He made his début in Stockholm in 1930 as Don Ottavio in Mozart's *Don Giovanni*, and in London in 1938. He sang at the Metropolitan Opera, New York, from 1938 to 1960, where he became a firm favourite with his interpretation of the Italian repertory. His roles included Cavaradossi in *Tosca*, Radamès in *Aïda*, Manrico in *Il trovatore*, Calaf in *Turandot* and Rodolfo in *La bohème*, most of which he recorded.

Blacher, Boris (1903-1975) German composer and teacher. He worked as a teacher of composition in Berlin and Dresden. Unusually among Germans, he was highly influenced by French composers, Les **Six** in particular, and also by jazz. Many of his works are for the theatre, and they include several adaptations of Shakespeare (*Romeo und Julia*, *Hamlet*). Blacher's style is mainly tonal, although late in life he experimented with **serialism**. He often employed short motifs, developing them with great wit and economy of instrumentation. The work that established him on the international scene was his *Variations on a Theme of Paganini* (1947), complementing those by Brahms, Rachmaninov and Lutosławski.

Blades, James (1901-) English percussionist. He trained as an engineer; his earliest musical posts were with various dance and popular bands. He was appointed principal percussionist with the **London Symphony Orchestra** in 1940. He has also played with many other orchestras and chamber groups, including the Melos Ensemble. With the English Opera Group he collaborated with Benjamin **Britten** on the particular percussion effects featured in Britten's *Church Parables*, dramatic works for performance in church (*Curlew River*, *The Burning Fiery Furnace*, *The Prodigal Son*).

He was professor of timpani and percussion at the Royal Academy of Music from 1960. He has broadcast and lectured extensively on his subject, and has written books on the history and technique of percussion instruments. He was awarded an OBE in 1972.

Blake, David (1936-) English composer. Blake's grounding in music mainly came through his contact with Hans Eisler, from whom he learned the techniques of the Second Viennese School. An interest in Far Eastern culture has also influenced the subject-matter of his work, which includes operas and song cycles as well as chamber music. Among his many commissions for major festivals is the choral piece *Lumina*, based on texts by Ezra Pound, written for the Leeds Festival. He has also written a striking violin concerto and an opera, *Toussaint*.

Blavet, Michel (1700-1768) French composer and one of the leading flautists of his age. He was one of the first composers of flute sonatas, successfully adapting the French violin sonata style. His *Recueils de pièces* achieved great popularity, containing many arrangements for flutes at all levels of difficulty, including duets for pupil and teacher. He wrote four stage works for the Count of Clermont's château at Berny, where he served from 1731 up to his death.

Blech, Harry (1910-) English violinist and conductor. For many years he led the Blech Quartet but later turned to conducting. His most celebrated ensemble is the **London Mozart Players**, which he founded in 1949, and of which Jane **Glover** is now conductor. He also founded the Haydn-Mozart Society; but these obvious affinities with the Viennese classical tradition have not prevented him from exploring a more contemporary repertory.

Bliss, Sir Arthur (1891-1975) English composer. He studied with E.J. Dent and Charles **Wood**, and his early style was influenced by his friendship with **Elgar**. Later he was drawn to the music of Stravinsky, and to that of Les **Six**. He was also a conductor and directed his own *Colour Symphony* at the Three Choirs Festival. His *Music for Strings* is in the same tradition as Elgar's *Introduction and Allegro*. He wrote film scores, incidental music and works for brass band and military band, in addition to works for various chamber ensembles. Among his ballets, *Checkmate* is the most frequently performed. He was appointed Master of the Queen's Music in 1953, and his fanfares have adorned many royal occasions. His music is tonal and accessible.

Blitheman, John (*c.*1525-1591) English composer, 12 of whose works survive: four settings of the plainsong *Eterne Rerum Conditor* and six of *Gloria Tibi Trinitas* (i.e. *In Nomine*) for organ, and two vocal works, one of them the extremely effective *In Pace*.

Blitzstein, Marc (1905-1964) American composer who wrote mainly for theatre, films and broadcasting. Consciously 'proletarian' in his approach, he orientated his work towards the creation of a 'music of the people'. *The Cradle Will Rock* (1936), a stage work which was a political piece concerning the struggle to establish a steelworkers' union in a company-dominated town, is his best-known work. His translation of *The Threepenny Opera* by Kurt **Weill** and Bertold Brecht is the version now most often heard.

Bloch, Ernest (1880-1959) Swiss-born composer who studied with Knorr in Frankfurt. He emigrated to the United States in 1916, but returned to Switzerland from 1930 to 1938. Much of his work up to that time has Jewish associations, of which the *Schelomo*, a Hebrew rhapsody for cello and orchestra (1915-16), is best known. Other works from this period include his early opera *Macbeth* (1904-9), the Jewish sacred service setting *Avodeth Hakodesh* (1930-3) and *Baal Shem* for violin and piano (1937-8). Bloch returned to the United States in 1939, where he remained until his death. In this final period he concentrated on larger abstract works such as the second and third quartets (1945 and 1952), and the *Concerto Symphonique* for piano and orchestra (1947-8).

block Hollow wooden percussion instrument which, when struck with a stick, produces a dry, knocking sound. Blocks are used for their unusual timbre and colouristic effect in many orchestral pieces, such as Constant **Lambert**'s cantata *The Rio Grande*. Blocks are also often to be found (chiefly for their novelty value) in dance bands and popular groups. Also known as a Chinese block, Korean temple block or temple block.

Blockx, Jan (1851-1912) Belgian composer. Influenced by **Grieg** and **Sinding** among others, Blockx is best remembered for his operas, which infuse a somewhat eclectic style with Belgian nationalism, partly attained through his studies of Flemish folk-songs which he married to a Wagnerian **leitmotiv** technique. Most of his works are settings in the Flemish language.

Blomdahl, Karl-Birger (1916-1968) Swedish composer and teacher, remembered particularly for his dissemination of the theories of **Hindemith** in Sweden. During the war years he held meetings for young composers known as *The Monday Group*, influential in moving Swedish music away from Romantic Impressionism. He wrote in many genres, and his music was performed in his own country and abroad, but is little heard today, although he had great success with his opera *Aniara* (1959), set in a space-ship. His style, though varied, frequently shows the influence of Hindemith's structural manner.

Blow, John (1649-1708) English composer and organist. In his youth he sang in the Chapel Royal and then became organist at Westminster Abbey in London. He taught **Purcell**, among others, while continuing his career, as organist and later composer to the Chapel Royal; he also worked at St Paul's Cathedral.

His output consisted of sacred works – more than 100 anthems and some church services – and a great number of secular songs. His only work for the stage was the masque *Venus and Adonis* (1685); he also produced much music for organ and harpsichord. He was closely associated with Purcell, and wrote a moving *Ode* on the latter's death in 1695.

blues Afro-American song form of a plaintive nature in which usually three-line stanzas are sung over four musical lines in **common time**. In its more developed accompanied form, it employs a standard chordal progression over a twelve-bar period (the twelve-bar blues), and has influenced a wide variety of dance and popular song styles such as **boogie**, **rock 'n' roll** and **rhythm and blues**. Melodically, unstable flattened third and seventh tones are prominent, commonly known as 'blue notes'. The blues possibly originates from field **hollers**.

Blüthner, Julius (1824-1910) Founder of a Leipzig firm of piano-makers which has become one of the most important in the 20th century. He patented a 'repetition action' in 1854 and is also celebrated for his Aliquot stringing, a system in which a sympathetic string is added to the normal trichord stringing, giving added resonance.

Boccherini, Luigi (1743-1805) Italian cellist and the most mature Italian composer of chamber music of the classical period. Born in Lucca, he travelled to Paris where, in 1767, his first works were published. His next, and final, move was to Madrid where in 1770 he was appointed to the service of Don Luis, the Spanish Infante. From 1786 he received patronage from Friedrich Wilhelm, Prince (later King) of Prussia. Most of his output is chamber music, including more than 100 string quintets, nearly 100 string quartets and more than 100 other chamber works. He also wrote some 29 symphonies; one opera (*La Clementina*) and orchestral and sacred works. His music is highly individual although its pervading charm, gentleness and even effeminacy led the contemporary violinist Giuseppe Puppo to term him 'Haydn's Wife'.

bodhran (Ireland) Frame drum about 60 cm in diameter and 12 cm deep, with a goatskin or deerskin head fixed to the ash rim with brass rivets. It is struck with a short, double-ended stick swivelled in the hand. Generally used as accompaniment to social dances.

Boehm, Theobald (1794-1881) German flautist and instrument-maker, inventor of the system of keywork used on the modern flute. It was devised in two stages, the 1832 Boehm keywork and the 1847 Boehm System. The system combines a large bore with large soundholes, covered not by the player's fingers, but by pads operated by keys. It made the instrument louder, with a larger range and fully chromatic, but compromised the flexibility and softness of tone of earlier flutes.

Boëllmann, Léon (1862-1897) French organist and composer. A pupil of **Gigout**,

Boëllmann worked mainly in Paris and enjoyed a modest success. He is most remembered for his *Suite gothique*, which ends with a celebrated toccata.

Boethius, Anicius Manlius Severinus (*c*.480-*c*.524) Roman mathematician and philosopher. His book on music theory, *De Institutione musica*, was the only Roman musical work known in the Middle Ages, and as such was the one on which medieval theorists based their system of modes and the Renaissance theorists their philosophy of the classification and function of music. In fact the book is an annotated translation of Nichomachus' lost *De musica* and Ptolemy's *Harmonica*.

Böhm, Karl (1894-1981) Austrian conductor. He studied at Vienna and Graz Conservatoires and made his conducting début in 1917. He was chief conductor of the Munich Opera from 1921 to 1927, and from 1933 was associated with the Vienna Philharmonic Orchestra. He was Director of the Vienna State Opera in 1943-5 and 1954-6 and achieved the honour of Austrian *Generalmusikdirektor*. He is most closely associated with the works of Mozart, Wagner and Richard **Strauss**, of whose *Die schweigsame Frau* (1935) and *Daphne* (1938) he conducted the first performances. His recordings include the complete Mozart symphonies, and three versions of *Così fan tutte*.

Boieldieu, Adrien (1775-1834) French composer who contributed greatly to the development of the **opéra comique** during the first quarter of the 19th century. His first opera, *La fille coupable*, was performed in 1793 and over the next decade he wrote 12 further works for the Parisian stage, including *Le calife de Bagdad* and *Ma tante Aurore*. In 1803 he was appointed director of the Imperial Opera at St Petersburg and remained in Russia for eight years. On returning to Paris he enjoyed further successes - most notably with *La dame blanche* - upholding the tradition of French comic opera amid the vogue for **Rossini**'s music. Known as 'the French Mozart', he wrote works that have great melodic appeal; his harmony is not always profound but his instrumentation is colourful and exciting.

Boismortier, Joseph Bodin de (1689-1755) French composer with a prolific output of chamber music geared towards the wealthy amateur. He was one of the first composers to become rich on sales of his music alone (that is, without relying on patronage). He had more than 100 sets of works published. He wrote much for flutes, including a set for five flutes with *basso continuo*. Sixteen of his sets are marked suitable for *musettes de court* (court bagpipes) and/or *vielles* (hurdy-gurdies). He was the first French writer of solo concerti. He wrote four stage works and a very entertaining collection, the *Recueil d'airs à boire et sérieux* for voices.

Boito, Arrigo (1842-1918) Italian composer and poet chiefly remembered for his collaboration with **Verdi**. On completing his studies in Milan he travelled to Paris where he met Victor Hugo, Berlioz, Rossini and Verdi. In 1880-1 he revised the libretto to Verdi's *Simon Boccanegra* and subsequently provided the composer with the texts for his two last and greatest operas, *Otello* and *Falstaff*. Boito was an accomplished operatic composer in his own right, creating both libretto and music for *Mefistofele* and leaving unfinished *Nerone*, which was performed posthumously in 1924.

bol (India) Syllables of the mnemonic system or **thekā** learned by drummers for rhythmic patterns of the **tablā** or **pakhāvaj** drums. Each *bol* indicates the exact manner in which the drum-head should be struck.

Bolcom, William (1938-) American composer and pianist who has held many posts in academic institutions, as both critic and composer-in-residence. His music is unusually direct and striking, strongly rooted in music-theatre and showing the influence of jazz and ragtime.

bolero (Sp.) Dance and song in moderate tempo and usually triple time, popular at the end of the 18th century and throughout the 19th. It is still danced in Andalusia, Castile and Majorca. The dance is normally performed by a couple, and is in three sections, with the music being in A-A-B form.

There is a Cuban version of the *bolero* which is in duple time, and out of which developed the conga.

The title *Bolero* has been used by several major composers, such as in Beethoven's *Bolero a solo*, and there are many examples in the opera repertory. **Ravel** wrote a *Bolero* which is extremely popular today.

Bolshoi Moscow theatre, first built in 1825 and used for all types of concerts as well as opera and ballet. A seminal force in Russian musical life, its productions of new national works have been numerous. Despite this, it has always been international in outlook as far as performers are concerned, and many of the world's best-known singers and conductors have performed there. The Bolshoi Ballet has become particularly celebrated.

bombarde 1. In the 14th and 15th centuries it was the French and English word for an alto-pitched **shawm**.

2. In Germany from the 1820s the word was taken up as *bombardon(e)* to refer to various bass cup-mouthpiece instruments, such as the bass horn or **ophicleide**. In England the *bombardon* at that time was the equivalent of the **tuba**, and in Italy *bombardino* is the **euphonium**.

3. In France, *bombarde* today refers to a double-reed instrument which accompanies the **bagpipe** in Brittany.

bonang (Java) Set of bronze knobbed gongs, forming part of the **gamelan** ensemble. They are suspended horizontally in two rows, on ropes fixed across a wooden frame, and struck with two long, padded sticks. There are three different sizes of *bonang* in a **gamelan**, each providing its own octave groupings.

Bond, Richard Capel See **Capel Bond, Richard**

Bondeville, Emmanuel (1898-1987) French composer. He studied at the Paris Conservatoire, and became director of the Eiffel Tower radio station and later music director of the French broadcasting service, Radio-Télévision Française. He was a director of the Monte Carlo Opera, the Opéra-Comique, and, from 1952 to 1970, the Paris Opéra. His works include operas (*L'école des maris*, 1935; *Madame Bovary*, 1951; *Antony and Cleopatra*, 1972), orchestral pieces (*Ophélie*; *Symphonie lyrique*), a piano sonata, and some songs.

bongo drum Small single-headed drum of Afro-Cuban origin which produces a high, clear sound. The bongos are generally played in pairs, tuned about a fourth apart, and may be seen in an increasing variety of types of music including Latin American dance bands and Western **jazz** fusion styles. The drums are played with the hands; subtle tone and pitch control are attained using varying pressure from the fingertips and palm of the hand.

Bongo drums

Bonnet, Joseph (1884-1944) French organist who studied with Alexandre **Guilmant** at the Paris Conservatoire and was appointed organist of St Eustace in 1906. He travelled widely as a recitalist. As well as composing many works for the organ, he edited unknown early organ music, including Frescobaldi's *Fiori musicali*.

Bononcini, Giovanni (1670-1747) Italian composer and cellist, son of Giovanni Maria **Bononcini** and prolific producer of operas in London in the 1720s and 1730s. His first instrumental works – three instrumental collections – were published when he was 15. It was in Rome in 1692 that he achieved his first international success with the opera *Il trionfo di Camilla*, which was produced throughout Europe and may well have contributed to the spread of the **galant** style.

He composed some 60 operas and other dramatic works, and 270 cantatas. They were popular for their tunefulness and conciseness, although some contemporary Londoners derided his ability to lull listeners to sleep and his music was condemned by 'some very fine Gentlemen for its too great simplicity'.

Bononcini, Giovanni Maria (1642-1678) Italian composer and music theorist, father of Giovanni **Bononcini**. He studied with Marco Ucellini in the tradition of the Modenese violinist-composers. His first nine *opere* are instrumental, including *sonate da chiesa* and *da camera*, which are perhaps the last dance suites actually intended for social dancing. He composed the first *cantata per camera*. His one treatise, *Musico prattico* (Venice, 1678), was an important step in the changeover from modal to tonal thinking.

Bonporti, Francesco Antonio (1672-1749) Italian composer. Four of his **inventions** were mistakenly attributed to **J.S. Bach** in the *Bach-Gesellschaft* edition and it is now thought that Bach's inventions were modelled on those of Bonporti. He published 12 volumes of chamber sonatas and was ordained a priest in 1697.

Bonynge, Richard (1930-) Australian conductor. Through his association with his wife Joan **Sutherland**, Bonynge is mainly known as a conductor of opera. He is most concerned with the revival of performance practices of the 18th century, and his recordings of Mozart have been important in re-establishing the art of ornamentation. He has conducted at many major opera houses and has recorded ballet music as well as opera. He was appointed musical director of the Australian Opera Company in 1976.

boogie-woogie Jazz piano style developed in the early part of this century and based on a twelve-bar **blues**. The style is characterized by an **ostinato** figure in the bass in 4/4 time, using quavers or dotted quavers. The right hand introduces syncopated elements above.

Borodin, Aleksandr Porfiryevich (1833-1887) Russian composer. Born in St Petersburg, the illegitimate son of a Russian prince, he was brought up by his mother and showed an early aptitude for music and chemistry. He studied medicine at St Petersburg, Heidelberg and elsewhere, and carried on an active career as a research chemist and government inspector of scientific facilities throughout Russia. In 1862 he became associate professor at the St Petersburg Academy of Medicine. In 1872 he founded a medical academy for women, and remained its director until his death.

Borodin studied music in whatever spare time was left to him after discharging his official duties. In 1862 **Balakirev** persuaded him to take up music seriously and he became a member of the group known as The Mighty Five, or the **Mighty Handful**. Less prolific as a composer than other members of the group, such as **Rimsky-Korsakov** or **Mussorgsky**, he nevertheless won great popularity, especially outside Russia, thanks to the interest of Liszt. His music often strikes a lyrical vein, rich in original melodies, Slavic-influenced, founded upon inventive harmonies that owe something to Mendelssohn yet bespeak great artistry in composition. His works include three symphonies (the last unfinished, but completed and orchestrated by **Glazunov**); the tone poem *In the Steppes of Central Asia*; two fine string quartets and a handful of piano pieces; and his masterpiece, the opera *Prince Igor*, which occupied him for 18 years, but had to be completed by Rimsky-Korsakov and Glazunov. Its Polovtsian Dances have become very widely known and were used as the basis for the musical *Kismet*.

Bortnyansky, Dmitri (1751-1825) Ukrainian composer. His two major contributions are to the repertory of opera and that of church music. His anthems in particular, stemming from his time as composer to the Imperial Chapel Choir, are skilful and lyrical in effect.

Bösendorfer, Ignaz (1796-1859) Founder of a Viennese firm of piano-makers, still trading today, though now owned by the American firm of Baldwin, and the most highly regarded manufacturer of Austrian pianos. The resilience of his pianos impressed Liszt; while other instruments collapsed under the strain of his playing, those of Bösendorfer survived. He employed both Viennese and English actions in his pianos and his modern concert grands are second only to **Steinway**'s in popularity. They are particularly renowned for their resonant bass register.

Boston Symphony Orchestra The main orchestra of Boston, Massachusetts. Founded in 1881, it began with mainly German players and its links with Europe have always been strong. The orchestra quickly established a high reputation and employed the best conductors available. From 1924 to 1949 its chief conductor was **Koussevitzky**, who commissioned many major works. More recently, **Münch**, **Leinsdorf** and **Ozawa** have been among its chief conductors. An offshoot of the orchestra is the Boston 'Pops', specializing in arrangements of the light classical repertory.

Boucourechliev, André (1925-) French composer and writer on music. He was involved with the Domaine Musical concerts in Paris in the 1950s and attracted attention with his pieces involving tape-recordings. He worked in studios in Milan and Paris, and contributed further tape pieces. His *Archipels* are memorable for their use of sound events mapped out on navigational charts which are followed by the performers. Despite these avant-garde activities, he has also published books on classical and Romantic composers.

Boughton, Rutland (1878-1960) English composer and writer. Boughton was as much known for his socialist views and plans for artistic communes as for his music. He planned an Arthurian cycle of operas to be performed in a festival at Glastonbury. His most famous opera, *The Immortal Hour*, was performed at Glastonbury in 1914, and subsequent operas were performed there and at Covent Garden. He gradually moved from a Wagnerian style towards a simpler, folk-like opera. As a writer, his Marxist views are striking and he has contributed stimulating books on Bach as well as on *The Music Drama of the Future*.

Boulanger, Lili (1893-1918) French composer and sister of Nadia **Boulanger**. Ill-health dogged her career and she died young, but she was a composer of great promise and the first woman to win the coveted Prix de Rome. Her winning entry, the cantata *Faust et Hélène*, shows allegiance to **Fauré**'s late style but also a striking individuality. She composed several psalm settings and left an unfinished opera based on Maeterlinck's *La princesse maleine*.

Boulanger, Nadia (1887-1979) French composer, conductor and renowned teacher. Sister of Lili **Boulanger**. She studied composition at the Paris Conservatoire (under **Fauré**), where she won many prizes. She was awarded the second Prix de Rome for her cantata *La sirène* (1908). She taught at several schools of music, including the Juilliard in the United States, the Paris Conservatoire, and the Ecole Normale de Musique, Paris. In

Nadia Boulanger

1937 she became the first woman to conduct an entire concert of the Royal Philharmonic Society, London.

Boulanger taught and influenced many outstanding composers and conductors, including **Berkeley**, **Carter**, **Copland**, **Piston** and **Thomson**.

Boulez, Pierre (1925-) French composer and conductor. He entered the Paris Conservatoire in 1942, studying composition with Olivier **Messiaen**. He also studied **twelve-note** technique with René **Leibowitz**, a pupil of **Schoenberg** and **Webern**. Under Leibowitz's influence, Boulez evolved a rigorous form of **serialism** in which not only pitches but also rhythms followed a strictly controlled sequence. His first two piano sonatas, his *Livre pour quattuor* (1948-9) for string quartet, and his composition *Le marteau sans maître* (1952-4; revised 1957) attracted much attention, and he became the centre of a circle of contemporary composers including **Stockhausen** and **Berio**. In 1953 he founded a series of Sunday concerts of contemporary music, which became known as the Domaine Musical. In 1966 he conducted Wagner's *Parsifal* at Bayreuth. He broke off his connections with Paris on political grounds, giving up the Domaine Musical concerts in 1967. He was principal guest conductor of the Cleveland Symphony Orchestra (1969-70) and chief conductor of the BBC Symphony Orchestra (1971-5) and the New York Philharmonic Orchestra (1971-77). In 1976 he returned to Bayreuth to conduct Patrice Chéreau's centenary production of Wagner's *Ring*, and three years later directed the first complete performance of Berg's *Lulu* at the Paris Opéra. In 1976 Boulez became director of the Institut de Recherche et de Coordination Acoustique/Musique (**IRCAM**), a Paris-based institute dedicated to research into modern composition techniques and funded by the French government. His works since then have included *Notations* (1980) and *Répons* (1981).

As a composer, Boulez has been an uncompromising adherent of strict serialism, a characteristic best seen in *Structures: Book I* (1952), for two pianos. But he has also been an original experimenter. *Le visage nuptial*, in its revised version for female soloists, women's chorus and orchestra (1951), uses choral speech, spoken *portamenti*, whispering and crying. *Pli selon pli*, a five-movement 'portrait of Mallarmé' for soprano and orchestra, was first composed in 1957-62 but, like many of his works, has been subject to continuous revision, in line with Boulez's view that a composition is never finished. Its five movements can be played in any order, except for the third, which must be placed centrally in the work.

Boult, Sir Adrian (1889-1983) English conductor who studied at Oxford and the Leipzig Conservatoire (1912-13), and joined Covent Garden in 1914. During his career he held conducting posts with the Bach Choir (1928-31), the City of

Sir Adrian Boult

Birmingham Symphony Orchestra (1923-30), the BBC Symphony Orchestra (1930-50) and the London Philharmonic Orchestra (1950-7). He championed British composers, and introduced much new music to London, such as **Berg's** *Wozzeck* (1934) and important works by Bartók, Stravinsky and American composers.

bourdon (Fr.) Sustained low note, such as a **drone** or pedal point. It is used to describe the lowest drone on the hurdy-gurdy, the free vibrating strings of the larger lutes, and the large pipes on an organ.

Bourgeois, Derek (1941-) English composer who studied at Cambridge and with Herbert **Howells** at the Royal College of Music. Bourgeois has written symphonies and chamber and organ music, but is best known for his choral works written for schools and amateur performers, and for his compositions for brass band. From 1971 he taught at Bristol University. He is now Director of the National Youth Orchestra.

Bourgeois, Louis (*c.*1510-*c.*1560) French composer and theorist, chiefly remembered as one of the music editors of the Calvinist Psalter, in which monophonic popular and church tunes were adapted to the new French translation of the Psalms for the Reformed Church.

Bourgeois was one of the many composers who used these tunes as the basis for polyphonic composition. His theoretical work *Le droict chemin de musique* (1550) displays his keenness for teaching practical music to children, and provides some very early evidence for *notes inégales.*

Bournemouth Symphony Orchestra Founded by Dan Godfrey in 1897, it was first called the Bournemouth Municipal Orchestra; it is the oldest professional orchestra in Britain. From the start it concentrated on English music, and such composers as **Elgar**, **Stanford**, and **Parry** were associated with it. The tradition of weekly concerts in the Winter Garden, which began in the 1910s, continues to this day, although there was a break before and during World War II. The name was changed in 1954. An associated chamber orchestra, the Bournemouth Sinfonietta, was founded in 1968. Both ensembles perform and broadcast frequently all over Europe and Britain. Since 1934 the directors have included Richard Austin, Rudolf **Schwarz**, Sir Charles **Groves**, Constantin **Silvestri**, Paavo Berglund, Rudolf Barshai and, since 1988, Andrew Lytton.

bouzouki/buzuq (Greece/Turkey) Long-necked lute (larger than the **saz**), traditionally having three double courses of strings tuned E-B′-E′ and movable frets. Before the 20th century it was used for solo improvisations on Turkish *maqamat* (see **maqam**), with the lower strings providing a drone, but the modern Greek *bouzouki* is designed for the more Western-style music which has been popular since the 1930s. It now has fixed metal frets and four double courses of strings tuned D-G-B′-E′, making chords easier to play.

Bouzouki

bow Arched piece of wood strung with horsehair. In its original form it had the shape of a bow as used in archery, and in many cultures the bow has retained this shape. It is used to play some form of string instrument by drawing the bow across the strings, producing a unique and sustained sound. The most widespread of these instruments is now the violin family of Western music, using a bow developed gradually from the mid-18th century and standardized by the work of François Tourte (1747-1835). The **Tourte bow** is made from Brazil-wood, which is lighter than the snakewood from which earlier bows were fashioned, curved inwards toward the hair and diminishing in thickness from the heel to the tip. This style of bow allows subtle dynamic variation and accentuation not afforded by earlier versions.

With the surge of interest in authentic performance practice of early and **Baroque** music, 'outcurve bows' are often used for the undifferentiated singing sound which results from their particular technical limitations.

Bowen, York (1884-1961) English composer and pianist. After studying at the Royal Academy of Music he established a reputation as a pianist of prodigious talent, as well as being a respected composer. He was one of the first English pianists correctly to interpret the music of Debussy and Ravel, as is testified by his important book *On Pedalling the Modern Pianoforte* (1936). His compositions include three piano concertos, as well as genre pieces and a fine oboe sonata.

Bowles, Paul (1910-) American composer, a pupil of Aaron **Copland**, Virgil **Thomson** and Nadia **Boulanger**. His work is mainly operatic and is influenced by jazz and the music of South America.

Bowman, James (1941-) English countertenor who studied at Oxford and made his stage début in 1967 as Oberon in Britten's *A Midsummer Night's Dream*. His wide repertory includes much 17th-century music and many of Handel's castrato roles as well as roles created for him by 20th-century composers: Priest Confessor in Maxwell Davies's *Taverner* and Voice of Apollo in Britten's *Death in Venice*, 1973. Bowman has a powerful voice and a remarkable stage presence.

Boyce, William (1711-1779) English composer. He was a Chorister of St Paul's Cathedral and studied with Maurice Greene. In 1734 he became organist of the Earl of Oxford's chapel, and in 1736 became both organist at St Michael's, Cornhill, and Composer to the Chapel Royal. He also composed much music for the Society of Apollo and for the Three Choirs Festival. His most serious and forward-looking opera, *Peleus and Thetis*, was produced in 1740, and 1747 saw the publication of his very popular *Twelve Sonatas for two Violins and Bass*. In 1755 he was made Master of the King's Musick, and composed a *Birthday Ode* and a *New Year Ode* practically every year thereafter. Among his 14 stage works *The Secular Masque* (*c.*1746) is particularly fine, while his 65 anthems include *O be Joyful in God* and *O Where shall Wisdom be Found?* (*c.*1769). His eight *Symphonies in Eight Parts* are overtures to odes.

Boyd, Anne (1946-) Australian composer. She studied at the New South Wales Conservatorium and in Britain, and became a lecturer at the University of Sussex. She has explored the music of the Far East and the Pacific Islands, and has taught at the University of Hong Kong since 1980. She is keenly interested in musical education. Her works include two string quartets; a quintet for wind, piano, and percussion, *The Metamorphosis of the Solitary Female Phoenix*; other pieces for strings; and theatre works (*The Rose Garden*, 1972; *The Little Mermaid*, 1974, for children).

Braga, Gaetano (1829-1907) Italian cellist and composer. Apart from several successful tours as a cellist, Braga was a composer of operas and later in life much in demand as a vocal coach. His salon piece *An Angel's Serenade* has become a popular classic.

Braham, John (1774-1856) English tenor of Portuguese Jewish extraction. As a boy soprano he had great success; **Cimarosa**, among others, composed for him. As a tenor he became one of the leading singers of his time, famed for the mellifluous use of the falsetto for the upper register, and for his stirring performances of patriotic songs.

Brahms, Johannes (1833-1897) German composer, pianist and conductor, born in Hamburg, the son of a double-bass player who taught him to play the violin, cello and horn well enough by the age of 15 to supplement the family income by playing in taverns and dance-halls. He studied composition with Eduard Marxsen, who soon recognized the boy's exceptional gifts. In 1849, the 16-year-old Brahms was engaged as accompanist for a tour by the Hungarian violinist Remenyi, and through him came to know **Joachim** and **Schumann**, who in a famous article headed *New Paths* proclaimed Brahms's genius. Immediately his music was accepted for publication, and solo engagements as a pianist poured in. With the tragic death of Schumann in 1856, Brahms developed a close friendship with his widow Clara, the famous pianist, who was influential in getting the young man a position at the court of Detmold. Here for some ten years he conducted the choir, was soloist at court concerts and piano-teacher to aristocratic young ladies, but had ample time for intense study of the classics and creative work. During these years he wrote several choral works, his first string sextet Op.18, the two orchestral Serenades, and the Piano Concerto No.1 in D minor, originally conceived as a symphony. In 1863 Brahms moved to Vienna, still regarded as the musical capital of central Europe. Having established himself as a pianist of first rank, he soon won respect for his compositions and was invited to become director of the Singakademie, but after one season resigned, realizing that his severe taste was not in tune with the easy-going Viennese. This choral experience prompted Brahms to compose his *German Requiem* which established his pre-eminence as a composer. Other important choral works followed – *Rinaldo*, *The Song of Destiny* and the *Alto Rhapsody*, as well as the charming set of *Love-Song Waltzes* for vocal quartet and piano duet, which won him widespread popularity.

In 1870 Brahms exulted in the victory of German arms over the French with his

Song of Triumph. In 1872 he was appointed director of the prestigious Viennese Society of the Friends of Music, and conductor of the finest choral concerts in Vienna, a post he held with great distinction for three years, introducing the music of Bach and Handel (until then little known to the Viennese), as well as pieces of his own such as the *Variations on the St Anthony Chorale* for two pianos or orchestra. Brahms had been working on a symphony since 1854, but, nervous of comparison with the great figures of the past, he regarded the form as 'no laughing matter'. In 1876 he at last completed the First in C minor, but despite the splendours of the large Romantic orchestra in the hands of Liszt and Wagner, Brahms asked for no more players than had Beethoven, in a work of severely classical proportions. Its success was immediate, and in the following year he sketched the pastoral, idyllic Symphony No.2 in D major. Music now poured from his pen: some of his loveliest songs, the piano rhapsodies (Op.79), the Violin Concerto for Joachim (1879), the Piano Concerto No.2 (1882), dedicated to his old teacher, Marxsen, the F major Quintet (Op.88), and at last, after an interval of six years, another symphony, No.3 in F major (1883), which more than any other expresses Brahms's inner feelings with its hidden messages and references to the music of Beethoven and Schumann.

In the following year he began to sketch out the Symphony No.4 in E minor (1885), a work of profound intensity and unusual form – it concludes with a passacaglia on a theme by Bach – which took many years to win the hearts of the public. Brahms's pre-eminent position was marked by many honours – a doctorate from Cambridge University in 1877, followed by many similar distinctions; in 1889 he was overjoyed to be given the freedom of his native Hamburg, and in 1893 the Viennese Society of the Friends of Music had a gold medal struck in his honour. At his death the whole musical world mourned the last of the great classical composers.

Brain, Dennis (1921-1957) British horn-player, son of Aubrey Brain. His tragic death in a car accident robbed the world of a horn-player who was perhaps England's finest. He recorded widely, and his recorded legacy includes chamber music as well as concertos. Probably best-known is the *Serenade for Tenor, Horn and Strings* by Benjamin **Britten**, with Peter **Pears**.

branle (Fr.) Family of dances, originating in France in the Middle Ages, and remaining popular up to the present day.

The many different types of *branle* – *simple, double, de Champagne, d'Ecosse* etc. – are all characterized by the dancers holding hands in a line or in a circle, and by a swinging, side-stepping motion.

During the 16th and 17th centuries many publications of dance music contained *branles*, beginning with the *Eighteen Basses Dances...* (1530) for lute published by **Attaignant** and continuing through Michael Praetorius's *Terpsichore* (1612) for instrumental ensemble to Robert Ballard's *Deuxième livre* (1614) for lute. **Arbeau**'s *Orchésographie* contains the largest surviving collection of descriptions of the steps of *branles*, including several 'mimed' *branles* in which dancers imitate horses, washerwomen, etc. The *branle* has survived (or resurfaced) in many parts of France.

The English and Italian equivalents are brawl and *brando* respectively.

Brant, Henry (1913-) American composer. Brant is in some ways an artistic descendant of Charles **Ives**. His experimental attitude to composition was established early in his career, and many of his pieces demand the spatial separation of instruments or groups of players. His compositions have been innovative in other ways too, using 'found objects' as well as conventional instruments. He has taught at several universities in the United States, and has composed in many genres. Perhaps his most celebrated piece is *The Grand Universal Circus* (1956).

brass band Although any large ensemble of **brass instruments** may be called a brass band, the term is used specifically to refer to the British 'competition' band, which has the standard line-up of one E♭ cornet, several B♭ cornets, one flugelhorn, three E♭ horns, two baritones, two euphoniums, two tenor trombones, one bass trombone, two E♭ basses and two B♭ basses. The National Brass Band Festival was established in 1860.

Many brass bands were originally founded to provide musical recreation for employees of mines and factories, especially in the north of England (where the movement has always been strong), whence come the most distinguished bands such as the Grimethorpe Colliery Band and the Brighouse and Rastrick Brass Band.

Many established composers have written music for brass band, including Elgar (*Severn Suite*, 1930), Holst (*A Moorside Suite*, 1929), Herbert **Howells** (*Three Figures*, 1960) and Harrison **Birtwistle** (*Grimethorpe Aria*).

brass instruments Family of musical instruments in which the sound is produced by the vibration of the player's lips setting a column of air in motion. The name derives from the fact that most modern representatives of the family are made of brass or similar metal, although certain instruments made of other materials (wood, clay and horn) could also be included in the definition.

The brass section of a modern orchestra generally includes French horns, trumpets, trombones and a tuba. For the instruments used in a British brass band see **brass band**. Other brass instruments in current use include the valve trombone, bugle and sousaphone.

The origin of brass instruments is ancient; simple horns can be easily constructed from an animal horn or a conch shell. The Roman army used large brass instruments called *tuba* and *buccina*. Brass instruments were used extensively in the Renaissance, namely the cornett, slide trumpet, sackbut and (natural) trumpet. Brass instruments have always had particular associations with the military (trumpets and bugles) and with the hunt (horns).

All brass instruments have the same method of sound production: the 'buzzing' or vibration of the player's lips is transferred via the mouthpiece to the air inside the instrument. The only notes that may properly be obtained from a natural instrument (that is one with an air column of fixed length) are those of the **harmonic series**. In order to fill in the gaps between the natural harmonics, various methods are employed to enable the player to shorten or lengthen the resonating length of the tube, such as valves (trumpet, tuba), a slide (trombone, slide trumpet), holes closed by fingers (cornett, serpent) or keys (keyed bugle, ophicleide).

The tonal characteristics of all brass instruments are loud, majestic and stirring, and it is for these properties that they have been used down the ages.

bravura (It.) Brilliance or virtuosity in vocal or instrumental music.

break Jazz term used to describe a brief solo by one or more of the instrumentalists. Usually the players improvise unaccompanied by the rhythm section. The word is also used to describe the unison playing of a planned **riff** which temporarily suspends the time of the piece.

Traditionally the break is used at the end of the **bridge** section or in the last bar and a half of a four-bar phrase.

breaking of the voice Process which occurs in adolescent men and, less dramatically, in women, whereby the voice becomes deeper and more mature. The term is particularly used of a boy's treble voice changing to a male alto, tenor, baritone or bass. The name has the connotation of a sudden, almost overnight change, which while true for a few people is somewhat misleading, because most people experience a gradual change.

Julian Bream

Bream, Julian (1933-) English guitarist and lutenist. His first guitar teacher was his father, and he later studied at the Royal College of Music. Since making his London début in 1950 he has travelled extensively and has given a number of first performances of important guitar pieces, such as the concerto by **Villa-Lobos**. His interest in the lute also dates from this period and both his solo performances of Dowland and his accompaniments to lute songs (recorded with Peter **Pears**) were revelatory in their day. Bream's expert and exciting playing has inspired many composers to write works for him, including Richard Rodney **Bennett**, **Walton** and **Britten**.

Brecht, Bertolt (1898-1956) German writer. Much of his work has been set to music, either in direct collaboration with a composer (such as **Weill**, **Hindemith**, Eisler and **Dessau**) or as a source of texts for other composers. Some of the collaborations are through-composed works, for example *Aufstieg und Fall der Stadt Mahagonny* (1927-9, with Weill), and others are plays with music, such as *Happy End* (1929, also with Weill).

In his early collaborations with Weill and Hindemith he performed the role of librettist, but in his later collaboration with Hanns Eisler, following his conversion to Marxism, the works they produced showed the music to be subordinate to the text, for example *Die Massnahme* (1930). During the time of his collaboration with Eisler he was in exile and relative obscurity in the United States. He returned to East Berlin in 1949, where he formed the theatre company *The Berliner Ensemble*. This was acclaimed as one of the world's greatest and Brecht came to be recognized as one of the major figures in 20th-century theatre.

Brendel, Alfred (1931-) Austrian pianist now resident in Britain. He studied at the Vienna Academy and with Edwin Fischer. He made his début in 1948. Brendel is especially esteemed for his recordings of the Viennese classics, although his repertory extends to Schoenberg and embraces the major Romantic composers. His playing has been supplemented by musicological studies, as is testified in his highly regarded writings on music as well as his master-classes both for television and for the major festivals of Europe, where he is much in demand. His playing demonstrates a respect for the composer's intentions and a deep feeling for style, as well as a sound palette rich in extremes and subtleties.

breve A note half the value of a long and twice that of a **semibreve**. In the 13th century it was the shortest note in use, hence its name (from the Latin *brevis*, short). It is only occasionally used in modern music. The American term is double whole note.

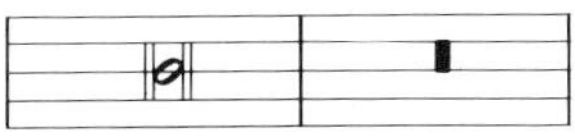

Breve Breve rest

Brian, Havergal (1876-1972) English composer, music critic and editor. Many of his compositions are scored for large choral and orchestral forces – the Gothic Symphony in E minor, for example, involving 16 horns – sometimes reminiscent of Richard Strauss in their complex textures and expansive, grandiose themes. In all, he wrote 32 symphonies and five operas in addition to several cantatas and part-songs, but the extravagant nature of his larger works meant that they received only occasional performances. In the 1950s, however, the BBC broadcast several of Brian's compositions, and this served to focus attention on many pieces previously little heard.

bridge 1. In string instruments, it is a wooden wedge raising the strings above the soundboard and allowing them to communicate their vibrations to the main body of the instrument.

2. In composition, a bridge (passage) is a short section joining together two larger sections in a full-scale work, often by means of a key change.

Bridge, Frank (1879-1941) English composer, conductor and accomplished violist. He studied under **Stanford** at the Royal College of Music, initially writing chamber music and songs, then turning to more substantial orchestral works. Among these, the three *Idylls* for string quartet and the symphonic poem *Summer* reflect the influence of his contemporary, **Delius**.

After World War I Bridge's style underwent considerable change in terms of harmonic language, rhythm and texture, and works from this period (for example the third and fourth string quartets) have been placed on a par with compositions by Schoenberg. Bridge played with several string quartets, conducted opera (Savoy Theatre, Covent Garden), and numbered **Britten** among his composition pupils.

Bridge, Sir John Frederick (1844-1924) English organist and composer. From 1869 he served at Manchester Cathedral, and at Westminster Abbey as deputy organist (1875-82) and organist (1882-1918). While at the Abbey he saw to the modernization of the organ and arranged the music for Queen Victoria's Jubilees in 1887 and 1897, and for the coronations of Edward VII and George V. From 1905 he was Professor of Music at London University. His compositions were mainly for the Church (oratorios) and for music festivals.

Bridgewater, Ernest Leslie (1893-1975) English pianist and conductor who held various musical posts in theatres and from 1935 to 1942 was engaged in the BBC light music section. He composed incidental music for films and the stage.

brindisi (It.) Popular song involving the drinking of a toast. A well-known operatic example is the chorus *Libiamo* from *La traviata*.

brio (It.) Spirit, vivacity; hence *con brio*, an expression mark directing the performer to play with brilliance and spirit. Also, *allegro con brio*.

Britten, Benjamin (1913-1976) English composer, pianist and conductor. He studied at the Royal College of Music with John **Ireland**, and with Frank **Bridge** who awakened an admiration for Alban Berg; other influences were Stravinsky, Bartók, and Mahler. Early in his career he made a strong impression with his *Sinfonietta* (1932), *Simple Symphony* (1934) and especially the *Variations on a Theme of Frank Bridge* (1937), played for the first time at the Salzburg Festival by the Boyd Neel String Orchestra. By 1936 Britten had already shown his gift for the voice with the orchestral song cycle *Our Hunting Fathers* (W.H. Auden), but this was greatly stimulated by his meeting in 1937 with the tenor Peter **Pears**, the start of a lifelong association, which produced the cycle *On This Island* (1937), *Les Illuminations* (1939), *Seven Sonnets of Michelangelo* (1940), the *Serenade for Tenor, Horn and Strings*, and many other songs and operatic roles.

Benjamin Britten

In 1939 Britten and Pears left England for the United States, where the premières of his Violin Concerto (1939) and *Sinfonia da Requiem* (1940) were given. While in America Britten came across Crabbe's poem *The Borough*, and, perhaps aware of his own position as a conscientious objector, was inspired by its theme of the hounding of an outcast to embark on his opera *Peter Grimes*, with the help of a grant from the Koussevitzky Foundation. He returned to England in 1942. With the successful production of *Peter Grimes* at Sadler's Wells in 1945, with Pears in the title-role, Britten thereafter concentrated on opera, with a stream of works: *The Rape of Lucretia* (1946); the comedy *Albert Herring* (1947); the all-male *Billy Budd* (1951); *Gloriana* (1953), an opera about Elizabeth I to mark the coronation of Elizabeth II; *The Turn of the Screw* (1954), based on a ghost story by Henry James; and *A Midsummer Night's Dream* (1960). Many of these were performed by the English Opera Group (later **English Music Theatre**), which Britten and Pears had founded in 1947 for the performance of chamber opera. This was followed in 1948 by the foundation of the **Aldeburgh Festival** on the Suffolk coast, which aimed to combine community music-making with the finest professional performances. These centred round his own outstanding gifts as a pianist, accompanist and conductor of much music other than his own – especially his favourites, Mozart, Schubert, Schumann, Mahler, and Elgar.

Other compositions included the *Young Person's Guide to the Orchestra* (1946), originally composed for an educational film; the choral *Spring Symphony* (1949); several song cycles; three string quartets; the *War Requiem* (1961) for the reopening of Coventry Cathedral; the *Church Parables*, and a *Cello Symphony* for **Rostropovich**. After completing the television opera *Owen Wingrave* in 1971, Britten returned to the stage for his last opera, *Death in Venice*, based on a story by Thomas Mann, in which Peter Pears gave a memorable interpretation. Shortly before his death in 1976, Britten became the first composer to be created a life peer, as Lord Britten of Lowestoft.

Britten's early instrumental works hold their place in the public's affection, but there is no doubt that he will be remembered as the greatest English composer for the voice since Purcell. His songs are the staple of every English singer, and his operas have a firm place in the repertory of opera houses throughout the world. With his outstanding gifts as a performer, he was a rare example of the complete all-round musician, an inspiration and a notable adornment to British musical life in the second half of this century.

Brixi, František (1732-1771) Most celebrated member of an extensive Czech family of musicians. The son of Simon Brixi, he was best known as a choirmaster and composer. His music draws heavily on the contemporary music of Italy and Vienna, and Alessandro **Scarlatti** and **Fux** may be cited as particularly important influences. Apart from writing more than 400 sacred works, he produced some school dramas, both serious and comic, as well as symphonies. Brixi was instrumental in bringing **Mozart** to Prague in the 1780s.

Broken chord

broken chord Type of melodic or accompanying figuration produced by playing the notes of a chord successively in any order, rather than simultaneously; the Alberti bass is a particular example of broken chord figuration.

broken consort Small 16th- and 17th-century instrumental group made up of a mixture of string and wind instruments.

Brott, Boris (1944-) Canadian violinist and conductor, son of the composer and conductor Alexander Brott. Apart from studying with his father, he also took lessons with **Monteux**, **Bernstein** and **Markevich**. He founded the Philharmonic Youth Orchestra of Montreal in 1959 and has since conducted in many countries. He has been principal conductor of the Northern Sinfonia. He has conducted the Royal Ballet, and gave the première at Covent Garden of Stravinsky's *The Soldier's Tale*. He is also widely known as a guest conductor as well as in the role of television presenter of programmes on music.

Brouwer, Leo (1939-) Cuban composer, guitarist and conductor. He has written many film scores, music for the guitar and *Hexahedrons* (music for any six instrumentalists or multiples of six).

Brown, Christopher (1943-) English composer. He studied at the Royal Academy of Music with **Berkeley** and at the Berlin Hochschule with **Blacher**. He is particularly noted for his vocal and choral works, which are designed to be easily assimilated by amateur performers: an outstanding example is his cantata *David* (1970), which was originally written for the Three Choirs Festival. He has also written two Masses (1967, 1974); a *Te Deum*; groups of songs such as *Wordsworth Songs*, *Snows of Winter*, and *Three Medieval Lyrics*; and an orchestral piece, *The Sun Rising* (1977). In 1969 he took up an appointment at the Royal Academy of Music. He is currently Director of Music at Clare College, Cambridge.

Brown, Earle (1926-) American composer, closely associated with the avant-garde New York School established in the early 1950s by John **Cage** and Morton **Feldman**.

After participating in the famous Darmstadt Summer Courses, Brown worked as a recording engineer for Capitol Records before becoming composer-in-residence at institutes in Baltimore and West Berlin. During the early 1950s, as one of the leaders of the American avant-garde, Brown developed the technique of graphic notation in pieces such as *November 1952* and *December 1952* and of open form in *Twenty-Five Pages* (1953) and *Available Forms I* (1961).

Brown, Iona (1941-) English violinist and conductor. She studied in Rome, Brussels, Vienna and with Henryk **Szeryng** in Paris. She became director of the **Academy of St Martin-in-the-Fields** in 1974 and has made numerous recordings with the orchestra, both as director and soloist: these include the complete series of Mozart's violin concertos, and his *Sinfonia concertante* with Josef **Suk** on the viola. In 1981 she was appointed artistic director of the Norwegian Chamber Orchestra, with which she toured Europe and the United States. She has been guest director of the **City of Birmingham Symphony Orchestra** and, from 1987, music director of the Los Angeles Chamber Orchestra. She has made solo appearances with many other orchestras, recording Bartók's Violin Concerto No.2 with the **Philharmonia** under Simon **Rattle**; she has also recorded the Violin Concerto by David **Blake**, which he dedicated to her. She was made an OBE in 1986.

Browne, John (*c.*1490-?) English composer and one-time clerk at Windsor. Little is known about his life but a number of his compositions are preserved, some of them in *The Eton Choirbook*. These works are rich and complex, and ahead of their time in an expressive use of dissonance. A few carols also survive.

Brubeck, Dave (1920-) American composer and jazz pianist with leanings towards classical music. He numbers both Schoenberg and Milhaud among his composition teachers. Brubeck has formed several ensembles, the most famous of which is his quartet, formed with the saxophonist Paul Desmond. Brubeck's compositions include the popular number *Take Five*, a piece in 5/4 time.

Dave Brubeck

Bruch, Max (1838-1920) German composer who was born in Cologne and studied there and in Bonn. His opera *Loreley*, first performed in 1863, reflects his roots in the Rhineland. He held various posts in Mannheim, Berlin and Koblenz, and was for some years conductor of the Liverpool Philharmonic Society. He wrote one other opera, *Hermione*, oratorios, symphonies and church music, but it is for his pieces for violin and orchestra that he is best remembered. They include several concertos, especially the Violin Concerto No.1, and the *Scottish Fantasy*, based on melodies he collected while he was working in Britain.

Bruckner, Anton (1824-1896) Austrian composer and organist, now regarded as one of the great symphonic composers of the 19th century. He was trained as a village school-teacher, like his father, and came late to music, developing his extraordinary skill as an organist, particularly in improvisation, which led to his being appointed organist at Linz Cathedral and later brought him international fame with acclaimed appearances in Paris and London. His earliest significant composition, the *Requiem* in D minor (1849), and other important church works reflected his life-long devotion to the Roman Catholic faith. In 1855 Bruckner gave up composition and for a period of six years pursued intense studies in counterpoint and orchestration with the celebrated teacher Simon Sechter; these, along with the overwhelming experience of the music of Wagner, transformed his approach to composition.

In 1863 he completed the first of his great cycle of symphonies, but with his simple peasant's outlook was ill-equipped to get them performed and accepted in the hothouse of Viennese musical politics. Conductors rejected them, and when he himself conducted, orchestral players laughed at his naive style. After meeting Wagner at the première of *Tristan und Isolde* in 1865, he dedicated his Symphony No.3 to him, and so earned the enmity of the influential critic Hanslick and the anti-Wagner camp. In 1868 he succeeded Sechter as a professor at the Vienna Conservatoire and was able to devote more time to composition, but it was not until 1881, with the first performance of the Symphony No.4, that Bruckner won any success. Lacking confidence, he reluctantly yielded to friendly and hostile advice by making wholesale revisions to his symphonies, leaving a minefield of problems, which still trouble scholars and conductors trying to establish ideal performing versions.

There are ten numbered symphonies if one includes what Bruckner called No.0, and the unfinished No.9, plus an unnumbered symphony in F minor (1863); their complicated history makes them difficult to date. By the end of the century Bruckner's music had won a firm place in the esteem of the Austrian and German public, touching depths of feeling grossly exploited by Hitler, who used it to create the mood for his Nazi rallies. Anglo-Saxon musicians and gramophone companies at first showed little interest in the combination of Schubertian themes and Wagnerian grandeur. Audiences were reluctant to sit through works lasting an hour or more, but since World War II they have taken Bruckner to their hearts as a major symphonist, with an honoured place in our concert life. The development of the LP also played an important part in bringing these works to the notice of the public.

Bruckner's choral music is of supreme importance. Motets such as *Ave Maria* (1861) and *Pange Lingua* (1868), the great *Te Deum* for soloists, chorus and orchestra and Masses such as the fine E minor (1866-82) with wind accompaniment, reveal a mastery of counterpoint enriched by his sensitive ear for melodic and harmonic expression, and inspired by his deep faith.

Brüggen, Frans (1934-) Dutch player of recorder and Baroque flute, and one of the great modern popularizers of these instruments. He studied at the Musieklyceum, Amsterdam, and has taught at the Royal Conservatoire, The Hague. In 1972-3 he was Erasmus professor of late Baroque music at Harvard University. Recordings include many with the harpsichordist Gustav **Leonhardt**. In 1986 he founded the Orchestra of the Eighteenth Century, and he is their principal conductor.

Brumel, Antoine (*c.*1460-*c.*1515) French composer. He became a cleric at Notre Dame de Chartres in 1483, master of the Innocents at St Peter, Geneva, in 1486 and thereafter was ordained. As a priest he worked at Laon Cathedral and Notre Dame in Paris, and in 1505 was appointed *maestro di cappella* to Alfonso I d'Este at Ferrara.

His 15 Masses form a major part of his output, and all are of high quality and craftsmanship. His *Missa 'Et ecce terrae motus'* is the earliest surviving Mass in 12 voice parts. His other Masses are scored for four voices. Among his secular songs his arrangement of **Ockeghem**'s *Fors seulement* is remarkable for its low ranges and rich sonorities.

Bruneau, Alfred (1857-1934) French composer and critic. A pupil of **Massenet**, Bruneau shared this composer's taste for Zola and for that author's realist doctrines. His music translates many features of Italian **verismo** into the French operatic medium. In Bruneau's day, *Messidor* (1897) and *L'ouragan* (1901) were well known, but in the early years of the century his work went out of favour as Zolaesque naturalism was replaced by more subtle aesthetics. As a writer, he produced many books and articles, including books on Fauré and Massenet.

Brunswick, Mark (1902-1971) American composer. His training was in France with Nadia **Boulanger** and in Vienna, where he came into contact with **Webern**. Among particular interests that have affected his music, 16th-century polyphony has been important and much of his work displays great contrapuntal facility. He also wrote verse and set many of his poems to music. Between 1946 and 1967 he was chairman of the music department at the City College of New York.

Bruscantini, Sesto (1919-) Italian baritone. He studied in Rome and made his début in 1946 in Puccini's *La bohème*. He appeared at La Scala, Milan, in 1949 and at Glyndebourne in 1951. He specialized in *buffo* roles such as Leporello in *Don Giovanni*, Dr Dulcamara in Donizetti's *L'elisir d'amore*, the cynical Alfonso in *Così fan tutte*, Dandini in Rossini's *La Cenerentola* and Figaro in *Il barbiere di Siviglia*. From 1961 he sang more dramatic roles, often in the United States, but continued with the *buffo* parts in London and elsewhere. His repertory was vast – well over 100 roles.

Bruson, Renato (1936-) Italian baritone. After studying in Padua he made his début in 1961 in *Il trovatore* at the Spoleto Festival. In 1968 he performed at the Metropolitan Opera in New York, in *Lucia di Lammermoor* and two Verdi operas, and in 1973 in San Francisco and Los Angeles, where he sang the title role in *Falstaff* in the famous production conducted by Giulini. He has appeared at the Royal Opera House, Covent Garden, since 1976, when he made his début in *Ballo in maschera*, followed by several other Verdi roles. He is considered a leading interpreter of the Verdi and Donizetti repertories. He has made many recordings and some films; he has also appeared in Chicago, Philadelphia, Vienna, Munich and in various festivals.

Brymer, Jack (1915-) English clarinettist. Although he originally trained as a schoolteacher, his career changed direction when **Beecham** appointed him to play in the **Royal Philharmonic Orchestra** in 1947. He has worked with many other orchestras and is much admired for his concerto and chamber playing. His tone is warm and vibrant, and his sense of style exemplary. He also gives entertaining lectures on the clarinet and on his experiences as a player.

Bucchi, Valentino (1916-1976) Italian composer who studied at the conservatoire in Florence before beginning a teaching career. His compositional activities have been accompanied throughout his career by work as a music critic and teacher. He employs an easily absorbed compositional style; his music is essentially **diatonic**, with easily followed contrapuntal movement. His numerous compositions include many operas, ballets, songs, film scores and orchestral pieces.

buffo, buffa (It.) Gust or puff, now used to mean comic. Thus *opera buffa* is comic opera, *basso buffo* a comic bass singer and *stile buffo* means in a comic style.

bugaku (Japan) Traditional court dance, and a term applied to **gagaku** when the music is used as an accompaniment to the dance. Movement in *bugaku* is extremely slow and is performed on a raised square stage in front of the orchestra. The dances correspond to the division of **gagaku** into 'music of the left' (*Tāgaku*) and 'music of the right' (*Komagaku*), and are accompanied by the music and ensemble, excluding stringed instruments, of the appropriate side. The dancers are dressed in elaborate costume, the dominant colour for left being red and for right being green. Generally the order of dances in a performance is fixed, the dance of the right following the dance of the left to form a pair.

bugle Military brass instrument traditionally used for signalling. Like the **post horn**, it is an instrument based on the notes of the harmonic series, forming a perfect fifth and octave from the bell note and then a major triad, using **harmonics** from the second to the sixth. Bugles are

Bugle

usually tuned in G or B♭ but occasionally in F.

The word is also used as a generic term for the family of brass instruments constructed after the principles of the **flugelhorn**.

buka (Java) Short, often unmeasured, introduction to a performance of a **gamelan** composition.

Bull, John (*c*.1562-1628) Welsh or English virginalist, organist and composer of keyboard and vocal music. In 1587 he became organist of Hereford Cathedral, and in 1586 a Gentleman of the Chapel Royal. In 1613 he left England never to return, going first to Brussels and in 1615 becoming organist of Antwerp Cathedral. His keyboard music is preserved largely in two sources, the Fitzwilliam Virginal Manuscript and the publication *Parthenia* (1612-13), and falls into four broad types: arrangements of popular songs, arrangements of **plainsong** and sacred models, fantasias on pre-existing polyphonic compositions, and dances, of which one of the **galliards** strongly resembles the British National Anthem and may have been the origin of the tune. He also wrote 16 sacred choral works and 200 canons, displaying his mastery of polyphony.

Bull, Ole (1810-1880) Norwegian violinist and composer, highly influential in the development of 19th-century Norwegian music. As a player he was influenced by the *hardanger* style of folk-fiddling of his native country, and he adopted the characteristic flatter bridge and longer bow of this style even when he performed classical music. This was much admired on his extensive European tours, where he was influenced also by Paganini. He embarked upon prodigiously busy concert tours in England, Germany and Russia and on his return to Norway was welcomed as a national hero. Bull's compositions are inseparable from his own personality as a violinist.

Buller, John (1927-) English composer. He began as a surveyor, but in 1959 studied music with Anthony **Milner**. In 1971-2 he composed a series of atmospheric pieces based on Joyce's *Finnegan's Wake*, which were broadcast a few years later. *Proença* (1977), for mezzo-soprano, electric guitar and orchestra, evokes the world of the troubadours in medieval Provence. He has also composed other compilations of voice and tape or instruments and tape (*Le terrazze*, 1974), and a string quartet.

bullroarer Australian aboriginal instrument consisting of an oblong wooden board, one of the two sides of which is carved in relief, making the surface uneven. The board is whirled around above the head on a string, producing a thunderous whirring, used in rituals to personify the sound of the supernatural itself.

Bülow, Hans Freiherr von (1830-1894) German conductor, pianist and composer. Bülow studied piano with Friedrich Wieck and **Liszt**, whose daughter Cosima he was to marry, and then toured extensively, giving first performances of many important works (including Tchaikovsky's Piano Concerto No.1 in Boston, 1875). He worked throughout Europe as a conductor; in Germany he was close to **Wagner**, presenting many influential operatic premières - *Tristan und Isolde* (1865) and *Die Meistersinger von Nürnberg* (1868). Cosima transferred her affections to Wagner in the late 1860s. Bülow composed several piano pieces and various orchestral works.

Bumbry, Grace (1937-) American mezzo-soprano who studied under Lotte **Lehmann**. She made her début at the

Paris Opéra in 1960 in *Aïda*, and was the first black singer to appear at Bayreuth (1961). Since 1970, she has also sung soprano roles. Bumbry is probably best known in the roles of Carmen and Salome and is considered to be a fine operatic singer with considerable stage presence.

bunraku (Japan) Puppet theatre with a **shamisen** lute accompanying the narrator-singer. The narrator portrays all the characters in the play, both male and female, old and young, and his intense singing style is generally known as **Gidayū-bushi**, after its most famous exponent. *Bunraku*, whose plots tend to be tragic, is characterized by extravagant gestures and heightened representation of all emotions. The puppets are animated by on-stage puppeteers. The performance is split into five main parts or *dan* and consists of *uta* (songs) and *odori* (dances). Its music has stereotyped melodic and rhythmic patterns.

Bürger, Gottfried August (1747-1794) German poet, important in the establishment of the early Romantic movement. He published old German folk ballads in a collection which was much in favour in the early 19th century. **Schubert** was one of several composers to set Bürger's work.

Burgon, Geoffrey (1941-) English composer. After playing the trumpet in the school jazz band he studied composition at the Guildhall School of Music with Peter **Wishart**. He performed as a trumpeter for several years, while continuing to compose. His first major success was the *Requiem* (1976), following his ballet scores *The Calm* (1974) and *Running Figures* (1975). Around this time he began writing for films and television, and the music for the series *Tinker, Tailor, Soldier, Spy* (1979) and *Brideshead Revisited* (1981) achieved enormous popular success, the *Nunc Dimittis* from the former becoming a best-selling record.

Burgon has also been drawn to early music and literature: *At the Round Earth's Imagined Corners* (1971) is a setting of Donne, while *Veni Spiritus* (1979) and *The Fall of Lucifer* (1977) have a medieval inspiration. More recent compositions include the song cycle *Title Divine* (1986), the ballet *The Trial of Prometheus* for the Royal Ballet (1988), much chamber and vocal music and the score for another television series, *The Chronicles of Narnia* (1988). His music is fluid and melodic, with strong elements of the mystical and theatrical.

Burkhard, Paul (1911-1977) Swiss composer and conductor, whose professional conducting career included posts as resident conductor in theatres in Berne and Zurich. He conducted his own works, mainly light operettas, throughout Europe and also wrote liturgical plays for school use. In addition he wrote film and television music, and incidental music for several plays. He is best remembered for the song *O mein Papa*.

Burkhard, Willy (1900-1955) Swiss composer. He studied in Switzerland and under Karg-Elert in Leipzig and later became a teacher of composition at the Zurich Conservatoire. Although his work shows allegiances to several other composers' styles, including those of Bartók and Hindemith, he retained an individual style, largely through his own enthusiasms for the Baroque and for church modes. He blended these influences with a highly developed **chromaticism** in works such as the oratorio *Das Jahr*. His later music embraced **serialism**.

Burleigh, Henry Thacker (1866-1949) Black American composer and singer. In the latter capacity he showed talent at an early age, and sang spirituals to **Dvořák** when he visited the United States. In 1911 he was employed as an editor at the Ricordi publishing house, and he published many arrangements of spirituals as well as original compositions.

burletta (It.) Musical farce. The term was originally used in England for Italian comic operas and then came to be applied to English imitations. The first English *burletta* was *Midas* by Kane O'Hara, first performed in Dublin in 1762. At first *burlettas* were popular entertainments featuring songs and comic dialogue, but by the beginning of the 19th century the term was applied to comedies of all sorts that featured music.

Burrows, Stuart (1933-) Welsh lyric tenor who began to study singing after winning a prize at the National Eisteddfod in 1954. He made his début with the **Welsh National Opera** in 1963 in Verdi's *Nabucco* and at Covent Garden in 1967. He has appeared regularly at the Metropolitan Opera, New York (since 1971), San Francisco, Salzburg, Vienna and Paris. He is particularly noted for his Mozart roles, including Tamino in *Die Zauberflöte*, Don Ottavio in *Don Giovanni*, and Ferrando in *Così fan tutte*. He has also been successful as Ernesto in Donizetti's *Don Pasquale*, Fenton in Verdi's *Falstaff* and other roles from the 19th-century Italian repertory. He has had his own television series, has made numerous recordings and given many recitals.

Burt, Francis (1926-) English composer. After studying with Howard **Ferguson** and Boris **Blacher**, Burt presented pieces at the Darmstadt festivals of the 1950s. He was appointed professor of composition at the Vienna Hochschule für Musik in 1977 and has produced many works for the stage, mainly performed in Germany.

Busch, Fritz (1890-1951) German conductor and pianist. He trained at the Cologne Conservatoire and then worked in opera houses throughout Germany (Aachen, Stuttgart, Dresden), conducting first performances of operas by Hindemith, Richard Strauss, Busoni and Weill. He resigned during the Nazi regime and subsequently worked in Scandinavia, Buenos Aires, New York and England, where he was the first conductor of the Glyndebourne Opera (1939-51).

Bush, Alan (1900-) English composer, pianist and teacher. Four years' training at the Royal Academy of Music were followed by private study under John **Ireland** (composition), and under **Schnabel** and **Moiseiwitsch** (piano) in Berlin (1929-31). Since 1925 he has been professor of composition at the Royal Academy of Music. His first success as a composer came in 1923 with the String Quartet in A minor. His Symphony No.1 (1940) exemplified his theory that all the notes should have a thematic relevance. Later he moved away from this compositional method; in his operas from the 1950s onwards he has voiced his strongly held communist sympathies, which motivate works such as *Wat Tyler* (1953), about the popular uprising in England in the 14th century, *Men of Blackmoor* (1960) and *Joe Hill* (1970), about the American union leader who was executed. In all, Bush has written seven operas, three symphonies and a piano concerto, as well as a variety of other orchestral pieces, chamber and vocal works. In 1936 Bush founded the Workers' Music Association.

Bush, Geoffrey (1920-) English composer. He studied at Balliol College, Oxford, and later lectured in Oxford and London. In 1969 he was visiting professor at King's College, London. One of his earliest works was the *Christmas Cantata*, written in Oxford (1947). He has also produced two symphonies (1954, 1957); operas (*Lord Arthur Savile's Crime*), choral works (a *Magnificat* and *Nunc Dimittis*, 1976), songs, chamber pieces (a wind quintet, a trio) and many other orchestral works. He is prolific in all fields and has a lively style based on conventional tonality.

Busnois, Antoine (*c.*1430-1492) French composer. In 1467 he entered the private chapel of Charles the Bold, Duke of Burgundy, and on the Duke's death served his heir, Mary of Burgundy, until her death in 1482. His works include two complete Mass cycles, one on the *L'homme armé* theme, and some 11 motets, including *In Hydraulis*, which pays homage to **Ockeghem**. His major output, however, was secular songs, more than 60 of which survive. The contemporary popularity of two of them is evident, for his *Je ne demande lialté* served as a basis for instrumental versions by Obrecht and Agricola, and his *Fortuna Desperata* was used as a **cantus firmus** by **Josquin** and **Senfl**.

Busoni, Ferruccio (1866-1924) Italian pianist and composer, who settled in Berlin. He was an infant prodigy and was passionately interested in the music of Bach. He is best known as an editor and transcriber of Bach's works, such as the famous piano arrangement of the *D minor Chaconne* for violin; his Bach transcriptions were published in a seven-volume edition. Most of his piano music requires a virtuoso Lisztian technique.

After the turn of the century his interests broadened to include modern music, and he championed the work of Bartók and Schoenberg as well as maintaining his keen appreciation of Bach and Mozart. The dichotomy between his excitable southern blood (on his father's side) and the cooler northern personality of his German mother seemed to find a reflection in much of his output which was never really resolved: for instance, in his piano concerto of 1904, and some operas, including *Die Brautwahl* (1912). His final important work, *Doktor Faust*, remained unfinished. Busoni held several teaching posts and was director of the Bologna Conservatoire.

Büsser, Paul Henri (1872-1973) French composer and conductor. He studied the organ with **Franck** and **Widor**, and composition with Ernest **Guiraud**. In the early years of the century he established a reputation as a conductor. Debussy admired his conducting, and Büsser orchestrated several of his works, including *Printemps* and the *Petite suite*. Several of his stage works were well received and he composed chamber and orchestral music as well as songs. His style is indebted to early Debussy, among others.

Bussotti, Sylvano (1931-) Italian composer who was also a writer, painter, and film and theatre director. Musically, he was initiated as a **serialist** but rapidly moved on to become more interested in the ideas of John **Cage**. His scores became highly graphic, with distorted staves and visual images sometimes replacing any semblance of conventional notation. The *Rara Requiem* (1969-70) is considered an important work, summing up Bussotti's career. His many music-theatre pieces (which include a *Passion According to Sade*) are equally thought-provoking, and contain all kinds of unconventional effects. Bussotti has also written extensively on contemporary music.

Butt, Dame Clara (1872-1936) English contralto. After studying in Bristol and at the Royal College of Music in London she made her début as Ursula in **Sullivan**'s *Golden Legend* (1892). Her immense popular acclaim was centred on her performances on the concert platform and she is perhaps best remembered for her interpretation of Elgar's *Sea Pictures* and the arrangement for contralto soloist and orchestra of *Land of Hope and Glory*. Her exceptionally powerful and resonant voice made her a unique and unforgettable concert performer.

Butterley, Nigel (1935-) Australian composer, active also as a conductor and pianist. His many interests are reflected in the lively variety of his compositions. His earlier style reflected the current vogue for the formalism of the music of **Hindemith**, but **plainsong**, **serialism** and **impressionism** have all in their own way influenced his style. Visits to Europe inspired *Laudes*, four impressions of cathedrals, and religious mysticism is a recurrent preoccupation. Among lighter pieces is a collaboration with Barry

Humphries entitled *First Day Covers*, but he has also written a wide range of more serious music.

Butterworth, Arthur (1923-) English composer and teacher, a pupil of Richard **Hall**. Although he experimented with **twelve-note composition**, most of his work is tonal, and is associated with the landscapes of his native northern England.

Butterworth, George (1885-1916) English composer and collector of folk-songs. After meeting Cecil **Sharp** and **Vaughan Williams** he became interested in the movement to revive English folk-music and incorporate folk-songs into compositions. His best-remembered orchestral compositions that demonstrate this are the rhapsody *A Shropshire Lad* and *The Banks of Green Willow*. His setting of six poems from Housman's *A Shropshire Lad* uses no direct folk-song quotations, although it is among the finest cycles of the English pastoral tradition. Butterworth was killed on the Somme during World War I.

Buxtehude, Dietrich (1637-1707) Danish composer and organist. Also known as Diderik Buxtehude, he was born at Oldesloe, Holstein, the son of a church organist. After holding posts as organist in Hälsingborg and Helsinger, in 1668 he succeeded Franz **Tunder** as organist at the Marienkirche in the north German town of Lübeck, retaining the post until his death. In 1673 Buxtehude revived Tunder's annual series of *Abendmusiken*, musical performances given in conjunction with church services on the five Sundays leading up to Christmas. Buxtehude's playing won such a following throughout Germany and the rest of Europe that the youthful **Handel** and **Mattheson** went to Lübeck to hear him perform, and **J.S. Bach** is supposed to have walked the 300 km from Arnstadt to Lübeck for the same purpose in 1706. Bach was one of many young composers of the time who were greatly influenced by Buxtehude's organ compositions and trio sonatas. Buxtehude also composed more than 100 cantatas, arias and other vocal works, and several suites and sets of variations for harpsichord.

buzuq (Turkey/Greece) Alternative spelling for **bouzouki**.

BWV Abbreviation of **Bach Werke-Verzeichnis**. See **J.S. Bach**

Byrd (Byrde), William (*c.*1543-1623) English organist and composer who studied under **Tallis** and held posts as organist at Lincoln Cathedral and at the Chapel Royal. Although he was a Catholic, he was nevertheless able to compose without fear of persecution – indeed his music found favour at the court of Elizabeth I, and for the rest of his life he was able to compose for both the Catholic and the Protestant Churches. Much of his output was sacred, including 17 *Cantiones Sacrae*, 200 Latin motets and Masses for three, four and five voices. He also wrote a wide variety of secular music, above all polyphonic songs and keyboard dance pieces. He was one of the founders of the English Madrigal School and as such profoundly influenced the development of English music. With Tallis, Byrd also held the monopoly on music printing granted to them by the Queen. A collection of his own and others' keyboard music was published in 1612-13, the first to be printed in England, under the title *Parthenia*.

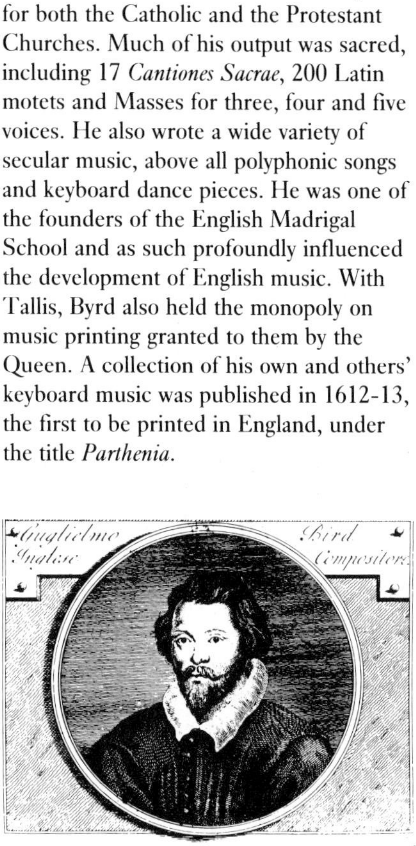

William Byrd

C

C Third note of the scale, one tone below D and and one semitone above B. The scale of C major has no sharps or flats in the key-signature.

C   C major has a blank key-signature

cabaletta (It.) A word of uncertain origin: it may be derived from *cavallo*, a horse, or a derivative, *cavaletta*, a grasshopper. The essential character of the *cabaletta* was the bounding, galloping rhythm of the accompaniment. Notable examples include the last section of the tenor aria *Parmi veder le lagrime* in Verdi's *Rigoletto*, although this is rarely heard, because like many *cabalettas* it is often cut in performance.

Caballé, Montserrat (1933-) Spanish soprano who studied at the Barcelona Conservatoire and made her operatic début with Basle Opera in 1956. Over the next decade she established her reputation in opera houses across Europe (Covent Garden, 1972, as Violetta). She has been an outstanding performer of the florid music of Bellini and Donizetti, rather than of roles where the emphasis is more on dramatic skills. She records extensively and appears often in recitals, most notably of Spanish songs.

Cabezón, Antonio de (1510-1566) Spanish organist and composer who was blind from early childhood. He studied in Valencia and entered the Royal Chapel in 1525, serving Queen Isabella until her death in 1539 and later Prince Philip (Philip II). His keyboard works can be divided into four main categories: settings of **plainsong** hymns and other chants for use in services; elaborate arrangements (*glosas*) of vocal **chansons**, **madrigals** and **motets**; arrangements of popular dances; and newly composed polyphonic works, many of them called *tientos*. These last were often marked as equally suitable for harp, **vihuela** or an ensemble of instruments.

caccia (It.) Musical and poetic genre that flourished in 14th-century Italy. The word, literally meaning chase, is similar to the English catch or round because the top two of the three voices, or sometimes all three voices, sing the same tune but enter one after the other. The text almost always tells of the hunt, with the intentional metaphor of the chase of love.

Caccini, Giulio (*c.*1545-1618) Italian singer and composer who pioneered the *stile* **recitativo** opera and the use of *basso* **continuo**. In the 1570s and 1580s he was closely involved with the Florentine Academy. It was there that the *stile recitativo* evolved, although Caccini's claim to have invented it himself was challenged by **Cavalieri**. For the most lavish of all the Florentine *intermedii* – that of 1589 – he composed the **madrigal** *Lo che dal ciel cader fare la luna*, for the accompaniment of which the **chitarrone** was said to be invented. He composed some of the music for one of the first operas ever performed, **Peri**'s *Euridice* (1600). His own setting of the same drama was the first opera to be published (in 1600). His collection of songs, *Le nuove musiche* (1601), contains a valuable introduction in which he explains his new monodic style and discusses the types of ornaments used by himself and other singers of the day. Of the songs in the collection the most famous is the first, *Amarilli mia bella*, which was adapted and arranged numerous times in the 17th century and is still in repertory.

cachucha (Sp.) Andalusian dance which originated in Cadiz in the early 19th century. It is a graceful dance in triple time, similar to the **bolero**. A famous but somewhat bastardized example occurs in Gilbert and Sullivan's *The Gondoliers*.

cadence Progression of two chords marking the end of a phrase, a section or an entire piece. There are four main types in tonal music.

First is the perfect cadence (authentic, final or full cadence; full close), consisting of a tonic chord approached from a dominant chord (e.g. V-I, or V_7-I). If one or both of the chords is an inversion, the cadence may be referred to as 'inverted'.

Second is the plagal cadence, consisting of a tonic chord approached from a subdominant chord (IV-I). This type is also known as an 'Amen cadence', because it is commonly used to harmonize the Amen at the end of hymns.

Third is the imperfect cadence (half cadence, half close), consisting of a dominant chord approached from any other chord (commonly I, II or IV). In American usage, 'imperfect' sometimes refers to cadences whose chords are not in root position (inverted cadences).

Fourth is the interrupted cadence (deceptive cadence, false close), consisting of a dominant chord resolving to some chord other than I, usually VI.

Of the cadences described here, the first two are suitable for use at the end of a piece (the perfect cadence is far more common in this context), and the second two serve as intermediate cadences.

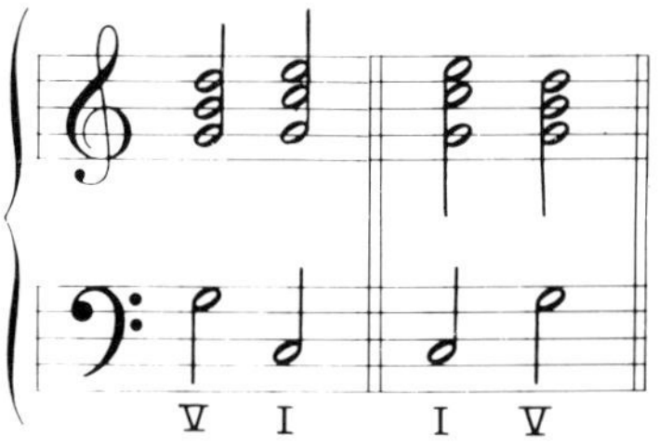

Perfect cadence   Imperfect cadence

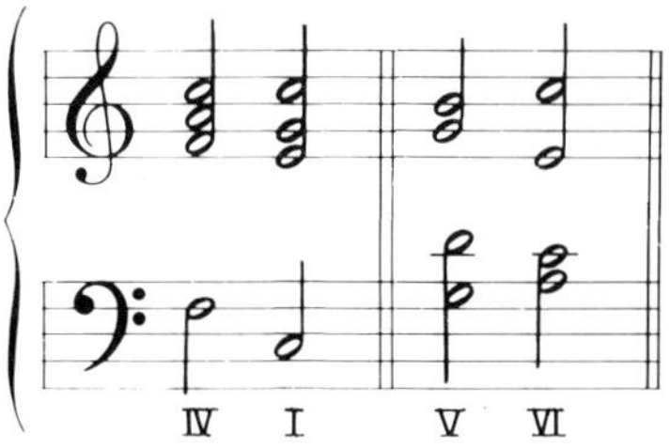

Plagal cadence   Interrupted cadence

Another important type is the Phrygian cadence, which originated in medieval music but continued to be used well into the Baroque era. Characterized by a falling semitone in the bass, it sounds like an imperfect cadence in a minor key.

In pre-tonal music, cadences depended not on harmonic progressions but on linear movement, and were characterized by melodic formulae. Many 20th-century composers have treated cadences in this way, or have avoided the tonal implications of traditional cadences by using modal progressions or dissonant chords.

cadenza Improvisatory passage, intended to show a solo performer's inventiveness and technical skill. It is mainly associated with the **concerto** and the operatic **aria**, and frequently occurs shortly before the final **cadence**. The **fermata** at the end of an aria was a cue for a cadenza in, for example, Mozart's operas, although this practice was later dropped and has only been revived in the last 15 years or so. Baroque and classical composers expected the soloist to provide his or her own cadenza, usually improvised around the thematic material of the movement, although Beethoven and Mozart both provided them for many of their concertos. Later composers, including Schumann and Brahms, usually wrote cadenzas as an integral part of a work and this has continued to be common practice in instrumental music. Composers of vocal music tended to leave the cadenzas unwritten or simply to sketch them in, although Verdi composed his own for his later operas. By the end of the 19th century, performers were rarely required to improvise. Modern performers of concertos often use original cadenzas, or those written by later composers and performers (such as Busoni's for Mozart's piano concertos and Joachim's for Beethoven's and Brahms's violin concertos).

Cadman, Charles Wakefield (1881-1946) American composer, pianist and teacher. His arrangements of American Indian music, set in a conservative 19th-century harmony, were very popular in their time; examples are his songs *At Dawning* and *Sky Blue Water*. He wrote one opera, *Shanemis or the Robin Woman*, produced by the Metropolitan Opera in 1918.

Cage, John (1912-) American composer. Born in Los Angeles, he studied with **Schoenberg** there and also with **Cowell**. Early in his career he wrote music for dance, and later was a notable collaborator with the Merce Cunningham Dance Company. The influence of Schoenberg resulted in some early **serial** music, but in about 1939 he moved towards experimentation with his 'prepared piano', which consisted of an ordinary piano with various objects fixed to or between the strings or the hammers; the slamming of the lid was occasionally incorporated. This provided the player with a range of percussive effects. Compositions using the prepared piano include *The Perilous Night* (1944) and the *Sonatas and Interludes* (1948). Under the influence of Zen Buddhism, Cage next explored the effect of chance in music, for example by switching on at random a portable radio while playing a prepared piano. His *Music of Changes* (1951) is **aleatory** to the point of tossing coins to decide the order in which the elements are played, while *Imaginary Landscape No.4* is scored for 12 radios. The aleatory technique was carried to an extreme in *4′ 33″*, in which the players do nothing at all for that period of time and the only sounds heard are those in the building - the point being that 'music' is all around, just as valid as the composer's.

Cage was also drawn to experiment with electronics, beginning with *Imaginary Landscape No.1* (1939) for variable-speed turntables. He continued to explore this direction throughout his career (*Cartridge Music*, 1960; *Roaratorio*, 1979). Cage's influence has been enormous; he has taught widely and has written several books expounding his theories.

Caix d'Hervelois, Louis de (*c*.1680-1760) One of the important school of French viol players/composers. From 1710 to 1750 he published six collections of music for viols and two for flutes. He is noted for the virtuosity and sensitivity of his pieces within a miniature framework. He appears to have eschewed membership of the Royal Bands and to have supported himself on private patronage.

cake-walk 1. A dance that originated among black slaves in the United States in the mid-19th century, of the same musical genre as **ragtime**. The strutting dance, mocking the mannerisms of white plantation owners, became very popular towards the end of the century; between 1889 and 1903 it became an international dance craze.

2. During the period that the cake-walk dance became popular, the musical elements evolved into a multithematic instrumental **march** featuring syncopated melodic rhythms. Debussy used this form in *Golliwog's Cake-Walk* from his *Children's Corner*.

calando (It.) Dropping or lowering. Instruction to a performer to decrease the volume, and sometimes the tempo, of the music.

Caldara, Antonio (*c.*1670-1736) Italian composer who wrote more than 90 operas and other stage works and 43 oratorios. He was born in Venice, probably a pupil of Legrenzi, and sang in the choir of S. Marco until 1699 when he moved to Mantua as *maestro di cappella* to Ferdinand Carlo, last Gonzaga Duke of Mantua. Other posts include appointments at the court of Prince Ruspoli in Rome, and *vicekapellmeister* to the Emperor in Vienna.

In 1708 his oratorio *Il martirio di S. Caterina* was performed at the Chancellery Cardinal Pietro Ottoboni in Rome, on which occasion he probably met Handel, Scarlatti and Corelli.

He wrote dramatic works each year for the Austrian Emperor's nameday and every other year for the Empress's birthday, as well as occasional smaller-scale works. An evolution can be detected in his operas and oratorios: they grew perhaps weaker, less dramatic and more easily assimilated. He also composed two volumes of instrumental works and some sacred music (including several masses and more than 500 canons).

Calinda, La Dance found in South America and the United States. It was considered indecent by white colonists, but it remained popular among blacks and Indians. Literary references to it, under slightly varying names, go back to the 17th century. **Delius** wrote an orchestral piece with this title.

Callas, Maria (1923-1977) Greek soprano. She was brought up in the United States,

Maria Callas

but moved to Greece in 1937, where she studied at the Athens Conservatoire. She made her début at the Athens Opera in 1941 as Tosca. Her career was launched when she was engaged by Zenatello for *La Gioconda* under **Serafin** in the Arena at Verona (1947). At first she excelled in heavy dramatic roles such as Turandot and Isolde, but under the influence of Serafin was encouraged to explore the dramatic coloratura repertory of the early 19th century in works by Bellini and Donizetti. This change of emphasis may also have been influenced by a rigorous course of slimming which, in the opinion of some critics, altered and diminished her vocal quality. However, she had a spectacular career, and for a while could command an engagement in any of the world's great theatres. She was an outstanding vocal actress, with an intensity and subtlety rarely seen in the opera house, and an agile and powerfully expressive voice. Her many recordings bear witness to her powers; her performance of *Tosca* with Di **Stefano** and **Gobbi**, conducted by De **Sabata**, is one of the greatest of the century. She gave up her career because of increasing vocal problems. Her last operatic appearance was at Covent Garden as Tosca in 1965.

Callcott, John Wall (1766-1821) English composer and theorist. A self-taught amateur, he became a popular composer of **glees** and a respected authority on musical theory, publishing a book, *Musical Grammar*, in 1806. He excelled in unaccompanied vocal music, but wrote little instrumental music. His most popular glees were *Forgive Blest Shade*, *The New Mariners* and *The Red Cross Knight*. He also composed solo songs and anthems.

calypso (Caribbean) Song-dance form which developed through the Trinidad carnival tradition during the 19th and 20th centuries, combining elements of African, French, Hispanic and British musical traditions.

The song form is thought to have its origins in the canboulay (stick burning/combat processions) of the early carnivals and the bawdy **calinda** songs performed by chantuelles which accompanied them. Bands from different neighbourhoods would compete on these occasions. Calypso lyrics generally contain elements of boasting and 'robber talk' (outrageous lies) stemming directly from these confrontations, and may also concern political, social and personal issues. Calypsonians commonly take heroic stage names, prefixed by Mighty, Lord, etc.

Pan calypso is the popular, instrumental dance form developed during the 1940s. See also **steel band**.

camera, da (It.) For the chamber, term that came into use during the **Baroque** period, applied to music considered suitable for performing in a room or chamber (as opposed to the church or the theatre). Since the late 18th century *musica da camera*, or chamber music, has come to imply music for one player to each part.

Camerata (It.) Name given to a group of intellectuals, musicians and literary men who frequented the palace of Count Giovanni de' **Bardi** in Florence in the 1570s and 1580s. The Camerata made music together and discussed poetry, philosophy, astrology and science. Musicians associated with the group included Giulio **Caccini**, Vincenzo **Galilei** and Pietro Strozzi. Galilei, with Bardi's encouragement, was particularly concerned with developing a style of music similar to that of ancient Greek drama.

The name *Camerata* was also used for a group under Jacopo Corsi whose experiments with musical drama in the 1590s led to the production of **Peri**'s *Daphne* (1597, now lost) and *Euridice* (1600).

Camidge, Matthew (1764-1844) English organist, composer and arranger of hymns and other sacred music. He was a chorister of the Chapel Royal, and in 1799 succeeded his father as organist of York Minster. In 1801 he became organist at St Michael-le-Belfry, where he remained until his retirement in 1842.

His *Musical Companion to the Psalms used in the Church of St Michael-le-Belfry* became widely known, and pioneered the use of Anglican chant. His first volume of *Cathedral Music* contains services and anthems, including *Lift up your Heads* and *O Save thy People*.

campana (It.) Bell. Campanella means little bell and has also been used as an alternative word for the glockenspiel. It is also the name of a study by Liszt (a piano adaptation of the piece of the same title for violin by Paganini), in which the sound of small bells is imitated.

campanology The art of bell-ringing.

Campion, Thomas (1567-1620) English poet, lawyer, composer and physician, sometimes spelt Campian. His earliest published compositions appeared in **Rosseter**'s *Ayres* of 1601, but his best-known songs occur in the four books of airs which he composed (*c*.1613-*c*.1617). The songs are elegant and poised, with a balance between music and text which is unequalled in the work of his contemporaries. In addition to his output of independent secular solo song, he produced songs for five masques. His lyrics were set by many other composers of the time, including **Pilkington** and **Ferrabosco**. Campion also wrote an important treatise on quantitative metre (1602) and a smaller theoretical work concerning the nature of **counterpoint** (1613).

can-can High-kicking dance popular in French music halls such as the Folies Bergère in the 19th century, and later adapted to the theatre, notably in **Offenbach**'s operetta *Orpheus in the Underworld.*

cancrizans (Lat.) Crab-like, a term indicating that a musical line is to be heard or played backwards, a technique also defined by the term 'retrograde'. Most often applied to the **cantus firmus** in medieval music and to one of the basic operations in **serial** music.

Cannabich, Johann Christian (1731-1798) German violinist, conductor and composer. A pupil of **Stamitz**, and later of **Jommelli**, he became leader (1759) and then director (1775) of the Mannheim orchestra, where he achieved a reputation as a fine conductor. His compositions include many operas and ballets, several symphonies and a variety of chamber music.

Cannon, Philip (1929-) English composer and conductor who studied under Imogen **Holst** at Dartington and then at the Royal College of Music with **Vaughan Williams** and Gordon **Jacob**. He became professor of composition at the Royal College of Music in 1960. Cannon has written various orchestral and choral pieces, three operas and several songs.

canon Strict method of composition whereby an entire piece is based on one or more melodies imitated exactly by one or more voices in unison or at different intervals.

There are several different types, determined by the delay of each successive entry (by a beat, a bar and so on), and by the pitch (at the unison, or a second, third, fourth, fifth, etc. away from the original).

Another important distinction is between the 'closed' and 'perpetual' types; the latter is represented by the famous Reading rota *Sumer is icumen in.*

In a two-part canon, the terms *dux* and *comes* are used for the leading and the following voices respectively. The *comes* may be an augmentation or a diminution of the *dux*; it may be an inversion of the *dux*; or it may imitate it in retrograde motion (i.e. working through the melody backwards - the earliest known example of this is Guillaume de Machaut's rondeau *Ma fin est mon commencement*). The combination of inversion and retrograde motion produces what is known as a 'mirror canon', in which the melody sung or played by the *comes* is produced by reading the printed music upside-down. Canons for many voices are known as group canons, and those for two parts against two are known as double canons.

Canon was a very important compositional technique in the works of the 15th-century Flemish masters, who made complex and sophisticated use of it in polyphonic sacred music. It was also used by **Josquin** in many canonic **chansons**, and by **Palestrina**, who habitually set the last *Agnus Dei* of his masses in canon. By the 17th century, canon had come to be regarded less as a creative than as a didactic means; it was the subject of much theoretical study, and formed an important part of a composer's training. Canon was used in popular music, however, in the English catches. In art music, the canon was restored to its former importance by J.S. Bach in his *Goldberg Variations* (which contain a series of canons at all intervals from unison to the ninth), the *Musical Offering* and *The Art of Fugue*. Haydn, Mozart and Beethoven all made use of the full range of canonic technique. Of the composers of the Romantic era, Brahms made the most notable use of canon, his interest in which was stimulated by his studies of Baroque and Renaissance music; his 13 canons, Op.113, show his mastery of the technique.

The 20th century has seen a resurgence of interest in canon, as augmentation, diminution and retrograde motion again became the basic technique in **serial** composition. Stravinsky, **Schoenberg**, **Berg** and **Webern** have all made extensive use of canon – Webern's Symphony Op.21 is composed in canon throughout – and **Messiaen** and **Boulez** have used 'rhythmic canon' in which the voices imitate rhythmic rather than melodic patterns, sometimes in retrograde.

cantabile (It.) Direction to indicate that a piece or line of music should be performed in a singing style, expressive of its melodic qualities.

cantata (It.) Literally 'sung' as opposed to **toccata**, 'touched', and **sonata**, 'sounded'. It is a vocal work with instrumental accompaniment, usually in several movements and based on a continuous narrative text which may be sacred or secular.

It originated in Italy in the early 17th century as a secular genre; it was usually for solo voice and could contain **strophic arias** or a mixture of **arioso** and **recitative** sections with instrumental ritornellos.

In the early 18th century cantatas generally consisted of two or three arias connected by recitative – Alessandro **Scarlatti** wrote more than 600 cantatas of this type. By the time of **J.S. Bach**, most Lutheran cantatas were settings of the poetic texts of Pastor E. Neumeister, based on scriptural passages. Bach's cantatas have an instrumental accompaniment of varying size, and may be for solo voice, such as *Ich habe genug*, or for soloists and chorus; they vary considerably in form, but usually close with a **chorale** setting.

After about 1750 the term came to be applied to a variety of works. Cantatas for special occasions were written by Haydn (*Birthday Cantata* for Prince Nikolaus Esterházy, 1763), Mozart (*Die Maurerfreude*, 1785), and Beethoven (*Der glorreiche Augenblick*, 1814) and by many later composers, but there was no consistent development of the form. It was one of the prescribed forms for the Prix de Rome, however; both Berlioz and Debussy wrote cantatas for this prestigious award (Berlioz succeeded in 1830 with *Sardanapale*; Debussy in 1884 with *L'enfant prodigue*). In the 20th century cantatas have been written by various composers including Boulanger, Hindemith, Bartók, Webern, Stravinsky and Britten.

cantatrice (Fr., It.) Female singer.

cante hondo (Sp.) Deep song; the vocal element of Spanish flamenco music, from the southern province of Andalusia. The particular timbre and pitch of the voice is throaty and hoarse, yet penetrating. It can be accompanied by guitar alone or by dance and guitar. An alternative spelling is *cante jondo*.

Cantelli, Guido (1920-1956) Italian conductor who studied at the Milan Conservatoire and held various conducting appointments in Italy, quickly establishing an international reputation with débuts in New York (1949) and Edinburgh (1950). During the early 1950s he worked with the **Philharmonia Orchestra**. He was identified by **Toscanini** as his artistic successor. Shortly after his appointment as musical director of La Scala, Milan, he was killed in an air crash; he left a number of outstanding recordings.

Canteloube, Marie-Joseph (1879-1957) French composer who studied under **d'Indy** and subsequently wrote his teacher's biography. His works include two operas and several vocal and instrumental pieces, but he is best known for his *Chants d'Auvergne*, collections of folk-songs in the local dialect for voice and piano or orchestra.

canticle From Latin *canticulum* or *canticum*, song. Song or lyrical passage from the Bible other than a psalm, used in the liturgies of both the Eastern and Western Churches. Canticles taken from the New Testament are called *cantica majora* (greater canticles). Three of these are used daily: the Benedicite is sung at morning prayer, and the Magnificat and Nunc Dimittis in the evening. Canticles taken from the Old Testament are called *cantica minora* (lesser canticles). In the Roman Catholic rite, these are sung at lauds, one for each day of the week.

The earliest form of music for the canticles was plainchant, and this is still used, mainly in Roman Catholic churches with a strong musical tradition. In the Anglican Church the canticles are sung either to Anglican chants or to specially composed settings, of which there are many, both unaccompanied and accompanied by elaborate organ parts. See also **plainsong**.

cantilena (Lat.) Term applied at different periods to various types of vocal music. It was used as a term for **plainsong** and, from the 9th century onwards, for secular **monophony**. From the end of the 13th century it was applied to **polyphonic** songs, such as those by Adam de la **Halle** and, in the 14th century, to settings of poetry by English musicians. *Cantilena* has been used more recently to describe a sustained lyrical melody, either vocal or instrumental.

cantillation Musical chanting of religious texts or prayers by a solo singer; the term is used particularly for such chanting in the Jewish synagogue, but is used also in connection with various Christian traditions.

Cantiones Sacrae (Lat.) Sacred Songs. It is most often found as the generic title of collections of Latin **motets** in the 16th and 17th centuries. Among the composers to use this title for their works were **Schütz**, **Byrd** and **Tallis**.

canto (It.) Song. An indication of a melody or prominent line in a vocal or instrumental composition. The term *col canto* is interchangeable with the more usual *colla voce* to note that the accompaniment must follow carefully the tempo, dynamics, etc. of the solo line during a particular section.

cantometrics Formal analytical procedure for the cross-cultural study of folk-song styles, devised principally by Alan Lomax in an attempt to show how worldwide variations in song style depend upon cultural context. In the published findings, songs of 233 cultures were rated by 37 musical parameters and statistically correlated with ethnographic data, so that universal relations between musical style and social organization were established.

cantor (Lat.) Singer. The term is used in sacred music, where it refers to the leader of singing in Jewish synagogues or Christian churches. In the Lutheran Church, cantor refers to the director of music in a church (not merely of the singing), of whom the most famous was probably **J.S. Bach**.

In modern Anglican churches the cantor is more commonly known as the precentor and leads the singing of psalms, the creed, responses, etc.

cantoris In an **antiphonal** choir (i.e. a choir divided into identically formed parts), the cantoris refers to the half of the choir that is seated in the stalls on the north side of the chancel, near the stall of the **cantor** or precentor. The second part of such a choir, which sits in the choir stalls facing the cantoris, is known as the **decani**.

cantrach (Scotland) Ancient mnemonic aid for acquiring the repertory of **pibroch**, the Highland bagpipe music, in which standard melodic motifs and their embellishments are represented by single syllables. The term is derived from the Gaelic *canntaireachd*.

cantus (Lat.) Song. In 12th-century usage, the original voice part in a **polyphonic** composition (the added one was called *discantus*, descant).

In the 16th century it came to replace the term *superius* for the top voice of a polyphonic composition. It was also used to describe any vocal composition as, for example, Canti A, Canti B and Canti C, the three volumes of the *Odhecaton* (1501).

Cantus figuratus and *cantus fractus* were used for melodies in measured notation; *cantus compositus* was an alternative term for polyphony.

cantus firmus (Lat.), **canto firmo** (It.) Fixed melody. Melody in long notes used as the basis for a contrapuntal composition. It refers particularly to the use of such melodies in **polyphonic** compositions of the 14th, 15th and 16th centuries, when it was the most important method of composition.

The *cantus firmus* usually appeared in the tenor voice; it was often derived from plainchant, but could be taken from other polyphonic compositions or even popular song.

From the 17th century *cantus firmus* declined as a method of composition but remained important as a compositional technique in German Protestant church music. *Cantus firmi* taken from chorale melodies formed the basis of chorale preludes for organ and cantata movements by **Buxtehude**, **Bach** and **Brahms**, among others.

canzona (It.) Song or ballad. The term can refer to either a vocal or an instrumental composition. Sometimes also written *canzone*. There are three main uses of the word.

1. The vocal *canzona* was a 16th-century Italian part-song, which involved the **polyphonic** setting of a particular Italian verse form. This poetic form is an important component of the early literature of the **madrigal** and proved popular with composers largely as a result of its flexibility of metre and structure.

2. The instrumental *canzona* evolved from its vocal predecessor. The Italian genre *canzon alla francese* originated in the French **chanson**, the rhythms of which were felt to be apt for instrumental transcription. By the end of the 16th century and the beginning of the 17th century, the genre had moved far away from its vocal origins.

3. Also used in the 18th century to refer to a light style of solo song.

canzonet Light song form popular in England and Italy from the end of the 16th century and the beginning of the 17th century. The canzonet was **polyphonic** and tuneful, and written either for several voices (with or without instruments) or for a solo voice and lute accompaniment. The term was loosely applied (some canzonets should be more properly classified as **madrigals**) and by the time of Haydn, the term was used for any song written in the English language.

canzonetta Tuneful song of the late 16th century, whose classification is often interchangeable with that of the **canzonet**. Later, *canzonetta* often referred to a short and simple song (which was not an **aria**) occurring in an opera; it was also occasionally applied to instrumental pieces.

Capel Bond, Richard (1730-1790) English organist and composer. He became organist to two churches in Coventry, St Michael and All Angels and Holy Trinity, in about 1750, and remained in these posts all his life. From there he was able to play an immensely important part in the development of musical life in the Midlands, organizing concerts and building up the Coventry Musical Society to include a choral section. Under his aegis, oratorio was first heard in many towns in the area, and he was instrumental in setting up the first Birmingham Festival (1768). Among his compositions are *Six Concerts in Seven Parts* (1766), the first and sixth of which are for trumpet and bassoon respectively and the middle four for strings and continuo; and *Six Anthems in Score* (1769).

Caplet, André (1878-1925) French composer and conductor who studied at the Paris Conservatoire, where he was awarded the Prix de Rome in 1901. In 1899 he became director at the Odéon and was later appointed conductor at the Boston Opera (1910-14). A close friend of **Debussy**, he orchestrated *Children's Corner* and *The Martyrdom of St Sebastian*, conducting the work's first performance. He wrote many songs, choral works and other pieces, most of which show some influence of Debussy.

capo, da (It.) From the beginning. Frequently found in all genres of music to indicate that the player should return to the beginning of the composition and perform it once more until the word *fine* appears; this is an instruction to end the performance. The term *da capo* is also often to be found in connection with the vocal **aria**. Its usual abbreviation is D.C.

capo tasto (It.) Device used to shorten the string length on fretted instruments such as the guitar to facilitate transposition without having to alter the fingering. The device consists simply of a bar, covered with either felt or leather, which clips on by various means to the neck of the instrument.

cappella (It.) Chapel. 1. In the 14th century, a group of clerical singers; after 1600 it came to mean any large group of musicians.

2. Originally used for music suitable for performance in church (*a cappella*), it came to mean any unaccompanied vocal music, whether sacred or secular.

Cappuccilli, Piero (1929-) Italian baritone. He studied with Donaggio and made his début in Leoncavallo's *I pagliacci* in 1957. His début at La Scala, Milan, was in 1964, since when he has become one of the foremost singers of the Italian repertory. He has sung Germont in *La traviata* (1967), Iago in *Otello* (1974) and Renato in *Un ballo in maschera* (1975) at the Royal Opera House, Covent Garden. He has also sung at Salzburg and many other European cities and in the United States and South America. His wide repertory includes the title-role in *Simon Boccanegra*, Posa in *Don Carlos* and virtually every other Verdi baritone part.

capriccio (It.) Whim or fancy. Used as a title for compositions since the 16th century. *Capriccios* are by definition miscellaneous in character, their one common feature being a disregard for established forms and procedures. There are distinct groups, however: the keyboard *capriccios* of the early 17th century, including those of **Frescobaldi**, which were important in the development of the **fugue**; dances and dance collections of the 17th and 18th centuries; and collections of **cadenza**-like virtuoso pieces or studies written in the 18th and early 19th centuries. A good example of such a collection is **Paganini**'s Op.1 (*c.*1810). Tchaikovsky, Rimsky-Korsakov and others also wrote *capriccios*, colourful works of free form.

caprice (Fr.) Equivalent of the Italian **capriccio**.

Carafa, Michele (1787-1872) Italian composer, born in Naples. He was mainly concerned with opera, becoming a lifelong friend of **Rossini**. His work had a mixed reception but was acclaimed in France and, accordingly, Carafa settled there. Although he composed prolifically, his work has not survived. 'He made the mistake', claimed Rossini, 'of having been born my contemporary.'

Cardew, Cornelius (1936-1981) Musician who formed the Scratch Orchestra in London in 1968, a group of mostly unskilled musicians who gathered to improvise, to play collective compositions and pieces by its members. He was a pioneer of the movement within art music which suggested that everyone might be a creative musician. His scores ask that inner reflection and considered sonic action should be integrated as musical composition. Later in his career, Cardew repudiated his early works and devoted himself to the projection of his Marxist views through his music.

Carey, Henry (1689-1743) English dramatist, poet and composer who took composition lessons in order to set his own poems to music. He had a burlesque and witty style, sometimes misunderstood. He wrote a number of stage works, most of them in a popularized operatic form. Many of his works gained great popularity, including *Britannia*, an opera which replaced the aria with **ballads**, and *Cephalus and Procris*, which was further lightened by a pantomime interlude. *Nancy*, written in 1739, was the most original of his works.

carillon Set of tuned bells, usually mounted in a tower, which work mechanically. The skill of tuning them has taken many years to perfect. The bells may be operated by a baton keyboard, or by perforated paper rolls or cassettes, and the music ranges from simple hymn tunes to specially composed pieces.

Carissimi, Giacomo (1605-1674) Italian composer. From 1625 he was organist at Tivoli Cathedral and from 1627 *maestro di cappella* at the Cathedral of S. Rufino, Tivoli. In 1629 he was appointed *maestro di cappella* of the Collegio Germanica, Rome, with responsibility for music at the church of S. Apollinare.

Carissimi was one of the first composers of **oratorios**, which he developed from the original form of an extended **motet** into a much longer work in several sections. The most famous of his 14 oratorios was *Jephte* (1650). He wrote more than 100 motets, some for large resources in the style of **Palestrina**, some for small resources with *basso continuo* after Viadana. His *Missa 'L'homme armé'* was probably the last of its type. He also wrote over 200 secular cantatas.

carmen (Lat.) Song (pl. **carmina**). Used in early music to denote the vocal or melodic line of a composition. It is often used in titles, e.g. *Carmen saeculare* (secular song). It was used by Carl **Orff** in his setting of early texts, *Carmina Burana* (Songs from Beuren).

carol The modern popular meaning of the word – a festive Christian song associated with Christmas – is only one of a number of meanings the term has had over the centuries; the Christmas association in particular is quite recent. Several types of carols can be distinguished.

The term itself derives from the medieval French *carole*, a round dance accompanied by a song, one of the most well-known of which is the anonymous tune to which Raimbault de Vaqueiras set the words *Kalenda Haya*.

The 15th-century English courtly carol has been described as the only indigenous English musical form. Several of these lively polyphonic works survive with words and music intact - there are many more of which only the words survive. The form is characterized by a refrain or burden, which is sung at the beginning and at the end, and repeated between the several verses. The text may celebrate a person or event, such as the well-known Agincourt song *Deo Gratias Anglia*, but many of them are for Christmas, such as *There is no rose of such vertu*.

Most European countries have a tradition of folk carols (French *Noëls*), some of very ancient origin, combining Christian with pre-Christian symbolism, such as in the English carols *The Holly and the Ivy* and *I Saw Three Ships*. Other 'traditional' carols may be of more recent origin, such as *God Rest ye Merry Gentlemen* and *Past Three O'Clock*.

The present interest in 'Christmas carols' dates from the end of the 19th century, with the revival of interest in folk carols, many of which were being collected and popularized at the time. New seasonal words were set to old tunes, such as J.M. Neale's *Good King Wenceslas* (to the tune of *Tempus Adeste Floribus* from *Piae Cantiones*) and G.R. Woodward's *Ding Dong Merrily on High* (to the tune of *Bransle de l'officiel* from Arbeau's *Orchésographie*). Many of the older composed 'carols' such as *Hark the Herald Angels Sing* and *While Shepherds Watched their Flocks by Night* are more properly Christmas hymns.

In recent years British composers have written many new Christmas carols, mainly for use in the highly popular carol services and concerts given annually. Among the most enduring modern carols are Benjamin **Britten**'s *A Ceremony of Carols*, Boris **Ord**'s *Adam Lay y-Bounden*, **Holst**'s *In the Deep Mid-Winter* and David **Willcocks**'s and John Rutter's contributions to the series *Carols for Choirs*.

Carpenter, John Alden (1876-1951) American composer who studied composition at Harvard. On graduating in 1897 he became a businessman but continued to compose, studying with **Elgar** in 1906 and later with Bernard Ziehn. His compositions are largely influenced by American popular music and include a jazz pantomime, *Krazy Kat* (1921); a ballet based on Oscar Wilde's *The Birthday of the Infanta* (1919); two symphonies; and several song cycles. His most important work is the ballet *Skyscrapers*; a depiction of modern life in the United States, it includes three saxophones and traffic lights operated by a keyboard.

Carreras, José (1946-) Spanish tenor who, after studying in Barcelona, made his début in Verdi's *Nabucco* and later won the Verdi Competition. He has since performed all over the world. After a serious illness in the late 1980s he has returned to top form and is ranked among the best operatic tenors today.

José Carreras

He has recorded extensively, especially the Verdi repertory; one of his finest roles is Don José in Bizet's *Carmen*.

Carrillo, Julian (1875-1965) Mexican musician of Indian origin who studied the violin, composition and acoustics at the conservatoire in Mexico City. As a violinist he led the Leipzig Gewandhaus Orchestra under **Nikisch**. At the same time he developed the theory and practice of **microtones** and incorporated them in orchestral pieces which were performed and recorded, attracting considerable attention. **Stokowski** commissioned from him a *Concerto for $\frac{1}{3}$ Tone Piano*, and this is complemented by symphonies and concertos, as well as instrumental pieces, both with and without microtones.

Carse, Adam (1878-1958) English composer and historian of instruments. Carse was educated at the Royal Academy of Music and later became professor of harmony there. His music is lightweight and it is more for his studies of instruments and their use that he is remembered. He wrote two important books tracing the history of the orchestra.

Carter, Elliott (1908-) American composer who studied with Walter **Piston** at Harvard University and with Nadia **Boulanger** in Paris (1932-5). In his early works he was a **neo-classicist**, showing the influence of **Stravinsky** in the ballet score *Pocahontas* (1938-9) and the *Holiday Overture* (1944). However, he moved away from neo-classicism with his piano sonata (1945-6) and the sonata for cello and piano (1948). In both of these works he concentrated on exploiting the character of the instrument itself, its tone colour and resonances. Since then, Carter has produced many works in different genres, including string quartets, *Variations for Orchestra* (1965), the Double Concerto for harpsichord, piano and two chamber orchestras (1961), and the Piano Concerto (1964-5). In more recent works, Carter has experimented with metre and rhythmic relationships, for both large and small ensembles: *A Symphony of Three Orchestras* (1976) and *Penthode* (1985).

In addition to his composition Carter has written widely, and a volume of his *Collected Writings* was published in New York in 1977.

Carulli, Fernando (1770-1841) Italian guitarist and composer of more than 400 works. Carulli was probably the first great guitar virtuoso, in an age when the guitar was not an accepted 'serious' instrument. He was originally a cellist, but gave this up in order to teach himself the guitar. After several foreign tours he settled in Paris in 1808 and began teaching. He also wrote a treatise on the art of accompanying on the guitar, as well as publishing many study pieces.

Caruso, Enrico (1873-1921) Italian tenor, considered to be the greatest of this century. Caruso made his operatic début in 1894 in Naples but achieved his first real triumph in 1901 in *L'elisir d'amore* at La Scala, Milan. Subsequently he sang in Britain, Spain, Germany, Austria and France, but performed most often for the Metropolitan Opera, New York (1902-20).

Caruso's voice was characterized by its baritone-like timbre, coupled with a smooth tenor range. His high notes were impeccable, his intonation exact and his breath control superb. Caruso excelled in lyric opera such as Puccini's *Tosca* as well as in lighter 19th-century opera. He was also a notable interpreter of Verdi. He made many recordings.

Cary, Tristram (1925-) English composer whose main interest lies with electronic music and who has done much to make the genre more widely known and accessible through his writing, teaching and composition. He founded the electronic studio at the Royal College of Music, the first of its kind in Britain. After a conventional music education at Trinity College of Music he became known in the 1950s through his music for film, television and theatre. He has also written chamber music and electronic music for performance in most accepted genres, and has published two books on electronic music.

Casadesus, Robert (1899-1972) French pianist and composer. As a student at the Paris Conservatoire he was awarded a first prize for piano. Casadesus travelled widely as a concert pianist and his many recordings include the complete works of Ravel. As a composer he wrote a number of works for the piano including *24 Préludes* (1924) and *Six Pièces* (1938), a work for two pianos intended for performance with his wife Gaby, with whom he formed a piano duo.

Casals, Pablo (or **Pau**) (1876-1973) Catalan cellist, conductor, pianist and composer. Casals's mastery of the cello led to a new public appreciation of the instrument in the first half of the 20th century. His technique combined a beautiful tone with technical surety, already apparent in recordings of the 1920s of trios by Beethoven, Brahms and Haydn made with **Thibaud** and **Cortot**. In 1919 Casals founded the Orguestra Pau Casals

Pablo Casals

in Barcelona, launching his career as a conductor. He gave many concerts in aid of the French Red Cross, but always refused to play in any country that recognized the Franco regime. In the 1950s, Casals began a new series of recordings, directed music festivals in Puerto Rico and Perpignan, worked each year at the Marlboro Festival, Vermont, coaching and conducting the Festival Orchestra, and gave master classes in many musical centres. In 1962 he launched a peace campaign with his own oratorio *El Pessebre*, which was performed worldwide. Casals was generally acknowledged in his lifetime as one of the greatest cellists in the world.

Casanova, André (1919-) French composer who originally studied law as well as music. His compositions include a piano concertino, first performed by Yvonne **Loriod** in 1959, as well as symphonies and operas.

Casella, Alfredo (1883-1947) Italian composer and pianist. He studied for a time in Paris with **Fauré**. Later influences included Debussy, Ravel, Bartók and Stravinsky. In 1915 he returned to Italy, where he was to have a decisive influence on Italian musical taste, partly by introducing French music to Italian audiences and partly by attracting students (both of piano and of composition), such as **Malipiero**, **Pizzetti** and **Respighi**. Together they formed the *Società italiana de musica moderna*, in which Casella was a driving force. His own music changed in style many times and is uneven in impact: it ranges from the witty *Pupazzetti* (1915) to opera (e.g. *La donna serpente*, 1932) and a *Missa Solemnis* (1944). His *Scarlattiana*, based on themes from sonatas by Domenico **Scarlatti**, is still performed, as are some of his piano pieces.

Cassadó, Gaspar (1897-1966) Catalan cellist and composer. He attended the Barcelona Conservatoire and in 1910 moved to Paris to study with **Casals**. Cassadó began his concert career in 1918, giving recitals with such celebrated pianists as Harold Bauer and **Rubinstein**. His compositions show the influence of Falla and Ravel and include string quartets, a piano trio and *Rapsodia catalana* for orchestra.

cassation Informal 18th-century instrumental form, most common in Austria and neighbouring regions. Usually of a light nature, cassations were not limited to 'serious' evening concerts, and they were often performed in the open air, as a sort of street entertainment. Cassations could be scored for full orchestra or smaller groups of instruments, and would have an indeterminate number of movements in **divertimento** style. The movements were often shorter, more numerous and of a lighter nature than in symphonic compositions. There are examples of writing in this genre by Mozart and Haydn.

Cassilly, Richard (1927-) American tenor. He studied in Baltimore and made his début in 1955 in New York, singing in **Menotti**'s opera *The Saint of Bleecker Street*. He sang with various companies in the United States before making his European début in 1965 in Geneva, after which he joined the Hamburg Opera. He first sang at the Royal Opera House, Covent Garden, in 1968. A powerful physical presence and strong acting ability make him ideal for such heroic roles as Florestan in Beethoven's *Fidelio*, Wagner's Siegmund (*Die Walküre*) and the title-roles in *Tannhäuser*, Verdi's *Otello* and Britten's *Peter Grimes*. He has sung in London, Vienna, Munich, Paris, Milan and New York.

Cassuto, Alvaro Leon (1938-) Portuguese composer and conductor. He studied composition in Lisbon, Hamburg and Darmstadt, and conducting at the Vienna Conservatoire. He has worked as assistant conductor of the Lisbon Gulbenkian Chamber Orchestra and the American Symphony Orchestra, and in 1970 became permanent conductor of the Radio Orchestra of Lisbon. Cassuto was the first Portuguese composer to write a **serial** work for orchestra, *Sinfonia Breve No.1* (1958). In 1969 he won the Koussevitzky prize for composition.

castanets (Sp.) Small hand-held percussion instrument usually used by dancers to provide their own rhythmic accompaniment in the **bolero, fandango** and other Spanish dance forms. They consist of two shell-shaped pieces of wood hinged together by a piece of string which the player winds round his or her thumb; the fingers tap out a rhythm, producing a clapping sound. Orchestral castanets may be mounted on a short handle.

Castelnuovo-Tedesco, Mario (1895-1968) American composer and pianist of Italian birth. After studying piano and composition at the Florence Conservatoire, he worked as a freelance throughout the interwar period. As a Jew he was forced to move to the United States in 1939, where he was to settle permanently. He was a prolific composer and an active teacher. His works, many based on Shakespeare's, are still largely unpublished and include eight operas (e.g. *The Importance of Being Earnest*, 1962), many film scores, ballets, oratorios, overtures, songs and chamber music.

Castiglioni, Niccolò (1932-) Italian composer. He studied piano and composition in Milan, at the Conservatoire, and in Salzburg under **Blacher**. He settled in the United States in 1967, and held a variety of teaching posts at American universities – Michigan, San Diego and Seattle. In the 1950s his works were broadly **serial**, with some elements of tonality; later they became more romantic in style. He has composed mainly for the theatre: the radio opera *Attraverso lo specchio* (Through the Looking-Glass, 1961), after Lewis Carroll, won the Italia Prize. He has also produced chamber works, sometimes with tape (*Eine kleine Weihnachtsmusik*, 1960). Other compositions include *Three Mystery Plays* (1968), cantatas, the *Symphony with Garden*, a Symphony in C and the opera *Oberon* (1980).

castrato (It.) Male singer castrated before puberty in order to preserve his alto or soprano voice into adulthood (also called *evirato*). The adult physique and undeveloped larynx combined to give power and brilliance to the sound of a boy's unbroken voice. This practice was common in Italy from the 16th to the early 19th centuries, becoming more popular in the 17th century with the rise of opera. Leading composers wrote parts for the *castrato*; Mozart, for example, in *Idomeneo* and *La clemenza di Tito* and Handel in many oratorios and operas. Italian churches often employed *castrati*; the Sistine Chapel used them from the late 16th century until 1903. The last famous *castrato* was probably Alessandro Moreschi (1858-1922).

Castro, Juan José (1895-1968) Argentinian composer and conductor who studied in Buenos Aires and, on winning the Europa prize, moved to Paris to study with Vincent **d'Indy** at the Schola Cantorum. As a conductor he held many posts including that of director of the Teatro Colón. His works include *Sinfonia Argentina*, operas and ballet music. His opera *Proserpina y el extranjero* was awarded the Verdi prize in 1951. He wrote five symphonies altogether, the last in 1956. His *Epitafio en ritmos y sonidos* for chorus and orchestra was composed in 1961, his Violin Concerto in 1962.

Catalani, Alfredo (1854-1893) Italian opera composer, important for his influence on the **verismo** school. He wrote many operas – *Loreley*, *Edmea*, and the most successful, *La Wally*, first performed at La Scala in 1892. His operas were popular in their day and he was highly regarded by **Toscanini**.

catch 17th- and 18th-century English **round** or **canon**, generally written for men's voices. Many, including some of Purcell's finest, were written to bawdy texts, and have only recently been considered suitable for revival. The first published collection of catches was Thomas **Ravenscroft**'s *Pammelia* (1609).

Causton, Thomas (*c.*1520-1569) English composer whose anthems and sacred services are in John Day's *Certain Notes set Forth in Foure and Three Parts*: the first published collection of English cathedral music (1565). His psalm settings are included in Day's *The Whole Psalmes in Foure Parts* of 1563. His style is simple and chordal with some interesting harmonic effects.

Cavalieri, Emilio de' (*c.*1550-1602) Italian composer and choreographer. He was stage manager of the Florentine *Intermedii* of 1589, the most lavish of those series ever conceived. He wrote several pieces for it, including the final chorus *O che nuovo miraculo*, which became one of the most popular pieces of its time. Many contemporary arrangements of it were made, with titles such as *Aria del grand duca*, *Aria di Fiorenza*, *Ballo di palazzo* etc. He was composer of the earliest surviving play set entirely to music, the *Rappresentatione di anima et di corpo... per recitar cantando* (1600). The printed score was the first to use a **figured bass**. He also claimed to be the inventor of the *stile recitativo*, although in this he was in competition with **Caccini**. His sacred compositions include some fine Lamentations and Responsories for Holy Week.

Cavalli, Francesco (1602-1676) Italian composer. His main works are his operas, of which he composed nearly 30 for the Venetian opera houses. He was the successor in this respect to Claudio **Monteverdi**. He entered the *cappella* of S. Marco in 1616, under Monteverdi's direction; in 1639 he became second organist and in 1665, first organist. It was, however, his operas to which he directed most of his energy. His first success was *Le nozze di Teti e di Peleo*. His greatest contemporary success came with *Gascione* (1649). His *Egisto, Callisto* and *Ormindo* have been revived in recent years, to acclaim.

cavatina Term applied to the opening or entrance aria of a character in an opera: for example, *Porgi amor*, the Countess's aria in Mozart's *Le nozze di Figaro*; *Largo al factotum*, Figaro's aria in Rossini's *Il barbiere di Siviglia*. Later, especially in its German form, *Cavatine*, it was applied to any sustained melodic piece, vocal or instrumental.

Cavendish, Michael (*c.*1565-1628) English composer of lute-songs and madrigals, published in a single volume in 1598. He contributed the madrigal *Come Gentle Swains* to the anthology *The Triumphs of Oriana* (1601), compiled in honour of Queen Elizabeth I.

cebell Musical genre, popular in England between 1690 and 1710, of pieces based on the *Descente de Cybelle*, a chorus with orchestral accompaniment from the last act of Lully's *Atys* (1676). Among the 21 surviving cebells are an open arrangement by John Bannister (1695), the anonymous contrafactum *Lord, How Men can Claret Drink*, and Purcell's *Trumpet Tune, called the cebell.* A cebell is characterized by its duple metre starting at the half bar and often having episodes with a running bass moving in crotchets or quavers. Alternative spellings are cibell and sebell.

Ceccato, Aldo (1934-) Italian conductor, mainly of opera, who studied for a time with **de Sabata**. He has conducted at most of the major opera houses of the world and was also principal conductor of the Detroit Symphony Orchestra during the 1970s.

Saint Cecilia (from a 14th century painting)

Cecilia, St Christian saint thought to have been murdered in Sicily by the Romans in the 2nd or 3rd century AD. She became associated with music in Italy in the 15th century after a misreading of a Latin text; she was soon being depicted in contemporary paintings with musical instruments, and the legend of her musical prowess grew. Music festivals commemorating St Cecilia began to appear annually in many European cities, the first on record being at Evreux, Normandy, in 1570. The Feast of St Cecilia is celebrated on 22 November.

cédez (Fr.) Instruction to a performer to slacken the pace of the music; it is equivalent to the Italian term *ritenuto.*

ceilidh (Scotland, Ireland) Gaelic, night-long, informal gathering for the performance of songs, instrumental music and dances.

celempung (Java) Plucked zither with 13 pairs of strings passing over a single bridge. The tapered box resonator stands on four legs.

celesta A keyboard instrument invented by Auguste Mustel in 1886. A piano-like action causes steel plates to be struck by hammers, producing a light, ethereal sound. **Tchaikovsky** used a celesta for *The Dance of the Sugar-plum Fairy* in his ballet *The Nutcracker*, 1892, as did **Bartók** in his *Music for Strings, Percussion and Celesta*, 1936. Its range may extend to five octaves upwards from C; music for celesta is written on two staves (as for piano), and an octave lower than it sounds.

Celibidache, Sergiu (1912-) Romanian conductor who studied in Berlin and in 1945 was appointed principal conductor of the Berlin Philharmonic Orchestra, a post he held until 1952. He has attracted much attention for his curious but effective baton technique and has been guest conductor in many countries including North and Latin America; most recently he has been attached to the Curtis Institute in Philadelphia.

Cellier, Alfred (1844-1891) English conductor and composer. He began his career as organist of St Alban's, Holborn, and later became conductor in several theatres in London and Manchester. As a composer, he is often compared to **Sullivan**; his best-known works are operettas – *Dorothy* (1886) and *The Mountebanks* (1892), to a libretto by W.S. Gilbert.

cello Common term for the violoncello, a bowed four-stringed instrument. The bass member of the violin family, it is pitched one octave below the **viola**, with strings tuned to C-G-D-A. Being large, the instrument is held between the knees of the player, supported on a spike known as a peg. Concertos for cello have been written by a variety of composers: Haydn, Schumann, Dvořák, Tchaikovsky (the *Rococo Variations*), Elgar, Walton and Lutosławski. Outstanding players of this century include Pablo **Casals**, Paul **Tortelier** and Jacqueline **du Pré**.

Celtic harp Instrument of the harp family, considerably smaller than the classical harp, having between 24 and 34 strings. It has a flat soundboard, rounded back and a hand-operated mechanism of blades or levers for tuning the strings. The tradition of harp playing had almost died out in Ireland by the early 19th century, when there was a revival of interest. Now it again holds a central position in the traditional music of Ireland in the accompaniment of song and as a solo instrument. The Celtic harp is sometimes also known as the Irish harp.

cembalo (It.) 1. An abbreviation of *clavicembalo* (harpsichord).
2. In Italian popular music, it denotes the tambourine.

cent Exact measure of a musical interval, by which 100 cents equal one tempered semitone, and consequently an octave comprises 1200 cents.

ceòl beag/ceòl meadhonach/ceòl mor (Scotland) Little, middle and big music, with reference to the Highland bagpipe repertory. *Ceòl beag* includes marches, strathspeys and reels; *ceòl meadhonach* includes Highland folk-songs, lullabies and slower marches; *ceòl mor* includes salutes to individuals, laments, special tunes in honour of important historical events and the **pibroch** repertory.

Certon, Pierre (?-1572) French composer influenced by **Josquin des Prés**. He held a number of appointments, including that of clerk at Notre Dame and the Sainte-Chapelle. He was at the latter from 1532 until his death. He composed parody Masses, motets and some chansons in the style of **Janequin**.

Cesti, Antonio (1623-1669) Italian composer and singer. In 1637 he was ordained a priest, but conflict between his musical and priestly duties, particularly with the success of his operas, caused him to renounce his vows in 1659. With *Orontea* (1649), *Alessandro vincitor di se stesso* (1651) and *Il Cesare amante* (1651) performed in Venice, his success was assured. From 1652 to 1657 and 1659 to 1665 he was at the court of Innsbruck, where many of his stage works were produced, including his largest, *Il pomo d'oro*. In 1668 he went to Florence as *maestro di cappella* to the Tuscan court.

His 15 stage works were written mainly for private theatres, and so their scale is grand, incorporating dance and often elaborate stage machinery. He also composed some 74 secular cantatas and five sacred choral works.

Chabrier, Emmanuel (1841-1894) French composer, largely self-taught but influential for subsequent generations of French composers, including **Debussy**, **Ravel** and **Poulenc**. Although he came under the spell of Wagner, his lasting achievement was to reorientate French music away from Germanic influences and to return to French ideals of conciseness and clarity, as well as encouraging musical **impressionism**. *España* (1883) is perhaps his best-known piece. He also wrote cantatas, songs and vocal music, several operas and operettas, including *Gwendoline* (1885) and *Le roi malgré lui* (1887), and much piano music of great charm and wide appeal.

chaconne Dance in triple time which became popular in Spain and Italy in the early 17th century, soon spreading to northern Europe. The dance typically features a basic progression of chords (I-V-IV-V) acting as melodic or harmonic ostinatos; some composers used this chord sequence to generate a series of melodic themes in the bass, which were repeated over and over again (i.e. ground **bass**). Other composers used a repeated theme but moved it through the instruments, or used a series of different melodies. **J.S. Bach** wrote a *chaconne* for solo violin; Dido's lament *When I am Laid in Earth* from Purcell's *Dido and Aeneas* is a good example of the vocal treatment of the form. See also **passacaglia**.

chacony Old English term for **chaconne**.

Chagrin, Francis (1905-1972) British composer of Romanian birth. He studied in Bucharest, with Nadia **Boulanger** and **Dukas** in Paris, and with Mátyás **Seiber** in London. He earned his living from composing film music, produced a small output of compositions showing a variety of modernist influences and conducted his own ensemble. He was instrumental in founding the Committee (later Society) for the Promotion of New Music (1943), set up to encourage young British composers.

Chailly, Luciano (1920-) Italian composer who first studied the violin in Ferrara and later composition in Milan. He has worked as artistic director at both La Scala, Milan, and at the Teatro Regio in Turin, and has taught at the Milan Conservatoire. His compositions include operas, ballets and chamber works, and show something of the influence of **Hindemith**, with whom he studied in 1948.

Chailly, Riccardo (1953-) Italian conductor, son of the composer Luciano Chailly. He studied in Milan and Siena and made his début in Milan conducting Massenet's *Werther* (1973). His Scala début was with Verdi's *I masnadieri* in 1978, and the same year he made his first appearance at the Royal Opera House, Covent Garden. After a spell with the London Philharmonic Orchestra, in 1986 he became music director of the Concertgebouw Orchestra in Amsterdam. His recordings include a fine version of Bruckner's Symphony No.4 (1990). One of the most gifted of the younger generation of conductors, he has already acquired a considerable reputation in both operatic and symphonic work.

Chaliapin, Fyodor Alternative transliteration of **Shaliapin**, Fyodor.

chalumeau (Fr.) 1. A reedpipe, or the chanter of a bagpipe.

2. The single-reed orchestral wind instrument from which the clarinet developed. The instrument was called for in the scores of **Fux** and others in Vienna from 1704, and it was also used in two concertos by Vivaldi.

3. Also commonly used for the lowest register of the clarinet.

chamber orchestra A small orchestra. Often used to describe the small orchestra of earlier periods; the term came into general use only in the 20th century, when composers chose to write for small and varied groups of players, ranging from ten to 30 or 40 musicians as opposed to the 80 or more of the full symphony orchestra.

chamber sonata Late 17th- and early 18th-century sonata intended to be played in a secular rather than sacred setting. After a prelude there would be a number of dance movements, for example an allemande, corrente, sarabande, gigue and gavotte. The chamber sonatas of **Corelli** (Op.2, 1685, and Op.4, 1692) are typical early examples. The Italian equivalent is *sonata da camera*. See also **church sonata**.

Chaminade, Cécile (1857-1944) French pianist and composer. She is best known for her songs and piano music (more than 200 works). Her other works include chamber music, a *symphonie dramatique*, *Les Amazones* (for chorus and orchestra), and an opera.

Champagne, Claude (1891-1965) Canadian composer, best known as the leader of a nationalist tradition in Canadian music, who incorporated the folk-music of his country into many types of composition. Fiddle music was a major influence, but he also had a rigorous academic training, mainly in France. He was one-time professor of music at McGill University and founded the Montreal Conservatoire. His music is influenced by the so-called Impressionist composers; several of his pieces for orchestra reflect the Canadian landscape.

change-ringing Ringing of a set of bells in an order determined by mathematical permutations rather than melody. Each bell is assigned a number (the bell with the highest pitch being number one), and the bells are then rung in various sequences. The basic principle is that bells adjacent in one sequence then change places in the next. The methods of mathematical permutation by which sequences avoid repetition have traditional names, e.g. 'Plain hunt', 'Plain bob', 'Grandsire' and 'Stedman'. Change-ringing originated in England in the 17th century. It enjoyed a revival in the second half of the 19th century, and now flourishes through out Britain.

changgo/changko (Korea) Double-headed, hourglass-shaped drum with lashed skin heads. The head to the right of the player is played with a stick, while that to the left is played with the palm of the hand or a small, round-headed mallet. It is the main percussion instrument in traditional Korean music, featuring in **sijo** and in **p'ansori**.

chanson (Fr.) Song, broadly any song with French text. It is most commonly used to refer to French **polyphonic** art-songs of the Middle Ages and Renaissance, but may describe the secular songs of the **troubadours** and **trouvères** of the 12th and 13th centuries; the *airs de cour* of the late 16th and 17th centuries; and popular songs of the 17th, 18th and 19th centuries, usually short **strophic** songs on amorous subjects, sung and sold in the streets. In the 19th and 20th centuries it came again to be applied to art music, and also to folk-song.

In the 14th century, *chansons* were usually in three parts, two of which were probably intended for instruments, and written in one of the poetic *formes fixes* (*ballade*, *rondeau*, *virelai*); these are typified in the work of **Machaut**. Towards the end of the 14th century there arose the Mannerist school (including Johannes **Ciconia** and Matteo da Perugia), the adherents of which wrote chansons of great rhythmic and contrapuntal complexity. The intricacies of Mannerist writing were replaced by a simpler style which culminated in the work of two Burgundians, Guillaume **Dufay** and Gilles **Binchois**, the finest *chanson* composers of the first half of the 15th century. These were in turn succeeded in the second half of the century by Antoine **Busnois** and Johannes **Ockeghem**, in both of whose works the treble-dominated style gave way to a more equal-voiced polyphonic style. This eventually led to the use of imitative counterpoint based on melodic motifs, which is found in the *chansons* of **Josquin des Prés** in the 16th century.

The 16th century also saw the gradual abandonment of the *formes fixes*, and the wide distribution of *chansons* through the publication of printed music. The Paris-based printer Pierre **Attaignant** printed

70 *chanson* collections between 1528 and 1549, most of them written in a new, simple homophonic style by French composers such as Claudin Sermisy and Clement **Janequin**. Later in the century the French firm Le Roy & Ballard succeeded Attaignant as the most important publisher of *chansons*; composers included Jacques **Arcadelt**, Claude **Goudimel** and Roland de **Lassus**. This period also saw the rise of the *chansons spirituelles*, with moralistic or sacred texts.

chant 1. A harmonized melody used in the Anglican rite for psalms and canticles; although in common time, it is often varied in metre to accommodate the text. See also **Gregorian chant**.

2. The French term for song or singing.

chanty Alternative spelling of **shanty**.

chapel-master Term used on the continent of Europe (but rarely in England) to describe a person in charge of music in a chapel, be it a private chapel at court, a collegiate chapel or a cathedral. A great many of the composers of the 16th and 17th centuries earned their livings as chapel-masters. The duties varied, but they invariably included conducting the choir and organizing music for the chapel services, and often playing the organ. The composition of music for the chapel was not necessarily part of the contract, but the job left time for the incumbent to compose, and indeed, he was most often expected to; a well-respected composer added greatly to the patron's prestige. The European equivalents are: (Ger.) *Kapellmeister*; (Fr.) *maître de chapelle*; (It.) *maestro di cappella*; (Sp.) *maestro de capilla*.

Chapel Royal Choir retained by successive monarchs in England to perform services for the Royal Family. At first it was largely a peripatetic body, travelling with the royal household, but in 1702 it was established permanently in St James's Palace, where it remains today.

The members of the choir were members of the royal household and their living conditions attracted singers of the highest standard. The size of the Chapel Royal has fluctuated throughout history, depending on the interest of the monarch of the time, but there would sometimes be as many as 32 men and 16 children. The size and ability of the choir encouraged many English composers to write works specifically for it: they include John **Dunstable**, William **Byrd**, John **Bull**, Orlando **Gibbons** and Thomas **Tomkins**.

The Chapel Royal has suffered a decline since 1714; today there are only six men and ten children (drawn from the City of London Boys' School).

Chapí, Ruperto (1851-1909) Spanish composer. He studied with Arrieta at the Madrid Conservatoire where, in 1869, he was awarded first prize in harmony. On leaving, he worked for a time as cornet player in a theatre orchestra, and most of his compositions are for the stage. His one-act opera *Les naves de Cortés* (1874) was awarded a three-year government grant, which enabled him to study in Rome, Milan and Paris. He wrote more than 100 other one-act operas (**zarzuelas**), including *La hija de Jefté* (1876) and *Musica classica* (1880).

character piece Short, 19th-century composition which embodies a specific programmatic idea or expresses a particular mood. Most character pieces are for piano solo and have titles that indicate their brevity and intention (bagatelle, impromptu, etc.)

Schubert's *Impromptus*, Mendelssohn's *Lieder ohne Worte* and many of Chopin's piano pieces are character pieces. Schumann developed the idea further by choosing separate names for individual pieces, highlighting their mood, and by grouping them together. Thus we have his *Novelletten*, *Nocturnes* and *Albumblätter* and the cycles *Papillons* and *Carnaval*. Debussy, with his carefully titled *Préludes*, is the direct inheritor of these ideas.

These characteristic pieces are most often in ternary (ABA) form, with A and B representing two contrasting moods within the general programmatic idea. Their precursors are to be found in the harpsichord suites of François **Couperin**, in which one basic motif can be heard to dominate a whole movement.

charleston Dance particularly associated with the 1920s. The charleston had its origins in African dance and was adapted by black Americans at the turn of the century. It was popularized through its inclusion in shows and musicals (for example, *Runnin' Wild*, 1923) and by the mid-1920s had become an international craze. Its complicated footwork and side-kicks were eventually incorporated and simplified in the quick-step.

Charleston

Charpentier, Gustave (1860-1956) French composer whose style was influenced by Wagner and Berlioz. He studied at the Paris Conservatoire under **Massenet** and was awarded the Prix de Rome for his cantata *Didon* in 1887. Most of his works were composed in the 1880s to 1890s, including *Impressions d'Italie* and *La vie du poète*. He is best known for his opera *Louise* (1900), which for the first time in opera dealt sympathetically with the life of the working class in Paris; it achieved an enormous success, which, however, was never to be repeated with any of his later works, although he lived for another 56 years. *Louise* was made into a film in 1936 under Charpentier's supervision.

Charpentier, Marc-Antoine (1645-1704) French composer who studied in Rome with **Carissimi**, where he learnt the Italian style. On returning to France he found himself opposed by **Lully** and at odds with the French nationalist style. In spite of Lully's jealousy he was employed by Molière to write incidental music for his troupe, which was to become the *Comédie française*. Charpentier was also favoured by the royal household and the Jesuits, who appointed him music master at their most important church, St Louis. He was honoured with the post of *maître de musique* at the Sainte-Chapelle in 1693. He composed a number of small-scale sacred dramas, oratorios, grand motets and one full-scale opera, *Médée*.

chasse (Fr.) Hunt. 1. Used to describe instruments originally used for hunting, e.g. *cor de chasse* – hunting horn.
2. A medieval piece whose text concerning hunting is reflected in the canonic nature of its composition. See also **caccia**.

Chausson, Ernest (1855-1899) French composer who, while influenced musically by César **Franck** and Wagner, was also deeply involved in contemporary literary movements and in painting. His reaction to fashionable trends in literature is shown in his memorable setting of the *Poème de l'amour et de la mer* for soprano and orchestra, which is a landmark in the setting of symbolist poetry. His assimilation of the wandering harmonies of Franck and Wagner is not always successful but there are many passages of striking originality in his works. Among the most successful are the Symphony in B♭ and the *Poème* for violin and orchestra.

Chávez, Carlos (1899-1978) Mexican composer. He was essentially self-taught, but met **Varèse** and others in New York in the 1920s. He was conductor of the Mexico Symphony Orchestra (1928-48) and director of the Mexican National Conservatoire (1928-35). He was instrumental both in stimulating music in his own country and in taking Mexican music abroad. The influence of pre-Columbian South America is apparent in several of his works, for example the *Sinfonia india* and the ballet *Xochipili-Macuilxochitl*, which was written for an ensemble of native instruments.

chef d'attaque (Fr.) Leader of the first violins in an orchestra.

chef d'orchestre (Fr.) Conductor of an orchestra.

Cheltenham International Festival Founded in 1945, the Cheltenham Festival takes place during the summer. Originally announced as a festival of British contemporary music, even though this has now become diluted with other events, it still maintains the original intention. It has been directed since 1969 by John Manduell and since the opening year, when Britten conducted the first concert performance of the *Sea Interludes* from *Peter Grimes*, hundreds of first performances of works by British composers have been given.

cheng (China) Sixteen-stringed, plucked zither. The strings are traditionally of silk, but more recently copper or steel strings have been used; they are stretched over movable bridges and are tuned to an anhemitonic pentatonic scale.

chengcheng (Indonesia) Pair of cymbals, a group of cymbals or a single large cymbal used mainly in the **gamelan** gong orchestra of Bali.

Cherkassky, Shura (1911-) Russian-born American pianist who studied with his mother and with Josef **Hofmann** at the Curtis Institute in Philadelphia. Cherkassky soon embarked on a series of world-wide concert tours. He is best known for his performances of the Romantic repertory and for his recordings of Soviet music.

Cherubini, Luigi (1760-1842) Italian composer, born in Florence. He lived in London for four years, and there produced two operas; later he moved to Paris and began to compose operas in a highly dramatic style. In due course he became director of the new Paris Conservatoire. In all he produced nearly 30 operas, which were to have an important influence on other composers and the development of the theatre. His opera *Les deux journées* was based on a similar story to that used by Beethoven for *Fidelio* and profoundly influenced that composer. His other works include a Symphony in D minor, composed in 1815 for the Philharmonic Society of London, which **Toscanini** recorded, and many sacred works, including several Masses and two Requiem Masses. Among his most important operas are *Lodoïska*, *Médée*, *Anacréon*, and *Faniska*.

chest of viols Set of instruments, usually stored in a cupboard or chest. In the 16th century this was a usual household item among the wealthy. The complete set (consort) of viols corresponded to the range of the bass to soprano voices, and consisted of two of each of three sizes, these being the treble, tenor and bass (also known as the viola da gamba).

chest voice The lower part of the vocal range in both women's and men's voices, in which the tone seems to come from the chest, although still produced by the larynx. In a woman's voice, it gives a powerful, almost masculine timbre, much favoured in the past, but now out of fashion: the contralto Clara **Butt** was a heroic exponent of this style.

Chevreuille, Raymond (1901-1976) Belgian composer. Besides composing he worked as an acoustical engineer for Belgian Radio, where he was also controller of French music broadcasts. Not surprisingly, his compositions include a number of scores for radio, such as *D'un diable de briquet*, for which he was awarded the Italia Prize in 1950.

Chicago Symphony Orchestra American symphony orchestra, founded in 1891 by Theodore Thomas and originally named the Chicago Orchestra. Between 1906 and 1912 it was named the Theodore Thomas Orchestra, and thereafter took its present name. It is the third oldest orchestra in the United States; it has toured widely and made a great number of recordings. It was raised to world class by the Hungarian-born conductor Fritz **Reiner**, who directed it between 1952 and 1963. Georg **Solti** took over the music direction in 1969. The recordings made under these two have contributed to the orchestra's pre-eminent status. Rafael **Kubelik** (1950-3) and Jean **Martinon** (1963-8) have also worked with it; the music director since 1989 has been Daniel **Barenboim**.

chiesa, da (It.) In Baroque music, sonatas or cantatas designated for use in church, as opposed to those marked *da camera* which were for secular use. Sonatas marked *da chiesa* included more serious abstract movements than those marked *da camera*, which had more movements based on stylized dance forms.

Child, William (1606-1697) English organist and composer, predominantly of church music. His works include many anthems, services and psalm settings, as well as some secular instrumental pieces and catches. Child was a court musician to King Charles II from the Restoration until the king's death.

Childs, Barney (1926-) American composer and teacher. Childs was largely self-taught, although in the 1950s he studied at Tanglewood with **Chávez** and **Copland**, and privately with Elliott **Carter**. His academic background was literary rather than musical and his compositions explore improvisatory and **aleatory** techniques. They include *Interbalances* (1960-3), works for wind ensemble, two symphonies and choral works.

ch'in/qin (China) Seven-stringed fretless zither, plucked with the finger-tips and nails. The body of the instrument is made of wood painted with many layers of protective lacquer. The open strings are tuned to an anhemitonic pentatonic scale and are pressed by the left hand, guided by 13 embedded studs, to change pitch. It is the oldest of the indigenous Chinese instruments and is used extensively as a solo instrument.

ching (Thailand) Small pair of teacup-shaped, hand-held cymbals used as time-markers, named after the sound they emit when hit together. They are employed in virtually all forms of traditional Thai music and especially in the **pi'phat** ensemble.

Chisholm, Erik (1904-1965) Scottish composer and conductor. He began his career as conductor of the Glasgow Grand Opera Society in 1930, where he introduced audiences to works outside the usual repertory, giving first performances of *Les troyens* and *Béatrice et Bénédict* by Berlioz. In 1946 he moved to South Africa, becoming professor of music at the University of Cape Town. He has composed operas, two symphonies and concertos for violin and for piano.

chitarra (It.) Guitar. See also **chitarrone**.

chitarrone Member of the **lute** family. It was larger than other lutes and was developed to play **continuo** parts. It had a double neck to carry a second set of strings of the bass notes. Historians disagree as to whether the *chitarrone* was synonymous with the **theorbo**, another double-necked or arch lute which appears in the music of that period. By 1600, the *chitarrone* was the favourite instrument for accompanying the human voice and there was also a certain amount of solo music written for it.

chiuso (It.) Closed. 1. Used in horn music to mean stopped, indicating that notes should be stopped with the hand.
2. A medieval term meaning the second-time ending in music, the first being called *aperto*.

choir 1. A group of singers.
2. Area of a church reserved for the choir in the above sense.
3. A group of similar instruments, sometimes forming part of a larger ensemble (e.g. brass choir).
4. An abbreviation for **choir organ**.

choir organ In England, the lowest manual of the organ, traditionally operating a set of pipes placed behind the player if the organ was in a gallery, but also used in other organs.
In the 19th century, sweet-toned solo stops rendered the manual less suitable for its original purpose of providing a foil to the other manuals.

chöömij (Mongolia) See **xoomij**

Chopin, Frédéric (1810-1849) Polish composer, mainly of piano music; son of a Frenchman who had settled in Poland. He began his musical career as a pianist, renowned for his soft tone and subtle nuances, and this early love for the piano was carried through to his compositions. He had begun to compose piano pieces before he was 20. In 1831 he settled in

Frédéric Chopin

Paris, where his performances were acclaimed and his compositions were well received by his audience. Particularly appealing were the dances of his native Poland, above all the **mazurka** and the **polonaise**, of which he wrote numerous examples.
In Paris he formed a relationship with the novelist George Sand (the pseudonym of Aurore Dudevant), and for more than ten years (from 1836) she sustained his creative genius and looked after him as his tuberculosis rendered him increasingly frail. Her house in the French countryside was a haven for him, although a trip they made to Majorca in 1838 was not a success because of the weather and his health. This period was intensely fruitful, and from it date some of the most memorable **nocturnes**, mazurkas, waltzes and ballades.
Chopin composed largely at the keyboard, and much of his music derives from pianistic ideas rather than abstract concepts. His reliance on the sustaining

pedal was as much a part of his compositional technique as it was a part of his piano playing. He was influenced by several other composers, but **Hummel** may be singled out, who showed Chopin new aspects of keyboard virtuosity; and **Bellini**, from whose operatic arias Chopin transferred the highly ornamented **bel canto** lines to the piano keyboard. These come out particularly in the *Nocturnes* and in the slow movements of the two piano concertos.

Among Chopin's best-known compositions are the 24 *Préludes* (1839), two sonatas (one containing the celebrated *Funeral March*), two sets of studies (including many known by names, such as *The Revolutionary*, the *Black Key* study and the *Winter Wind*), the *Polonaise-fantaisie* (Op.61) and the *Berceuse* (Op.57). There is also a small amount of music for other instruments, including a cello sonata and some songs. Chopin became one of the major forces in 19th-century piano music and his influence was profound, not only on **Liszt** and the later 19th-century French school such as Debussy and **Fauré**, but also on Wagner, Tchaikovsky and many 20th-century composers.

choragus Official post at the University of Oxford dating from 1626. The choragus was appointed to conduct music practices twice a week.

chorale Hymn of the German Protestant Church. Luther was very influential in building up the repertory of chorales and favoured vernacular texts and simple, tuneful melodies. Many were adaptations of **Gregorian** hymns and medieval German religious songs.

Written for congregational use, chorales have simple tunes, many based on secular songs, but often have complex contrapuntal harmonizations. One of the first important collections was that published by Lukas Osiander in 1586. It was different from many previous collections in that Osiander placed the melody at the top of the texture, rather than in the tenor line. Many chorale melodies are familiar today, such as *Nun danket alle Gott* and *Jesu meine Freude*. **J.S. Bach** made a great many chorale harmonizations and also used chorales as a basis for many other types of composition, such as chorale **fantasias**, chorale **fugues** and chorale **motets**.

chord Group of two or more notes sounded together; the basic element in harmony. Chords are named according to the **intervals** of which they are formed (e.g. six-four chord, containing a fourth and a sixth above the lowest note) and, in a harmonic context, according to the degree of the scale on which they are built (e.g. dominant seventh, a chord built on the **dominant** and containing the seventh above it).

The common chords of traditional harmony are **triads**, consisting of a third and a fifth above the bass. These may be used in **inversion**, giving a six-three chord (first inversion) or a six-four chord (second inversion). Other notes, such as the seventh or ninth above the root, may be added. In modern music, chords may be formed by any combination of intervals, including some highly dissonant ones.

Triads in: root position, first inversion and second inversion

chording 1. The spacing of **chords**.

2. In performance, the art of balancing and tuning chords in voices or instruments for perfection of attack, ensemble and clarity of harmony and tone.

chordophone Generic term for instruments in which the sound is produced by means of stretched strings fixed at both ends. It includes all classes of **zithers**, **lutes**, **guitars**, **violins**, **viols** and **harps**.

chord symbol 1. The symbol written below a stave or system of notation which identifies the **chord**. Roman numerals are usually assigned to each chord, indicating which degree of the scale the chord is built on. Major chords are conventionally assigned upper-case symbols; minor chords, lower-case. Lower-case letters a, b, and c denote root position, first and second inversion respectively, whereas superior numbers indicate intervals other than those of the basic **triad** occurring in the chord.

2. In music for guitars and guitar-like instruments, it refers to the grids that represent the strings and frets, with dots to indicate where the fingers should be placed for each different chord; or just the names of the chords. These may be written underneath text alone, or underneath text and a piano part.

choreographic poem Extended piece of music composed in the form and spirit of a dance, e.g. **Ravel**'s *La valse*.

choreometrics Analytical method for the cross-cultural study of dance, developed by Alan **Lomax** and Irmgard Bartenieff from a similar system devised for song styles (**cantometrics**). It attempts to show how various types of dance movement are related to the dynamic qualities of everyday life in different cultures.

choro (Port.) Term loosely used to describe many kinds of ensemble music in which one instrument dominates the others in a virtuoso manner. Originally a Brazilian term for a group of serenaders, and then for their music (*musicas de choro*), the *choro* is often used by **Villa-Lobos** and other Brazilian composers.

chorus Group of singers who perform together either in unison or in parts, often accompanying soloists or as an adjunct to a group of instruments. By extension, this term also refers to a work written for several voices, such as the *Hallelujah Chorus* in Handel's *Messiah*.

Chorzempa, Daniel (1944-) American organist who studied at the University of Minnesota and at Cologne. He has received much critical acclaim for his recitals on the piano and harpsichord in addition to his organ-playing. His repertory is wide and his playing notable for its colour and energy. His performances of the works of Liszt are especially admired.

Chou Wen-Chung (1923-) Chinese-born American composer and teacher. He moved to the United States in 1946 and originally studied architecture before going on to study music at the New England Conservatoire, Columbia University and privately with **Varèse**. His music combines Chinese melodic patterns with Western orchestration and he is influenced by Chinese philosophy, painting and poetry. This is most obvious in *The Willows are New*, and in *Yü Ko* and *Metaphors* for wind ensemble, based on the *I Ching*.

Christoff, Boris (1914-) Bulgarian bass who studied in Sofia, Rome and Salzburg and made his début in **Mussorgsky**'s *Boris Godunov*, a work with which he has been associated ever since. His extraordinary acting ability is matched by an excellent diction and depth of tone. His performance of Verdi is highly esteemed.

chromaticism In its broadest sense, a term that refers to the use of notes not belonging to the key in which a piece or passage is written. Melodically, it applies to **motifs** based on sequences of adjacent semitones; in this sense it was a feature of ancient Greek music.

From the late Middle Ages, chromaticism was regarded mainly as an expressive means within an essentially diatonic framework, as used by the Italian madrigalists.

In the Baroque period, composers often used chromatic motifs, and chromatic chords such as the diminished seventh. In the works of the Romantic composers, particularly **Wagner**, chromaticism came into its own. Further developments were the whole-tone language of **Debussy** and, ultimately, the **twelve-note** technique of **Schoenberg**.

chromatic scale Sequence of twelve consecutive semitones. An instrument on which the chromatic scale is available is said to be chromatic and can play in any key.

Chromatic scale

Chung, Kyung-Wha (1948-) Korean violinist who studied at the Juilliard School in New York and in 1968 made her début there with the New York Philharmonic Orchestra. She has frequently performed as a soloist and in chamber ensembles in Europe and is much admired for her vibrant and warm tone. Her recordings include many concertos and the solo violin music of J.S. Bach.

church cantata English equivalent of the Italian *cantata da* **chiesa**.

church modes Eight modes (referring both to scale and to melodic type) under which **Gregorian chant** was classified.

The authentic modes were those that can now be obtained by playing D-D′, E-E′, F-F′ and G-G′ on the white notes of a keyboard instrument; D, E, F and G were the **finals** of the modes.

The plagal modes were obtained by beginning a fourth below the final of the authentic modes. In the 16th century the notes A and C′ were added, giving four more modes (two authentic, two plagal).

Although their meaning was different, the names most commonly given to these modes today are borrowed from ancient Greek modes: Dorian (D-D′), Phrygian (E-E′), Lydian (F-F′), Mixolydian (G-G′), Aeolian (A-A′) and Ionian (C-C′); the plagal modes take the prefix 'hypo-'. See also **modes**.

church sonata (Italian: *sonata da* **chiesa**) Sonata that was considered suitable for church use (as opposed to a **chamber sonata**). The term came into use in the second half of the 17th century. Generally the form consisted of four movements in two pairs – slow, fast, slow, fast – the slow movements acting as introductions to the fast ones. There is some evidence that as plainsong declined, church sonatas were played in its place at services.

ciaccona (It.) Equivalent of the French **chaconne**.

cibell Alternative spelling of **cebell**.

Ciccolini, Aldo (1925-) Italian-born pianist. When only nine he enrolled at the Naples Conservatoire and at the age of 22 became professor of piano there. In 1942 he made his début with Chopin's F minor concerto, and subsequently went on to win many prizes, including the St Cecilia prize in 1948. He moved to France in 1949, and is much admired for his performances of the French repertory, especially Ravel and Debussy. His recordings include the complete works of Erik **Satie** and the **Saint-Saëns** piano concertos.

Ciconia, Johannes (*c.*1335-1411) French composer who, working in both France and Italy, fused the French *ars nova* with the Italian 14th-century style. The 'Ciconia style' continued to be apparent in music for some 20 years after his death. His surviving works include eight Glorias and four Credos for the Mass, 12 motets, three French songs (including *Le ray du soleil*), 15 Italian songs and four songs in the 14th-century madrigal style. He also wrote three musical treatises. One is lost, but his *Nova Musica* and its later reworking, *De Proportionibus*, survive. They contain distilled teachings of Pythagoras,

Boethius, Jehan de Murs and Marchetto di Padova.

Cilea, Francesco (1866-1950) Italian composer and teacher who studied at the Naples Conservatoire from 1881 to 1889. After two rather unsuccessful attempts at composing opera (*Gina*, 1889, and *La Tilda*, 1892), he supported himself by teaching, first at the Naples Conservatoire and then at the Reale Istituto Musicale in Florence. He went on to compose three more operas, *L'arlesiana* (1897), *Adriana Lecouvreur* (1902) and *Gloria* (1907). *Adriana Lecouvreur* achieved a certain success and is still performed.

Cimarosa, Domenico (1749-1801) Italian opera composer, educated at the Conservatorio di S. Maria di Loreto, where he developed as a gifted singer and composer. His first opera, *Le stravaganze del conte*, was heard in Naples in 1772. By the mid-1780s, Cimarosa had established himself as one of the most popular **opera buffa** composers of his day. He was *maestro di cappella* at the court of Catherine II in St Petersburg from 1787 to 1791, and spent a year in Vienna. There he composed his most famous opera, *Il matrimonio segreto* (The Secret Marriage), which the audience applauded so enthusiastically that it was repeated from the beginning at its first performance in 1792. He returned to Naples in 1793. In addition to his vast output of nearly 70 operas, Cimarosa also composed sacred works, including five oratorios and numerous Masses; concertos and keyboard sonatas.

cimbalon Hungarian **dulcimer**. The smaller and older variety is similar to the English instrument. A larger, recently invented version allows chromatic notes to be obtained and is fitted with a damper pedal. The cimbalon has been adopted by dance bands; it has also been used by Stravinsky, for *Les noces* and *Renard*; by **Kodály** in *Háry János*; and by **Boulez** in *Eclat*, among others.

Cimbalon

cinema organ Type of organ used in cinemas between 1925 and 1950, at first to accompany silent films; later it became a notable feature of the large cinemas which were hugely popular in the 1930s, and was used for entertainment during intermissions. The instrument often featured some unusual **stops** producing novelty sounds (e.g. a motor-horn). It is also known as a theatre organ.

cipher Name given to the continued sounding of an organ pipe caused by a mechanical fault.

cipher notation System of notation in which numbers are used as a substitute for staff notation, advocated by Rousseau among others in the 18th century.

cither, cithern Alternative spellings of **cittern**.

cittern Small-bodied stringed instrument of the same family as the **lute** and **guitar**, differing from these in that it had metal rather than gut strings. It was plucked with a quill or plectrum rather than the fingers, and was used widely throughout Renaissance Europe for music of all kinds.

The cittern was developed in Italy in the late 15th century from the citole, and passed out of use in the mid-18th century with the development of new metal-strung instruments. It is now being made and played again because of a revival of interest in medieval and Renaissance music. Alternative spellings are cither and cithern.

City of Birmingham Symphony Orchestra (CBSO) Orchestra that started life as the City of Birmingham Orchestra in 1920, when **Elgar** conducted its first concert with a programme of his own works. Its first permanent conductor was Adrian **Boult** (1923-30). The orchestra was renamed in 1948 and gave its first London concert that year. Supported by the Birmingham City Council, the CBSO gave a regular Thursday evening and Sunday afternoon series as well as touring the Midlands area. The Sunday series has now been dropped, but there is still a Thursday evening concert series in Birmingham Town Hall.

The orchestra rose to prominence under Louis **Frémaux** (1969-78). It developed unusual programmes and made a large number of recordings. The CBSO's reputation has been greatly enhanced since the appointment of Simon **Rattle** as its conductor in 1980.

Civil, Alan (1929-1989) English horn-player. He studied in Hamburg and England, and became the principal horn of the Royal Philharmonic, the Philharmonia and (from 1966) the BBC Symphony Orchestra. He also worked with small ensembles such as the London Wind Players, the Music Group of London and the London Wind Quintet. He performed all over the world and made recordings of most of the important horn concertos. In 1966 he became a professor at the Royal College of Music. He played and recorded some early music on his own collection of natural horns. Among his compositions are a wind quintet and a symphony for brass and percussion.

claribel Sweet-sounding 8-foot (2.5 m) wooden organ stop known also as clarabella or claribel-flute.

clarinet Woodwind instrument with a cylindrical barrel and single reed, usually made of cane, which was developed in the late 17th century from the **chalumeau** by J.C. Denner. In expert hands (especially in **jazz**) it has a range of over three octaves and great flexibility; it can produce a wide range of dynamics from a whispering *ppp* to a brilliant and penetrating *fff*. It was first used in military bands, but by the end of the 18th century it was in general use as a valuable solo and orchestral instrument, and was introduced into operatic and symphonic scores by Mozart and Haydn. Because it was difficult to play chromatic notes in tune, the clarinet was made in several keys, those in common use at the beginning of the 19th century being pitched in A, B♭, and C. As the demands of orchestral technique grew, high instruments in D, E♭ and F were added, although of these only the E♭ is now in general use. Other types included the bass clarinet in B♭ and A, and the basset-horn in F.

In the 1840s the Boehm system for the flute, with an elaborate mechanical key arrangement, was adapted to the clarinet and greatly eased the problems of tuning. Other types include the alto E♭, often used in military bands, the rare G clarinet used in the Austrian traditional

Clarinet

Schrammelmusik, and the contrabass clarinet in B♭. The C clarinet figures in many scores up to the time of Mahler, but dropped out of use at the beginning of the 20th century; however, a new instrument made of plastic has been successfully designed in England by Graham Lyons, primarily for educational use.

Mozart was one of the first composers to realize the possibilities of the clarinet as a solo instrument, when he heard the great virtuoso of the time, Anton **Stadler**. He composed for him the Clarinet Trio K498 (*Kegelstadt*) in 1786, the Clarinet Quintet K581 in 1789 and the Clarinet Concerto K688 in 1791, chiefly for the obsolete basset clarinet, which had a deeper low register. Other outstanding works include concertos by **Stamitz, Weber, Spohr, Stanford, Nielsen, Copland,** Stravinsky and **Goldschmidt;** sonatas by Brahms, **Hindemith, Bax, Ireland, Bernstein, Poulenc** and **Martinů**, and numerous chamber works for the clarinet with other instruments. The clarinet is an important instrument in jazz groups, especially in the hands of such players as the Americans Benny Goodman and Harry James, and the English Tony Coe (who plays an old C clarinet).

clarino 1. The high register of the **clarinet.** 2. A virtuoso method of trumpet-playing practised by trumpeters in the 17th and 18th centuries, trained specially and exclusively in the art of producing the highest harmonics, where they form a continuous scale. Such players were able to play the very difficult trumpet parts in, for example, **J.S. Bach**'s cantatas. Various piccolo trumpets in high keys have now been developed for the performance of these high parts.

Clarke, Jeremiah (1674-1707) English composer and organist. He began his career as chorister of the Chapel Royal and was appointed organist of Winchester College in 1692. At various times he was also vicar-choral at St Paul's Cathedral and organist at the Chapel Royal. His compositions include anthems, odes, harpsichord pieces and incidental music for the stage. His best-known work is the *Trumpet Voluntary*, often wrongly attributed to **Purcell.**

Clarke-Whitfield, John (1770-1836) English composer and organist who held a number of appointments as church organist before becoming Professor of Music at Cambridge in 1841. His compositions are conservative in style and show the influence of Handel. His two **oratorios**, *The Crucifixion* and *The Resurrection*, were well known in their day. He also edited the music of Handel and Purcell.

clarsach Small Celtic harp used for the accompaniment of folk-song. The Gaelic name is *clairseach.*

classical Strictly, the music of the late 18th and early 19th centuries, particularly that of Haydn, Mozart and Beethoven. The term is also applied to art music of all periods as opposed to popular, folk or jazz music.

claves Cylindrical hardwood blocks originating in Cuba and the Antilles. They are struck together, with the cupped palm of the hand providing resonance. They were introduced into concert works by **Varèse** and used since by **Copland** and **Berio** (in *Circles*), among others.

clavicembalo (It.) Alternative term for **harpsichord.**

clavichord Stringed keyboard instrument in which the strings are activated from below by brass blades or 'tangents', which are fixed upright on the key levers. The

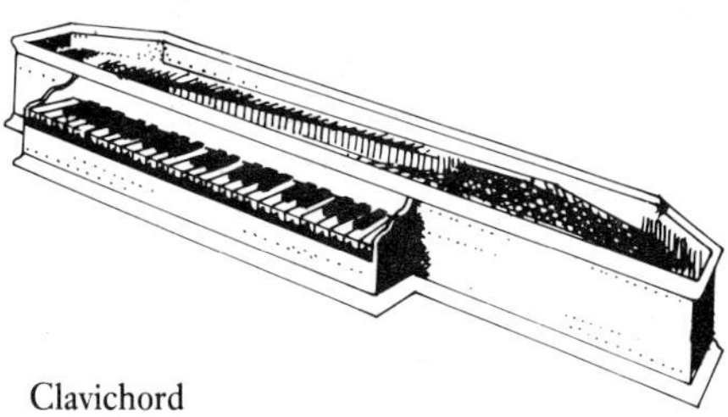

Clavichord

clavichord first appeared in the 15th century, and in some countries was in use until the early 19th century. It is a quiet but expressive instrument which many people used in preference even to the early piano. **J.S. Bach** is said to have preferred the clavichord to any other keyboard instrument, apart from the organ.

There are two kinds of clavichord: 'fretted' and 'unfretted'. In the unfretted variety, each note has its own string (or pair of strings). However, on the earlier fretted clavichord, two or more notes shared the same string, with the tangent striking it a little nearer or further away from the bridge. This made the earlier instrument very compact.

clavicytherium Upright harpsichord. The first recorded use of the term is *c.*1460. The world's oldest surviving keyboard instrument is a clavicytherium from the late 15th century, now in the Royal College of Music, London. The advantages of the upright soundboard are that the instrument takes up less space and the sound is projected better into the room, but the fact that the jacks cannot return to their resting place under their own weight tends to give a heavy, uneven action, so the instrument has never proved as popular as the horizontal harpsichord. Clavicytheria nevertheless continued to be made until the 18th century.

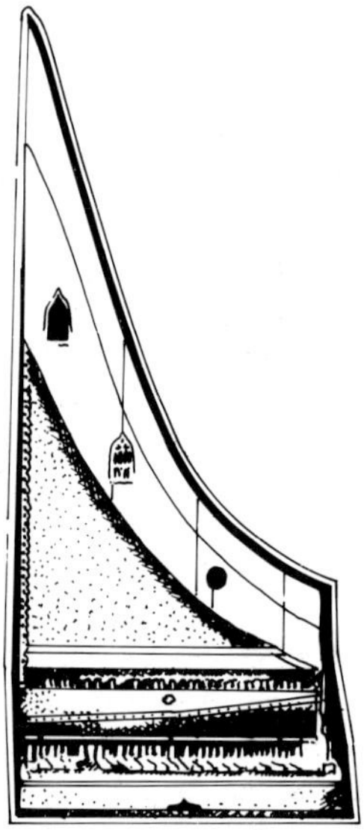

Clavicytherium

clavier (Fr.) Keyboard of an instrument. In the Baroque period it was a generic term in German (also as *Klavier*) for keyboard instruments (clavichord, harpsichord, spinet, organ), as in **J.S. Bach**'s *Das wohltemperirte Clavier*; sometimes it was used to denote the clavichord in particular. In modern German, *Klavier* means piano.

clef Symbol placed at the beginning of a stave which sets the pitch represented by the lines in relation to itself. Three types are generally used today: the G (or treble) clef, the F (or bass) clef, and the C clef; their position on the stave indicates the note after which they are named. The clefs originally consisted of the letters G, F and C; the signs now in use are stylizations of these. In music after 1750, the G and F clefs are invariably used in the same positions. The C clef is commonly used in either of two positions: on the middle line of the stave it is referred to as the alto clef, and on the fourth line it is referred to as the tenor clef.

G clef F clef C clef

Clementi, Muzio (1752-1832) Italian composer, keyboard player and teacher. He travelled to London in 1766, where he made his début in 1770. He is most important as a composer of piano sonatas. **Beethoven** thought highly of him in this capacity, and he is now considered to be the first composer to write successfully for the piano, with its specific qualities (as opposed to the harpsichord). His *Gradus ad Parnassum* (a series of 100 piano *études*, published in 1817) is particularly well remembered.

Cleveland Orchestra American orchestra founded in 1918 and resident at Severance Hall since 1931. Conductors have included Nicolai Sokolov (1918-33), George **Szell** (1946-70) and Lorin **Maazel** (from 1972). It was Szell who expanded the size of the orchestra and raised it to its present eminence. The recordings made with him include a wide range of works, from Haydn to Mendelssohn, Mahler, Debussy, Dvořák, **Kodály** and **Walton**. The present principal conductor is Christoph von **Dohnányi** (from 1984); the orchestra continues to make numerous fine recordings (some with guest conductors such as **Boulez**), and is generally considered to be of world standard.

Cliburn, Van (1934-) American pianist who studied with Rosina Lhévinne at the Juilliard School in New York after having made his début at the age of four. He went on to win a great number of prestigious awards, including first prize at the Tchaikovsky Competition in Moscow in 1958. He is best known for his performances of the Romantic repertory and for the competition he founded in 1962 in Texas.

close Alternative term for **cadence**.

close harmony Use of chords that are spaced so that the parts lie as close together as possible: in four-part harmony there is no more than a twelfth between the outer parts. See also **barber shop**.

cluster Group of notes, adjacent or close together, and usually strongly dissonant, forming a **chord**; also known as a tone-cluster. Clusters are most often used in keyboard music, where they may easily be played with the fist or forearm. They were used first by Henry **Cowell**, and later by **Bartók**, **Ives**, **Stockhausen** and **Ligeti**.

Coates, Albert (1882-1953) English conductor and composer who studied conducting with **Nikisch** at the Leipzig Conservatoire. After being conductor of Elberfeld Opera (1906-8) he held appointments at Dresden and St Petersburg. On his return to England, Coates worked regularly with the London Symphony Orchestra, with whom he conducted the first performance of **Bax's** First Symphony. His compositions include the operas *Samuel Pepys* and *Pickwick*.

Coates, Eric (1886-1957) English composer and viola player. After studying at the Royal Academy of Music, Coates joined the Queen's Hall Orchestra as principal viola (1912). From 1919 he concentrated solely on composition, and his works, although light in mood, are generally admired for their craftsmanship. They include more than 100 songs, several orchestral suites and marches. The best known of his works are *Calling All Workers*, *The Knightsbridge March*, and the *Dam Busters March* from the 1954 film.

cobza (Romania) Plucked lute found in parts of Moldavia. It has a pear-shaped wooden resonator with a very short neck terminating in a large rectangular peg-box, bent back from the fingerboard. Its eight to twelve strings are tuned in fourths or fifths and are set in four courses of two or three strings each. It usually accompanies the violin.

coda (It.) Section at the end of a composition which is not an integral part of the structure but serves to round off the piece. In a **polyphonic** work, it may involve some of the voices continuing against held notes in one or more of the others, particularly against a pedal point.

In a **fugue**, the coda is anything that is played after the last complete statement of the subject. In **sonata form**, the coda is anything that occurs after the **recapitulation** (assuming that the recapitulation is an exact repeat of the **exposition**). **Beethoven** often wrote very lengthy codas which used thematic material in such a way as to be like second development sections. After Beethoven the coda became a standard feature of sonata form.

codetta (It.) Short **coda**. It usually refers to material added to a section of a movement (particularly the **exposition** of a **sonata**) rather than to a complete movement. In a **fugue** it refers to a passage linking two entries of the theme.

Cohen, Harriet (1895-1967) English pianist who studied with Matthay and at the Royal Academy of Music. She was well known for her performances of Bach, and also gave several first performances of contemporary works, including the piano concerto by **Vaughan Williams** and many piano solos by **Bax**. In 1948 a hand injury cut short her concert career, although she continued to play left-handed until 1961. Her recordings include **Elgar**'s Piano Quintet and piano music by Bax. In 1961 the Harriet Cohen International Prizes were founded.

col (It.) With the, an abbreviation of *con il*. This is also written as *coll'* and *colla*, for example *colla destra, sinistra* (with the right, left hand).

Cole, Hugo (1917-) English composer. After gaining a degree in the natural sciences, he entered the Royal College of Music in 1944 to study the cello and composition; he also studied with Nadia **Boulanger** in Paris. His music can be said to be neo-classical in style, and has a clear, fresh quality which makes it particularly attractive for young performers. Among his operas are *The Tunnel, The Falcon*, and some children's operas including *The Fair Traders* (1971). He has also composed concertos, choral works (*Baron Munchhausen*, 1963), chamber music (*Winter Meetings*, 1975) and some songs. In 1964 he became music critic of *The Guardian*.

Coleman, Edward (?-1669) English composer and counter-tenor. He sang in *The Siege of Rhodes*, the first English opera (1656), and was employed at the court of Charles II. His compositions include songs published in the volumes entitled *Select Musicall Ayres and Dialogues* (1653-69).

Colgrass, Michael (1932-) American percussionist and composer. He studied at the University of Illinois, and after graduating won a number of prestigious awards. His compositions include works for percussion, music theatre and songs. They display acquaintance with a wide variety of styles, including **atonality** and **jazz**.

col legno (It.) In string-instrument playing, striking the strings with the bow-stick instead of playing with the hair of the bow.

colophony Rosin for the bow of a stringed instrument.

coloratura (It.) Colouring, a term common in 18th- and 19th-century writing and applying to elaborate decoration, notated or improvised, of a vocal part. It also applies to a singer with a high range and fluid style capable of performing virtuosic arias, such as those for the role of the Queen of the Night in Mozart's *Die Zauberflöte*.

colotomic Originally used by the ethnomusicologist Jaap Kunst to describe the timing structure of Javanese **gamelan**, in which particular gongs mark off sections or subdivisions of a complete time or metrical cycle. Many instruments in Far-Eastern cultures (e.g. Tibet, Korea, Japan and Indonesia) are said to have a colotomic function when, by virtue of a particular rhythmic event, they punctuate phrases or cycles.

colour organ Organ in which the projection of visible colours is in some way connected with various sound colours. A. Wallace Rimington (1854-1918) invented a colour organ which projected colours to music played on another instrument, intensifying the colour in higher octaves. Since then several other variants have been produced, some giving a visual representation of rhythm. None has been really successful, probably because of the fallacious nature of direct parallels between colour and sound.

combination tones Acoustical phenomena, consisting of a third tone heard when two loud tones are sounded together. They are produced not by external factors but by the workings of the inner ear, and are thus sometimes described as subjective tones.

come (It.) As; used in music in phrases such as *come prima*: as before.

comma of Pythagoras Minute difference in pitch between twelve perfect fifths and seven octaves if the intervals are pure. On a well-tempered instrument there should be no difference.

commodo (It.) Comfortable. The term describes a tempo and is used as a qualification to other tempo marks, as in *allegro commodo*. An alternative spelling is *comodo*.

common chords Major and minor **triads**. In American usage, major triads only.

common metre Standard poetic metre in hymns corresponding to a quatrain in which the first and third lines are of eight syllables, and the second and fourth lines are of six, all in iambic rhythm.

common time 4/4 time, indicated in the time signature by a letter C. This is derived from the half-circle used in medieval music to denote duple division of breve and semibreve; it does not stand for common.

Common time

community singing Massed singing of popular songs or chants by the public at a meeting or sporting event. It has existed for many centuries in one form or another. Psalms were at one time sung by crowds outside churches, and even today hymns are sometimes sung at football matches. Community singing is also an important activity in school music in many countries.

compass Range of an instrument or voice, or the range of notes used in an instrumental or vocal part.

composer's counterpoint Alternative term for **free counterpoint**.

composition Act of writing a piece of music. Originally composers were anonymous; no idea of self-expression was connected with their work. In the Western world, composition began as the addition of new music and words to the **alleluia** of the anonymous **plainsong** and composers often remained unknown. Later composers began to acknowledge their art, taking control of the various parameters of a piece of music. In the Renaissance, **instrumentation** was often not the concern of the composer; pieces were described as 'apt for voices or viols'. In the **Baroque** era, embellishment was often considered the job of the performer, and composers wrote 'skeleton' movements over which **ornamentation** was presumed. Later the trend was for more and more precision on the part of the composer - tampering with notated intentions was discouraged rather than expected.

In the 20th century, composers have again involved the performer, introducing **aleatory** techniques and elements of improvisation with a greater or lesser degree of control.

composition pedal Foot-operated lever of an organ that activates a pre-selected combination of stops.

composition piston Thumb-button or toe-stud on an organ which the player can use to activate a pre-selected combination of stops.

compound interval **Interval** that is larger than an **octave**. For example, the interval between C in one octave and F in the next octave above is a compound interval, and can be described as an eleventh or as a compound fourth.

compound time Time signature that divides each main beat into three, such as 6/8 (two beats of three quavers each), 6/4 (two beats of three crotchets each), or 12/8 (four beats of three quavers each), as opposed to **simple time**, in which the beat divides into two.

comprimario (It.) Operatic role of secondary importance, or the singer performing this part.

con (It.) With. Used to link a qualifying term to a principal instruction, e.g. *allegro con brio*, quickly with spirit. Depending on the subsequent word, it may be written *cogli*, *coi*, *col*, *coll'*, *colla* or *colle*.

concert 1. Musical performance, usually by a large group of musicians playing to an audience. A solo or duo performance is normally termed a **recital**, except in pop and rock music, where even solo performers give concerts. Public concerts, with admission by ticket, became established during the late 17th century, and the demand for this type of performance led to the building of many purpose-built concert halls from the 18th century onwards.

2. Term applied in early times to an ensemble, and revived by Trevor **Pinnock** for his group the **English Concert**.

concertante (It.) Acting together. It signifies music with a **concerto**-like element. **Sinfonia concertante** indicates music in symphonic style, but with soloists, in the manner of a **concerto grosso**. In keyboard **sonatas**, the term implies an essential, or **obbligato**, string part, rather than an optional one.

concert band Band consisting of woodwind, brass and percussion (but without strings), which is popular in the United States. It is similar to the British **military band**. **Schoenberg** and **Hindemith**, as well as many American composers, have written works for this instrumentation. See also **wind band**.

Concertgebouw The leading orchestra of the Netherlands, and one of the finest in the world, it was founded in 1888 when the concert hall of that name was opened in Amsterdam. Willem **Mengelberg** was principal conductor from 1895 until World War II, when he was forced to step down; he was responsible for shaping it into an ensemble of the highest quality. He was succeeded by Eugen **Jochum**, who left Germany during the Nazi regime. From 1961 to 1988 the chief conductor was Bernard **Haitink**, who maintained the orchestra's status and with it made numerous recordings of the classical and Romantic repertory, particularly Beethoven, Bruckner, Mahler and Strauss. The present chief conductor is Riccardo **Chailly**.

concertina Portable, bellows-operated, free-reed instrument. The English concertina, developed by Charles Wheatstone in 1829, has two hexagonal

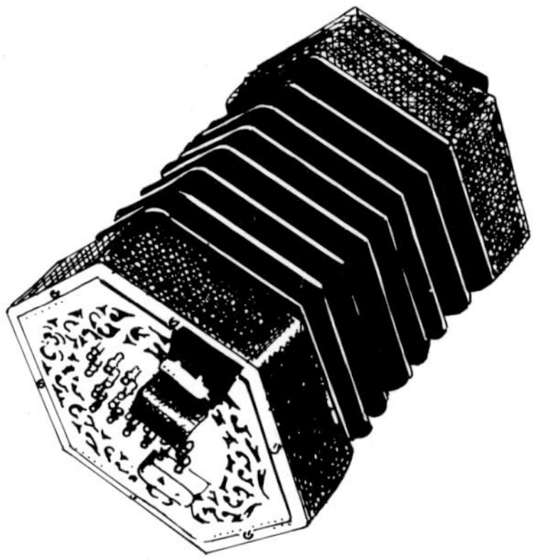

Concertina

heads connected by an expandable bellows, each casing containing a keyboard of buttons, which correspond to individual notes.

The German concertina, constructed by Carl Friedrich Uhlig in 1834, has rectangular ends and five buttons on each side, which control different pitches depending on whether the bellows are moving in or out.

Although the extensive Victorian repertory for the concertina, by composers such as Giulio Regondi, is not often heard nowadays, the instrument has remained popular among folk musicians. Charles **Ives** and Percy **Grainger** have composed for it.

concertino (It.) In a **concerto grosso**, the small group of soloists, as opposed to the **ripieno**, or full body of strings. In the 19th and 20th centuries, it has also been used to indicate a small-scale (and usually rather light) **concerto**.

concertize American musicians' and promoters' term for arranging a **concert** or concert tour.

concertmaster Derived from the German *Konzertmeister*, the American term for the **leader** of an orchestra, who is responsible for deciding on bowing for the strings, for performing solo passages, and for communication between conductor and players.

concerto (pl. **concerti**) (It.) Derived from the verb *concertare*, to compete. Its earliest use was in the late 16th century when concerto pieces employed opposed groups of singers or players. Giovanni **Gabrieli**, organist of St Mark's, Venice, was famous for his ecclesiastical concerti which used different groups of musicians in the various galleries of the church. At about the same time, **Monteverdi** wrote concerto **madrigals**: secular pieces similarly involving various groups.

In its late **Baroque** and **classical** form a concerto is a work for solo instrument(s) and orchestra, usually in three movements, fast-slow-fast. The soloist(s) is given virtuoso material, contrasting with the simpler orchestral parts, and an unaccompanied **cadenza** (originally improvised, but from the mid-19th century onwards usually notated by the composer) at the end of the first movement may give further opportunity for virtuosity.

concerto grosso (It.) Type of orchestral work pioneered by **Corelli** (and others) during the 1680s and 1690s, contrasting a small group of string players (**concertino**) with the full string section (**ripieno**). The *concerto grosso* was developed from the **trio sonata** (two violins with continuo) by reinforcing sections of the music with full strings, and the form became very popular during the first part of the 18th century, particularly in England, where **Handel** composed many pieces based on the Corelli model. The *concerto grosso* subsequently fell into disuse, although 20th-century composers such as **Bloch** and **Martinů** have resurrected the form.

concert overture One-movement orchestral work composed specifically for the concert hall, rather than as an introduction to an opera or oratorio. The practice began in the early 19th century, prompted by the performance in the concert hall of theatrical overtures. Notable pioneers were Berlioz, with his overtures *Waverley*, *Rob Roy* and *Le Corsair*, and Mendelssohn with his *Hebrides* and *Ruy Blas* overtures, who set a trend for overtures of historical, descriptive, or literary inspiration.

concert pitch Following the (almost) universally accepted international agreement on a pitch standard in 1939, this has been set at A′ = 440 hertz (cycles per second). This is a semitone higher than the A′ = 415 Hz, used nowadays by most players in 'authentic' performances of **Baroque** music, but is on the whole lower than the standard pitch used in the 19th century.

concord Interval or chord that is considered to be harmonious and musically stable, unlike a **discord**, which demands resolution by moving to a concord. In medieval music theory, concordance was restricted to perfect intervals (fourths, fifths and octaves), but for many centuries major and minor thirds and sixths have also been included.

conducting Direction of an **ensemble** of musicians by hand (or foot) indications, which have varied somewhat through the centuries.

In ancient Greece the practice of giving an audible beat was known, and existed in performances well into the 18th century; it is still sometimes used for training amateur ensembles or choirs. Pitch has also been indicated by hand movements, singers being given hand signs to indicate the rise and fall of the melody – a practice which survives in the teaching methods of **Kodály**, based on the methods of John Curwen (1816-80).

Renaissance woodcuts commonly show directors of music using a long staff to indicate the time, and in the **Baroque** era the tendency was for shorter sticks (although **Lully** was celebrated for the long stick with which he injured his foot and subsequently died). When the **continuo** section of the orchestra finally disappeared, the **baton** became popular and this has lasted until today, although some conductors merely use their hands. Since the 19th century conductors have also indicated phrasing and encouraged particular moods. Although the conductor's art in its final form is seen on the concert platform, his rehearsal technique, rather than his baton technique, is of paramount importance.

conductus (Lat.) Medieval song. The earliest pieces called *conductus* are found in a mid-12th-century manuscript from Norman Sicily. The songs appear to have been used for processional and recessional purposes. Some *conducti* are set for two to four voices, and this form was developed by the Parisian composers of the late 12th and early 13th centuries (the Notre Dame School), such as Pérotin. These works were composed in a wide variety of styles, from pieces in which there is one note per syllable of text, to other pieces containing long **melismas** to certain syllables. The form dropped out of use from the mid-13th century, when the **motet** became the most popular form of composition.

conjunct motion Applied to a melody in which the movement is from one note of a diatonic scale to an adjacent note (a step). If the melody proceeds by larger intervals, it moves by **disjunct motion** (a leap). See also **contrary motion**.

Connell, Elizabeth (1946-) Irish soprano. She studied at the London Opera Centre and with Kraus, and in 1972 won the Maggie Teyte Prize. Her début was in 1972, at the Wexford Festival; she sang mezzo roles to begin with, including that of Eboli in Verdi's *Don Carlos*. She joined Australian Opera in 1973 and then English National Opera. Her début at the Royal Opera House, Covent Garden, was in 1976 in *I lombardi*. Since 1983 she has been singing soprano roles. She has appeared in Europe (Bayreuth, La Scala, Salzburg, Rome, Munich, Vienna) and the United States (Philadelphia, New York and elsewhere) and has made several recordings. Her roles include Fiordiligi in *Così fan tutte*, Leonora in *Il trovatore*, Norma, Lady Macbeth and Leonore in *Fidelio*, which she sang in London in 1986.

Connolly, Justin (1933-) English composer, who studied and now teaches at the Royal College of Music. His style was influenced by Elliott **Carter**, particularly his use of small intervallic units to construct large, dense structures. Among his most important works are *Cinquepaces* (1965-6), *Tetramorph* (1972) and *Anima* (1974).

consecutive intervals In harmony, any interval that occurs in the same two parts in two adjacent chords. In conventional harmony, consecutive perfect fifths and octaves are considered to give a poor effect, although they are found in the works of Bach, and composers from Debussy onwards have used them with effective results. The medieval practice of **organum**, or harmonizing of a plainchant, consisted almost entirely of adding parts consecutive to the original.

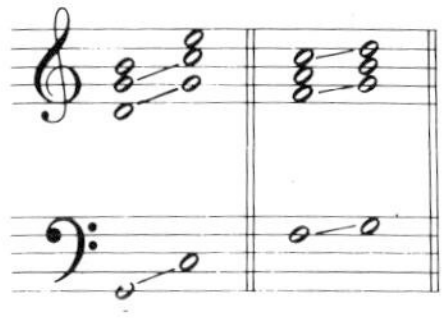

Consecutive octaves and fifths

conservatoire (Fr.) Conservatory, conservatorium. Place of musical training, originally an orphanage. During the 18th century those in Venice and Naples were renowned for their excellent standards of performance. In more recent times, the word has come to mean a place of higher education, where performers are trained for orchestral or concert careers, such as the Paris Conservatoire de Musique, equivalent to the Royal College or Royal Academy of Music in London. The Italian equivalent is *conservatorio*.

console Control desk of an organ, including keyboard, pedals, pistons and organ stops. There is no standard arrangement of a console, either with regard to keyboard size or the arrangement of stop-knobs, and therefore an organist has to master each new organ individually. If the console is separated from the organ, and operated by electric action, it is known as a detached console.

consonance In acoustical physics, a consonance consists of any two (or more) frequencies which relate to each other as small whole numbers, such as the perfect fifth (3:2) or fourth (4:3). Perceived consonance is, however, largely a social or psychological judgement, and can be used about any group of sounds that are heard as stable and harmonious, i.e. that do not demand resolution.

consort Small ensemble of voices or instruments before about 1700. The whole consort was a group composed entirely of one type of instrument, e.g. a consort of viols. The broken consort signified various different types of instrument in combination. A common Elizabethan broken consort consisted of treble **viol**, **recorder**, bass viol, **lute**, **cittern** and **bandora**.

Constant, Marius (1925-) Romanian-born French composer and conductor, who studied at the Paris Conservatoire after World War II with **Messiaen**, **Boulanger** and **Honegger**. As a conductor, he became the musical director for dance at the Paris Opéra in 1971. His most important compositions include the ballets *Cyrano de Bergerac* (1959) and *Nana* (1976). He is also known as an arranger and orchestrator.

continental fingering In piano-playing, the standard system of indicating fingering, in which the thumb is represented by 1, and the fingers as 2-5. The English system, where the thumb was marked + and the fingers 1-4, is now obsolete.

continuo Abbreviation of *basso continuo* (continuous bass). In the scores of **Baroque** composers (e.g. **Bach** and **Handel**), the bass part was performed by the harpsichord or organ and often with additional instruments such as a viola da gamba and/or lute; later a cello and double-bass, or in fact any bass instrument, such as the bassoon. Players read from a single line of music, providing harmony which was indicated with figures written above the notes (the **figured bass**).

The use of continuo began around 1600 when organs were used to accompany sacred choral pieces. The organist was provided merely with a figured **bass** line which he would then fill out to provide any missing harmonies and support the inner voices. This organ line was, in effect, an abbreviated score. Continuo also became important with the growth of **recitative** in the first operas and **monodies**. A much greater emphasis was given to the expression of words by the solo human voice, and the continuo provided the harmonic support. It was also vital in the Baroque **trio sonatas** and **concerti grossi** for providing the harmony beneath one or more solo melodic instruments. The use of continuo carried on throughout the Baroque and into the early **classical** period, when a harpsichord or fortepiano played with an orchestra, as in **Haydn**'s and **Mozart**'s choral works, concertos and symphonies. However, the continuo line was largely redundant by that period because the inner harmonies were taken by other instruments in the orchestra.

The practice of playing continuo in classical works has ceased, except for performances by groups aiming to achieve 'authentic' performances.

contrabasso (It.) See **double-bass**

contrafagotto (It.) Double-bassoon, which sounds an octave lower than the standard **bassoon**, reaching down to B^1 (below the **double-bass**). The modern form was developed by Wilhelm Heckel in 1877-9. The distinctive buzzing quality of its lowest register has been used to great effect by Mahler and Strauss.

contralto Lowest type of female voice, ranging from G-G′, and with a sombre, rich tone. In choirs, the male voice of this range is termed **alto**.

contrary motion In harmony, two parts that move in opposite directions, as opposed to **similar motion**, in which the parts move up or down together.

contredanse (Fr.) Originating in England as a country dance, this became the most popular French dance of the 18th century. In its final form, it consisted of a binary form melody, in duple time, and a set pattern of steps which was danced nine times. Many tunes were used, including *Greensleeves*, which became *Les manches vertes* in France. **Beethoven** composed a set of 12 *contredanses* for orchestra in 1802.

Converse, Frederick Shepherd (1871-1940) Boston-based American teacher and composer, who studied with **Rheinberger** in Munich. From 1903 to 1907, he taught at Harvard College, devoting himself to composition and to the administration of the Boston Opera Company. He composed six symphonies, and his operas *The Pipe of Desire* (1905) and *The Sacrifice* (1910) enjoyed great success. After World War I he became head of the theory department at New England Conservatoire.

Conversi, Girolamo (*fl.*1571-1584) Italian composer, known principally for his six-part **madrigals** (settings of Petrarch, Castiglione and others, Venice, 1571-5) and his **canzoni** (Venice, 1572), which combine the popular **villanella** form with the more sophisticated madrigal.

Cooke, Arnold (1906-) English composer, born in Yorkshire, a pupil of **Hindemith**. His work is characterized by fluent instrumental writing, and the use of contrapuntal technique in a diatonic idiom. He was principal professor of composition at Trinity College of Music. His works include six symphonies (the last dating from 1984), concertos, a ballet, and a number of solo and chamber works.

Cooke, Benjamin (*c.*1695-1743) English music publisher, active in London between 1726 and 1743. His most notable publication was the complete works of **Corelli** (1732), printed unusually in full score, rather than in parts. Cooke also played a vital role in the re-establishment of music at the Chapel Royal after the Restoration, in his capacity as Master of the Children.

Cooke, Benjamin (1734-1793) English organist and composer, son of the above, and a pupil of **Pepusch**. From 1752 he was conductor at the Academy of Ancient Music in London. His output included church music, glees and many works for organ.

Cooke, Henry (*c.*1615-1672) English composer and singer, who introduced into the Chapel Royal Italian influences, such as a more improvised and highly ornamented style than was then prevalent in England. His singing was favourably remarked upon by Pepys and Playford, the latter calling him 'that Orpheus of our time'. His compositions are of lesser interest.

coperto (It.) On the snare drum, instruction to the player to cover the upper (or batter) head with a cloth, giving a muffled sound. More generally, it is used to indicate that any drum should be covered with a cloth, e.g. for funeral music.

Copland, Aaron (1900-) American composer, whose work evokes a specifically American spirit. He studied in New York and then with Nadia **Boulanger** in Paris for four years. His earliest compositions were strongly influenced by jazz rhythms and harmonies (*Music for the Theatre*, 1925; *Piano Concerto*, 1926). On his return to New York he took an active interest in the promotion of contemporary music, and also taught. At this period he made the conscious decision to create recognizably American music, an aim which he triumphantly achieved, and which reached its apogee with *Fanfare for the Common Man* (1942).

An attraction to the music of Hispanic America resulted in an orchestral sketch of a Mexican night-club, *El salón México* (1936), irresistible in its rhythmic vitality. More serious, although hardly more formal, ballets followed: *Billy the Kid* (1938), *Rodeo* (1942) and, his masterpiece in the genre, *Appalachian Spring* (1944), composed for Martha Graham's ballet company – all harking back to America's past. His opera *The Tender Land* (1942) is in the same vein. An element of folk-music runs through these works, with a Shaker hymn-tune providing the underlying theme for *Appalachian Spring*.

Aaron Copland

The influence of **Stravinsky** was also potent in Copland's work; it is felt particularly in a major work, his third and last symphony (1946). From about the early 1950s he began to experiment with **serial** techniques, and his work became more cerebral and less popular in style (*Inscape*, 1967; *Duo* for flute and piano, 1971).

Other compositions include *Quiet City* (1939); the *Lincoln Portrait* (1942), with speaker; *Connotations* (1962); *Music for a Great City* (1964); a clarinet concerto; arrangements of songs; piano and chamber music. He also produced a large body of film music – of *Mice and Men* (1939); *The Heiress* (1948); *Something Wild* (1961). He has written several books, and has also been a highly effective teacher.

Coprario, Giovanni (John Cooper) (*c.*1575-1626) English composer, who visited Italy and thereafter Italianized his name. His instrumental works, particularly his fantasias for viols, make striking use of advanced Italian dissonant harmony and **chromaticism**. Charles I appointed him Composer-In-Ordinary in 1625.

cor (Fr.) A horn. See **French horn**

cor anglais (Fr.) Not a horn, nor is it English (originally *anglé*, angled); it is a tenor double-reeded woodwind instrument of the **oboe** family, with a large bulb-shaped bell. It is a transposing instrument, sounding a perfect fifth lower than written, with a lowest note of E and a range of about two and a half octaves. Although tenor oboes have existed from the late 17th century, the modern instrument was developed by Brod in Paris in 1839.

Cor anglais

corda (It.) A string. On bowed instruments, the instruction *corda vuota* means an open string, and *corda soprano* the highest string. On the piano, *una corda* instructs the player to use the soft pedal, so that in instruments whose mechanism works in this way the hammer strikes only one string. *Tre corde* cancels this, causing the hammer to strike all three strings.

Corelli, Arcangelo (1653-1713) Italian performer and composer. He studied in Bologna, and spent most of his life in Rome, where he was in great demand as a violinist; he was also a fine teacher of the violin. He composed only instrumental music, publishing four sets of **trio sonatas**, a set of solo violin sonatas and his best-known set of 12 **concerti grossi** (which include the famous *Christmas Concerto*). His patrons included Queen Christina of Sweden, to whom he dedicated a set of trio sonatas (1681). He was at the centre of musical life in Rome until he retired in 1708 to devote himself to composition. Although his music never had the incisive rhythmic quality of that of **Vivaldi** or **Bach**, he was a popular and widely influential composer who died a very wealthy man.

Corelli, Franco (1921-) Italian tenor, born in Ancona, who, after studying in Milan, Florence and Spoleto, made his operatic début as Don José in *Carmen* at Spoleto in 1951. He sang regularly at La Scala, Milan, and established himself as one of the world's leading Italian heroic tenors, his dark-timbred voice being suited as much to **spinto** as to **verismo** roles.

Franco Corelli

Corigliano, John (1938-) American composer whose output includes various chamber and orchestral works, notably *The Naked Carmen*, an arrangement of **Bizet**'s *Carmen* for rock groups and **Moog** synthesizer.

cornamuse In English the name refers to a now obsolete reed instrument common in the 16th century. In its French (*cornemuse*) and Italian (*cornamusa*) forms it refers simply to the **bagpipes**. **Verdi** wrote for it in *Otello*, but suggested that the part might equally be taken by two **oboes**.

Cornelius, Peter (1824-1874) German composer, author and friend of Liszt and Wagner. Cornelius was a firm disciple of the New German School. His comic opera

Der Barbier von Bagdad was produced by Liszt at Weimar in 1858, but because of organized opposition it was withdrawn, with the result that Liszt resigned as court conductor. Cornelius wrote two other operas, *Der Cid* and *Gunlöd*, and many other vocal works, including a Christmas hymn for baritone and chorus, known in England as *Three Kings from Persian Lands Afar.*

cornet 1. A brass instrument in B♭, also known as *cornet-à-pistons* (Fr.), similar to the modern trumpet but with a slightly more conical bore and mellower tone. The cornet first appeared about 1828 and its orchestral début was probably in Rossini's

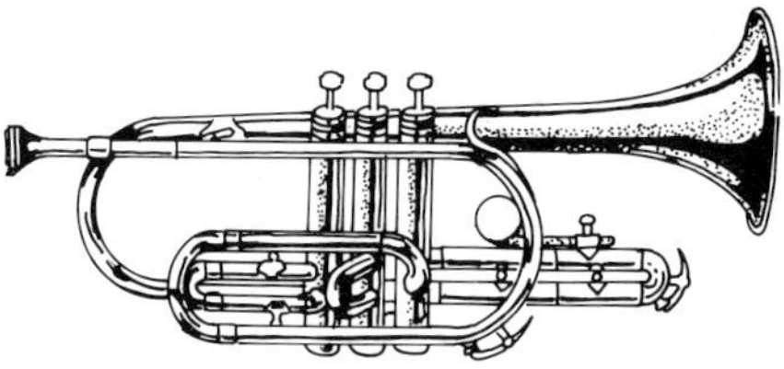

Cornet

William Tell the following year. Its agility and flexibility were exploited in brilliant popular solos during the latter part of the 19th century, and for a time its popularity was such that it threatened to oust the trumpet from the orchestra. Tchaikovsky and Berlioz used it in some works. A smaller, soprano instrument in E♭ is used also in English brass bands.

2. An important organ stop, invariably a mutation rather than a reed. In England the stop was mounted at the top of the organ (hence, mounted cornet) and was extensively used by 18th-century composers such as John **Stanley** and Maurice **Greene**.

cornet-à-pistons (Fr.) Equivalent of the English **cornet**.

cornett A wind instrument that appeared as early as the 13th century but rose to prominence in the late 16th and early 17th centuries. The cornett is approximately two feet long, slightly curved, and made from wood covered with leather. It has seven finger-holes and is played with a cup mouthpiece similar to that on a brass instrument. The sound produced is something like a gently played trumpet or horn, but it has a facility in articulation and expression that makes it sound at times like a wordless soprano voice. Cornetts were used in the 16th century in church music to support the choir, often alongside **sackbuts**. This combination of instruments was specifically named for the opening toccata of **Monteverdi**'s *Orfeo*, and was frequently used in the Venetian music of the two **Gabrielis**; also by **J.S. Bach** in certain cantatas to double the treble line.

The less common mute cornett is a straight instrument, turned in wood with no leather covering. There is no separate mouthpiece but merely a conical recess cut into the narrow end of the tube. The sound is less bright than that of the curved cornett. This instrument was very popular in chamber ensembles in 16th-century Italy.

Cornish, William Alternative spelling of **Cornyshe, William**.

corno (It.) A horn. See also **French horn**.

corno di bassetto (It.) 1. A **basset-horn**. George Bernard Shaw adopted the Italian form as a pseudonym for his music criticisms in *The Star* in the 1880s and 1890s.

2. An organ stop.

cornopean Early type of **cornet**, but more usually the name of an organ stop, often found on the swell organ of English organs.

Cornyshe, William (*c.*1465-1523) English composer, actor and playwright who became a member of the Chapel Royal in 1496 and Master of the Children of the Chapel Royal in 1509. As pageant-master at the court of Henry VIII he was responsible for organizing many masques, pageants and banquets. His compositions include some particularly cheerful part-songs. Some of his church music was included in *The Eton Choirbook.*

Coronation Anthem Anthem written for a coronation, often for chorus and orchestra. One of the first was *My Heart is Inditing,* composed by **Purcell** for the coronation of James II in 1685.

The title often refers to the four anthems for chorus and orchestra by **Handel,** written for the coronation of George II in 1727: *Zadok the Priest, The King Shall Rejoice, My Heart is Inditing* and *Let Thy Hand Be Strengthened.*

Correa de Arauxo, Francisco (1576-1654) Spanish composer and organist whose life centred on Seville, where he was organist at S. Salvador. All his work survives in one collection, which also includes an important theoretical treatise on the change from the Renaissance **modes** to **Baroque** tonality. His work, with its complex rhythms and extravagant embellishments, marks the beginning of the Spanish Baroque. His name is alternatively spelled Araujo or Azavedo.

Corrette, Michel (1709-1795) French composer and organist whose works include concertos for harpsichord, flute, organ and **hurdy-gurdy**, as well as sacred music and organ solos. He also wrote treatises instructing in the art of playing various instruments.

Cortot, Alfred (1877-1962) Swiss-born pianist and conductor who spent most of his life in France. He trained at the Paris Conservatoire and made his début as a pianist in 1896, followed by a period as an assistant at **Bayreuth**. He was an active Wagner propagandist and in 1902 conducted the first performance in France of *Götterdämmerung.* From 1905 Cortot toured widely as a solo recitalist and with **Thibaut** and **Casals** as a trio. His editions of Schumann, Chopin and Liszt are widely used today. He made many recordings which have become classics in their field, particularly of the works of Chopin.

Cossotto, Fiorenza (1935-) Italian mezzo-soprano. She studied with Campogalliani and Della Torre in Turin, and made her début at La Scala, Milan, in 1957. She sang Neris in Cherubini's *Médée* with Maria Callas at Covent Garden in 1959. She has appeared in Barcelona, Vienna, Paris and the United States. She has sung regularly with the Chicago Lyric Opera, the Metropolitan Opera, New York (notably as Amneris in Verdi's *Aïda* in 1968) and in most of the main Italian opera-houses. Other important roles are Azucena in Verdi's *Il trovatore,* Santuzza in Mascagni's *Cavalleria rusticana* and Adalgisa in Bellini's *Norma.*

Costa, Sir Michael (1806-1884) Conductor and composer born in Naples, who went to England at the age of 21 and remained to achieve prominence as a conductor of opera, oratorio and orchestral works. As a composer his best-received works were the oratorios *Naaman* and *Eli* and a number of operas. He was knighted in 1869.

Cotrubas, Ileana (1939-) Romanian soprano who studied in Bucharest. Her vibrant, Slavic timbre first came to wider notice when she won first prize in the highly esteemed 'sHertogenbosch Competition in the Netherlands. She made her Glyndebourne début in 1969 as Mélisande and her Covent Garden début as Tatyana in *Eugene Onegin* in 1971. However, it was at La Scala in 1975 that she rose to stardom almost overnight when she understudied Mirella Freni as Mimì in *La bohème.* She has excelled in such roles as Susanna in *Le nozze di Figaro,* Norina in Donizetti's *Don Pasquale,* Violetta in *La traviata* and Gilda in *Rigoletto,* and has also been highly popular as a recitalist. She recently announced her retirement from the stage, although she still sings in concerts and recitals occasionally.

couched harp Alternative term for **spinet.**

counterpoint Derived from the Latin *punctus contra punctum*, note against note, or, by extension, melody against melody. It denotes music of two or more lines that sound simultaneously. Counterpoint is the horizontal element of texture in music, the vertical element being **harmony**. In counterpoint, the individual melodies are treated more or less equally (as opposed to those styles in which the treble or bass lines are prominent).

After counterpoint first began to be used, in the 13th century, it evolved a complex system of rules governing the **intervals** and **dissonances** that could appear between the parts. **Palestrina**'s Masses are good examples of late 16th-century counterpoint, and **J.S. Bach**'s fugues show how far it had developed by the 18th century. Counterpoint continued to be used throughout the 18th and 19th centuries, but has found a new importance in the 20th century with the development of the serial or **twelve-tone** system by **Schoenberg**, in which the emphasis on the individual lines has led to the virtual disappearance of any traditional harmonic element.

counter-subject One of the **melodies** in a **fugue**, heard against the main subject and normally contrasting with it.

counter-tenor Alternative term for the male **alto** or adult male voice with the range of a female **contralto**. This is usually produced by developing the falsetto register.

country dance Generic term that covers a whole series of figure dances originating on the English village green. The music for such dances included folk-tunes and was typically constructed in eight-bar phrases. Country dances were popular among all classes during the reign of Elizabeth I, and both dance steps and music were described in detail by John Playford in his *English Dancing Master*, published in various editions from 1651 to 1728. Around 1700 many of these dances became popular in France as **contredanses**. In the early 19th century, however, the **waltz** and **quadrille** superseded the country dance in the English ballroom, but it has seen a revival in the 20th century, largely because of the efforts of folklorists such as Cecil **Sharp**.

coup d'archet (Fr.) Bow stroke.

Couperin, François (1668-1733) French composer and keyboard player, the most famous member of a family of musicians, and known as *le grand*. He was organist at St-Gervais in Paris, a post that was promised to him when he was only ten years of age. His compositions include several vocal works for the Church in an unusual style using a combination of Italian **recitative** and **aria** with French **ornamentation** and **instrumentation**. He is, however, best known for his four books of harpsichord suites or *ordres* (1713-30). There are 220 pieces altogether, grouped into 27 'orders', some of which contain as few as four and others as many as 23 items. Most of them depict people, animals, moods or types of personality. Many are cast in dance form (**courante**, **allemande**, gavotte, **minuet** etc.) He also composed two organ Masses, 12 trios (*L'apothéose de Corelli*, 1724; *L'apothéose de Lully*, 1725), and two suites for bass viol. His treatise *L'art de toucher le clavecin* was written in 1717.

Couperin, Louis (1626-1661) French composer, violist and keyboard player. In about 1650 he and his two brothers were heard by Chambonnières and taken to Paris. Louis became the organist of St-Gervais, a post held by the Couperin family for the next 175 years. He was an uncle of the better-known François **Couperin**. His keyboard music shows the influence of Chambonnières and **Froberger**.

coupler A mechanical device in organs and harpsichords for connecting one keyboard to another so that their notes sound together. An octave coupler couples notes an octave above on the same keyboard.

couplet (Fr.) 1. Denotes a **strophic** song, often in a light or humorous vein, in which the same music recurs for each verse.
2. The forerunner of the **episode** in **rondo** form (or the French **rondeau** as cultivated by **Couperin** and others), referring to the sections between recurrences of the main theme.
3. An alternative term for **duplet**.

courante (Fr.) **Baroque** dance movement in triple time which by about 1630 had become a regular part of the solo **suite**, following the **allemande**. Two versions, considered French and Italian, co-existed, although most composers used the titles *courante* and *corrente* (It.) interchangeably. The true Italian type is in a fast 3/4 or 3/8 time, whereas the French *courante* was a slower 3/2, its pulse nearer to that of the **sarabande**, and with many cross-rhythms between two groups of three and three groups of two. Both types are usually binary in form, beginning on the upbeat and ending on the strong beat of the bar.

cow-bell Everyday cow-bell of mountainous central Europe, sometimes specified in orchestral works, particularly by Mahler in his sixth symphony. With the clapper removed and played with a drumstick, it often appears in the popular music of Latin America.

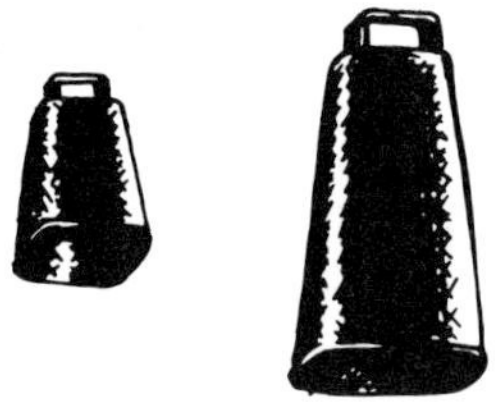

Cow-bells

Cowell, Henry (1897-1965) American pianist, theorist and composer who was highly individual, experimenting with original instrumental effects and trying to find the common ground between the Eastern and Western musical arts. He wrote over 20 symphonies and a great amount of music in all genres exemplifying all his experimental techniques.

Cowen, Sir Frederick (1852-1935) Jamaican-born conductor and composer who went to England as a baby; at the age of six he published a waltz, and at eight an operetta. After making a name for himself as a young pianist, he went on to conduct the Hallé Orchestra in Manchester. His compositions ranged widely from popular Victorian ballads to more serious art songs, operas and oratorios, of which *Ruth* (1887) is best known. He was knighted in 1911.

cow-horn A lip-vibrated wind instrument traditionally made from the horn of a cow and played by herdsmen. Where **Wagner** calls for such instruments in *Der Ring des Nibelungen*, they are usually played on specially made straight brass instruments with a perfectly conical bore.

Cowie, Edward (1943-) English composer and painter. After studying at the University of Southampton and with Alexander **Goehr**, Cowie was appointed as composer-in-residence and lecturer at the University of Lancaster. His composition, although using no strikingly avant-garde techniques, has a highly original language and is deeply influenced by his interest in ornithology and landscape. The Lancashire coast inspired many pieces, including *Leighton Moss* and *Stimmungsbild: Hest Bank*. His large orchestral piece *Leviathan* was given its first performance at a Henry Wood Promenade Concert and his opera *Commedia* was also premièred in London. He has for some years been Professor of Music in the Department of Performing Arts at Wollongong, Australia, and his more recent pieces (and paintings) reflect his experience of the Australian landscape.

Craft, Robert Lawson (1923-) American conductor and writer, best known for his long association with Igor **Stravinsky** as both pupil and interpreter of his music and thoughts. He has written several important books about this relationship, as well as other essays and criticism; he has also been closely associated with the music of **Webern** and **Schoenberg**.

Cramer, Johann Baptist (1771-1858) Son of the violinist Wilhelm **Cramer** and piano pupil of **Clementi**, he became a celebrated pianist, touring Europe widely. Of his prolific output as a composer (100 sonatas and numerous concertos), only the piano studies are in use today; these were greatly admired by Beethoven, who left an illuminating guide to their performance. In 1824 Cramer founded the piano-makers and music publishing company Cramer & Co., which is still in business.

Cramer, Wilhelm (1745-1799) Violinist born in Mannheim, who went to London at the age of 27 and soon attained celebrity as a soloist and as leader of orchestras.

Crawford, Ruth Porter (1901-1953) American composer who studied at the American Conservatoire in Chicago and went on to teach there. She later studied composition in New York with Charles Seeger, whom she married. An interest in American folk-songs led her to transcribe several thousand of them from recordings and to write piano accompaniments to some 300 more. Her compositions include a string quartet (1931) and a violin sonata (1927).

Creighton (Creyghton), Robert (*c.*1636-1734) Canon and precentor of Wells Cathedral from 1674, who wrote anthems and settings of the liturgy. He lent his name to the 'Creyghtonian seventh' after his practice of preceding a final perfect **cadence** by a **subdominant chord** with an added **seventh**.

crescendo (It.) Increasing in loudness, a direction often indicated on a score by a graphic marking consisting of a pair of diverging horizontal lines.

Crespin, Régine (1927-) French soprano who studied at the Paris Conservatoire and made her début in Mulhouse in 1950 as Elsa in *Lohengrin*. She was particularly noted for her Marschallin in *Der Rosenkavalier*. From 1977 Crespin has taken mezzo-soprano roles.

Creston, Paul (1906-1985) American composer and organist of Italian origin (he changed his name from Giuseppe Guttoveggio), self-taught in harmony and composition. He was organist at St Malachy's, New York, 1934-67. Compositions include five symphonies and concertos for many instruments, including saxophone and accordion.

Cristofori, Bartolomeo (1655-1731) Italian harpsichord-maker who in Florence in about 1700 invented the *gravicembalo col piano e forte*, the forerunner of the modern piano. Instead of the strings being plucked, they were hit by a series of hammers. By 1720 he had improved the design by graduating the force of the fall of the hammers and putting a damper above instead of under the strings. Today only three Cristofori pianos survive.

croche (Fr.) French name for a **quaver**. *Monsieur Croche* was the pseudonym under which **Debussy** wrote some of his music criticism.

Croft, William (1678-1727) English organist and composer who collaborated with **Blow** and others in *Ayres for the Harpsichord or Spinet*. He composed many fine anthems and a burial service, and also wrote the hymn tune *St Anne*, to which is usually sung *O God our Help in Ages Past*.

crook Detachable pieces of tubing of different lengths attached to a brass instrument to vary the basic pitch. Before the invention of valves, horn- and trumpet-players could put their instruments into different keys according to the crook, which would be known, for example, as an A crook, or a B♭ bass crook. Crooks continued to be used, despite the invention of valves, well into the 20th century, partly because each had a characteristic tone.

croon Originally a term meaning to sing softly – for example, to a baby. However, since the 1930s it has been used to refer to a particular style of soft, mostly sentimental, singing, usually by a man and often with dance-band accompaniment. The most famous crooner was Bing Crosby.

Cross, Joan (1900-) English soprano. She studied with Gustav **Holst** and Dawson Freer at Trinity School of Music. After singing in various opera choruses she became principal soprano at Sadler's Wells, where she was also director. She remains best known for the roles she created in the operas of Benjamin **Britten**, which included Ellen Orford in *Peter Grimes*, Lady Billows in *Albert Herring* and Mrs Grose in *The Turn of the Screw*. A tireless champion of English opera, Cross was a founder member of the English Opera Group in 1946, and of the Opera School in London, which later became the National School of Opera.

Crosse, Gordon (1937-) English composer who studied composition with **Wellesz** at Oxford University in 1961. His music is both declamatory and lyrical, following more in the style of **Britten** than the European avant-garde. His earliest works, however, were written in **serial** form and influenced by **Webern**. Crosse was composer-in-residence at King's College, Cambridge, in 1973. His output includes several works for children, four operas (including *Potter Thompson*, 1973), two symphonies, several chamber concertos (*Wildboy*, 1978), vocal music (*The World Within*, 1976, after Emily Brontë) and a string quartet.

cross fingering Referring to wind instruments with side-holes, a cross fingering is one in which open and closed holes alternate. This is in contrast to a 'normal' fingering in which all open holes are at the lower end of the instrument and all closed at the upper end. Whereas normal fingerings produce most of the **diatonic** tones of the octave, cross fingering is necessary to produce semitones and tones of the higher octave. Its effectiveness is reduced in relation to the remoteness of the key from the basic key in which the instrument is pitched.

Cross fingerings are largely avoided on modern-day instruments, such as the flute, oboe and clarinet, through the use of elaborate systems of **key** mechanisms, which have overcome the difficulties of playing in more remote musical **keys** .

Crossley, Paul (1944-) English pianist. He studied with Fanny Waterman, and with **Messiaen** and his wife Yvonne **Loriod**. He has made a speciality of the music of Messiaen and **Tippett** – two of the latter's piano sonatas were written for him – and is a keen promoter of contemporary music. He has made two television series (1986, 1990) analysing seminal 20th-century works and exploring the creative processes of their composers. He is currently artistic director of the **London Sinfonietta**. His recordings include the solo piano works of **Janáček**, **Fauré**, **Ravel** and **Poulenc**.

cross relation An alternative term for **false relation**.

Crotch, William (1775-1847) English composer and organist; also a painter. A child prodigy to rival Mozart, he began to play in public before he was three. Besides the organ, he was also proficient on the piano and violin. He studied in Cambridge and Oxford, where he became organist to Christ Church Cathedral at the age of 15. He became a professor there in 1797, and was the first person ever to lecture on music history. In 1807 he moved to London, where he continued to lecture, to teach and to compose. He became principal of the Royal Academy of Music on its foundation in 1822. He was instrumental in reviving interest in early Church music.

Although the parallel with Mozart did not develop, Crotch was nevertheless a fluent composer in a variety of styles; his first great success was an oratorio, *Palestine* (1812), in the manner of Handel. Another oratorio was *The Captivity of Judah* (1834). He also wrote three organ concertos, Anglican chants and other sacred music, songs and piano music. He was a prolific writer, on other subjects as well as music – one of his most important books was *Elements of Musical Composition.*

crotchet A note that is half the value of a **minim** and twice that of a **quaver**. In American usage it is called a quarter-note. As the denominator in a time signature, the crotchet is represented by the number 4.

Crotchet Crotchet rest (either of the above)

Cruft, Adrian (1921-1987) English composer who studied at the Royal College of Music under Sir Adrian **Boult**, Gordon **Jacob** and Edmund **Rubbra**. He had a varied career as double-bass player, teacher, conductor and composer, and became chairman of the Composers' Guild in 1967. His music is **diatonic** and straightforward in idiom, often written specifically for children and amateurs. His output includes settings of the canticles, cantatas, orchestral works and chamber music.

Cruft, Eugene (1887-1976) English double-bass player and father of Adrian **Cruft**. He played in most of the leading London orchestras and was the orchestral organizing secretary for the coronations of George VI and Elizabeth II.

Crumb, George (1929-) American composer who studied at the Universities of Illinois and Michigan. His musical output includes many settings of verse by Lorca, such as the four books of *Madrigals* (1965-9) and *Ancient Voices of Children* (1970). His music is characterized by an imaginative use of vocal and instrumental colour, and by the inclusion of theatrical elements such as dance and the use of masks. He has also taught at the Universities of Colorado and Pennsylvania.

crumhorn A woodwind instrument that has a double reed enclosed in a cap and a curved or crook-shaped bottom. The crumhorn flourished during the 16th century as a **consort** instrument. Its tone was soft, albeit buzzing, and blended with most other instruments of the time. There were at least five regular sizes of crumhorn, ranging from the small treble to the great bass, although all had the limited pitch range of a ninth and an equally limited dynamic range.

Little is known of the instrumentation of the music of the period, and it is assumed that the crumhorn played as important a role as any other instrument of the day in both sacred and secular **polyphonic** compositions. It is almost certain, however, that by the 17th century it was used less and less because of its limitations, and was soon replaced by the more versatile recorder and oboe.

Crusell, Bernhard (1775-1838) Finnish clarinettist and composer who studied with Tausch and Lefèvre before becoming a court musician in Stockholm in 1793. His many compositions for clarinet, originally intended for an eleven-keyed instrument, are still performed today. Crusell was also an accomplished linguist, and in 1837 was awarded the Swedish Academy's Gold Medal for his translations of French, German and Italian operas for the Swedish stage.

crwth (Welsh) A bowed lyre. Usually, the bowed lyre that was used throughout Britain from Anglo-Saxon times but had retreated to Wales by the 16th century, where it remained in continuous use up to the 19th century. The *crwth* in medieval illustrations has only three strings, whereas the later Welsh instrument usually had six strings in three courses.

csárdás A 19th-century Hungarian dance. It is in **duple time** and has a slow section, *lassu*, followed by a fast one, *friss*. Johann Strauss incorporated a *csárdás* into his operetta *Die Fledermaus*, and Bartók included the form in several of his instrumental works. It is also found in ballet music, for example, Tchaikovsky's *Swan Lake* and Delibes's *Coppélia*.

cuckoo Small one-holed wind instrument designed to imitate the call of the cuckoo. Leopold **Mozart** used it in his *Toy Symphony*.

Cuénod, Hugues (1902-) Swiss tenor who studied at the Basle Conservatoire and in Vienna. He was well known as an interpreter of humorous character roles and appeared in the main European opera houses. He had a high, light tenor voice and made fine recordings of lute-songs, works by **Couperin**, and of the Evangelist role in J.S. Bach's *St Matthew Passion*.

Cui, Cesar (1835-1918) Russian composer and critic who studied at St Petersburg, where he became a professor at the Academy of Military Engineering. He started composing after meeting **Balakirev** in 1856, and subsequently became a member of the group of composers known as the **Mighty Handful**. Balakirev himself helped with the orchestration of Cui's first pieces. Cui composed a large number of works, including 15 operas (among them *The Prisoner of the Caucasus*, *Angelo*, *The Saracen*, and *Mam'zelle Fifi*), and completed **Mussorgsky**'s *Sorochintsy Fair*. He was most at ease composing miniatures, both songs and short piano pieces, in which he showed the influence of **Chopin** who had fascinated him since childhood. He is now best remembered for his critical writings.

cuivré, cuivrez (Fr.) Ringing, indicating a brassy sound. The term is most often used with regard to the **French horn**.

curtal Name used in England from the late 16th century to the early 18th century for both the dulcian and the **bassoon**.

Curwen, John (1816-1880) English educationist, who first clarified and popularized the **tonic sol-fa** system of teaching music. Finding himself in the position of having to teach it without knowing it himself, he learnt music from a book published in 1835 by a schoolmistress in Norwich, Sarah Glover. He decided to polish and revise the system, and found himself working on it for the rest of his life. He felt strongly that music was a valuable part of a general education, and wrote many books and articles on his work. A logical step from this was to found his own publishing house, J. Curwen and Sons (1863), and in 1869 he set up the Tonic Sol-fa College. The Curwen Institute, an offshoot of this, was founded in 1973. Curwen's method greatly influenced **Kodály** in the development of his system of teaching sight-singing.

Curzon, Sir Clifford (1907-1982) English pianist who entered the Royal Academy of Music in 1919 to study with Charles Reddie. Later teachers included **Schnabel** and **Boulanger**. In his youth, Curzon was associated with a wide-ranging repertory, giving world premières of English works including **Berkeley**'s *Sonata* and **Rawsthorne**'s Concerto No.2. He later concentrated on performing classical works, especially those of **Mozart**, in which he was outstanding. After World War II he played in every important European and American musical centre. He was made a CBE in 1958 and knighted in 1977.

Cutting, Francis (*fl.*1583-*c.*1603) English lutenist and composer, known to have worked in London and thought to have come from East Anglia. Eleven of his typically light-hearted pieces for the six-course lute are to be found in Barley's *A New Booke of Tablature* (London, 1596). Cutting's last work was written no later than 1603.

cyclic form Composition in which thematic material heard at the beginning of a work is reintroduced in the last movement. Haydn's Symphony No.32 in D and Brahms's Symphony No.3 both have finales that close with the work's opening material, following the principle of strict cyclic form.

The term can also be used where thematic material is more loosely linked or repeated across more than one movement. **Mendelssohn**, **Schumann** and **Liszt** in particular were greatly concerned with the cross-reference of thematic material between movements, in an attempt to create more cohesion and continuity in multi-movement form, as was **Berlioz** in his *Symphonie fantastique*. Among others, **Franck**, **d'Indy**, **Saint-Saëns** and **Fauré** were also fond of using cyclic form.

cymbals (Ger. *Becken*; It. *piatti*; Fr. *cymbales*) One of the oldest of instruments, in use for at least 3,000 years. In ancient times they were used in religious ceremonies, and on occasions of festive joy – 'Praise him upon the loud cymbals; praise him upon the high-sounding cymbals', said the psalmist, who was probably describing rather small versions; in fact what we now call **antique cymbals** (crotales), based on specimens found at Herculaneum, are only 10 to 15 cm in diameter. The modern cymbal owes much to the work of an Armenian family with the name Zildjian, which actually means cymbal-maker, who still guard a 'secret' process discovered in the 17th century by a forebear in Constantinople. It is a large metal-alloy plate, slightly convex so that only the edges touch when two are clashed together; there is a dome in the centre, with a leather strap by which it is held. They are usually made in matched pairs, ranging in size from about 40 to 50 cm. When struck together there must be a sideways movement to avoid the dull hollow sound produced by an air-lock of the two domes.

Apart from the great climactic crash, the expert player can produce an astonishing variety of tone and dynamics, sometimes scraping, sometimes barely touching the

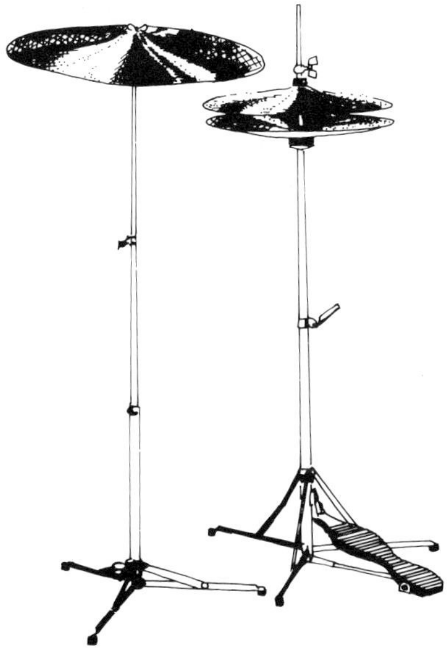

Two types of cymbal

rims, or even just pulling them apart. The sound is damped by pulling the cymbals back against the chest. A single cymbal may be suspended and struck in a variety of ways – scraped with a triangle beater, caressed with a wire brush, or rolled with a variety of drum-sticks. The contemporary composer is usually precise in his or her instructions, but in the past they were often vague – even Debussy, who wrote for the cymbals with astonishing imagination in *La mer*, but leaves the mode of execution to the players. The cymbal player needs nerve as well as skill – he cannot play wrong notes, but bad timing is a disaster.

Czerny, Karl (1791-1857) Austrian pianist, composer and piano teacher who is best known for his hundreds of piano studies and exercises, especially his *Complete Theoretical and Practical Pianoforte School*, Op.500. Czerny could play the piano by the age of three, and became a much-admired pianist in his day. At ten he became a pupil of Beethoven and was subsequently renowned for his interpretations of Beethoven's piano works, all of which he could play from memory. After 1805 Czerny gave up the life of a travelling virtuoso to spend his time in Vienna as a composer and piano teacher, who counted the young Franz Liszt among his numerous pupils.

D

D 1. Fourth note of the scale, one tone above C and one tone below E. The scale of D major has two sharps in the key-signature.
2. The works of **Schubert** are given D-numbers, being categorized by the chronology established by Otto Deutsch. For example, Piano Quintet D667 (*The Trout*).

D D major

da capo (Abbreviated to D.C.) From the beginning, an indication that the performer should start again from the beginning of a piece. *Da capo al fine* indicates that the performer should continue up to the word *fine* (end), or *da capo al segno* up to the sign in the score.

Dalayrac, Nicholas-Marie (1753-1809) French composer of songs, string quartets and more than 50 operas, including *Nina* (1786) and *La maison à vendre* (1800).

d'Albert, Eugen (1864-1932) German pianist and composer, born in Glasgow, but of French descent. He won the Mendelssohn Scholarship (1861) to study in Vienna under Liszt. After a career as a concert pianist he became director of the Berlin Hochschule (1907). He composed numerous instrumental works and 20 operas, including *Der Tiefland* (1903).

Dalcroze, Emile Jacques- See **Jacques-Dalcroze, Emile**

Dale, Benjamin (1855-1943) British composer of sonatas for piano, violin and viola, songs, and choral and orchestral works. In later years he was involved with educational work for the Royal Academy of Music and Associated Board.

Dallapiccola, Luigi (1904-1975) Italian pianist and composer. He studied in Trieste and at the Cherubini Conservatoire, Florence, and was first influenced by Mozart, Wagner and Monteverdi. He was the earliest Italian exponent of the **twelve-note** technique, following his exposure to its Viennese practitioners, Schoenberg, Berg and Webern. The fruits of these experiments can be heard in the work of the late 1930s, notably in his choral piece *Canti di prigionia* (1938-41), and in the first of his three operas, *Volo di notte* (1940). His later compositions reflect a **polyphonic** style, which came to the fore in his *Piccola musica notturna* (1954). Other works include *Il prigioniero* and *Ulisse* (operas), two ballets, choral and solo vocal music (*Commiato*, 1972), and a variety of orchestral and chamber works. From the early 1930s to the 1960s he taught in the United States.

Damase, Jean-Michel (1928-) French composer and pianist who studied at the Paris Conservatoire. His works include the ballet *La Croqueuse de diamants* (1950) and compositions for piano, violin and harp.

Dämpfer German equivalent of **mute**.

damper pedal Alternative term for the soft pedal of a piano, which either applies a damping cloth to the strings, or moves the action sideways so that the hammers strike one string instead of two or three. (This is indicated by the instruction *una corda*.)

Damrosch, Leopold (1832-1885) German composer and conductor who did much to enhance the reputation of New York's Metropolitan Opera House. He was a violinist in the Weimar court orchestra, and became a close friend of its conductor, **Liszt**. Damrosch moved to the United States in 1871 and became co-founder and first conductor of the New York Oratorio Society. At the Metropolitan Opera House he organized and conducted a season of German opera, which included the first US performance of Wagner's *Die Walküre*.

Damrosch, Walter (1862-1950) Born in Germany, the younger son of Leopold **Damrosch**, he followed his father to the United States and introduced many important works there. He succeeded his father as conductor at the New York Oratorio in 1885, and became an assistant conductor at the Metropolitan Opera House. He conducted the first US performance of Wagner's *Parsifal* there in 1896, and in 1900 formed a touring opera company which performed Wagner's operas, some for the first time. As conductor of the New York Symphony Orchestra (1903-27) he directed the first US performances of works by such composers as Bruckner and Mahler. Among his compositions are five operas, including *The Scarlet Letter* (1896) and *Cyrano de Bergerac* (1913).

dance band See **swing**

dance poem Description sometimes given by composers to a major orchestral work intended for ballet and having a narrative interest. See also **choreographic poem**; **symphonic poem**.

Dancla, Charles (1817-1907) French violinist and composer who became a tutor at the Paris Conservatoire in 1857. Among his compositions are four symphonies, six violin concertos and works for string quartet.

Dandrieu, Jean-François (1682-1738) French priest and composer who wrote mainly for the keyboard. He became a member of the Chapel Royal in 1724. He wrote a set of symphonies, *Les caractères de la guerre*, and three volumes of harpsichord pieces.

Dankworth, John (1927-) English composer and jazz musician. He began by playing clarinet in a jazz band; he went to the Royal Academy of Music to study, then spent some time in the United States. On his return he founded the Johnny Dankworth Seven and later (1953) his own large jazz orchestra. By now he was playing the alto saxophone. He married the singer Cleo Laine in 1960, and has toured extensively with her and the orchestra. Since the mid-1980s the two have promoted various series of concerts and events at their home in Wavenham, Bucks. Dankworth is a prolific composer. The opera-ballet *Lysistrata* (1964) blends jazz and symphonic styles; *Zodiac Variations* was written for his own orchestra; there is also a string quartet, a piano concerto, and film scores (*The Servant*; *Darling*; *10 Rillington Place* are among the best known).

danmono (Japan) Compositions for **koto** which comprise several *dan* or sections. Each *dan* contains 104 beats, except for the first which has an extra four beats. Pieces are known by the number of *dan* they contain, e.g. *Rokudan* (*roku* means six), *Hachidan* (*hachi* means eight), etc. *Danmono* begin slowly with a gradual acceleration through all the *dan* until the last few bars; they begin and end quietly, rising to a climax towards the end of the last section. The two most common tunings are *hirajoshi* and *kumoijoshi*, derived from the popular **in** and **yō** scales. See **Japanese scales**

dan tranh (Vietnam) Horizontal plucked zither which has 16 steel strings stretched over movable bridges. Similar to the Japanese **koto**, the Chinese **cheng** and the Korean **kayagŭm**.

Daquin, Louis Claude (1694-1772) French composer famous for his *Le coucou* for harpsichord. A child prodigy, Daquin played for Louis XIV at the age of only six. He succeeded **Dandrieu** as organist at the Sainte-Chapelle in 1739. His name is sometimes spelled D'Acquin.

Dargason English folk-tune used from the 16th century onwards as a country dance, as such incorporated into **Holst**'s *St Paul's Suite*.

Dargomizhsky, Alexander Sergeyvich (1813-1869) Russian pianist and composer who studied with **Glinka** and became associated with the **Mighty Handful**. His works include the operas *Rusalka* (1856) and *The Stone Guest* (1872), treating the same theme as Mozart's *Don Giovanni*, which was completed after his death by **Cui** and orchestrated by **Rimsky-Korsakov**. He also produced orchestral fantasies on fairy-tale themes (*Baba-Yaga*, about the witch who features in Russian children's stories).

dastgah (Persia) Classical form consisting of a modal system which acts as a basis for solo instrumental improvisation. A performance of a *dastgah* entails the exposition of several tunes chosen from a set repertory of about ten to 30 melodies, or *gusheh*, in any given mode or **maqam**, of which there are 12. The tunes chosen embrace the characteristics of a single mode, selected to convey the particular sentiment of the *dastgah* performance.

David, Félicien César (1810-1876) French composer whose passion for Eastern music coloured his own work and influenced **Gounod**, **Bizet** and **Delibes**. His symphonic ode *Le désert* (1844) for chorus and orchestra was admired for its Oriental coloration. He also composed operas, including *La perle du Brésil* (1851) and *Lalla Roukh* (1862), and works for string quintet.

David, Ferdinand (1810-1873) German violinist and composer who also taught at Leipzig Conservatoire. He was a close friend of **Mendelssohn**, who brought him to Leipzig at the age of 26 to be concertmaster of the Gewandhaus Orchestra, one of the greatest orchestras of the day; he held this post until his death. Mendelssohn's Violin Concerto (1845) was composed for him. Among his many works were an opera, concertos for violin, and chamber music.

Davies, Hugh (1943-) English composer associated with avant-garde electronic music. He studied at Oxford University and became an assistant to **Stockhausen** in 1964. In 1967 he was appointed director of London University's electronic music workshops. He has devised and built a variety of unique instruments and sound sculptures. His compositions include *Meldoci Gestures* (1978) for flute or violin, cello and piano; *Strata* (1987) for his own instrument, the concert Aeolian harp, and tape; and other combinations of tape and electronic effects with live performers. He is also a writer, and has contributed over 300 articles on 20th-century instruments to the *New Grove Dictionary of Instruments*.

Davies, Sir Peter Maxwell (1934-) British composer of highly individual music, often characterized by angular melodies and complex rhythms. He attended Manchester University and the Royal Manchester College of Music. His fellow students included Harrison **Birtwistle** and Alexander **Goehr**, later (like Davies himself) to become prominent members of Britain's avant-garde. After studying in Italy with **Petrassi** and at Princeton with Roger **Sessions**, Davies spent a year in Australia as resident composer at Adelaide University. In 1967 he became director of the Pierrot Players, a chamber ensemble performing contemporary music. Re-formed by him into the Fires of London in 1971, this group served as a major vehicle for his gifts as a composer until it was disbanded in 1987. From his days with the Pierrot Players comes one of his most notable theatre pieces, *Eight Songs for a Mad King* (1969), a work in eight movements for actor-singer and chamber ensemble including a train whistle, chains and a didjeridoo. Other theatre pieces include *Miss Donnithorne's Maggot* (1974), *Le jongleur de Notre Dame* (1978), which features a children's band, and *The Number 11 Bus* (1983-4). The dramatic potential of his music was fully realized in his opera *Taverner* (1962-70). Davies has had a rewarding association with the poet George Mackay Brown, whose poetry was set in such works as *Solstice of Light* (1979), for choir and organ, and whose work inspired Davies's own libretto for his chamber opera *The Martyrdom of St Magnus* (1976-7). From 1979 to 1984 Davies was director of Dartington Hall music summer school. In 1985 he became associate conductor/composer with the Scottish Chamber Orchestra, for which some of his most recent works, such as his oboe concerto (1987), have been written. His many other compositions include three symphonies, *St Thomas' Wake* (a foxtrot for orchestra, 1969), choral pieces, chamber music, piano works, and film scores (for Ken Russell's *The Devils* and *The Boy Friend*, both 1971). He has also made transcriptions and realizations of Renaissance and Baroque pieces. He was knighted in 1987.

Davies, Sir Walford (1869-1941) Welsh composer and organist who wrote the famous *Royal Air Force March Past* in 1918. He encouraged musical festivals, composing his oratorio *Everyman* for the Leeds Festival in 1904, and his *Solemn Melody* for organ and strings for the tercentenary of Milton's birth in 1908. He was made Master of the King's Music in 1934. His main compositions were sacred choral works, although other works included violin sonatas, orchestral overtures and music for children. Davies was also a pioneer of music broadcasting for schools.

Davis, Andrew (1944-) English conductor. He studied the organ at Cambridge, and conducting in Rome with Ferrara. In 1970 he became associate conductor of the BBC Scottish Symphony Orchestra. He came to prominence when he took over at very short notice a concert broadcast by the BBC Symphony Orchestra. He held a post at the New Philharmonia Orchestra before becoming music director of the Toronto Symphony Orchestra in 1975. His opera début was at **Glyndebourne** in 1973 with Strauss's *Capriccio*. He has also been principal guest conductor with the **Royal Liverpool Philharmonic** and has made broadcasts and recordings (including Shostakovich's Symphony No.10 with the London Philharmonic Orchestra). In 1989 he was appointed chief conductor of the **BBC** Symphony Orchestra in succession to John **Pritchard**.

Davis, Carl (1937-) American composer and conductor best known for his film and television scores. He studied composition at the New England Conservatory, Boston, and in 1959 joined New York Center Opera as a répétiteur. He settled in London the next year and began by writing for radio. Television projects followed, notably *The Naked Civil Servant* and *The World at War*. A commission to compose the music for a television survey of silent films led in due course (1980) to his highly successful score for the newly restored film epic *Napoleon* by Abel Gance, when a large live orchestra accompanied the screening of the film. Another silent film score is for D.W. Griffith's *Intolerance*; he has also written the music for the film *The French Lieutenant's Woman* (from the novel by John Fowles) and the ballet *A Simple Man*, on the life of the painter L.S. Lowry. In 1989 he conducted **Weill**'s *Street Scene* at the **English National Opera**. His music successfully blends the classical with the popular idiom.

Davis, Sir Colin (1927-) British conductor and former clarinettist. He founded and was the conductor of the Chelsea Opera Group in the 1950s and has since held many important conducting posts. He was music director of the **Sadler's Wells** Opera, and was chief conductor of the BBC Symphony Orchestra, 1967-74. He is chief guest conductor of the Boston Symphony Orchestra and music director of the Bavarian Radio Symphony Orchestra. He first came to prominence when he took over a concert performance of Mozart's *Don Giovanni* because Klemperer fell ill. He is an outstanding interpreter of the music of Berlioz, **Tippett**, and Mozart, and has made numerous fine recordings with the leading orchestras of the world, including the **London Symphony** and the **Concertgebouw**. From 1971-86 he was musical director of the Royal Opera House, Covent Garden; during this time he conducted the world première of Tippett's *The Ice Break*, which was dedicated to him.

Davy, John (1763-1824) British composer, violinist and organist. He wrote music for light opera and theatre, including the song *The Bay of Biscay*, and incidental music for Shakespeare's *The Tempest*.

Davy, Richard (1467-1507) English composer and priest who was appointed choirmaster of Magdalen College, Oxford, in 1491. There he composed a respected *St Matthew Passion* and six antiphons. He also wrote several motets, and began a Magnificat in 1500, which was never completed.

Dawson, Peter (1882-1961) Australian bass-baritone who studied under Charles Santley (1834-1922) in London. He made his Covent Garden début in 1909, but

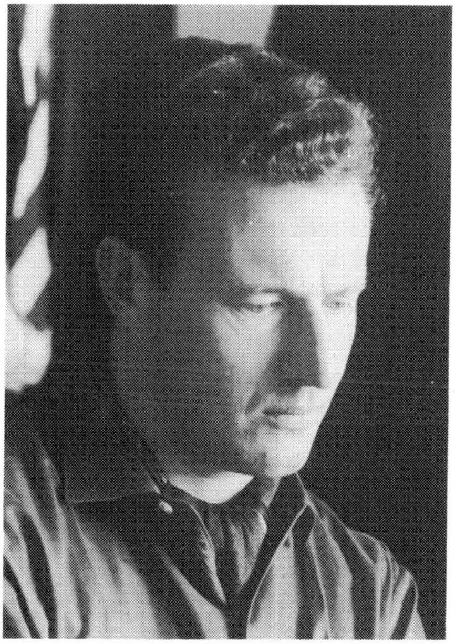

Sir Colin Davis

went on to pursue a career in more popular song. He made many recordings (starting in 1904, the early days of the gramophone), including the well-known *The Road to Mandalay*, and sold something in the region of 13 million records. Dawson remained an extremely popular singer for more than half a century.

dbyangs (Tibet) General term for singing, melody, etc., especially religious song. More specifically, it refers to a sustained style of singing in Buddhist ritual in which the vowel sounds of each syllable in certain sacred texts are modified according to the **neumatic** score (*dbyangs-yig*). Each sound is extended for some length of time, so that the sense of ordinary time is lost; it is also subject to a variety of tonal inflections, glides and tremolo. In some traditions, special techniques including voice constriction and multiphonics are used.

dead march A funeral march.

debayashi (Japan) On-stage ensemble in the **kabuki** theatre and largely responsible for performing its **nagauta** music. The ensemble is generally placed at the back of the stage on tiers, with **shamisen** (lute) and singers above, and with the drum and flute (**hayashi**) ensemble at floor level. The number of players on the stage varies according to the plot. A subsection of the *debayashi*, the *chobo*, may be found in plays deriving from the **bunraku** puppet theatre, and consists of **Gidayū** singers and **shamisen** players behind a bamboo curtain.

Debussy, Claude (1862-1918) French composer whose ability to paint musical pictures with great delicacy and detail led to his being described as an impressionist, despite the fact that he laid great stress on the demands of form. A brilliant exponent of orchestral and pianistic colouring, he pioneered many technical innovations of composition, such as the use of modal harmonies and shimmering mystical whole-tone and oriental scales. His exploring spirit blazed a trail that many others followed, including **Bartók**, **Messiaen** and **Boulez**, making him arguably the most influential composer of the 20th century.

Born in Paris, Debussy received little formal education. From 1872 he attended the Paris Conservatoire, where he proved a wayward pianist and a rebellious student, impatient with prevailing academic theories. In the summers of 1880 and 1881 he went to Russia, serving as pianist to Nadiezhda von Meck, Tchaikovsky's patron. In 1884 he won the Prix de Rome with his cantata *L'enfant prodigue*. Required to study in Rome, he took the opportunity of meeting Liszt and Verdi and heard Wagner's opera *Lohengrin*, which much impressed him. In 1887-8 he wrote his second choral work, *La damoiselle élue*, for soprano, mezzo-soprano, female chorus and orchestra.

He attended the Bayreuth festivals of 1888 and 1889, but other influences eventually ousted Wagner. At the Paris Exposition of 1889 he heard a Balinese **gamelan** orchestra for the first time and was startled by its impact and the harmonic avenues that it opened up to him. His friendship with poets such as Mallarmé and the Symbolists and his meeting with Erik **Satie** in 1890 went hand in hand with a feeling that he was a *musicien français*. In 1893 he wrote a string quartet in F, his only essay in the genre. His first major success, *Prélude à l'après-midi d'un faune*, an orchestral evocation of the atmosphere conjured up in a poem by Mallarmé, came in 1894. Its apparent formlessness caused a great stir among critics. In 1902 *Pelléas et Mélisande*, an opera based on a Symbolist play by Maeterlinck, was staged at the Opéra-Comique, a decade after Debussy had begun it. In 1905 his three symphonic sketches comprising *La mer* received their première. They were followed by three orchestral *Images* (1905-12) and the ballet *Jeux* (1913), written for the Ballets Russes.

Besides the works already cited, Debussy produced a wealth of piano music of the highest quality. It includes the *Suite bergamasque* (1890, revised 1905); the three movements *Pour le piano* (1896-1901); *Estampes* (1903); *L'île joyeuse* (1904), two books each of *Images*, *Préludes*, and *Etudes*; and the ever-popular *Children's Corner* suite (1906-8). He also wrote songs and chamber pieces.

decani (Lat.) Of the dean. Section of the choir that is positioned on the south side (that is, the dean's side) of the chancel in a cathedral. See also **cantoris**.

decrescendo (It.) Instruction indicating that the music is to become quieter, represented graphically by a pair of converging lines.

Defesch, William (1687-1761) Flemish composer who moved to London in 1733. He studied the organ, violin and cello, and became choirmaster at Antwerp cathedral in 1731. Among his compositions are the oratorios *Judith* and *Joseph*, performed in London (1732), and several Masses, songs and instrumental sonatas.

degree Note of the **diatonic** scale relative to other notes. Alternative names for the

1st to 7th degrees (major or minor scales) are tonic, supertonic, mediant, subdominant, dominant, submediant and leading note.

Delage, Maurice (1879-1961) French composer, a pupil of **Ravel** at the Paris Conservatoire. Delage blended elements of an impressionistic style with themes from Indian music, of which he made a study. He introduced an exotic flavour to his works, particularly in his ballet *Les bâtisseurs de ponts*, the symphonic poem *Conte par la mer* and *Quatre poèmes hindous* for violin and orchestra. In 1926 he completed an orchestral version of Debussy's *Chansons de Bilitis*.

Delalande, Michel Richard (1657-1726) French composer who was well known at Versailles for the grand **Baroque** style of his ecclesiastical compositions. He became Musician at Court to Louis XIV, taught the king's daughters, and composed music for the Sainte-Chapelle. He wrote 42 motets and other devotional pieces, as well as several ballets for performance at the court in Versailles.

Delannoy, Marcel (1898-1962) French composer who abandoned a career as an architect to take up music. He was largely self-taught, but was influenced by **Honegger**, adopting some of his neo-Romantic styles. Among his compositions are the operas *Le poirier de misère* (1927) and *Puck* (1949). He also wrote a ballet-cantata, *Le fou de la dame*.

Delden, Lex van (1919-) Dutch composer of chamber and choral music, children's ballets and seven symphonies. Delden's *In Memoriam* for orchestra was written for the Dutch flood victims of 1953.

Delibes, Léo (1836-1891) French composer who began as an organist. He studied under Adolphe **Adam**, composer of *Giselle*, and worked at the Paris Opéra as a chorus-master; from that time he was attracted to the stage and his works were almost entirely theatrical. His *Coppélia* (1870), based on a Hoffmann story about a doll that apparently comes to life, is one of the most popular and frequently performed ballets, even today. He also wrote another tuneful ballet of great charm, *Sylvia* (1876), this time on a classical theme. Other works include choruses, songs and operas, the most important of which is *Lakmé* (1883), on an Oriental theme. The *Bell Song* from this work is frequently performed as a showpiece by coloratura sopranos.

Delius, Frederick (1862-1934) English composer of Prussian parentage, who left his native Bradford in 1882 to manage an orange plantation in Florida. However, he neglected his duties in order to study music with Thomas Ward, an organist. While in Florida, Delius was profoundly influenced by negro melodies.

On returning to Europe, Delius studied composition in Leipzig, meeting **Grieg** and other Scandinavian musicians. He then moved to Paris, where he completed the *Florida Suite* and *Appalachia* and became friendly with the painters and writers of the period. He settled in the French

Frederick Delius

countryside and there composed the majority of his best-known music, from the 1890s onward. In the 1920s he became incapacitated by paralysis and blindness, but continued to work with the aid of his amanuensis, Eric **Fenby**. He completed several works with Fenby, including his Violin Sonata No.3 and *Idyll* (1932).

Delius's compositions clearly reflect the natural landscapes that were his inspiration – for example, the tonal impressions for full orchestra, *Brigg Fair* (1907), *In a Summer Garden* (1908) and *North Country Sketches* (1914). He also wrote several operas, including *A Village Romeo and Juliet* (1901), *Fennimore and Gerda* (1908-10) and *The Magic Fountain* (1893). His short orchestral work *On Hearing the First Cuckoo in Spring* (1912) is one of his most well-known pieces.

Della Casa, Lisa (1919-) Swiss soprano who studied under Margarete Haeser in Zurich. She made her début in Solothurn-Biel in 1941 in *Madama Butterfly*. Della Casa has sung world-wide and is best known for her performances of **Strauss** and **Mozart**.

Deller, Alfred (1912-1979) British counter-tenor who founded the Deller Consort (1950) to revive English lute songs and **madrigals**. Composers such as **Britten, Fricker, Mellers, Ridout** and **Rubbra** wrote pieces for him.

Dello Joio, Norman (1913-) American composer and organist noted for his command of melody. He has written for the stage and has composed some respected operatic works, including *The Ruby* (1953) and *The Lamentation of Saul* (1954). His work shows the influence of **Gregorian chant** and Italian opera. He studied with **Hindemith** and **Wagenaar** in New York (1940-1) and was appointed musical director of the Loring Dance Players in 1941.

Del Mar, Norman (1919-) British conductor associated with 20th-century British music. He founded the Chelsea Symphony Orchestra (1944) and was conductor of the Yorkshire Symphony Orchestra (1954-5) and the BBC Scottish Symphony Orchestra (1960-5). He conducted the first performance of Benjamin **Britten**'s *Let's Make An Opera!* and has published a three-volume study of the works of Richard **Strauss**.

Del Monaco, Mario (1915-1982) Italian tenor who studied at Pesaro Conservatoire. After singing in Milan and London he joined the New York Metropolitan Opera (1951-9). He was the most famous Italian tenor of his generation, an outstanding interpreter of the title-role in Verdi's *Otello* and the other leading roles of the Italian repertory. He had a voice of great power and vigour.

Del Tredici, David (1937-) American composer and conductor best known for his works based on the *Alice* books of Lewis Carroll. He studied in California and at Princeton, and has taught at Harvard, Boston and (since 1984) New York City University. He has won a Guggenheim Foundation award and has had commissions from various American musical foundations. The *Alice* cycle for soprano and orchestra, begun in 1969, includes *An Alice Symphony*, *The Lobster Quadrille*, *Final Alice*, *Adventures Underground*, *In Wonderland*, *The Annotated Alice*, and *The Child Alice* (1981). Some of these works also include a folk-group.

Other compositions are a piano duet, songs, and fantasies: *Syzygy* for soprano and small orchestra; *The Last Gospel* (1967) for rock group, orchestra and chorus. His music is characterized by great density of scoring, often with different tempos played simultaneously.

Delvincourt, Claude (1888-1954) French composer who became director of the conservatoires in Versailles (1932) and Paris (1941). Among his works are piano solos and duets, songs and operas.

demisemiquaver Note with half the time value of a **semiquaver**, and a thirty-second that of a **semibreve**. In American usage, it is known as a thirty-second note.

Demisemiquaver and its rest

Demus, Jörg (1928-) Austrian pianist and recitalist who often appears as accompanist to artists such as **Suk**. He is also celebrated for his recitals and recordings of music played on early pianos.

Denisov, Edison Vasilievich (1929-) Soviet composer who was persuaded by **Shostakovich** to abandon mathematics and study at the Moscow Conservatoire (1951-6). He became a tutor there in 1959 and composed at the Experimental Studio of Electronic Music in Moscow from 1958. He combined elements of Russian folk-music with modern styles in compositions that range from *Peinture* for orchestra to *Crescendo e Diminuendo* for the harpsichord.

Denza, Luigi (1846-1922) Italian composer of the opera *Wallenstein* (1876) and of more than 600 songs, including the famous Neapolitan *Funiculi, funiculà*, composed to celebrate the opening of a funicular railway. This song was borrowed by Richard **Strauss** for his *Aus Italien* (1887). He studied at the Naples Conservatoire under **Mercadante**, and in 1898 became professor of singing at the Royal Academy of Music, London.

Dering (or Deering), Richard (*c.*1580-1630) British composer and organist who worked at the court of Charles I. He is said to have been one of the first organists to use the basso **continuo** method. His compositions include *Cantiones Sacrae* for several voices, church music, motets, fancies and other pieces for viols.

Dernesch, Helga (1939-) Austrian soprano, now mezzo-soprano, who studied at the Vienna Conservatoire (1957-61). She was notable as a performer in operas by Wagner (Brünnhilde in the *Ring* at Salzburg, 1969), and also Strauss. In 1979 she began to appear in mezzo roles, and has been successful in such parts as Herodias in Strauss's *Salome*, which she sang in 1988 in London and Los Angeles, and Fricka in the *Ring*. She has performed in most European and American opera-houses.

descant Originally (from about the 12th century) referred to a second part composed in counterpoint to a piece of **plainsong**. In this sense musicologists favour the spelling discant.

In the 13th century the term was extended to become a virtual synonym for **polyphony** in general, most of which was in two parts. As polyphony became more complex, the word discant came to describe an additional accompanying part written above the other two.

The modern uses of the word (now more usually spelled descant) denote firstly a high part freely composed or extemporized above a composed melody, such as a hymn or carol, and secondly the highest-pitched member of a family of instruments that is in normal use – for example, a descant recorder.

Dessau, Paul (1894-1979) German composer and conductor associated with Bertolt **Brecht**. He studied in Berlin and became an opera tutor at Hamburg, 1913. In 1918 he became conductor of the Cologne Opera, and in 1926 he conducted at the Berlin State Opera. He left Germany when the Nazis came to power, and lived in the United States (1939-45). He wrote music for Brecht's *Mutter Courage* (1926), *Der gute Mensch von Sezuan* (1947) and *Mann ist Mann* (1951), while Brecht provided librettos for his operas *Die Verurteilung des Lukullus* (1951, revised) and *Puntila* (1957). His choral work *Deutsches Miserere* was also to a text by Brecht.

Destinn, Emmy (1878-1930) Czech soprano. She studied in Prague and made her début in Dresden in 1897 as Santuzza in Mascagni's *Cavalleria rusticana*. In 1901 she sang Senta in Wagner's *Der fliegende Holländer* at Bayreuth, the first time it had been produced there. She appeared many times at the Royal Opera House, Covent Garden, from 1904 until World War I (her début was as Donna Anna in Mozart's *Don Giovanni*), singing the title-role in the first *Madama Butterfly* staged in England, in 1905. Her career at the Metropolitan Opera, New York (1908-16), was notable; there she created the role of Minnie in Puccini's *La fanciulla del West*, and her Verdi heroines were also outstanding. She made over 200 recordings, from which it is possible to appreciate her warm, flexible tone.

détaché (Fr.) Detached or separated. A bowing style in string playing that produces separated notes. *Grand détaché* means played with the whole of the bow, *petit détaché* at the point of the bow. Both are usually played on the string, as opposed to **staccato** which is usually off the string.

Deutsche, deutsche Tanz (Ger.) Country dance in 3/4 time. Sets of such dances were composed by Beethoven, Mozart, Schubert and others.

development Section of a movement in **sonata form** in which the thematic material is developed and expanded, before its restatement in the original form.

dhrupad (India) Solemn vocal style which originated in the northern Indian courts of the 15th century, using Hindu texts on noble themes. Although less florid than the currently popular **khyāl**, it is the most demanding Indian genre, particularly when a greatly extended **ālāp** or introduction is included. The song consists of two or four long sections, the first of which **(sthāyī)** is repeated as a refrain between subsequent improvisations. It is accompanied by the **pakhāvaj** drum.

Diabelli, Anton (1781-1858) Austrian composer who became a partner in Peter Cappi's publishing business. Cappi withdrew in 1824, and Diabelli & Co. was formed, publishing works by such composers as Beethoven, Schubert, **Czerny** and Liszt.

Diabelli studied singing with Michael **Haydn** at Salzburg before moving to Munich to become a priest. But he abandoned the priesthood in 1803 and settled in Vienna. His first independent publication was the *Vaterländischer Künstlerverein*, a collection of variations by 50 composers on one of his own waltz compositions, including 33 variations by **Beethoven**: the *Diabelli Variations*, Op.120.

diabolus in musica (Lat.) The devil in music. One of the names given to the interval of an augmented fourth. It is also known as a tritone.

Diaghilev, Sergei (1872-1929) Russian impresario who studied law and music at St Petersburg. In Paris (1909) he organized

Sergei Diaghilev

the highly successful Ballets Russes company. Among the many talented artists associated with the company were Nijinsky, the dancer; Fokine, the choreographer; and Picasso. He encouraged many composers to write for him, including **Stravinsky, Ravel, Debussy** and **Prokofiev**.

Diamond, David (1915-) American composer who was noted in the 1940s for his new lyricism and his combination of romantic colours and a neo-classical discipline.

He studied at the Cleveland Institute, the Dalcroze Institute in New York, and at the Paris Conservatoire with the influential tutor Nadia **Boulanger**. He wrote eight symphonies, some concertos, and a series of *Rounds* for string orchestra. He also wrote six string quartets and other chamber pieces. His later symphonies – the Sixth (1954) and *Sinfonia Concertante* (1955) – reflect a difficult and violent style which is seen by some critics as heralding a transitional phase in his work.

diapason (Greek) Through all. Foundation stops (open and stopped) of an organ, which give the instrument its distinctive tone.

diapason normal Former standard of pitch in which the note A has a frequency of 435 hertz.

diaphonic song (Yugoslavia) Part-song type, from the western region of Croatia and the Istrian peninsula, characterized by its narrow interval style which is thought to be of ancient origin. In rural areas these songs usually occur as duets. The voice parts are of equal importance and are closely intertwined, with intervals of major and minor seconds (not considered dissonant) predominating. However, the voices may occasionally be less interdependent, as in instances of parallel part movement, counterpoint and drone singing. Unique to this region is an unusual scale, known as the Istrian, approximating to E, F, G, A♭, B♭ and C♭.

diaphony Simple **organum**, usually with only two voices.

diatonic To do with any given major or minor **scale**.

A diatonic scale is any of the major or minor scales, as opposed to the **chromatic scales**.

A diatonic harmony is one in which the prevailing major or minor scales are used without significant recourse to notes outside those scales.

A diatonic **interval** is one between two notes of the same scale.

Diaz, Alirio (1923-) Venezuelan guitarist. He is prominent as a soloist throughout Europe and the United States. Since 1954, Diaz has taught at the Accademia Chigiana in Siena, Italy.

Dibdin, Charles (1745-1814) British composer, singer and author. In 1798 he began his series of 'table entertainments' at which he recited, sang and accompanied. One of the most successful, *The Oddities*, contained the song *Tom Bowling*. Many other songs, including sea-songs, and works for harpsichord formed part of his repertory.

Dichtung (Ger.) Poem. For example, *symphonische Dichtung*, **symphonic poem**.

Dickinson, Peter (1934-) English composer and pianist who has written many songs and a series of impressionistic pieces for strings, orchestra and piano. Many of his pieces represent experimental combinations of instruments, in particular his *Winter Afternoons* (1971) for six solo voices and double bass, *Solo* (1976) for baritone, tape and viola da gamba, and *The Unicorns* (1982) for soprano and brass band. He studied the organ at Queen's College, Cambridge, and was elected to the Juilliard School in 1958. He was a pianist with the New York City Ballet and lectured at London and Birmingham Universities. From 1974 he was professor of music at Keele University.

diction Enunciation in singing.

diddling Practice of singing dance tunes to nonsense syllables in the absence (or prohibition) of instrumental resources. Also known as mouth music.

didjeridu (Australia) Wind instrument of the North Australian Aborigines, consisting of a straight end-blown tube at least a metre long. It is generally played with 'circular breathing' techniques (i.e. blowing out through the mouth while breathing in through the nose), using the cheeks as a bagpipe-like air reservoir to maintain a continuous sound. The didjeridu is capable of producing sounds approximating to bird calls, trills, croaks, etc. Also spelled didjeridoo.

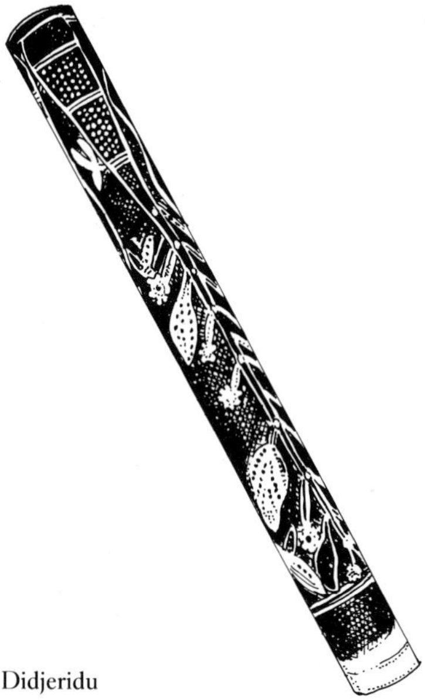

Didjeridu

Diepenbrock, Alphons (1862-1921) Dutch composer and friend of Mahler who became an important teacher. His sacred works, including two settings of the *Te Deum* and a *Stabat Mater*, reflect the influences of Wagner and Palestrina. He also wrote music for the theatre (notably for Sophocles' *Electra*) and a number of songs.

Dieren, Bernard van (1887-1936) Dutch composer of complex **polyphonic** and impressionistic work, who was much admired by British intellectuals including Gray, Gerald Cooper and the Sitwells. Born in Rotterdam, he trained in the sciences, but in 1909 moved to London as a correspondent of the *Nieuwe Rotterdamsche Courant*. He became interested in musical composition and wrote music criticism for this and for other periodicals. His compositions include a *Chinese Symphony* (1914) for soloists, chorus and orchestra; a comic opera, *The Tailor* (1917); and a volume of critical essays, *Down Among the Dead Men* (1935). He also wrote five quartets, a solo violin sonata, piano pieces and some songs.

Dies Irae (Lat.) Day of Wrath, the sacred piece that forms the second section of the Requiem Mass. It appeared in 19th-century symphonic works, such as Berlioz's *Symphonie fantastique* and Saint-Saëns's *Danse macabre*.

difference tone **Combination tone** that is created by the sounding together of two loud notes. The difference tone is that which is heard to be below the two notes in pitch. Its companion, the **summation tone**, is heard at a higher pitch than the original two.

digital recording In analogue recording and reproduction of music with magnetic tape or LP records, the shape of the original sound-waves created by the music is retained throughout the process, and is therefore liable to distortion and deterioration at every stage from microphone to loudspeaker. In digital recording the sound-waves are measured many thousands of times per second, and the measurements stored as numbers in a series of pulses (pulse code modulation), that can be recorded on tape, broadcast, sent over low-grade land-line or transferred to a compact disc (CD) as a sequence of minute indentations. These are scanned and converted to the original sound-waves, which are then reproduced through loudspeaker or headphones.

The essential advantage of PCM, digital recording and compact discs is that the transference and storage of information can be in a low-grade form, because it is a series of numbers and not an analogue of the original sound-waves.

dim. Abbreviation of **diminuendo**.

diminished Perfect or minor **intervals** that have been reduced by a semitone. **Triads** are diminished if the 5th is reduced by a semitone.

diminuendo (It.) Getting quieter. See also **decrescendo**.

diminution Shortening of note-values, often by half, as a method of ornamenting a melody or phrase.

d'Indy, Vincent (1851-1931) French composer who founded the Schola Cantorum in Paris with Charles Bordes and **Guilmant** (1894). He was an influential admirer of Debussy and of Wagner's *Ring des Nibelungen*, and he did much to assist **Lamoureux** (who introduced Wagner's works in Paris).

He became a pupil of **Franck** at the Paris Conservatoire in 1872. **Duparc** had first introduced him to Wagner's work and in 1876 he attended the first Bayreuth Festival. In 1900 the Schola Cantorum became a general music school and d'Indy wrote a treatise on teaching method, the *Cours de composition* (1906). He taught **Auric, Roussel** and **Satie**. In 1911 he became sole director of his school.

His richly-orchestrated compositions include the operas *Le chant de la cloche* (1879), *Fervaal* (1897), *L'étranger* (1903) and *La légende de St Christophe* (1920). He also wrote two symphonies and a number of tone-poems for orchestra, *Wallenstein* (1882), *Symphonie sur un chant montagnard* (1886) and *Jour d'été à la montagne* (1905).

dirge Funeral composition, usually vocal, performed at a burial.

discant Alternative spelling of **descant**.

discord Feeling of 'restlessness' or 'dissatisfaction' created by a chord that needs to be resolved. Sometimes what was perceived as a discord in a past age may be accepted as a concord in a succeeding era, or vice versa. See **resolution**; **suspension**.

disjunct motion In harmony, the progress of a single part by leap, as opposed to by step (called conjunct motion). See also **contrary motion**; **parallel motion**; **similar motion**.

dissonance Sounding together of notes to produce **discord**.

Di Stefano, Giuseppe See **Stefano, Giuseppe di**

Distler, Hugo (1908-1942) German composer who studied the organ in Leipzig and became organist at the Jakobkirche there (1931). In 1921 he became an organist in Lübeck and was appointed professor of composition at the Stuttgart Conservatoire in 1937. His compositions are devotional and include more than 50 motets, settings of the *Passion* and *Nativity*, and an oratorio. He also wrote a string quartet and a harpsichord concerto.

Dittersdorf, Carl Ditters von (1739-1799) Austrian composer of operas and symphonies. He is known to have played in Vienna in a string quartet with **Vanhal**, Haydn and Mozart. He travelled to Italy with **Gluck** (1763), achieving great success as a violinist, and also became *Kapellmeister* to the Bishops of Grosswardein (1765) and Breslau (1769). His major works include the opera *Doktor und Apotheker*, and 12 symphonies based on Ovid's *Metamorphoses*. He also wrote 115 other symphonies, 40 operas, 35 concertos and a great deal of other music.

divertimento (It.) Diversion. Work for an instrumental ensemble in several movements which is predominantly light-hearted in character.

divertissement Term that is used mainly in connection with ballet, in which it means a group of dances that are outside the main narrative of the plot. In a musical sense it can refer either to music played between acts, or to pieces based on familiar tunes performed as light entertainment.

divisi (It.) Divided. Indication that a single section of the strings in an orchestra, such as the first violins or cellos, should divide into two or more parts to play a single chord or a more extended passage. It is contradicted by the marking **unisoni.**

Dixieland Style of jazz playing which was originated in the United States by a group of white Southerners, based on the music played by black musicians in the **New Orleans style**.

dodecaphonic Alternative term for **twelve-note** composition.

Dodgson, Stephen (1924-) English composer and musical broadcaster, who studied under R.O. Morris. Among his compositions are symphonic works, including a *Symphony for Wind* (1947), a guitar concerto, *Epigrams from a Garden* (1977) for contralto and clarinets, and various songs and piano pieces.

doh/do Name for the tonic note in any key in **tonic sol-fa**, represented by the symbol d. Also the name for the note C in systems with fixed pitch, such as **solfège**.

Dohnányi, Christoph von (1929-) German conductor of Hungarian descent, grandson of Ernst von **Dohnányi**. He studied in Berlin, Munich and in the United States with **Bernstein**, and won the Richard Strauss Prize for conducting in 1951. He joined the Frankfurt Opera in 1952 as chorus-master, moving to major appointments in Lübeck, Kassel, Frankfurt again and, in 1975, Hamburg. He was chief conductor of the West German Radio Orchestra (1964-9). In 1984 he became principal conductor of the **Cleveland Symphony Orchestra**. He has worked in many major opera-houses, including Vienna, San Francisco, the Metropolitan, New York, and at Covent Garden, where he first appeared in 1975, recently conducting Wagner's *Die Meistersinger* there (1990). He conducted the world premières of **Henze**'s *Der junge Lord* (1965) and *The Bassarids* (1966). His readings are marked by great attention to detail allied to an infectious energy.

Dohnányi, Ernst von (1877-1960) Hungarian pianist with a Viennese repertory, who abandoned a successful career in order to compose. He is best known outside his home country for his *Variations on a Nursery Song*, completed in 1916. He also composed two symphonies, two concertos each for piano and for violin, and some chamber works. Dohnányi was widely respected in Hungary, and became an influential tutor at the Budapest Academy and eventually the conductor of the Budapest Philharmonic Orchestra in 1927. Later he was appointed director of the Hungarian Broadcasting Services.

Ernst von Dohnányi

doina (Romania) Lyrical song form, in free rhythm, which incorporates improvisation of a highly ornamental and recitative-like nature on the skeleton of a tune using traditional formulaic patterns. Increasingly popular outside Romania are instrumental *doinas*, particularly those that feature the **nai** panpipes.

Dolmetsch, Arnold (1858-1940) British maker and restorer of antique instruments and performer of early music, of Swiss descent. He settled in England (1914) and set up his own workshop for harpsichords, viols, lutes and recorders; he also arranged annual festivals of ancient music and was the writer of the first important book on the interpretation of early music. His son, Carl Dolmetsch (1911-), continues his father's work.

dominant Fifth note of the major or minor **scale** above the **tonic**, or the fourth below it. In harmony, the dominant may be said to be the second most important note of the scale after the tonic. See also **secondary dominant**.

Domingo, Placido (1941-) Spanish tenor who, after studying in Mexico, made his début at the Metropolitan Opera House, New York, in 1968. He has toured the world extensively and has appeared in more than 40 roles. He is now one of the best-known and most popular tenors in the world, taking as his main repertory the heroic Italian roles: he excels in the title-role of *Otello*, as Rodolfo in *La bohème*, Cavaradossi in *Tosca*, and Radamès in *Aïda*. He scored a notable success as Don José in *Carmen*. Since 1973 he has also turned to conducting. He has appeared in a film of *Otello*, and has made many recordings, including songs outside the classical repertory.

Placido Domingo

dompe Alternative spelling of **dump**.

Donatoni, Franco (1927-) Italian composer noted for his experimentation with a number of varying styles, and for the composition *Black and White* for two pianos, in which the performers are given no actual notes to play or tempos to follow, just advice about which fingers to use. He has taught in many conservatoires since 1954. Among his compositions are *Per orchestra*, *Strophes* and *Sezioni* for orchestra, three *Improvisations* for piano, and works for strings, brass and percussion.

Donizetti, Gaetano (1797-1848) Italian composer of more than 60 operas. He was born in Bergamo and studied locally under Johann Simon **Mayr**. His first success came at 21 with *Enrico di Borgogna*. The influence of Rossini, Bellini and even Verdi can be discerned in his mature works, the first of which to be widely acclaimed was *Anna Bolena* (1830), one of several based on episodes from English history. This was followed by *L'elisir d'amore* (1832), a wonderfully comic work of perennial appeal; *Lucrezia Borgia* (1833); and *Lucia di Lammermoor* (1835), based on Scott's novel, in which the role of the eponymous heroine provides a superb vehicle for the **coloratura** soprano. In 1839 he went to Paris, where he produced *La fille du régiment* and *La favorite* the following year. The success of *Linda di Chamounix* in 1842 led to his appointment as *Kapellmeister* to the Austrian court. *Don Pasquale*, another delightful comedy, was premièred in Paris in 1843. Other notable works are *Maria*

Stuarda, *Roberto Devereux* and *Caterina Cornaro*. Donizetti's operas provide ample scope for vocal fireworks as well as dramatic and comic opportunities, and remain deservedly popular.

Doppel (Ger.) Double.

Doppelschlag (Ger.) Double stroke, the German equivalent of **turn**.

doppio (It.) Double, for example, *doppio movimento*, at double the preceding speed.

Dorati, Antal (1906-1988) Hungarian composer and conductor who recorded an important collection of Haydn's symphonies with the Philharmonia Hungarica. He studied in Budapest with **Kodály** and **Bartók**. He conducted for several major ballet companies, including the American Ballet Theatre (1941). In 1948 he became an American citizen and continued to conduct, with the Minneapolis Symphony Orchestra (1949), the BBC Symphony Orchestra (1962), the Stockholm Symphony Orchestra (1966), the National Symphony Orchestra of Washington (1970), the Royal Philharmonic (1976) and the Detroit Symphony Orchestra (1977). His compositions include symphonies, a violin concerto, ballets, cantatas and music for strings.

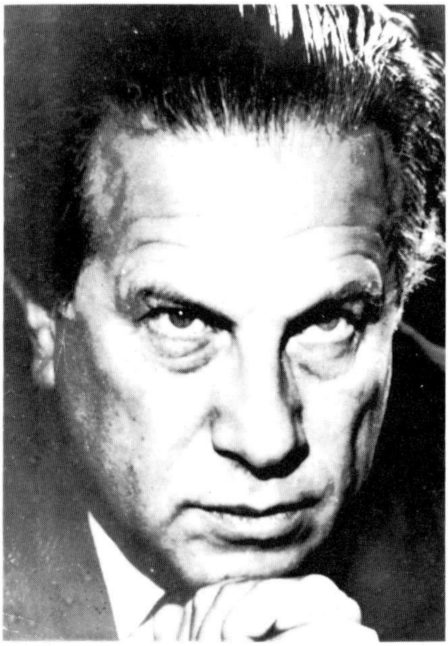

Antal Dorati

Dorian mode First of the Ambrosian **modes**, which are also known as the authentic modes. On the keyboard it can be played as a white-note scale starting on the note D.

dot Indication that the time-value of a note is to be altered. A dot above or under a note normally indicates that the notes are to be played **staccato**. If a dot is placed after a note it means that the time-value of the note should be extended by half. In 1769, Leopold **Mozart** introduced the double dot to indicate that the time-value of the note was to be extended by half and half again.

In French Baroque music, dots (above or below the note) have a special significance as denoting *notes égales*.

In jazz jargon, 'dots' refer to written music.

Dots indicate different things, depending on their position

double 1. The practice of being able and equipped to play two instruments alternately in the same piece. In jazz music, for instance, some clarinettists double on saxophone, and orchestral flautists often double on piccolo.

2. The duplication of a melody or voice by more than one instrument.

3. Used to indicate an instrument of low pitch, such as the double bassoon, double harp, double-bass, etc. See also **doublé**.

doublé (Fr.) Doubled. Form of variation in which the strain of a dance is repeated in a more ornamented version.

double bar Pair of bar lines placed close together to indicate that a piece of music, or a section of it, has come to an end. It may be followed or preceded by a repeat sign.

double-bass Largest string instrument, originally of the **viol** family, with a flat rather than curved back. The earliest examples had five strings, tuned F, A, D, F♯, A. Later these were reduced to three, tuned A, D, E. Around the middle of the 19th century, a fourth string was added, tuned to E. Later in the century, a fifth string was added, tuned to B. Some four-string instruments have an extension on the bottom string taking it to C. It is an important element in small jazz ensembles, played **pizzicato**. Also known as contrabass.

Double-bass

double counterpoint **Invertible counterpoint** in two parts.

double flat Accidental (♭♭) that lowers the pitch of a note by two semitones.

double-reed See **reed instrument**

double sharp Accidental (♯♯ or X) that raises the pitch of a note by two semitones.

double stopping Production of two notes by means of the player's stopping (i.e. fingering) two strings simultaneously on a bowed stringed instrument.

double suspension In harmony, the suspension of two parts to act as a temporary discord against the following chord.

double tonguing Technique whereby a brass or woodwind player articulates very quickly with the tongue against the embouchure, making the sounds T-K or D-G.

double-whole-note American alternative for **breve**.

doux (Fr.) Gentle in volume or sweet in tone, or both.

Dowland, John (1563-1626) English composer, probably born in Westminster. Little is known of his early life, except that he visited Paris in 1580 as the servant of the ambassador, Sir Henry Cobham, and was converted to Catholicism. This prompted Elizabeth I to reject him as a prospective court musician in 1554. Instead, he visited Venice and Florence under the patronage of the Duke of Brunswick and, in 1597, completed his *First Booke of Songs*. In 1598 he was appointed lutenist to Christian IV of Denmark, composing his *Second* (1600) and *Third and Last Booke of Songs* (1603) while holding this position. He was dismissed in 1606, returning to England to be made one of King James I's musicians in 1612.

Dowland's songs – one of his finest is *Flow my Teares* – and his compositions for solo lute are enriched by continental influences as well as by traditional melodies. He is widely regarded today as an important figure in the development of lutine harmonies.

downbeat Alludes to the downward motion of a conductor's baton or hand and refers to the first or stressed beats of a bar. See also **upbeat**.

downbow Motion of the bow in the playing of stringed instruments in which the player pulls the bow from the heel towards the point. The sign indicating a downbow is derived from the N for *Nobilis*.

Downes, Edward (1924-) British conductor and horn-player who studied with Scherchen. He was associate conductor at the Royal Opera (1952-69), music director of the Australian Opera (1972-6), and has been guest conductor with many leading symphony orchestras. Since 1980 he has been principal conductor of the BBC Philharmonic Orchestra in Manchester. He is noted as the first English conductor since World War II to present Wagner's *Der Ring des Nibelungen* (in 1967). He has also conducted several important premières of new works such as Maxwell **Davies's** *Taverner* (1972) and **Bennett's** *Victory* (1970).

Downes, Ralph (1904-) British organist who has appeared as a recitalist on many occasions. As a noted organ designer, he was responsible for the organ at the Royal Festival Hall, London.

Draghi, Giovanni Battista (1640-1710) Italian composer and harpsichordist who moved to England and became organist to Queen Catherine of Braganza at the court of Charles II, and taught music to the future Queen Anne. His compositions include a setting of Dryden's ode *From Harmony, From Heavenly Harmony*, his *Song for St Cecilia's Day* (1687), and a number of pieces for harpsichord and organ.

Dragonetti, Domenico (1763-1846) Italian double-bass player and composer. At the age of 13 he was admitted to the opera orchestra at Venice. His works include several concertos for double-bass. From 1794 he settled in London, where he formed a partnership with the cellist Lindley.

dramma per musica (It.) Play through music. 17th-century term for **opera**.

Drdla, Frantisek (1868-1944) Czech composer and violinist who became a member of the Vienna Court Opera orchestra. He composed two operettas, songs, piano pieces and works for the violin and piano such as *Serenade* and *Souvenir*, which are still popular today.

Dresden Amen Threefold version of the sung Amen, associated with the Royal Chapel of Dresden. Using a traditional melody, this particular setting was composed (*c.*1764) by J.G. **Naumann**.

Drigo, Riccardo (1846-1930) Italian composer and conductor who is best known for the *Serenade* from his ballet *Les millions d'Arléquin* (1900). He was conductor at the St Petersburg Court Opera from 1876 and became the principal conductor at the Maryinsky Theatre in 1886. He composed operatic works as well as ballets and chamber pieces.

drone Three lower pipes of the **bagpipe** that provide a continuous, fixed chord above which the melody is played on the chanter. A drone is also evident in many forms of Eastern music. The term is also used to indicate a similar effect in other music.

Druckman, Jacob Raphael (1928-) American composer who was awarded a Pulitzer Prize (1972) for his orchestral composition *Windows*. He studied at the Juilliard School (1949-56) with **Copland**, Mennin and **Wagenaar**. In 1957 he studied in Paris and finally moved to the Columbia-Princeton Electronic Music Center, 1965. He has also been associated with electronic music studios at other universities. Among his compositions are impressionistic orchestral pieces including *Chiaroscuro* (1976) and *Lamia* (1974) for soprano and orchestra. He also worked extensively with tape, notably in his *Animus* in three parts (1966, 1968, 1969).

drum Popular term for the family of membranophones which includes in

Western music the following instruments: kettledrums (timpani), bass drum, bongos, snare drum, tabor, tambourine, tenor drum. Some drums have a specific pitch (e.g. the kettledrums are tuneable either by taps which are positioned at points around the side of the instrument to change the tension of the membrane and thus the pitch of the note produced, or by pedals, which perform the same function). Other drums are of indefinite pitch.

drumstick Wooden stick used to strike a drum. Drumsticks come in many shapes and sizes, and the head of the stick may be hard or soft.

Dubensky, Arkady (1890-1966) Russian composer and violinist who was notable for the unusual combinations of instruments demanded by his compositions. He studied at the Moscow Conservatoire and became leader of the Moscow Imperial Opera Orchestra. In 1921 he moved to the United States and joined the New York Symphony Orchestra. His compositions include a fugue for 18 violins, *Fantasy on Negro Themes* for tuba and orchestra, an overture for 18 toy trumpets, and a concerto for three trombones, tuba and orchestra.

Dubois, Théodore (1837-1924) French composer and organist who composed a number of operas, ballets, cantatas and orchestral pieces, and was an influential teacher. He studied at the Paris Conservatoire and became professor of harmony there in 1871. In 1877 he became organist at La Madeleine, returning to the Conservatoire as director in 1896. He resigned this post in 1905 in support of **Ravel**, who had been refused the chance to compete for the Prix de Rome by a prejudiced jury. He is best known for his sacred music and writings on harmony and counterpoint.

due corde (It.) Two strings. In violin music, indicates that a section is to be played on two strings rather than one, to give an undulating effect. In piano music, the term indicates that the pedal is to be partly raised to allow two strings to be struck; it can then be fully raised to allow three to be struck.

duet Composition for two performers (vocal or instrumental), with or without accompaniment. For example, a piano duet is a work for two pianists at one keyboard (as opposed to a duet for two pianos).

Dufay, Guillaume (*c.*1400-1474) French composer, regarded by both his contemporaries and modern experts as probably the greatest of the 15th century. After singing in the choir at Cambrai Cathedral, he spent his 20s and 30s in Italy, singing in the Papal chapel and discharging the duties of curate in Savoy. In 1434 he met the Franco-Flemish composer **Binchois**. Back in Cambrai on a fairly regular basis from 1439, Dufay served as a cleric at the cathedral. Nearly 200 works by him survive, including eight complete Masses and more than 80 songs. He may have been the first to use a secular folk-tune such as *L'homme armé* as the *cantus firmus* (core melody) of a Mass. His warm harmonies and expressive melodies prefigure the music of the Renaissance. He is also said to have composed the earliest Requiem, now lost.

Dukas, Paul (1865-1935) French composer and widely respected critic, who wrote the first piano sonata by a major French composer (the piano sonata in E♭ minor, 1901), and who developed some of **Debussy**'s techniques in his work.

He studied at the Paris Conservatoire (1882-9), became a professor of composition there in 1909, and devoted his time to musical criticism. In the 1920s his confidence failed him and he destroyed much of his work. He passed his later years assisting **Saint-Saëns** in the completion of Guiraud's opera *Frédégonde* and editing some operas by **Rameau**. His most famous composition is the orchestral scherzo *The Sorcerer's Apprentice* (1897). He also composed operas – including the acclaimed *Ariane et Barbe-bleue* (1907) – and the ballet *La péri* (1912). He was admired for his orchestration, and highly regarded as a teacher and critic.

Duke, Vernon (1903-1969) Russian-born composer whose original name was Vladimir Dukelsky. He became an American citizen (1922) and, under his new name, composed for the cinema, sometimes working with Harberg. His song *April in Paris* for the 1952 film of the same name has become a classic. He studied music at the Kiev Conservatoire with **Glière**. His ballet *Zéphyr et Flore* was produced by Diaghilev's Ballets Russes in 1925. He wrote other ballets, concertos for the piano, violin and cello, and a harpsichord sonata.

dulcimer Instrument with a set of strings stretched over a sound-board which are struck by hammers. The Hungarian **cimbalon** is the only type of dulcimer still in use.

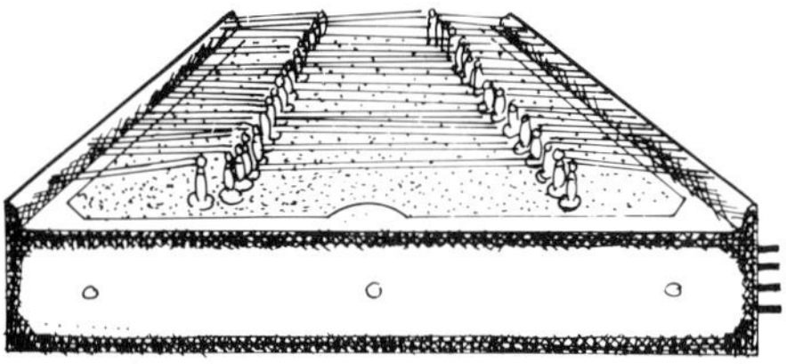

Dulcimer

dumka Lament of Slavonic folk-origin which takes the form of a slow piece alternating with more animated sections. The form was used by **Dvořák** in his piano trio *Dumky* (1891).

dump Name used in the 16th and 17th centuries for a doleful piece of English music. An alternative spelling is dompe.

dung-chen (Tibet) Large, straight trumpet which is typically two to three metres long and constructed with telescopic sections of copper or brass, and a mouthpiece. Although it probably has military origins, it is now used in pairs in Buddhist ritual to provide drones and occasional two- or three-note patterns.

Dunhill, Thomas (1877-1946) British composer, teacher and writer who was a pupil of **Stanford**. Dunhill is best remembered for his didactic compositions, mostly for the piano. Other works include a symphonic operetta *Tantivy Towers* (1931), *Elegiac Voices* (1933), a symphony, chamber music and songs.

Duni, Egidio (1708-1775) Italian-born composer who settled in Paris in 1757. He became a leading composer of **opéras-comiques** such as *Le caprice amoureux*, *Le milicien* and *Les sabots*.

Dunstable, John (*c.*1385-1453) English composer and mathematician who was known throughout Europe. His work has been discovered in early French and Italian manuscript collections. He was one of the first composers to use an instrumental accompaniment for devotional music. He was in the service of the Duke of Bedford, who was Regent of France (1422-35), and he was able to travel widely. His compositions – notably his setting of *O rosa bella* – reflect the influences of **Dufay** and **Binchois**. He wrote a number of Masses, as well as other choral pieces, and was an authoritative author of astronomical texts.

duo 1. Composition for two voices or instruments.

2. Name given to the players who perform such a composition. See also **duet**.

Duparc, Henri Fouques (1848-1933) French pianist and composer whose settings of Baudelaire's poems, particularly *L'invitation au voyage*, brought new emphasis to the importance of song texts. Educated under **Franck** at the Jesuit College of Vaugirard, he joined Franck's collective of composers and travelled to Weimar to study Teutonic styles. He was strongly influenced by Wagner, whom he met at Liszt's house in 1869. His interest in literature dictated his choice of texts for his songs, but he wrote only 16, and very few other pieces, as he became seriously ill at the age of 36 and stopped composing.

duplet Group of two notes that occupy a time of three. Also known as a couplet, marked with a figure 2.

Duplet

duple time Time signature that indicates two beats in the bar, such as 2/4 or 6/8.

Duplex-coupler piano Piano with two keyboards tuned an octave apart. Designed in 1921 by Emanuel Moor (1863-1931).

du Pré, Jacqueline (1945-1987) British cellist who studied with **Tortelier** and **Rostropovich**. She gained a world-wide reputation as a soloist but was stricken in 1972 with multiple sclerosis, which later brought about her untimely death. When she was no longer able to play she taught extensively. In 1967 she married Daniel **Barenboim**, the pianist and conductor. She recorded widely, and is especially associated with **Elgar**'s Cello Concerto.

Dupré, Marcel (1886-1971) French composer and organist. He studied at the Paris Conservatoire and gained the Prix de Rome (1914) as a pupil of **Widor**. He became the first organist to present the complete cycle of Bach's organ music. As director of the Paris Conservatoire (1954-6) he edited the organ works of Liszt, Schumann, Bach and Handel. His compositions include many organ works, including two organ symphonies, other symphonic pieces, and a violin sonata.

dur (Ger.) Equivalent of the English major, referring to the major key.

Durante, Francesco (1684-1755) Italian composer associated with the Neapolitan School. He studied with **Scarlatti** and became *maestro di cappella* at the Conservatorio de S. Maria di Loreto in 1742. His compositions include devotional music and pieces for the harpsichord and strings. He was an influential tutor, numbering **Piccinni**, **Pergolesi** and **Jommelli** among his pupils.

Durchführung (Ger.) Equivalent of the English **development**.

durchkomponiert (Ger.) Through-composed. Term used for a work, especially a song in a continuous form, that does not repeat itself in successive stanzas.

Durey, Louis (1888-1979) French composer who attended the Schola Cantorum, Paris, and joined Les **Six** (1920), abandoning them a year later. His works include three string quartets and other chamber compositions, songs, choral music and an opera (*L'occasion*).

Durkó, Zsolt (1934-) Hungarian composer, pupil of **Petrassi** and Farkas. Among his works are *Hungarian Rhapsody* for two clarinets and orchestra (1964), *Altamira* (1968) and the music drama *Mozes* (1977).

Duruflé, Maurice (1902-1986) French organist and composer who was a pupil of **Vierne**, and later became a professor at the Paris Conservatoire (1943). His compositions include *Prélude et fugue sur le nom Alain* (1942) for the organ, *Cum Jubilo* (1967) and *Requiem* (1947) for organ, orchestra and choir, as well as some fine unaccompanied motets.

Dussek, Johann Ladislav (1760-1812) Bohemian pianist and composer, a pupil of C.P.E. **Bach** and friend of Haydn. He was a prolific composer, writing 28 piano sonatas and 15 concertos, 38 violin and 16 flute sonatas, as well as pieces for two pianos, a ballad opera and a Mass. An alternative spelling of his name is Jan Dusik.

Dutilleux, Henri (1916-) French composer noted for his technical skills and use of dissonant styles as well as his development of styles initiated by **Ravel** and **Roussel**. He studied at the Paris Conservatoire and was awarded the Prix de Rome in 1938. He became a broadcaster in 1944, and in 1961 was appointed professor of composition at the Ecole Normale de Musique. His compositions include two symphonies (1950, 1958), a ballet, *Le loup* (1953), sonatas for the piano and oboe, string quartets, music for film, and more recently a violin concerto.

Dvořák, Antonin (1841-1904) Czech (Bohemian) composer, the most renowned of his nation. Born in a village near Prague, he went to study violin in that city (1857) and became a viola player in **Smetana**'s orchestra at the Opera, taking part in the première of *The Bartered Bride* and absorbing the influence of the composer. He was also strongly influenced by Wagner in his early years. His first two symphonies are now rarely heard, but he achieved recognition with his third (1873), which won the Austrian State prize, and his fourth; these brought encouragement from Brahms. A few years later (in 1877) he produced his first choral work, *Stabat Mater*, and in the following year published his first set of *Slavonic Dances* for piano duet, which he also orchestrated; the nationalistic element which he celebrated in these pieces, and in the *String Sextet* of the same year, was a development of his earlier use of Czech folk idiom. These Czech forms – the **dumka**, the polka, the **furiant** – appeared again and again in works of all genres: a set of *Slavonic Rhapsodies* (1878), the Symphony No.6 (1880), a further set of *Slavonic Dances* (1886) and the *Dumky Piano Trio* (1891).

As Dvořák's fame spread abroad, he was invited to England in 1884, the first of nine visits, when he conducted his own compositions, many of them newly commissioned by Birmingham (the cantata *The Spectre's Bride*, 1884), the Philharmonic Society in London (Symphony No.7, 1885) and Leeds (the oratorio *St Ludmilla*, 1886); an honorary doctorate was also conferred on him by Cambridge University. In 1891 he went to the United States as director of the National Conservatory, New York. He spent three years there, absorbing American musical idioms both black and Amerindian; while clearly the work of a Czech, his Symphony No.9 *From the New World* shows some of these influences, as well as the atmosphere of Longfellow's famous poems about the Amerindian Hiawatha; the same rhythmic vitality is to be found in String Quartet No.12, *The American*. The fame of these works has tended to obscure the superb qualities of his other works, particularly the symphonies No.7 in D minor and No.8 in G, and the wide range of chamber music. The *Cello Concerto* (1895) is a masterly achievement, especially considering the

Antonin Dvořák

problems of balance with such a solo instrument.

On his return to Prague he composed more chamber works (the two fine string quartets of 1895 and 1896), and a number of symphonic poems, but concentrated on opera in his last years. He wrote ten operas, but only *Rusalka* (1901) has achieved lasting popularity, although *Kate and the Devil* (1899) and *Armida* (1904) are occasionally staged. *Rusalka*, the tale of a water-nymph who longs to become human in order to consummate her love for a prince, contains the famous aria *O Silver Moon*, one of the most lyrical passages in an outstandingly beautiful score. Dvořák's music is characterized by warmth, colour and emotional intensity, built on a powerful sense of form, which owed much to the example and encouragement of Brahms. It is an irony of fate that in many respects Dvořák's great popularity today exceeds that of his model and mentor.

Dykes, John Bacchus (1823-1876) British composer and Anglican clergyman who composed many hymn tunes, along with other church music. He assisted in compiling *Hymns Ancient & Modern* and composed some hymns himself, including *Nearer my God to Thee* and *Jesu, Lover of my Soul.*

dynamics Graduations of volume in music.

Dyson, Sir George (1883-1964) English composer and organist, best known for his composition *The Canterbury Pilgrims* (1931) which is a cantata setting of Chaucer's text (modernized), first performed in Winchester in 1941. He studied at the Royal College of Music before travelling to Italy and Germany on a scholarship (1904-8). He taught music at English public schools, including Rugby and Winchester, and became director of the Royal College of Music in 1937. He was knighted in 1941. Among his other compositions are the orchestral works *St Paul's Voyage to Melita* (1933) and *Quo Vadis* (1939).

Dzerzhinsky, Ivan Ivanovich (1909-1978) Russian operatic composer whose work is considered to be technically naive and dependent for its form and melodic character upon Russian folk-songs. But when **Shostakovich** fell from favour with the Soviet government in 1936 for producing works in which *Pravda* detected 'petty-bourgeois sensationalism', Dzerzhinsky's work was used as a model of correctness, perhaps because of the closeness of its ties with traditional music. He produced a number of operas, including *Quiet Flows the Don* (1935), *Virgin Soil Upturned* (1937), *Blood of the People* (1941) and *Grigory Melekhov* (1967). He also composed for the piano and orchestra.

E

E Fifth note of the scale, one tone above D and one semitone below F. The scale of E major has four sharps in the key-signature.

E E major

Eastwood, Thomas (1922-) English composer who studied in Turkey, in Berlin with **Blacher** and in London with Stein. His *String Trio* won first prize at the 1949 Cheltenham Festival. He has concentrated on theatrical and broadcast works: *Christopher Sly* (1960) is an opera based on Shakespeare's *The Taming of the Shrew*; the opera *The Rebel* was written for television in 1969. He has composed incidental music for many plays, especially those staged by the Royal Court Theatre in London: Osborne's *Look Back in Anger*, Wycherley's *The Country Wife*, and *Héloïse and Abélard* among them. His scores for radio and television include *Mary Queen of Scots* and *A Picture of Katherine Mansfield*. He has also composed a concerto for violin and viola, *Amphora* for guitar, and choral works (*Three American Settings*, 1972).

Edinburgh International Festival Annual international festival of the arts held in three weeks in August and September. Main festival activities include concert performances, recitals and operas, although there is also a very active 'fringe' festival involving many less formal performances, especially of plays and revues. The festival was founded in 1947 under Rudolf Bing, and his successors have included Ian Hunter (1949-61), Robert Ponsonby (1961-6), Peter Diamand (1966-78), John Drummond (1979-85) and Frank Dunlop (since 1986). Almost all the major world orchestras have appeared at Edinburgh.

Edwards, Ross (1943-) Australian composer who studied at the New South Wales Conservatorium and with Maxwell **Davies**, **Meale** and **Veress**. He has written three string quartets, the second of which was commissioned by the Australian Musica Viva Society for the bicentenary of Captain Cook's discovery of the continent. He has also composed much other chamber music, including a wind quintet, and orchestral music (*Etude*; *Choros* for piano and orchestra, 1971). He is drawn to the techniques of medieval music, and this informs the music for his nativity play *Quem quaeritis*.

Egk, Werner (1901-1983) German composer. He studied in Frankfurt, and in Munich with **Orff**. He then spent two years in Italy. His earliest works were scores for radio; his first major composition was an oratorio, *Furchtlosigkeit und Wohlwollen* (1931), followed by an opera, *Columbus* (1932), for radio. He was invited to write the *Olympische Festmusik* for the famous Olympic Games of 1936 in Berlin, for which he was given a medal. His first opera for the stage was *Die Zaubergeige* (The Magic Fiddle), performed in 1937; this led to a post as guest conductor of the Berlin Staatsoper, which he held until 1941. He was director of the Berlin Hochschule (1950-3) and in 1968 was made president of the German Music Council.

Among his many stage works are *Peer Gynt* (opera, 1938), *Joan von Zarissa* (opera, 1940, on the Don Juan theme), *Abraxas* (ballet, 1948, on the Faust legend), *Siebzehn Tage und Vier Minuten* (opera, 1966, a revision of an earlier work), *Der Revisor* (opera, 1957, based on Gogol) and *Irische Legende* (opera, 1970, based on Yeats). His orchestral suites were often taken from his operas and ballets. He also composed choral works, songs, and a piano sonata (1947). His fluid, lively style was influenced by Debussy and Stravinsky, among others.

Einem, Gottfried von (1918-) Austrian composer. His earliest posts were as a coach at Berlin and Bayreuth. His opposition to the Nazi regime led to his arrest; later he was able to help many vulnerable people escape, and his strong views on freedom and justice for all mankind were central to many of his works. From 1941 to 1943 he studied with **Blacher**, who was also out of favour with the regime. His first work for the stage was a ballet, *Prinzessin Turandot* (1944). He worked at the Dresden Staatsoper for a while, producing his first opera, *Dantons Tod*, in 1947. This brought him wide recognition, and he joined the board of the Salzburg Festival and the Konzerthausgesellschaft, Vienna. He was director of the Vienna Festival, 1960-4, and then became professor of composition at the Vienna Hochschule. His second opera, *Der Prozess* (The Trial, 1953), was based on Kafka but also reflected his wartime experiences. His next, *Der Zerrissene* (1964), was a comedy. *Der Besuch der alten Dame* (The Visit of the Old Lady, 1971) was a great success; it was given in English at Glyndebourne in 1973. His last opera was based on Schiller: *Kabale und Liebe* (1976). He also composed several ballets, two symphonies (the *Philadelphia* and the *Vienna*), concertos for piano and for violin, some large-scale choral music (the oratorio *An die Nach geborenen*, 1975), the song-cycle *Rosa Mystica* for baritone and orchestra (1972), songs and chamber music.

Einleitung (Ger.) Introduction; prelude.

eisteddfod Competitive festival of music and literature that originated in Wales. One form of *eisteddfod* is an annual international festival held in Llangollen, Wales, where choirs and dancers from all over the world compete. The present festival was started in 1947.

A second type is the National Eisteddfod, founded in 1880, which is held in a different Welsh town every year, to assess the accomplishments of the bards (poets). Festivals of this kind date back to the Middle Ages, although the term *eisteddfod* was not used until the 18th century.

Elder, Mark (1947-) English conductor and bassoonist who studied at Cambridge University. In 1970 he acted as assistant to Raymond **Leppard** at **Glyndebourne**. Conducting posts have included Covent Garden and Australian Opera (1972-4) and he was appointed principal conductor of the **English National Opera** in 1979, where he has been responsible (with David Pountney, the artistic director) for the adoption into the repertory of many challenging 20th-century operas. Elder is especially noted for his interpretations of Richard Strauss.

electronic music Music which is produced or changed by electrophonic instruments. Often the musical elements are assembled on magnetic tape, using electronic sound-mixing equipment, synthesizers and computerized instruments (such as drum machines). Sometimes electronic instruments and computers are used in live performance in conjunction with conventional musicians. One form of popular electronically-produced music that has come to the fore recently is known as house music, in which motifs, tunes and rhythms previously recorded (and often the copyright of someone else) are 'sampled' electronically and then put together to form a coherent composition.

electronic organ Organ in which signals created by electronic oscillators are amplified and converted into sound by a loudspeaker. A modern electronic organ usually has two or three manuals and an electronic rhythm section, and can produce a wide variety of sounds.

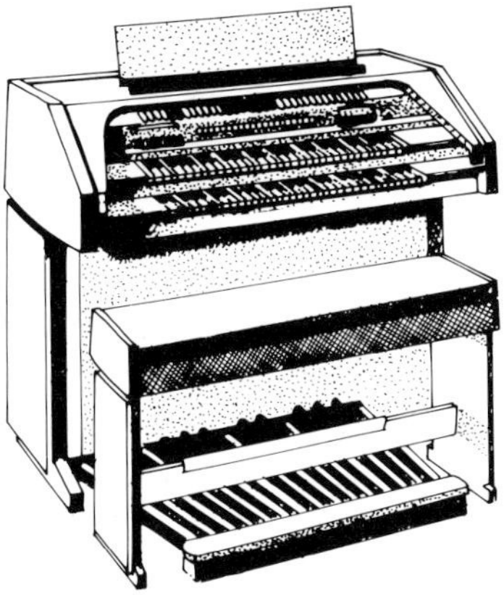

Electronic organ

electrophonic Describing musical instruments in which the notes are transmitted through electric circuits to amplifiers. Instruments such as the electric guitar, violin and piano are electrophonic instruments.

elegy Vocal or instrumental piece of reflective or mournful quality, named after the poetic form of the same nature. **Berlioz**'s *Elégie en prose* from *Neuf mélodies irlandaises* (1830), which he dedicated to Harriet Smithson, is an example of this type of composition.

Elgar, Sir Edward (1857-1934) English composer and conductor, born in Broadheath, a tiny village in Worcestershire, where the house is now kept as a museum. His father had a small music shop in Worcester, worked as a piano-tuner, was organist at the Roman Catholic church, and played in local orchestras. Edward learned the violin, the piano and organ from his father, but in composition was largely self-taught. Without family resources or a rich patron he was forced to leave school at the age of 15. After a desultory few months in a lawyer's office he left to start his career as a musician, playing in local bands and teaching. His earliest compositions were for the church or for family gatherings, for which he learned the cello, the bassoon, and the double-bass – he used many of the tunes in mature compositions such as *The Wand of Youth*.

His early light orchestral works were played in Birmingham, and at the Crystal Palace in London, but he was still no more than a minor local celebrity. In 1889 he married one of his pupils – Alice Roberts, daughter of the late Major-General Roberts of the Indian Army. Undeterred by her family's disapproval she set about fostering her husband's great gifts as a composer. He turned to the lucrative oratorio market and with *The Black Knight* (1892), *Lux Christi* (1896) and *Caractacus* (1898) made a powerful impact, particularly through the brilliance of his writing for orchestra. This was reinforced by the performance in London in 1899 under Hans **Richter** of his *Enigma Variations*, a unique collection of musical portraits of his friends based on a theme whose secret was never divulged. The following year he completed *The Dream of Gerontius*, a setting of the poem by Cardinal Newman. Despite a disastrous, under-rehearsed première in Birmingham under Richter, a performance in Germany in 1901 revealed this to be a choral masterpiece. Honours were now showered upon him, and in 1901 Elgar was awarded a doctorate of music by Cambridge University. In 1903 he completed *The Apostles* to his own text, intended to be the first of a great oratorio trilogy on the life of Christ, though only

Sir Edward Elgar

the second part, *The Kingdom*, was added in 1906. Elgar's rich melodic vein captured the affection of a vast public in such works as the *Overture, Cockaigne* (1901) and his *Pomp and Circumstance Marches*, and as a result he was commissioned by Covent Garden to write an ode to celebrate the coronation of King Edward VII. The King himself suggested that words (by A.C.Benson) be added to the great tune of the first march, which we now know as *Land of Hope and Glory*. In 1904 his national fame was recognized with a knighthood, and a three-day festival of his music was held in London, an honour never before accorded to a native musician. Elgar's first symphony was completed in 1908; its première in Manchester under its dedicatee Hans Richter was such a success that within the following 12 months it received over a hundred performances. With the violin concerto, first played by Fritz **Kreisler** in 1910, the Symphony No.2 (1910), and the symphonic study *Falstaff* (1913), Elgar now commanded an international reputation.

In the closing years of World War I, as though needing to express more intimate feelings, Elgar turned to chamber music with the Violin Sonata and String Quartet (1918), and the Piano Quintet (1919). This elegiac mood was echoed in the Cello Concerto, which was soon established as an essential part of that instrument's meagre concerto repertory.

In 1920 Elgar was deeply affected by the death of his wife, in some ways the motive force of his genius. In the following years he composed few works of importance: the surface impression of Edwardian grandeur offered little appeal to audiences still numbed by the horrors of the war, or to critics dazzled by the new music of Stravinsky, Schoenberg and their followers, although there was some compensation in being appointed Master of the King's Musick in 1924.

In his final years he took advantage of the development of recording to leave an imcomparable archive of works performed under his direction; this greatly speeded the reappraisal of his music that has placed him among the leading composers of the century. Perhaps the most telling feature of this has been the enthusiasm of foreign conductors, notably in Russia, for music which was once regarded as quintessentially English.

Elizalde, Federico (1907-1979) Spanish composer and pianist. After a number of successes on the jazz scene in England during the 1920s, he became conductor of the Manila Symphony Orchestra in 1930 and President of the Manila Broadcasting Company in 1948. His best-known work is the opera *Paul Gauguin*, which reflects the influences of his tutor, **Bloch**.

Ellington, Duke (Edward Kennedy) (1899-1974) American jazz conductor, composer, orchestrator and pianist who came to have a seminal influence on the development of jazz music.

Ellington was born in Washington D.C., but achieved his first success at New York's Cotton Club. He wrote hundreds of pieces during his career, for his own band, and also for stage and screen, providing film scores for *Anatomy of a Murder*, *Paris Blues* and *Assault on a Queen*. He developed many styles of composition, extending pieces such as *Black, Brown and Beige* (1943) beyond the usual 32-bar format to allow his themes to develop unhindered. He also experimented with vocal works, adapting songs from Shakespeare's plays in *Such Sweet Thunder*, and using the voice of Adelaide Hall as an instrument in *Creole Love Call*. Among his other works, *Take the 'A'-Train* and *Mood Indigo* are possibly the most enduring.

Ellis, Osian (1928-) Welsh harpist and singer. Born in Ffynnongroew, now in Clwyd, he attended the Royal Academy of Music. He has gained a great reputation both inside and outside Wales as an exponent of Welsh folk-song, especially the form known as **penillion**, in which the words of a poem are sung as a composed or improvised **descant** to a traditional melody or *alaw*, played on a harp. Ellis's reputation has also spread to the field of better-known music. He is a member of the British chamber group, the Melos Ensemble, and was a close friend of **Britten**, who wrote his *Harp Suite* Op.83 for him.

Eloy, Jean-Claude (1938-) French composer who studied under **Milhaud** at the Paris Conservatoire and **Boulez** at the Basle Academy of Music. Much of his orchestral work, particularly his *Polychromes I & II* (1964) and *Faisceaux-Diffractions* (1970), display the influence of his tutors in their polychromatic style. His work has become popular in the United States following his visit there in 1967.

embouchure (Fr.) Mouthpiece, meaning the position and application of the lips to the mouthpiece of a wind instrument.

enchaînez (Fr.) From *enchaîner*, to link together. Indication that the next movement or section of a piece should follow its predecessor without a break.

Encina, Juan del (1468-*c*.1530) Spanish poet and composer of romances and villancios. Most of these were reprinted in Barbieri's *Cancionero* (1890). Encina is known to have entered the service of the Duke of Alba from 1492. He then moved to Rome as a cleric and became the Archdeacon of Málaga in 1509, and finally the Prior of León in 1519.

encore (Fr.) Again. Used in English as a call to a performer to repeat all or part of a work just played or sung. On some occasions an encore is not a repetition, but a different piece. The word is not used in French for such an occasion: instead the Latin *bis* is used.

en dehors (Fr.) Outside. An indication that a melody or instrument should stand out.

Enescu, George (1881-1955) Hailed as the 'father of Romanian national music', Enescu blended themes from folk-songs with powerful romantic colours in his work, particularly in his two *Romanian Rhapsodies* (1901 and 1902). Born in Liveni-Virnav, Enescu became an accomplished violinist and recitalist, studying in Vienna and entering the Paris Conservatoire in 1897. While there, he conducted his own work and became one of **Menuhin**'s tutors. He wrote an opera and five symphonies.

English Chamber Orchestra British chamber orchestra, founded by Arnold Goldsbrough and Lawrence Leonard in 1948 (when it was known as the Goldsbrough Orchestra). It changed its name in 1960 when the repertory progressed beyond 18th-century music.

Although primarily known for its classical music, the English Chamber Orchestra has been associated with Benjamin **Britten** and the **Aldeburgh Festival**, and has performed many premières of the works of British composers. It has no permanent conductor, but regular conductors have included Colin **Davis**, Daniel **Barenboim**, Raymond **Leppard** and Pinchas **Zukerman**.

English Concert Ensemble founded in 1973 by Trevor **Pinnock** to perform early music on authentic instruments, following the practice of the period. Their performances and recordings of the **Baroque** repertory are greatly admired: they have recorded all the Brandenburg Concertos of J.S. Bach, much of Handel's music and works by Vivaldi, Purcell, Albinoni and Corelli. They have also performed Haydn's works with success.

English horn Alternative term for **cor anglais**.

English Music Theatre Company Founded in 1947 by Benjamin **Britten**, John Piper and Eric Crozier, when it was called the English Opera Group. Its main objectives were to create and perform new operas and to encourage poets and playwrights to write librettos in collaboration with composers. Since its foundation it has been responsible for establishing and directing the **Aldeburgh Festival** (1948). Among the new works it has produced are Britten's *Albert Herring* (1947), *The Turn of the Screw* (1954) and *Death in Venice* (1973); Lennox **Berkeley**'s *A Dinner Engagement* (1954) and *Ruth* (1956), and Harrison **Birtwistle**'s *Punch and Judy* (1968).

In 1964 the group became the first British opera company to tour the Soviet Union. The management of the company was taken over in 1961 by Covent Garden, and in 1975 it was reorganized under its present name.

English National Opera British opera company based in London, which before 1974 was known as Sadler's Wells Opera. The original Sadler's Wells Theatre was built in 1765; musical performances were held there, and in the 19th century the occasional opera was also produced. At one stage the theatre operated as a music hall until it fell into disuse. In 1931 it became the northern branch of the Old Vic Theatre for the alternate production of classical drama and opera. From 1935 plays were confined to the Old Vic and opera to Sadler's Wells. In 1948 Norman Tucker began his long association with the company. Sadler's Wells expanded and many new operas and existing operas were produced, all performed in English.

The company moved to the Coliseum Theatre in 1968 under the direction of Stephen Arlen. At its new home there were several adventurous productions such as Berlioz's *Damnation de Faust*, Prokofiev's *War and Peace*, and the *Ring* cycle conducted by Reginald **Goodall**. The company's musical directors have included Sir Alexander **Gibson**, Sir Colin **Davis**, Sir Charles **Mackerras**, Sir Charles **Groves** and Mark **Elder**. Since the early 1980s the repertory, under the aegis of the Elder/David Pountney partnership, has expanded to include less frequently performed works such as Prokofiev's *The Gambler* and *The Love for Three Oranges*; Janáček's *The Cunning Little Vixen* and *The Makropoulos Case*. Light opera has also been a great success, notably Jonathan Miller's production of Gilbert and Sullivan's *The Mikado*.

English Opera Group The earliest name for the **English Music Theatre Company**.

enharmonic interval Note that has changed its name but not its pitch. For example, when F♯ becomes G♭ or B♯ becomes C.

ensemble (Fr.) Together. 1. A group of performers, either vocalists or instrumentalists, of no fixed number.

2. Used to describe a group's ability to play together – they are either good ensemble or bad ensemble.

3. An item in an opera in which two or more soloists sing together, such as a duet, trio or quartet.

entr'acte (Fr.) Music played between the acts of plays and operas. See also **intermezzo**.

entrée (Fr.) Dance or group of dances unified by subject in French 17th-century *ballet de cour.* The term thus often signified a scene. In later *tragédie lyrique* and opera-ballet it was used for the instrumental march or air at the start of the **divertissement** of songs and dances found in most acts.

epicedium Mournful funeral ode such as **Blow**'s *The Queen's Epicedium* (1695) on the death of Queen Mary II, based on a poem by George Herbert.

episode Incidental passage in a composition which is a digression from the main theme or themes. For example, in a **rondo** it is a contrasting section between recurrences of the main theme, whereas in a **fugue** it is a passage that does not contain a complete entry of the subject. It may, however, be derived from the main thematic material.

éponge (Fr.) Sponge. *Baguettes d'éponge* refers to drumsticks with sponge heads.

equale (It.) Equal. Voices or instruments of equal pitch. The term was used specifically for formal funeral music such as Beethoven's three *Equali* (1812) for trombone quartet.

equal voices 1. A vocal composition written for voices of equal or comparable range, such as two sopranos or three tenors.

2. It has come to mean more loosely music for only female or only male voices.

Erb, Donald James (1927-) American composer, born in Youngstown, Ohio, who studied at Ohio State University, the Cleveland Institute, and at the Paris Conservatoire with **Boulanger**. He created a style of composition that used tape recorders and electronic sound mixers in conjunction with traditional instruments.

Erbse, Heimo (1924-) German composer who was influenced by the tonal and variable rhythm techniques of his tutor Boris **Blacher**. He studied in Weimar from 1945 and entered the Berlin Hochschule in 1950. He became a producer of opera and a singing tutor in 1947. His compositions include the operas *Julietta* and *Der Herr in Grau*, as well as pieces for chorus, orchestra and wind instruments.

erh-hu (China) Two-stringed fiddle with a hexagonal sound box. Both the neck and body are made of wood, and one side of the hexagon is covered with snakeskin. The strings are attached to the top of the neck and to the sound box, forming an angle with the neck, there being no bridge. It is bowed held vertically and used in the orchestra of the traditional Chinese opera, as well as being a popular solo instrument.

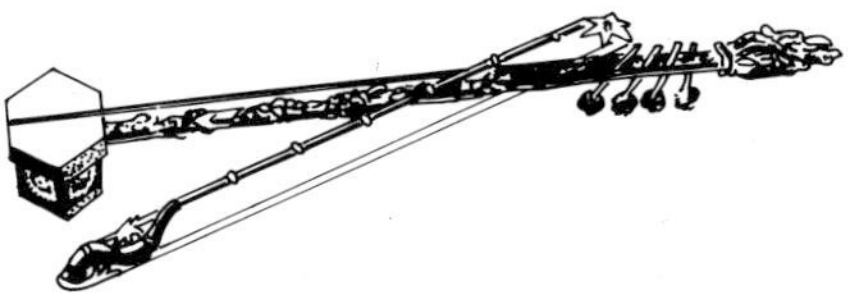

Erh-hu

Erickson, Robert (1917-) Avant-garde American composer, influenced by dodecaphonic forms and by the patterns of *musique concrète.* Erickson studied and taught at the San Francisco Conservatory (1957) and San Diego University (1967).

He was influenced by **Krenek**'s theories of free **atonality** and abandoned the **twelve-note** form in 1957 to concentrate on freer techniques. This new freedom is shown in his *Chamber Concerto* (1960) and in *High Flyer* (1969).

Erkel, Ferenc (1810-1893) Hungarian conductor and nationalist composer who enjoyed as much adulation from Hungarians as **Smetana** from his Czech compatriots. He became conductor of the Budapest National Theatre (1838) and founded the Budapest Philharmonic Orchestra (1840). As a professor at the Hungarian National Academy of Music he encouraged composers in the use of ethnic idioms, and always strove to preserve a national musical identity among his pupils. His opera *Hunyady László* (1844) was a great success, as was his *Bánk Bán* (1844-52), which is still played on the national holiday. He also composed the music for the Hungarian national anthem.

Ernst, Heinrich Wilhelm (1814-1865) Moravian composer and violinist who modelled his style on the legendary **Paganini**. He studied at the Vienna Conservatoire before moving to Paris in 1832. He toured Europe as a performer before settling in London in 1855. He composed a number of concertos and other pieces for violin.

Eschenbach, Christoph (1940-) German pianist. He studied in Cologne and Hamburg, and won a prize at the Munich International Competition, 1962, and at the Clara Haskil Competition in Lucerne, 1965. He made his début in London in 1966. He gave the première of **Henze**'s Piano Concerto No.2 (1968), which was dedicated to him. He has performed all over the world, including at the Salzburg Festival, and is considered an outstanding interpreter of the Viennese classical composers. His repertory is extensive and ranges from the **Baroque** to the contemporary. In 1973 he made his début as a conductor.

Escher, Rudolph (1912-1980) Dutch composer who developed an interesting arrangement of orchestral players in some of his pieces. He studied composition in Rotterdam (1931) with **Pijper** and began work in 1961 at the Delft studio for electronic music and later at the Utrecht State University. He was a respected critic and published books on the French impressionist composers, including Debussy and Ravel. His compositions include two symphonies, the tone poem *Le tombeau de Ravel* (1952) and the spectacular *Summer Rites at Noon* (1973) for two orchestras arranged as the **cantoris** and **decani** halves of a choir.

Esplá, Oscar (1886-1976) Spanish composer who trained as an engineer but left the profession to devote his time to composition. His works include operas, symphonic pieces, choral works and chamber music, and reflect the patterns and rhythms of Spanish folk music. Esplá did not receive any formal musical training, and a measure of his independence can be seen in his creation of a new scale, the 'Levantine', equivalent to the scale C-D♭-E♭-E-F-G♭-A♭-B♭.

Esposito, Michele (1855-1929) Italian composer and pianist who founded and conducted the Dublin Orchestral Society (1899). He studied at the Naples Conservatoire and then moved to Paris (1878). In 1882 he moved again to Dublin, and was appointed professor of piano at the Royal Irish Academy of Music. Among his compositions are the operetta *The Postbag* (1902), the *Irish Symphony* (1902) and music for strings and orchestra. He returned to Italy shortly before his death.

estampie (Fr.) Instrumental piece or dance of the 13th and 14th centuries, related to **troubadour** forms. The *estampie* consisted of between four and seven sections (known as *puncta*), each of which is stated twice, with a different ending the second time.

estinto (It.) Extinct, indication that a passage is to be performed extremely softly, in an almost toneless manner.

estudiantina (Sp.) Piece of music played in a light-hearted manner, generally performed by wandering students to a street audience.

etherophone Alternative term for **thérémin**.

ethnomusicology Study of the music of world cultures, especially primitive and non-Western systems of music, in relation to their anthropological and historical development. In the 1880s it was known as comparative musicology, but in the 1930s this type of research was renamed by Jaap Kunst, a specialist in Indonesian music.

Etler, Alvin Derald (1913-1973) American composer and oboist who wrote pieces for electronic performance as well as for conventional orchestral settings. He studied at the Cleveland Institute of Music (1931) and at Yale University (1942) with **Hindemith**. He became oboist for the Indianapolis Symphony Orchestra (1938) and followed a career as a lecturer in several academic institutions. Among his compositions are many works for wind instruments, concertos for orchestra, for violin and wind quintet, for orchestra and brass quintet and for orchestra and strings.

étouffez (Fr.) Direction to deaden or dampen the tone on instruments that are liable to vibrate after being sounded, such as the harp, kettledrum or cymbals.

étude (Fr.) **Study** or exercise. For example, Chopin's Op.25 for piano.

euphonium Also known as a tenor tuba, a four-valved brass instrument of the **tuba** family, with a wide, conical bore, sounding in B♭. It was invented by Sommer of Weimar, Germany, in 1843 and is now used mainly in brass and military bands.

Euphonium

eurhythmics System of teaching music, especially rhythmic music, by bodily movement. It was invented by Emile **Jacques-Dalcroze**, who set up an institute for it in Dresden (1910). Apart from being helpful to performers of ballet and modern dancing, it has proved valuable to general physical and mental education.

Evans, Sir Geraint (1922-) Welsh baritone who studied at the Guildhall School of Music and in Hamburg (with Theo Hermann) and Geneva (with Fernando Carpi). He made his début at Covent Garden in 1948 in *Die Meistersinger von Nürnberg* (Wagner). He has since sung all the major roles for his voice, including Figaro, Papageno, Masetto and Leporello. He has created several roles, including Mr Flint in *Billy Budd* and Antenor in *Troilus and Cressida*, and has produced some fine comic performances (notably Dr Dulcamara in Donizetti's *L'elisir d'amore*). His voice is warm with a wide range. Evans was awarded the CBE in 1959 and was knighted in 1969; he retired in 1984. He is considered to be one of the greatest baritones of his day.

Ewing, Maria (1950-) American soprano/mezzo-soprano. She studied in Cleveland and New York, and made her début as Cherubino in Mozart's *Le nozze di Figaro* at the Metropolitan Opera in 1976. She appeared at La Scala in Debussy's *Pelléas et Mélisande*, and at **Glyndebourne** many times in the 1980s, as Dorabella in *Così fan tutte*, Rosina in *Il barbiere di Siviglia* and as a mesmerizing Carmen. In 1988, for her début at the Royal Opera House, Covent Garden, she took on the taxing soprano role of Salome in Peter Hall's sensational production of Strauss's opera, and scored a notable success. In 1990 she sang her first Tosca in Los Angeles. She has also made many concert appearances and recitals. Gifted with a highly individual voice, she has a fine acting ability and a vivid stage presence.

exercise 1. A vocal or instrumental piece of little or no artistic value, which is intended to develop technique, such as a five-finger exercise for piano. The French equivalent is **étude**.

2. A form of 18th-century keyboard suite. As an example, some of D. **Scarlatti**'s early sonatas were published under the Italian equivalent of the term.

3. A composition which candidates are expected to write for a music degree.

exposition Part of a fugue or **sonata** movement in which the original theme or themes are stated before the middle or development section begins.

expressionism Term borrowed from the visual arts and applied to a movement in music that originated in Germany and Austria in the period 1910 to 1930. It was partly a reaction to French impressionist painting. Although there is a technical meaning to expressionism in art, it is difficult to see how its tenets may be applied to music. However, the style can be characterized as being harshly dissonant and **atonal**, with extremes of melodic and rhythmic effects.

The two composers most closely associated with expressionism are Arnold **Schoenberg** and Alban **Berg**.

extemporization Alternative term for **improvisation**.

extension organ Alternative term for **unit organ**.

F

F 1. Sixth note of the scale, one semitone above E and one tone below G. The scale of F major has one flat in the key-signature.

F F major

2. Abbreviation of Fanna, used as a prefix to indicate the numbers of **Vivaldi**'s works catalogued by Antonio Fanna (1968). A later catalogue by Peter Ryom superseded Fanna's in 1973.

fa In **tonic sol-fa**, name given to the subdominant note in any key, represented by the symbol f. Also the note F in fixed **doh** systems.

faburden 1. In the late 14th and early 15th centuries, a method of improvising three-voice parallel harmony to **plainsong**, with the melody at the top of the texture; originally the faburden was the part below the middle.

2. In modern usage, a part added to a hymn and sung by a choir's sopranos and tenors. The congregation sings the tune itself, and the remaining voices of the choir sing their parts much as usual. This is also known as **descant**.

See also **fauxbourdon**.

facile (Fr., It.) Easy. It is applied, for example, to a solo passage written for a virtuoso performer so that he or she performs fluently without any signs of labouring.

fado Popular Portuguese song performed in streets and cafés, accompanied by the guitar and enlivened by dancing. Following its popularity in Lisbon during the 1850s it spread to the provinces.

fagott (Ger.), **fagotto** (It.) From a word meaning bundle of sticks: a **bassoon**. Also refers to a 16-foot reed organ stop that produces a bassoon tone.

fah Alternative spelling of **fa**.

Fall, Leo (1873-1925) Austrian composer who enjoyed some success in France, Germany and England with his light operettas. He studied at the Vienna Conservatoire and then in Berlin, Hamburg and Cologne. Among his works are two serious operas and the operettas *Der Rebell* (1905), *Die Dollarprinzessin* (1907), *The Eternal Waltz* (first performed in London, 1912) and *Madame Pompadour* (1922).

Falla, Manuel de (1876-1946) Spanish composer and pianist who reflected the themes from Andalusian folk music in his earlier works and adopted neo-classical styles in his later compositions.

Falla first received musical instruction from his family and relatives. He studied the piano at the Madrid Academy with Trago (1898-9) and composition under Pedrell (1902), and composed his first pieces, two **zarzuelas**, at this time. In 1905 he completed his opera *La vida breve* and won the Madrid Academy of Fine Arts Prize. His four *Pièces espagnoles* were first performed in Paris (1909) and then in London (1911). In 1916 he completed his most important work, *Noches en los jardines de España* (Nights in the Gardens of Spain) for piano and orchestra, an atmospheric piece which reflected the influences of Debussy and **Ravel**. His most famous work, the ballet *El sombrero de tres picos* (The Three-Cornered Hat), was completed in 1919 and produced in London by **Diaghilev**. Other works include *El amor brujo* (1915), *Fantasia bética* (1919), *El retablo de maese Pedro* (1923) and *L'Atlántida*.

false relation Special effect of harmony in which two different versions of the same note (for instance, E♯ and E♭) occur simultaneously or in immediate succession in different parts. Composers of the 16th and early 17th centuries accepted simultaneous false relations, and they were still being used by English composers in the latter half of the 17th century, mainly as a result of tradition and as a means of expression. Also known as cross relation.

fancy English 16th- and early 17th-century term for a composition for lute, keyboard or instrumental ensemble. The fancy had no distinct form, but always made considerable use of **counterpoint**, and was generally divided into a number of sections, played without a break and not connected thematically. In the latter part of the 17th century the sections became more distinct, and in the works of Henry **Purcell**, John Jenkins and Matthew **Locke** they were often interspersed with dance movements. See also **fantasia**.

fandango (Sp.) Spanish dance in moderately fast triple time, with guitar and castanets prominent in the accompaniment. Spanish composers have incorporated the form into some of their orchestral works. A slower form also exists, and was used by **Gluck** in his ballet *Don Juan* and later by **Mozart** in the finale of Act III in *Le nozze di Figaro*.

fanfare Flourish for trumpets or other brass instruments, usually by way of an introduction or at the head of a procession. Fanfares have been used in operas such as Beethoven's *Fidelio*, Bizet's *Carmen* and Verdi's *Otello*.

fantasia Composition in which the composer's imagination is given free rein without being subject to the rules of structure or form. The term was first used by 16th-century lutenists such as Luis de **Milan** (1535) and Francesco da Milano (1536). It may also be a composition based on a selected theme from another composer's work, such as a folk-song, popular tune or operatic air. See also **fancy**.

farandole (Fr.) Dance form which originated in Provence, performed by groups of people in the streets and accompanied by pipe and tabor. The music is in 6/8 time. A farandole appears in Bizet's *L'arlésienne* (1872), but its form is not traditionally correct, although it is based on an authentic Provence tune.

Farmer, John (late 16th century) English composer who became the organist of Christ Church, Dublin. Little is known about his life, other than that he moved to London in 1599. He wrote a series of canons in 1591 and composed a collection of madrigals in 1599, including *Fair Phyllis I Saw Sitting All Alone*. He also wrote pieces for Thomas East's *Whole Booke of Psalmes*.

Farnaby, Giles (1566-1640) English composer of keyboard music, madrigals, psalms and canzonets. In 1594 he moved from London, his birthplace, to Lincolnshire, and is known to have taught the children of Sir Nicholas Saunderson. While there, he composed his *Canzonets to Foure Voices* (1598). In 1614 he returned to London and continued to write. He contributed more than 60 pieces to the Fitzwilliam Virginal Book, including *A Dreame, a Toye*, and *His Humour*.

Farrant, Richard (*c.*1530-1580) English composer who became organist and master of the choristers at St George's Chapel, Windsor, and a member of the Chapel Royal. He composed anthems, including *Hide Not Thou Thy Face*, *Call to Remembrance* and songs for the court.

Farrar, Geraldine (1882-1967) American soprano. She studied in Boston, New York, Paris and Berlin, and made her début in Berlin in 1901 as Marguerite in Gounod's *Faust*. She then studied with Lilli Lehmann before returning to the United States to join the Metropolitan Opera in 1906, where her début was as Juliette in Gounod's *Roméo et Juliette*. She remained a star of the Metropolitan until 1922, when she retired; during this time she sang nearly 30 roles and enjoyed her greatest successes as Zerlina in Mozart's *Don Giovanni*, the title-roles in Puccini's *Madama Butterfly* and *Manon Lescaut*, and another Puccini role which she created, the title-role in *Suor Angelica* (1918). She also appeared in several films.

farruca (Sp.) Lively and energetic Andalusian dance with heel-stamping accompaniment, of gypsy origins. It was used by **Falla** for the miller's dance in *The Three-Cornered Hat* (1919).

Fasch, Johann Friedrich (1688-1758) German composer who founded Leipzig's Gewandhaus concerts. He studied in Leipzig at the Thomas-schule (1701-7) and became *Kapellmeister* to the court of Zerbst, 1722. Among his compositions are three operas, concertos, chamber and church music.

fasola (US) Notation and style of hymnodic singing which originated in the New England region. Fasola Folk are those people who practise this form. The name originates from the combination of names given to the different notes of the scale fa-sol-la, deriving from **Guido**nian solmization via the Elizabethan diatonic major scale fa-sol-la-fa-sol-la-mi. Spiritual hymnody in this style reached its heyday with the foundation of the Singing Schools in the late 18th century and may be split into four categories: those deriving from European folk-tunes; those with psalm tunes for the melody; revivalist hymns; and fuguing tunes. Songs are learned by heart, each singer learning all parts, at first to the syllables fa-sol-la, etc. Singers may exchange parts at will during a performance. In some rural southern states of America songs in this style are still sung and often known, after the title of published collections, as *Sacred Harp* songs. See also **shape note**.

Fassbaender, Brigitte (1939-) German mezzo-soprano. She studied with her father, the baritone Willi Domgraf-Fassbänder, and at Nuremberg, and made her début in 1961 at Munich as Nicklausse in Offenbach's *Les contes d'Hoffmann*. She has been a member of the Munich company since then, with frequent visits to the United States and London. Her Covent Garden début was in 1971 as Octavian in Strauss's *Der Rosenkavalier*; she also sang this role for her début at the Metropolitan Opera, New York, in 1974. She is particularly admired in *travesti* roles such as Octavian and Cherubino (*Le nozze di Figaro*), but is equally successful as Carmen, Eboli in Verdi's *Don Carlos* and Dorabella in Mozart's *Così fan tutte*. She has also been a memorable Countess Geschwitz in **Berg's** *Lulu*.

Fauré, Gabriel (1845-1924) French composer and organist who blended Germanic idioms with a French style in compositions that were striking for their originality and harmonic sensitivity. His *Requiem Mass* (1887) grew in popularity in the 1950s and is now his most famous work; he is also highly regarded for his songs.

Gabriel Fauré

Fauré studied at Louis Niedermeyer's school from 1854, and while there worked under **Saint-Saëns**. In 1866 he became organist at Rennes and remained there until the outbreak of the Franco-Prussian War (1870), in which he fought. In 1871 he became an organist at St Sulpice, Paris, and started his teaching career at the Niedermeyer School. He became assistant (1877) and then chief (1896) organist and choirmaster at La Madeleine, and a professor of composition at the Paris Conservatoire (1896). His pupils included **Boulanger**, **Ravel** and **Enescu**. In 1905 he became director of the Conservatoire.

Apart from his Requiem he wrote the operas *Prométhée* (1900) and his masterpiece, *Pénélope* (1913), both of which reflect the influence of Wagner. He also wrote several widely acclaimed song cycles, including *La bonne chanson* (1891) and *Le jardin clos* (1915). His orchestral pieces include *Pavane* (1887), *Masques et bergamasques* (1920), *Ballade* (1881) and *Fantasie* for piano and orchestra (1919).

fauxbourdon Technique for improvising on a chant. See also **faburden**.

Fayrfax, Robert (1464-1521) English composer who was a member of the Chapel Royal by 1509. He was much admired, and was still in Henry VIII's service at the Field of the Cloth of Gold in 1520. He composed Masses, motets and other devotional pieces.

feierlich (Ger.) Solemn.

Feldman, Morton (1926-1987) American composer whose work was influenced by **Cage**, **Brown** and **Tudor**. He attempted to reflect the physical canvases of art in musical paintings, and his love of Jackson Pollock's work is a clue to the temperament of his compositions. Feldman studied with Riegger and was appointed Edgard Varèse Professor at the State University and a director of the Center for Creative and Performing Arts in New York.

Among his compositions is *Projection* (1951), which contains an element of flexibility in its form that needs to be interpreted by the performers. Feldman also composed *The Swallows of Salangan* (1962) for chorus and 16 instruments, *Durations* I, II, III and IV (1960-2) for various combinations of players, and a number of works for smaller ensembles.

feminine cadence Cadence in which the concluding chord is reached on a weak instead of a strong beat.

Fenby, Eric (1906-) English musicologist, composer and conductor. He studied with Keeton, and worked with a number of amateur choral and orchestral groups before spending six years (1928-34) with the composer Frederick **Delius**, who by this time was severely incapacitated. At Delius's retreat in the French countryside Fenby worked as amanuensis, writing out the scores for the *Songs of Farewell* and *Song of Summer*, among other compositions. He was adviser to the publishers Boosey and Hawkes, and from 1948 to 1962 director of music at the North Riding Training College in Yorkshire. In 1964 he was appointed professor of composition at the Royal Academy of Music. His memoirs of his time with Delius (*Delius as I Knew Him*,

1936) are sympathetic and revealing; he has also written a definitive study of Delius's music. His own compositions include orchestral, church and brass band music, and some film scores (notably *Jamaica Inn*). He has conducted important recordings of music by Delius with the **Royal Philharmonic Orchestra**.

Ferguson, Howard (1908-) Northern Irish composer who studied the piano with Samuel in 1922, and entered the Royal College of Music in 1923 to study composition with Morris. He later became a professor at the Royal Academy. Among his compositions are the ballet *Chauntecleer*, four *Diversions on Ulster Airs* for orchestra, a sonata and concerto for piano, two violin sonatas, and *Amore Langueo* for soloist, choir and orchestra.

fermata (It.) Pause, indicated by a sign prolonging a note or a rest beyond its normal length.

Fernandez, Oscar Lorenzo (1897-1948) Brazilian composer and teacher who wrote in the Brazilian tradition, drawing upon folk styles and emphasizing a nationalist theme. He wrote chamber pieces, ballets and orchestral works, and is best known for his opera *Malazarte* and his symphonic suite *Trio brasiliero*.

Ferneyhough, Brian (1943-) English composer of complex works who has experimented with electronic instruments. He studied at the Birmingham School of Music from 1960, and at the Royal Academy of Music. He moved to the Netherlands and studied with Ton de **Leeuw** (1968). He emigrated to Switzerland in 1969 and studied at the Basle Conservatoire with Klaus **Huber**, teaching in Germany from 1973. Among his compositions are a sonata for clarinet and bass clarinet, pieces for wind instruments and sonatas for string quartet.

Ferrabosco, Alfonso (1543-1588) Italian composer who lived in Italy and England and composed much devotional music. In 1546 he was appointed *maestro di cappella* at the Basilica Vaticana in Rome. In the 1560s he moved to England, entering the service of Elizabeth I. He left England in 1578 to serve the Duke of Savoy.

He published two volumes of Italian **madrigals** in 1587, but composed many more madrigals, motets and pieces for instrumental consort. Some of these are known to have influenced William **Byrd**, who competed with Ferrabosco in a setting of the plainsong *Miserere* for instruments.

Ferras, Christian (1933-) French violinist. He studied at the Nice Conservatory and in Paris with Calvet, making his début at the age of 13. He later studied with George **Enescu**. He won the prestigious Scheveningen International Competition in 1948, among other prizes. He has played all over the world, and has been particularly successful in eastern Europe. His repertory is concentrated on French music, together with the great concertos of the nineteenth century; he has made an exceptionally fine recording of Berg's Violin Concerto. His powerfully emotional style is combined with great beauty of tone.

Ferrier, Kathleen (1912-1953) English contralto who studied with such teachers as J.E. Hutchinson and Roy Henderson. Ferrier began her musical career as a concert singer. Her concert repertory included *Messiah* (Handel) and *The Dream of Gerontius* (Elgar). She made her opera début in 1946 (Glyndebourne, première of **Britten**'s *The Rape of Lucretia*). She also performed under such conductors as Bruno **Walter** and Sir John **Barbirolli**. Ferrier made many recordings and became one of the most popular and well-loved singers of her time. Her most famous role was that of Orfeo in Gluck's opera *Orfeo ed Euridice*.

Festa, Constanzo (*c*.1490-1545) Italian composer who became a singer in the choir of Pope Leo X in 1517. He composed numerous madrigals, Masses and other sacred polyphonic pieces. His *Te Deum* is still performed at the election of a new pope.

Festing, Michael Christian (*c.*1680-1752) English composer and violinist who studied under **Geminiani**. He joined the King's Musicians in 1735 and became director of the Italian Opera in 1737. He composed symphonic pieces, concertos and sonatas for the violin, songs, odes and a cantata.

Fibich, Zdeněk (1850-1900) Bohemian composer and conductor, best known for his serenade *At Twilight* and for his spoken orchestral melodrama *Hippodamia*. He was a pupil of **Moscheles** and Jadassohn at the Leipzig Conservatoire from 1865 and became a tutor at Wilno in 1870, returning to Prague in 1874 to become an assistant conductor at the National Theatre. Most of his compositions were written after 1881 and include more than 500 pieces, which range from the operas *Šarká* (1897), *The Tempest* and *Hedy* (based on Byron's *Don Juan*), to symphonies, symphonic poems and chamber pieces. His *Moods, Impressions and Reminiscences*, a major set of piano pieces, are autobiographical, describing a love affair in the late 1880s. He also wrote piano suites and other orchestral and piano melodramas (*Queen Emma*) for piano, later orchestrated.

fiddle Colloquial term for members of the violin family and their medieval predecessors, the vielle and **rebec**. The instruments have a variety of shapes and sizes, and the family includes the single-stringed folk instruments of Ethiopia, the square-bodied *morinchur* of Mongolia and the *sarangi* of India.

Field, John (1782-1837) Irish composer and pianist who was admired by Liszt and Mendelssohn and who developed the **nocturne**, a short piece for the piano, further explored by **Chopin**. He studied in Dublin with T. **Giordani** and was apprenticed to **Clementi** in London, who took him to France, Germany and Russia in order to demonstrate his pianos. He settled in Russia in 1803, appearing in Moscow as a performer – where his delicate and sensitive playing was widely admired – and becoming a teacher. He remained in Russia for the rest of his life. Field composed more than 20 nocturnes and seven piano concertos, as well as numerous other works for the piano: variations, rondos, sonatas, fantasies and romances. The *Air russe varié* was written for piano duet, and he also produced a piano quintet.

fife Simple and obsolete form of high-pitched flute, with finger-holes and no keys, normally used in military bands. The name now applies to a military flute with six finger-holes and several keys which is used in drum and fife bands; it is not identical to the orchestral flute or piccolo.

fifteenth Diapason organ stop in which two-foot pipes produce notes two octaves (15 steps of the diatonic scale) above those played on a manual keyboard.

fifth **Interval** of five notes (counting the first and last notes). For example, a perfect fifth is C-G or D-A; a semitone less gives a diminished fifth (C-G♭), and an augmented fifth has one semitone more (C-G♯).

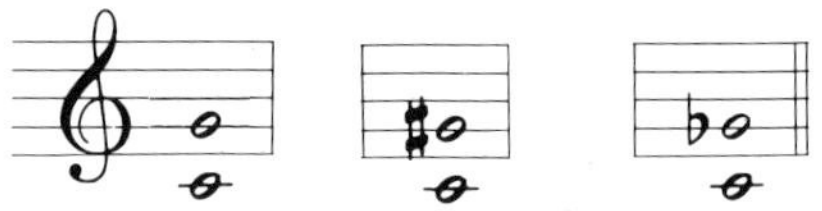

Perfect 5th　　Augmented 5th　　Diminished 5th

figured bass System of shorthand notation for keyboard instruments indicating the harmony above a written-out bass part by means of figures. The original system, which was practised in the 17th and 18th centuries, was to help players of keyboard and plucked instruments (lute, chitarrone) to play **continuo** parts without a score.

The basic principle of this method is that notes forming the harmony are indicated by the interval they make with the bass and are written as numbers. For example, if the key is C major, and the bass note C, the figure 5 would indicate G, and 5♯ would indicate G♯. However, the choice of the octave in which this G or G♯ is to be placed is left to the performer. In addition, some conventional abbreviations are used to assist the composer or copyist, and also to make reading easier for the player.

film music In the early days of the cinema at the beginning of the 20th century, silent films were shown to the accompaniment of a piano, organ or small orchestra. The music chosen for the films corresponded to the mood of the various scenes depicted on the screen. With the introduction of talking films came the integrated sound-track, which demanded the commissioning of new scores or an adaptation of existing works. Some early scores for the cinema included works by **Bliss** (*Things to Come*, 1933), **Shostakovich** (*New Babylon*, 1929), **Prokofiev** (*Alexander Nevsky*, 1938) and **Auric** (*A Poet's Blood*, 1930). **Vaughan Williams** made a valuable contribution to film music, culminating in the music for *Scott of the Antarctic* (1948), as did William **Walton** who wrote the music for *Henry V* (1944), *Hamlet* (1948) and *Richard III* (1956). In recent years the contribution of an atmospheric score to the overall impact of a film has been more widely recognized, and such composers as Carl **Davis**, John **Dankworth**, Bernard **Herrmann** and Tom **Eastwood** specialize in this exacting but lucrative field.

fin (Fr.) End.

final Tonic note on which the scales of authentic **modes** end.

finale (Fr.) Final movement of any instrumental work having several movements. It also refers to the last number in an act of an opera in which the music is divided into more or less separate pieces. This assumes that such a number is on a large scale: for example, the great ensemble piece at the end of Act II in Mozart's *Le nozze di Figaro* is a finale, whereas the aria at the end of Act I is not.

fine (It.) End. Used occasionally by composers at the end of a score to show that a composition is complete. It is also used before the end of a score where an earlier portion is to be repeated to form the closing section. See also **da capo**.

Fine, Irving (1914-1962) American composer and critic whose work reflects an evolution of style from **neo-classical** methods to use of the **twelve-note** technique. He studied at Harvard from 1933. He moved to Cambridge, England, then to Paris as a pupil of **Boulanger**. In 1946 he returned to Harvard to become a professor of music, and six years later became chairman of the School of Creative Arts at Brandeis University.

Among his compositions are *Music for the Modern Dance* (1941), three choruses from *Alice in Wonderland* (1942), *The Hourglass* (1949) for chorus and orchestra, the orchestral 'diversion' *Blue Towers* (1959), and other pieces for strings and orchestra.

fingerboard Part of the neck of a stringed instrument on to which the fingers press the strings in order to stop them. See also **stopping**.

finger-holes Holes in the tube of a wind instrument that are opened and closed with the fingers. Finger-holes are used (sometimes with keys) on a variety of instruments, such as flutes, clarinets, oboes, recorders, bagpipes and some horns. Opening the finger-holes provides a method of shortening the tube of the instrument, which in turn reduces the length of the column of vibrating air within it, thus raising the pitch.

fingering Use of fingers on musical instruments to produce notes in various ways. It is also an indication on paper to show which fingers to use to produce a particular note or sequence of notes. For instance, in piano-playing, the thumb is indicated as 1 and the other fingers are 2-5. This is sometimes called continental fingering, as opposed to English fingering in which the thumb is marked with a + and the other fingers as 1-4.

When playing instruments of the violin family, the thumb is not used, and the fingers are numbered 1-4. Exceptions to this are the cello and double-bass, which require the use of the thumb in the higher positions.

Finney, Ross Lee (1906-) American composer who used **tonal** and **serial** techniques in his work but also borrowed from earlier traditions of American music. He studied at the University of Minnesota and moved to Paris in 1927 as a pupil of **Boulanger**. In 1931 he studied with **Berg** in Vienna. He became a tutor at Smith College in 1929 and established the electronic music studio at the University of Michigan in 1947.

Finney adopted themes from the *Ainsworth Psalter* in his cantata *Pilgrim Psalms* (1945) and developed folk-melodies in his piano concerto and in his *Barber-shop Ballad* (1937). He also composed six string quartets, *Communiqué* for orchestra (1943) and a number of sonatas.

Finnissy, Michael (1946-) English composer who studied composition at the Royal College of Music and later moved to Italy to continue his research. He formed a music department at the London School of Contemporary Dance, and taught there from 1969. He is a frequent lecturer and has taught at the Chelsea School of Art and at Dartington's Summer School. Among his compositions are many works for musical theatre, *Medea* (1973) and *Circle, Chorus, and Formal Act* (1973), and for voice and ensemble, *Horrorzone* (1966). He also composed for orchestra – *Transformations of the Vampire* (1971) – and for the piano.

Finzi, Gerald (1901-1956) English composer with a gentle, pastoral, melodic style, noted particularly for his songs. He studied at York with Bairstow (1918-22) and later with Morris in London. In 1930 he became a tutor at the Royal Academy, but left during World War II to work in the Ministry of War Transport (1941-5). Finzi was inspired by English literature; his compositions include settings of poems by Thomas Hardy, Christina Rossetti and John Milton and songs by Shakespeare. Other works have a depth and sensitivity that stem from literary associations, particularly in his *Intimations of Immortality* for tenor, chorus and orchestra (1950), the cantata *Dies Natalis* (1940) and the song-cycle *To a Poet.* He also composed concertos for the cello and clarinet, as well as works for voices and orchestra.

fioritura (It.) Decoration of a plain melodic passage with ornaments, either according to the composer's notation or improvised by the performer.

fipple Piece of wood that diverts the air blown through a mouthpiece of an instrument of the fipple flute family, of which the chief member is the **recorder**.

Firkušný, Rudolf (1912-) Czech-born American pianist. He studied with Janáček in Brno, and in Prague; he also studied composition with Josef **Suk**. He made his début in Prague in 1922, and in England in 1933. He toured all over the world, including Australia and the United States, where he taught for a time at the Juilliard School and at Aspen, Colorado. As well as the classical and Romantic repertory he is particularly associated with the piano music of Dvořák and **Janáček**, which he has recorded extensively. He has given the first performances of Samuel **Barber**'s Piano Concerto (1962) and works by **Menotti, Martinů** and **Ginastera,** and has also performed and recorded many piano trios. He has composed piano works and a string quartet.

Fischer, Annie (1914-) Hungarian pianist who studied at the Franz Liszt

Conservatoire and under such teachers as Székeley and **Dohnányi**. She made her début in Budapest in 1922 and has toured worldwide. Her Mozart performances and recordings have been particularly admired.

Fischer, Johann Kaspar Ferdinand (*c.*1670-1746) German composer and organist who became *Kapellmeister* to the court of the Markgraf in Baden. His works include *Ariadne Musica Neo-organoedum* (1702), a collection of 20 preludes and fugues in different keys for the organ, as well as other pieces for the keyboard.

Fischer-Dieskau, Dietrich (1925-) German baritone and conductor who studied at the Berlin Hochschule für Musik. By the 1950s he was acknowledged to be one of the greatest living exponents of *Lieder*, and his recordings of the Schubert cycles are supreme examples of his artistry. Operatic roles have included Posa (*La Forza del Destino*), Falstaff, Don Giovanni, Mandryka in Strauss's *Arabella*, and Wozzeck. He took up conducting in 1975.

Fisher, Sylvia (1910-) Australian soprano. She studied in Melbourne and moved to London in 1947. Her début at Covent Garden was as Leonore in Beethoven's *Fidelio* (1949), and for ten years she was the company's principal dramatic soprano, her most successful roles being the Marschallin in Strauss's *Der Rosenkavalier*, Sieglinde in *Die Walküre* and the Kostelnička in Janáček's *Jenůfa*. She also sang Ellen Orford in **Britten**'s *Peter Grimes*. After 1963 she sang with the **English Opera Group** in several other Britten works: Mrs Wingrave, a role she created, in *Owen Wingrave* (1971, for television), Queen Elizabeth I in *Gloriana*, Mrs Grose in *The Turn of the Screw* and the Chorus in *The Rape of Lucretia*.

Fitelberg, Jerzy (1903-1951) Polish composer, son of Gregorz Fitelberg who founded the Young Poland collective of composers in Berlin (1905). Jerzy studied in Berlin but moved to Paris in 1933 and to the United States in 1940. His compositions include string quartets, concertos for the violin and cello, wind quintets, and other works for chamber orchestra.

flageolet Type of **recorder** used in the 17th, 18th and 19th centuries. The English version had six finger-holes; the French had four, and two thumb-holes. An example of the use of the instrument may be found in Handel's opera *Rinaldo*, first performed in London, 1711.

In modern usage, flageolet is an alternative name for the **tin whistle**.

Flagstad, Kirsten (1895-1962) Norwegian soprano, the outstanding Wagnerian interpreter of her day. She studied in Oslo and acquired a wide operatic repertory; she did not venture outside Scandinavia until 1933, when she made her first appearance at Bayreuth. The following year she sang Sieglinde in *Die Walküre* and Gutrune in *Götterdämmerung*; her success there led to her New York début at the Metropolitan in 1935, again as Sieglinde, and this was quickly followed by Brünnhilde, Isolde (in *Tristan und Isolde*) and Kundry (in *Parsifal*). The astonishing power and ease of her pure, radiant voice in these arduous roles quickly earned her unstinting admiration. In London, where she sang Isolde, Brünnhilde and Senta (*Der fliegende Holländer*) in 1936-7 at Covent Garden, her reception was equally enthusiastic, and she performed there regularly for many years.

She sang little during the period of World War II, but returned triumphantly to Covent Garden in 1948 as Isolde, her voice undiminished; it was the role she chose for her last stage appearance in 1951. In 1950 she gave the first performance of Richard Strauss's *Four Last Songs* in London. After her retirement she became director of the Norwegian National Opera (1959-60). She made many superb recordings, of songs by **Grieg** and **Sibelius** as well as of her operatic roles: the finest of these is her *Tristan und Isolde* with **Furtwängler**, in which the glories of the voice are allied to a matchless power to move the listener.

flam Double stroke, as distinct from a **roll**, played on a side drum.

flamenco (Sp.) Andalusian song and dance of gypsy origin, often with the accompaniment of guitars. The song is often a ballad, and the dance is in a highly rhythmic style, punctuated by the tapping of the toes and heels of the shoes of the dancers. The accompanying guitarists (often improvising) display an unusual technique in that they use the body of the instrument to produce percussive effects.

Flanagan, William (1923-1969) American composer; also music and theatre critic for the *New York Herald Tribune*. He studied at the Eastman School of Music under **Honegger** and worked with **Diamond** and **Copland**. He also collaborated with Ned **Rorem** as a promoter of American songs, and with Edward Albee, writing music for four of his plays, including *The Sandbox* and *The Death of Bessie Smith*.

Flanagan's compositions include the opera *Bartelby* (1957), a setting of A.E. Housman's poetry in the song cycle *The Weeping Pleiades* and choral works. His compositions for orchestra include the charming and lyrical *A Concert Ode* (1951), *Notations* (1960) and *Narrative for Orchestra* (1964).

flat 1. The sign (♭) placed before a note or in a key signature to reduce the pitch of that note by one semitone.

2. Used when a singer or instrumentalist is singing or playing flat, that is, slightly lower than the written note, often producing a discord.

flat keys Keys that have flats in their key-signatures. Such keys are: B♭ with two flats, E♭ with three flats, A♭ with four flats, D♭ with five flats, and G♭ with six flats. The relative minor keys have, in each case, the same signatures as the major keys given.

Flatterzunge (Ger.) Flutter-tonguing. Technique of playing the flute or clarinet that produces a fluttering, bird-like sound. See also **double tonguing**.

flautando (It.) Flute-like tone produced on a violin when drawing the bow lightly over the strings near the end of the fingerboard.

flautist Player of the **flute**. In the United States, the word is usually spelled flutist.

flauto (It.) **Flute**.

flebile (It.) Plaintive, mournful.

flexatone Instrument that is similar to the musical saw. It consists of a steel blade against which two knobs vibrate when the instrument is shaken (but not bowed). Thumb pressure on the blade is used to alter the pitch.

flicorno (It.) Brass instrument used in military bands which is similar to the **saxhorn** and **flugelhorn**. It is found in various sizes: soprano (flugelhorn), basso, basso grave and contrabasso.

florid Any musical passage that is highly ornamented, especially one in which a theme or melody is elaborated.

Flöte (Ger.) **Flute**.

Flothuis, Marius Hendrikus (1914-) Dutch composer and musicologist who studied in Amsterdam and became the assistant manager of the Concertgebouw Orchestra in 1937. In 1945 he became music critic of the Amsterdam newspaper *Het vrije Volk* and he has written a number of books on English composers, Monteverdi and Mozart. Among his compositions are concertos for piano, violin, flute and horn, *Hymnus* for soprano and orchestra, a *Sinfonietta Concertante* for clarinet, saxophone and chamber orchestra, a cello sonata and some songs.

Flotow, Friedrich von (1812-1883) German composer. His initial success in the world of opera, with works that combined gaiety with some sentimentality, was not sustained. He studied at the Paris Conservatoire under Reich and was influenced by **Offenbach**, with whom he produced operas for grand occasions. He wrote ballets, chamber music and 18 operas, including *Le naufrage de la Méduse*, successful in Paris when it first appeared in 1839, *Alessandro Stradella* (1845), popular in Hamburg for a time, and *Martha* (1847), the only one of his works still performed.

flourish Fanfare of trumpets. In modern musical terminology it is a florid passage used as an embellishment rather than as a theme.

Floyd, Carlisle (1926-) American composer noted for his ambitious attempts to translate powerful literary stories into opera. He studied at Spartanburg and Syracuse Universities and took piano tuition from **Firkušný**. He now teaches at the University of Tallahassee. Floyd's operas were composed to his own libretti and include *Susannah* (1955), a skilful combination of the biblical tale and the plot of Somerset Maugham's novel *Rain*, *Wuthering Heights* (1958), *Of Mice and Men* (1970) and *Bilby's Doll* (1976).

flue-pipe Organ pipe into which air is made to enter directly to produce sound in a similar manner to a whistle or recorder. The pipe has an open mouthpiece, as opposed to reed stops which have vibrating metal tongues. An alternative term is flue-stop.

flugelhorn Brass instrument similar to the keyed **bugle** and alto **saxhorn**. It has a trumpet-like mouthpiece and a horn-like conical bore, and is used in British brass bands as an alto in B♭, being played with the cornets, with which it has an identical range. It is also made in two other pitches, soprano and tenor.

flute General name for various types of woodwind instrument. Some of the oldest flutes were made of bone and date back to 10,000 BC, when successful attempts were made to reproduce the sounds of nature, such as the call of an owl.

In the 18th and 19th centuries flutes were made of wood. **Boehm** invented the modern version, improving its system of keys and thus its range and intonation; the instrument has changed little since 1847. The modern flute is made of metal (nickel, silver, gold or platinum), and is held horizontally (hence the name transverse flute). Air is blown into the tube through the mouth-hole (the **embouchure**). The pitch of the resulting sound is altered by covering or uncovering a combination of finger-holes.

Other varieties of flute include the nose-blown flute, where the player plugs one nostril and blows with the other; the

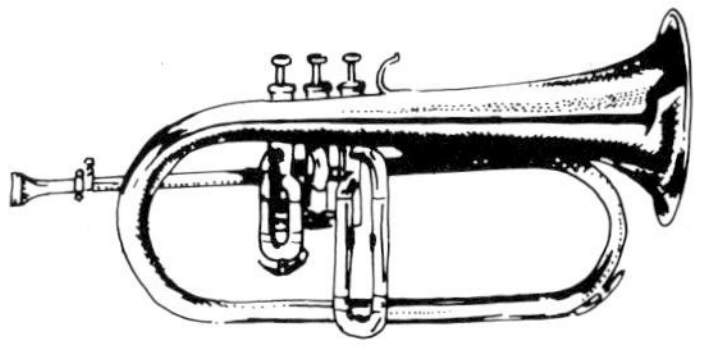

Flugelhorn

Flute

piccolo, a smaller version of the flute, sounding an octave higher; the alto flute, pitched a fourth or fifth lower than the standard instrument, and the bass flute, an octave lower.

Apart from its use in an orchestra and a military band, the flute is also used as a solo instrument. Sonatas for the flute and keyboard were composed by Bach; Handel and Vivaldi also composed much flute music. Mozart wrote flute concertos. In the early 20th century several French composers found it particularly attractive, among them **Poulenc** (a sonata), **Honegger** and above all **Debussy** (*Syrinx*, 1913, flute solo; *Prélude à l'après-midi d'un faune*, which features three flutes). **Nielsen**, **Arnold** and **Boulez** have also composed for the flute.

flute-à-bec (Fr.) Beak-flute, equivalent of the English **recorder**.

flutist American alternative for flautist.

Foldes, Andor (1913-) Hungarian composer and pianist who was considered one of the finest performers of the work of **Bartók**. He studied at the Budapest Academy with **Dohnányi** and in 1933 was awarded the International Liszt Prize. He toured Europe as a virtuoso pianist and in 1948 settled in the United States, writing books on piano technique and composing a certain amount for the piano.

folk-music Body of songs, tunes and dances that have been handed down from generation to generation and accepted in several different versions or corruptions as part of the oral tradition of a region, nation or people.

Interest in folk-music arose towards the end of the 19th century, when the phrase was coined. Many composers and academics have transcribed the folk-music of various areas. In England these include Cecil **Sharp** and **Vaughan Williams**. **Bartók** and **Kodály** made a very important contribution to the field with their work in central Europe. These two, **Dvořák**, Vaughan Williams and **Holst** have used folk-tunes as the basis for compositions (Dvořák's *Slavonic Dances*; Vaughan Williams's *English Folk-Song Suite*).

Recently, in popular music, the term has been used (outside its strict meaning) for music based on folk-tunes and forms, often used as protest songs. The songs of Woody Guthrie and Bob Dylan are examples.

foot Unit of length used to measure the pitch of an organ stop, based on the length of the lowest pipe. For example, an 8-foot pipe refers to the approximate pitch length of the pipe sounding C below the bass clef on the keyboard. Therefore, a pipe 4 feet long produces C an octave higher, and a 16-foot pipe C an octave lower and so on.

Foote, Arthur (1853-1937) American composer and organist. He was one of the New England group of composers that strove to bring to the United States some of the methods of composition that they had been taught in European conservatoires. Foote studied music at Harvard and became organist at the First Unitarian Church, Boston (1878). He was one of the founders of the American Guild of Organists and became its president in 1909.

Among his compositions are orchestral works as well as organ pieces, choral pieces and songs. He also wrote cantatas on Longfellow's *The Farewell of Hiawatha* (1885) and *The Wreck of the Hesperus* (1887).

Ford, Thomas (*c*.1580-1648) English composer and lutenist who wrote one of the best-known English lute songs, *Since First I Saw your Face*. He entered the service of the Prince of Wales, remaining when the prince became King Charles I in 1625. Many of his compositions – airs, madrigals and anthems – were published in a collection entitled *Musicke of Sundry Kindes* in 1607.

forlana (It.) Dance-form in 6/8 or 6/4 time. A typical example of its use is in

Bach's *Overture* (Suite) in C (undated), and Ravel's *Le tombeau de Couperin* (1917) for piano.

form The organization of the elements of a piece of music. The principal forms are binary, **ternary**, **rondo**, **sonata-form**, **ritornello** and **variation**.

formalism School of thought based in the Soviet Union during the early part of the 20th century, embracing literature, language studies and philosophy. The movement maintained that art (music, literature, etc.) is best understood by an intellectual examination of its form rather than its content, its 'message'. Composers such as **Prokofiev** and **Shostakovich** were criticized by Soviet authorities for their unconventional forms, rather than for not following the tenets of Socialist Realism.

forte, fortissimo (It.) Loud, very loud. Instruction to players to play loudly, or very loudly. Abbreviated to f or ff.

fortepiano (It.) Early Italian alternative term for pianoforte. Also an instruction to play loudly and immediately drop to **piano**, indicated by fp.

Fortner, Wolfgang (1907-) German composer and teacher. He studied in Leipzig, where he absorbed the influence of the Protestant tradition; his earliest works were for the Church. He taught in Heidelberg and founded the chamber orchestra (1935) and the Musica Viva concerts (1947). He also worked in Munich, Darmstadt, Detmold and Freiburg, and held many notable appointments. He was considered an outstanding teacher (**Henze** was a pupil). His compositions reflect a variety of influences, with Hindemith and Stravinsky paramount. His ballets and operas show his dramatic gifts: *Die weisse Rose*, 1950; *Bluthochzeit* (Blood Wedding, after Lorca, 1957); *Don Perlimplin*, also after Lorca, 1962; *Carmen*, 1971; *Elisabeth Tudor*, 1972. He has also composed choral and solo vocal music (the cantata *The Creation*, 1955), suites, concertos for organ, for piano and for violin, works for electronic and conventional instruments and a *Madrigal* for 12 cellos (1979).

Foss, Lukas (1922-) German composer and conductor (original name Fuchs), widely respected for his romantic lyricism and combination of American and European styles.

He studied in Berlin, then at the Paris Conservatoire, and later at the Curtis Institute, where he worked with Scalero and **Hindemith**. He became professor of music at the University of California in 1953. From 1963 to 1970 he was conductor of the Buffalo Symphony Orchestra. Foss's compositions reflect a movement of style that leads from the influences of the German Romantic tradition and a Mahlerian temperament in his earlier works to a later 'New World poetic' that is more often associated with **Copland**. *The Prairie* for orchestra, chorus and soloists (1944) is a powerful indication of his earlier influences, while the opera *The Jumping Frog of Calaveras County* (1950) displays the vivacity of his later style. His other compositions include the oratorio *A Parable of Death* (1952), the orchestral piece *Recordare* (1948), *Cave of the Winds* for wind quintet and multiphones (1972) and *Round a Common Centre* for chorus and ensemble (1979).

Foster, Stephen (1826-1864) American composer of more than 200 songs which have entered the fabric of American culture and are regarded as authentic 'folk-songs'. Songs such as *Oh! Susanna* (1845), *Camptown Races* (1850), *My Old Kentucky Home* (1853), *Jeanie with the Light Brown Hair* (1854) and *Beautiful Dreamer* (1864) serve as an eloquent voice for United States sentimentality. Self-taught, Foster began writing at an early age and fell prey to unscrupulous publishers. *Oh! Susanna* grossed $15,000 but Foster received nothing. With the minstrel craze at its height in the 1850s, Foster began to receive commissions and his income increased. He formed a potentially fruitful but short-lived partnership with George Cooper, a lyricist.

Foulds, John (1880-1939) English composer and conductor. He first worked with the **Hallé Orchestra** under **Richter**, but left in 1906 to concentrate on composition. He was music director of the YMCA in London, 1918, and became conductor of the London University Musical Society in 1921. His *World Requiem*, written to commemorate the dead of World War I, was performed annually in the Royal Albert Hall for many years. Other works include the tone poem *Epithalamium*; *Music Pictures*; *Holiday Sketches*; the *Keltic Suite*; a cello concerto, and a concert opera, *A Vision of Dante*.

Fournier, Pierre (1906-1986) French cellist. He studied at the Paris Conservatoire, where he taught from 1941 to 1949. In 1925 he participated in the first performance of **Fauré**'s String Quartet. A number of works have been composed for him, including **Poulenc**'s Cello Sonata and a revised version of **Martinů**'s Cello Concerto. His wide repertory includes much contemporary music. In later years he has played many chamber works: his recordings include the Cello Concertos of Elgar and Dvořák; he has also recorded the complete Beethoven piano trios (with **Szeryng** and **Kempff**) and the complete piano and cello music (with Kempff). In 1963 he was made an Officier of the Légion d'Honneur.

fourth Interval of four notes (counting both the first and the last note) or five semitones. A perfect fourth, for example, is C-F, and an augmented fourth has one semitone more, C-F♯. The diminished fourth, C-F♭, is one semitone less than the perfect.

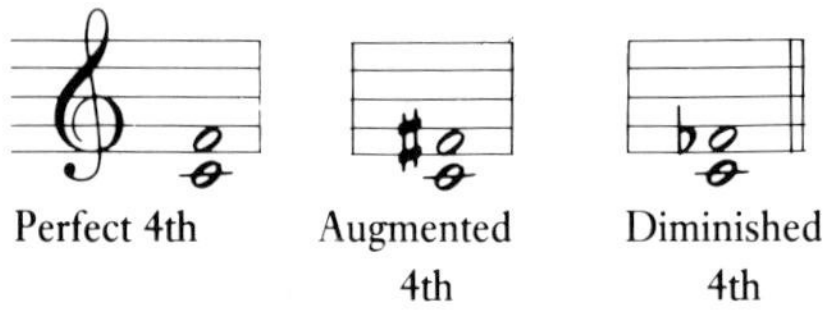

Fou Ts'ong (1934-) British pianist of Chinese birth. He studied with Mario Paci, and won a prize in the 1953 Bucharest Piano Competition and the 1955 International Chopin Contest in Warsaw. He then studied at the Warsaw Conservatoire. He settled in London in 1958, from where he has made extensive tours all over the world. His sensitive style is well suited to the music of Chopin and Debussy; he has also performed Mozart and Handel with great success.

foxtrot American ballroom dance dating from about 1912, and cultivated mainly by jazz bands. It developed into two forms, one moderately fast and the other slow, and its popularity spread throughout the United States and Europe during the 1930s and 1940s.

Françaix, Jean (1912-) French composer and pianist noted for his concise style and skills as a performer. He studied composition with **Boulanger** at the Paris Conservatoire. He became a respected pianist and completed several successful tours of Europe. Among Françaix's compositions are the oratorio *Apocalypse de St Jean* (1933), a comic opera *Le Diable boiteux* (1937) and a full-scale opera, *La main de gloire* (1945). He also wrote ballets, a concertino for orchestra and piano, a piano concerto (1936), and a quintet for flute, harp and string trio, as well as other chamber works.

Franck, César (1822-1890) Belgian composer, pianist and organist whose talents were not fully recognized in his lifetime. Franck's orchestral works reveal the powerful and precise temperament of the organ as well as more romantic and sentimental elements contained within a cyclic form.

He studied at the Liège Conservatoire and in 1837 at the Paris Conservatoire with

Reicha. His first orchestral work, the oratorio *Ruth*, was performed at the Paris Conservatoire in 1846. In 1858 he became organist at the church of Ste-Clotilde and caught the attention of Liszt with his brilliant technique. In 1872 he became professor of the organ at the Conservatoire, where his pupils included **d'Indy**, Bréville, **Chausson** and Bordes. His pupils organized the first performance of his Symphony in D minor (1888) in Paris and encouraged his efforts at composition.

Most of his finest compositions were completed in the 1870s and include devotional works such as the oratorios *Rédemption* and *Les Béatitudes* (1873-5), the symphonic pieces *Les Eolides* (1877) and *Variations symphoniques*, with piano (1885, considered to be his finest work), a piano quintet and the powerful *Prélude, choral et fugue* and *Prélude, aria et finale* for piano.

Franck, Melchior (*c.*1579-1639) German composer who became *Kapellmeister* to the Duke of Coburg. He composed songs, church music and instrumental pieces. A modern edition of some of his instrumental works is in *Denkmaler Deutscher Tonkunst XVI* (1904).

Francoeur, François (1698-1787) French composer and violinist. He became music director of the Paris Opéra (1739) and in 1772 music director at the court of Louis XV. He composed violin sonatas, operas and ballets.

Frankel, Benjamin (1906-1973) English composer and conductor who wrote incidental music for more than one hundred films. He studied in Germany and at the Guildhall, London. He worked as a café musician during World War II and as a jazz violinist. He started on his composing career by arranging popular scores and in 1946 became a tutor at the Guildhall. Apart from film music, Frankel wrote a violin concerto (1951), five string quartets, eight symphonies and sonatas for the violin and viola.

Franz, Robert (1815-1892) German composer of choral music and a series of highly-regarded songs. He studied in Dessau (1835) and was appointed organist at Ulrichskirche in Halle. In 1859 he became the musical director of Halle University. In 1868 illness forced him into semi-retirement, but he managed to edit works by Bach and Handel.

He composed more than 200 songs of a quality that was noted by Liszt and Schumann. He also wrote additional accompaniments to Bach's *St Matthew Passion* and *Magnificat* and Handel's *Messiah*.

Frederick the Great (Frederick II), King of Prussia (1712-1786) Composer and flautist as well as an outstanding military leader. He maintained a very fine musical establishment at his court in Berlin; C.P.E. **Bach** was a member of it for almost 30 years, and accompanied the king on the harpsichord when he played his own flute compositions. Frederick founded the Berlin Opera and wrote a great deal of flute music, both sonatas and concertos. One of his themes was taken up by **J.S. Bach** and used in his *Musical Offering*, which he dedicated to the king.

free counterpoint Counterpoint that is built up without reference to the specific rules of such composition. Free counterpoint is also known as composer's counterpoint and is often defined by contrast with student's (or **strict counterpoint**).

free fantasia In **sonata form**, an alternative term for **development**.

French horn Brass instrument with tube bent into a circular form. In its early form it could produce only the natural harmonics and was used mainly for playing hunting fanfares. In the early 18th century, when composers began to write for the instrument, they were still restricted to the natural harmonics. A number of developments transformed it into the

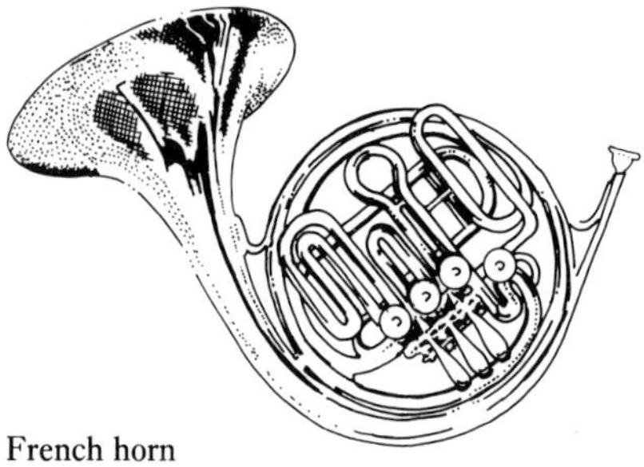

French horn

flexible instrument of today: first, the use of crooks – different lengths of tubing which could be changed to alter the fundamental pitch of the instrument, which was then described as a horn in D, F and so on, according to the crook. A player at that time might use as many as ten crooks. Secondly, the discovery in the late 18th century that the hand in the bell could modify the pitch (stopped notes) enabled the player to produce a complete scale, although some of the notes were muffled. This also produced the characteristic tone of the instrument. Thirdly, the evolution of valves in France during the 1820s, whereby the varied lengths of tubing were produced by piston valves instead of crooks, allowed the production of a complete chromatic scale throughout the compass. Fourthly, the development in Germany of double or even triple horns eased the task of the player. The horn is a **transposing** instrument: the modern instrument is usually pitched in B♭/F though the part is notated in F. Apart from its natural place in the orchestra, it is also used for particular effects: for Siegfried's hunting call in the *Ring*, and in Strauss's *Don Quixote*. Sonatas have been composed for horn by Beethoven and Hindemith, and trios by Brahms and Berkeley, as well as the more familiar concertos by Mozart, Haydn and Strauss. It is also used in military brass bands. See also **flugelhorn** and **saxhorn.**

French sixth Augmented sixth chord, consisting of a major third, augmented fourth and augmented sixth above the bass (for example, A♭-C-D-F♯).

Freni, Mirella (1935-) Italian soprano. She studied with Campogalliani and made her début in Modena as Micaëla in *Carmen* (1955). She sang in various Italian cities and in Amsterdam before her first appearance at Glyndebourne in 1960, as Zerlina in Mozart's *Don Giovanni*. In the following two years she sang Susanna in Mozart's *Le nozze di Figaro* and Adina in Donizetti's *L'elisir d'amore*. Her début at the Royal Opera House, Covent Garden, was in 1961 and at La Scala, Milan, in 1962; she has also sung at the Metropolitan, New York. Her roles were at first drawn from the lighter lyric repertory, including Violetta in *La traviata* and Mimì in *La bohème*. Since about 1970 she has been singing weightier Verdi and Puccini roles: Aïda, Desdemona in *Otello*, Amelia in *Simon Boccanegra*, and Madama Butterfly. A singer of great popularity and charm, she has made many fine recordings of the Italian repertory (*Simon Boccanegra* with Abbado; *Manon Lescaut* with Domingo and Sinopoli; *Madama Butterfly* with Carreras and Sinopoli).

frequency Measure of the pitch of a note in terms of the number of vibrations per second of the vibrating body producing it. The higher the frequency of sound, the higher is its pitch; the lower the frequency, the lower its pitch. Frequency is measured in hertz (cycles per second).

Frescobaldi, Girolamo (1583-1643) Italian composer and respected virtuoso organist. He studied with Luzzaschi in Ferrara and was appointed organist at St Peter's, Rome, in 1608 after a year in Antwerp. He also served the Grand Duke of Tuscany in Florence (1628-33). While in Rome, he taught the German organist **Froberger** and influenced both his playing and his composition.

Frescobaldi composed a series of madrigals and motets and some brilliant toccatas, notably those in his second book of keyboard pieces (1627), and fugues. His collection of organ works, *Fiori musicali* (1635), including *ricercari*, *canzoni* and variations, is still widely performed.

fret Small strip of wood, gut or metal fixed onto the fingerboard of certain string instruments (e.g. the lute, viol, guitar, mandoline, banjo and ukulele, but not those of the violin family). The performer presses his or her finger against a fret to shorten the length of the vibrating string, and thus raise its pitch.

Frick, Gottlob (1906-) German bass. He studied at Stuttgart and first sang with the Stuttgart Opera in 1927. His solo début was as Daland in Wagner's *Der fliegende Holländer* in 1934, in Coburg. He joined the Dresden Staatsoper in 1941 and the Berlin Städtische Oper in 1950. His début at Covent Garden was in 1951, and he appeared there many times; he also sang at the Metropolitan (New York), Salzburg and Bayreuth. With his powerful dark voice he specialized in Wagnerian villains – Hunding, Hagen and Fasolt in the *Ring* – and nobler characters, Gurnemanz in *Parsifal* being a particularly fine interpretation. Other roles included Sarastro in Mozart's *Die Zauberflöte,* Rocco in Beethoven's *Fidelio,* Caspar in Weber's *Der Freischütz* and Philip II in Verdi's *Don Carlos* – one of his few excursions outside the German repertory. He retired in 1970.

Fricker, Peter Racine (1920-1990) English composer who reflected the influences of Stravinsky and Bartók in his richly-patterned work. In 1953 he became director of music at Morley College, succeeding **Tippett**, and a professor of composition at the Royal College in 1956. In 1964 he was appointed visiting professor of music and composer in residence at the University of California. In 1947 his wind quintet won the Alfred Clements Prize and he was awarded the Koussevitsky Prize for his Symphony No.1, 1950. Among his other compositions are three symphonies, a violin concerto, *Fanfare for Europe* (1972) for trumpet, a large number of choral works that range from his *A Cappella Madrigals* (1947) to the oratorio *The Vision of Judgement* (1957) for soloists, choir and orchestra, the *Sinfonia in Memoriam*

Peter Fricker

Benjamin Britten (1977), the *Laudi Concertati* for organ and orchestra (1979) and other pieces for full and chamber orchestra, organ and piano.

Frid, Géza (1904-) Hungarian composer and pianist who studied at the Budapest Academy (1912) with **Kodály** and **Bartók**. He moved to Amsterdam in 1929 and became a Dutch citizen in 1948. His compositions include a symphony, a concerto and sonata for the piano and string quartets.

Friml, Rudolph (1879-1972) Czech composer who studied at the Prague Conservatoire. He visited the United States as a pianist with the virtuoso violinist and composer Jan **Kubelík** in 1901. He settled in the United States and performed his first piano concerto with the New York Symphony Orchestra in 1906. Friml composed a series of piano works and some chamber music, as well as a number of popular operettas including *Katinka* (1916), *Rose Marie* (1923) and *The Vagabond King* (1925).

Froberger, Johann Jacob (1616-1667) German composer and organist who was appointed organist at the court of Vienna in 1637 and studied with **Frescobaldi** in Italy

(1638-42). He travelled extensively, visiting Paris, Brussels, Rome and London. He composed a number of organ and harpsichord pieces.

frottola (It.) Late 15th- and early 16th-century Italian song originating in Mantua, for a group of several voices or a solo voice and instruments. It was set to poems of varying metres, and successive stanzas were sung to repetitions of the same music. The *frottola* was an important predecessor to the **madrigal**.

Frühbeck de Burgos, Rafael (1933-) Spanish conductor of German parentage. He studied the violin in Bilbao and Madrid, then turned to conducting with a *zarzuela* company. He went to Munich to study conducting further, then became conductor of the Bilbao Symphony Orchestra in 1958. He was appointed chief conductor of the Spanish National Orchestra in Madrid in 1962. He has also held posts in Düsseldorf and elsewhere, and became music director of the Montreal Symphony Orchestra in 1975. He has toured in Europe, Israel, the United States, and has also toured Spain with the New Philharmonia Orchestra, conducting choral works by Beethoven, Brahms, Haydn, Mendelssohn, and Walton. His recordings include *Carmina Burana* with the New Philharmonia, and works by Falla and other Spanish composers. He has received many honours, including the Gran Cruz del Mérito Civil.

Fry, William (1813-1864) American composer and critic notable for his opera *Leonora* (1845), which is considered to be the first important American operatic composition.

Fry was largely self-taught. In 1846 he moved to London and then Paris and became the music correspondent to the *New York Tribune*. On his return to the United States (1852) he continued to write, advancing the work and reinforcing the confidence of other American composers. He composed some symphonic pieces and a selection of choral music.

fuga (It.) Italian equivalent of the English **fugue**.

fugato (It.) Composition or passage using the technique of **imitation**, whereby a theme is brought in by successive voices, though not necessarily with the tonal conventions of the **fugue** proper.

fughetta (It.) Little fugue. Unlike the **fugato**, it is formally a proper **fugue**, although greatly condensed.

fugue Contrapuntal composition founded on a short theme (known as the **subject**), and written for two or more voices (so-called, whether the work is vocal or instrumental) or parts.

Common to all fugues is the **exposition**, in which the parts enter in turn with the subject, in **tonic** key, and then with its transposed form (known as the **answer**) in the **dominant**. The answer may reply literally, imitating exactly the shape of the subject.

In the course of the fugue, there are often several complete entries of all voices (with the order of entry changing). The complete entries are separated by episodes. When each subject has been announced, the subject or answer passes to another thematic element called the counter-subject. Once all voices have entered, the fugal exposition is complete.

After all the initial entries of the subject and answer, there is generally an episode derived from the material already heard or completely independent, leading to a further entry of the subject. The remainder of the fugue is made alternately of episodes and entries, which may include treatment of the subject in **canon**. Towards the end of the fugue, overlapping entries (known as stretto) may occur when the answer enters before the subject is completed. A **codetta** is a linking passage between the subject and the answer.

The most famous exposition of fugue structure is **Bach's** *The Art of Fugue*.

Fuleihan, Anis (1901-1970) American composer and pianist who wrote an early concerto for the **thérémin** flute, an electronic instrument. Fuleihan was born in Cyprus and moved to the United States in 1915. His first appearance as a pianist was with the New York Symphony Orchestra in 1919. During the 1920s he composed ballets for two companies. In 1947 he became professor of music at Indiana University and he returned to the Middle East to become the director of the National Conservatoire in Beirut (1953). Fuleihan conducted the Tunis Orchestra (1963-5) and then returned to Illinois University to teach. Among his other compositions were two symphonies, concertos for the violin, piano, cello and bassoon and *Cyprus Serenades* for orchestra.

full anthem **Anthem** that is written for full chorus throughout, as opposed to the **verse anthem**, which includes sections featuring smaller groups (solo, duet, quartet, etc.).

full orchestra Orchestra that consists of the usual four sections (strings, woodwind, brass and percussion) and is up to normal concert-hall strength. See **orchestra**

full organ The terms *organo pleno* (It.) and *plein jeu* (Fr.) have the same meaning and indicate that an organ passage should be played using the full extent of the instrument's power.

full score **Score** that shows all the parts at once. See also **orchestral score**; **vocal score**.

fundamental First partial of a **harmonic series**. It is the note produced by playing the open string or the open-ended organ pipe.

fuoco (It.) Fire. *Con fuoco* indicates that the playing of a particular passage should be vigorous and powerful.

furiant Lively Czech dance with changing rhythms, often used by **Dvořák** in place of a **scherzo**.

Furtwängler, Wilhelm (1886-1954) German composer and the leading German conductor of his generation. He was noted for his interpretations of Beethoven, Bruckner and Wagner. He studied in Munich under **Rheinberger** and conducted in Zurich and Lübeck, before succeeding **Nikisch** as conductor of both the Leipzig Gewandhaus Orchestra and the Berlin Philharmonic in 1922. He was a frequent conductor at **Bayreuth** during the 1930s and 1940s, and also conducted at the Salzburg Festival. In 1946 his career recovered after difficulties in the war years and he again toured widely as a conductor. Furtwängler composed three symphonies, a *Te Deum*, a piano concerto and some chamber music.

futurism Attempt by the Italian poet Marinetti and the painter-musician Luigi **Russolo** to combine traditional sounds of music with sounds of explosions, shrieks, screams and groans. The Futurist movement began in Rome in 1909, at which time it received the support of Mussolini, and it continued until the late 1930s. Marinetti (*Futurismo e fascismo*, 1924) and Russolo (*L'arte dei rumori*, 1916) both wrote books on the subject. The composer Francesco Pratella (1880-1955) was a strong advocate of musical futurism.

Fux, Johann Joseph (1660-1741) Austrian composer and organist who rose to prominence in Vienna, where he commanded the respect of both court and clergy. Fux entered the Jesuit University in Graz in 1680 and was employed as an organist by the Primate of Hungary, resident in Vienna. Emperor Leopold I was impressed with his compositions and sent Fux to study in Rome in 1698. On his return to Vienna (1700) Leopold's successor, Joseph I, appointed him court composer. He became choirmaster at the church of St Stephen (1705) and *Kapellmeister* (1715).

He was a prolific composer, completing 19 operas including *Constanza e fortezza*, written to celebrate the coronation of the Emperor Charles VI as King of Bohemia (1723), 50 Masses, oratorios, partitas and other instrumental works. He also wrote a seminal treatise on counterpoint, *Gradus ad Parnassum* (1725).

G

G Seventh note of the scale, one tone above F and one tone below A. The scale of G major has one sharp in the key-signature.

G G major

Gabrieli, Andrea (1533-1586) Italian composer and organist associated with the most magnificent era of the Venetian school. He developed the *cori spezzati* style, which positioned instruments and singers at various points within the chapel to create separate centres of sound.

Gabrieli studied with **Willaert**. He toured Germany in 1562 and was greatly influenced by **Lassus**. He succeeded **Merulo** as organist at St Mark's in 1566. His pupils included his nephew Giovanni **Gabrieli**, **Hassler** and **Sweelinck**.

He composed a series of motets, psalms and madrigals as well as Masses and instrumental pieces, including the motets *Cantiones Ecclesiasticae* (1576) and *Cantiones Sacrae* (1565). Also of interest are his madrigals *Jiustinianae* (1571), musical caricatures of various Venetian figures. Perhaps his greatest work, however, was published after his death, notably the *Canzoni alla francese* (1605) and various *ricercari* (1589-96).

Gabrieli, Giovanni (1557-1612) Italian organist and one of the great composers of ceremonial music and of *Sacrae Symphoniae* – motets with instrumental accompaniment. Some critics believe his *Sonata Pian e Forte* (1587) to be one of the earliest instances of music to contain expression marks.

He studied with his uncle Andrea **Gabrieli** and followed him to Germany, becoming a musician with **Lassus** at the Bavarian court before returning to Venice in 1584. He succeeded Andrea as organist of St Mark's, Venice, in 1585, composing, and teaching such figures as **Schütz**.

Gabrieli's compositions include various *canzone*, toccatas and motets, including *Angelus ad Pastores* (1587), *O Magnum Mysterium* (1587), *Hodie Christus Natus Est* (1597) and *Jubilate Deo* (four versions, 1597-1615).

Gade, Niels (Wilhelm) (1817-1890) Danish composer, organist and violinist with the Royal Orchestra whose work reflects the influences of **Mendelssohn** and **Schumann**, as well as national characteristics. Gade visited Italy and Germany, becoming the assistant conductor of the Gewandhaus Orchestra in Leipzig (1844) and befriending **Mendelssohn**. He returned to Copenhagen in 1848 and was appointed *Kapellmeister* to the court there in 1861. He visited England in 1876 and conducted at the Birmingham Festival. He received a Doctorate in 1879 and was eventually made a Commander of the Order of Dannebrog. Among Gade's compositions are eight symphonies, six overtures, including *In the Highlands* (1844) and

Michelangelo (1861), cantatas, the opera-ballet *The Fairy Spell*, music for the piano and for strings, and a series of songs.

gagaku (Japan) Refined music, a general term for imperial court orchestral music of Japan. It may be purely orchestral (**kangen**), or used to accompany dance (**bugaku**). The repertory is divided into two main categories, Old Music (Kogaku) and New Music (Shingaku). These categories are divided into a further two classes according to their origin: **Togaku** (music of the left) denotes the repertory imported from China, while **Komagaku** (music of the right) is imported from Korea and Manchuria. There is a slight difference in the instrumentation of *Togaku* and *Komagaku*, although they both share oboes (**hichiriki**), mouth-organs (**shō**), flutes and drums. The *Togaku* orchestra, when performing *kangen*, adds the lute (**biwa**) and a form of zither. *Komagaku* is generally used only for *bugaku* accompaniment and not as an independent orchestral form.

gaida General name for various bagpipes in Southern and Eastern Europe (also oboes in Iberia and North Africa – see **zurna**). In Bulgaria, where it is particularly common, the sheepskin or goatskin windbag is filled by a mouthpiece (not by bellows, as in parts of Yugoslavia, Czechoslovakia and Poland) and has one or two chanters in addition to a drone pipe. It occurs in three sizes, the largest being used to accompany the male voice. In ensembles including a frame drum, it accompanies dances on festive occasions. An alternative transliteration is *gaita*.

gaillarde Alternative spelling of **galliard**.

gaku-biwa (Japan) Type of **biwa** or lute.

Gál, Hans (1890-1987) Austrian composer and musicologist. He studied in Vienna and later taught there, writing five operas, of which *Die heilige Ente* (1923) was the most successful. He left Austria because of the Nazi regime and settled in Edinburgh, where he taught at the university and was involved in the musical life of the city. He produced four symphonies, concertos for violin and for piano, much choral music and some fine chamber pieces, rather in the mould of Brahms and Strauss. He also wrote studies of several composers, including Schubert and Brahms.

galanteries Extra dances or other musical pieces added to those in the standard Baroque suite. The most frequently used were bourrées, **minuets** and gavottes.

galant style (Fr. *style galant*, It. *stile galante*) Term used in the 18th century to describe music with regular melodic phrases and light accompaniment, with delicate feeling and graceful formality. Used in the titles of opera-ballets by Campra (1697) and **Rameau** (1735) and of paintings by Watteau, the description has been applied to the works of F. **Couperin**, **Telemann**, D. **Scarlatti**, **Galuppi**, **Soler** and J.C. **Bach**.

Galilei, Vincenzo (*c.*1520-1591) Italian composer, lutenist and father of the astronomer Galileo Galilei. He wrote some important theoretical texts and was a member of a group of poets and musicians whose discussions influenced the early development of opera. This group, the **Camerata**, met at **Bardi**'s Florentine villa and included the composers **Peri**, **Caccini** and **Cavalieri**. They debated the revival of Greek drama and assisted the development of early forms of declamatory song for the solo voice, important in the evolution of opera.

Galilei wrote a treatise on style and tuning, *Dialogo della musica antica e della moderna* (1581), and a book on lute-playing, *Il fronimo* (1568). Among his compositions are a number of **madrigals** and lute pieces.

galliard Lively 16th-century dance in triple time, often linked thematically with the **pavane** (England), or passamezzo (Italy). It is now obsolete, but was revived by **Vaughan Williams** in *Job, A Masque for Dancing* (1930).

Galli-Curci, Amelita (1882-1963) Italian **coloratura** soprano. She studied piano at Milan Conservatoire, but was mostly self-taught as a singer. Her début in Italy was in 1906, and thereafter her career took her to various countries in Europe and Latin America, although she never sang opera in Britain. In 1916 she made her United States début in Chicago as Gilda in Verdi's *Rigoletto*, and sang many roles with the company, including Rosina in *Il barbiere di Siviglia*, Violetta in *La traviata* and the title-roles in Donizetti's *Lucia di Lammermoor* and *Linda di Chamounix*. She sang with the Metropolitan Opera from 1921, but by 1930 developed throat problems and eventually retired. Her many recordings reveal her unforced, limpid tone and graceful style.

galop Quick ballroom dance in duple time with a leap or hop at the end of each phrase. The dance first appeared under this name in Paris (1829), but it originated in Germany, where it was known as a *galopp*.

Galuppi, Baldassare (1706-1785) Venetian composer who found success in Italy and England with comic operas that influenced the development of that genre. He studied with **Lotti** and became choirmaster of St Mark's, Venice, and director of the *Conservatorio degli Incurabili* in 1762. He visited London in 1741 and St Petersburg in 1765-7.

Galuppi composed oratorios, devotional music and sonatas for harpsichord as well as more than 100 operas, including *Adriano in Siria* (1740), *Scipione in Cartagine* (1742), *Il filosofo di campagna* (1754) and *Il re pastore* (1762).

Galway, James (1939-) British flautist, born in Northern Ireland. He studied at the Royal College of Music and the Guildhall School in London, and later in Paris. After a career as an orchestral player, culminating in membership of the Berlin Philharmonic, he went solo in 1975, quickly gaining great popularity with his technical virtuosity, the expressiveness of his playing and his engaging personality. With his gold flute he has made many recordings, ranging from Bach and Mozart to contemporary music. Works have been dedicated to him by Thea **Musgrave** (*Orpheus*) and others. He has written an autobiography, and has frequently appeared on television.

gamaka (India) Standard embellishments used to characterize individual notes. It is the primary means by which subtlety of expression is achieved in all melodic styles, and includes all varieties of glides, bends and vibrati.

gamba Shorthand term for **viola da gamba**. Also, an open metal organ stop imitating the tone of the *viola da gamba*, ranging over 4-, 8- and 16-foot pipes.

gambang (Java) Type of xylophone and the only instrument in the **gamelan** ensemble with keys made of wood. The keys, spanning two to four octaves, are laid over a wooden box frame and are hit with two sticks made of buffalo horn tipped with small, padded discs.

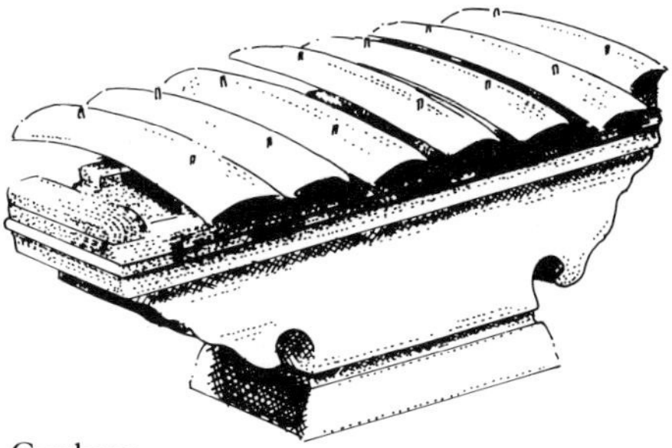

Gambang

gambuh (Bali) Archaic theatrical form, with plots taken from the literature of 14th-century court life in East Java. The ensemble is unusual because it includes the large, wailing **suling** flutes. Otherwise, it is a small ensemble consisting of **rebab**, a pair of drums, gongs, cymbals and bells. Although *gambuh* is not frequently performed, it has provided the foundation for all Balinese dance and drama, and many of the more popular small **gamelans** are derived from the *gambuh* ensemble.

gamelan (Indonesia) Generic name for a musical ensemble or orchestra, derived from the Javanese word *gamel* meaning 'hammer' and therefore suggesting the percussive method of playing. A *gamelan* may vary in size from just a few instruments to as many as 80. The fundamental instruments common to both Balinese and Javanese gamelans are keyed metallophones, which elaborate with intricate interlocking patterns a fixed, repeated melody of equal note length; and knobbed gongs, whose function, being **colotomic**, subdivides binarily the temporal cycle of the melody.

In Java there are two kinds of *gamelan* playing, the 'loud style' which makes use of the louder bronze instruments and is led by a drummer, and the 'soft style' which, led by a two-string bowed lute (**rebab**), may additionally feature a flute (**suling**), a wooden-keyed xylophone (**gambang**), a female singer and a male chorus.

In contrast to the generally sedate character of the Javanese *gamelan*, the Balinese *gamelan* is more brilliant and more rhythmically dynamic, making greater use of melodic interplay between pairs or quartets of keyed metallophones and often adding sets of small cymbals.

gamut 1. The entire range of musical pitches, from the highest to the lowest.

2. Formerly, it was the name for one particular note, the G on the bottom line of the bass stave (from *gamma*, the lowest note of the **hexachord**, plus *ut*, the first note of the scale).

3. It also came to be used to mean the scale.

gangsa (Bali) Single-octave metallophone of the **gamelan** orchestra, with bronze keys suspended over a sound box, the ends of each resting on cushions. The instrument is struck with a single mallet. Built in pairs or quartets, *gangsas* play complex interlocking parts which together elaborate the melodic line of the composition. Half of the number of *gangsas* are 'female' and tuned slightly lower than their 'male' counterparts, so that when played together they produce the distinctive shimmering effect of the **gamelan**. Equivalent to the Javanese **saron**.

Ganze-Note (or Ganze Taktnote) (Ger.) Equivalent of the English **semibreve**.

gapped scale Any scale having fewer than seven notes. For example, the **pentatonic** scale, which has five notes.

García, Manuel (1775-1832) Spanish tenor, one of the best-known of his day. He was a student at the choir school in Seville, making his début in 1798. He went to Paris in 1808, and then to Naples and Rome; he was the first Count Almaviva in Rossini's *Il barbiere di Siviglia* (1816), and became famous for his Rossini interpretations. He spent much time in Paris at the Théâtre Italien, and in London, singing and putting on his own works (he composed many operas and operettas). He took a company to New York in 1825 – the first such tour by an Italian troupe; it included his three famous children, Manuel García II, Pauline **Viardot** and Maria **Malibran**.

Gardelli, Lamberto (1915-) Italian conductor and composer of four operatic works. He studied in Pesaro and Rome and became a singing tutor and rehearsal director at the Rome Opera in 1940. He conducted in Rome, making his début there in 1945, in Stockholm (1946), Budapest (1961) and at Glyndebourne (1964). Gardelli has also conducted at Covent Garden and in New York.

Garden, Mary (1874-1967) American soprano of Scottish origin. She studied in

Chicago and Paris, where she made an unexpected début in the title-role of Charpentier's *Louise* in 1900 when the leading soprano was taken ill. She created the role of Mélisande in Debussy's *Pelléas et Mélisande* in 1902. She sang in London (1902) and in New York (1907), where she gave the first American performance of Massenet's *Thaïs*. In 1910 she joined the Chicago opera company, and sang with it until 1931. During her brief but financially disastrous directorship in 1921-2, the première took place of Prokofiev's *The Love for Three Oranges*. Her repertory encompassed not only the major French operas of the time but also Verdi (*La traviata*), Strauss (*Salome*) and Honegger (*Judith*).

Gardiner, Henry Balfour (1877-1950) English composer who strove to bring recognition to the work of Gustav **Holst**. He studied at Oxford and in Frankfurt with Ivan Knorr and was appointed music-master of Winchester College. He promoted performances of contemporary English music (1910-20) and became its most enthusiastic and influential champion.

Among Gardiner's compositions are the *Shepherd Fennel's Dance* for orchestra (1911), pieces for choir and orchestra such as *News from Whydah* (1912), a symphony and chamber works.

Gardiner, John Eliot (1943-) British conductor, specializing in early music. He studied with Thurston Dart and George Hurst, and in Paris with Nadia **Boulanger**. While a student at Cambridge he founded the Monteverdi Choir, and later the Monteverdi Orchestra. He made a special study of the works of **Rameau**, conducting the first ever performance of *Les boréades* at Aix in 1982. His Covent Garden début was in 1973 with Gluck's *Iphigénie en Tauride*; his New York début followed in 1979. He founded the English Baroque Soloists in 1978, dedicated to historically **authentic** performances of Handel, Bach and other Baroque and early classical masters. He has been director of the Göttingen Festival and musical director of the Lyons Opéra (1982-7).

Gasparini, Francesco (1668-1727) Italian composer who contributed to the practice of **figured bass** accompaniment with a treatise on the harpsichord, *L'armonico practico al cimbalo* (1708). He studied with **Corelli** and **Pasquini** and became choirmaster at the Ospedale della Pietà in Venice, 1701. In 1725 he was appointed *maestro di cappella* at St John Lateran in Rome. Gasparini composed oratorios and other devotional pieces, cantatas and a number of operatic works, including *Amleto* (1705).

Gassmann, Florian (1729-1774) German composer who studied with Padre **Martini** in Bologna and was employed as a court musician to Count Leonardo Veneri in Venice. In 1763 he moved to Vienna to succeed **Gluck** as a composer of ballets. In 1772 he founded the *Tonkünstler Sozietät*, a benevolent trust for the dependants of musicians.

Gassmann composed 20 operas, including *La contessina* (1770) and *L'amore artigiano* (1779), 54 symphonies, as well as works for the chamber and chapel. His music was admired by his pupil **Salieri** and by **Mozart**.

Gastoldi, Giovanni Giacomo (*c.*1552-1609) Italian composer whose *Balletti a cinque voci con li suoi versi per cantare, sonare, e ballare* (1591) heavily influenced **Hassler** and **Morley**, who imitated its style in his *First Booke of Balletts to Five Voices* (1595). Gastoldi was appointed a singer at the ducal palace in Mantua in 1581 and composed a number of **madrigals**, Latin psalms and Masses.

gat (India) Short, fixed composition set in any tempo and any **tala** in an instrumental **rāga**, accompanied by **tablā**. It follows the **ālāp** and **jor** sections and is used as the basis for extensive improvisation, its theme recurring as a kind of refrain.

gatra (Java) Smallest melodic unit in Javanese compositional theory. It consists of a set of four sonic events, including silences if they occur, and recognizable as set patterns with a specific melodic contour.

Gaultier, Denis (1603-1672) French composer and lutenist who composed elaborate conceits for the lute in collections of dances, notably *La rhétorique des Dieux* (*c.*1652). His style of composition influenced later harpsichordists, who like **Froberger** and **Chambonnières** imitated his use of **broken chords** and **arpeggios**.

Gauntlett, Henry John (1805-1876) English composer and organist who composed hundreds of hymn tunes, including *Once in Royal David's City*. He became organist at Southwark Cathedral in 1827 and lectured at the London Institute (1837-43) on aspects of the organ's construction.

Gaveaux, Pierre (1761-1825) French composer and singer who left a career as a tenor at the Opéra-Comique to compose for the same theatre. About 30 of his operas were performed there in the 1790s, including *Léonore* (1798), to a libretto by Bouilly from which **Beethoven** constructed *Fidelio*.

Gedda, Nicolai (1925-) Swedish tenor. He studied in Leipzig and at the Stockholm Conservatoire, making his début in 1952. He sang at La Scala, Milan, later that year, and in Paris in 1954. His first appearance at Covent Garden was in 1955, as the Duke of Mantua in Verdi's *Rigoletto*, and at the Metropolitan Opera, New York, in 1957. He first performed the title-role in Berlioz's *Benvenuto Cellini* in 1961, and has become closely associated with it. His repertory, a great deal of which he has recorded, is extremely varied and includes not only operas but songs, notably those of Fauré. He is considered a supreme interpreter of French opera, although he is outstanding in all areas. One unexpected but notable recorded performance is of Elgar's *Dream of Gerontius*.

Geminiani, Francesco (1687-1762) Italian composer and violinist who published *The Art of Playing on the Violin* (1751). He also wrote *A Treatise of Good Taste* (1749), *The Art of Playing the Guitar*, and *The Art of Accompaniment*. He studied with A. **Scarlatti** and **Corelli** and became a member of the Naples opera orchestra in 1711. He toured England in 1714 as a soloist and won wide acclaim. He lived in Dublin (1733-40) and spent the intervening years living and working in Paris and London.

Geminiani's compositions include 18 *concerti grossi*, 24 violin sonatas, and pieces for the cello and harpsichord. He also composed the ballet *La foresta incantanta* (1754).

gendèr (Indonesia) Family of metallophones with a range of two or more octaves, made of thin bronze keys suspended over individual tubular resonators. The instrument is struck with two mallets or padded discs on short sticks, and produces a mellow, non-percussive sound. There are two or more *gendèrs* in each **gamelan**, which together play interlocking parts, elaborating the melodic line. The shadow puppet play **wayang kulit** is accompanied by its own quartet of *gendèrs*.

Javanese gendèr

gending/ghending (Indonesia) Generic term for composition.

Genée, Richard (1823-1895) German composer and conductor, notable for his libretto *Die Fledermaus* (1872), for which Johann **Strauss** composed the music.

He conducted for many orchestras, including the *Theater an der Wien* orchestra in Vienna (1868-78). He also composed several successful operettas.

Genzmer, Harald (1909-) German composer who studied at the Berlin Conservatoire with **Hindemith** and became a professor of composition at the Hochschule für Musik, Freiburg, in 1946. He studied and composed for electronic instruments, including the trautonium. Among Genzmer's compositions are the *Bremer Symphony* (1942), concertos for orchestra, strings, piano, cello, flute, oboe and trautonium, and a number of choral pieces and sonatas.

Gerhard, Roberto (1896-1970) Spanish composer of Franco-Swiss descent who became identified with the Spanish idiom and later with the methods of **Britten** and **Tippett**. He studied with **Granados** and Pedrell at Barcelona and with **Schoenberg** in Vienna and at the Berlin Conservatory (1924). He was appointed a tutor and music librarian at the Catalan Library in Barcelona in 1929, but when civil war broke out in Spain he moved to England and settled in Cambridge in 1940. He was later to become an important figure in innovative English music.

Gerhard's compositions reveal an impressionist influence, gleaned from a study of **Debussy**, as well as the **serialism** associated with Schoenberg. They nonetheless still retain a Spanish flavour and preserve an air of stylistic independence and subtlety. The serialism displayed in his second symphony (1959), for example, is very individual and conventionally harmonic. His ballet suites, *Alegrías* (1944) and *Don Quixote* (1941), and the opera *The Duenna* (1947) also betray a similar independence. Gerhard completed four symphonies as well as several concertos and other chamber pieces.

German, Sir Edward [G. E. Jones] (1862-1936) Welsh composer who had great success with his incidental pieces for Shakespeare's plays, including *Richard III* (1889), *Henry VIII* (1892), *Romeo and Juliet* (1895) and *As You Like It* (1897). He studied at the Royal Academy of Music and began playing in theatre orchestras as a violinist. In 1888 he became conductor and musical director at the Globe Theatre and began composing for the stage. He was made a Fellow of the Royal Academy in 1895 and was knighted in 1928.

German composed several light operettas, including the popular *Merrie England* (1902), *The Princess of Kensington* (1903) and *Fallen Fairies* (1909). He also produced some orchestral pieces, including two symphonies and the *Welsh Rhapsody* (1904), as well as pieces for the theatre.

Germani, Fernando (1906-) Italian composer and organist who is widely respected for his bold recitals and for his edition of the works of **Frescobaldi**. He studied at the Rome Conservatory and at the Papal School of Church Music. In 1936 he travelled to the United States to become an organ tutor at the Curtis Institute, Philadelphia. He became an organist at St Peter's, Rome, in 1948.

German sixth Form of **augmented sixth**.

German sixth

Gershwin, George (1898-1937) American composer and pianist whose parents emigrated from Russia in 1893 to settle in Brooklyn, New York. He began his career in Tin Pan Alley, the centre of the popular music industry; he wrote several songs during this period, including *Swanee* (1916), an early success that boosted the career of Al Jolson. In 1919 he wrote his

George Gershwin

first stage musical, *La La Lucille*, which captured the public imagination. For the next 40 years Broadway persistently demanded more Gershwin compositions. Among his most enduring stage shows were *Primrose* (1924), *Lady Be Good* (1924), *Tell Me More* (1925), *Oh, Kay* (1926), *Strike Up the Band* (1927), *Funny Face* (1927) and *Girl Crazy* (1930). Some shows, such as *Funny Face*, *Shall We Dance* and *The Goldwyn Follies*, were later made into film musicals. Numerous other musicals benefited from Gershwin songs: among the many he composed, often with his brother Ira as lyricist, are *Embraceable You*, *The Way You Look Tonight*, *I Got Rhythm*, *Let's Call the Whole Thing Off* and *The Man I Love*.

In 1924 he produced a 'serious' work, the *Rhapsody in Blue* for piano and jazz ensemble. It was orchestrated by Ferde **Grofe**, although Gershwin himself scored later pieces. The *Concerto in F* for piano was commissioned by Walter **Damrosch** the following year; the orchestral piece *An American in Paris* (1928), an ingenious rhapsodic instrumental work, was hailed by several critics as an important link between jazz and the concert hall. It formed the basis for the score of the film of the same title, which also featured five of his songs. His opera *Porgy and Bess* (1935), written for a black cast and including the beautiful lullaby *Summertime*, enjoys an established place in the repertory.

Gershwin was able to combine jazz idioms with conventional orchestrations to produce an archetypal musical expression of 20th-century American culture.

Gesualdo, Carlo, Prince of Venosa (1560-1613) Italian nobleman who composed devotional works and six books of **madrigals**, considered to be of a very advanced chromatic complexity and sensitivity to their text. He murdered his first wife and her lover, but escaped severe punishment and married for the second time, into the house of Este. He played at the court of the Estensi at Ferrara from 1594 to 1596 and composed four books of madrigals in this time. He returned to Naples in 1597. A violent, passionate man, he spent the latter part of his life suffering from severe depression. His fifth and sixth books of madrigals were published in 1611.

Gevaert, François-Auguste (1828-1908) Belgian composer and historian who published several important works on instrumentation and contributed greatly to modern understanding of ancient music. He studied at the Ghent Conservatoire and won the Prix de Rome in 1847. He travelled throughout Europe, finding success in Paris with his operas before becoming musical director of the Paris Opéra in 1867. In 1871 he was appointed Director of the Brussels Conservatoire. Gevaert composed a number of operas and operettas and wrote a treatise on orchestration, *Nouveau traité général d'instrumentation* (1885). He also published collections of earlier music, including *Gloire d'Italie* (1868) and *Chansons du XVe siècle* (1875).

geza (Japan) Lower place, referring to the off-stage ensemble in the **kabuki** theatre, found behind a slatted screen, down-stage right. The ensemble provides music, sound effects, noise and signals not covered by the on-stage **debayashi** ensemble, often underlining and punctuating dialogue and action. The *geza* ensemble comprises melody instruments including **shamisen**, **koto**, **shakuhachi**, a **noh** flute, and a large selection of percussion instruments, including drums (*taiko*, *ō-tsuzumi*), gongs, chimes, bells and xylophones.

ghazal (India) Light classical genre of 19th-century origin, now very popular among Muslims of northern India and Pakistan. It consists of an Urdu text on a romantic theme, set to a short, simple melody.

Ghedini, Giorgio Federico (1892-1965) Italian composer who produced several transcriptions of works by Bach, Monteverdi and Frescobaldi. He studied at the Turin and Bologna conservatoires and became assistant conductor at the Teatro Regio, Turin. In 1937 he was appointed professor of harmony and composition at the Turin Conservatoire but moved to Parma (1938) and then to Milan Conservatoire (1942) where he became director in 1951.

Among his compositions are eight operas, including *Billy Budd* (1949), which was produced at least a year before **Britten**'s opera of the same name. He also wrote a symphony, concertos for the piano, violin and viola, as well as chamber music, choral works, songs and film scores.

ghending (India) See **gending**

Ghiaurov, Nicolai (1929-) Bulgarian bass. He studied in Sofia, Leningrad and Moscow, and first sang in 1955 as Don Basilio in *Il barbiere di Siviglia*. He has sung at Covent Garden, the Metropolitan (New York), Salzburg, Paris and Vienna. Gifted with a true heavy bass in the Russian style, he is also able to sing baritone roles. His greatest successes have been as Méphistophélès in Gounod's *Faust*, King Philip in Verdi's *Don Carlos* and above all the title-role in Mussorgsky's *Boris Godunov*, in which his forceful acting is an added dimension. His recordings include several Verdi operas.

Giannini, Vittorio (1903-1966) American composer who combined the influences of Verdi, Puccini and the vigour and fullness of Richard Strauss in his operatic work. He studied at the Milan Conservatoire and at the Juilliard School, New York. His compositions include the symphony *In Memoriam Theodore Roosevelt* (1935), concertos for the piano and organ, a *Stabat Mater* and nine operas, including *Lucidia* (1934), *The Scarlet Letter* (1938) and *The Servant of Two Masters* (performed in 1967).

Giardini, Felice de (1716-1796) Italian composer and violinist who produced a number of operas and a large amount of music for strings. He was a member of the Milan Cathedral Choir and played in opera orchestras in Rome and Naples. He toured Germany (1748) and England (1751) as a virtuoso performer, settling in London as the leader of the orchestra at the Italian opera in 1756. He contributed to three choral festivals in the 1770s and in 1790 he founded a comic opera company at the Haymarket Theatre.

Gibbons, Orlando (1583-1625) English composer and organist whose works form an important contribution to sacred music in English. His style reflects an exchange of ideas between the solo voice and other voices or instruments which verges on the **polyphonic** form. In 1596 Gibbons became a chorister at King's College, Cambridge. He was appointed organist at the Chapel Royal in 1604. While in the service of James I, he performed as a chamber musician and later became organist at Westminster Abbey (1623).

Among his compositions are the anthems *O Lord in Thy Wrath* in six parts, much admired for its intensity, and *This is the Record of John* which has an accompaniment for viols rather than the usual organ. His **madrigals** (such as *The Silver Swan*) were published in a collection entitled *Madrigals and Motets of Five Parts* (1612). He also composed many keyboard works and a number of **fantasies**, **pavanes** and **galliards** for instrumental consort (viols).

Gibbs, Cecil Armstrong (1889-1960) English composer. After studying at Cambridge with Dent and Wood he taught for a while in Sussex. His music for a school play, *Crossing* (1919), brought him into close touch with the poet Walter de la Mare. The conductor on this occasion was Adrian **Boult**, who was so impressed by the music that he suggested Gibbs should enter the Royal College of Music. He studied under both Boult and **Vaughan Williams**, and later taught there. He was active as a festival adjudicator in Britain for nearly 30 years (1923-52). His lifelong friendship with De la Mare resulted in some of his most beautiful songs, settings of the poet's works (including *Peacock Pie*); other fine songs set the poetry of Mordaunt Currie and others. He also composed much choral music, designed for amateur choirs; orchestral suites and dances; operas (*The Blue Peter*, *Twelfth Night*); incidental music for the stage; and piano music, including the outstandingly successful slow waltz *Dusk* (1946).

Gibson, Sir Alexander (1926-) Scottish conductor who studied in Glasgow at the Royal Scottish Academy of Music and in Salzburg and Siena. He became music director at **Sadler's Wells** in 1957, and principal conductor of the **Scottish National Orchestra** in 1959, a post he held until 1984; during this period the orchestra gave many new works, including the first British performance of Stockhausen's *Gruppen* (1961). In 1962 he was co-founder of **Scottish Opera**, and as artistic director built it into a very fine ensemble during his 25 years' tenure, conducting a warmly received *Ring* cycle and Berlioz's *Les troyens* and giving several premières. He has conducted in the United States (principal guest conductor, Houston Symphony Orchestra) and Europe, but it is the revitalization of music in Scotland that is his greatest achievement. His repertory includes Dvořák, Elgar and Sibelius, a cycle of whose works he recorded in 1990 with the **Royal Philharmonic Orchestra**.

Gidayu-bushi (Japan) Narrative vocal form, named after its most celebrated exponent and used in the **bunraku** puppet theatre. It was later adopted by the **kabuki** theatre. Accompanied by the **shamisen** lute, it consists of heightened speech and intense extremes of vocal expression. *Gidayu kyogen* are plays written for the puppet theatre, recited in the *Gidayu-bushi* style. There are regular *Gidayu-bushi* competitions in Japan.

Gielen, Michael (1927-) Austrian composer, conductor and pianist who was born in Germany and has travelled widely as a conductor. He studied in Buenos Aires and became a tutor at the Teatro Colón in 1947. In 1951 he moved to Vienna to join the staff of the Vienna State Opera and was appointed resident conductor in 1954. He became chief conductor of the Royal Swedish Opera in 1960 and a conductor for the West German Radio Orchestra at Cologne in 1965. In 1969 he was appointed director of the National Orchestra of Belgium. He was musical director of the Frankfurt Opera for ten years (from 1978). He has also conducted in New York and with the BBC and Cincinnati Symphony Orchestras. Among his compositions are choral pieces and works for the chamber orchestra.

Gieseking, Walter (1895-1956) German pianist who studied in Hanover and when he was 20 gave a series of recitals of Beethoven's sonatas. He performed the première of **Pfitzner**'s Piano Concerto in 1923, and was noted for playing contemporary music, including that of **Schoenberg** and **Szymanowski**. Although he recorded all of Mozart's solo piano works and most of Beethoven's, as well as outstanding versions of the concertos, his qualities of clarity and sensitivity were supremely well suited to the piano music of Ravel and Debussy, all of which he also recorded.

Gigli, Beniamino (1890-1957) Italian tenor, considered one of the greatest of the century. He studied in Rome under Rasati, and made his début in 1914. He sang Faust in **Boito**'s *Mefistofele* many times; at La Scala in 1918 the performance, under **Toscanini**, was in memory of the composer, who had recently died. He went to New York in 1920 and sang at the Metropolitan Opera for 12 seasons, where his reputation was unrivalled, notably in *La bohème*, *L'africaine* and *La Gioconda*. At Covent Garden in 1930 he sang another of his finest roles, Giordano's *Andrea Chénier*; after the war he returned there for many appearances, establishing himself as a great favourite. He made numerous recordings, from which his beautiful sweet tone can be appreciated.

Gigout, Eugène (1844-1925) French composer and organist who enjoyed considerable acclaim as a virtuoso performer. He studied at the Ecole Niedermeyer with **Saint-Saëns** from 1855, and was appointed a professor there after graduation. He became organist at St Augustin in 1863 and held the post until his death. In 1885 he founded an organ school and in 1911 became a professor of the organ at the Paris Conservatoire. Gigout's compositions include many works for the organ, toccatas, fugues, anthems and concertos, noted for both their power and their technical brilliance, and liturgical pieces based on Gregorian chant.

Gilbert, Henry (1868-1928) American composer who studied in Boston with **MacDowell** and became heavily influenced by folk-music and by the traditional melodies of the black population. His work reveals a romanticism inherited from MacDowell and a melodic structure gleaned from **negro spirituals**.

Gilbert's compositions include a *Comedy Overture for Negro Themes* (1905), *Three American Dances* (1911) and *Negro Rhapsody* (1913). He also wrote a number of symphonic pieces and prologues as well as a ballet, *Dance in Place Congo* (1918).

Gilels, Emil (1916-1985) Russian pianist who began his studies in Odessa. In 1933 he won first prize at an important Moscow competition, and studied there for a further two years. He won several other major prizes, and taught at the Moscow Conservatoire. After the war he began an international career, touring Europe and the United States. His début in England was in 1959. His immaculate technique was allied to a sense of power and energy which was ideally suited to Beethoven and Bartók; he was also capable of great delicacy and finesse. His recorded repertory is extensive and ranges from the Baroque to the 20th century.

Giles, Nathaniel (1558-1633) English composer of anthems and services. He was choirmaster at Worcester Cathedral and from 1585 at St George's Chapel, Windsor, where he was also one of the organists. In 1597 he was appointed Gentleman and Master of the Children of the Chapel Royal.

Gillis, Don (1912-1978) American composer who wrote comic and serious pieces and never forgot the popular idiom to which he was introduced as a brass-player at college. He studied at the Texas Christian University and joined Fort Worth Radio in 1932 as a composer and arranger. In 1944 he was appointed Programme Director and Producer of the National Broadcasting Company in New York, where he worked with **Toscanini**. He was chairman of the Southern Methodist University music department from 1967 and chairman of fine arts at Dallas Baptist College from 1968.

Among his compositions are ten

symphonies, including the *Symphony No.5+*, subtitled *Symphony for Fun* (1946), *No.8, The Man who Invented Music* (1950), and *A Short Short Symphony* (1975), some comic operas and an oratorio, *The Crucifixion*.

Gilson, Paul (1865-1942) Belgian composer and critic who sensed a lack of direction in Belgian music at the turn of the century and attempted to inspire young composers. He studied at the Brussels Conservatoire with **Gevaert** in 1887 and became music critic for *Le soir* in 1906. He helped to produce *La revue musicale belge*, 1924, with which he attempted to encourage his musical contemporaries. He became an inspector of music in Belgian schools in 1908. Gilson's compositions include operas, cantatas, overtures and organ works.

gimel Alternative spelling of **gymel**.

Ginastera, Alberto (1916-1983) Argentinian composer whose style developed from naive nationalistic influences to a mature grasp of **serialist** techniques. He is still highly regarded for his operatic works.

Ginastera studied at the Williams Conservatoire in Buenos Aires (1928) and at the National Conservatoire from 1936 with Athos Palma. He moved to New York in 1942, where he studied with **Copland**; he returned to Argentina in 1948. He founded the Centre for Advanced Musical Studies in Buenos Aires and became its director in 1963. In 1971 he moved to Switzerland. Among his compositions are the operas *Don Rodrigo* (1964), *Bomarzo* (1967), and *Beatrix Cenci* (1971), the ballets *Estancia* (1941) and *Variaciones concertantes* (1953), an *Argentine Concerto* (1961) for piano and orchestra, another piano concerto (1972), three string quartets and other choral and chamber pieces.

giocoso (It.) Jocose. Indication that the music is to be played in a merry or playful style.

Giordani, Giuseppe (*c.*1753-1798) Italian composer commonly known as Giordaniello. After his studies at the Conservatoire in Naples he wrote many operas for Mantua (including *Ritorno d'Ulisse*, 1782, and *La Vestale*, 1786), Florence, Pisa and Rome (including *Ifigenia in Aulide*, 1786). He also wrote oratorios, beginning with *La fuga in Egitto* (*c.*1775), and in 1791 became choirmaster at Fermo Cathedral.

Giordani, Tommaso (1730-1806) Italian composer and conductor. After leaving his native Naples (*c.*1745) to perform Italian operas with his family, he spent some years in London (1753-6 and 1768-83) composing for the King's Theatre in the Haymarket and for the Vauxhall Pleasure Gardens, and Dublin (1764-8 and 1783-1806), where he worked as an impresario (1783-4) and music director of the Theatre Royal in Crow Street (1788). He composed more than 50 operatic pieces in Italian and English, including the comic operas *Il acio* (1782) and *The Cottage Festival* (1796), as well as many songs (including some for the first performance of Sheridan's *The Critic*, 1799) and many solo chamber and orchestral pieces, such as the very successful keyboard *Six Concertos* (Op.14, 1775), in the **galant** style. The popular song *Caro mio ben,* often ascribed to Tommaso, was probably written by Giuseppe **Giordani**.

Giordaniello Nickname of the Italian composer Giuseppe **Giordani**.

Giordano, Umberto (1867-1948) Italian composer of opera with a bold, expressive style; he had some early success which he was unable to sustain. He studied at the Naples Conservatoire from 1880 and achieved his first success with the opera *Mala vita* in Rome in 1892. This work exploited a **verismo** style which met the demands of the audience for realism in opera, a style which he abandoned in his later pieces. Subsequent operas were far more romantic, notably *Regina Diaz* (which failed on its appearance in Naples in 1894) and *Fedora* (1898). His most successful and enduring work is *Andrea Chenier* (Milan, 1896), a tragedy set in the French Revolution. Other, later operas have disappeared from the repertory.

Giovannelli, Ruggiero (1560-1625) Italian composer who was appointed *maestro di cappella* at St Peter's, Rome, succeeding **Palestrina** in 1594. In 1599 he became a member of the Sistine Choir. He composed several madrigals, four of which were translated by **Morley** in his *Madrigalls to Five Voices* (1598), a 12-part Mass and other Masses and motets.

Giovanni da Cascia (*fl.*1340s) Florentine composer active in Verona (and possibly Milan) in the mid-14th century. His works include 16 two-voice madrigals and three three-voice **cacce** in florid style. He was also known as Johannes de Florentia or da Firenze.

Gipps, Ruth (1921-) English composer, pianist, oboist and conductor who studied at the Royal College of Music with **Vaughan Williams** and Morris. She became an oboist with various orchestras and a concert pianist. In 1948 she became choirmaster with the City of Birmingham Choir and conducted the London Repertory Orchestra from 1955. In 1961 she founded the Chanticleer Orchestra and became a professor of composition at the Royal College of Music in 1967. Gipps composed five symphonies, concertos for the oboe, piano, violin and viola, the cantata *Goblin Market*, a tone poem for wind instruments and other choral works.

giraffe piano Form of upright piano made in Germany in the 19th century, but now obsolete. It is fundamentally a grand piano, the body of which stands on end. The bass strings on the left are encased in an elongated box not unlike the neck of a giraffe in appearance.

Gis (Ger.) Equivalent of the English G♯.

Giraffe piano

gittern Medieval form of guitar with four strings, played with a **plectrum**. The body and neck of the gittern were carved from the same block of wood, with a hole beneath the fingerboard for the performer's thumb. It survived in England until the late 17th century.

Giuliani, Mauro (Giuseppe Sergio Pantaleo) (1781-1828) Italian composer and guitarist who was largely self-taught, but who toured widely as a virtuoso performer. In 1806 he settled in Vienna and while there befriended **Beethoven**. In 1814 he was made *virtuoso onorario di camera* for Napoleon's second wife. He settled in Naples after accumulating crippling debts in the Austrian capital.

Giuliani composed more than 200 pieces for guitar, including three concertos, chamber pieces and numerous songs.

Giulini, Carlo Maria (1914-) Outstanding Italian orchestral and operatic conductor, noted for his impassioned yet disciplined style and his association with the works of Verdi. Having studied at the Accademia di S. Cecilia in Rome, he made his opera-conducting début at Bergamo in

1951 in a performance of Verdi's *La traviata* and for the next five years held the post of music director at La Scala, Milan. Following his British début, conducting the **Glyndebourne** Company in a performance of Verdi's *Falstaff* at the 1955 Edinburgh Festival, he began a long association with the Philharmonia Orchestra. From 1958 to 1967 he was a guest conductor at Covent Garden, where in 1958 he conducted a memorable performance of Verdi's *Don Carlos*. He returned to Covent Garden in 1982 to conduct *Falstaff*. From 1969 to 1972 he shared with Sir Georg **Solti** the conductorship of the Chicago Symphony Orchestra, and from 1978 to 1984 he was conductor of the Los Angeles Philharmonic Orchestra.

giusto (It.) Just, or proper. Used to indicate moderation or exactness of tempo.

Glanville-Hicks, Peggy (1912-1990) Australian composer who worked in the United States between 1922 and 1959 to encourage concert performances of contemporary pieces. She studied with Fritz Hart at the Melbourne Conservatoire (1929-31). In 1932 she moved to Europe and studied at the Royal College of Music, London, in Vienna and in Paris. In 1942 she settled in New York, composing and later working as music critic for the *New York Herald Tribune* (1948-58) and organizing concerts of contemporary music.

Glanville-Hicks's compositions reflect a combination of **serial** techniques with ancient and oriental idioms. They include the opera *Nausicaa* (1961), the ballets *Tragic Celebration* (1964) and *Saul and the Witch of Endor* (1964) and the *Etruscan Concerto* for piano and orchestra.

Glass, Philip (1937-) American composer who studied at the University of Chicago and at the Juilliard School. Later he worked under **Boulanger** at the Paris Conservatoire (1964-6). In 1966 he met the Indian **sitār** virtuoso and composer Ravi **Shankar** and abandoned the styles of composition that he had developed to embrace Indian idioms. He later adopted the **minimalist** style – short repetitive melodies with steady driving rhythmic and static harmonies. His works include the operas *Einstein on the Beach* (1975), *Akhnaten* (1985), the ballet *Glass Pieces* (1982); instrumental works such as *Music in 5ths*, *Music in Similar Motion* (1969) and *Music with Changing Parts* (1970), as well as incidental music and film scores, including music for John Irvin's *Hamburger Hill*. He is an immensely popular and successful composer who has also been involved in popular music groups. When *Akhnaten* was produced at the **English National Opera** it scored a great success and attracted wide audiences, for many of whom this was their first experience of opera.

glass harmonica Instrument consisting of glass vessels, partly filled with liquid, and tuned to produce musical notes when rubbed round the rim with dampened fingers. In 1763 Benjamin Franklin invented a machine which he called musical glasses. It consisted of graded sizes of glass half-globes that were attached to a spindle in a trough of water. A pedal was used to revolve the spindle, and by touching the half-globes with the fingers notes were produced. Mozart composed a quintet for it in 1791.

Glazunov, Alexander Konstantinovich (1865-1936) Russian composer whose work reveals the dominant influences of Liszt and Wagner. In his earlier years he was associated with the group of Russian nationalist composers, the **Mighty Handful**.

He studied privately with **Rimsky-Korsakov** from 1880 and became a tutor at the St Petersburg Conservatoire in 1899. His first symphony, in E♭ major, was performed in 1882 conducted by **Balakirev**, and was a great success. A series of Russian concerts at the Paris Exhibition of 1899 included two of

Glazunov's symphonies and his tone poem *Stenka Razin* (1885). In 1906 he was appointed director of the St Petersburg Conservatoire. His ballet *The Seasons* (1899) was adopted by Pavlova. Another ballet, *Raymonda*, is a staple of the Bolshoi's repertory.

Glazunov completed nine symphonies, all of which reflect the temperament of the Russian school, concertos for the piano, violin, cello, saxophone and strings, six orchestral suites, chamber music and a number of choral works including the *Hymn to Pushkin* (1899).

glee Light-hearted choral composition for unaccompanied male voices that was especially popular in England in the 17th, 18th and early 19th centuries. The glee is written in sections, which vary according to the mood of the line of poetry set. The Glee Club of London, founded in 1783 and lasting until 1857, gave performances of glees, **madrigals**, **motets**, **canons** and **catches**. In the United States, glee clubs exist in universities today, but these groups sing many forms of music, not just glees.

Glière, Reinhold Moritzovich (1875-1956) Soviet composer and conductor, best known for his ballet *The Red Poppy* (1926), based on the events of the Russian Revolution. It exhibits a powerful social realism. Glière studied at Kiev (1891) and at the Moscow Conservatoire (1894) with **Arensky**. In 1905 he entered the Berlin Conservatoire. He was appointed director of the Kiev Conservatoire in 1913 and a tutor of composition in Moscow in 1920. In 1939 he became chairman of the Organizing Committee of Soviet Composers.

Among his powerful, nationalistic compositions are three symphonies, the *March of the Red Army* (1924) and the *Victory Overture*. His later pieces sometimes reflect the influences of Eastern Soviet folk-music, particularly his opera *Shah Senem* (1934) and the symphonic poems *Cossacks of Zaporozhy* (1921) and *Trizna* (1915). He also wrote chamber music, 175 works for the piano, and songs.

Glinka, Mikhail Ivanovich (1804-1857) Russian composer regarded by Tchaikovsky as 'the acorn from which the oak of Russian music sprang' and revered by successive schools of Soviet composers.

While at school in St Petersburg he took piano tuition from John **Field**. In 1828 he studied composition with Zamboni and went to Milan, Vienna and Berlin, where he studied with Siegfried Dehn in 1833. On his return to St Petersburg in 1836 he was appointed *Kapellmeister* to the Imperial Chapel. In 1844 he visited Paris and met **Berlioz**, and travelled in Spain and other countries before returning to Russia in 1847.

Glinka's compositions developed a strong Russian temperament. His first opera, *Ivan Susanin* (*A Life for the Tsar*, 1836), with its clarity and simplicity, was a reaction against the prevailing supremacy of Italian opera. His second, *Ruslan and Ludmilla* (1842), was powerfully Russian, betraying oriental colours and folk melodies from the Eastern steppes. A similar atmosphere pervades his instrumental fantasy *Kamarinskaya* (1848). His *Jota aragonesa* (1845) is based upon Spanish rhythms, but most of his works, including many song-cycles and piano pieces, are steeped in Russian idioms.

glissando Sliding scale played on a piano or harp, not by fingering, but by sliding over the keys or strings. On a piano or similar keyboard instrument, a glissando can be played only in C major, by sliding the fingers over adjacent keys.

On bowed instruments a glissando is played on one string by sliding the finger up or down while bowing. Glissando passages can be played on a trombone by not interrupting the breath while the slide is moved to another position. They can also be played on clarinet (for instance, in **Gershwin**'s *Rhapsody in Blue*) and on pedal timpani.

Globokar, Vinko (1934-) Yugoslav composer and virtuoso trombonist whose extraordinary command of this instrument enabled him to perform the avant-garde pieces that his tutor **Berio** composed for him. He was born in France and studied at the Ljubljana Conservatoire from 1949 and at the Paris Conservatoire with Liebowitz, Lafosse and Berio (1959-63). He became a trombone tutor at Cologne's Musikhochschule in 1968. Among his compositions are *Plan* (1965), *Fluide* (1967), *Etude Pour Folklora I & II* (1968) and *La Ronde* (1970) for various combinations of instruments, as well as choral and chamber pieces.

Glock, Sir William (1908-) English critic, administrator and pianist. He studied at Cambridge and with **Schnabel** in Berlin, and began a career as a concert pianist with some success. He became a critic in 1934, chiefly for the *Observer*. After the war he concentrated on musical education, founding the Dartington Summer School, of which he was music director until 1979. In 1959 he became controller of music at the **BBC**, and held the post for 13 years; during this time his imaginative planning of Third Programme broadcasts, juxtaposing contemporary music with familiar favourites, and his revitalization of the Promenade Concerts consolidated his reputation as an outstanding administrator. He was knighted in 1970 and retired in 1973; he was artistic director of the Bath Festival, 1976-80.

glockenspiel Percussion instrument, consisting of a set of tuned steel plates played either with two hammers, one held in each hand, or with a mechanism operated by a piano keyboard. It has a range of two and a half octaves and produces a bell-like sound.

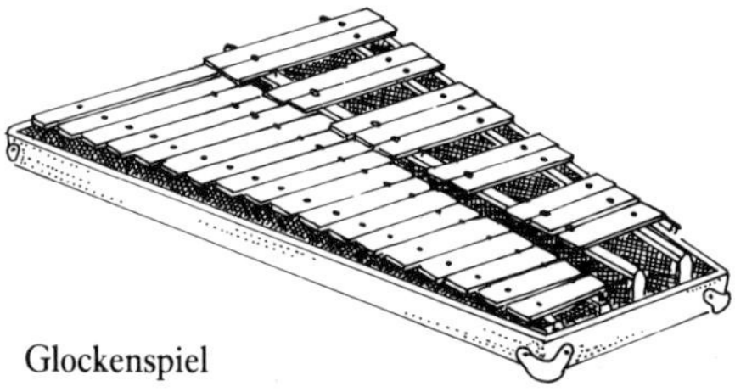

Glockenspiel

Glossop, Peter (1928-) Outstanding English operatic baritone. He joined the chorus of the **Sadler's Wells** Opera in 1952. With the recognition of his vocal gifts he was soon promoted to leading roles. In 1961 he won the first international opera competition in Sofia, Bulgaria, and made his Covent Garden début in 1962. Around this time he studied with the great Italian baritone Tito **Gobbi**, and was soon in demand in the leading opera-houses of the world. In 1964 he was awarded the Verdi gold medal, and made his début at La Scala, Milan, in 1965. After his début in 1967 at the Metropolitan, New York, he sang there each season for many years. He sang first in Vienna in 1968. Glossop has been particularly admired, especially in Italy, for his performances of Verdi's baritone roles, though his repertory covers a wide field, including Britten's *Billy Budd*, which he recorded with the composer conducting.

Glover, Jane (1949-) British conductor, musicologist and broadcaster. She made her début as a conductor at the Wexford Festival in 1975. In 1980 she became chorus-master at Glyndebourne and has also conducted there. In 1983 she was appointed musical director of the London Choral Society and in 1984 she became artistic director of the **London Mozart Players**. In 1988 she became the second woman to conduct at the Royal Opera House, Covent Garden. She has edited operas by Monteverdi and Cavalli and has made BBC television series on the history of the orchestra and the life of Mozart.

Gluck, Christoph Willibald von (1714-1787) Bohemian-born German composer of opera whose most positive innovation was the abandonment of **da capo** arias, where convention made nonsense of dramatic continuity, replacing them with more intense natural declamation and a more seamless texture.

Gluck entered a Jesuit school in 1726 and Prague University in 1732. He earned a living performing on the violin and piano and teaching until he was appointed to the court of Prince Lobkowitz at Vienna in 1736. In 1737 he moved to Milan with Prince Melzi to continue his study with Giovanni **Sammartini**, and wrote his first opera, *Artaserse* (1741). He travelled to London in 1745 at the height of his success, where he met **Handel**. He visited other countries before being appointed director of the court musicians by Joseph, Prince of Saxe-Hildburghausen, in Vienna in 1754. In 1773 he composed *Iphigénie en Aulide* for the Paris opera company. He returned to Vienna in 1779.

His early operas reflect Italian styles, whereas later ones, including *La Cythère assiégée* (1759), *L'ivrogne corrigé* (1760), *Orfeo ed Euridice* (1762), *Alceste* (1767) and *Iphigénie en Tauride* (1779), are in the French manner. *Orfeo ed Euridice*, *Alceste* and *Paride ed Elena* (1770) reflect a new style which subordinates virtuosity to dramatic truth and seeks to use the music of opera to express the poetry of its libretto. Their narratives are direct and continuity is maintained through the abandonment of traditional **secco** recitatives in favour of the sustained dramatic tempo of classical Greek drama.

Glyndebourne Name of the house and estate of John Christie (1882-1962) where the Glyndebourne Festival Opera was founded in 1934. The first operas to be performed were *Le nozze di Figaro* and *Così fan tutte*.

Up to the beginning of World War II the repertory was mostly devoted to the works of Mozart, though the first English performance of Verdi's *Macbeth* was given in 1938. The music director was Fritz **Busch**, the producer Carl Ebert and the manager Rudolf Bing, who between them set high standards, attracting internationally acclaimed singers. During the postwar years several premières were given, including **Britten**'s *Rape of Lucretia* (1946) and *Albert Herring* (1947), and the repertory was extended to include Strauss, early opera and more Verdi. The Royal Philharmonic and London Philharmonic Orchestras have appeared for the opera company. Music directors have included Vittorio **Gui**, who was responsible for the inclusion of several of Rossini's operas, John **Pritchard** and Bernard **Haitink**. The touring company was set up in 1968 to take productions to various British venues.

Gnecchi, Vittorio (1876-1954) Italian composer memorable for his quarrel with Richard **Strauss** whom he accused of plagiarism, Strauss's *Elektra* (1909) resembling his own *Cassandra* (1905). He studied at the Milan Conservatoire and produced several successful operatic works, including *Cassandra* and *La Rosiera* (1927).

Gobbi, Tito (1915-1984) Italian baritone who studied in Rome and made his début in 1935 as Rodolfo in Bellini's *La sonnambula*. Gobbi sang at Covent Garden, San Francisco and Chicago, as well as at all the Italian opera houses and in Vienna. His repertory covered nearly 100 operas and he made many films. Gobbi was best known for his interpretations of **Verdi** and **Puccini**, especially the villainous Baron Scarpia in *Tosca*, and was also a fine actor. In 1965 he turned to opera production and published his autobiography in 1979.

Godard, Benjamin (1849-1895) French composer and violinist who studied at the Paris Conservatoire from 1836 and in 1885 founded and conducted the *Concerts modernes* in Paris. Among his compositions are two concertos for violin, a symphony and works for the piano. He also wrote eight operas which are now forgotten, chamber pieces and more than a hundred songs.

Godowsky, Leopold (1870-1938) Polish composer and pianist who became an American citizen in 1891. He studied at the Berlin Hochschule with **Saint-Saëns** in 1887 and toured the United States as a performer. He became a piano tutor in Philadelphia in 1890, and in 1894 was appointed director of the piano school at the Chicago Conservatoire. He toured in Europe as a tutor and recitalist, returning to America in 1912. Godowsky's compositions include *53 Studies on Chopin, Etudes* and *Triakontameron* (all for the piano) and three symphonic pieces.

Goehr, Alexander (1932-) English composer who employs **serial** techniques and was strongly influenced by Schoenberg and his pupils. He is a member of the Manchester School of composers, which includes Peter Maxwell **Davies**, Harrison **Birtwistle** and John **Ogdon**. The son of the German conductor Walter Goehr, he studied composition with Richard **Hall** at the Royal Manchester College of Music. In 1957 he began studies at the Paris Conservatoire with **Messiaen**. He joined the BBC in 1960 and became composer in residence at the New England Conservatoire in 1968. He held academic posts in the music departments of Yale, Leeds and Cambridge Universities and is now Professor of Music at Cambridge. Among his compositions are the opera *Arden muss sterben* (1966), orchestral works, including a *Little Symphony* (1963), *Pastorals* (1965), a *Symphony in One Movement* (1970) and various romances for strings, as well as choral and vocal works (notably *5 Poems and an Epigram of William Blake*, 1964) and chamber pieces.

Goetz, Hermann (1840-1876) German composer who studied at the Stern Conservatoire, Berlin, in 1860 and became organist at Winterthur in 1863. He composed the successful opera *The Taming of the Shrew* (1874). He settled in Zurich and started work on a second opera, *Francesca da Rimini*. However, he died before it was finished, Ernest Frank taking up and completing his work. He also composed *Frühlingsoverture* for orchestra, a symphony, and concertos for the piano and the violin as well as chamber pieces and songs.

Goldberg, Johann (1727-1756) German composer and keyboard player who studied with **Bach** from 1742 and became a chamber musician at the court of Count Brühl in 1751. He composed two concertos for the keyboard and music for the flute and harpsichord. Bach's 30 variations for harpsichord were dedicated to him and are known as the *Goldberg Variations*.

Goldmark, Karl (Károly) (1830-1915) Hungarian composer and violinist. He studied at the Vienna Conservatoire and remained in Vienna as a tutor, composer and critic. He became a friend of **Brahms** during this time and was undoubtedly influenced by him. In 1848 he joined a theatre orchestra at Györ in Hungary. Goldmark's compositions include six operas (of which *The Queen of Sheba*, 1875, and *Merlin*, 1886, are the best known), the symphonic poem *Rustic Wedding* (1876) and two overtures, *Im Frühling* and *Sakuntala*. He also composed concertos and choral works, pieces for the piano and a number of songs.

Goldmark, Rubin (1872-1936) American composer and nephew of Karl Goldmark, who studied at the New York Conservatoire and later at the Vienna Conservatoire. He returned to New York to study at the National Conservatoire with **Dvořák**. In 1895 he became director of the Colorado College Conservatoire and was appointed director of the composition department at the Juilliard School in 1924. While there he taught **Copland** and **Gershwin**. Goldmark's compositions include a *Requiem* for orchestra, a *Negro Rhapsody*, *Hiawatha* and other chamber pieces.

Goldschmidt, Berthold (1903-) German-born British composer and conductor who in 1964 conducted the first performance of **Mahler's** Symphony No.10, in the performing version prepared by Deryck Cooke with his and others' advice. After studying at Hamburg University and with **Schreker** in Berlin he joined the Berlin State Opera in 1925 and took part in the first performance of **Berg's**

Wozzeck. He moved to England in 1935 and was music director for the Ballets Joos. Later he joined the German service of the BBC. In 1947 he was appointed chorus-master of the **Glyndebourne** Opera and conducted Verdi's *Macbeth* at the first Edinburgh Festival. His opera *Der gewaltigen Hahnrei* (1932) was produced in Mannheim and scheduled for performance in Berlin the following year, but was cancelled when the Nazis came to power. His other opera, *Beatrice Cenci*, based on the play by Shelley, won a prize at the Festival of Britain in 1951. His other compositions include concertos for clarinet, violin and cello, as well as three string quartets, a clarinet quartet, songs, choral and piano music.

Gombert, Nicholas (*c.*1500-*c.*1556) Flemish composer and follower of **Josquin des Prés**. He served Emperor Charles V until 1540 and won a high reputation for his **motets**, **Masses** and **chansons**. He was admired for his use of the **polyphonic** style, which developed through his 160 motets into a distinctive form in which voices imitate each other in a complex relationship of melodies.

gong Circular percussion instrument made of bronze, with a rim. It is struck with a mallet covered with various materials according to the quality of sound required.

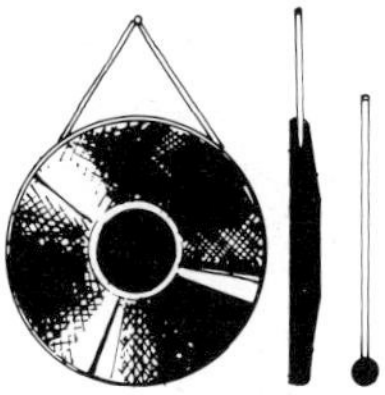

Gong

gong-ageng (Indonesia) Largest form of gong which hangs in an imposing frame at the back of the larger **gamelans** and serves as the primary **colotomic** or time-marking instrument in the *gamelan*.

gongan (Indonesia) Complete melodic period or phrase ending with a stroke on the largest gong, usually the **gong-ageng**. It is the fundamental **colotomic** or time-marking event in a **gamelan** composition and usually consists of multiples of eight beats. The *gongan* is subdivided by other time-marking gongs, such as the **kenong**, **kempul** and **ketuk**.

Goodall, Sir Reginald (1901-1990) British conductor, noted above all for his Wagner interpretations. He studied at the Royal College of Music, and spent much time in Munich and Vienna, where he developed a love of Bruckner and Wagner. After assisting **Coates** and **Sargent** he obtained a post at **Sadler's Wells Opera**, where he conducted the première of **Britten**'s *Peter Grimes* in 1945. Soon afterwards he joined the music staff at the Royal Opera House, Covent Garden, where his wide repertory encompassed **Massenet**'s *Manon*, **Berg**'s *Wozzeck*, Beethoven's *Fidelio* and Britten's *Gloriana*. In 1954 he conducted his first *Walküre*. His career entered the doldrums for a while, and he spent the next years coaching singers in Wagnerian roles (in a little room high in the Royal Opera House which naturally came to be referred to as Valhalla). In 1968 a brilliant performance of *Die Meistersinger von Nürnberg* with the **English National Opera** established him in his rightful place as a supreme Wagnerian, and his accounts of *Parsifal* (1971), the *Ring* cycle (1973) and *Tristan und Isolde* (1979) were acclaimed with universal enthusiasm and later recorded. He was knighted in 1985.

Goossens, Sir Eugene (1893-1962) English composer and violinist who encouraged the performance of new music and enjoyed a successful career as an international conductor. He studied at the Bruges Conservatoire, the Liverpool College of Music and at the Royal College of Music with **Stanford**. He conducted many orchestras in London, where he was an assistant to **Beecham** (1916-20), as well as in the United States and Australia. He was knighted in 1955. His compositions include the opera *Judith* (1929), which has

Sir Eugene Goossens

a libretto by Arnold Bennett, a symphony and *Sinfonietta* (1922) for orchestra, and choral works such as *Silence* (1922) and the oratorio *Apocalypse* (1952). He also wrote chamber music.

Goossens, Leon (1897-1988) The leading oboist of his generation, who transformed the style and technique of his instrument. Born in Liverpool, he came from a famous Belgian musical family: his grandfather and father were conductors of the Carl Rosa touring opera company; his brother Eugene **Goossens** was an internationally known composer and conductor; his brother Adolphe, a horn-player, was killed in World War I; his sisters Marie and Sidonie were leading harpists in London orchestras. Leon Goossens studied at the Royal College of Music; his ears were opened to the possibilities of the oboe by the playing of the Belgian Henri du Busscher, whose place he was to take as principal of the Queen's Hall orchestra at the age of 17. In 1924 he joined the Covent Garden Orchestra, and in 1932 was a founder-member of **Beecham**'s **London Philharmonic**. Goossens transformed what had been the harsh, unyielding tone of his instrument by modifying the shape and thickness of the reed to produce the sweet, expressive sound for which he became internationally famous as the first solo oboist of distinction. Elgar, Gordon **Jacob**, **Vaughan Williams** and Leon's brother Eugene composed important works for him. It was said that as a member of Beecham's orchestra he taught the conductor the art of phrasing. He was made CBE in 1950.

gopak Russian folk-dance with music of a lively character, in duple time. It originated in the Ukraine. An alternative spelling is hopak.

Gossec, François (1734-1829) Belgian composer who wrote many pieces that glorified the ideals of the French Revolution. He was a chorister at Antwerp Cathedral and taught himself composition. In 1751 he moved to Paris and became friends with **Rameau**, who secured him a post as conductor of concerts organized by La Pouplinière. He was appointed musician to the court of Louis-Joseph de Bourbon, Prince de Condé, in 1762. In 1773 he was made a director of the *Concert spirituel* and a second conductor at the Paris Opéra. He became a professor of composition at the Paris Conservatoire in 1795.

Gossec composed more than 30 symphonies and 15 operas, as well as ballets and devotional pieces, including the *Messe des morts* (1780), which experimented with complicated arrangements of instruments and voices.

Gotovac, Jakov (1895-1982) Yugoslav composer and conductor who studied in Split and at the Vienna Academy and became conductor of the Croatian Opera in 1923. His compositions include the opera *Ero the Joker* (1935), which reflects the folk-music of his country, and a number of chamber and choral works.

Gottschalk, Louis Moreau (1829-1869) American composer, conductor and pianist who studied with **Hallé** and **Berlioz** in Paris and began a career as a virtuoso pianist. He toured widely as a popular performer and conductor. A scandal involving one of his female students in 1867 forced him to move to South America, and he embarked upon an arduous schedule of tours in order to remain solvent. He wrote two symphonies and works for the chamber and stage, some of which have been lost, although recordings have been made of others. His compositions for the piano, including *The Aeolian Harp* and *The Dying Poet*, are still performed.

Goudimel, Claude (*c.*1520-1572) French composer who wrote a number of **Masses** and **motets** before his conversion to Protestantism, when he abandoned the ornate style of his earlier sacred works to compose simple psalms and spiritual songs for the Huguenot community. He was killed by Catholics at Lyons in the St Bartholomew's Day Massacre of 1572.

Gould, Glenn (1932-1982) Canadian pianist who studied at the Toronto Royal Conservatoire. He made his début at the age of 14. Gould had an extremely wide repertory and toured all over the world, including the USSR. He was an outstanding interpreter of Bach, among others. He was somewhat eccentric, and in 1964 decided to give up playing in public and confine his work to the recording studio; a large body of fine recordings is still available.

Gould, Morton (1913-) American composer, pianist and conductor who is highly regarded for his skills as an orchestrator. His compositions reflect a fusion of the idiom of popular American music with the form and structure of classical works. He has also experimented with jazz, as in his *Boogie-Woogie Etudes* for piano (1943). Gould studied at the Institute of Music and Art, New York, and followed a career as a broadcaster working for NBC and CBS. His compositions include three symphonies, a concerto for tap dancer and orchestra, *Cowboy Rhapsody* (1944), an orchestration of *The Battle Hymn of the Republic* (1951), *Lincoln Legend* (1941) and *Fall River Legend* (1947). He has also written several Broadway musicals, including *Delightfully Dangerous* and *Billion Dollar Baby* (1945).

Gounod, Charles (1818-1893) French composer, organist and conductor whose work is still widely respected today and has retained a place in the international repertory. After a classical education, during which he received piano instruction from his mother, he entered the Paris Conservatoire, studying with **Halévy** and Lesueur. He was organist at the Eglise des Missions Etrangères, Paris, for a while. His earlier compositions reflect his ecclesiastical background, comprising mainly Masses and oratorios. He won the Prix de Rome in 1839 and visited Austria and Germany. In 1870 he moved to England to be the first conductor of the Royal Albert Hall Choral Society, renamed the Royal Choral Society in 1888; this appointment lasted only two seasons. His most famous composition is his opera *Faust* (1859), which is still popular today. Other operas include *Philémon et Baucis* (1860), *La reine de Saba* (1862), *Mireille* (1864), *Roméo et Juliette* (1867), and *Le tribut de Zamora* (1881). He also wrote some orchestral pieces, including two symphonies and choral works; many of these reflect the influence of **Palestrina**, whose work he studied while in Rome.

Gow, Nathaniel (1763-1831) Scottish composer, violinist and trumpeter who became leader of the Edinburgh Assembly Orchestra in 1791. He composed many dance pieces, and as a publisher produced several collections of his own work and that of others. He wrote *Caller Herring* as a harpsichord piece combining the tones of cathedral bells with the cries of Edinburgh's fishwives.

Grabu, Louis (?-*c.*1694) French composer and violinist who settled in England in

1665. He then served as Master of the King's Musick to Charles II from 1666 to 1674. He composed for the stage, completing music for Dryden's nationalist opera *Albion and Albanus* in 1685.

grace note Ornamental note considered additional to a melody or harmony, not included in the notated rhythm. It is always printed in small type on a score.

Grace note

Gradual Responsorial chant following the reading of the Epistle and coming before the Gospel in the **Mass**. It is coupled with the **Alleluia** or Tract, and its text is taken from one of the psalms.

gradulka Bulgarian fiddle, held vertically and rested on the knee, as opposed to being held horizontally and rested against the chest or shoulder like a modern **violin**.

Grainger, Percy (1882-1961) Australian-born composer and pianist who became an American citizen in 1919. He was admired by **Britten** and others, chiefly for his experiments with folk melodies, which he arranged for the orchestra in an original and striking style. His use of English instead of Italian to mark the dynamics of his scores is unusual.

Grainger studied in Melbourne, Frankfurt and later at the Berlin Conservatoire, where he was a pupil of **Busoni**. In 1900 he toured England as a recitalist and settled there; he became a friend of **Grieg**, by whom he was invited to Norway to study his Piano Concerto in A Minor. He came to the attention of **Delius** with his arrangement of the folk melody *Brigg Fair*, which Delius himself was later to rhapsodize. In 1915 he performed in the United States and moved there shortly afterwards. He was appointed chairman of the music department of New York University in 1932.

Grainger's best-known compositions include *Country Gardens* (1925), *Handel in the Strand* (1911), *Shepherd's Hey* (1922) and the *Rosenkavalier Ramble* for piano. He also composed *Shallow Brown* for chorus and orchestra (1927), *Over the Hills and Far Away* (1928) and *Molly on the Shore* (1921) for orchestra.

grama (India) Ancient name for basic scale forms used in the Sanskritic tradition of northern Indian music. Each is characterized by a unique set of intervals (**shrutis**) governed by certain rules.

Granados, Enrique (1867-1916) Spanish composer of music in the nationalistic idiom, and also a virtuoso pianist. He studied composition with Pedrell in Barcelona and the piano with de **Beriot** in Paris. He returned to Barcelona to found his own piano school and the Society of Classical Concerts in 1900.

Among his compositions are the operas *Maria del Carmen* (1898), *Gaziel* (1906), *Liliana* (1911) and *Goyescas* (1916), which has a memorable intermezzo; a series of orchestral suites including *Elisenda*, *Suite arabe* and *La nit del mor*, and works for voice and piano. His piano pieces and songs are, perhaps, the most brilliant: the piano suite *Goyescas*, from which he derived the opera, is based upon the paintings of Goya and is a virtuoso piece that remains very popular. The songs *Canciones amatorias* and his *Allegro de concierto* reflect a deeply poetic and elegant character.

gran cassa (It.) Equivalent of the English bass **drum**.

Grandi, Alessandro (?-1637) Italian composer of sacred music in the concerto style, as well as of solo cantatas, motets and accompanied madrigals. He became choirmaster at Ferrara Cathedral in 1615 and from 1617 singer and later assistant director to **Monteverdi** at St Mark's, Venice. In 1625 he was appointed *maestro di cappella* at S. Maria Maggiore, Bergamo.

grand jeu (Fr.) Organ stop that brings the whole instrument into play.

grand opera Style of opera established in Paris in the late 1820s, which was built around grandiose plots and made use of large ensemble scenes, expanded orchestral resources and colourful pageantry. It catered for the newly prosperous and relatively uncultured bourgeois classes of that time. Later these characteristics became less pronounced and grand opera merged with comic opera. Among the operas of this genre were **Rossini**'s *Guillaume Tell* (1829) and **Meyerbeer**'s *Les Huguenots* (1836).

grand piano **Piano** whose shape was originally derived from the **harpsichord**. Its strings are laid out horizontally, and each string corresponds in position to the relevant key on the keyboard.

Grand piano

Granjany, Marcel (1891-1975) French composer and harpist who studied at the Paris Conservatoire and began a career as a recitalist in 1908. He served with the French Army and after World War I taught at the Fontainebleau Summer School. In 1936 he moved to America, becoming director of the harp department at the Juilliard School and the Conservatoire de Musique de Québec in 1938. In 1956 he was appointed a tutor at the Manhattan School of Music. His compositions for harp are technically demanding but lyrical and passionate. They include *Colorado Trail*, *Divertissement* and a *Rhapsody*. He also composed *Poème* for harp, horn and orchestra, and an *Aria in Classic Style* for harp and strings.

graphic notation Musical notation used by some contemporary composers. It offers a visual abstract pattern which the performer should interpret in music.

Graun, Carl Heinrich (1704-1757) German composer who worked as a tenor at the Brunswick Opera from 1725 and was appointed second *Kapellmeister* there in 1726. He entered the service of Crown Prince **Frederick** of Prussia in 1735 and was appointed conductor of the Berlin Royal Opera by him on his coronation in 1740.

Graun composed more than 30 operas in the Italian style, including *Rodelinda* (1741), *Montezuma* and *Ezio* (1755) and a Passion, *Der Tod Jesu* (1755).

grave (Fr., It.) Indicates a slow, serious tempo.

gravicembalo (It.) Alternative term for **harpsichord**.

grazia (It.) Grace. Used alone to indicate the character of a piece or passage, or more often in combination with a tempo indication such as *allegro grazioso*, or *andantino grazioso*.

great organ Principal manual keyboard of the organ.

great service Anglican musical service of the late 16th and 17th centuries. Among the composers of this type of work were William **Byrd**, Orlando **Gibbons** and Thomas **Weelkes**.

Grechaninov, Alexander Tikhonovich (1864-1956) Russian composer and pianist. He studied at the Moscow Conservatoire with Safonov and at the St

Petersburg Conservatoire with **Rimsky-Korsakov**. In 1925 he moved to France and then to the United States in 1939, settling in New York. His compositions include five symphonies, operas, cantatas, sonatas for violin, cello and clarinet, more than 200 songs and a number of choral works, including litanies and Masses for both the Russian Orthodox and the Roman Catholic Churches. His *Missa Oecumenica* (1944) was intended to bridge the cultural divide between these two devotional forms.

Greene, Maurice (1695-1755) English composer and organist at St Paul's Cathedral, London, from 1718. He became organist and composer at the Chapel Royal in 1727. In 1735 he was appointed Master of the King's Musick and a professor of music at Cambridge University. He was a friend of Handel, a notable collector of English church music and a composer of oratorios, organ works, songs and anthems such as *Lord let me know mine End*, which was published as part of a collection in his *Forty Select Anthems*, 1743.

Gregorian chant Official repertory of **plainsong** traditionally associated with Pope Gregory I (St Gregory, *c*.540-*c*.604), which became standard in the Roman Catholic Church. The term is often used as an alternative for plainchant. Gregorian chant differs from its predecessor, **Ambrosian chant**, in that it used four more modes and one dominant tone as a reciting note. Gregorian chant was superseded as the major Western musical form in about the 10th century with the rise of harmonized forms based around the **cantus firmus**.

Gregorian tones Chants of the Gregorian psalmody sung in groups corresponding to the eight church **modes** (four authentic and four plagal).

Grétry, André-Ernest-Modeste (1741-1813) Belgian composer of operas who exploited the French style, with its accentuation of the dramatic, and who published several treatises concerning the composition of operatic music. He studied in Rome from 1759 and composed the intermezzo *La vendemmiatrice* there (1761). In 1767 he moved to Paris and found success with his light comic operas. He was appointed an inspector of the Paris Conservatoire in 1795. His more serious and tragic works, however, were less well received.

Grétry composed more than 50 operas, including *Richard Coeur-de-Lion* (1784), his masterpiece; *Le tableau parlant* (1769), *Zémire et Azor* (1771) and *L'amant jaloux* (1778). He also wrote a requiem, motets and songs, as well as six sonatas for the piano and a flute concerto.

Grieg, Edvard (1843-1907) Norwegian composer, pianist and conductor who developed a unique style within a nationalistic idiom. He studied with his mother, and entered the Leipzig Conservatoire in 1858. His first concert performance was in Bergen in 1863, and following this he settled in Copenhagen, visiting Rome in 1865 where he completed the overture *In Autumn* (1865). In 1867 he returned to Norway and worked with

Edvard Grieg

Richard Nordraak, who was attempting to establish a national school of music. On another visit to Rome (1870) he met Liszt, who greatly admired his work. The Norwegian Government and Ibsen commissioned him to write incidental music to the play *Peer Gynt* (1876) and it was this piece that brought him international acclaim. He toured in England with his wife, giving recitals, and met both **Delius** and **Grainger**.

Grieg's compositions for orchestra include two revised suites from *Peer Gynt* (1888, 1891), the Piano Concerto in A Minor (1869) for which he is most widely known today, the *Holberg Suite* (1884) and a set of *Symphonic Dances* (1898). He wrote a Sonata in E Minor for piano and a number of ballads and songs, including *Ich liebe dich* and the choral works *Landjaenning* and *Foran Sydens Kloster* (1871).

Griffes, Charles Tomlinson (1884-1920) American composer who combined an impressionistic style with reflections of Amerindian and Japanese themes, and later developed a polytonal approach to composition.

He studied in Berlin at the Stern Conservatoire with **Humperdinck** from 1903 and taught there, as well as working as an accompanist and recitalist, until 1907. Among his compositions are *Nocturne* (1919), *The White Peacock* (1919), *The Pleasure Dome of Kubla Khan* (1919) for orchestra, a series of dance-dramas including *The Kairn of Koridwen* (1916), *Tone Pictures* (1914) and *Four Roman Sketches* (1916) for piano, and some chamber pieces, including *Two Sketches Based on Indian Themes* (1918).

Grigny, Nicholas de (1672-1703) French composer who was appointed organist at Rheims Cathedral in 1694. He composed liturgical pieces for the organ in his *Livre d'orgue* (1699), which was later copied by **Bach**.

Grofé, Ferde (1892-1972) American composer and conductor who was acclaimed as an orchestrator and developed the idiom of symphonic jazz. Admired for his skills as an arranger, he was employed by the bandleader Paul Whiteman to exploit this increasingly popular idiom, and orchestrated **Gershwin**'s *Rhapsody in Blue* in 1924.

All his compositions are symphonic jazz pieces, and include the *Grand Canyon Suite* (1931), *Broadway at Night* (1937) and *Symphony in Steel* (1937), notable for its use of four pairs of shoes, brooms, a locomotive bell and a compressed air tank. Among his other suites for orchestra are *Mississippi Suite*, *Hollywood Suite*, *Death Valley Suite* and *Aviation Suite*.

grosse caisse (Fr.) Equivalent of the English bass **drum**.

grosses Orchester (Ger.) Equivalent of the English full orchestra.

grosse Trommel (Ger.) Equivalent of the English bass **drum**.

ground Melodic figure used as a **bass** (2.) in a composition, constantly repeated (although sometimes repeated transposed) while the upper parts proceed in free style. Sometimes also called ground bass.

Groven, Eivind (1901-1977) Norwegian composer and collector of national folk-music, noted for his work regarding the tuning of instruments to natural intervals. He composed two symphonies, several symphonic poems, pieces for the piano and choral works, and arranged many folk-songs for orchestra.

Groves, Sir Charles (1915-) English conductor who studied at the Royal College of Music before joining the BBC as a chorus-master. He became conductor of the BBC Northern Orchestra (1944) and of the **Bournemouth Symphony Orchestra** (as it was called after 1954) in 1951. He was musical director of the **Welsh National Opera** for a short period (1961-3) before taking up the musical directorship of the **Royal Liverpool Philharmonic Orchestra**, where he remained until 1977. He was briefly musical director of the **English National Opera** (1978-9) before his retirement. His conducting of choral performances was particularly notable, and he was a leading interpreter of English music, notably Elgar and Delius. He was knighted in 1973.

Gruber, Heinz Karl (1943-) Austrian composer and double-bass player who was a member of the Vienna Boys' Choir and studied at the Vienna Hochschule under Ratz, Jelinek and von **Einem**. He has played double-bass in several orchestras including that of Austrian Radio. He has composed in a **serial** manner and has used tape; from about 1970 his compositions have reverted to tonality. His best-known works are his *Concerto for Orchestra* (1964) and *Frankenstein!!* for baritone and orchestra (1977); he has also composed suites for various instruments, a Mass and a violin concerto.

Gruberová, Edita (1946-) Czech coloratura soprano. She studied in Prague and Vienna and made her début in 1968. She has sung in Vienna and in many Austrian and German opera-houses; she has also appeared at Glyndebourne, Covent Garden and the Metropolitan Opera, New York. Her secure upper register and stylish presence are admirably suited to the demands of the Queen of the Night in *Die Zauberflöte*, a role she has sung often; she is also outstanding as Gilda in Verdi's *Rigoletto*, Zerbinetta in Strauss's *Ariadne auf Naxos* and Olympia in Offenbach's *Les contes d'Hoffmann*.

Gruenberg, Erich (1924-) British violinist of Austrian origin. He studied in Vienna and in Israel, where he settled for a while; he made his London début in 1947 and became a British citizen in 1950. He was leader of several orchestras, including the **London Symphony Orchestra** (from 1972) and the **Royal Philharmonic Orchestra**. He was noted as a fine player with chamber ensembles: the London String Quartet and the Rubbra-Gruenberg-Pleeth Trio. He has been particularly successful in contemporary music.

Gruenberg, Louis (1884-1964) American composer and pianist, born in Russia, who was captivated by the free rhythms and melodies of jazz. He studied in New York, Vienna and at the Berlin Conservatoire with **Busoni** and Koch. From 1912 he toured with the Berlin Philharmonic Orchestra as a pianist, but returned to the United States to become a professor of composition at the Chicago College of Music in 1930. Gruenberg's compositions include four symphonies, the operas *Emperor Jones* (1933) and *Volpone* (1945), a jazz suite for orchestra (1925) and concertos for the piano and violin. He also wrote chamber pieces and works for piano which reflect the influences of jazz music.

Grumiaux, Arthur (1921-1986) Belgian violinist who studied at the Brussels Conservatoire and in Paris. His début came just before World War II in 1939; he played in Britain for the first time in 1945. He became professor of violin at the Brussels Conservatoire in 1949. The discipline and purity of his playing are to be heard in his numerous recordings, which include all the Bach partitas and sonatas for unaccompanied violin and the sonatas of Mozart and Beethoven. In his repertory were also concertos by Berg, Stravinsky, Walton and Bartók.

gruppetto (It.) Equivalent of the English **turn**.

Guarneri (or Guarnerius) Italian family of violin- and cello-makers of the 17th and 18th centuries. Andrea Guarneri (*c.*1626-1698) lived in Cremona, where (along with Antonio **Stradivari**) he was instructed in the art of violin-making by Nicola **Amati**. Of Andrea's sons, Pietro Giovanni Guarneri (1655-1720) broke away from the family business in Cremona and set up as a violin-maker in Mantua, whereas Giuseppe Giovanni Battista Guarneri (1666-1739) developed an individual style of making violins. The most important member of the family was Bartolomeo Giuseppe Guarneri (1698-1744), known as del Gesù. A nephew of Andrea, Bartolomeo worked all his life at Cremona, producing instruments second in quality only to those made by Stradivari.

Guarnieri, Camargo (1907-) Brazilian composer and conductor whose work illustrates the influences of folk-music and is rich in colour and variety. He seldom quotes directly from folk-songs, preferring to reflect them in melodies of his own devising. He studied in Paris in 1938, becoming a pupil of **Koechlin**. On returning to Brazil, he became a professor at the São Paulo Conservatoire and a conductor with the São Paulo Philharmonic Society. He was awarded first prize at the Caracas Music Festival (1957) for his *Choros* for piano and orchestra. His compositions include three symphonies, the suite *Brasiliana* and *Dansa brasileira* for orchestra, and concertos for the piano and violin. He has also written songs and chamber pieces.

Guglielmi Family of Italian opera composers active between 1750 and 1830. Pietro Alessandro (1728-1804) studied with his father, Jacopo, and later with Durante in Naples, where he worked from 1776 to 1793, when he became choirmaster at St Peter's in Rome. He wrote more than 100 operas, including *Il re pastore* (1765), several oratorios, cantatas, sonatas and quartets. His son, Pietro Carlo, known as Guglielmini (*c.*1763-1817), wrote more than 40 operas, mainly in his native Naples.

Gui, Vittorio (1885-1975) Italian composer and conductor, noted for his revival of a number of operas by Rossini. He studied at the Liceo di S. Cecilia in Rome. While there he conducted a performance of *La Gioconda* by **Ponchielli** and came to the notice of **Toscanini**, who appointed him as an assistant in Milan in 1923. He conducted for various Italian opera houses, founded the Stabile Orchestra of Florence in 1928 and participated in the foundation of the Maggio Musicale Fiorentino in 1933. He was also music director at Glyndebourne, and was a guest conductor with several other orchestras. Gui's compositions include symphonic pieces and the opera *La Fata Malerba* (1927).

Guido d'Arezzo (*c.*995-*c.*1033) Monk, musical theorist and teacher who reformed musical notation by adding a third and fourth line to the staff and devising a system of **solmization** using the syllables *ut*, *re*, *mi*, *fa*, *sol*, *la* as a means of learning notes in the sequence of a hexachord (six-note scale). These were the first syllables on each line of a hymn to John the Baptist, supposedly written by Guido. Born in Paris and educated at the Benedictine abbey of Pomposa, he was appointed in about 1025 to teach in the cathedral school of Arezzo and commissioned to write down his theories in the *Micrologus de disciplina artis musicae*. In about 1029 he moved to the Camaldolese monastery at Avellana. The Guidonian hand, a diagram of a left hand attributed to him and used as a means of teaching notes, is not in fact mentioned in his writings.

Guilmant, Alexandre (1837-1911) French composer and organist who studied in Paris with Lemmens and at the Brussels Conservatoire. He became the organist at La Trinité, Paris, in 1871. As a virtuoso performer he toured widely, visiting both England and the United States. He founded the Schola Cantorum with Bordes and **d'Indy** and acted as organ tutor there. In 1896 he was appointed professor of organ studies at the Paris Conservatoire.

He wrote organ symphonies, eight sonatas and other works such as toccatas and fugues. In addition he edited volumes of ancient music for the organ, collecting them in the *Archives des maîtres de l'orgue* (1898).

Guiraud, Ernest (1837-1892) French composer who wrote an important treatise on instrumentation (1892), completed the controversial recitatives for **Bizet**'s *Carmen* (1875) and orchestrated *Les contes d'Hoffmann* by **Offenbach** (1881). He studied at the Paris Conservatoire and became a professor of composition there in 1880. He composed several operas including *Piccolino* (1876), and the ballet *Gretna Green* (1873).

guitar Plucked string instrument. There are various types of guitar, of which the principal one originated in Spain and is often known as the Spanish guitar. This normally has six strings, tuned E, A, D, G, B, E, and has a range of three octaves and a fifth from E below middle C. The guitar has a flat back, a waisted bodyshape, and the sound-hole in the sound-board is often decoratively carved. The fingerboard is fretted.

The 20th-century classical guitar, as it is now called, has gained in popularity as a result of the teaching and playing of the Spanish virtuoso Andrés **Segovia**. Among more recent composers who have written music for the guitar are **Villa-Lobos**, **Falla**, **Roussel** and **Britten**. The Spanish composer **Rodrigo** is especially known for his *Concierto de Aranjuez* (1939) for guitar and orchestra. See also **Hawaiian guitar**.

Guitar

Gulda, Friedrich (1930-) Austrian pianist who studied in Vienna and made his début in 1944. He went to New York in 1950 and quickly became recognized for his austere readings of the classics: Mozart, Beethoven and Schubert. Meanwhile he had developed a deep interest in jazz and had appeared at various American jazz venues; in 1962 he began playing mixed jazz and classical programmes with the idea of stretching the minds of his audiences. He founded the Eurojazz Orchestra and started a competition in 1966. The International Music Forum at Ossiach, southern Austria, was also his brainchild. He has composed a variety of works (which are not widely known), and among his recordings are several Mozart concertos.

Gundry, Inglis (1905-) English composer who studied at Oxford and the Royal College of Music, where he was a pupil of **Vaughan Williams**. His compositions include five operas, symphonic pieces, and chamber music.

Gungl, Joseph (1810-1889) Hungarian composer and bandmaster who founded his own band in Berlin (1843) and toured the United States in 1849. He was appointed *Kapellmeister* to the Emperor of Austria in 1876 and composed more than 300 marches and dances for his band.

Guridi, Jesús (1886-1961) Spanish composer and organist who studied at the Schola Cantorum, Paris, with **d'Indy**, and became a professor of organ and later director of the Madrid Conservatoire. He composed a number of operas, choral works and pieces for the organ, all of which reflect in some measure the flavour of Basque folk-music.

Gurlitt, Manfred (1890-1973) German composer and conductor who studied with **Humperdinck** at the Berlin Conservatoire and conducted orchestras in Essen (1911), Augsburg (1912) and Bremen (1914). He left Germany in 1939 after the Nazi authorities banned his compositions; he settled in Tokyo.

He composed the opera *Wozzeck* (1928), an evocative version of Büchner's play, in the same period as **Berg**'s version. He also wrote the *Goya Symphony* (1938) and *Shakespeare Symphony* (1954) for orchestra and chorus, and a number of chamber pieces and songs.

Gurney, Ivor (1890-1937) English composer, poet and organist who sang in the choir at Gloucester Cathedral and became organist there in 1906 as a pupil of Brewer. He studied composition under Stanford at the Royal College of Music from 1911.

He spent much time setting his own poetry and that of A.E. Housman to music, and composed 82 songs and a number of sensitive song-cycles, including *Ludlow and Teme* and *The Western Playland.*

gusla Slavonic one-stringed bowed instrument. The bow is an ordinary stick with a small branch attached to it into which the hair is wound. The instrument is played resting on the knee, and it is used to accompany narrative songs sung by the player. An alternative spelling is gusle.

gusli Russian **zither** used in folk-music as an accompaniment to singers. It was used in **Rimsky-Korsakov**'s ballet-opera *Sadko* (1867).

Guy, Barry (1947-) English composer and double-bass player who studied at the Guildhall School of Music with **Orr** and Buxton and became a leading performer with a number of chamber orchestras. He founded the London Jazz Composers' Orchestra in response to calls from other musicians. His compositions reflect both his interest in jazz and his own technical skill as a performer. They include *Eos* (1977) and *Anna* (1974) for double-bass and orchestra, *Songs for Tomorrow* for orchestra (1975) and *Play* (1976) for chamber ensemble.

Guy, Helen See **Hardelot, Guy d'**

gymel Vocal composition in two parts, both of the same range. A characteristic feature is the use of parallel thirds. The term first appeared in the 15th century, when it was used to refer to a divided voice-part in a **polyphonic** composition, but examples are found as early as the 13th century. An alternative spelling is gimel.

Gyrowetz, Adalbert (1763-1850) Bohemian composer whose work was admired by Mozart. He worked in association with Haydn, whose style influenced him greatly. He read law in Prague but abandoned the legal profession to study music in Naples and at the Paris Conservatoire. In 1798 he moved to London, but returned to Vienna in 1804 and became *Kapellmeister* to the two court theatre orchestras. He composed 60 symphonic works, 30 operas and 40 ballets, as well as a large amount of work for chamber orchestras.

H

H German symbol for the note B♮.

Hába, Alois (1893-1973) Czech composer and violinist who was influenced by Oriental and Moravian folk-music and by the atonal technique of **Schoenberg**. His own **microtonal** style has influenced many present-day composers.

After 1921 he developed a microtonal technique which he taught as director of music at the Prague Conservatoire (1923). His opera *Matka* (1929) is in quarter-tones, and his third operatic piece, *Prijd Kralovtsvi Tve* (1934), uses one-sixth tones. Both place great demands upon performers. The use of these tones in orchestral works such as his *Fantasy for Piano* (1954), in string quartets and pieces for the chamber, necessitates the adaptation of various instruments including the clarinet, trumpet and piano; the microtonal piano has different black keys for sharps and flats.

habanera Dance and song form, introduced into Spain from Africa via Cuba. It is a moderate 2/4 time and has a basic rhythm of four quavers, the first of which is dotted. Its rhythm is clearly exemplified in the famous habanera of **Bizet**'s opera *Carmen* (1875).

Hadley, Henry (1871-1937) American composer and conductor who championed US music and helped to found the National Association of American Composers and Conductors. He studied composition at the conservatoires of New England and Vienna and conducted various European orchestras, before returning to the United States. He then conducted for the Seattle (1909) and San Francisco (1911) Symphony Orchestras, and the New York Philharmonic (1920). His compositions include four symphonies, several operas including *Cleopatra's Night* (1920) and *A Night in Old Paris* (1925), the tone poem *Salome*, chamber music and works for chorus.

Hadley, Patrick (1899-1973) English composer of music for voice and orchestra who was inspired mainly by literary themes and influenced by **Delius** and **Vaughan Williams**. He studied at Cambridge and at the Royal College of Music, where he became a tutor in 1925. In 1946 he was appointed Professor of Music at Cambridge University. His compositions include *Ephemera* (1929), *Scene from Hardy's The Woodlanders* (1926), *La Belle Dame sans Merci* (1935) and *Lines from Shelley's 'The Cenci'* (1951).

Haebler, Ingrid (1929-) Austrian pianist who studied in Salzburg, Vienna, Geneva and Paris. She won several prizes, including the Harriet Cohen Beethoven Medal (1957). Her career has taken her all over the world, to Russia, Japan and Australia as well as to many European festivals. She is considered a player of delicacy and refinement and has made numerous recordings of the Mozart and Schubert repertories.

haegŭm/haekum (Korea) Popular two-stringed fiddle with a curved neck. It is held vertically and played with a horse-hair bow inserted between the strings, which are made of twisted silk.

Haendel, Ida (1924-) British violinist of Polish origin. She studied in Warsaw, where she won various prizes. In 1937 she gave her first performance in London, where she settled; her American début was in 1946. She moved to Canada in 1952. She has made many recordings – the concertos of Beethoven and Brahms as well as less frequently heard works. In 1957 she gave the first performance of *Tartiniana Seconda* by **Dallapiccola.**

Hageman, Richard (1882-1966) American composer who was born in the Netherlands and studied at the Brussels Conservatoire. He became chief conductor of the Amsterdam Royal Opera in 1900 and emigrated to the United States in 1907, where he conducted at the New York Metropolitan from 1912. His compositions include the opera *Caponsacci* (1932), a series of songs and film music.

Hahn, Reynaldo (1874-1947) French composer and conductor, born in Venezuela, who studied the works of Mozart and was influenced by him in his own operatic compositions. He studied composition at the Paris Conservatoire from 1886 with **Massenet** and **Dubois**. In 1945 he became director of the Paris Opéra. He composed ballets, cantatas, operettas and chamber music, as well as the opera *Ciboulette* (1923) and the musical comedy *Mozart* (1925). He also wrote a series of songs (including the famous *Si mes vers avaient des ailes*) and settings of poems by Verlaine.

Haitink, Bernard (1929-) Outstanding Dutch conductor and violinist who studied at Amsterdam Conservatoire. He began his musical career as a violinist in the Netherlands radio orchestra and from 1967 to 1979 conducted the Concertgebouw orchestra and the London Philharmonic Orchestra (1967-77). From 1978 he was

Bernard Haitink

music director at **Glyndebourne**. His repertory has included *Don Carlos*, *The Rake's Progress*, *Don Giovanni* and *Lohengrin*. He was appointed music director of the Royal Opera House, Covent Garden, in 1987. Haitink has made many recordings and was awarded an honorary KBE in 1978.

Halévy, Fromental (1799-1862) French composer who studied at the Paris Conservatoire with **Cherubini** and in Italy. He won the Prix de Rome in 1819. He returned to Paris in 1926, became a chorus-master at the Opéra and taught at the Conservatoire, where he became a professor of composition in 1840. **Bizet** and **Gounod** were among his students. In 1854 he was appointed permanent secretary to the Académie des Beaux-Arts. He composed more than 30 operas, including *La juive* (1835), which was his greatest success, as well as ballets, cantatas and songs.

half close Alternative term for **interrupted cadence**.

Halffter, Christobal (1930-) Spanish composer and nephew of Ernesto and

Rodolpho **Halffter**. He studied with Conrado del Campo and **Tansman**, and was appointed professor of composition at the Madrid Academy in 1960. He has composed a number of orchestral pieces, including *Sequences* (1965), *Requiem por la libertad imaginada* (1971) and *Elegies for the Death of three Spanish Poets* (1974). Choral works and pieces for voice and orchestra, notably the *In expectatione resurrectionis Domini* (1965) for baritone, male choir and orchestra, are also among his compositions.

Halffter, Ernesto (1905-) Spanish composer and conductor who studied at the Madrid Academy with **Falla** and whose *L'Atlántida* was completed in 1927. He founded a chamber orchestra in Seville and composed the opera *The Death of Carmen* as well as other orchestral pieces.

Halffter, Rodolfo (1900-) Spanish composer who settled in Mexico after the Spanish Civil War. He was privately tutored by **Falla** and studied the works of **Schoenberg**, whose influence can be heard in his compositions, notably in the *Overtura concertante* (1932) for piano and orchestra. He has also composed ballets and a violin concerto (1940).

Hall, Richard (1903-1982) English composer who became an influential professor of composition at the Royal Manchester College of Music in 1938. Among his students were **Birtwistle**, Maxwell **Davies** and **Goehr**. His compositions include a number of orchestral fantasies, four symphonies, a piano concerto and some chamber pieces. He reveals the influence of **twelve-note** technique in some of his work.

Hallelujah Praise Jehovah, used in choruses in Restoration anthems and in oratorios such as **Handel**'s *Messiah* (1741).

Hallé Orchestra One of the leading British orchestras, based in Manchester, which grew out of the so-called Gentlemen's Concerts organized by prosperous German merchants. Charles Halle was a German pianist and conductor, who adopted the French version of his name when he settled in Manchester. Originally invited as a pianist, he was asked to form an orchestra to play each day at the 1856 Art Treasures Exhibition. When the exhibition was over he determined to keep the orchestra together to satisfy the demand that their daily concerts had awakened. The first concert of the new orchestra took place on 30 January 1858, and it soon became the premier musical institution of the north of England. Sir Charles Hallé died in 1895, and after a disappointing period under Frederick Cowen, Hans **Richter**, the eminent Wagnerian conductor, was appointed and ushered in one of the orchestra's greatest periods (1895-1911). Later conductors of distinction included Sir Hamilton **Harty** (1920-33), Sir Thomas **Beecham** (guest conductor during World War I) and Sir Malcolm **Sargent** (1933-9), but it was Sir John **Barbirolli** (1943-70) above all who turned the Hallé into an international orchestra, with his many fine recordings. His successors have included the Scottish conductor James **Loughran** and the Polish-born Stanislaw Skrowaczewski.

halling Lively Norwegian dance, which sometimes involves somersaults, originating from the Hallingdal district. It is usually in 2/4 time at a moderately quick pace. **Grieg** uses the *halling* in his second volume of *Lyric Pieces* Op.71 No.5 (1883).

Hambraeus, Bengt (1928-) Swedish avant-garde composer and organist who is best known for his *Rota* for three orchestras, percussion and tape recorder (1962) and for his early use of electronic techniques. He studied at Uppsala University from 1947 and in Darmstadt with **Messiaen** and **Krenek**. In 1957 he began a career in broadcasting with the Swedish Broadcasting Company and became their director of chamber music in 1965. He was appointed professor of composition at McGill University,

Montreal (1972), and has composed at the electronic music studios in Cologne, Munich and Milan. He championed the works of **Boulez, Nono** and **Stockhausen** and has written a number of complex *Constellation* pieces for instruments and electronic voices.

Hamilton, Iain (1922-) Scottish composer and pianist who reflects the influences of **Bartók** and **Berg**, as well as later **serial** techniques in his work. His search for inspiration from foreign schools of composition has distressed some Scottish audiences, particularly at the Edinburgh Festival which commissioned his *Sinfonia* (1958) to commemorate Robert Burns's bicentenary. Other critics have acclaimed his virtuoso handling of orchestration.

Among his compositions are the operas *The Catiline Conspiracy* (1974), *The Royal Hunt of the Sun* (1967) and *Anna Karenina* (1979); the ballet *Clerk Saunders* (1951) and pieces for the orchestra which include two symphonies, two violin concertos and two piano concertos. He has also composed a large body of work for chorus, various voices and chamber ensembles.

Hammerstein II, Oscar (1895-1960) American librettist and producer who wrote some of the most enduring musicals. His adaptation of **Bizet**'s *Carmen* for the stage was critically acclaimed and other musical productions have reached wide audiences in both their stage and screen versions. He and Rodgers commissioned **Copland**'s only operatic work, *The Tender Land* (1954).

His compositions were most successful when he worked in collaboration with other songwriters, notably Romberg and Friml, Jerome **Kern**, with whom he wrote *Show Boat* (1927), and Richard **Rodgers**, with whom he wrote *Oklahoma!* (1943), *Carousel* (1945), *South Pacific* (1949), *The King and I* (1951) and *The Sound of Music* (1959).

Hammond, Dame Joan (1912-) New Zealand soprano and champion golfer. She

Oscar Hammerstein II

studied in Sydney, where she played the violin in the Symphony Orchestra, and made her début as a singer in 1929. Nine years later she appeared for the first time in London and Vienna. Her Covent Garden career began in 1948 with Leonora in Verdi's *Il trovatore*. Other Verdi and Puccini roles followed, notably Tosca and Madama Butterfly. She took the title-role in the first British production of Dvořák's *Rusalka* at Sadler's Wells in 1959. On a tour of the USSR she sang Tatiana in Tchaikovsky's *Eugene Onegin*, the first of several Russian roles. She also sang the choral works of Bach, Beethoven and Verdi. Her recording of *O my beloved Daddy* from Puccini's *Gianni Schicchi* sold more than a million copies.

Handel, George Frideric (1685-1759) German composer who lived in England from 1726 and whose style dominated English music for the next century. His greatest works, the dramatic oratorios and operas, are characteristically noble, and all his compositions reflect a combination of the traditions from which he developed his own style. German ideals of contrapuntal techniques are blended with Italian solo styles and elements of the English choral tradition to produce a melodically and technically masterful quality. Despite his apparent plagiarism of other composers' work – a common practice during a period in which pasticcios were popular – Handel 'took other men's pebbles and turned them into diamonds', a contemporary remarked.

Although his father was unwilling to allow him a musical education, he did tolerate Handel's study under Zachau, the local organist at St Michael's Church, Halle. He studied law at Halle University and began to study music seriously only when his father died in 1703. He joined the Hamburg Opera Orchestra, conducted by **Keiser**, as second violinist and completed the opera *Almira* which Keiser had started in 1705 and the opera *Nero* (1705). In 1706 Handel visited Italy and was exposed, through meetings with **Corelli** and A. **Scarlatti** in Rome, to Italian styles of composition which he soon mastered, much to the admiration of contemporary Italian musicians. His opera *Agrippina* was produced in Venice in 1709 and at its first performance he met the younger brother of the Elector of Hanover. The following year he was appointed *Kapellmeister* to the court of the Elector of Hanover. It was the success in London of his opera *Rinaldo* (1711) that prompted him to move to England, and to compose the operas *Il pastor fido* (1712), *Silla* (1714) and *Amadigi* (1715) in the same style.

When his former patron, the Elector of Hanover, was crowned King George I of England in 1714 he was given a life pension of six hundred pounds and composed the *Water Music Suite* for a royal water party in 1717. In 1718 he became musical director to the Duke of Chandos, as well as director of the Royal Academy of Music at the King's Theatre, Haymarket, which sought to produce Italian **opera seria**. He wrote 14 operas for this venture, until the theatre closed in 1728, as well as 15 solo sonatas, eight suites for the harpsichord, and nine trio sonatas. George II was crowned in 1727 to the sound of four of Handel's anthems including *Zadok the Priest* (1727), which has since been played at every British coronation.

The declining popularity of the Italian operatic style, caused in part by the dramatic success of *The Beggar's Opera* by John Gay, led Handel to compose dramatic oratorios, including *Esther* (1732), *Deborah* (1733), *Saul* (1733) and *Israel in Egypt* (1739), which reflected the fullness and richness of the *opera seria* style but released him from the restrictions of the genre. He conducted many of these himself, despite seriously deteriorating health. He suffered a stroke in 1737, but still carried on composing and wrote another series of oratorios, including *Messiah* (1742), *Samson* (1743), *Judas Maccabaeus* (1746) and *Solomon* (1748). In 1751 he succumbed to blindness, but continued conducting performances of his oratorios and revised some of his scores. He was buried in Westminster Abbey.

Among his many other compositions are the oratorio *La Resurrezione* (1708), two *Te Deum* works: for the Peace of Utrecht (1713) and for the Duke of Chandos (1718); six concertos for the oboe (1729), 12 for the organ (1738), *Music for the Royal Fireworks* (1749), 12 *concerti grossi* (1739) and numerous chamber pieces, songs and cantatas for two or more voices.

Handl, Jacob (1550-1591) Slovenian composer who experimented in the **motet** form with the Venetian style, blending the voices of three or four choirs at different locations in the chapel. He became *Kapellmeister* to the Bishop of Olmutz in 1579 and later cantor at St Johann's, Prague. He composed 16 Masses, numerous motets which appear in the collection *Opus Musicum* (1586-91), and other devotional pieces. Four books of secular motets entitled *Harmoniae Morales* appeared between 1589 and 1596.

Handley, Vernon (1930-) English conductor who studied at the Guildhall School of Music. He later taught at the Royal College of Music and conducted its orchestra. In 1970 he came to prominence when he took over at the last minute a concert given by the **London**

Philharmonic Orchestra in Swansea. He has frequently broadcast on BBC radio and has made numerous recordings with the London Philharmonic Orchestra, specializing in English music of the first half of the 20th century.

Hanslick, Eduard (1825-1904) German critic of great influence, who was a perceptive though critical commentator on Wagner and his ideas; he was rewarded by being satirized in Wagner's opera *Die Meistersinger von Nürnberg* as the pedant Beckmesser, a character originally called Hans Lick. His views on music in the late 19th century are nevertheless of great value, and often highly informative. His compositions have little significance today.

Hanson, Howard (1896-1981) American composer of Swedish origin whose work reflects Nordic images and themes. His compositions have a poetic quality which allies them closely with those of **Sibelius** and **Franck**. He studied composition with Goetschius at the Institute of Musical Art, New York, and won the Prix de Rome in 1921. He became director of the Eastman School of Music, New York, in 1924. In 1925 he established the Rochester Festivals at which contemporary American composers exhibited their work. He became a director of the Institute of American Music at Rochester University in 1964. Among his compositions are six symphonies, orchestral suites and symphonic poems such as *Summer Seascape* (1959). His choral work includes the *Lament for Beowulf* (1926) and the *Song of Human Rights* (1963). He also composed chamber music and the opera *Merry Mount*, first performed in New York in 1934.

hardänger fiddle (Scandinavia) Short-necked, low-bridged fiddle with sympathetic strings, used for playing dance music. The low bridge makes it ideal for providing its own chordal accompaniment.

Hardelot, Guy d' (1858-1936) Pen-name of Helen Rhodes (née Guy), a French composer who studied at the Paris Conservatoire and toured the United States as a singer. She composed a number of songs which found their way into the repertories of singers such as Dame Nellie **Melba**, Emma Calvé (with whom she toured in 1896) and Victor Maurel.

harmonica Modern term for mouth organ, a small wind instrument with metal reeds (one to each note), enclosed in slots in a narrow box. Air is blown into or sucked out of the box by the player. The notes sounded depend on the position of the box in the mouth and the use of the player's tongue. As a musical instrument, it is sometimes considered a toy, although when played by a virtuoso it can produce very moving music. Larry **Adler** is the most notable exponent of the harmonica, and compositions by **Vaughan Williams** and Darius **Milhaud** have been written for him.

harmonic series, harmonics When a string or column of air vibrates, as well as the whole, simple fractions simultaneously vibrate to produce overtones in a harmonic series. By varying the pressure of the lips the brass player can select these harmonics, heard at their simplest in the notes of the

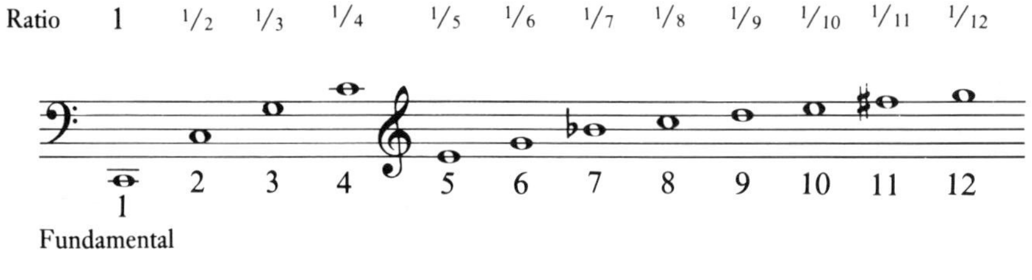

Harmonic series: the seventh and eleventh harmonics are out of tune and avoided.

bugle. The string players may also select them, by touching the string at the appropriate point to bring out the fractional rather than the whole vibrating string. The characteristic timbre or quality of an instrument depends largely on the relative strength of the fundamental and the individual overtones – the saxophone having one of the fullest combinations, the flute one of the weakest.

Harmoniemusik (Ger.) Music for woodwind, brass and percussion.

harmonium Small, portable keyboard instrument, the sound of which is produced by reeds, played by wind coming from pedal-operated bellows worked by the player's feet. In later models the bellows are operated by an electric motor. The harmonium was invented in the early 19th century, and in some instances has been used as a substitute for an organ, especially for hymn-singing.

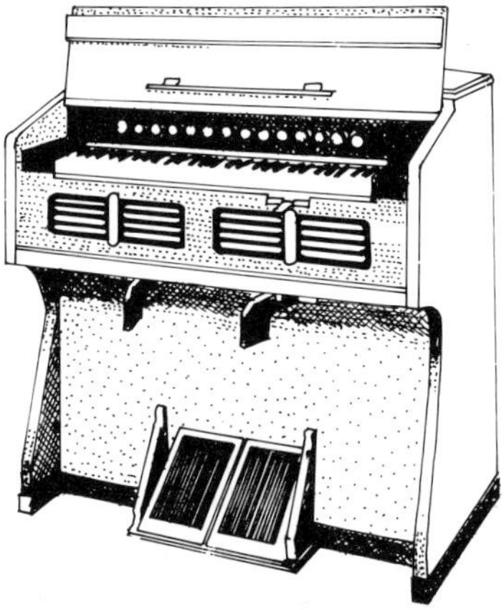

Harmonium

harmony Whereas **counterpoint** is concerned with a horizontal approach to music (interweaving melodies), harmony is the vertical aspect, concerned with **chords** and chord progressions. There is evidence that harmony was used before the 9th century AD, but it is generally agreed that the real beginning of harmonic music occurred with the first written appearance of parallel fourths and fifths, in about the 9th century.

The study of harmony concerns the structure of individual chords, the relationship of one chord to another and the construction of music, with particular regard to the succession of chords which support or surround the melodic line.

Harnoncourt, Nikolaus (1929-) Austrian conductor and cellist who studied in Vienna and played with the Symphony Orchestra there for 17 years. His interest in early music grew over this period, and he frequently took part in performances in which he played the viola da **gamba**. He founded the early music group the Vienna Concentus Musicus in 1953; they developed a wide repertory of Bach, Monteverdi, Handel and other **Baroque** works as well as earlier music, played in **authentic** style with original instruments. The ensemble has gained an impressive reputation in Europe and America, and they have made many excellent recordings (Bach cantatas, Monteverdi operas and so on). Harnoncourt is also a fine Mozart conductor and has made recordings with various orchestras of the classical repertory.

harp Stringed instrument with a series of strings of different lengths stretched parallel across a frame. The strings produce notes of fixed pitch: the longer the string, the lower the note produced. The strings are vibrated by plucking with the fingers.

The harp was among the earliest stringed instruments. It is referred to in the Old Testament, and is shown in Egyptian tomb paintings and appears on a *bas-relief* found in Nineveh dating from the 7th century BC.

The modern concert harp, developed by Erard around 1810, has a range of six and a half octaves, with seven pedals, each of which can be put into three different positions. Each pedal controls the pitch of all strings of the same note in the scale, regardless of the octave, so one pedal sets all the A strings as A♯, A♭, or A♮; another all the B strings and so on. You

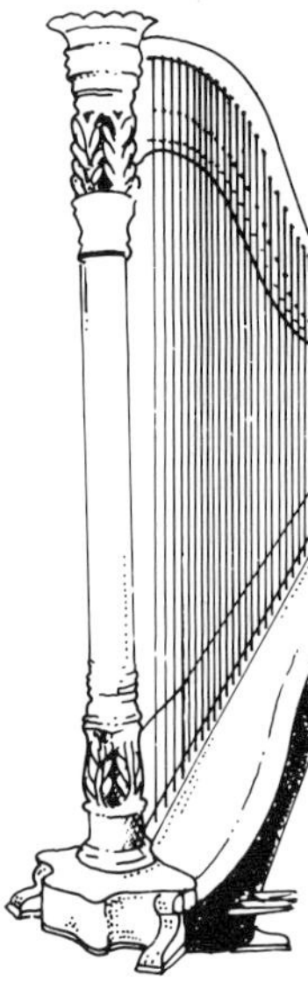

Harp

cannot have A♯ on one string and A♭ on another. A complete chromatic scale is therefore not possible on the pedal harp. The chromatic harp, which today is a rarity, has a string for each note. The harp came into general orchestral use in the early part of the 19th century, but was regarded as inappropriate for symphonies. It played an important part in opera and ballet music: Wagner was bold enough to demand twelve instruments for one passage in the *Ring*, although he admitted that he did not understand harp technique. It was left to French composers such as Ravel and Debussy to reveal its charm, grace and subtlety of tone, as both a solo and an orchestral instrument.

harpsichord Keyboard instrument usually shaped like a grand piano. A note is sounded by plucking the strings with a quill plectrum (as opposed to a piano, in which the strings are struck by hammers). The square-shaped **virginal** and **spinet** are instruments of the same type but smaller in size.

Harpsichords often have two keyboards, which may offer a different tone colour. The tone may also be modified by stops: handpulls which activate dampers to produce a sound like a lute, or couplers to add lower octaves. The harpsichord was displaced by the piano in the early years of the 19th century, but has enjoyed a revival in this century, not only for authentic performances, as for **Scarlatti**, Bach and Handel, but also in the esteem of composers such as **Poulenc** and **Falla**, who wrote harpsichord concertos.

Harpsichord

harp stop Device on a harpsichord that dampens the strings so that the sound produced resembles that of a harp.

Harrell, Lynn (1944-) American cellist. He studied at the Juilliard School, where he later taught, and made his début at the age of 16. He joined the Cleveland Orchestra in 1965, where he was principal cellist. He first played in London in 1975. He has appeared at many festivals and other venues in the United States and has made several recordings, including the Dvořák and Saint-Saëns concertos; he has also commissioned a concerto from Donald **Erb**.

Harris, Roy (1898-1979) American composer who is considered to be the leading American symphonist of the

1930s. His style is bold, angular and irregular and reflects the influences of folk-music and hymn melodies. Some critics find points of comparison between his work and that of **Janáček**, but it is essentially American in its buoyancy and momentum.

He studied at the Paris Conservatoire with Nadia **Boulanger** (1926) and returned to the United States to teach at the Westminster Choir School, Princeton. He became a tutor at the Juilliard School and Cornell University, and in 1940 was appointed composer in residence at the University of California.

His compositions include 16 symphonies, the overture *When Johnny Comes Marching Home* (1935), the *Farewell to Pioneers* (1936) and a concerto for amplified piano (1968), as well as chamber pieces. He also wrote choral works, including *Songs for Occupations* (1934), *Symphony for Voices* (1936), a Mass for male choir and a number of works for various voices and orchestra.

Harris, Sir William (1883-1973) English composer and organist who is best known for his composition *The Hound of Heaven* (1919) for baritone, choir and orchestra. He studied at the Royal College of Music with Parratt and **Stanford**, and became an organist at New College and later at Christ Church, Oxford (1919-28). In 1921 he became a professor of the organ and harmony at the Royal College of Music, and was appointed organist at St George's Chapel, Windsor, in 1933. He was knighted in 1934.

Harrison, Julius (1885-1963) English conductor and composer who studied at the Birmingham and Midland Institute with **Bantock** and conducted his first performance at Covent Garden in 1913. He went on to conduct various orchestras before becoming a professor of composition at the Royal Academy of Music. Among his compositions are the cantata *Cleopatra*, *Cornish Sketches* and *Bredon Hill*, as well as a Mass and a *Requiem* and works for violin, orchestra and voice.

Harrison, Lou (1917-) American composer who has experimented with various musical forms, as well as with **atonal** techniques and **serial** procedures. He studied at the San Francisco State College and organized concerts with John **Cage**. He became a tutor at Mills College in 1936, but left in 1939 to study with **Schoenberg**. In 1943 he moved to New York, where he enjoyed success as a ballet composer and critic.

His compositions include the atonal and serialist opera *Rapunzel* (1954), the puppet opera *Young Caesar* (1971), several ballets (including *Johnny Appleseed*, 1940), a series of harpsichord sonatas and works for percussion instruments, the sextet *Schoenbergiana*, a violin concerto and *Four Strict Songs* for eight baritones and orchestra in pure **intonation**.

Harsányi, Tibor (1898-1954) Hungarian composer who studied at the Budapest Academy of Music with **Kodály** and settled in Paris in 1924. He composed operas, ballets, symphonic pieces and chamber music.

Hartmann, Karl Amadeus (1905-1963) German composer who studied at the Munich Academy of Music with Haas and **Webern**, but refused to perform publicly or to compose for the Nazi authorities. In 1945 he organized the Musica Viva concerts in Munich, which became showcases for new composers. His own compositions reflected the influences of **Berg** and Stravinsky and include eight symphonies, the opera *Des Simplicius Simplicissimus Jugend* (1949), and concertos for the piano, viola and violin.

Harty, Sir Hamilton (1879-1941) Irish composer, organist and conductor. In 1900 he moved to London, where he continued to find success as an accompanist and later as a composer. He conducted for both the Covent Garden and the London Symphony Orchestras, and was eventually appointed conductor of the Halle Orchestra in 1920. He was knighted in 1925 and received the Gold Medal of the Royal Philharmonic Society in 1934.

His compositions include the questionable modern arrangements of Handel's *Water Music Suite* and *Music for the Royal Fireworks*, the lyrical *Irish Symphony* (1924), *Ode to a Nightingale* (1907) for soprano and orchestra, a violin concerto and symphonic poems, notably *With the Wild Geese* (1910).

Harvey, Jonathan (1939-) English composer who studied at the Universities of Glasgow and Cambridge. **Stockhausen** heard his work in Darmstadt in 1966 and suggested a further period of study with **Babbitt** in 1969. In 1970 he was appointed senior lecturer in music at Southampton University.

Among his compositions, some of which incorporate the use of tape recordings, are *Benedictus* (1970), *Inner Light III* (1975), a symphony for orchestra (1966), several cantatas for voice and instruments or orchestra, and a number of pieces for the chamber orchestra including *Inner Light I* (1973) for instruments and tape.

Harwood, Elizabeth (1938-1990) English soprano who studied in Manchester and at the Royal College of Music. Her début was in 1961 at Glyndebourne; the following year she joined the Sadler's Wells company, where she sang the lighter Mozart roles (Susanna in *Le nozze di Figaro*, Constanze in *Die Entführung aus dem Serail*) and Adèle in Rossini's *Le comte Ory*. She first sang with Scottish Opera in 1967 and at Covent Garden in 1968. She sang at Salzburg, La Scala and the Metropolitan, New York (her début there was in 1975). Other roles in which she shone are Fiordiligi in *Così fan tutte*, the Countess in *Le nozze di Figaro*, Sophie in *Der Rosenkavalier* and Donna Elvira in *Don Giovanni*. She made recordings of both operas and oratorios.

Haskil, Clara (1895-1960) Romanian pianist who studied at the Paris Conservatoire under **Fauré** and **Cortot** and in Berlin with **Busoni**. She made her début in 1902 and was best known for her performances of Mozart, Beethoven, and the early Romantic repertory.

Hasse, Johann Adolph (1699-1783) German opera composer who enjoyed considerable success in his day with his elegant and graceful style. When only 19 he sang as a tenor at the Hamburg Opera and he composed his first opera, *Antioco* (1721), at the age of 22. In 1724 he studied with A. **Scarlatti** in Naples and completed several popular operas in the Italian style. He spent some time in Venice before returning to Germany to become director of the Dresden Opera (1731). He moved to Vienna in 1763 and continued to compose in the Italian manner, despite some controversy. In 1775 he left permanently for Italy, living in Venice until his death.

He composed more than 100 operatic pieces, as well as Masses and oratorios, but most of his manuscripts were destroyed.

Hassler, Hans Leo (1564-1612) German composer and organist who studied in Venice with A. **Gabrieli** and became organist to Octavian Fugger at Augsburg in 1585, moving on to take up similar posts at Nuremberg (1600) and Dresden (1608). He wrote in the Venetian polychoral manner and composed a number of polyphonic *Lieder*, as well as madrigals and motets.

Haubenstock-Ramati, Roman (1919-) Polish composer who studied at Cracow University and became musical director of Cracow Radio in 1947. He was appointed director of the music library and a professor of music at the Tel Aviv Academy in 1950.

He was influenced by *musique concrète* and worked for some time in France on his electronic pieces. In order to write music for electronic instruments he experimented with new methods of notation and developed an early form of graphic score. His compositions include an opera (*America*), a symphony entitled *K* and the symphonic poems *Les symphonies de timbres* and *Petite musique de nuit*. He has also written chamber music and some choral pieces.

Hauer, Joseph Matthias (1883-1959) Austrian composer who was largely self-taught. His stylistic independence is reflected in his invention of a **twelve-note** system, developed quite separately from that of **Schoenberg**. He wrote the opera *Salammbo* and concertos for the piano and violin, as well as a series of songs. All his work illustrates his dodecaphonic technique.

Haussmann, Valentin (*c*.1570-*c*.1614) German composer and organist at Gerbstedt, near Merseburg. He wrote secular songs, madrigals and dances as well as devotional motets and instrumental pieces. He also published works by **Vecchi** and **Gastoldi** with German texts and undoubtedly assisted in the development of early music by this cross-fertilization of national influences.

hautbois (Fr.) **Oboe**.

hautboy Obsolete English name for **oboe**.

Hawaiian guitar Type of guitar differing from the normal instrument in the tuning of the strings, and in the fact that the strings are stopped not with the fingers, but with a small metal bar (the steel). This forms a movable nut passing across the strings. By sliding the steel, tuning can be reproduced at any pitch, and this makes possible the sliding thirds which are a feature of music for this instrument. The Hawaiian style of dance music played on the Hawaiian guitar was popular before World War II.

Hawaiian guitar

hayashi (Japan) Generic term for drum and flute ensemble. When used in festivals to play folk music, it consists of three drums - **ō-daiko** and two *taiko* – with a six- or seven-holed flute, and is often accompanied by a small, suspended brass gong. In **noh** drama, there are again three drums – *ō-tsuzumi*, *ko-tsuzumi* (see **tsuzumi**) and *taiko* – with a seven-holed flute, the *nohkan* or *noh* flute. In both **kabuki** and **nagauta**, the *hayashi* is borrowed from the *noh* ensemble, but more drums are often added.

Haydn, (Franz) Joseph (1732-1809) Austrian composer whose work displays a masterful balance between contrapuntal and harmonic elements and an energy that does not break the pattern and texture of his music. He was an important figure in the development of both the symphony and the string quartet, being regarded as in a sense the 'father' of both genres, for although he did not create them he took them both to new levels of development and refinement.

As a boy, Haydn showed early musical promise and at the age of eight he was sent by his father to Vienna as a chorister in St Stephen's Cathedral. When his voice broke he became a servant and accompanist to the composer Porpora in order to earn a living. He wrote his first quartets (1755) at this time. In 1757 he became musical director to Count Morzin and composed his first symphony in that year. His symphonies *Le matin*, *Le midi* and *Le soir* were composed in 1761. Also in 1761 he was appointed *Vize-Kapellmeister* by Prince Paul Eszterházy at Eisenstadt, and then *Kapellmeister* at the family's residence at Eszterháza, where he remained until 1790. He had married in 1760, but the marriage was never particularly happy.

During his years at the Eszterháza palace Haydn's work was internationally recognized. He published a great deal of work and received commissions from Cadiz for the oratorio *The Seven Words of the Saviour on the Cross* (1784) and from the Concert de la Loge Olympique in Paris for six symphonies (Nos.82-7). He also befriended **Mozart** and each composer reflects the influence of the other during this period. Haydn was later to recall these years as being among his most fruitful.

In 1791 Haydn visited England and was hailed as a genius. He wrote four symphonies; he heard Handel's *Messiah* at Westminster Abbey and was deeply impressed. He returned to Vienna in 1792 and became **Beethoven**'s tutor for a while before returning to England to compose six more symphonies. During his two periods in England he was warmly received and treated with great honour; he also embarked on a serious love affair at the age of almost 60. In 1796 he again went back to Vienna and wrote six settings of the Mass (1796-1802), the oratorio *Die Schöpfung* (The Creation) (1798) and *Die Jahreszeiten* (The Seasons) (1801). Both of these works reveal the influence of Handel. The 'London' symphonies, 12 in number altogether, by which he is best remembered, include No.94 *The Surprise*, No.96 *The Miracle* (1791), No.101 *The Clock* (1794) and No.104 *The London*. At this time his health deteriorated and he appeared less and less in public. He died during the French occupation of Vienna.

Haydn composed more than 104 symphonies, 13 keyboard concertos and at least 17 concertos for other instruments. He also completed 18 operas, eight oratorios, 12 Masses, 84 string quartets, 31 piano trios, 52 keyboard sonatas, 125 songs and a further 377 arrangements of airs.

Haydn, Michael (1737-1806) Austrian composer who was somewhat overshadowed by his brother, Franz Joseph **Haydn**, but who revealed in his religious compositions a masterful dignity and structural complexity. He was a chorister and deputy organist at St Stephen's Cathedral, Vienna, from 1745, and in 1757 became choirmaster to the Bishop of Grosswardein in Hungary. He taught himself composition using **Fux**'s *Gradus ad Parnassum* as a guide. In 1762 he was appointed *Konzertmeister* to the Archbishop of Salzburg and organist at his cathedral. He composed more than 50 symphonies, concertos for violin, horn, trumpet, harpsichord, flute and viola. In addition he wrote a large amount of devotional music, including over 30 Masses, oratorios and shorter works for the chapel.

Head, Michael (1900-1976) English composer and pianist who became a professor of piano at the Royal Academy of Music in 1927. He wrote a number of light operas, cantatas and songs.

head voice The high register of the voice, which seems to come out of the head, though it is doubtful whether the head actually acts as a resonator. See also **chest voice**.

heckelclarina Instrument similar to a clarinet, but with a conical bore, invented by the German firm of Heckel. It was used for the playing of the shepherd's pipe in Act III of Wagner's *Tristan und Isolde* (1865).

Heckelclarina

heckelphone Double-reed instrument invented by the German firm of Heckel. It is similar to an **oboe**, but sounds an octave lower in pitch.

Heifetz, Jascha (1901-1987) Lithuanian-born American violinist widely regarded as the 20th century's most dazzlingly brilliant exponent of the instrument. He was admired more as a virtuoso with a faultless technique than as a musician of passion. He began playing the violin at the age of five and studied at the Imperial Conservatoire, St Petersburg (now

Leningrad), Russia. He emigrated to the United States in 1917, on the outbreak of the Soviet Revolution, becoming an American citizen in 1925. He played the classics as well as many showpieces by such composers as Pablo de **Sarasate** and Fritz **Kreisler**. He also commissioned many new works, including the **Walton** and **Schoenberg** violin concertos. He retired from the concert platform in 1972.

Heike-biwa (Japan) Type of **biwa** or lute.

helicon Brass instrument and a member of the **tuba** family, similar to the **bombardon** but made in a circular form so that it may be carried over the shoulder when marching in a military band.

Helicon

Heller, Stephen (1813-1888) Hungarian composer and pianist who studied at the Vienna Academy and settled in Paris in 1838. He toured Europe as a virtuoso performer and met both **Chopin** and **Liszt**. He visited England in 1850 and 1862, and wrote more than 100 short pieces for the piano and chamber ensemble.

Hely-Hutchinson, Victor (1901-1947) South African composer, pianist and conductor who spent most of his time in England. He studied at Eton, Oxford and the Royal College of Music and became a lecturer in music at Cape Town University in 1922. He returned to England in 1926 to join the BBC. Until 1934, when he was appointed a professor of music at Birmingham University, he was head of music for the Midland Region. He became director of music for the BBC in 1947. His compositions include *A Carol Symphony* and settings of Edward Lear's *Nonsense Songs*, as well as chamber works.

hemidemisemiquaver Note having half the time value of a **demisemiquaver** and a sixty-fourth that of a **semibreve**.

Hemidemisemiquaver and its rest

hemiola Change of metre, whereby six units are momentarily grouped in two groups of three, instead of three groups of two, usually at a cadence in **Baroque** music.

Hemsley, Thomas (1927-) English baritone whose début in 1951 was opposite Kirsten **Flagstad** in Purcell's *Dido and Aeneas*. He sang with various German and Swiss opera companies before appearing at **Bayreuth** in 1968 as Beckmesser in *Die Meistersinger von Nürnberg*. He did not sing at Covent Garden until 1970, although he had appeared often at Glyndebourne, Sadler's Wells and with the **English Opera Group**. He sang Demetrius at the première of **Britten's** *A Midsummer Night's Dream* (1960), and Magnus at that of **Tippett's** *The Knot Garden* (1970). He has also given admired readings of *Lieder* – especially Wolf's *Songbooks* and Schubert's *Winterreise* – and of oratorios.

Henry, Pierre (1927-) French composer noted for the fluency of his compositions in an electronic medium and for his pioneering experiments with Henri Barraud. Henry studied at the Paris Conservatoire with **Boulanger** and **Messiaen** and became a director of the Groupe de Recherches de Musique Concrète at the French Radio Studios in 1950. He worked with Pierre **Schaeffer** on electronic composition and founded the first private electronic studio in France at Apsone in 1958. His compositions, all electronic, include *Le voile d'Orphée* (1953), *La messe de Liverpool* (1967) and *Gymkhana* (1970).

Henschel, Sir George (1850-1934) German-born composer, pianist, conductor and singer, who became a British citizen in 1890. His début as a pianist was in 1862, and he studied at the Leipzig Conservatoire in 1867 and later at the Berlin Conservatoire. He also had a well-developed baritone voice and in 1868 played the part of Hans Sachs in a production of Wagner's *Die Meistersinger*. He was the first conductor of the Boston Symphony Orchestra (1881). As a singer he accompanied himself and made a number of recordings. His compositions include three operas, choral works, songs and chamber music. He left a valuable reminiscence of his friendship with **Brahms**.

Henze, Hans Werner (1926-) German composer. He studied at the Brunswick State Music School (1942) and at Heidelberg University (1946); during the war he had deserted from the German army. He worked in Darmstadt with **Leibowitz**, studying **Schoenberg**'s **twelve-note** system, and again with Leibowitz in Paris. In 1950 he became musical director of the Hessian State Opera Ballet company but moved to Italy in 1953.

His earlier works reflect the influences of Schoenberg and **Stravinsky**, whereas later pieces are infused with the atmosphere and richness of Italian styles. Among his compositions are the lyrical drama *Boulevard Solitude* (1951), the operas *König Hirsch* (1952) with its Mediterranean gloss, *Der Prinz von Homberg* (1960) and *Der Junge Lord* (1965), which satirized German society. His opera *The Bassarids* (1966) was produced for the Salzburg Festival.

After 1945, Henze declared his affiliation to the extreme Left. He paid an extended visit to Cuba in 1969, and his later compositions are coloured by revolutionary fervour, including *The Raft of the Medusa* which ends with the percussive chant of 'Ho! Ho! Ho-Chi-Minh!' Henze wrote a large amount of orchestral music including six symphonies, but his main preoccupation has been with choral compositions, ballets (*Ondine*, 1958; *Orpheus*, 1979) and above all opera (*We come to the River*, 1976; *The English Cat*, 1983; *Tre operi di burattini*, 1984).

Herbert, Victor (1859-1924) Irish composer, cellist and conductor who studied at the Stuttgart Conservatoire and became a principal cellist with the Stuttgart Court Orchestra in 1883. In 1886 he moved to the United States and became principal cellist at the New York Metropolitan in 1877. He conducted the Pittsburgh Symphony Orchestra, 1898.

His compositions include more than 30 operettas, including *Naughty Marietta* (1910) and *Babes in Toyland* (1903), two more serious operas, *Madeleine* (1914) and *Natoma* (1911), the *Irish Rhapsody* (1892) for orchestra and other chamber pieces.

heroic tenor The powerful type of tenor voice best suited to heroic rather than lyrical or comic parts. In German, such a type (*Heldentenor*) is classed as a category of character as well as a voice. **Wagner**ian roles such as those in *Tannhäuser*, *Lohengrin*, *Tristan*, *Die Walküre* and *Siegfried* demand such a voice.

Herold, Ferdinand (1791-1833) French composer who studied piano with his father, with C.P.E. **Bach** and later with Louis Adam at the Paris Conservatoire (1806-10). In 1812 he won the Prix de Rome and was appointed pianist to Queen

Caroline in Naples (1820). He was accompanist at the Théâtre des Italiens until 1827, when he became a choirmaster at the Opéra in Paris.

He composed more than 20 *opéras-comiques*, including *La Clochette* (1817) and *Marie* (1826), as well as ballets (*La fille mal gardée* is his best known) and cantatas.

Herrmann, Bernard (1911-1975) American composer and conductor who wrote the memorable score for Alfred Hitchcock's film *Psycho*. He studied at the Juilliard School with **Wagenaar**, and founded the New Chamber Orchestra in 1931. He became musical director of CBS (1934) and conductor of the CBS Symphony Orchestra (1940). Both Hitchcock and Orson Welles commissioned him to compose music for films, among them *Citizen Kane*, *The Magnificent Ambersons*, *Marnie* and *Fahrenheit 451*. He also composed the opera *Wuthering Heights* (1952), two symphonies, the orchestral suite *For the Fallen* (1943), choral works (including the cantata *Moby Dick*, 1938) and some chamber music.

Hertel, Johann Wilhelm (1727-1789) German composer and violinist who studied with **Benda** and became *Kapellmeister* to the court of Schwerin in 1775. He composed many symphonies, concertos and sonatas, as well as several volumes of chamber music.

Hervé (1825-1892) Pen-name of Florimond Ronger, a French composer, organist and singer who studied under **Auber** at the Paris Conservatoire and became a conductor with several opera orchestras. He composed more than 100 operettas, including *L'oeil crevé* (1867), *Chilpéric* (1868) and *Le petit Faust* (1869), and sometimes appeared in them himself. In 1870 he moved to London to conduct at the Empire Theatre. He also composed for the orchestra and wrote his own librettos.

Heseltine, Philip English composer who worked under the pen-name of Peter **Warlock**.

Hess, Dame Myra (1890-1965) English pianist. She studied at the Guildhall School of Music and at the Royal Academy of Music under Matthay, and made her début at 17, playing Beethoven's Piano Concerto No.4. This launched her on an international career. From 1922 she often appeared in the United States, and gained great popularity there; indeed, she was throughout her life a most warmly admired, even loved personality. During the entire course of World War II she organized a series of lunchtime concerts at the National Gallery in Trafalgar Square, for which she was often unpaid; these performances did much to boost morale, and for this enterprise she was made DBE. Her recording of J.S. Bach's *Jesu, Joy of Man's Desiring* was a best-seller. Her wide repertory encompassed Baroque (Bach and Scarlatti), classical (Mozart and Beethoven concertos) and Romantic music (Chopin, Brahms, Schumann and Debussy), although she also tackled contemporary music such as works by Howard **Ferguson** with success.

heterophony Single melody existing in different simultaneous forms. Although heterophony occurs in Western classical compositions, the term is often used in non-Western or folk music contexts – for example, when an instrument embellishes a vocal melody – or when variations, intentional or accidental, occur between individual participants in a **monodic** chorus.

hexachord Scale of six notes which **Guido d'Arezzo** (in the 11th century) named Ut, Re, Mi, Fa, Sol, La. There are three hexachords beginning on the notes G, C and F, and the same names were used for the notes of each. The G hexachord was called hard (*durum*), the C natural (*naturale*) and the F soft (*molle*). The German names for major (*dur*) and minor (*moll*) are derived from the Latin names for two of these hexachords.

hichiriki (Japan) Short, double-reed woodwind instrument of Chinese origin, traditionally considered to be imbued with supernatural properties. It is made of bamboo wrapped in strands of cherry bark, lacquered inside, with seven finger-holes on top and two thumb-holes behind, and is found in Shinto ceremonial music and in the **gagaku** court orchestra.

high fidelity Often abbreviated to hi-fi, a method of electronic sound reproduction of high quality without distortion.

Hill, Alfred (1870-1960) Australian composer and conductor who studied at the Leipzig Conservatoire and played in the Gewandhaus Orchestra as a violinist before settling in New Zealand. He became fascinated by Maori music and collected some traditional pieces. In 1915 he was appointed professor of composition and harmony at the New South Wales Conservatorium. His compositions reflect the influence of Maori culture, particularly in his *Maori Symphony* (1900) and *Maori Rhapsody* and the cantata *Hinemoa* (1895). He also wrote several operas, symphonies and string quartets.

Hiller, Ferdinand (1811-1885) German composer, pianist and conductor who became an exponent of **Beethoven**'s piano works and who had some success in Paris with his operas, written mainly in the French style. He studied with **Hummel** and visited Beethoven with him in 1827. In 1828 he moved to Paris as a virtuoso pianist and performed Beethoven's Piano Concerto No.5 at his début. He conducted in Frankfurt, Düsseldorf and Cologne and founded the Cologne Conservatoire in 1850. In 1852 he was appointed director of the Italian opera in Paris.

His compositions include six operas, three symphonies, two oratorios, concertos for the piano and violin and pieces for chamber ensemble.

Hiller, Johann Adam (1728-1804) German composer and conductor who was one of the originators of the **Singspiel**, an opera form with spoken dialogue. He studied at the conservatoires of Dresden and Leipzig and from 1758 became a leading figure in the musical life of the city. He was the conductor of the Gewandhaus Concerts, which he founded in 1781. He conducted various other orchestras until 1789, when he became a cantor at the Thomasschule. Among his compositions are a number of *Singspiel* operas, including *Der Teufel ist los* (1766), and some church music.

Hilton, John (*c.*1560-1608) English composer, lay-clerk at Lincoln Cathedral (1584) and organist at Trinity College, Cambridge, from 1594. He composed anthems and motets, as well as the **madrigal** *Fair Oriana, Beauty's Queen* which was included in **Morley**'s collection *The Triumphs of Oriana*, presented to Elizabeth I in 1601.

Hilton, John (1599-1657) English composer and organist, son of John **Hilton**. Born perhaps at Cambridge, Hilton became organist of the church of St Margaret's, Westminster, in 1628. He published a set of balletts under the title *Ayres, or Fa La's* and an extremely popular collection of rounds and canons known as *Catch as Catch Can*.

Himmel, Friedrich Heinrich (1765-1814) German composer who studied at the Dresden Conservatoire and in Italy. In 1795 he became *Kapellmeister* to the court at Berlin. He visited England, Austria and Russia, producing operas successfully in several cities. Among his compositions are a number of operas and operettas in Italian and German, the *Liederspiel Frohsinn und Schwarmerei* (1801) and the opera *Fanchon, das Leiermädchen* (1804). He also wrote works for piano and for orchestra, as well as songs, oratorios and Masses.

Hindemith, Paul (1895-1963) German composer, violinist and violist who began as a startling innovator and ended by being regarded as a conservative by the avant-garde. His compositions were tonal, and held dissonance and consonance in constant tension despite a rhythmic energy.

He studied composition and violin at the Hoch Conservatoire in Frankfurt from 1913. In 1915 he became leader of the Frankfurt Opera Orchestra. He served in the German Army (1917-19) but continued to compose, and eventually returned to the Opera orchestra. His second string quartet was performed at Donaueschingen in 1921; the players, led by Licco Amar, included Hindemith himself on viola. The Amar Quartet thus came into being, strictly for the performance of modern works, and Hindemith performed with and provided material for it until 1929. These years were very productive and his opera *Cardillac* (1926), with its echoes of Handel's style, was a success.

In 1927 he was appointed a professor of composition at the Berlin Hochschule. He also sent compositions to the conductors **Furtwängler** and **Klemperer**, including his opera *Neues vom Tage* (1929), which featured a soprano singing in a bathtub. In 1933 he began work on his opera *Mathis der Maler*, only to fall foul of the Nazi authorities, who viewed him as a musical degenerate. Despite the protestation of Furtwängler, the opera was banned by Goebbels.

Hindemith resigned from the Berlin Hochschule in 1937 and moved to New York, where he was appointed visiting professor at Yale University in 1940. He also taught at the Tanglewood Festivals, where his pupils included Leonard **Bernstein** and Lukas **Foss**. One of his most important works from this period is the Requiem *When Lilacs Last in the Dooryard Bloom'd*, a setting of Whitman poems. After the war he returned to Europe and toured extensively, revising some of his scores and lecturing in Berlin at the Hochschule. He conducted for various orchestras, taught at the Universities of Yale and Zurich, and composed his later, introspective compositions, among them

Paul Hindemith

the opera *Die Harmonie der Welt* (1957). Another major work with an American theme is the opera *The Long Christmas Dinner* (1960), from a Wilder play.

His compositions completed in the 1920s include the song cycle *Das Marienleben* (1923), the operas *Mörder, Hoffnung der Frauen* (Murder, Hope of Women, 1919), *Sancta Susanna* (1921) and *Das Nusch-nuschi* (1920), six chamber sonatas, four quartets, many sonatas for various instruments and pieces for the chamber ensemble. They are individual in style, but still based upon traditional influences. One of these influences is found in the linear counterpoint of Bach and is described by Hindemith in his important treatise *The Craft of Composition* (1937). Later pieces reflect his notion of *Gebrauchsmusik* (music for use), and have a degree of technical simplicity. Other works, like the ballets *Nobilissima Visione* (1938) and *The Four Temperaments* (1940), are more clearly tonal.

Hob. Abbreviation of Hoboken, after Anthony van Hoboken (1887-1983), the Dutch musicologist who compiled the definitive catalogue of **Haydn**'s works. References to this cataloguing system are given as Hob., followed by a roman and an arabic numeral.

hocket Device used in medieval vocal and instrumental music consisting of phrases broken up by rests, in such a way that when one part is silent, another fills the gap. The term is derived from the Latin *hoquetus* (hiccup). **Machaut**'s *Hoquetus David* is a piece in which this technique is predominant.

Hoddinott, Alun (1929-) Welsh composer whose work reflects the influence of **serialism** in a casual manner and is both richly romantic and carefully patterned. He studied at the University College of South Wales and became a lecturer at Cardiff College of Music and Drama in 1951. He returned to University College as a lecturer, becoming professor of music in 1976 (the department has now closed). He founded the Cardiff Festival of 20th-Century Music in 1967 and is its artistic director. He won the Arnold Bax Medal for composers in 1957.

He has been influenced by the music of **Rawsthorne** and Bartók, and is a prolific composer, who has concentrated on opera in recent years (*The Beach of Falesa*; *The Magician*; *What the Old Man Does is Always Right*; *The Rajah's Diamond*). His other compositions include five symphonies; orchestral works such as *Fugal Overture* (1953), *Night Music* (1966) and *French Suite* (1977); and concertos for harp, piano, violin, horn, and organ. He has also composed much choral music (*St Paul on Malta*, cantata, 1971), instrumental music and many songs, as well as film and television music.

hoe-down American get-together for folk-dancing, originating in the 19th century and including such dances as jigs and reels. A hoe-down is featured in Aaron **Copland**'s ballet *Rodeo* (1942).

Hoffding, Finn (1899-) Danish composer who studied in Copenhagen and at the Vienna Conservatoire with Joseph **Marx**, and became a professor of composition at the Royal Danish Conservatoire in 1931. He founded the Copenhagen Folk Music School (1935) with Jørgen **Bentzon**. His compositions include the opera *The Emperor's New Clothes* and chamber pieces which reveal the influences of folk-music.

Hoffmann, Ernst Theodor Amadeus (1776-1822) German composer, conductor and writer who was the hero of **Offenbach**'s *Les contes d'Hoffmann* (1881) and was most successful as an author of intriguing tales and essays. His character Kreisler the *Kapellmeister*, who appears in his *Fantasiestücke in Callots Manier* (1814), was the inspiration behind Schumann's *Kreisleriana*.

He studied law but continued his musical education and became conductor of the Bamberg Theatre Orchestra in 1808, after some time in the civil service. He also conducted many other orchestras, notably in Leipzig and Dresden. Among his compositions are ten operas, including *Undine* (1816), a symphony, ballet scores, piano sonatas and chamber music.

Hoffmeister, Franz Anton (1754-1812) German composer and publisher who founded the Bureau de Musique with Kühnel at Leipzig, 1800. In Vienna he was a friend of Mozart. He wrote a large number of works for clarinet, flute and strings, as well as songs and devotional music.

Hofmann, Joseph (1876-1957) Polish composer and pianist who became an American citizen in 1926. As a performer he was a masterful exponent of Chopin's works. He was a child prodigy and made his first solo appearance with the Berlin Philharmonic Orchestra when only nine years old. He toured Europe and the United States until stopped by the Society for the Prevention of Cruelty to Children. He studied with **Rubinstein** for a while before returning to the United States in 1898 to embark on another series of tours. In 1925 he became director of the Curtis Institute, Philadelphia.

His compositions include five piano concertos that reflect his sensitivity to romantic themes, equally manifest in his playing. He also wrote a symphony, sonatas and other pieces for the piano.

Hogwood, Christopher (1941-) English harpsichordist and conductor who studied at Cambridge, with **Puyana** and **Leonhardt**, and in Prague. While at Cambridge he became associated with David **Munrow**, and with him founded the Early Music Consort (1967). In 1973 he formed the **Academy of Ancient Music** to give **authentic** performances of Baroque and classical music; with them and as a soloist he has made many recordings of Bach, Handel, Rameau and Couperin. He has also made appearances all over the world as a conductor, and was appointed to the Boston Handel and Haydn Society in 1986. In addition, he has written several musicological studies.

Holborne, Anthony (?-1602) English composer of whose life little is known. He worked with the **cittern** and composed an exquisite series of pieces for it. In 1597 he published *The Cittharn Schoole*, with 57 pieces for cittern and bass viol. His other compositions were published in the collection *Pavans, Galliards, Almans and other Short Ayres* (1599). Compositions by Holborne also appear in John Dowland's *Variety of Lute Lessons* (1610).

Holbrooke, Joseph (1878-1958) English composer and pianist who challenged the musical establishment both by his background and with his views. From an early age he worked as a music-hall pianist. He was admitted to the Royal Academy of Music in 1893. He studied there with Corder until he returned to the stage with a travelling pantomime which he conducted and performed in. He composed a number of serious pieces, including the symphonic poem *Byron and the Raven* (1900), which became popular at music festivals. He also wrote three Celtic operas – *The Children of Don* (1912), *Dylan* (1913) and *Bronwen* (1929) – as well as orchestral variations on the themes *Auld Lang Syne* and *Three Blind Mice*.

holler Long, wavering one- or two-line call used by black agricultural workers in the United States and the Caribbean. It may have been used as a signalling device, and was often sung in African dialect. Features such as falsetto breaks and falling motifs at the end of lines are characteristic of the **blues** style of singing, and suggest the field holler may have been a contributory precursor of the blues.

Höller, Karl (1907-) German composer who became a teacher at the Hoch Conservatoire in Frankfurt in 1937. He was appointed a professor at the Munich Conservatoire in 1947, and composed *Variations on a Theme of Sweelinck* for orchestra as well as a symphony, concertos for the violin, cello and organ, and chamber pieces.

Holliger, Heinz (1939-) Swiss composer and oboist who has experimented with unusual combinations of instruments, and more latterly with electronic techniques. He studied at the conservatoires in Berne, Basle and Paris (1952-63) and became first oboist with the Basle Orchestra in 1959. His compositions include many works for the oboe with other instruments, such as *Trio* (1966) for oboe, viola and harp, and *Siebengesang* for oboe, voices and orchestra (1967), a work which exhibits the tones of the oboe magnified and distorted by electronic means. He has also composed *Pneuma* (1970) for 34 wind instruments, percussion, voices and radio and *Der magische Tanzer* (1965) for two singers, two actors, two dancers, choir, orchestra and tape.

Holloway, Robin (1943-) English composer of romantic and occasionally introspective works which reflect an individual understanding of harmony and melody. He studied at St Paul's Cathedral Choir School and then at Cambridge and Oxford. He returned to Cambridge as a research student at Gonville and Caius College, and became a Fellow there in 1969. In 1974 he was appointed a lecturer in music at Cambridge.

Among his compositions are the opera

Clarissa (written in 1976, though not performed until 1990, by the English National Opera), *Souvenirs de Schumann* (1970) for orchestra, the symphonic poem *Domination of Black* (1973), *Romanza* (1978) for small orchestra, and choral music, including *The Consolation of Music* (1979) for unaccompanied choir and *Five Madrigals* (1973). He has also written extensively for chamber orchestra and for voice and piano, his most sensitive songs being *Songs for Eliot's Sweeney Agonistes* (1965), *The Leaves Cry* (1974) and *A Poor Soul Sat Sighing* (1977).

Holmboe, Vagn (1909-) Danish composer who was influenced by the folk-melodies he collected. His style is expansive and essentially rugged, although his grasp of melody tends to smooth an otherwise primitive tendency. He studied at the Royal Conservatoire, Copenhagen, with **Hoffding** (1927) and at the Berlin Hochschule with **Toch**. He collected Danish folk-melodies and became a critic for the periodical *Politiken* in 1947. In 1950 he was appointed a professor of composition at the Danish Conservatoire. His compositions include ten symphonies, two operas and a *Requiem for Nietzsche*. He also wrote a number of chamber pieces and 14 motets.

Holst, Gustav (1874-1934) English composer of Swedish origin who freed himself from Teutonic traditions and wrote colourful, exotic music that is both demonstrative and impressionistic and which developed from classical to polytonal forms.

He studied the piano with his father, and in 1893 was admitted to the Royal College of Music after the first performance of his opera *Lansdowne Castle* (1893). He studied composition with **Stanford** and was a friend of **Vaughan Williams**. Soon afterwards some of his early works were performed, the best known of which include the *Cotswold Symphony* (1902) and *Mystic Trumpeter* (1903).

He went on to become a music teacher,

Gustav Holst

first at James Allen's Girls' School in Dulwich and then at St Paul's School for Girls (1905), composing his *St Paul's Suite* for strings in that year. He also began collecting English folk-melodies and cultivating an interest in both Sanskrit literature and Hindu scales. *Somerset Rhapsody* (1907) was to reflect the influence of folk-music, while his Eastern preoccupations produced the *Choral Hymns from the Rig Veda* in 1911. In 1907 he became director of music at Morley College and continued to compose.

After World War I Holst began to experiment with larger orchestras and choirs. In 1917 he began his choral work *The Hymn of Jesus*, and two years later the first performance of *The Planets* suite met with success. He joined the teaching staff at the University of Reading and the Royal College of Music shortly afterwards. His compositions at this time include the *Choral Symphony* (1925), based on poems by Keats, *At the Boar's Head* (1925) and *Egdon Heath* (1927), a masterful orchestral setting of a picturesque theme. His later works reveal a deeper lyricism which is particularly notable in *Twelve Songs by Humbert Wolfe* (1929) and *Choral Fantasia* (1931).

Holst's compositions include a large body of choral work, chamber music, hymns and songs. His orchestral pieces number over 20 suites, a form which he exploited with ease, in addition to concertos, sonatas and smaller ensemble works.

Holst, Imogen (1907-1984) English conductor and editor, the daughter of Gustav **Holst**. She studied at the Royal College of Music. She edited and conducted recordings of several of her father's works and wrote books on him, on **Britten** (for whom she acted as musical assistant), and on **Byrd**. She was also for a time director of the **Aldeburgh** Festival.

Holzbauer, Ignaz (1711-1783) Austrian composer, who featured largely in the musical scene at Mannheim in the late 18th century. He studied in Vienna and became *Kapellmeister* to a noble family in Moravia before returning to Vienna as director of the court theatre. In around 1744 he went to Milan and Venice, and became *Kapellmeister* at Mannheim in 1753, where he remained until 1778. This was his most productive period; he composed operas and pantomimes, of which the most successful was *Günther von Schwarzburg* (1777). *Nitteti* (1758) and *Alessandro nell'Indie* (1759) were written for Italian theatres, and are the only other operas to have survived. He also wrote church music – 17 Masses, 37 motets and four oratorios – and 65 symphonies, many sonatas and other chamber music. His music was admired by Mozart and the English musicologist Dr Burney.

homage Composition dedicated to a composer and written in his or her style. For example, **Falla**'s *Homenaje*, for guitar, is in honour of **Debussy**.

homophonic Music in which the parts move in step together, without strong linear independence, as in a hymn tune.

Honegger, Arthur (1892-1955) Swiss composer of neo-romantic and tonal works with a deep sense of power and passion. He studied at the Conservatoires in Zurich (1909) and Paris (1911) and joined Les **Six**, a group of French composers formed in 1917; he was the most serious member of the group. The successful oratorio *Le roi David* was composed in 1921 and the masterful *Pacific 231*, a portrait of a steam engine, in 1924. He composed prolifically, completing five symphonies, including the fifth (1951), which has three movements each ending on the note 'D'; the symphonic movement *Rugby* (1928); the oratorio *Jeanne d'Arc au bûcher* (1938); the operas *Antigone* (1927), with a libretto by Cocteau, and *L'Aiglon* (1937), which he wrote in collaboration with **Ibert**; numerous ballets; film scores (more than 40) and incidental music for plays and radio; three string quartets and a variety of other chamber music; and over 60 songs. He also wrote an illuminating autobiography, *I Am a Composer*.

Arthur Honegger

Hopkins, Antony (1921-) English composer and pianist who became a respected broadcaster with his educational radio series *Talking About Music*, which has run for over 30 years. He studied at the Royal College of Music and became director of the Intimate Opera Company in 1952. He has composed several chamber operas, including *Three's Company*, and music for radio, theatre and film.

Hopkinson, Francis (1737-1791) American composer, harpsichordist and statesman who was one of the signatories of the Declaration of Independence in 1776. He wrote the first piece of art (classical) music by an American, *My Days Have Been So Wondrous Free* (1759). He also dedicated a series of harpsichord pieces to George Washington and composed the oratorial entertainment *The Temple of Minerva*, none of which survives today.

Horenstein, Jascha (1899-1973) American conductor of Russian and Austrian parentage. He studied in Vienna with **Schreker**, and spent some time in Berlin assisting **Furtwängler**. In 1923 he made his début in Vienna and appeared as a guest conductor with the Berlin Philharmonic over the next few years. He moved to Düsseldorf in 1928, and spent five years at the Opera there; he left Germany in 1933 at the onset of the Nazi regime. After a period of touring in Europe he settled in the United States in 1940. His first performance at Covent Garden was in 1961, when he conducted Beethoven's *Fidelio*. His repertory included many 20th-century operas (Berg's *Wozzeck*; Janáček's *From the House of the Dead*) and the symphonies of Mahler and Bruckner, of which he made several recordings.

horn Alternative term for **French horn**. It is also used in American **jazz** parlance for any wind instrument.

Horn, Charles Edward (1786-1849) English composer who acted and sang on the London stage from 1809. He moved to the United States in 1833 and had some success with his operatic productions in New York. In 1843 he returned briefly to England, but settled for the rest of his life in Boston after 1847. He wrote a number of choral and operatic works, including the song *Cherry Ripe*, which are still popular among choral societies today.

Horn, Karl Friedrich (1762-1830) German composer and organist, and father of Charles **Horn**. He settled in London (1782) and was appointed music master to Queen Charlotte and the Royal Household in 1811. He became the organist at St George's Chapel, Windsor, in 1823. His compositions include a number of piano sonatas and an edition of **Bach**'s *Well-Tempered Clavier*, which he produced with Samuel **Wesley**.

Horne, Marilyn (1934-) American mezzo-soprano who studied in California and made her début there in 1954. In the same year she sang the title-role on the sound-track of Otto Preminger's film *Carmen Jones*, the all-black version of Bizet's *Carmen*, dubbing the voice of the leading lady, Dorothy Dandridge. She sang in Europe, in San Francisco, and at Covent Garden in 1964 as Marie in **Berg**'s *Wozzeck*. In 1962 she first sang with Joan **Sutherland**, and thereafter the two had a famous partnership in such works as Bellini's *Norma* (Horne singing Adalgisa) and Rossini's *Semiramide* (Horne as Arsace). Her Metropolitan début was as Adalgisa in 1970. Her other roles include Carmen and Orfeo in Gluck's *Orfeo ed Euridice*, and she has recorded an extensive range from *bel canto* to Wagner, revealing her astonishing versatility.

hornpipe Lively English dance, so-called because it was first accompanied on a pipe of the same name which was made from an animal's horn. Originally it was in 3/2 time, although the later form is in 2/4. It was known as the sailor's hornpipe, and an example appeared in the operetta *Ruddigore* by **Sullivan** (1887).

Horovitz, Joseph (1926-) Austrian-born composer, conductor and teacher who settled in England as a child, and studied at Oxford and the Royal College of Music. He became an assistant director of the Intimate Opera Company in 1952, and a professor of composition at the Royal College in 1961. He has composed two operatic works, 11 ballets, concertos for various instruments and a series of popular parodies for the music festivals organized by Gerard Hoffnung in London.

Horowitz, Vladimir (1904-1989) Russian pianist who studied at the Kiev Conservatoire and made his début in Kharkov in 1921, and in London and New York in 1928. He emigrated to the United States in 1940 and made many recordings, gaining an international reputation as a virtuoso pianist. His concert career was halted by illness several times, but he performed until the 1970s, and emerged from retirement on special occasions, returning to Russia to perform in 1986. His numerous recordings, above all of the Romantic repertory, reveal not only his superlative technique but his powerfully emotional interpretive abilities. Apart from Liszt, Schumann and Chopin he has recorded Bach, Mozart, Rachmaninov, and Scriabin, bringing to them all the same careful preparation and faultless articulation.

hot Lively and exciting, especially associated with **jazz** music.

Hotter, Hans (1909-) German bass-baritone. He studied in Munich, and played the organ before beginning his career as an opera-singer. His early performances were in Prague, Breslau and Hamburg; he returned to Munich in 1940. After the war he appeared at Covent Garden in the title-role of *Don Giovanni*, on tour with the Vienna State Opera. The following year he sang Hans Sachs in *Die Meistersinger von Nürnberg*, the first of what came to be recognized as supreme Wagner interpretations – he was engaged at Bayreuth in 1952, and over the next two decades established himself as the pre-eminent Wotan in the *Ring* cycle. He created several Strauss roles, and made a number of fine recordings. He produced the *Ring* cycle at Covent Garden (1961) and was notable as a *Lieder* singer.

Hotteterre, Jacques Martin (?-1760) French composer and flautist who came

Vladimir Horowitz

from a large family of woodwind instrument-makers and performers. He studied in Rome and is believed to be the first musician to play a transverse flute, at the Paris Opéra in 1697. He composed a number of flute pieces, suites for two flutes and pieces for the musette (a small bagpipe).

Hovhaness, Alan (1911-) American composer and organist who was deeply influenced by Eastern music. His works reflect a combination of Western elements with a modal, Oriental harmony and the tones of Oriental instruments. This is clearly heard in his *Fantasy on Japanese Footprints* (1965).

He studied at the New England Conservatoire and at the Tanglewood Studios with **Martinů**. In 1948 he became a tutor at the Boston Conservatoire, and settled in New York in 1952. His compositions include more than 20 symphonies, operatic works, the suite *Mysterious Mountain* for orchestra and the now well-known *And God Created Great Whales*, which features the recorded call of the humpbacked whale.

Howarth, Elgar (1935-) English conductor, trumpeter and composer who studied in Manchester and played with various brass groups, including the Philip **Jones** Brass Ensemble. He was principal trumpet at the Royal Philharmonic Orchestra, 1963-8. In 1973 he became director of the **London Sinfonietta**, where he continued the policy of promoting new music, such as works by **Ligeti**, **Xenakis** and **Birtwistle**. He has toured Europe, and has conducted the **London Symphony** and the **Royal Philharmonic** Orchestras, as well as broadcast performances with the BBC Symphony Orchestra. He has written works for his own instrument, and arranged many pieces for brass ensemble.

Howells, Herbert (1892-1983) English composer and organist. His compositions reveal the influences of **Vaughan Williams** and **Elgar**, although not to the detriment of his individual creativity.

He entered the Royal College of Music in 1912, where he studied composition with **Stanford**. He became an organist at St John's College, Cambridge, in 1941 and was appointed a professor of music at London University in 1954. He composed both devotional and secular music, including the picturesque *Pastoral Rhapsody* (1923) for orchestra and *Pageantry Suite* (1943) for brass band. His choral works suggest the boisterous nature of country pursuits as in the *Kent Yeoman's Wooing Song* (1933), and a more sublime eloquence in sacred works such as *Hymnus Paradisi* (1950) and *Missa Sabrinensis* (1953).

hsaing-waing (Burma) Largest and most common Burmese percussion ensemble, taking its name from the 21-piece drum-chime which leads the group. The instrumentation depends upon the function of the music – whether for monastic rituals, dramas, festivals or state visits. A full professional ensemble may include two types of gong chime, an oboe, barrel drums, slit drum, clappers, large cymbals and hand cymbals.

hsiao/xiao (China) Set of well-tempered pipes, blown across the open end, similar to panpipes. There are usually 16 pipes mounted in a row, ascending from left to right by the interval of a semitone. They are set into a bottomless wooden case which is painted red and ornamented with a dragon or a phoenix.

Huber, Klaus (1924-) Swiss composer and violinist who studied in Berlin with **Blacher**. He became a tutor at the Zurich Conservatoire in 1950 and a professor of harmony at the Basle Conservatoire in 1961. His compositions include *Tenebrae* for orchestra and a number of chamber pieces.

Hughes, Arwel (1909-1988) Welsh composer and conductor who studied at the Royal College of Music with **Vaughan Williams** and was appointed conductor of the BBC Welsh Orchestra in 1950. His compositions include the opera *Menna* (1951) and other works for orchestra and chamber ensembles. His son Owain Arwel Hughes is a conductor who makes frequent television and radio broadcasts.

Hughes, Herbert (1882-1937) Irish composer who studied at the Royal College of Music and became the music critic for the *Daily Telegraph* in 1911. He was an important collector of Irish folk-music and a competent arranger of this music in orchestral settings.

Hullah, John Pyke (1812-1884) English composer and organist who visited Paris in 1839 to study G.L. Wilhelm's method of teaching singing from sight. He introduced this method into English schools in 1841. From 1844 he was a professor of vocal music at Queen's College and Bedford College, London University, and in 1872 became a schools inspector. He composed a number of devotional pieces and several song cycles, as well as the opera *The Village Coquette* (which had a libretto by Charles Dickens).

Hume, Tobias (?-1645) English composer and master of the viola da **gamba**. He wrote a series of works for the lyra viol, *The First Part of Ayres* (1605), which includes the first recorded instruction – *con legno* (with the back of the bow). His only other collection of pieces, *Captain Hume's Poeticall Musicke*, followed in 1607.

Humfrey (or **Humphrey**), **Pelham** (1647-1674) English composer who became a chorister at the Chapel Royal and studied with **Lully** in Paris by order of Charles II. He returned to London in 1666 and was appointed a Gentleman of the Chapel Royal and Master of the Children there in 1672. He composed a series of secular and devotional songs, anthems and motets, and provided a score for Shakespeare's *The Tempest*.

Hummel, Johann Nepomuk (1778-1837) Austrian composer and pianist of great ability whose improvisational skills were considered to be greater than Beethoven's. His compositions are noted for their elegance and polish, and influenced Chopin with their lightness and decoration. He studied with Mozart while still a boy and toured Germany, the Low Countries and England as a virtuoso performer. In 1804 he was appointed *Kapellmeister* to the court of Eszterházy and then at Stuttgart (1816). He conducted the German Opera in London from 1833.

Among his compositions are some now forgotten operatic pieces and more than 100 instrumental works, including concertos and sonatas. He also wrote the influential tutorial book *Piano School* (1828).

humoresque Instrumental composition of capricious or fantastic rather than humorous character. It was a term used particularly by **Dvořák** and **Schumann**.

Humperdinck, Engelbert (1854-1921) German composer whose operatic work reveals the influence of **Wagner** in its orchestration and moral sensibilities. He studied at the Cologne Conservatoire with **Hiller** and moved to Munich to compose. On a visit to Italy in 1879 he met Wagner and assisted him in the production of *Parsifal* at Bayreuth. He became a professor of harmony at the Barcelona Conservatoire in 1885, and returned to take up a similar post at the Hoch Conservatoire in 1890. He also became a music critic for the *Frankfurter Zeitung* in that year. In 1893 his opera *Hänsel und Gretel* was produced in Weimar and was an immediate success. It is still widely performed today.

Humperdinck's principal compositions include other operas such as *Dornroschen* (1902) and *Königskinder* (1910), but none of them matched the success of his first. He also wrote some incidental pieces for the theatre, including *The Merchant of Venice* (1905), *The Winter's Tale* (1906) and *As You Like It* (1907).

Hunter, Rita (1933-) English soprano. She studied in Liverpool and with Dame Eva **Turner**. Her début in 1960 was as Marcellina in *Le nozze di Figaro*; she quickly moved on to more substantial roles such as Senta in Wagner's *Der fliegende Holländer* and two Verdi roles, Leonora in *Il trovatore* and Amelia in *Un ballo in maschera*. Her Brünnhilde in the English-language *Ring* cycle at the English National Opera (beginning in 1970) was a revelation, and she scored an outstanding success, blending effortless power with a touching quality. She has also been successful in the title-role of Bellini's *Norma*. She was made DBE in 1980 and later settled in Australia, where she has become a firm favourite.

hurdy-gurdy Mechanical violin consisting of six strings vibrated by a wheel turned with a handle. The tune is played on the top string by means of a keyboard, the lower strings remaining unchanged in pitch and therefore acting as a drone. Both Mozart and Haydn wrote compositions for the instrument. It is also known as a barrel organ or street piano, because like

Hurdy-gurdy

them it is operated by a handle. An alternative term for the hurdy-gurdy is organistrum.

Hurford, Peter (1930-) English organist and administrator. He studied at Cambridge and in Paris with Marchal. He was master of music at St Albans Abbey for over 20 years (1958-79) and founded the International Organ Festival there in 1963. He has specialized in the 18th-century French repertory and in Bach. In a search for authenticity he had the St Albans organ rebuilt, although he has also given many recitals on modern instruments in which he takes advantage of their up-to-date technology, and has himself suggested new features to be incorporated in organ design. He has also been active as a teacher and has composed several works.

Hurlstone, William (1876-1906) English composer and pianist who studied with **Stanford** at the Royal College of Music and became a tutor of counterpoint there in 1905. His compositions include *Fantasy-Variations on a Swedish Air* (1903) for orchestra, the ballad *Alfred the Great* and works for the piano, songs, and chamber pieces.

hyangak (Korea) Native court music and music originating from China before the T'ang dynasty. The main instruments of the orchestra include a *p'iri* (oboe), a *taegŭm* (flute), a *haegŭm* (bowed fiddle), a *changgo* (drum) and often an *ajaeng* (bowed zither). See also **aak**; **tangak**.

hydraulis Ancient type of organ invented in Egypt by Ctesibius in the 3rd century BC, and used by the Greeks and Romans. The pipes were played by wind forced through them by the pressure of water, and for this reason it is also sometimes known as a water-organ.

hymn Song of praise to God or to a saint in the Christian Church, either to a **plainsong** melody or more usually now as a four-part harmonization of a simple melody intended for congregational singing.

The hymn formed part of the earliest devotional music, formally established in the 4th century by St Ambrose of Milan. Between the 16th and 17th centuries the English hymn emerged and many fine tunes were composed, most of which are still used today. Charles Wesley (1757-1834), the English composer, wrote more than 6,000 hymns.

I

Ibert, Jacques (1890-1962) French composer noted for his lightness of touch and wit. From 1909 he studied at the Paris Conservatoire, and was appointed director of the French Academy in Rome in 1937. He returned to France in 1955 to become an assistant director at the Paris Opéra and the Opéra-Comique.

He composed a number of light operas including *Angélique* (1927) and *Gonzague* (1930), and collaborated with **Honegger** on the opera *L'Aiglon* (1937). He wrote two orchestral pieces which reflect the influences of the New World, the *Louisville Concerto* (1953) and the *Bostoniana* symphony (1955), as well as *The Italian Straw Hat* (1929) and *Escales* (1922), a descriptive piece which journeys between the ports of Valencia, Tunis and Palermo. Ballet scores, chamber pieces and works for voice and piano, including *The Little White Donkey* (1940), are also among his compositions.

idée fixe (Fr.) Term used by **Berlioz** for a theme, above all in the *Symphonie fantastique*, 1830-1, which recurs obsessively in varying forms in the course of the composition as an allusion to the artist's vision of his beloved. See also **leitmotif**.

idiophone Any musical instrument that is self-sounding, such as cymbals, xylophones, bells, gongs, rattles and tambourines. In other words, when an idiophone is hit, rattled or stroked, it produces a sound from its own material, without strings or membranes. Drums are not in this category: they are **membranophones**.

idyll Composition that describes a peaceful, pastoral picture, such as Wagner's *Siegfried Idyll* (1857).

illustrative music Piece that describes or refers to non-musical sources such as a poem, play, picture, landscape or a particular emotional experience. Examples of this type of music are Beethoven's Symphony No.6, *Pastoral* (1807-8), and the tone poem *Till Eulenspiegel* (1896) by Richard Strauss. See also **programme music**.

Imbrie, Andrew (1921-) American composer and pianist whose works display a lucid, neo-classical style. He studied composition with **Sessions** and piano with Ormstein, and lectured at the University of California from 1948. He spent several years (1947-9 and 1968-9) composing in Rome and was appointed a professor of music at the University of California in 1960.

His compositions include the opera *Three Against Christmas* (1962), symphonies, *Shaggy Dog* (1947) for wind quintet and piano, and *Divertimento for Six Instruments* (1948) for flute, bassoon, trumpet, violin, cello and piano. He has also written concertos and sonatas for the piano and violin, chamber pieces, and works for voice and orchestra, notably *Drum Taps* for chorus and orchestra.

imitation Device in a composition in which a voice or instrument repeats a theme or motif previously stated by another. An imitation may be either deferred until the first statement has been completed or made to overlap it (**stretto**). **Canon** and **fugue** employ imitation according to strict and regular patterns.

imperfect cadence **Cadence** made up of the chord progression I-V, giving the impression that the phrase is unresolved and is therefore to continue.

impressionism Term borrowed from the visual arts, in which it was applied to such painters as Monet and Renoir of the late 19th and early 20th centuries. Although **Debussy** did not approve, he was identified as the leader of musical impressionism after his composition *Prélude à l'après-midi d'un faune* was performed (1894). Its influence can also be seen in the works of **Ravel, Dukas, Delius** and **Falla**.

impromptu Music, usually for piano, written in such a way as to suggest that it is an **improvisation. Schubert** composed eight (including D899 and D935) for piano in 1827 and **Chopin** composed several, including Op.29 (1837) and Op.36 (1840).

improvisation (extemporization) Art of playing or singing music not written down by a composer, but following directly from the player's imagination. Improvised cadenzas were expected of singers and instrumental soloists in the 17th and 18th centuries, and to a certain extent survived into the 19th century. Skill in improvisation is an important aspect of an organist's training.

in (Japan) One of the two principal scales of folk origin. See **Japanese scales**

incipit (Lat.) It begins, indication of the first few bars of a musical work as quoted in an index or catalogue.

indeterminacy In the 1950s, a type of music emerged in which some modern composers left certain elements to the choice of the performer. Karlheinz **Stockhausen** was active in this particular form of music, best exemplified in two of his works: *Gruppen* (1955-7), for three orchestras, and *Zyklus* (1959), for one percussion player who may begin on any page of the score. See also **aleatory**.

Ingegneri, Marc'Antonio (1547-1592) Italian composer, singer and instrumentalist who was one of **Monteverdi**'s tutors. He studied with Ruffo and became choirmaster at Cremona Cathedral by 1572. He composed several books of Masses and motets, at least eight books of madrigals, and a set of 27 *Responsories for Holy Week* (which were attributed to **Palestrina** until 1897).

Inghelbrecht, Désiré-Emile (1880-1965) French composer, conductor and author of the books *The Conductor's World* (1953) and *The Composer's World* (1954). He conducted the Swedish Ballet Orchestra in Paris and became an assistant conductor at the Pasdeloup concerts. In 1924 he conducted at the Opéra-Comique, and in 1945 at the Paris Opéra and with the French National Radio Orchestra. His compositions include the ballet *El Greco*, choral and orchestral works, as well as chamber pieces.

in modo di (It.) In the manner of.

In nomine Instrumental composition of the late 16th or the 17th century for viols or keyboard based on a **plainsong** melody used as a **cantus firmus.** The melody is that of the chant *Gloria tibi Trinitas*, as used in a Mass by **Taverner**. Part of the Benedictus of the Mass begins with the words 'In Nomine Domini'.

instrument Any device used for the production of musical sound. The usual practical classification is into percussion, wind and string instruments. However, this type of classification can be imprecise because the piano, for instance, uses strings but is percussive in mechanism. To avoid such ambiguity, Erich von

Hornbostel and Curt Sachs published in 1914 a classification, according to what it is that actually makes the sound, into aerophones, **chordophones**, **idiophones** and **membranophones**.

instrumentation Art of writing music for instruments in a manner suited to the nature of each instrument. See also **orchestration**.

Intendant (Ger.) Superintendent or administrative director of a German opera-house or theatre.

interlude Piece of music inserted between longer pieces or between the acts of plays. In 16th- and 17th-century France such an entr'acte was called *intermède* – in Italy *intermedio*.

intermezzo 1. An instrumental piece in the middle of an opera, performed when the stage is empty, as in *Cavalleria rusticana* by **Mascagni** (1890).

2. A short instrumental piece for piano, such as *Three Intermezzos for Piano* (1892) by Brahms.

3. A comic operatic piece played as an interlude between acts of a serious opera in the 18th century. The most notable example is **Pergolesi**'s *La serva padrona* (1732).

interrupted cadence **Cadence** in which the dominant chord is followed by an unexpected chord – usually the submediant.

interval Distance in pitch between two notes, whether sounded simultaneously or in succession. There are two main divisions: simple intervals, in which the distance is an octave or less, and compound intervals, in which the distance exceeds an octave.

In the major scale (say, the scale of C major), the following simple intervals exist: second (C-D), third (C-E), fourth (C-F), fifth (C-G), sixth (C-A), seventh (C-B) and octave (C-C′). Of these the fourth, fifth and octave are spoken of as perfect intervals, and the second, third, sixth and seventh as major intervals. If a major interval is decreased by one semitone, it becomes a minor interval (e.g. C-A♭). The perfect intervals may be increased or decreased to the extent of a semitone, and are then termed augmented or diminished (e.g. C-G♯ and C-G♭, respectively).

When the two notes of an interval belong to the same scale, it is known as a diatonic interval.

intonation 1. The act of intoning, the singing of the opening phrase of a piece (for example, in church service responses) by a singer in authority so as to ensure that the right melody will be sung by the group and at the proper pitch.

2. The degree of accuracy that a singer or instrumentalist is able to achieve as regards pitch. Thus, a singer with good intonation is able to pitch a note very accurately.

intrada Used in the 16th and 17th centuries for the opening number of a suite of dances, with a festive and martial style, and occasionally so applied in modern composition. Beethoven applied the term to the short overture *Wellington's Victory* (1813).

introit Opening item of the Proper of the Mass, accompanying the entrance of the priests and choir. It was introduced by Pope Celestine I in the early 5th century.

inventions Title given to **J.S. Bach**'s two sets of short keyboard pieces composed strictly in two and three parts respectively, and possibly designed as technical studies. He called the three-part set 'symphonies', but there is no distinct difference between these and the two-part inventions.

inversion 1. The process of changing the position of the notes in a chord. For instance, the chord of C major is said to be in the root position in the form of C-E-G. Its first inversion is in the form E-G-C, its second inversion is in the form G-C-E.

2. The act of writing a melody 'upside-down', which means that the intervals remain the same but the movement is in the opposite direction.

3. The process of changing over the upper and lower melodies in invertible **counterpoint**.

Root position

First inversion

Second inversion

inverted mordent Ornament that indicates that three notes are to be played in the time-value of the principal note, consisting of the principal note, plus the note below it and the principal note repeated. An alternative term is lower mordent. See also **upper mordent**.

invertible counterpoint Two melodies in **counterpoint** may be inverted by the upper becoming the lower and vice versa.

Ionian mode In the 16th century, Henricus Glareanus, a Swiss theorist, recognized two authentic **modes**, one being **Aeolian** and the other Ionian. The Ionian mode is represented by the white keys of the piano beginning from C, and corresponds exactly to the modern C major scale.

Ippolitov-Ivanov, Mikhail Mikhailovich (1859-1935) Russian composer and conductor who studied at the St Petersburg Conservatoire with **Rimsky-Korsakov** and became head of the Tbilisi Conservatoire in 1883. His *Caucasian Sketches* for orchestra were published in 1895, and his reputation spread to the capital. After the revolution in 1917, he was appointed director of the Moscow Conservatoire and in 1925 a conductor of the Moscow Opera.

His compositions reflect his Soviet patriotism, notably in his *Song of Stalin* and other marches and songs. He also composed operas, including *Ruth* (1887), *Treachery* (1909) and *The Last Barricade* (1934), symphonic pieces, sonatas, cantatas, *An Evening in Georgia* for harp and wind instruments, and chamber music. In 1931 he completed **Mussorgsky**'s opera *The Marriage*.

IRCAM (Institut de Recherche et de Coordination Acoustique/Musique) Institute established in Paris in 1977 (after a long gestation period) to provide facilities for composers of contemporary music. It forms part of the Centre Pompidou. The first director was Pierre **Boulez**. The organization is in four sections, three covering natural sound, electronic music and computer composition, and the fourth being a 'mobile unit'. Concerts are given under its aegis.

Ireland, John (1879-1962) English composer and pianist who wrote works that were inspired by the landscape, nature and a meditative temperament. He studied at the Royal College of Music with **Stanford** in 1893, and mixed with such contemporaries as Gustav **Holst** and **Vaughan Williams**. He was also influenced by French composers (Debussy,

John Ireland

Ravel) and Stravinsky. He taught composition at the college (until 1939), and was organist at St Luke's, Chelsea, until 1926. After destroying all of his early work (pre-1908), he concentrated on the composition of picturesque orchestral pieces such as *The Forgotten Rite* (1913), *Mai-Dun* (1921), *A London Overture* (1936) and a *Concertino Pastorale* for strings (1939).

He wrote many piano pieces, including an admired piano concerto (1930) and *Legend* for piano and orchestra; *These Things Shall Be* for chorus and orchestra, hymns and church service settings, as well as deeply poetic and sensitive songs which released English song composition from the grip of Teutonic styles (*Five Poems of Thomas Hardy*, 1926; *Songs Sacred and Profane*, 1931).

Irish harp Alternative term for **Celtic harp**.

isometric Describing rhythmic structures that are measured in units of equal length. This includes all Western compositions that use the same time signature throughout.

isorhythmic One of the most important structural devices of the 14th and 15th centuries used by composers of **polyphonic** music. It consisted of a reiterated rhythmic pattern imposed on a melody or phrase, which might be repeated several times. The pitch of the notes may, however, differ.

istesso tempo (It.) At the same tempo, a direction given where a change in time-signature is indicated, but the composer wishes the music to continue at the same pace or beat in the new rhythm.

Italian sixth Form of **augmented sixth** chord with a major third (e.g., A♭-C-F♯).

Ives, Charles (1874-1954) American composer of exceptional inventiveness, who borrowed many themes from other composers but who created in such an individual way that he is acknowledged as a great innovator. Idioms developed by him long before can be identified in the subsequent works of **Stravinsky** and **Hindemith**. He is also credited as an influence by many American composers writing today.

Ives was born in Danbury, Connecticut, and his music reflects his love for New England and its musical traditions (for instance, the singing of hymns at open-air camp meetings). His first pieces, such as *Variations on America* (1891), were composed before he began to study music at Yale University, where his well-developed and individual sense of composition put great strain on his relationship with his tutor, Horatio Parker. He earned his living as an insurance executive, and composed mainly at weekends. His most productive period began with his second symphony in 1897 and his third in 1904. He composed very little after 1917, but revised many of his manuscripts so chaotically that performers faced grave difficulties later.

His compositions include the *Concord Sonata* (1915) for piano, *Three Places in New England* (1914) and *The Holidays Symphony* (1913). He also wrote shorter pieces, 11 volumes of chamber music, and more than 200 songs including *Evening* and *Soliloquy*, which reflect a more lyrical style. In the 1920s he planned a *Universe Symphony* for several different orchestras and huge choirs positioned in valleys and on mountain peaks.

J

jack Mechanism in the **virginal, harpsichord** and similar instruments by which the strings are plucked.

Jacob, Gordon (1895-1984) English composer, conductor and teacher who wrote much instrumental music that is highly polished and traditional in style. He studied at the Royal College of Music with **Stanford** and **Boult** and became a professor of theory, composition and orchestration. He transcribed **Vaughan Williams**'s *English Folk-Songs* for full orchestra in 1927.

His compositions include two symphonies, a sinfonietta (1942), concertos for various instruments and ballets, as well as numerous arrangements of pieces by other composers and from popular songs and rhymes, among them the *Passacaglia on a Well-Known Theme* (the theme being *Oranges and Lemons*).

Jacobi, Frederick (1891-1952) American composer, conductor and pianist who made a study of Amerindian music and the music of the Jewish litany, and incorporated both these styles into his work. He studied composition with **Goldmark** in New York and later at the Berlin Hochschule. In 1913 he became assistant conductor at the New York Metropolitan and from 1936 taught at the Juilliard School. His compositions include *Sabbath Evening Service* (1952), *Indian Dances* for orchestra, the opera *The Prodigal Son* (1943), concertos for the violin, piano and cello, chamber music and songs.

Jacques-Dalcroze, Emile (1865-1950) Swiss composer, notable for his development of eurhythmics, a new connection between musical rhythm and physical movement. Dalcroze studied at Geneva, Vienna (where he worked with **Bruckner**) and Paris. He composed operatic works including the popular *Sancho Panza* (1897) and experimented with music for strings. In 1915 he founded the Institut Jacques-Dalcroze in Geneva to promote eurhythmics as an influence in ballet and gymnastics.

jam session Improvised performance by jazz musicians.

Janáček, Leoš (1854-1928) Czech (Moravian) composer, organist and conductor whose earlier work reflects the

Leoš Janáček

styles of Smetana and Dvořák but whose later compositions (from *Jenůfa* onwards) display a shattered and fragmented structure in which the natural rhythms of speech are explored. After Dvořák and Smetana he is the most important Czech composer.

He studied at the Augustinian monastery in Brno as a chorister and became a teacher; he entered the Prague Organ School in 1874 and spent a year there, returning to Brno to take up his teaching duties and conduct choral groups. Later that year he became a student at the Leipzig Conservatoire, working hard under Leo Grill; he also visited Vienna for a few weeks, but was lonely and had very little money, so was unable to derive much benefit from the musical life of these two cities.

On his return to Brno in 1881 he married and was able to set up an organ school, of which he remained the director until 1919. He extended his teaching activities to other schools and edited a musical journal. He had already composed some minor works and begun work on his first opera, *Šárka*; at this point he began to study and collect Moravian folk-music, and made arrangements of some of it. His second opera achieved some success, being given six performances. However, he realized that the story would fit a much more ambitious work, and started on its composition; this was *Jenůfa* (1904), his first great work, a highly dramatic piece with a strong psychological background. Although it was well received, it was not presented in Prague until 1916.

After 1904 Janáček cut down his teaching to some extent and concentrated on writing music. His next opera was *Osud* (Fate, 1907), followed by *The Excursions of Mr Brouček* (begun in 1908; premièred in 1920). Several choral works date from this time, and some piano music. It was not until after the success of *Jenůfa* in Prague when he was over 60 that he was stimulated to produce his exciting later works; another factor behind this new creativity was his platonic love for a young married woman. The rhapsody *Taras Bulba* (1918), the song-cycle *The Diary of One Who Disappeared* (1919), the wind sextet *Mládi* (Youth, 1924) and two pieces of 1926, the *Sinfonietta* and the *Glagolitic Mass*, were the most important of the orchestral and vocal pieces; the three operas *Katya Kabanova* (1921), *The Cunning Little Vixen* (1924) and *The Makropoulos Case* (1926) are among the most substantial and admired works in the 20th-century repertory. His last opera, *From the House of the Dead*, was barely finished before his death.

Janequin, Clément (1475-1560) French composer who worked as a singer and choirmaster in Bordeaux (1505) and Angers (1534) before enrolling at the University in Paris (1549) and eventually receiving a court appointment. Ordained a priest before 1526, he published only two Masses and one book of motets (now lost), but is more famous for his 250-plus *chansons* – mostly in four parts – including *La guerre* and *Le chant des oiseaux*. He also composed *chansons spirituelles* (1556) and French metrical psalms, notably the 82 *Pseaumes de David* (1559) – which may indicate Huguenot sympathies in his later years. The alternative spelling Jannequin is also found.

janissaries European Christian prisoners forced into the Turkish army between the 14th and the 19th centuries. They were formed into bands with predominantly percussion instruments, including the **jingling johnny**: this gave rise to the description Turkish or janissary music. In Mozart's opera *Die Entführung aus dem Serail* there are examples of this characteristic percussion effect.

Jannequin, Clément Alternative spelling of Clément **Janequin**.

Janowitz, Gundula (1937-) German soprano who studied in Graz and made her début in Vienna in 1960. The following year she sang Pamina in *Die Zauberflöte* and

Mimì in *La bohème*; she also appeared at Bayreuth. The roles for which she is best known include the Countess in *Le nozze di Figaro*, Donna Anna in *Don Giovanni* and Agathe in Weber's *Der Freischütz*. She has also sung Sieglinde in *Die Walküre* and the title-roles in *Ariadne auf Naxos* and *Aïda*, and is a fine *Lieder* singer. She has performed in New York, London, Salzburg and Berlin and has made a number of recordings.

Japanese scales **In** and **yō** are the two principal scales of folk origin. *In* is essentially a hemitonic **pentatonic**, with two auxiliary tones, corresponding to E, F, (G), A, B, C, (D), and produces what is recognized as the distinctive character of much Japanese music. This scale is used extensively in **shakuhachi**, **shamisen** and **koto** music, the *koto*'s open strings being tuned to two forms of the scale.

Yō is an anhemitonic pentatonic scale, again with two auxiliary tones, corresponding to A, (B), C, D, E, (F), G.

Ryo and **ritsu** are the two basic pentatonic scales in Buddhist music theory and **gagaku** court music. *Ryo*, including four chromatic auxiliary or 'passing' tones, corresponds to D, E, F♯, (G/G♯), A, B, (C/C♯), and *ritsu*, with a pair of auxiliary tones, corresponds to E, F♯, (G), A, B, C♯, (D).

Jarnach, Philipp (1892-1982) German composer of Spanish origin, born in France. He studied in Paris and came to know Debussy and Ravel. During World War I he lived in Zurich, where he met and was influenced by **Busoni**. Afterwards he moved to Berlin, and on Busoni's death completed the unfinished score of his *Doktor Faust*. In Berlin he also became friendly with Schoenberg. In 1927 he went to teach at Cologne and in 1949 in Hamburg. He was awarded many honours and prizes, and was considered one of the leading composers of interwar Germany. His works include the symphonic variations *Musik mit Mozart* (1935), two piano sonatas (of which the second is particularly admired) and other piano pieces, songs and chamber works.

Järnefelt, Armas (1869-1958) Finnish composer and conductor who became a Swedish citizen in 1910. He studied in Helsinki, Berlin and at the Paris Conservatoire and became the conductor of the Viipuri Orchestra in 1898. In 1907 he conducted the Stockholm Royal Opera Orchestra and in 1940 was appointed a professor at Helsinki University. He composed the popular *Praeludium* for orchestra and *Berceuse* for piano, as well as songs and choral works.

Jarre, Maurice (1924-) French composer of film scores. He studied in Paris with **Honegger**, and played percussion for the Renaud-Barrault stage company. He became music director of the theatre in Vilar, and wrote the music for several productions there. His compositions include several in a serial manner, a *Passacaglia in Memory of Honegger* (1964) among them. He composed the ballet *Notre Dame de Paris* in 1964, an opera for radio and another ballet (for television); at the same time he was becoming more involved in writing film music, and eventually he moved to Hollywood. Two of his most evocative scores are for *Lawrence of Arabia* and *Dr Zhivago* (*Lara's Theme* from the latter achieved enormous popularity).

jazz Form of popular music that originated in New Orleans in the latter part of the 19th century among the black population. It developed out of ragtime and blues, which emerged from negro spirituals and work-songs in the 1860s.

Jazz relies for its effects mainly on syncopated rhythm and improvisation on a melodic theme. It uses a special combination of instruments, including plucked string instruments, saxophones, double-bass and muted brass. The distinctive style of black New Orleans jazz (later known as 'traditional' jazz) was followed by the Dixieland style of the white southerners. In the 1930s this was replaced by big-band swing, and in the 1940s came bebop, followed by the cool jazz of the 1950s. Jazz has influenced many composers, including **Stravinsky** (*Scherzo à la Russe*, for jazz ensemble, 1944), **Gershwin** (*Rhapsody in Blue*, 1924), **Copland** (*Billy the Kid*, 1938), and **Lambert** (*The Rio Grande*, 1929). Jazz has also contributed to many styles of popular music.

Jensen, Adolph (1837-1879) German composer and pianist who studied with Ehlhert and Liszt and who performed and taught in Berlin and Copenhagen. He composed a large number of songs, cantatas, choruses and other choral works, as well as the opera *Turandot*, which he never completed.

jhala (India) Section following the **jor** in an instrumental **rāga**. It is a stylistic treatment of the *jor* in which the drone strings are rapidly strummed between the main melody notes. Its driving rhythms can also make it an exciting way of concluding a **gat**.

jig Popular 16th-century English dance in binary form, usually in 6/8 or 12/8 time. It was the fourth of the dances regularly found in the classical **suite**. The jig's popularity spread to France and Italy, where it was called *gigue* and *giga*, respectively.

jingling johnny Obsolete percussion instrument, formerly used in military bands, shaped in the form of a tree, pavilion roof, or Turkish crescent hung with bells. It is sometimes called a Chinese pavilion.

jiuta (Japan) Important ensemble form which originally referred to the **shamisen** music of Kyoto, but became well known as an ensemble form with **koto** and *shamisen* in combination. It includes a third instrument, at one time a bowed fiddle, but later replaced by the **shakuhachi** flute. See also **tegotomono**.

Joachim, Joseph (1831-1907) Hungarian composer and violinist whose playing was admired by **Mendelssohn** and **Brahms**, who dedicated his violin concerto to him. He was a child prodigy, performing from the age of seven, and studied in Vienna with **Boehm** before entering the Leipzig Conservatoire in 1843. He performed at the Gewandhaus Concerts and in 1849 became the leader of Liszt's Weimar Court Orchestra. In 1869 he was appointed director of the Berlin Hochschule. Joachim toured widely as a soloist, visiting England in 1887, and achieved great success as an interpreter of Beethoven and Brahms.

His compositions include an orchestration of Schubert's *Grand Duo* (1855), the *Hungarian Concerto* for violin and orchestra, five overtures and a number of songs.

Jochum, Eugen (1902-1987) German conductor who studied in Augsburg and at Munich, making his début there in 1926. He was conductor of the Kiel Opera for several seasons, then moved to Mannheim, Duisburg and Berlin. There he became musical director of Berlin Radio and first conducted the Philharmonic Orchestra. In 1934 he went to Hamburg to take charge of the opera and the Philharmonic Orchestra; he was able to stay there during the war and to give concerts, conducting works of which the Nazis disapproved. He also formed a close association with the Concertgebouw Orchestra in Amsterdam, which continued well into the 1960s. In 1949 he founded the Bavarian Radio Symphony Orchestra in Munich. He was noted above all for his warmly romantic Bruckner performances and recorded all his symphonies, as well as all those of Beethoven and many of Haydn's.

jod See **jor**

jo-ha-kyū (Japan) Important structural concept in Japanese music, concerned with tripartite division. For example, in **gagaku**, *jo* is the introduction, *ha* is the 'breaking apart' or exposition, and *kyū* is the 'rushing to finish'. This can apply to both the whole composition and individual sections. In **noh** drama, a composition consists of five main units or *dan*. These are divided into *jo* (first dan), *ha* (second to fourth dan), and *kyū* (fifth, concluding dan).

Johnson, Robert Sherlaw (1932-) English composer, lecturer and pianist who became an authority on the works of **Messiaen**. He studied at Durham University and entered the Royal Academy of Music in 1953. In 1957 he studied with Nadia **Boulanger** at the Paris Conservatoire. Among his compositions are the opera *The Lambton Worm* (1978), works for soprano, piano and tape, including *Praises of Heaven and Earth* (1969), *Green Whispers of Gold* (1971) and *Where the Wild Things Are* (1974), originally intended for soprano and tape but later adopted for operatic performance. He has also written a number of religious pieces, including *The Festival Mass of the Resurrection* (1974) for chorus and orchestra.

Jolivet, André (1905-1974) French composer who, with **Messiaen**, Lesur and Baudrier, founded the *Jeune France* group of composers which set out to re-establish a more humanized style of composition. He studied at the University of Paris with **Varèse** from 1928, and became a musical director of the Comédie Française in 1942. He was appointed a professor of composition at the Paris Conservatoire in 1965. His compositions reflect his interest in the sonorities of instruments and are transparent and dissonant. They display the influence of **Schoenberg** as well as of polytonal and Oriental idioms.

Among his compositions are three symphonies and a number of concertos, including the *Concerto for Ondes Martenot* (1947) and the *Suite française* (1957), as well as the opera *Dolores* (1942) and works for chamber orchestra. His devotional compositions include *Le coeur de la matière* (1965) and other works for voice and orchestra.

Jommelli, Niccolò (1714-1774) Italian composer who studied at Naples and Rome, and who subsequently went to Bologna and Venice to compose. He visited Vienna in 1748 and became *Kapellmeister* to the court at Stuttgart in 1753. In 1769 he moved back to Naples but found little success there. While in Vienna he became a friend of Metastasio and used a number of his texts in his operatic compositions. He developed, from the Neapolitan tradition, a style that accentuated the dramatic elements of opera and which avoided the digressions of arias as much as possible. He composed more than 60 operas, including *L'errore amoroso* (1737), *Ifigenia in Aulide* (1751) and *Ifigenia in Tauride* (1771), as well as a large body of devotional music.

Jones, Daniel (1912-) Composer, pianist and conductor, the doyen of Welsh musicians. He was a prolific composer even as a child. After taking a degree and doctorate in English at Swansea University he studied at the Royal Academy of Music, where he won the Mendelssohn Prize for composition. During war service in intelligence he showed his unusual aptitude for languages by compiling a Chinese dictionary.

His works range over a wide field, and include 12 symphonies which were recorded and broadcast complete by the BBC in 1990; the operas *The Knife* (1962) and *Orestes* (1967); the oratorio *St Peter* and the cantata *The Country Beyond the Stars*; concertos for violin and for cello; nine string quartets, and numerous other chamber and orchestral works, including a sonata for three kettledrums. In 1954 he wrote the prize-winning incidental music and songs for the radio production of *Under Milk Wood* by Dylan Thomas, a close friend since their childhood together in Swansea. He devised the principle of complex metres, where a group of bars of varied time signatures recurs throughout a movement. He was awarded the OBE in 1968.

Jones, Dame Gwyneth (1936-) Welsh operatic soprano who studied at the Royal College of Music, in Siena, Zurich and Geneva. She began as a mezzo, making her début as Orfeo in Gluck's *Orfeo ed Euridice* in 1962 at Zurich. She joined the Royal Opera, Covent Garden, in 1963, singing Lady Macbeth in Verdi's *Macbeth*. The first of many Wagner roles was Sieglinde in *Die Walküre* in 1965; the following year she performed at Vienna and at Bayreuth, where she has returned often. Her greatest success is in the role of Brünnhilde in the *Ring* cycle, which she performed in the 1976 Bayreuth centenary production and has given several times since. She is an exciting Tosca and Turandot (Puccini), Elektra, Marschallin and Salome (Strauss), and has sung all over the world. She was made DBE in 1986.

Jones, Philip (1928-) English trumpeter who studied at the Royal College of Music. He has played first trumpet with most of the major orchestras (the Royal Philharmonic, the Philharmonia, the London Philharmonic, the Northern Philharmonic and the BBC Symphony Orchestras). In 1951 he founded the Philip Jones Brass Ensemble, a group which gained an enormous following world-wide and made many recordings. It specialized in early music (the **Gabrielis** in particular) and specially commissioned new works, and also performed at ceremonial functions. It ceased its activities in 1987. Jones was appointed principal of Trinity College of Music in 1988.

Jones, Sydney (1861-1946) English composer who concentrated on light opera and operetta. His *Geisha* (1896) was successful in London and transferred to the New York Metropolitan in the same year. Another success was *The Gaiety Girl*.

Jongen, Joseph (1873-1953) Belgian composer, organist and pianist who studied at the Liège Conservatoire and became a tutor there in 1903. He was appointed a professor of counterpoint and a director at the Brussels Conservatoire in 1920. He composed the ballet *S'Arka*, a number of concertos for the piano, violin, cello and harp, as well as a symphony and chamber music.

jongleur Medieval minstrel, whose accomplishments could include juggling, but who was also a story-teller, singer and instrumentalist. Jongleurs were often called upon to assist **troubadours** (who were generally more creative artists), although on occasions they did reverse roles.

Joplin, Scott (1868-1917) American composer and **ragtime** pianist whose work has aroused new interest due to the efforts of the American pianist Joshua **Rifkin** and because of the film *The Sting*, which used his composition *The Entertainer* and several popular arrangements of some of his other rags. His early jazz style is notable for its use of complete compositions which do not allow a performer to improvise.

Joplin worked as a pianist in a number of brothels in Chicago and St Louis before moving to New York, where he composed many of his best-known pieces, including *Maple Leaf Rag* and *The Entertainer*. He also composed the first ragtime operas, *A Guest of Honour* (1903) and *Treemonisha* (1911), but the massive failure of these projects destroyed his confidence.

jor/jod (India) Transitional section in a **rāga** following the **ālāp**, in which the melodic outline of the *ālāp* is played in strict time and without embellishment. In this way the soloist sets the tempo before the entry of the **tablā** or **pakhāvaj**.

jōruri (Japan) Musical narrative style, derived from Japanese epic poetry, which was sung originally with **biwa** accompaniment by blind priests. Now it is generally sung with **shamisen** accompaniment, particularly in the *bunraku* puppet theatre.

Josephs, Wilfred (1927-) English composer who first studied dentistry at

Newcastle University and then music at the Guildhall School, London. He entered the Paris Conservatoire in 1958 and studied with Deutsch. In 1963 he won first prize in the International Milan Competition with his *Requiem*. His compositions include a large number of works for film and television (including the series *The Great War* and *I, Claudius*), as well as nine symphonies and other orchestral pieces. Among them are *Monkchester Dances* (1961), *Variations on a Theme of Beethoven* (1969), *The Four Horsemen of the Apocalypse* (1974) and *The Ants* (1955). He has also composed the television opera *The Appointment* (1968), another opera, *Rebecca* (1983), a number of choral and vocal works, and music for chamber orchestra.

Josquin des Prés (1440-1521) Most renowned of the Franco-Flemish composers of the early Renaissance. Josquin's style is considered to represent a bridge between the later Middle Ages and the Renaissance, with its use of expressive phrasing and division of the choir into contrasting groups. His music is smoother and sweeter than that of earlier periods, with a greater variety of rhythm and melody. He is also the first composer whose music attempts to express the emotional content of the material he sets. He was a prolific composer, writing more than 20 Masses, 80 motets and around 70 *chansons*; his *Princeps Musicorum* was admired by Martin Luther for its technical brilliance.

He was born in north-east France and was a pupil of the influential **Ockeghem**, on whose death he wrote a moving lament. He became a singer at Milan Cathedral in 1459, and later joined the establishment of the Sforza dukes of Milan. He travelled to Rome to join the Papal Chapel in 1486, and afterwards moved to Ferrara to serve the Este family. He then returned to France to join the Chapel of Louis XII. His last post was as a canon of the church at Condé. Alternative forms of his name are des Prez, Desprez.

Joubert, John (1927-) South African composer who studied at the South African College of Music and at the Royal Academy of Music in London. He became a lecturer and musicologist at the universities of Hull and Birmingham, and a composer of evocative and sometimes picturesque music in the English tradition. His works include *Herefordshire Canticles* (1979) and the opera *Silas Marner* (1961), as well as various symphonic works and concertos, choral pieces and sacred music.

Joyce, Eileen (1912-) Australian pianist who studied in Leipzig and with **Schnabel** before moving to London. She became very well known for her renderings of the Romantic repertory and of popular light pieces; when giving a recital she would wear a dress of the colour she thought appropriate to the relevant composer. She also recorded works by 20th-century composers, including Shostakovich, and later turned to the harpsichord, often giving concerts with other harpsichord-players. She has appeared in several films, including one based on her own life.

Jubilate Canticle from the Anglican service of Matins which includes the text of Psalm 100 (*O be joyful to the Lord*). Occasionally it is set for concert and ceremonial purposes, as an expression of rejoicing. In addition, its settings for soloists, chorus and orchestra include Purcell's *Te Deum and Jubilate* for St Cecilia's Day (1694) and Handel's *Utrecht Te Deum and Jubilate* (1713).

Juilliard School Leading American teaching institute for the performing arts, located in New York. It was originally established in 1905 as the Institute of Musical Art. In 1919 the wealthy New York businessman Augustus D. Juilliard died, leaving some $20,000,000 to a foundation for the advancement of musical education in America. In 1926 the Institute of Musical Art and the Juilliard Foundation came under the same board of directors and the IMA became known as the

Juilliard School of Music. The school and the foundation formally merged under that name in 1946. In 1952 dance was added to the music syllabus, with a drama department opening there in 1968. The name was changed in 1968 to the Juilliard School in order to reflect the broader base of the teaching offered. The Juilliard School moved into its present buildings within the Lincoln Center arts complex in 1969.

Jürgens, Jürgen (1925-) German conductor who studied in Frankfurt and Freiburg before becoming director of the Hamburg Monteverdi Choir in 1955. The choir specializes in early music, by Monteverdi, **Josquin des Prés**, **Schütz** and Bach; however, it ranges up to the 20th century, with works by **Henze** and **Dallapiccola** in its repertory. Jürgens has made a particular study of Monteverdi and Alessandro Scarlatti and has edited some of their works. He became music director at Hamburg University in 1966. He has made extensive recordings with the choir, mostly of early works.

Jurinac, Sena (1921-) Yugoslav soprano who studied in Zagreb. Her début there was as Mimì in Puccini's *La bohème*; she first appeared in Vienna in 1945, and in Salzburg two years later. She sang Dorabella in *Così fan tutte* at Edinburgh in 1948, then Fiordiligi in the same opera at Glyndebourne in 1950, and was warmly admired in both roles. A voice of great purity and a radiant stage presence made her a memorable Countess in *Le nozze di Figaro*, Marschallin in *Der Rosenkavalier* and Donna Anna and Donna Elvira in *Don Giovanni*; she has also performed the title-roles in *Tosca*, *Madama Butterfly*, Janáček's *Jenůfa* and the role of Marie in Berg's *Wozzeck* with great ardour and conviction. She has recorded a considerable part of her repertory.

just intonation Method of tuning or performing in which the notes of the scale of a key are correctly tuned according to their mathematical relationship. This, however, does not allow modulation to other keys with exact intonation; for this tempered tuning is needed, whereby the notes of all scales are slightly out of tune, a distortion perceptible only to the most acute musical ears. Orchestral instruments tend to play with just tuning; this can lead to problems when accompanying keyboard instruments, which usually have tempered tuning.

K

K When followed by a number, it stands for **Köchel**, and identifies a work in the Köchel catalogue of Mozart's compositions.

Kabalevsky, Dmitri (1904-1987) Russian composer, conductor and pianist who studied in Moscow with **Miaskovsky**. In 1939 he was appointed professor of composition at Moscow Conservatoire. He was also active in music publishing. He was greatly involved with the Soviet war effort, his compositions encompassing Soviet Realism and hymns of patriotism. In 1948 he conducted in Moscow with Vladimir **Ashkenazy** as soloist. He travelled throughout Europe and the United States. In 1972 he was awarded an honorary degree by the International Society of Musical Education. Kabalevsky was prolific in all fields of composition. Although best known in his own country for his songs and hymns, his chamber music and operas have received much wider acclaim. His earliest opera was *Colas Breugnon* (1938); others are *The Taras Family*, *Nikita Vershinin*, *Spring Songs* and *The Sisters* (the last two being operettas). His orchestral music includes four symphonies, three piano concertos, a violin and two cello concertos; choral works include *Leninists* (1959), a *Requiem* (1962) and *Letter to the 30th Century* (1972).

kabuki (Japan) Popular theatre which involves narrative, songs and dance sequences. Traditionally *kabuki* is an all-male domain, although originally it was performed by women. It incorporates both musical and theatrical elements of various Japanese entertainment forms, such as **noh** drama and the **bunraku** puppet theatre. Most *kabuki* plays fall into one of two categories: *jidaimono*, historical plays, based on 11th- to 16th-century heroic characters; and *sewamono*, domestic, middle-class dramas. See also **debayashi**; **geza**.

Kadosa, Pál (1903-1983) Hungarian pianist and composer who studied in Budapest with **Kodály** and taught at the Fodor Music School. By the early 1930s he had achieved international acclaim with his Piano Concerto No.1. He was appointed head of piano at the Budapest Academy in 1945. Although he owes much of his style to **Bartók**, there are undeniable elements of traditional Hungarian rhythms and melody. This combination of old and new is in evidence in the seven *Attila Jozsef* songs (1964). Kadosa was made an honorary member of the British **Royal Academy of Music** in 1967.

kāfī (India) One of the ten parent scales (**thāt**) in Hindustani music, corresponding to C, D, E♭, F, G, A, B♭, C′ (the same notes as the Western **Dorian** mode).

Kagel, Mauricio (1931-) Argentinian-born multi-media artist and self-taught composer. He settled in Cologne in 1957 to pursue interests in film, drama and art, as well as composition. *Musica para la torre* (1952) is one of the last purely musical works he composed, and he has taken references from Dada and other modernist movements for his more recent compositions. His iconoclasm has aroused much critical debate. While pieces such as *Pas de cinq* combine music and theatre, even more recent works such as *Der Schall* (1968) show a heterogeneous use of household objects and car horns in a characteristically detailed score.

kagok (Korea) Long lyric song form, consisting of a cycle of courtly songs with instrumental preludes, interludes and postludes. Each five-line stanza is sung in a highly melismatic style, with syllables drawn out in virtuosic sequences, making it one of the most difficult vocal genres in Korean music. It is usually accompanied by a small instrumental ensemble, including **kŏmun'go**, **taegŭm**, **piri**, **haegŭm** and **changgo**.

Kajanus, Robert (1856-1933) Finnish conductor and composer who studied in Paris with Svendsen (1879-80). Although he founded an orchestral school and the first permanent orchestra in Helsinki, he is best known for his pioneering work on behalf of **Sibelius** and Finnish music in general, bringing them to a wider audience in Europe; he is, however, alleged to have made alterations to Sibelius's scores, which did not please the composer. Kajanus has left some fine interpretations of Sibelius's work in his early 1930s recordings with the London Symphony Orchestra.

kakegoe (Japan) Calls made by the drummers in **noh** drama to mark the subdivision of a musical line or rhythmic phrase – an integral part of the *noh* ensemble sound. It also refers to the audience calls in **kabuki** theatre, in which set cries are used to mark the appreciation of certain theatrical devices, complex dance routines, etc.

kakko (Japan) Small horizontal drum with two lashed heads of deerskin. Both heads are struck with two light drumsticks. The *kakko* is used in the **gagaku** court orchestra and assists in leading the ensemble by marking time with three basic set patterns, of which two are rolls and one a single tap with the right-hand stick.

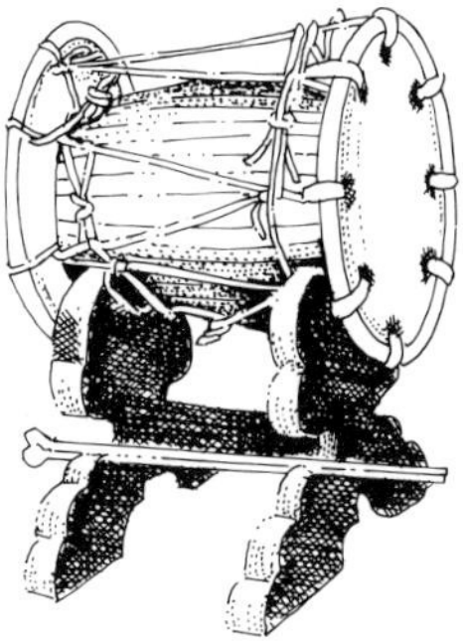

Kakko

Kalevala Group of Finnish epic songs from the Kaleva region of Finland, handed down orally for centuries and published in the 19th century. **Sibelius** was inspired by them, as exemplified in such works as *Kullervo* (1893), *Pohjola's Daughter* (1906) and *The Swan of Tuonela* (1893).

Kálmán, Emmerich (1882-1953) Hungarian composer and critic who studied in Budapest with **Bartók** and **Kodály**. It is for his light operas, such as *The Gay Hussar* (1908) and *Countess Maritza* (1924), rather than for his more serious compositions that he is most remembered. He combined the best elements of Viennese operetta with contemporary Hungarian themes and achieved great success throughout Europe and the United States. He moved to America in 1940.

kalyan (India) One of the ten parent scales (**thāt**) in Hindustani music, corresponding to C, D, E, F♯, G, A, B, C′, and similar to the Western **Lydian** mode.

Kaminski, Heinrich (1886-1946) German composer of Polish descent. He studied in Heidelberg and Berlin, but was largely self-taught. In 1914 he moved to a village in Bavaria and remained there for the rest of his life, apart from a three-year teaching post in Berlin. His music was not generally well received, especially after the advent of the Nazi regime, and is somewhat difficult to appreciate; it grew out of his belief in the spiritual aspect of musical composition.

Although he wrote two operas he is best remembered for his *Concerto Grosso* for double orchestra (1922). His other works include a number of choral pieces, songs, chamber music and some works for organ and for piano.

Kammer (Ger.) Chamber. Hence *Kammermusik*, chamber music.

Kanawa, Dame Kiri Te (1944-) New Zealand soprano who studied under Vera Rosza and at the London Opera Centre. She made her début in 1970 at Covent Garden and has since sung many leading roles there, at Glyndebourne, the Metropolitan (New York), San Francisco, all the great European houses (Paris, Vienna, La Scala) and at the Salzburg Festival. She has established herself as a major recording and performing artist. Perhaps her greatest role is that of Elvira in Mozart's *Don Giovanni*; other memorable interpretations are as the Countess in *Le nozze di Figaro*; the Marschallin in *Der Rosenkavalier*; and Arabella in the opera of that title. She also gives recitals and recently has recorded outside the classical repertory (*West Side Story*). She was made a DBE in 1982. Te Kanawa's voice is vibrant and mellow and she tends towards a style of fresh simplicity.

kangen (Japan) **Gagaku** court music that is performed in a purely orchestral context without dance or song. It refers only to music of Chinese origin (**Tōgaku**) and employs three sets of instruments: *sankan* (wind instruments), including *ryūteki* (flute), **hichiriki** (oboe) and **shō** (mouth organ); *nigen* (stringed instruments) – a zither and a **biwa** (lute); *sanko* (percussion) – *taiko*, **kakko** (drums) and **shōko** (gong).

Kapelle (Ger.) Originally a term for the musical establishment of a king's or prince's chapel. Later it referred to any orchestra or other musical body.

Kapellmeister (Ger.) Originally a choirmaster, or a musician in charge of a court chapel. By the 19th century, it was used to refer to the musical director of an orchestra.

Karajan, Herbert von (1908-1989) Austrian conductor and pianist. Born in Salzburg, he studied with Paumgartner and in Vienna. He hired an orchestra for his début as a conductor in Salzburg, and made a great impression with a demanding programme that included Strauss's *Don Juan* and Tchaikovsky's Symphony No.5. In 1935 he joined the Nazi Party and was appointed *Kapellmeister* in Aachen. He conducted *Tristan und Isolde* in Vienna in 1937 and quickly established himself as a leading conductor. After the war he was banned for a while from public performance as a former Nazi, but was able to make records under the patronage of Walter Legge. He soon established an international reputation with his work with the Philharmonia Orchestra, and was allowed to take a full part in musical life. In 1954 he was made conductor of the Berlin Philharmonic in succession to Furtwängler, and in 1956 Director of the Vienna Opera, a post he held for six stormy years. He often conducted at the annual Salzburg Festival and founded his own Easter Salzburg Festival in 1963. No other conductor has achieved such dominance; not only did he hold important positions as a conductor, but produced opera, founded his own production company for television films, and made a vast range of recordings.

Herbert von Karajan

He was undoubtedly a master conductor, with a remarkable memory and a relentless, even ruthless approach to rehearsal and performance. However, musicians and critics were by no means unanimous in their praise – his style was often held to be too voluptuous, too preoccupied with beautiful smooth tone rather than with clear phrasing and rhythmic articulation.

katarimono (Japan) Generic name for a narrative song accompanied by the **shamisen** lute. Of the wide variety of *katarimono* styles that exist, often named after their founder, the most celebrated is Gidayū-bushi, used principally in the **bunraku** puppet theatre.

Katchen, Julius (1926-1969) American pianist of Russian descent. He studied in New York and made his radio début at the age of 11; in the same year he played with the Philadelphia and the New York Philharmonic Orchestras. Later he studied in Paris and settled there; his début as an adult brought him to wide attention throughout Europe, and he was contracted to make the first British long-playing recording. His repertory, much of which he recorded, was extensive and embraced Russian, French, American and British composers as well as the works of Mozart, Beethoven and above all Brahms.

Katin, Peter (1930-) British pianist who studied at the Royal Academy of Music at the age of 12 with Harold Craxton. His début was at the Wigmore Hall in 1948. In addition to touring extensively, Katin has done much to help young musicians. He is credited with a masterly understanding of Mozart and of the Romanticism of such composers as Chopin.

Kay, Hershy (1919-) American composer who was self-taught, although he studied orchestration with Randall Thompson. He wrote numerous ballets, including several for George Balanchine's company, the New York City Ballet; much of this music consisted of orchestrated versions of folk-songs and other composers' work, such as Noël Coward (*Grand Tour*, 1971) or Sousa (*Stars and Stripes*, 1958). He has also written film and stage scores.

Kay, Ulysses (1917-) American musician and composer who studied piano, saxophone and violin on the advice of his uncle, Joseph 'King' Oliver, the New Orleans jazz-band leader. He studied with **Hindemith** at Yale, and during World War II he played in a United States Navy band and jazz orchestra. Eventually he was made professor at City University, New York. Acclaimed even in his twenties, Kay wrote the music for the film of *The Quiet One* (1948) and many other film and television scores.

kayagŭm/kayakeum (Korea) Indigenous zither with 12 movable bridges and a relatively thin body. Strings are plucked with the right hand while the left hand twists and presses them down beyond the bridges, giving a wide variety of sound effects. It is used in both court and social music, especially the solo instrumental form **sanjo**.

Kb. (Ger.) Abbreviation of *Kontrabass* (**double-bass**).

kecak (Bali) See **ketjak**.

Keeffe, Bernard (1925-) English conductor, singer and broadcaster who after war service with the Intelligence Corps studied theory at Cambridge with **Orr** and **Ord**, singing with Lucie Manen and conducting with **Goldschmidt**. After singing with the Glyndebourne Opera and in musical plays in London and the Edinburgh Festival, he joined the BBC music staff in 1956, becoming head of radio opera. From 1960 to 1962 he was Controller of Opera Planning at Covent Garden, then returned to the BBC as conductor with the BBC Scottish Orchestra in Glasgow. In 1964 he returned to London and as conductor and presenter pioneered the development of music documentaries on BBC TV with many highly acclaimed programmes – his *Elgar and the Orchestra* was selected as music programme of the year. As well as conducting concerts and broadcasts with the leading orchestras, including the Robert Mayer concerts for children, he has written and presented many talks and features for radio and television, prepared translations of five operas and other vocal works, and from 1966 to 1989 was professor of conducting at Trinity College of Music.

Keiser, Reinhard (1674-1739) German composer who studied in Leipzig with Schelle and in Hamburg with Kusser. He was a highly prolific composer of operas (he produced more than 100, the first of which, *Basilius*, was initially performed in 1693). His importance to German opera is widely recognized, and his immediate influence extended especially to the young Handel and helped to make Hamburg a centre for opera. He is believed to have brought the Italian **aria** style to German opera, most notably in his *Die verdammte Staat-Sucht* (1703). *Der Carneval von Venedig* (1707-8) was one of his most successful operas, using the Hamburg dialect (as opposed to Italian) in its comic scenes and arias. Keiser also wrote sacred music.

Kelemen, Milko (1924-) Yugoslav composer who studied with Sulek in Yugoslavia, and with **Messiaen** and Aubin in Paris. His work has been mostly in the field of electronic music (following a scholarship to the Siemens Electronic Studio, 1966-8). In 1961 he founded the Zagreb Biennial Festival of New Music, thereby bringing avant-garde composition and music to Yugoslavia virtually single-handed. His compositions include the opera *The Plague*, and a bassoon concerto.

Kell, Reginald (1906-1981) English clarinettist who studied at the Royal Academy of Music with Haydn Draper. From 1935 to 1948 he taught clarinet at the Royal Academy, and took Draper's post on his retirement. Kell pioneered an unusual vibrato technique which has since proved very influential. He was principal clarinettist in many orchestras, including the London Symphony Orchestra (1936-9). In 1948 he emigrated to the United States, and in 1968 published *The Kell Method*.

Keller, Hans (1919-1985) British critic and musicologist of Austrian origin. He studied violin in Vienna but had to escape from Austria in 1938. He played with a number of orchestras and chamber ensembles in Britain, at the same time contributing criticism to various journals, and in 1959 joined the music staff of the BBC. He broadcast frequently and continued to write on a wide range of topics; in the 1950s he devised his 'functional analysis' method of studying a piece of music.

Kelly, Michael (1762-1826) Irish tenor, who sang in the first performance of Mozart's *Le nozze di Figaro*. Kelly's studies and work took him throughout Europe, especially to Naples, Venice and Vienna (where he met Mozart). Returning to England in 1787, Kelly was the leading tenor at Drury Lane and then sang throughout the country. Although he aspired to be a composer in later life, it is for his voice that he is chiefly remembered, and for his illuminating reminiscences, a valuable source of information on Mozart and operatic life in the 18th century.

Kempe, Rudolf (1910-1976) German conductor and oboist whose conducting début was with the Leipzig opera in 1935. After World War II he had a series of appointments, beginning as general music director of Dresden and later the Bavarian Staatsoper (1952-4). His conducting début in Britain was at Covent Garden in 1953 with *Arabella*, after which he made numerous visits until 1960. Greatly admired for his masterful conducting of Wagner's *Ring*, he was much loved by performers. After Sir Thomas **Beecham**'s death in 1961 he became principal conductor of the Royal Philharmonic Orchestra, and in 1970 was honoured with the title of 'Conductor for life'.

Kempff, Wilhelm (1895-) German pianist who entered the Berlin Hochschule at the age of nine. He studied composition with Robert Kahn and piano with Heinrich Barth. His concert career began in 1916 and he toured extensively with the Berlin Cathedral Choir. Although he played in South America (1918-21), it was not until 1964 that he toured the United States. His début in Britain was in 1951.

In 1957 Kempff began the first of an annual series of master classes teaching Beethoven at Positano, demonstrating his gift for interpreting this composer above all others. He also composed stage and orchestral works and songs.

kempul (Java) Set of fairly large, hanging, knobbed gongs. Along with the **kenong** and **ketuk** gongs, it performs a **colotomic** function in the **gamelan** ensemble, subdividing the musical phrase into shorter periods.

kendang (Indonesia) Pair of barrel drums with two lashed heads, of which the *kendang lanang* is the higher-pitched or 'male' and the *kendang wadon* is the lower-pitched or 'female'. In many **gamelan** ensembles the *kendang* players may lead, or conduct the performance.

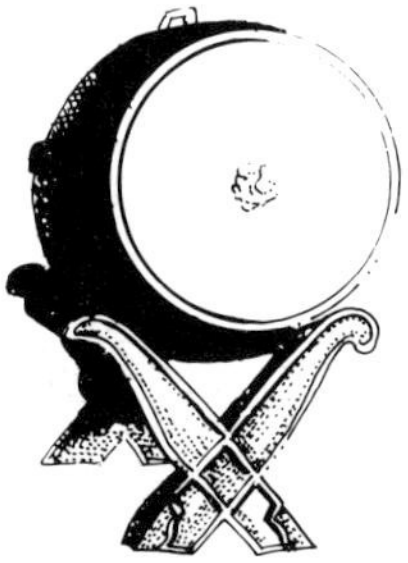

Kendang

Kennedy, Nigel (1956-) English violinist who studied at the Menuhin School and at the Juilliard School in New York. He has achieved unparalleled popularity, not only through the brilliance of his playing but through his unconventional appearance and mode of behaviour, which emulate those of a pop singer. His recordings of Vivaldi's *Four Seasons* and Bruch's Violin Concerto No. 1 have had a tremendous appeal, to young people in particular – not only have they been high in the classical Top Twenty list since their release (in 1989 and 1990 respectively) but have even featured among the popular music best-sellers.

kenong (Java) Large knobbed gong which hangs in a wooden frame. It performs a similar function to the **kempul** and **ketuk** gongs.

Kenong

Kent bugle Brass instrument with valves, roughly the size and pitch of a bugle. It was related to the **ophicleide** and has now been superseded by the **cornet**. It is also known as a key bugle or keyed bugle.

Kentner, Louis (1905-1987) British pianist of Hungarian birth who studied under **Kodály** and Szekely. He gave the first performance in Europe of **Bartók**'s Piano Concerto No.3 (1946), and was considered one of the major exponents of Bartók's compositions. He settled in London in 1935; there he performed an extensive repertory of Beethoven and Schubert, and began to favour contemporary English composers. **Walton**'s violin sonata was composed specially for Kentner and his brother-in-law, Yehudi **Menuhin**. Kentner has himself composed several works including the *Serenade for Orchestra* and many songs. He was awarded the CBE in 1978.

Kern, Jerome (1885-1945) American pianist and composer, a most prolific song-writer for the stage. He wrote more than 1,000 songs for more than 100 shows and films. Following a brief stay in Europe in the early 1900s, where Kern studied composition in Germany, he returned to the United States where his first song was published (1903). His first success was the musical comedy *The Red Petticoat* (1911). This followed a spell as a rehearsal pianist on Broadway. *The Red Petticoat* was followed by a series of hit musicals on Broadway, and his style was already becoming influential on composers of the era such as George Gershwin. During World War I Kern wrote four musicals of which *Oh Boy* (1917) proved the most successful. In 1939 he went to Hollywood and produced songs for many films.

His success is largely attributable to the popularity of his brand of musical comedy, which effectively superseded European light opera. Kern is best remembered for the musical *Showboat* (1927), with words written by Oscar **Hammerstein** II and including the song *Ol' Man River.*

Kertész, István (1929-1973) Hungarian-born conductor. He studied at the Franz Liszt Academy, Budapest, with **Kodály** and **Weiner**. In 1953 Kertész became resident conductor at Györ and went on to become conductor and *répétiteur* with the Budapest Opera, 1955. Following the Hungarian Uprising (1956), he moved to Germany. From 1964 he was general music director at Cologne. In 1965 he became principal conductor with the London Symphony Orchestra. Kertész had a great love of the works of **Bartók**, **Stravinsky** and **Britten**, and conducted the German première of Britten's *Billy Budd.* He was accidentally drowned while swimming.

Ketèlbey, Albert William (1875-1959) British composer who composed a piano concerto at the age of 11. By the age of 16 Ketèlbey had been appointed Organist of St John's, Wimbledon. He was appointed to the Vaudeville Theatre at the age of 22. He composed songs, anthems, and pieces for many different instruments. He wrote many popular narrative pieces, such as *In a Monastery Garden* (1915) and *In a Persian Market.* He also composed music for the silent films of the time, including *Wonder Worker* (1915).

kethuk See **ketuk**

ketjak/kecak (Bali) Popular choral and theatrical form, performed by concentric circles of seated men who can number as many as 200. It is based on the legends of the monkey armies from the *Ramayana* epic. It is essentially a vocal **gamelan**, each circle of men energetically chanting onomatopoeic sounds (the most common being 'cak', giving the form its name), in interlocking rhythmic parts, with coincidental arm gestures.

kettledrum (It. *timpani*; Fr. *timbales*; Ger. *Pauken*) Drum with a single head, that used to be of calf-skin, but is now usually synthetic. Of ancient origin, thought to be Egyptian, it produces notes of definite pitch, which can be adjusted by handles, or pedals, which alter the tension of the head. Pedal timpani allow rapid changes of pitch, even while being played, and can produce a glissando. Sticks of different weight and material will produce tones of varied character and volume, which also may vary

Kettledrum

according to the place where the head is struck. Kettledrums are commonly available in four sizes, covering a wide range; in classical times, orchestras usually had only two drums, but today composers may ask for as many as six or eight, with more than one player.

ketuk/kethuk (Java) Small horizontal gong hung by rope in a wooden frame. Often referred to as the 'kettle', it is struck with a padded stick which produces a rather dead sound in comparison to other Javanese gongs. It performs a similar function to the **kenong** and **kempul** gongs.

key 1. The lever on a keyboard instrument such as piano, harpsichord or organ, or a woodwind instrument, which when depressed by a finger or foot produces a note of a certain pitch.

2. The prevailing tonality of a composition, which may be major or minor. The keynote is the first note of the scale upon which the tonality is based, defined by the **key signature**. The key may be changed during the course of a piece by **modulation**. See also **scale**; **modes**.

keyboard Framework of finger-operated levers or switches that conventionally consists of a row of long, broad keys surmounted by another row of shorter, narrow keys in a contrasting colour. By convention on modern instruments the long, broad keys are white, whereas the shorter keys are black, although on some older instruments, such as an authentic harpsichord or a copy of one, the colours may be reversed. The long keys play natural notes, the black keys notes altered by sharps or flats. Instruments have been devised – for example by Aloys **Haba** – with double black notes, giving microtonally different pitches (for example, to D♯ and E♭). In general, however, keyboard instruments follow tempered tuning; see **just intonation**.

On an organ a keyboard is often referred to as a manual to distinguish it from a pedal keyboard, which is played with the feet. On electronic instruments the keys of a keyboard activate switches which send an electric current through circuits called oscillators to produce a sound.

The description of a work as being for keyboard means that it can be played on any keyboard instrument (piano, organ, harpsichord, etc.).

keyboard instrument Any musical instrument operated by striking keys (and, where applicable, pedals). They include the organ, virginals, clavichord, harpsichord, piano, celesta, keyed glockenspiel, carillon and the 20th-century electronic instruments such as the electronic organ and the synthesizer. See also **keyboard**.

key bugle/keyed bugle Alternative term for **Kent bugle**.

key-signature In written music, an indication placed at the start of a composition, after the **clef**, but before the **time-signature** (and at key changes during a composition) which indicates the prevailing **key**. It takes the form of a series of sharps (♯) or flats (♭), in a given order (for sharp keys, the order is F, C, G, D, A, E, B; for flat keys the order is the reverse: B, E, A, D, G, C, F). Each note indicated in this way shows that each time this note appears in the music it should be played sharp or flat. If there are no sharps or flats shown, the key is taken to be C major or A minor. Deviations from the prevailing key and the sharpened or flattened notes in the minor keys are marked by **accidentals**.

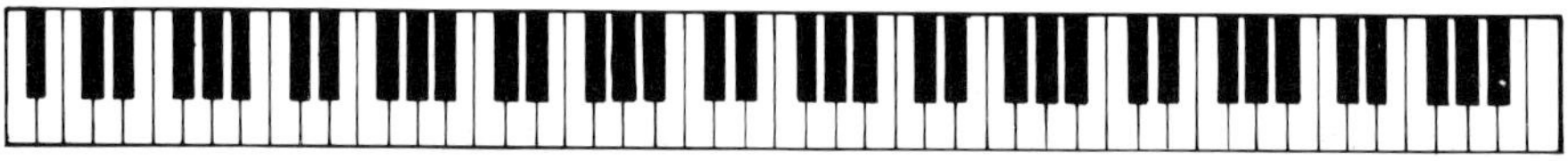

Keyboard

Sharp keys (above), flat keys (below).

Khachaturian, Aram (1903-1978) Soviet composer of Armenian origin who first studied at the Moscow Conservatoire under such teachers as Shebalin and **Miaskovsky**. He later became senior lecturer in instrumentation at the Academy. Although he did not turn to composition until later in his career, he was prolific, writing symphonies, music for ballet (*Spartacus*, 1956), orchestra (*Masquerade*, 1944) and chorus (*Mig Istorii*, 1971, a choral work dedicated to the memory of Lenin), chamber, piano and incidental music and music for films (*Lenin*, 1948-9). His work draws heavily on the traditional music of the Caucasus. Later in life he came to conduct his own works, and in 1968 he toured the United States as conductor of the National Symphony Orchestra.

khaen/khene (Thailand/Laos) Bamboo mouth-organ of north-east Thailand, consisting of two rows of six to 16 bamboo pipes, reaching lengths of 1m (3ft) or more, each with a metal reed. They are fixed in order of size into a central windchest, held cupped in the player's hands, with finger-holes above. There are four sizes, but the 16-pipe version, with a two-octave range, is the most common. In Laos there is a system of modes (*lai*) used for improvisations, while melodies are often played in parallel fourths, fifths or octaves. The instrument is capable of playing both chords and a melody simultaneously, and often produces a drone.

Khaen

khamāj (India) One of the ten parent scales (**thāt**) in Hindustani music, corresponding to C, D, E, F, G, A, B♭, C′. It is therefore the same as the Western **Mixolydian** mode.

khene (Thailand/Laos) See **khaen**

Khrennikov, Tikhon (1913-) Soviet composer who studied at the Gnesin Music School, Moscow, and with Shebalin at the Moscow Conservatoire. His début as composer/pianist of the Piano Concerto Op.1 in 1933 brought him much acclaim. He began a long association with the Vakhtangov Theatre, composing scores such as that for *Much Ado about Nothing* (1936). Moving from theatre to opera in the 1930s, Khrennikov wrote *V Buryu* (1939). He became an outspoken advocate of Soviet trends of socialist realism in music and the arts. Khrennikov was made head of the Soviet Composers Union during the late 1940s in the purge which accused **Prokofiev** among others of anti-Soviet beliefs and practices. On his 60th birthday he was made a Hero of the Soviet Union.

khyāl (India) Principal classical vocal genre in northern Indian music, which developed from **dhrupad** during the 18th and 19th centuries. The genre is more ornate than *dhrupad*, with musical virtuosity tending to supersede textual enunciation. Its two sections (**sthāyi** and **antarā**) form the basis of extensive melodic and rhythmic improvisations, including **sargams**. Having virtually dropped the *dhrupad*, many *khyāl* singers now include a slow **ālāp** in the *dhrupad* style.

Kilpinen, Yrjö (1892-1959) Finnish song-writer who studied at the Finnish Music Institute and later in Vienna and Berlin. In 1948 he was elected to the Finnish Academy. He composed over 800 songs to texts in German, Swedish and Finnish, and could be said to be in the great tradition of *Lieder* composers. In the 1930s his songs were brought to the notice of a wide audience by the advocacy of the German baritone Gerhard Hüsch, who regularly included them in his recitals and recorded them.

kinnor Biblical form of lyre, supposedly played by King David. Knowledge about the instrument is limited, although it would appear that the kinnor was played by hand and was similar to the Greek **kithara**.

Kinnor

Kipnis, Alexander (1896-1978) American bass of Ukrainian birth who studied music at the Warsaw Conservatoire and in Berlin. In 1919 Kipnis joined the Charlottenburg Opera and later the Staatsoper in Berlin. He often sang at the Bayreuth and Salzburg festivals as well as at leading opera-houses around the world, including a season at Glyndebourne where he sang Sarastro in Mozart's *Die Zauberflöte*. He became an American citizen in 1934, and sang at the Chicago and New York Metropolitan opera-houses. Kipnis possessed a remarkable voice, of great depth and colour, and though he excelled in the music of Wagner and Verdi, as well as his native Russian repertory, he also left recordings of *Lieder*.

Kirchner, Leon (1919-) American composer, conductor and pianist who studied at Los Angeles City College and later at the University of California with **Schoenberg**. Before World War II he spent some time working with Roger **Sessions**, and after 1945 he took up various teaching posts.

As a conductor Kirchner is well known for his interpretations of Mozart and Schubert. As a composer, he has received many awards, including the Pulitzer Prize for his *Third Quartet with Electronic Tape* (1966).

Kirkby, Emma (1949-) English soprano who studied at Oxford. She specializes in Renaissance and Baroque music, to which her distinctively pure, high voice is ideally suited. She made her début in 1974 and has sung with a number of early music groups: the London Baroque Players, Anthony Rooley's Consort of Musicke and Christopher Hogwood's **Academy of Ancient Music**. She has made recordings of the early repertory with these ensembles.

Kirkpatrick, Ralph (1911-1984) American harpsichord player, scholar and editor who studied piano from the age of six, turning to the harpsichord in 1930 while at Harvard. He also studied in Paris with Nadia **Boulanger** and **Landowska**. After his European début, performing Bach's *Goldberg Variations* to great acclaim in Berlin, he toured Europe and the United States. He was well known for his repertory of 18th-century keyboard music, including all of Bach's keyboard works and Domenico **Scarlatti**'s sonatas. His catalogue of all Scarlatti's sonatas forms the basis of the standard Kk numbering system.

kithara Ancient Greek instrument similar to the **lyre**. It had between three and

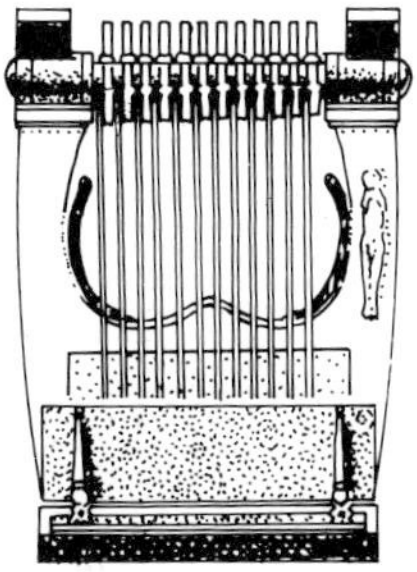

Kithara

twelve strings that were plucked, a large square resonator at the base and an upper crossbar.

Kjerulf, Halfdan (1815-1868) Norwegian composer and pianist who did not formally study music until 1849 (with Carl Arnold at Christiania – now Oslo), long after his first compositions (*Six Songs*, Op.1) were published. He then travelled to Copenhagen and Leipzig and studied with Richter at the Leipzig Conservatoire. His songs show varied influences, including those of Schumann and Schubert, but it is his links with folk-music that have made Kjerulf so crucial to the development of Norwegian music, paving the way for later Norwegian composers, particularly **Grieg**.

Klavier (Ger.) Originally used to describe any keyboard instrument, but in modern usage it generally refers to the piano. In French and English (and formerly in German) the word is spelled *clavier*.

Klavierauszug (Ger.) Score of a work arranged for piano; a piano score.

Klebe, Giselher (1925-) German composer who studied with Kurt von Wolfurt, and with Rufer and Boris **Blacher**. From 1946 to 1949 he worked for Berlin Radio as a programmer. However, it was his orchestral compositions, such as *Die Zwitschermaschine* (1950), that brought him acclaim. In 1957 Klebe was elected to the Royal Academy of the Arts, Berlin.

Klebe has composed operas (*Die Räuber, Jacobowsky und der Oberst, Das Mädchen aus Domrémy* and several others) as well as **twelve-note** instrumental pieces.

Klecki Alternative spelling of the name of Paul **Kletzki**.

Kleftic/Klephtic song (Greece) Songs which relate to the heroic deeds of the Klefts in battles against the Turks. They are unmeasured (although some have instrumental interludes in 7/8), highly ornate and melismatic, with an imitative accompaniment usually played by a trio of clarinet, violin and lute.

Kleiber, Carlos (1930-) Argentinian conductor of Austrian descent, the son of Erich **Kleiber**. He studied in Buenos Aires and in Munich. In 1954 he became a conductor at Potsdam and quickly moved to other notable companies, including Düsseldorf, Zurich and Stuttgart. Since then he has avoided taking resident posts, as he requires the freedom to rehearse at length; he insists on strict discipline but his passionate commitment is greatly admired by the orchestras he conducts. He has frequently appeared in Munich at the Bavarian State Opera, and at Vienna and Bayreuth. His Covent Garden début was in 1974 with *Der Rosenkavalier*. His repertory is not wide; it includes Strauss and Wagner, Berg's *Wozzeck* and Verdi's *Otello*. He has stated that he is happy to conduct only occasionally.

Kleiber, Erich (1890-1956) Austrian conductor. He learned the violin, and joined the Prague Conservatoire on the strength of his compositions. He made his conducting début at the Deutsches Theater there; appointments followed in Darmstadt (1912), Wuppertal (1919), Düsseldorf (1921) and Mannheim (1922). In August 1923, at short notice, he conducted for the first time at the Berlin Staatsoper, a highly successful performance of Beethoven's *Fidelio*. On the strength of this he was immediately appointed Generalmusikdirektor, at the age of 33. During his 12 years in Berlin he established the Staatsoper as one of the leading theatres of the world, especially with his performances of contemporary operas such as Janáček's *Jenůfa* (1924) and Berg's *Wozzeck* (1925). In 1935 as Nazi power grew he left Germany, and worked for many years in both North and South America. After the war he returned to Europe, and spent several memorable seasons conducting at Covent Garden. His mastery is preserved in his legendary recordings of Mozart's *Le nozze di Figaro* and Strauss's *Der Rosenkavalier*, as well as symphonies by Beethoven. Kleiber was an indefatigable worker and a brilliant rehearser, who believed in thorough preparation rather than improvised effects. He had a vivid theatrical instinct, which gave great vitality, wit and charm to his performances. His perfectionist demands made life difficult for administrators, but won nothing but respect and affection from the artists he worked with.

Klemperer, Otto (1885-1973) German conductor and composer born in Breslau. He studied in Frankfurt, and with **Pfitzner** in Berlin. While assisting at a performance of Mahler's Symphony No.2 he met the composer, who later gave him an introduction that opened many doors. In 1907 he was appointed chorus-master in Prague, and made his début conducting Weber's *Der Freischütz*. Appointments followed in Hamburg (1910); Barmen (1913); Strasbourg (1914); Cologne (1917); Wiesbaden (1924); and, in 1927, as Director of the Kroll Opera in Berlin, where he introduced revolutionary productions of contemporary works such as Janáček's *From the House of the Dead*, Hindemith's *Cardillac*, and Schoenberg's *Erwartung*. As a Jew he was unable to remain in Germany and left for America, where he directed the Los Angeles Philharmonic from 1933 to 1939. Despite severe ill-health he continued an international career after the war, at the Budapest Opera and later in London in a

Otto Klemperer

celebrated partnership with Walter Legge and the Philharmonia Orchestra, preserved in many outstanding recordings. As a young conductor, Klemperer was famous for his radical approach to contemporary music and opera, and for his 'objective' treatment of the classics. In his last years he attained a high reputation for his majestic interpretations, particularly of Beethoven and Mahler symphonies. His compositions are regarded with somewhat less enthusiasm than his conducting.

Klephtic song See **Kleftic**

Kletzki, Paul (1900-1973) Polish conductor, composer and violinist who studied at the Warsaw Conservatoire and the Berlin Academy. During World War I he joined the Lotz Philharmonic Orchestra and in 1923 made his conducting début in Berlin, conducting his own compositions. Kletzki left Berlin (1933) for Italy, where he taught composition and orchestration in Milan. In 1937 he was appointed musical director of the Kharkov Philharmonic

Orchestra. He settled in Switzerland in 1947, becoming musical director of the Suisse Romande Orchestra in 1967.

He wrote about 50 compositions, including four symphonies, string quartets and chamber music. Although many compositions were destroyed during World War II, recordings of many of his concerts remain. An alternative spelling of his name is Klecki.

Klien, Walter (1928-) Austrian pianist who studied piano, composition and conducting in Frankfurt, Graz, and finally at the Vienna Academy with Josef Dichler and **Hindemith** (1950-3). After winning several prizes in the early 1950s he toured Europe, Africa and the Americas, making his début in the United States in 1969. Klien has made many recordings which have justly earned him much critical acclaim, including all of Schubert's piano sonatas; he is also noted for his performances of contemporary music.

Knussen, Oliver (1952-) English composer and conductor, the son of Stuart Knussen, the celebrated double-bass player. Composing from the age of six, Knussen studied with John Lambert until 1968 and later with Gunther **Schüller**. At the age of 15 he received much publicity when he conducted his own Symphony No.1. Later works such as *Océan de terre* (1972-3) have been well received. He has written two other symphonies, *Masks* (1969) for flute, various songs, dances and a cantata. His operas *Where the Wild Things Are* (1980) and *Higglety Pigglety Pop!* (1985) have both been performed at Glyndebourne. In recent years he has been one of the artistic directors of the Aldeburgh Festival (with Murray **Perahia** and Steuart Bedford).

Kochanski, Pau (1887-1934) Polish violinist who studied with Emil Mynarski as early as 1894. At the age of 14 he was appointed first violin with the Warsaw Philharmonia. In 1913 he was appointed professor at the Imperial Conservatoire, St Petersburg, and it was there that he first met and promoted the violin concertos of **Szymanowski**. He also collaborated with Szymanowski on works such as *Mity* (1915) and the Concerto No.1 (1916). He emigrated to the United States in 1921, appearing with the New York Symphony Orchestra. In 1924, while still making concert appearances, Kochanski joined the staff of the Juilliard School.

Köchel, Ludwig von (1800-1877) Austrian music bibliographer, best known for his **Mozart** catalogue. Born in Vienna, Köchel studied at the University of Vienna and by 1827 was tutor to the four sons of Archduke Carl. Devoted to the works of Mozart, Köchel was prompted to order the previously uncatalogued compositions into a chronological list. The catalogue that Köchel subsequently produced featured the first few bars of each work, which for the first time were given a catalogue number, any manuscript source and finally a reference to the contemporary biography by Kahn. Mozart himself began cataloguing his works after 1784, but Köchel had to contend with the ordering of 450 compositions, many undated. The catalogue, *Chronologisch-thematisches Verzeichnis sämtlicher Tonwerke Wolfgang Amadeus Mozarts*, was first published in 1862. It has been constantly revised and remains a standard text on the subject.

Kodály, Zoltán (1882-1967) Hungarian composer and educationist who studied at Budapest University and at the Liszt Academy of Music with Koessler. He early developed an intense interest in Hungarian folk-music, and in collaboration with Béla **Bartók** amassed a huge collection, often with the aid of a primitive recording machine. In 1907 Kodály was appointed to the staff of the Liszt Academy and in 1911 was made professor of composition. With Bartók he founded the New Hungarian Music Society, and later embarked on the publication of their folk-song collection in response to a government commission. Throughout his

Zoltán Kodály

life he took great interest in musical education; this culminated in the development of the Kodály Method of aural training and sight-singing, which is taught in all Hungarian primary schools, and in many others all over the world. Kodály's compositions owe much to folk-music but preserve more of its charm and melodious appeal than Bartók's more austere treatment. They range over many fields; his opera *Háry János* is a universal favourite, while orchestral works such as the *Dances of Galánta* (1933) and the *Peacock Variations* (1939) appear frequently in concert programmes. There are two string quartets, several solo sonatas, and other chamber music. He composed a great deal for children, but perhaps his most popular work is in the field of choral music: his arrangements of folk-songs are rarely absent from choral programmes, and large-scale works such as *Psalmus Hungaricus* (1923), for chorus and orchestra, and the unaccompanied *Jesus and the Traders* (1934) are major works of the repertory.

Koechlin, Charles (1867-1950) French composer and teacher who studied at the Paris Conservatoire from 1890, and, from 1896, composition there with **Fauré**. With other pupils, including **Ravel**, he founded the Société Musicale Indépendante with the intention of promoting new music. By the end of World War I, Koechlin was prominent in Parisian music circles. By the 1930s he had become a notable critic and theorist, which overshadowed his compositional work. However, a cycle based on Rudyard Kipling's *Jungle Book* occupied him until World War II. Koechlin's wide-ranging influences are shown by the many pieces written in homage to female film stars of the 1930s, works such as *Five Dances for Ginger* (1937). He destroyed many of his manuscripts before the works could be performed, however.

Kogan, Leonid (1924-1982) Soviet violinist who studied at the Central Music School at the age of ten and later at the Moscow Conservatoire, where he became a tutor. His reputation as a violinist spread while he was still a student, and he made his performing début in Moscow at the age of 17. He travelled widely throughout Europe and the Americas in the 1950s, and was awarded the Lenin Prize in 1965. His repertory includes all of Bach's solo works as well as **Paganini**'s caprices and many classical concertos.

Kokkonen, Joonas (1921-) Finnish composer who studied at the Sibelius Academy and read musicology at Helsinki University. He returned to the Sibelius Academy as a lecturer and in 1959 as professor of composition. Kokkonen has composed for the stage and orchestra, as well as chamber music and choral works. The opera *The Last Temptations* (1975) proved to be a major break from his earlier works, influenced as they were by strongly Finnish elements, and Bartók.

Kollo, René (1937-) German tenor. He began as a singer of light music, but studied in Berlin and made his début as an opera singer in 1965. He sang at Brunswick and Düsseldorf, and at Bayreuth for the first time in 1969 in *Der fliegende Holländer*. From this point he began to specialize in the Wagner *Heldentenor* roles, singing Parsifal,

Lohengrin, Siegmund and eventually Siegfried in the 1976 centenary production of the *Ring* cycle at Bayreuth. His voice is held by some to be a little light for these roles, but he acquits himself nobly; he also sings the more lyrical repertory, such as Lensky in Tchaikovsky's *Eugene Onegin* and Tamino in *Die Zauberflöte*. He has made a number of recordings, *Tristan und Isolde* among them.

Komagaku (Japan) Music of the right, in **gagaku** court music. Influenced by Korean and Manchurian forms, it is associated with the colour green. It is differentiated from **Togaku**, or 'music of the left', that of Chinese origin, by its instrumentation and absence of stringed instruments. *Komagaku* is used to accompany **bugaku** dance and never as a separate orchestral form or **kangen**.

kŏmun'go (Korea) Ancient plucked **zither** with six strings of twisted silk. Three strings, tuned by adjusting pegs, pass over fixed bridges whereas the remaining three pass over movable bridges.

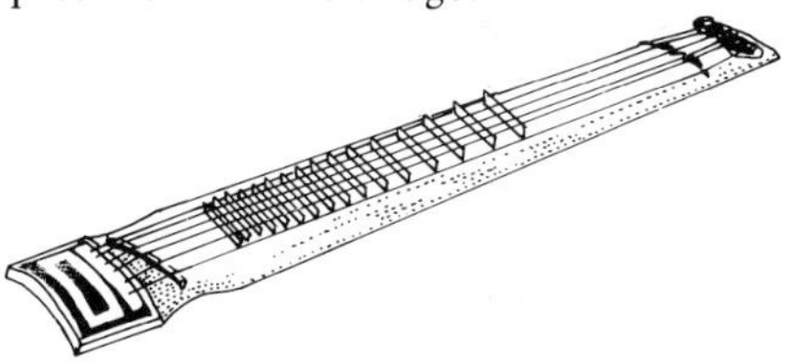

Kŏmun'go

Kontarsky, Aloys (1931-) German pianist who studied at the Cologne Musikhochschule with F. Maurits Frank (1952-7). In 1955 he and his brother Alfons gained acclaim by winning the prize for piano duo in Munich's Radio Festival. Following this, the brothers toured extensively together. While their repertory includes work by Mozart and Debussy, it is Kontarsky's abiding interest in modern music that has brought him much respect, with performances, many of them premières, of the works of **Stockhausen**, **Zimmermann** and **Kagel**, among others. In 1960 he joined the staff of the Darmstadt New Music Festivals.

Kontrabass (Ger.) German equivalent of **double-bass**.

Kontrafagott (Ger.) German equivalent of double bassoon.

Konzertmeister (Ger.) The **leader** of an orchestra.

kora (Africa) Stringed instrument with a sound-box, large bridge and 21 strings. The sound-box is a large half-calabash with skin stretched over it and a sound-hole. Strictly, it should be referred to as a harp-lute, because the size of the bridge combined with the placing of the strings, ten on one side and eleven on the other, bring it as much into line with the harp family as with the lute. Strings are tuned differently according to the geographical area in which the instrument is found.

Korngold, Erich (1897-1957) Austrian-born American composer, son of a well-known Viennese critic, and pupil of **Zemlinsky**. He displayed prodigious gifts as a child; at the age of 13 he had a work performed at the Opera. He followed this with a piano concerto and further operas including *Die tote Stadt* (1920), which was widely performed. His rich romantic style was out of tune with the fashions of the 1920s and 1930s but found its natural home in Hollywood, and won for the composer two Oscars for film scores, one of which was *Robin Hood*. After World War II he composed many orchestral pieces, including a Violin Concerto (1945) and a symphony.

Kostelanetz, André (1901-1980) American conductor, Russian by birth. After studying at the St Petersburg Conservatoire, he left for the United States (1922), where he was appointed as a rehearsal accompanist at the Metropolitan Opera, New York, and conductor of the CBS Radio Network (1930). As well as becoming involved with American cinema and radio broadcasting, he organized concerts for the American forces in World

War II. He is chiefly remembered for his popular concerts of classical music, conducted in a typically vivacious style, and for his arrangements of light music.

koto (Japan) Horizontal plucked zither, about 2m (6ft) long, with 13 silk strings and movable bridges. The body is constructed from two pieces of paulownia wood, of which one is hollowed out to form a sound-box. The inside of the instrument is carved with special patterns to improve the tone. The strings are plucked with ivory picks, *tsume*, which are fitted on to the middle three fingers of the right hand. Strings may be played open or may be pressed down, or twisted with fingers of the left hand to produce variations in pitch of up to a whole tone. See also **danmono**.

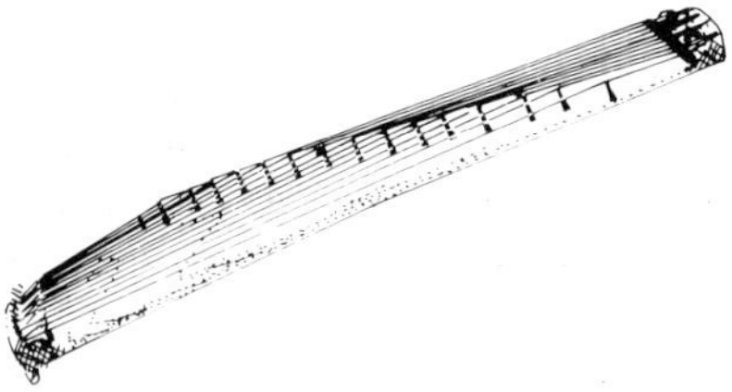

Koto

Koussevitzky, Serge (1874-1951) Russian-born double-bass virtuoso and conductor. Engaged as a player by the Bolshoi Theatre at the age of 20, he developed into an outstanding solo bass player. Upon his second marriage he launched himself on a second career as a conductor, engaging the Berlin Philharmonic for his début in January 1907. He also founded a music-publishing house encouraging the younger school of Russian composers. He founded his own orchestra in St Petersburg and gave an annual season of concerts, in which he introduced many new works. After the Revolution he settled in Paris; in 1924 he was appointed conductor of the **Boston Symphony Orchestra**, a post he was to hold until his death. Under his autocratic rule, the Boston orchestra attained an international reputation. Koussevitzky continued to present new music, and aided the careers of many American composers, especially through the establishment of the Berkshire Music Foundation. In memory of his wife he set up in 1943 the Natalie Koussevitzky Foundation, which enabled Benjamin **Britten** to complete his opera *Peter Grimes*. Koussevitzky excelled in the performance of colourful rhapsodic music, particularly of the Russian school, but his interpretation of the classics was often criticized as wayward and romantic. His recordings of Tchaikovsky and Sibelius give a fine impression of his gifts.

Kovacevich, Stephen See **Bishop-Kovacevich, Stephen**

krakowiak Polish dance in quick 2/4 time originating in the region of Kraków (Cracow), sometimes introduced into ballrooms and ballets in the 19th century under the name *Cracovienne*. Originally it was danced by assembled groups of dancers with improvised singing. Chopin composed *Krakowiak* (1828), a concerto rondo for orchestra.

Krauss, Clemens (1893-1954) Austrian conductor who was a member of the Vienna Boys' Choir. After studies with Reinhold at the Vienna Conservatoire he was appointed chorus-master of the Brno Theatre. Further appointments were at Stettin and Graz, until in 1922 he was appointed a conductor at the Vienna Opera. He was appointed music director in Frankfurt in 1924, Vienna in 1929, Berlin in 1935, and Munich again from 1937 to 1944. After the war he returned as director in Vienna until his death in 1954. Krauss was an outstanding opera conductor, famous for his baton technique and subtle control of orchestras and singers. As a close friend of Richard **Strauss**, he provided the libretto for *Capriccio*, and conducted the premières of four of his operas: *Arabella* (1933), *Friedenstag* (1938), *Capriccio* (1942) and (after Strauss's death) *Die Liebe der Danae* (1952).

Krebs, Johann Ludwig (1713-1780) German composer and organist who entered the Thomasschule, Leipzig, in 1726, where he studied the lute, violin and organ, for part of the time as a pupil of **Bach**. He was organist to the Marienkirche, Zwickau (starting 1737). He acted as organist at Zeitz Castle for 12 years, followed by a spell at the castle of Prince Friedrich of Altenberg, where he composed the Concerto in A minor for two harpsichords. Despite difficulties in attributing some of the early work, many of his organ pieces including a fugue based on the name B-A-C-H are undoubtedly entirely his own, while others are based on Bach's work. Many of his organ compositions were posthumously published, whereas other pieces for clavier and lute were circulated widely during his own lifetime.

Kreisler, Fritz (1875-1962) Austrian-born violinist and composer. After studies in Vienna and Paris he appeared in public at the age of 13 as a soloist. Later he abandoned his music for the study of medicine, and then joined the Austrian army. Upon resuming his musical career

Fritz Kreisler

he won immediate success, and went on to become one of the world's finest players, especially of the classics, where his poised vibrant tone was matched with an elegant sense of style. He was the dedicatee of **Elgar**'s violin concerto and gave the first performance in 1910. He spent several years in the United States but became a French citizen in 1938. He is also remembered for his short, charming compositions, which figure in most violinists' repertory; these were often pastiches of the classics and were attributed to well-known names. They include *Caprice viennois*, *Liebeslied*, and *Tambourin chinois*. His recordings preserve his masterly playing, especially his superb account of the Beethoven sonatas with Hans Rupp.

Krenek, Ernst (1900-) Austrian-born composer who studied in Vienna and in Berlin with **Schreker**. After a sensational success with his jazz-inspired opera *Jonny spielt auf* (Leipzig, 1927), he went on to complete eight operas and attained an international reputation for his monumental opera *Karl V*, composed in a **serial** technique. He moved to the United States in 1938, and for a while earned his living as a teacher. In this period he experimented with electronic music and composed the *San Fernando Sequence* for soprano, electronic tape and chamber ensemble. His other music ranged over a wide field; it included six symphonies and numerous other orchestral works, seven string quartets and six piano sonatas.

Kreutzer, Conradin (1780-1849) German composer and conductor. While in Stuttgart in 1812, his opera *Konradin von Schwaben* was staged and he was appointed court conductor on the strength of this. Although employed as *Kapellmeister* to Prince Carl Egon, he became a conductor in Vienna following the success of another opera, *Libussa* (1822). The period spent in Vienna marked the height of Kreutzer's success with operas such as *Der Verschwender*. Although he became musical director in Hamburg and his operas reached a large audience throughout Germany, the rise of **Wagner** in the mid-1840s inevitably overshadowed this success.

Kreutzer, Rodolphe (1766-1831) French violinist, composer and teacher who was himself taught violin and composition from 1778 by Anton **Stamitz**. At the age of 14 he played a concerto in Paris composed by his tutor. On the strength of his growing reputation, he was appointed first violin with the Chapelle du Roi. Beethoven dedicated his Violin Sonata Op.47 to him. During the 1780s he composed sacred music and performed his own violin concertos. Moving to Paris in 1789, he wrote his first opera, *Jeanne d'Arc*, performed in 1790. This was the first of more than 40 operas; he also wrote studies and violin sonatas.

Krieger, Johann Philipp (1649-1725) German composer and organist who studied with Johann Dretzel and Gabriel Schütz in Nuremberg. He is believed to have been extraordinarily precocious, composing arias and performing at the age of nine. In 1670 he was appointed chamber composer to the Bayreuth court and travelled to Italy, where he studied the clavier and composition. In 1677 he became court organist in Halle, and *Kapellmeister* to the court of Weissenfels in 1680. Krieger is considered by many to have been one of the foremost composers of his day, with a canon of more than 2,000 sacred cantatas alone.

Krips, Josef (1902-1974) Austrian conductor and violinist who became chorus-master and *répétiteur* at the Volksoper while still studying at the Vienna Academy. Krips went on to work with the opera companies at Aussig (1924) and Dortmund (1925). In 1933, following a lengthy period as musical director in Karlsruhe, he became conductor of the Vienna Staatsoper and was then made professor at the Academy in 1935. Following World War II Krips was able to resume his post with the Vienna Staatsoper. He relaunched the famous Salzburg Festival in 1946 with a memorable production of Mozart's *Don Giovanni*. A tour of Europe in the 1940s was followed by a series of posts, including those of conductor of the London Symphony Orchestra (1950-4) and the San Francisco Symphony Orchestra (1963-70). Krips also made many fine recordings.

Kubelík, Rafael (1914-) Czech composer and conductor who later took Swiss nationality. After a period of study at the Prague Conservatoire, Kubelík made his conducting début in 1934 with the Czech Philharmonic Orchestra. In 1950 he was appointed musical director of the Chicago Symphony Orchestra and introduced many modern works into its repertory. He premièred **Bloch**'s *Suite hébraïque* in 1953. From 1955 to 1958 Kubelík was musical director at Covent Garden, where he performed the original version of **Mussorgsky**'s *Boris Godunov* as well as giving the British première of **Janáček**'s *Jen fa*. The post of chief conductor of the Bavarian Radio Symphony Orchestra gave him the opportunity to record many pieces, including works by Janáček and Schoenberg. He also performed all of

Rafael Kubelík

Mahler's symphonies. Kubelík has composed several operas, perhaps the most famous being *Veronika* (1947), several concertos and a Requiem.

Kuhlau, Friedrich (1786-1832) German-born Danish composer and pianist. Kuhlau studied theory and composition with Schwenke in Hamburg, where his first compositions for flute and piano were composed and published. Kuhlau was forced to flee Napoleon's invasion and travelled to Copenhagen. In 1811 he performed his own Piano Concerto Op.7 to great acclaim, and in 1813 became court musician. A year later his stage work *The Robbers' Castle* proved successful and in 1817 his first opera was performed. Kuhlau also wrote the incidental music for the frequently revived play *The Fairy's Mound.*

Kuhnau, Johann (1660-1722) German composer, keyboard player and theorist who studied at the Kreuzschule in Dresden with Salomon Krügner. He became cantor and organist of the Johanneskirche and studied law at the University of Leipzig. In 1701 Kuhnau was appointed cantor to the Thomaskirche and taught several subjects, including singing, at the Thomasschule. Throughout the early 1700s he directed music at Leipzig's various churches. As a composer, Kuhnau is chiefly remembered for his many keyboard sonatas, such as the biblical narratives *Biblische Historien* (1700). He is also thought to have composed more than 100 secular songs, now lost.

Kullak, Theodor (1818-1882) German pianist and teacher. His first piano recital was in Berlin at the age of 11, performed in front of the king. While reading medicine in Berlin in 1837 he studied music with Siegfried Dehn. He was later to study with **Czerny** in Vienna and in 1843 became Prussian court pianist after a period as teacher to Vienna's nobility. In 1850 with Stern and Marx he founded the Berlin Conservatoire, and in 1855 established the Neue Akademie.

kumiuta (Japan) Suite of songs, consisting of a fixed sequence of short and often unrelated poems, accompanied by either the **koto** zither or the **shamisen** lute. These suites often consisted of *kouta* (short songs) with wistful or romantic sentiments which lent themselves very well to use at geisha parties.

Kurtág, György (1926-) Hungarian composer, born in Romania. He studied in Hungary with **Kadosa**, **Weiner** and **Veress**, and in Paris with **Messiaen**. From 1958 Kurtág was coach and tutor to the Bartók Secondary Music School and to the National Philharmonia. In 1967 he was appointed professor of piano and chamber music to the Budapest Academy. Kurtág's output has been far from prolific, and works such as String Quartet Op.1 (1959) owe a debt to the modernism of his education as well as more traditional Renaissance and Baroque elements. Kurtág's most highly regarded work is almost certainly *The Sayings of Peter Bornemisza* (1963-8), a concerto for soprano and piano, based on an old Hungarian sermon. Other works include *In Memory of a Winter Sunset*, *Four Capriccios*, *Splitter* (two versions – for cimbalon and piano), a number of songs and some incidental music.

Kurtz, Efrem (1900-) American conductor of Russian birth. He studied in St Petersburg, Riga and Berlin, where he made his début in 1921. In his early years he was associated with ballet, accompanying Pavlova and directing the Ballets Russes de Monte Carlo before and during World War II. He became an American citizen in 1944 and worked with the Kansas City and Houston Symphony Orchestras. After 1954 he toured widely, giving concerts in the USSR and opera in Italy. From 1955 to 1957 he was joint conductor of the Liverpool Philharmonic Orchestra. His wide repertory included much Russian music.

Kurz, Selma (1874-1933) Austrian soprano who made her début in Hamburg in 1895 in the title-role of Ambroise **Thomas**'s *Mignon*. In 1899 she played the role at the Vienna Court Opera at the invitation of **Mahler**. It was in Vienna that she was most successful; she performed the title-role in *Tosca* before moving to such coloratura roles as Violetta in *La traviata*, in which her clear voice came to the fore. She appeared to rapt audiences at Covent Garden for three successive seasons from 1904 as Gilda in *Rigoletto*.

kyemyŏnjo (Korea) One of the most commonly used **pentatonic** modes, corresponding to the notes A, C, D, E, G.

L

L Abbreviation of Longo, used to number the works of Domenico **Scarlatti** in Alessandro Longo's catalogue of Scarlatti's works (1906-8). See also Ralph **Kirkpatrick**.

la Sixth note of the scale as named in **tonic sol-fa**.

Lablache, Luigi (1794-1858) Italian bass of French origin, the most renowned of his day. He studied in Naples and made his début there, moving to Palermo in 1813. His first appearance at La Scala, Milan, was in 1817 as Dandini in Rossini's *La Cenerentola*; he sang there for several years, visiting Rome and Vienna, where he sang at Beethoven's funeral. He became a member of the S. Carlo opera in Naples, where he created various Bellini and Donizetti parts (including the title-role in the latter's *Don Pasquale*, which gave full rein to his comic talent). His London and Paris débuts in 1830 were tremendously successful and he returned to both cities almost every year until the early 1850s; in 1854 he joined the Covent Garden company. His roles included the title-role in *Marino Faliero*, Henry VIII in *Anna Bolena* (both by Donizetti) and Leporello in *Don Giovanni*.

Labroca, Mario (1896-1973) Italian composer and critic who studied with **Respighi** and **Malipiero** at Parma and championed new music, working with various organizations such as the International Society for Contemporary Music. He was director of the Florence Maggio Musicale festival from 1936 to 1944, and spent two years at La Scala before directing the music department of Italian Radio (1949-58). He organized many festivals, taught at Perugia and wrote much criticism. His works include a piano suite (1921), two operas for children, a *Sinfonietta* (1927), three string quartets, songs, cantatas and a *Stabat Mater* (1933).

la Halle (or **Hale), Adam de** (*c.*1237-1287) French **trouvère** poet and composer. Very little biographical information survives, but he is believed to have been born in Arras and to have studied in Paris. These studies are mentioned in his song *Le jeu d'Adam* (1276-7). Soon after this time he travelled to Italy, where he served the Count of Artois. While in Italy he composed the pastoral *Le jeu de Robin et de Marion* (1285). La Halle wrote in many of the styles of the day, composing *chansons* and the famous *jeux partis*, an early comic 'opera' form, as well as **polyphonic** works and motets.

Lalande, Michel Richard de Alternative spelling of **Delalande**, Michel Richard.

Lalo, Edouard (1823-1892) French composer who studied violin with Habeneck at the Paris Conservatoire, as well as taking composition lessons privately. During the 1830s Lalo spent time teaching, but he also played the violin in concerts given by **Berlioz**. He composed some symphonies and some songs, the best of which, along with some violin pieces, were published in *Six Romances Populaires*. Lalo also composed chamber music, a neglected medium in the 1850s, and in 1855 founded the Armingaud-Jacquard Quartet to play classical quartets. His own String Quartet was published in 1859. In 1866 Lalo wrote his first opera, *Fiesque*. Although it was never performed, he was to draw upon it extensively for later works such as the Symphony in G Minor and the *Divertissement* (1872). It was not until the mid-1870s that Lalo was to achieve widespread acclaim with several orchestral compositions, such as the flamboyant *Symphonie espagnole* (1875). Throughout the 1870s he devoted himself almost entirely to orchestral works, except for music written to accompany a libretto by Edouard Blau called *Le Roi d'Ys*. This was eventually performed as a complete opera in 1888, when it was hailed as a masterpiece by French audiences.

Lambert, Constant (1905-1951) English conductor, composer and musicologist. He won a scholarship to the Royal College of Music at the age of 17 and was taught by R.O. Morris. It was at this time that he showed an early love for French and Russian music. In 1926 he performed (with Edith Sitwell) in Walton's *Façade*, a work dedicated to Lambert. At this time he also met Diaghilev, who commissioned the

Constant Lambert

ballet *Romeo and Juliet*. It was also in the mid-1920s that he was to become greatly influenced by jazz, the orchestral work *Elegiac Blues* (1927) being dedicated to the film star Florence Mills. *Rio Grande*, based on a poem by Sacheverell Sitwell, was broadcast by the BBC and premièred in performance by the Hallé Orchestra (1929). In 1931 Lambert was appointed music director of the Sadler's Wells Ballet (later the Royal Ballet) and remained there until after World War II, receiving praise for his conducting ability. He also composed ballet scores for the company (*Horoscope*, 1937; *Tiresias*, 1951). In the 1930s and 1940s he made several guest appearances with the Hallé and other orchestras and made more than 50 broadcasts, including the première of Satie's *Socrates*. He also wrote a provocative and influential book, *Music Ho! A Study of Music in Decline* (1934).

lament Scottish or Irish music played on the **bagpipes**, normally on the occasion of a funeral or some other sorrowful event. It is also a composition written to commemorate the death of a distinguished person. Early laments were those composed on the deaths of Charlemagne (814) and Richard I (1199). More recent examples include **Ravel**'s *Le tombeau de Couperin* (1917) and **Stravinsky**'s *Elegy for J.F. Kennedy* (1964).

Lamoureux, Charles (1834-1899) French conductor and violinist who studied at the Paris Conservatoire with Girard. He financed a performance of Handel's *Messiah* (1873) as well as Bach's *St Matthew Passion* (1874). The popularity of these enabled him to start the Société Française de l'Harmonie Sacrée in the same year. He conducted performances of works by Handel, **Massenet** and others. He was appointed conductor of the Paris Opéra (1877-9). He became conductor of the Société des Nouveaux-Concerts (1881) and became a champion of the music of **Wagner** in Paris, producing *Lohengrin* in 1887. The Nouveaux-Concerts became the

Lamoureux Orchestra, which continued after his death and was an important element in Parisian musical life. It made numerous recordings.

Landi, Steffano (*c.*1587-1639) Italian composer, singer and teacher. In 1610 he was appointed organist to one church, and in 1611 singer to another. In 1618 Landi was appointed *maestro di cappella* by the Bishop of Padua, who became dedicatee of Landi's published book of madrigals. In the following year Landi completed his first opera, *La morte d'Orfeo*. In 1620, on his return to Rome, Landi's first book of arias was published. In Rome, he held a variety of posts, as teacher, clerical composer and again as *maestro di cappella*. In 1629 he was honoured with an appointment to the Papal choir. Following this, in the early 1630s, Landi's best-remembered opera *Il Sant' Alessio* was performed. He also composed many more arias.

Landini (or **Landino**), **Francesco** (*c.*1325-1397) Italian instrumentalist and composer. Few details of his early life in Florence are recorded. However, he is known to have lost his sight at an early age. He composed and wrote poetry as well as building organs. He is believed to have been organist at the monastery of Santa Trinita (1361) and as a virtuoso became known as '*Francesco degli organi*'. He is also thought to have been organist at San Lorenzo for many years. In the 1370s he is known to have built organs in both SS. Annunziata and Florence Cathedral. Many of his works, both secular and sacred, survive, those from the late 14th century displaying popular French influences. In Florence he was considered the most famous exponent of **ars nova**.

Landowska, Wanda (1879-1959) Polish keyboard player who studied at the Warsaw Conservatoire. In 1896 she studied composition with Urban in Berlin. She researched extensively into 17th- and 18th-century composition and its performance, and became convinced of the value of the harpsichord – at that time an underestimated instrument. She made her harpsichord début in 1903. Landowska travelled extensively, giving master-classes in the harpsichord. In 1923 she toured the United States with an instrument built to her own specification. It was on this occasion that she made her first recordings. In the mid-1920s she was performing her own compositions. In 1940 she travelled to Switzerland and later to the United States, where she toured and continued her recordings until she was in her 70s.

Langlais, Jean (1907-) French composer and organist who studied in Paris with **Dupré** and went on to win the Paris Conservatoire's Premier Prix in 1930. It was there that he was to study composition with **Dukas**, alongside **Messiaen**. In the early 1930s he became organist of St Pierre de Montrouge, and after World War II became organist of St Clothilde. Most of Langlais's compositions have been religious organ works, loosely based on **plainsong**.

Langridge, Philip (1939-) English tenor. He began by studying violin, and took up singing in 1962 at the Royal Academy of Music under Boyce. His début was in 1964 at Glyndebourne, and he has sung there in many Mozart roles (Idomeneo, Don Ottavio in *Don Giovanni*). He has also sung frequently at the English National Opera, creating the role of Orpheus in **Birtwistle**'s *The Mask of Orpheus* (1986). At the Royal Opera, Covent Garden, he has sung the title-role in Britten's *Peter Grimes* (1990); he has also appeared at the Metropolitan, New York, La Scala and Vienna, and has made many recordings, of the Baroque repertory as well as contemporary music.

Lanner, Joseph (1801-1843) Austrian dance composer and violinist. Lanner was self-taught, and in 1813 joined Pamer's dance orchestra in Vienna, playing alongside Johann **Strauss** the Elder. In 1818 he formed a trio, joined later by Johann Strauss as violinist. By 1820 the group had grown to a quintet, becoming a full and unwieldy orchestra within the decade. It was therefore disbanded into two smaller orchestras led by Lanner and Strauss, each with its own fervent followers. Lanner and Strauss composed an enormous volume of waltzes and dances. Lanner alone composed 207 light orchestral works, thereby helping to establish the waltz as the most popular dance of 19th-century Vienna.

largamente (It.) Indication that a movement or phrase is to be played in a broad manner. See also **largo**.

larghetto (It.) Indication that the music should be played at a tempo not quite so slow as **largo**.

largo (It.) Indication that the music should be played slowly, in a broad manner.

Larrocha, Alicia de (1923-) Spanish pianist who gave her first performances at the age of five, going on to study with Marshall at Barcelona, where she was to return as director of the academy in 1959. Her concerto début was at the age of 12 with the Madrid Symphony Orchestra. After World War II she toured extensively in Europe and, in 1955, the United States. She is valued for her interpretations of Mozart and of the 19th-century repertory, but it is as a performer of Spanish music that she is renowned. She has made many fine recordings of the piano works of Albéniz, Granados and Falla, including an authoritative performance of Falla's *Nights in the Gardens of Spain*.

Larsson, Lars-Erik (1908-1986) Swedish composer. He entered the Stockholm Conservatoire in 1925, where he studied composition and conducting. His Symphony No.1 was published while he was still a student (1927-8). In 1929 he travelled to Vienna to study with **Berg**, and his works from 1932 feature the tentative use of the **twelve-note** technique. His *Sinfonietta* (1932) was much admired, and in the late 1930s he was appointed to the Swedish Radio Orchestra as conductor, where he concentrated exclusively on film and radio scores. In 1947 he was appointed professor of composition at the Stockholm Conservatoire and later became director at Uppsala University. By the 1960s he had begun to experiment with works such as *Adagio for Strings* (1960), with his own twelve-note scale. He also composed 12 concertinos, one for each main orchestral instrument plus the piano.

La Rue, Pierre de (*c.*1460-1518) Flemish tenor and composer. In 1483 he joined Siena Cathedral choir, and in the 1490s he entered the chapel of Maximilian of Austria, remaining there under Maximilian's successor. He held various posts (both ecclesiastical and courtly) in Europe until his return to the Netherlands in 1508. He became singer to the court at Mechelen and attended the court of Archduke Karl. Although La Rue is known to have been an important composer in his day, few of his compositions date from the period spent in Italy. The majority of his works are Masses dating from the 1500s. He also composed *chansons*.

Lassus, Roland de (Orlando di Lasso) (1532-1594) Franco-Flemish composer. He travelled widely in Europe, in the service of various European households and courts. Lassus's first compositions are believed to date from a period spent at the Accademia de' Sereni in Naples. In the mid-1500s he travelled to Antwerp, where his first collection of **madrigals** and **motets** was printed. In 1555 a volume of five-part madrigals was published. More madrigals, five- and six-part motets and, it is believed, a Mass, were all printed before 1556. Throughout the 1550s and 1560s, with visits to Italy and Paris, his reputation grew. In 1575 his motet *Cantantibus Organis* won the Evreux prize. His five-volume work *Patrocinium Musices* was published during this time, and in the 1580s he had Masses, motets, psalms, *chansons*, drinking songs and even German *Lieder* published, all of which showed the influence of his travels. At his death Lassus left a staggering 2,000 works, both sacred and secular, with more than 100 settings of the Magnificat alone.

lauda, laude (It.) Song of praise, widely used in Italy between the 13th and 19th centuries. It is a religious work for several voices, with its own distinctive poetry, sung by a religious confraternity called *laudisti*. It is said that this type of work contributed to the emergence of the **oratorio** in the 17th century.

Lawes, Henry (1596-1662) English composer and singer, elder brother of William **Lawes**. In 1631 he was appointed musician to Charles I. It was at this time that he met and composed for many of the famous poets of the day, including Milton, Herrick, Suckling, Lovelace and Waller. He was employed in many courtly masques, collaborating with his brother in *The Triumph of the Prince d'Amour* (1636). In the 1650s Lawes was also involved in composing for the operas *First Dayes Entertainment at Rutland House* and *The Siege of Rhodes*. He also wrote many ecclesiastical pieces but it is for his songs (more than 400 in total) that he is best remembered. These are collected in surviving editions of *Ayres and Dialogues*, published in the 1650s.

Lawes, William (1602-1645) English composer who was taught by his father and John **Coprario**. It seems likely that he performed with the young Charles I, who was also taught by Coprario. He was appointed musician to Prince, later King, Charles. From the early 1630s he composed many songs and instrumental music for the court. Unlike those of his brother Henry, none of his works was published in his own lifetime. *Choice Psalmes* (1648) contains 40 of his works. Lawes's chamber music was written for the violin. Today his stage music is better remembered than his vocal settings, and he is believed to have been the first English composer to feature continuity passages in dramatic works. Lawes may be considered a direct precursor of later English composers such as **Purcell**, whose success overshadowed his own.

Lawrence, Ashley (1934-1990) British ballet conductor, born in New Zealand. He studied in Auckland and at the Royal College of Music, and joined the Royal Ballet at Covent Garden in 1962. He became music director of the Berlin Deutsche Oper ballet company (1967), and of the Stuttgart Ballet (1969). At the same time he held the post of principal conductor of the BBC Concert Orchestra (1971-89), which broadcast light music; this he conducted with delicacy, charm and enjoyment. In 1972 he returned to Covent Garden and became music director of the Royal Ballet (1973-87). He was especially considerate of the needs of dancers with regard to speeds and other possible traps, for which he was greatly esteemed; he did much to raise the level of ballet-music performance generally.

leader Principal first violinist in an orchestra, string quartet or other chamber music ensemble. The orchestral leader plays any required solo passages, collaborates with the conductor and has certain administrative responsibilities. He or she also determines the bowing to be used by the string section. In the United States, the term is used as an alternative for conductor.

leading-motif English equivalent of **Leitmotif**.

leading note Seventh note of a major or ascending minor scale, leading to the tonic a semitone above.

Leclair, Jean-Marie (1697-1764) French composer and violinist. He is believed to have begun as a ballet-master in Turin and to have studied violin under Somis. In the early 1720s Leclair came under the patronage of Joseph Bonnier and his Op.1 earned him a considerable reputation. A manuscript from 1721 contains ten sonatas written by Leclair. From then on many of his works for violin were published and he travelled extensively, holding several posts in various courts. In his 50th year Leclair wrote his first opera, *Scylla et Glaucus*, first performed at the Royal Academy, Paris. Leclair's surviving work shows him to be one of the most important violin composers of the 18th century, who popularized the instrument in France both through his compositions and by his performances.

Lees, Benjamin (1924-) American composer of Chinese birth, who studied at the University of California with Halsey Stevens. After a lengthy period of study with George **Antheil** he was awarded a Guggenheim fellowship and travelled to Helsinki, Vienna and Longpont, France. In 1956 he returned to the United States to establish himself as a teacher and composer. Lees has toured in the Soviet Union and has received commissions to write many works for various groups. Although his early compositions show the influence of such composers as **Prokofiev** and **Bartók**, more recent works such as *Medea of Corinth* (1970) show his individuality.

Leeuw, Ton de (1926-) Dutch teacher and composer. He studied with **Badings**, **Messiaen** and **Hartmann**. On his return to Amsterdam in 1950 he studied ethnomusicology with Jaap Kunst. He has studied music in India and Iran, and has taught ethnomusicology and music at Amsterdam University. Leeuw's first published compositions were well received: works such as *Treurmuziek in memoriam Willem Pijper* (1946) show the influence of **Bartók**, whereas later compositions, such as *Sonata for two pianos* (1950), show that of **Pijper**. As well as a radio oratorio, *Job* (1956), Leeuw has composed an opera, *The Dream* (1956), based on *haiku*. By the late 1960s Leeuw's works were deeply concerned with the notion of physical space, performers being spread out or changing position in mid-performance.

Lefanu, Nicola (1947-) English composer, daughter of Elizabeth Maconchy, who studied at Oxford University and the Royal College of Music. Following her graduation she studied with Maxwell **Davies** at Dartington and in Siena. She was later appointed lecturer at King's College, London. She has won many awards for her compositions such as *Antiworld* (1972) and *Dawnpath* (1977). Her most important recent works include the radiophonic opera *The Story of Mary O'Neill* (1986, broadcast 1989), *Wind Among the Pines*; *Five Images of Norfolk* (1987) and a string quartet (1988) in which she makes expressive use of quarter-tones.

legato (It.) Bound, or tied, indication that the music is to be played smoothly, one note leading gently to the next. It is the opposite of **staccato**.

leger line Short line written below or above the stave to indicate those notes that fall outside its compass.

legno (It.) Indication (*col legno*) that a passage for a string instrument is to be played by striking the strings with the stick (back) of the bow.

legong (Indonesia) Dance-theatre form, traditionally accompanied by the **gamelan** *pelegongan* in Bali. *Legong* is danced by three girls, one of whom is the principal dancer. They are trained from an early age and are dressed in magnificently elaborate costumes. The gamelan ensemble provides sudden rapid *ostinati* contrasting with long melodic periods.

Legrand, Michel (1932-) French composer and conductor who studied at the Paris Conservatoire with Henri Chaland and Nadia **Boulanger** from the age of 11. He was drawn towards jazz and popular music from an early age, earning a living from arranging music and writing scores for television and the cinema. He travelled to New York, where he conducted Maurice Chevalier's shows in the mid-1950s. His work has won him many awards, including Oscars for the scores of films such as *Summer of '42*.

Lehár, Franz (1870-1948) Austrian composer and conductor. Hungarian by birth, he is known as this century's foremost composer of operettas. He was taught by his father before joining Prague Conservatoire at the age of 12. In 1885 he obtained private lessons from **Fibich**, and it was at this time that he met Dvořák, whose work was to influence him greatly. His earlier works include the march *Jetzt gehts los!*, the operettas *Wiener Frauen*, *Zigeunerliebe* and *Der Restelbinder* and his most famous, *The Merry Widow* (1905). His other successes include *The Land of Smiles*, *The Count of Luxembourg*, *Paganini*, and *Giuditta*. The voice and charm of the tenor Richard **Tauber** contributed greatly to their success.

Lehmann, Liza (1862-1918) English soprano and composer. She studied singing with Jenny **Lind** in London and composition in Rome and Wiesbaden. Her début was in the Monday Popular Concerts in 1885. At the time of her retirement (1894) she had published various songs, but from this point she was to concentrate on composition. She is remembered for *In a Persian Garden* (1896), a setting of poems by Omar Khayyam as a song-cycle for four solo voices, including her best-known song *Myself When Young*.

Lehmann, Lotte (1888-1976) German soprano who studied in Berlin with Mathilde Mallinger, the first Eva in Wagner's *Die Meistersinger von Nürnberg*. Her début was in 1910 in Hamburg; in 1914 she sang Sophie in *Der Rosenkavalier* with the Beecham company in London. From 1916 to 1938 she established a great reputation in Vienna, creating the Strauss roles of the Dyer's Wife in *Die Frau ohne Schatten* and Christine in *Intermezzo*. In

Franz Lehár (seated) with Richard Tauber

1924 she first sang the Marschallin in *Der Rosenkavalier*, a part in which she became pre-eminent throughout her career. This first Marschallin was at Covent Garden, where her popularity was immense over a long period in roles such as the Countess in *Le nozze di Figaro*, Leonore in Beethoven's *Fidelio* and many Wagner roles. Her United States début was in 1930 at the Chicago Opera, where she sang Sieglinde in *Die Walküre*, repeating the role for her Metropolitan début in 1934. She also developed an extensive *Lieder* repertory. She retired in 1951 and settled in California, teaching and writing. Her recordings, especially an incomparable *Rosenkavalier*, reveal her beautiful, generous tone and elegant phrasing.

Leibowitz, René (1913-1972) Polish-French composer, teacher and conductor. For three formative years from 1930 Leibowitz studied in Berlin with **Webern** and **Schoenberg**, and travelled to Paris to study with **Ravel**, where he remained throughout the war years. His début came in 1937 and from this point he travelled extensively as a conductor. In 1947 he organized the International Festival of Chamber Music in Paris which was to première music by Schoenberg, Webern and **Berg**. Although these composers were disregarded in Paris until the 1940s, credit must be given to Leibowitz for championing and publicizing their **twelve-note** technique and compositions.

Leider, Frida (1888-1975) German operatic soprano. She studied in Berlin and made her début at Halle in 1915, as Venus in Wagner's *Tannhäuser*. In 1923 she joined the Berlin State Opera, singing Mozart and Verdi roles and quickly gaining a reputation in Strauss and above all Wagner. Her début in London was in 1924, as Isolde; she returned there for many years, where her Brünnhilde, Kundry and other Wagnerian parts were greatly admired. She sang at Bayreuth from 1928 and in that year sang in the United States for the first time (as Brünnhilde). Her Metropolitan début was as Isolde in 1933. Her deep, rich voice is heard to great effect on her numerous recordings, which include some of her finest Wagnerian roles.

Leigh, Walter (1905-1942) English composer who studied with E.J. Dent at Cambridge. After graduating (1926) he studied with **Hindemith** at the Berlin Hochschule. During this period he had his first works published. In the early 1930s Leigh became director of the Musical Theatre, Cambridge. He was killed during World War II, leaving several works for the stage, including two musical comedies, *The Pride of the Regiment* (1931) and *The Jolly Roger* (1933).

Leighton, Kenneth (1929-1989) English composer who studied classics and then composition at Oxford. Later he studied in Rome with Goffredo **Petrassi**. He won many awards, including one in 1956 for his *Fantasia Contrapuntistica*. In 1956 he was appointed to the faculty of Edinburgh University as lecturer in composition, moving to Oxford in 1968. Leighton wrote vocal, orchestral and chamber music, all typified by the use of a characteristic lyrical romanticism.

Leinsdorf, Erich (1912-) Austrian conductor who studied with Paul Emerich at the Vienna Academy. In 1932 he made his début as a pianist in Stravinsky's *Les noces*. In 1934 he travelled to Salzburg to serve as assistant to Bruno **Walter**. He remained in Salzburg until 1937, associated with both **Toscanini** and Walter. He conducted in France and Italy before accepting the post of assistant conductor at the Metropolitan Opera, New York, where he made his début with *Die Walküre* in 1938. He has become known as an expert interpreter of Wagner. In 1962 he was appointed to the Boston Symphony Orchestra as director and conductor. He has recorded extensively in the operatic and symphonic repertories.

Leitmotif (Ger.) Leading-motif. Theme associated with an object or idea, or an aspect of a character in an opera, quoted at appropriate moments or worked up symphonically. The chief exponent of the *Leitmotif* was **Wagner**.

lent, lento (It.) Slow.

Lenya, Lotte (1898-1981) American actress and singer of Austrian origin. She trained as a dancer and worked first in Zurich, where she met Wedekind. She moved to Berlin and in 1926 married Kurt **Weill**. Her reputation was established as a singer in the Brecht-Weill pieces *The Rise and Fall of the City of Mahagonny*, *The Threepenny Opera* and *The Seven Deadly Sins*. After Weill's death she made many recordings and performed many of the works from his Berlin period; at the same time she acted on the stage and in films, memorably evil in a small part in one of the James Bond films, *From Russia with Love* (1963).

Leoncavallo, Ruggiero (1857-1919) Italian composer who entered Naples Conservatoire in 1866. He graduated a decade later, having been taught by Rossi. While at Bologna University in the late 1870s he became interested in the Renaissance, and wrote the opera *Tomaso Chatterton*. His greatest success was the opera *I pagliacci* (The Clowns), a work in the *verismo* style for which he wrote both words and music; it was first performed in 1892, conducted by **Toscanini**. He wrote several other operas including *La bohème* (1897, unfortunately overshadowed by **Puccini**'s version, staged a short time earlier), *Roman von Berlin* (1904), *Maia* (1910) and *Malbruck* (1910). He also wrote songs, including *Mattinata* (which was recorded by **Caruso**). He never achieved another success comparable to that of *Pagliacci*, but the opera *Zazà* (1900) was well received.

Leonhardt, Gustav (1928-) Dutch keyboard-player and conductor. He studied organ and harpsichord with Müller in Basle after World War II. His début was in Vienna in 1950. He became professor of harpsichord at the Vienna Academy from 1952 to 1955, as well as at the Amsterdam Conservatoire. In 1955 he founded the Leonhardt Consort, dedicated to playing chamber music on authentic instruments. In the mid-1950s he toured extensively in Europe and the United States as both harpsichordist and lecturer. Leonhardt's repertory includes keyboard compositions from the 16th to the 18th centuries, performed on original instruments in a quest for **authenticity**.

Leppard, Raymond (1927-) English harpsichordist and conductor. He studied at Cambridge with Middleton and **Ord** until 1952. In that year he made his conducting début at the Wigmore Hall, London, and earned a reputation for his performances of 17th- and 18th-century music. In the late 1950s he was appointed lecturer at Cambridge University. In 1962 at Glyndebourne he conducted what was to become the first of a series of early Italian opera revivals, including **Monteverdi**'s *L'Orfeo*. In the following year he began his involvement with the English Chamber Orchestra. From 1973 to 1980 he was principal conductor of the BBC Northern Symphony Orchestra. In 1984 he became principal conductor of the St Louis Symphony Orchestra.

Levine, James (1943-) American pianist and conductor who appeared as a soloist at the age of ten. He was tutored by Walter Levin; at the Juilliard School he studied conducting with Jean Morel. At the age of 21 he was offered the post of assistant conductor of the Cleveland Orchestra; while there he also taught at the Aspen Music School, at Oakland University and elsewhere. His début at the Metropolitan Opera, New York, came in 1971 when he conducted *Tosca*; he was appointed principal conductor in 1973 and musical director in 1975. He has also conducted at Salzburg, Vienna, and at Bayreuth (1982). Levine's conducting repertory ranges from 18th-century to modern avant-garde composers; he also directs from the piano. Among his notable recordings is a series of Mozart symphonies with the Vienna Philharmonic, and Wagner's *Die Walküre* with the Metropolitan Orchestra (1988).

Lewis, Sir Anthony (1915-1983) English composer, conductor and musicologist. He was appointed to the BBC, organizing chamber music broadcasts in the pre-war period; after World War II he rejoined the BBC as a key planner for what would become the Third Programme. In 1947 he was appointed professor at Birmingham University, producing many rarely heard works, including Handel's Italian operas translated into English by Lewis's colleagues. In the 1940s Lewis made the first recordings of works by **Lully** and **Monteverdi** and **Purcell**'s *The Fairy Queen*. In 1950 he was appointed secretary and later chairman of the Purcell Society. In the same year he organized the publication of *Musica Britannica*, overseeing the first 30 volumes. In 1968 Lewis was appointed to the post of principal of the Royal Academy of Music and received a knighthood in 1972. His published compositions have included an *Elegy* (1947) and a Horn Concerto (1959).

Lewis, Richard (1914-) English tenor. After studying at the Manchester College of Music and the Royal College, he made his British début in **Britten**'s *Serenade* (1947). A performance of *The Rape of Lucretia* at Glyndebourne, also in 1947, marked his operatic début. In the same year he appeared at Covent Garden in Britten's *Peter Grimes*, and often appeared there subsequently. He also undertook the role of Aaron in the British première of Schoenberg's *Moses und Aaron*. He made his American début in San Francisco in 1953. He has frequently appeared in concerts and operas in all parts of the world, and has made many fine recordings.

Liadov Alternative spelling of **Lyadov**.

libretto (It.) Written text of an opera, oratorio or cantata, originally contained in a small booklet for the benefit of the audience. The role of a librettist was to adapt or translate an existing play, poem, novel or folk-tale in conjunction with the composer, who would provide the music. The most successful partnerships between librettists and composers have included those of Da Ponte and **Mozart**, Boito and **Verdi**, Gilbert and **Sullivan**, Hofmannsthal and Richard **Strauss**.

licenza (It.) Licence, freedom. *Con alcuna licenza* indicates that the performer has some freedom in such matters as speed and rhythm.

Lidholm, Ingvar (1921-) Swedish composer. At the outbreak of World War II, Lidholm studied violin and theory at Stockholm's Royal College of Music under Barkel, Brandel, Mann and **Rosenberg**. In 1956 he was appointed to the post of director of chamber music for Swedish Radio; in 1965 he joined the faculty of the Stockholm Royal College of Music. Publications from the 1970s such as the *Three Aspects of New Music* firmly link Lidholm to the canon of new music appearing in Scandinavia, and his own compositional work features constructivist methods.

Liebermann, Rolf (1910-) Swiss composer and opera director. He studied composition with Vladimir Vogel, from whom he learned about **twelve-note** compositional developments. After World War II, Liebermann was appointed to Swiss Radio as producer and manager. In 1957 he became musical director of North German Radio, Hamburg, and later **Intendant** of the Hamburg State Opera. He was appointed artistic director in 1962. Under him the Hamburg State Opera gained a reputation for its première performances of new commissioned works. On the strength of this he was appointed to the Paris Opéra from 1973 to 1980. As a composer he is known for several operas, including *Die Schule der Frauen* (1955) and *A Concerto for Jazzband and Orchestra* (1954).

Lied German song. The most important characteristic of the *Lied* is that its piano part is not merely a decorative support to the song, but an integral and equal part of it. The greatest and most prolific composer of *Lieder* was **Schubert**, whose songs, over 600 in number, achieve a rare expressive intensity and lyricism. Other fine *Lieder* composers include **Schumann**, **Brahms**, **Wolf**, **Pfitzner**, **Marx**, **Reger**, Richard **Strauss** and **Kilpinen**.

ligature 1. A slur over several notes to show that they are to be phrased as one melodic unit, played in one bow stroke, or sung to one syllable.

2. A metal band that secures the reed to the mouthpiece in instruments of the clarinet family.

Ligeti, György (1923-) Hungarian composer who studied composition at the Kolozsvár Conservatoire with Farkas during World War II, followed by a period of private study with **Kadosa** in Budapest. In 1949 he resumed his studies with Farkas as well as **Veress** at Budapest. He went to Vienna in 1956 because of the Hungarian uprising, and there met many leading avant-garde composers, including **Stockhausen** and Eimert, who invited him to study at the Cologne Electronic Music

Studio in 1957 on the strength of his experimental compositions. During this period he composed one of his major works, *Visions* (which later became *Apparitions*), first performed at the 1960 Cologne ISCM Festival. His compositional development was most affected by his move to the West, with the subsequent destruction of formal rhythm and pitch structures in a move towards greater expression in his work. *Atmosphères* (1961), with its wide variety of noises, effects and timbres, laid the foundations for later works. An outstanding composition is the fantasy opera *Le grand macabre* (1978); other works include *Melodien* (1971); *Poème symphonique* (1962), which uses 100 metronomes set at different tempi; a piano concerto (1983); piano studies (1985); choral and chamber music.

Lilburn, Douglas (1915-) New Zealand composer who won the Grainger Prize for his overture *In the Forest* (1936). He studied in London with **Vaughan Williams** (1937-40); on his return to New Zealand, he was appointed to the faculty of Victoria University, Wellington, becoming professor in 1963. In 1970 he was made professor of the University Electronic Music Studio, after he had established Australasia's first ever such studio in the 1960s. Lilburn's early compositions evoked the landscapes of New Zealand. The influences of Vaughan Williams are unmistakable in his Symphony No.2 (1951). In the same year, he composed his *Elegy* in response to the poets of the Central Otago region. More recently he has produced electronic works. Lilburn's work is considered central to the development of post-war music in New Zealand.

Lill, John (1944-) English pianist who studied at the Royal College of Music and with **Kempff**. His début in London was in 1963, in New York in 1969; after winning the 1970 Moscow Tchaikovsky Competition his reputation was assured. He has played all over the world and has made many recordings, particularly of Beethoven and Brahms concertos. He also includes the grand Romantic works of Liszt, Chopin and Rachmaninov in his repertory, and with his muscular technique has had great success with the Prokofiev concertos. He is a deeply thoughtful interpreter of Beethoven sonatas.

Lind, Jenny (1820-1887) Swedish soprano, nicknamed the Swedish Nightingale. She studied in Stockholm and with Isak Berg and made her operatic début in 1838 as Agathe in *Der Freischütz*; she took the title-role in Weber's *Euryanthe* in the same year. She appeared regularly for the next three years in a variety of major roles. In 1841 she began to lose her voice from overwork and a poor method. In Paris she went to Manuel **García** for advice, and after careful study was able to return to the stage with enhanced success. In the mid-1840s Lind sang throughout Europe and appeared in a performance of *Norma* for her Viennese début in 1846. Her British début was in *Robert le Diable* before Queen Victoria in 1847. Lind's subsequent popularity was matched by her reception in the United States, where she toured in 1850-2. In 1852 she married Otto Goldschmidt, her accompanist, and moved to England in 1858. In 1883 Lind was appointed to the Royal College of Music as professor of singing. She is best remembered for her performances in *Norma*, as Amina in *La sonnambula* and in Spontini's *Robert le Diable*.

lining out Practice in sacred music whereby the priest or precentor recites a line of text before it is sung by the congregation. The precentor may speak, chant or sing each line.

Linley, Thomas (1733-1795) English composer and teacher. He studied with Thomas Chilcot, organist at Bath Abbey, and later with William **Boyce** and, it is believed, Domenico Paradisi. From the mid-1750s Linley was director of many of Bath's concerts until the 1770s, when his success led to an appointment with the

Drury Lane Theatre, London, as joint director and later manager. Linley's opera *The Royal Merchant* was produced at Covent Garden in 1767, and *The Duenna* in 1775. He also wrote songs for many other comic operas and dramas.

Linley, Thomas (1756-1778) English composer and violinist, son of Thomas **Linley**. Of precocious ability, Linley performed a violin concerto at the age of seven at Bristol. From then until he was 12, he studied with his father and **Boyce**, then with Nardini in Florence, where he met Mozart in 1770. On his return to England he performed extensively in Bath and London, becoming leader at Drury Lane from 1773 to 1778.

Lipatti, Dinu (1917-1950) Romanian pianist and composer who studied piano with Florica Musicescu at the Budapest Conservatoire from 1928 to 1932. Winning the second prize at the 1934 Vienna International Competition amid great critical debate, he travelled to Paris to study piano with **Cortot**, conducting with Münch, and composition with Nadia **Boulanger**, with whom he made his initial recordings, of Brahms's waltzes for piano duet. His tours giving recitals in Germany and Italy were cut short by World War II. Later he taught at the Geneva Conservatoire. He was an outstanding interpreter of Chopin and Schumann, and made some fine recordings during his last years, although seriously ill.

Lipkin, Malcolm (1932-) English composer who studied under Bernard Stevens at the Royal College of Music (1949-53) and with **Seiber**. His Piano Concerto (1957), first performed at the Cheltenham Festival, was well received and in 1967 he was appointed to the music faculty of Oxford University as tutor for external studies. In 1975 he joined the faculty of Kent University. He has written choral as well as orchestral pieces, notably a setting of Psalm 96 (1969), and a *Prelude and Dance* for cello and piano in memory of Jacqueline **du Pré**.

lira Generic name given to various old bowed stringed instruments, such as the **rebec** and **crwth**.

lira da braccio (It.) Bowed stringed instrument, current in the late 16th and early 17th centuries, which evolved from the fiddle. It had seven strings, five stopped on the fingerboard, and two unstopped **drones** tuned an octave apart. As the name implies, it was played on the arm.

Lira da braccio

Lira da gamba

lira da gamba (It.) Larger version of the **lira da braccio** that was held between the knees. The number of strings, including drones, varied from 11 to 15.

Liszt, Franz (Ferenc) (1811-1886) Hungarian composer who was also a piano virtuoso and highly influential teacher and conductor. Liszt appeared in public and began to compose at the age of eight. When he was ten years old he moved to Vienna to study with **Czerny**, and impressed Beethoven with his playing. He moved to Paris in 1823 and embarked on a fabulous career as the leading piano virtuoso of his day, in demand all over Europe. From 1848 to 1859 he was music director at the court of Weimar and made it an important centre for the production of new music by composers such as Berlioz and **Wagner** – he gave the first performance of *Lohengrin* in 1850. His romantic looks and style fascinated audiences and attracted women; he lived with the Countess d'Agoult and fathered Cosima, who was to be the wife of Hans von **Bülow** and later Wagner. From 1848 to 1861 he lived with Princess Sayn-Wittgenstein. However, he never married and in 1865 took minor orders in the Roman Catholic Church, thereafter being referred to as 'Abbé'. Despite the extravagant demands and difficult life of the travelling virtuoso, Liszt was a prolific composer in several fields. His piano music reflected his astonishing technique and set new standards of virtuosity that few could equal, though the musical content swung from flashy display in his fantasias on operatic themes to works of great imagination and power, such as the one-movement B minor piano sonata and the collection *Années de pèlerinage*. Although initially he was helped by **Raff** in his instrumentation, Liszt was a major force in the development of Romantic orchestral music, with a profound influence on later composers such as Wagner and Richard Strauss. He composed the *Faust* and *Dante* symphonies, and an uneven series of 14 **symphonic poems** (a form he invented), of which *Les Préludes* and *Orpheus* are outstanding. His religious beliefs inspired many large-scale choral works such as *The Legend of St Elizabeth*, *Christus*, and the *Grand Coronation Mass*. Many of his 55 songs are regularly performed, and his piano transcriptions capture his remarkable virtuosity, as well as his respect for other composers. As in his lifetime, Liszt still provokes controversy – some praise his development of cyclic form, imaginative harmony, and radical innovations like the whole-tone scale that prefigured developments in the 20th century, while others cannot abide the flashy style, the chromatic sentimentality and the rhapsodic form. History has often tried to write Liszt off, but his reputation as an erratic genius still survives.

litany Supplicatory chant consisting of a series of petitions with an infrequently changing response to each. Among the best-known litanies are those of the Roman Catholic Church; they include the Litany of Saints, sung on Holy Saturday and during Rogation-tide, and the litany sung in honour of the Virgin Mary. Cranmer's litany of the mid-16th century is still used in Anglican churches, but excludes references to the saints.

Liverpool Philharmonic Orchestra See **Royal Liverpool Philharmonic Orchestra**

Lloyd, Charles Harford (1849-1919) English organist and composer who studied at Oxford and founded Oxford's Musical Club, becoming its president in 1872. In 1876 he was appointed organist of Gloucester Cathedral and conductor of Gloucester's Choral and Philharmonic Societies. In 1882 he was appointed organist of Christ Church, Oxford, and from 1887 taught organ at the Royal College of Music until 1892, when he was appointed to the post of music instructor at Eton. From 1914 he was organist at the Chapel Royal, St James's. Lloyd has left many compositions both religious and secular, including orchestral works such as *Hero and Leander* (1884).

Lloyd, George (1913-) English composer who studied composition with Harry

Farjeon. His first opera, *Iernin* (1934), was performed in his native Cornwall and *The Serf* was performed at Covent Garden in 1938. His third opera, *John Socman*, was featured at the Festival of Britain in 1951. The libretti of all three operas were written by his father. Lloyd has written other orchestral and choral works including nine symphonies, four piano and two violin concertos and *The Vigil of Venus* (1980) for soprano, tenor, chorus and orchestra. He was awarded the OBE in 1970.

Lloyd, Robert (1940-) English bass who studied at Oxford and at the London Opera Centre. He joined the Sadler's Wells company in 1969 and the Royal Opera, Covent Garden, in 1972. He has also sung in Paris, Aix, La Scala, San Francisco and in other American houses. His roles include Sarastro in *Die Zauberflöte*, Fasolt in Wagner's *Das Rheingold*, the title-role in Mussorgsky's *Boris Godunov* and Gurnemanz in Wagner's *Parsifal*.

Lloyd Webber, Andrew (1948-) English composer who studied briefly at the Royal College of Music before teaming up with Tim Rice to write popular songs. Their first successful musical was *Joseph and the Amazing Technicolour Dreamcoat* (1968), based on a biblical story, first staged in its full length at the Edinburgh Festival. His second successful work with Tim Rice was *Jesus Christ Superstar* (1970), of which a best-selling recording was made; it has been staged all over the world and was made into a film. Throughout the 1970s Lloyd Webber wrote film scores and has had other stage hits, including *Evita* (1978), *Cats* (1981) and *Phantom of the Opera* (1987). He has also written a *Requiem* (1984).

Lloyd Webber, Julian (1951-) English cellist, brother of Andrew **Lloyd Webber**. He studied with Pierre **Fournier** in Geneva in 1973. His début in Britain was at the Wigmore Hall in 1971. Lloyd Webber has toured extensively as a solo cellist, as well as making recordings of **Delius**'s cello compositions and modern British works.

Julian Lloyd Webber

Locatelli, Pietro Antonio (1695-1764) Italian violinist and composer, who studied in Italy, possibly with **Corelli** in Rome. He performed extensively in Italy and was appointed *virtuoso da camera* to the Governor of Mantua from 1725 to 1735. In 1729, Locatelli is known to have settled in Amsterdam, revising his Concerti Grossi Op.1 (1721), teaching and participating in regular concert appearances. His playing was known for its virtuosity; he used a short bow and was famous for the deft use of double stopping. His composition owes much to his formative years spent in Venice, influenced largely by **Vivaldi** and Valentini.

Locke (or Lock), Matthew (*c.*1622-1677) English composer who studied at Exeter Cathedral as a chorister with Edward Gibbons and William Wake. He was commissioned to write music for Shirley's masque *Cupid and Death* (1653) and in 1656 wrote some of the music for what is arguably the first English opera, *The Siege of Rhodes*, now lost, and for other plays of the 1650s and 1660s. Locke is remembered primarily for his chamber and dramatic music, his chamber music owing much to the traditional consort music of

Lawes and Simpson. *The Broken Consort*, for instance, dates from 1661 and was intended for his eight chamber musicians.

Lockhart, James (1930-) Scottish pianist, accompanist, organist, and conductor who studied at Edinburgh University and the Royal College of Music. He held positions as organist and choirmaster at St Giles Cathedral, Edinburgh, and between 1951 and 1954 in major churches in London. He worked as a conductor with the Yorkshire Symphony Orchestra (1954-5), Münster Opera (1955-6), Munich Opera (1956-7) and Glyndebourne (1957-9). He conducted the first British stage production of Berg's *Lulu* in 1971 with the Welsh National Opera, and was music director there, 1972-3. He also became music director of Kassel Opera. He is a guest conductor with the BBC Concert Orchestra, and Director of Opera at the Royal College of Music.

loco (It.) Indication that a passage is to be played in the register indicated by written notes, rather than an octave higher or lower as in a preceding passage.

Loeillet, Jean Baptiste (1680-1730) Flemish-born harpsichordist and flautist. He is known to have settled in London in 1705 after studying in Ghent and Paris. From 1705 to 1710 he played oboe and flute at the Queen's Theatre, Haymarket, and Drury Lane. He is believed to have introduced and certainly popularized the German transverse flute in England and was a major collector of flutes and violins. He has left several suites of lessons and sonatas in the tradition of **Corelli** and **Vivaldi**.

Loewe, Frederick (1901-1988) American composer of musicals and songs, Austrian by birth. He studied piano with **Busoni** and **d'Albert** in Berlin, and performed his first solo with the Berlin Philharmonic Orchestra at the age of 13. In 1924 he emigrated to the United States, where he unsuccessfully pursued a career as a

Frederick Loewe

concert pianist. It was in New York that he found a new direction as a composer when he collaborated with the librettist Alan Jay Lerner, writing some of the world's most successful musicals including *Brigadoon* (1947), *Paint Your Wagon* (1951), the Pulitzer Prize-winning *My Fair Lady* (1956) and *Camelot* (1960).

Löhr, Hermann (1871-1943) English composer, born in Plymouth, who studied at the Royal College of Music. He was the composer of many popular ballads, such as *Little Grey Home in the West* (1911) and *Where My Caravan has Rested.*

Lomax, Alan (1915-) American ethnomusicologist who studied music and anthropology at the universities of Harvard, Texas and Columbia. After working at the Archive of American Folksong (1937), he became director of Folk Music at Decca Records (1946-9). Since then he has carried out research in the United States, Great Britain, Haiti, Italy and Spain, and has promoted folk-song through festivals, radio broadcasts and lecturing. In 1963 he was appointed director of the **Cantometrics** Project at Columbia University, the results of which he published in *Folk Song Style and Culture* (1968). Other publications include a biography of Ferdinand 'Jelly Roll' Morton (*Mister Jelly Roll*, 1950) and numerous anthologies and bibliographies of folk-song and poetry.

Lombardy rhythm Alternative term for the **Scotch snap**.

London Mozart Players Chamber orchestra founded in 1949 by the violinist Harry **Blech** specifically to perform Mozart, Haydn, Beethoven and Schubert. It became a popular institution at the Royal Festival Hall, where it performed regularly. After 1969 the repertory was considerably broadened, and the orchestra played under a variety of guest conductors. Since 1983 the music director has been Jane **Glover**.

London Philharmonic Orchestra British orchestra founded in 1932 by Sir Thomas **Beecham** at a low point in London orchestral playing, with the aim of creating an ensemble of the standard of the great philharmonic orchestras in Berlin and Vienna. Having followed his well-tried formula of buying the best players, Beecham and the new orchestra made a tremendous impact at the opening concert on 7 October 1932 with brilliant performances of Berlioz's overture *Le carnaval romain* and Strauss's *Ein Heldenleben*. As well as giving superb concerts, the orchestra often played for the Beecham opera season at Covent Garden, and made gramophone recordings which stand comparison with those of today and have often been reissued in LP form. In 1939, after Beecham's departure for America, the orchestra decided to govern itself, and under the management of Thomas Russell made an important contribution to morale throughout World War II by giving concerts all over the country, often in difficult circumstances. After the war the orchestra struggled to regain its earlier glory, working under such conductors as Edouard van Beinum, Victor de **Sabata**, William **Steinberg**, and later Sir Adrian **Boult**. More recently Bernard **Haitink**, Georg **Solti** and Klaus **Tennstedt** have raised the orchestra to international status. In 1990 it was announced that it was to be the resident orchestra of the South Bank complex in London.

London Sinfonietta Orchestra founded in 1968 by David **Atherton** and Nicholas Snowman to perform contemporary music. It plays regularly at festivals all over the world and gives annual seasons in London. Many works by such composers as **Birtwistle**, **Berio**, **Henze**, **Gerhard** and **Stockhausen** have been commissioned or have been premièred by it. Its conductors have included Atherton, Elgar **Howarth** and Simon **Rattle**. There is also an associate choir, and it is the orchestra for the avant-garde Opera Factory, whose director is David Freeman.

London Symphony Orchestra British orchestra founded in 1904 by members of Henry **Wood**'s Queen's Hall Orchestra, who left when Wood announced they would no longer be able to send deputies. The first concert was given at 3pm on 9 June 1904 under the direction of the eminent German Hans **Richter**, who was principal conductor until 1911. He opened the very long programme with Wagner's prelude to *Die Meistersinger* and included Elgar's *Enigma Variations*. This marked the beginning of a long association of Elgar with the orchestra. For many years it was the main British orchestra, often playing for opera at Covent Garden, for the Three Choirs Festival and for regular series of London concerts. The standard of playing deteriorated in the 1920s, and the orchestra struggled to survive when in 1932-3 some of the best players were poached by the BBC and London Philharmonic Orchestras. After the war its fortunes revived under the direction of such conductors as Josef **Krips** (1950-4), Pierre **Monteux** (1961-4), István **Kertesz** (1965-8), André **Previn** (1968-79), Claudio **Abbado** and Michael **Tilson Thomas**.

Loraine, Alain Original name of the conductor Gerard **Victory**.

Lorengar, Pilar (1928-) Spanish soprano who studied at Madrid, and made her concert début in 1952. She appeared in leading roles in the Aix-en-Provence Festival, in New York, at Covent Garden for several seasons in *La traviata* (Verdi), and from 1956 for four seasons in *Die Zauberflöte* (Mozart) at Glyndebourne. She has sung many different roles at the Deutsche Oper in Berlin. Her Metropolitan début in 1963 as Donna Elvira in Mozart's *Don Giovanni* enhanced her reputation. She has a wide repertory including all the Mozart and many Verdi roles; she has also sung in Puccini's *Tosca* and as Eva in Wagner's *Die Meistersinger*.

Loriod, Yvonne (1924-) French pianist who studied at the Paris Conservatoire and took composition lessons with **Messiaen** and **Milhaud**. The Conservatoire awarded her seven first prizes. After appearing in the first performance of Messiaen's *Visions de l'Amen*, she toured extensively in Germany and Austria. She is married to Messiaen and has appeared in all of his first performances of new works. Loriod's American début was in the first performance of the *Turangalîla-Symphonie* in 1949. Loriod has recorded the piano works of Messiaen as well as those of **Boulez** and Barraqué.

Lortzing, Albert (1801-1851) German composer and singer. He studied piano as a child and appeared in his parents' theatre company; there he learnt much about stagecraft, which was useful to him when he later came to compose operas. Most of his work is for the stage – comic operas of the *Singspiel* type, of which the best-known are *Zar und Zimmermann* (1837), *Der Wildschütz* (1842), *Undine* (1845) and *Der Waffenschmied* (1846). He wrote over 20 of these works, while continuing as an actor and singer with his parents' company; he also composed incidental music for the theatre, an overture, an oratorio, a cantata and various songs and choral works.

Los Angeles, Victoria de (1923-) Spanish soprano who studied at the Barcelona Conservatoire. She made her operatic début in 1945 at the Teatro Liceo and in 1947 won the prestigious International Singing Competition in Geneva. At this time her repertory included *La bohème*, *Tannhäuser*, *Lohengrin* and *Der Freischütz*. In the immediate post-war years her reputation spread, after she made a BBC broadcast of *La vida breve* in 1948. She made her Covent Garden début in 1950, and appeared there for over a decade in a variety of roles, including the title-role in Puccini's *Madama Butterfly*. She also appeared at the Metropolitan Opera, New York, and in the mid-1960s in Buenos Aires. She retired from opera appearances in 1969, but her outstanding artistry is preserved in many fine recordings.

Lott, Felicity (1947-) English soprano who studied at the Royal Academy of Music and made her début in 1973. She sang with the English National Opera from 1975; her roles included Pamina in *Die Zauberflöte*, Fiordiligi in *Così fan tutte* and Natasha in Prokofiev's *War and Peace*. At Glyndebourne she sang Ann Truelove in Stravinsky's *The Rake's Progress*, and made a particular impact in Strauss parts – Octavian in *Der Rosenkavalier*, the title-role in *Arabella* and the Countess in *Capriccio*. At the Royal Opera, Covent Garden, she has been successful as the Marschallin in *Der Rosenkavalier*, Helena in Britten's *A Midsummer Night's Dream* and Ellen Orford in his *Peter Grimes*. Recently she has essayed her first Wagner role, as Eva in *Die Meistersinger von Nürnberg* (1990). She has appeared in New York, Chicago and many leading European houses.

Lotti, Antonio (*c*.1667-1740) Italian composer and organist who studied in his teens with Legrenzi in Venice, producing the opera *Giustino* at the age of 16. By the end of the 1680s Lotti was an established alto at S. Marco, becoming first organist there in 1704, a post he held until 1736 when he became music-master. During his time at S. Marco Lotti composed many ecclesiastical works for the choir as well as writing secular choral works, motets and music for the theatres of Venice. His opera *Il trionfo dell'innocenza* appeared in 1692. During a two-year period in Dresden he wrote three operas. Lotti returned to Venice in 1719, again to S. Marco, where his *Miserere* of 1733 was to be performed well into the 19th century.

Loughran, James (1931-) Scottish conductor. He won a British conducting competition in 1961 and joined the Bournemouth Symphony Orchestra. In 1963 he appeared at Sadler's Wells and in 1964 at Covent Garden, where he conducted *Aïda*. In 1965 Loughran was appointed chief conductor of the Scottish Symphony Orchestra. In 1970 he joined the Hallé Orchestra, making his New York début two years later. In 1979 Loughran was made principal conductor of the Bamberg Symphony Orchestra. Loughran has in more recent years conducted first performances of a number of British works.

James Loughran

Lourié, Arthur Vincent (1892-1966) Russian composer who studied at the St Petersburg Conservatoire. He composed the sacred work *Corona Carmina Sacrorum* and following the 1917 Revolution was made music commissar to the Conservatoire. Lourié travelled to the United States in 1941, taking citizenship after World War II. Initial experiments in **atonality**, in which his compositions dispensed with staves, were succeeded by modal works such as the *Sonata Liturgica* (1928), harking back to more classical idioms.

lower mordent Alternative term for **inverted mordent**.

lü/lülü (China) Chinese theoretical scale-modal system of twelve pitches within an octave, whose frequencies are related to one another by specific ratios.

Lucier, Alvin (1931-) American composer who studied theory at Yale with **Porter** and then at Brandeis University with **Shapero** and **Berger**. He later taught at Brandeis and at Wesleyan University. Lucier's work has been influenced by the electronic experiments of the Cologne Studio and European composers of the 1960s. His works from this period, such as *Shelter 999*, rely heavily on arbitrary environmental sounds. In 1970 Lucier was commissioned to write a piece for the Osaka Expo which utilized hundreds of tape recorders to give a collage of sound.

Ludwig, Christa (1928-) German mezzo-soprano. Her career began with her début at Frankfurt in *Die Fledermaus*; she appeared at Darmstadt for the 1952-4 seasons and in 1954 as Cherubino in *Le nozze di Figaro* at Salzburg. In the following year she sang at Hanover. In 1955 she was appointed to the Vienna Staatsoper, where she has since made many appearances. Ludwig's New York début came in 1959 and she appeared a decade later in *Aïda* at Covent Garden. Ludwig is notable for a variety of Verdi, Strauss and Wagner roles.

Her numerous recordings, especially of Mahler's orchestral songs, do justice to her warm, full tone.

Luening, Otto (1900-) American composer. His family settled in Munich, where he studied and made his début playing the flute in 1916. Further study in Switzerland followed during World War I, under **Jarnach** and **Busoni,** who were to have a considerable influence on him. He moved to Chicago in 1920, where he conducted, played in chamber ensembles and wrote incidental music for films. He began teaching in 1932, at the University of Arizona, then at Bennington, Columbia and at the Juilliard School. His earliest compositions were somewhat serial in structure; later they became rather more romantic, until in the 1950s he fused the two styles in his works for electronic performance. He founded the electronic music centre at Columbia with Ussachevsky. Besides opera, ballet and television scores (*Evangeline*, 1930; *Carlsbad Caverns*, 1955) he has written a number of fantasias and scenes for orchestra, and a great deal of chamber music of all kinds.

Lully (Lulli), Jean-Baptiste (1632-1687) Italian-born composer, known as a leading exponent of the French **Baroque** style. Lully joined the household of Mlle de Montpensier in 1646, where his dancing as well as guitar and violin performances were notable. He received a good grounding in operatic, concert and popular music performances. Through these concerts he probably became aware of contemporary Italian music and developed a passion for the theatre. It is believed that in the late 1640s Lully studied with the Italian violinist Lazzarini. In 1652 he was appointed to the court of Louis XIV; here he was exposed to many court performances, rose through the ranks to compose instrumental music for court ballets and himself danced for the King. At this time, Lully's reputation stood high and by 1661 he was appointed composer to the King. Lully composed music for many ballets until 1671, collaborating with France's chief dramatists, such as Molière, with whom he wrote *Le bourgeois gentilhomme* in 1670. In 1672, facing much competition, Lully helped to establish what was to become a new form of opera, his musical dramas, which preceded the later comic opera format. Having established a theatre with full royal backing, Lully gathered many of France's best musicians and himself acted as director, manager and conductor, collaborating with the librettist Philippe Quinault. Lully's overtures became famous, a typical example being that featured in the ballet *Alcidiane* (1658).

Throughout this period, Lully came under increasing pressure to dispense with Quinault, who was out of favour with Louis XIV's court. Operas such as *Psyché* (1671) were written with Thomas Corneille. *Bellérophon* (1679) proved to be a great success and for more than a decade Lully wrote one opera a year.

Lully composed *ballets de cour*, pastorals and stage tragedies, his early vocal works being influenced by Italian trends. His comic works were based largely on Italian burlesque. Although Lully was not offered ecclesiastical posts at the court, he wrote many motets and a *Te Deum* for the court chapel.

Lumsdaine, David (1931-) Australian-born British composer who studied at the Royal College of Music as well as taking private lessons with **Seiber**. In 1970 he was appointed to the faculty of Durham University where he established an electronic music workshop. In 1980 he took up a lectureship at King's College, London. Lumsdaine's work is rooted in **serial** composition and in the sounds of his environment. Works from the mid-1960s, such as *Annotations on Auschwitz* (1964), showed his increasing preoccupation with modern historical issues. The influence of his electronic studio is evident in pieces such as *Kaliban Impromptu* (1972).

Lumsden, Sir David (1928-) English keyboard player and choirmaster. He studied at Cambridge with **Ord** and Dart, and founded the Nottingham Bach Society (1954). He became organist at New College, Oxford, and took up a post as lecturer there in 1959, conducting the choir and enhancing its already high reputation. He taught at the Royal Academy of Music (1960-2) and in 1978 was appointed as principal of the Royal Scottish Academy of Music in Glasgow. He is particularly interested in Renaissance and church music and has published several editions. He was appointed principal of the Royal Academy of Music in 1982, and knighted in 1985.

Lupu, Radu (1945-) Romanian pianist who made his début in 1957, and in 1963 studied at the Moscow Conservatoire on a scholarship. He has won many international competitions, including the Leeds Piano Competition in 1969. That year he appeared in London, where his playing was widely admired. Lupu is considered to be an outstanding interpreter of the 19th-century Romantic composers, above all Schumann and Brahms, and he has also made highly-praised recordings of Mozart's sonatas.

lute Plucked string instrument with a pear-shaped body and a round vaulted back. One of the earliest known lutes was the Mesopotamian lute, dating back to 2000 BC. The lute was introduced into Europe during the Crusades, and continued to be a popular instrument until the 18th century, when the **harpsichord** superseded it in popular use.

The early instruments usually had four courses of strings and were plucked with a quill. By the 16th century the instrument had gained an extra course of strings. The tuning of the average-sized 16th-century lute was G, C, F, A, D, G (the lowest string sounding G below middle C). Other tunings were adopted in the 17th century. Music for the lute is played from a **tablature** of letters or figures.

The lute has been used for various compositions, such as dance movements,

A type of lute

variations and contrapuntal **ricercari** and fantasias. The most notable English lutenists were Francis **Cutting** (*c.*1583-*c.*1603) and John **Dowland** (1591-1641). **J. S. Bach**'s repertory for lute included four suites and other pieces. Today Julian **Bream**, the leading modern exponent of the lute, has revived popular interest in the instrument.

Lutosławski, Witold (1913-) Polish composer who played the piano and violin as a child, and studied at the Warsaw Conservatoire from 1932 to 1937. He began his career as a pianist, often playing in cafés in Warsaw, and later took up conducting and teaching throughout Europe and the United States. Outstanding among his early compositions was *Variations on a Theme of Paganini* (1941) for two pianos, which he arranged for orchestra in 1979. His early compositions were influenced by **Szymanowski** and Bartók, and under ideological pressure incorporated rhythmic and melodic elements from folk-music, culminating in the fine *Concerto for Orchestra* (1954), which displayed complete mastery of orchestral technique. This gave rare strength to his later development, when he turned to the **twelve-note** system.

In 1960 in *Venetian Games* he adopted **aleatory** methods as a subsidiary feature of his style, although he retained control over the texture and harmony. This method led to one of his finest and most influential works, *Livre pour Orchestre* (1968), first heard in the United Kingdom in 1972 under the direction of Bernard **Keeffe**. Other important works are the Cello Concerto (1970), *Mi-parti* (1976), *Novelette* (1980), Double Concerto for oboe and harp (1980), Symphony No.3 (1983), *Chain I* (1983) and *Chain II* (1985) for violin and orchestra. His vocal music includes the striking *Three Poems for Henri Michaux* for chorus, wind, two pianos, harp and percussion (1963), and *Paroles tissées* for tenor and 20 solo instruments (1965).

Lutosławski's imaginative expansion of new techniques, built on his mastery of traditional elements, makes him one of the outstanding composers of his time.

Lutyens, Elisabeth (1906-1983) English composer who studied in Paris and from 1926 to 1930 at the Royal College of Music. The romanticism of her early works such as *The Birthday of the Infanta*, a ballet first performed in 1932, was replaced in later years by the **serialism** of works such as Chamber Concerto No.1. The British musical establishment's inability to embrace the ideas of **Schoenberg** and **Webern** made it very hard for her to become accepted, even though pieces such as *O Saisons, O Châteaux* of 1946 showed her newly crystallized **dodecaphonic** system to the full.

Works throughout the 1940s and 1950s, such as the String Quartet No. 6, showed the growth in confidence of Lutyens's compositional techniques, but it was not until the 1960s that she was fully understood and accepted. Lutyens's work of the 1960s, such as *The Valley of Hatsu-Se* (1965), show a confident marriage of text and atmosphere. By the mid-1960s she had begun to pare down her compositions to an insistent simplicity. Lutyens's evocation of textual atmosphere is best illustrated by her increasing corpus of works commissioned for cinema and radio. In 1965 she wrote her first opera, *The Numbered*, and in 1969 was awarded a CBE.

Luxon, Benjamin (1937-) English baritone who, after studying at the Guildhall School of Music in London, made appearances with the English Opera Group, most notably as Owen Wingrave in Britten's television opera of that name in 1970. After a 1972 appearance at Glyndebourne in *Ulysses* he appeared at Covent Garden in *Taverner* and again in 1974 in *Eugene Onegin*. Also in 1974 Luxon made his début with the English National Opera and in 1977 appeared in the title-role of *Don Giovanni* at Glyndebourne. Luxon's recordings include many *Lieder*, folk and Victorian popular songs as well as opera.

Lyadov (Liadov), Anatol Konstantinovich (1855-1914) Russian teacher, conductor and composer. In 1870 he joined the Conservatoire of St Petersburg, where he excelled at the piano; he studied counterpoint with Johannsen and composition with **Rimsky-Korsakov**. By 1878 he was teaching there. Famous pupils included **Prokofiev**, **Stravinsky** and **Miaskovsky**. During the 1890s he made many concert appearances as a conductor and in 1897 published the first of several folk-song collections. Many of Lyadov's compositions owe much to traditional folk-songs, including works such as his *Eight Russian Folk-Songs* (1906). He had a reputation for indolence, confirmed by his failure to meet the commission from **Diaghilev** for the music to the ballet *The Firebird*, which eventually went to Stravinsky and made his reputation.

Lyapunov (Liapunov), Sergey Mikhailovich (1859-1924) Russian pianist and composer who attended the Moscow Conservatoire (1878-83), studying composition with **Tchaikovsky**. In 1884 Lyapunov went to St Petersburg, where he studied with **Balakirev**. Both of them were commissioned to collect traditional folk-songs. Lyapunov's compositions of the 1890s and 1900s owe much to his familiarity with these traditional songs. In 1894 Lyapunov replaced **Rimsky-Korsakov** as assistant director of the Imperial Chapel and in 1910 was appointed piano and theory tutor at St

Petersburg Conservatoire. In 1919 he emigrated to Paris after touring extensively as a conductor and concert pianist.

Lydian mode One of the ecclesiastical **modes**, represented by the scale beginning on F on the white notes of the piano keyboard. See also **mode**.

Lympany, Moura (1916-) English pianist who studied in Liège, at the Royal College of Music and with Matthay. She made her début in 1928, aged 12. Her reputation grew from the 1930s and 1940s, when she toured Europe extensively. She has made a special study of modern English music, performing works by **Arnell**, **Rawsthorne** and **Scott** among others; she has also established herself as a specialist in **Khachaturian**, **Rachmaninov** and other Russian composers. Her recordings include many Rachmaninov works.

lyre The most important instrument of ancient Greece and Egypt, the lyre was

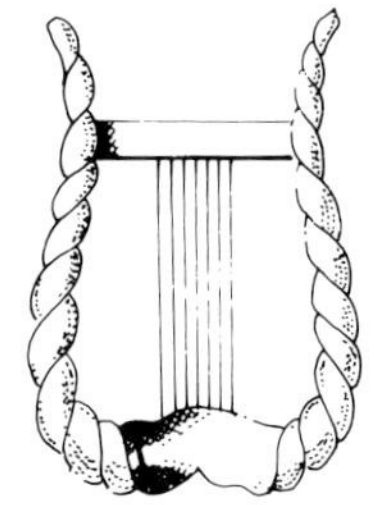

Lyre

depicted in Sumerian art around 3000 BC. The number of strings to the instrument varied. They were stretched on a framework with a hollow sound-box at the bottom and plucked by the fingertips of the left hand and a plectrum held in the right. See also **crwth**; **kithara**; **lira da braccio**.

M

Maazel, Lorin (1930-) French-born American conductor and violinist, who has often played concertos and directed the orchestra simultaneously. A child prodigy, he conducted at the New York World's Fair and the Hollywood Bowl at the age of only nine. He has held many important conducting posts around the world, including the Berlin Radio Orchestra (1965-75) and the Deutsche Oper, Berlin. From 1972 to 1982 he was musical director of the Cleveland Orchestra. In 1982 he became the first American to direct the Vienna Staatsoper, but resigned in 1988. Since 1986 he has been music director of the Pittsburgh Symphony Orchestra. His numerous recordings concentrate on the late 19th- and early 20th-century repertory: Dvořák, Rachmaninov, Strauss, Ravel, Zemlinsky, and a lively recording of a New Year's Day concert in Vienna of the Strauss family's works.

McCabe, John (1939-) British composer and pianist who trained at Manchester University before attending the Royal Manchester College of Music, studying composition under Pitfield. He also studied in Germany under **Genzmer**. His works include three symphonies, three piano concertos, a clarinet concerto, two violin concertos, *Notturni ed Alba* (1970), *Time Remembered* (1973), *Reflections of a Summer Night* (cantata, 1977), *Les soirs bleus* for soprano and small ensemble (1979), several ballets, chamber music, and piano and organ music. Recent important compositions are the *Concerto for Orchestra* (1982), *Fire at Durilgai* (1988), and *Cloudcatcher Fells* for brass (1985). As a performer his outstanding achievement was the recording of the sonatas of Haydn. He was appointed Principal of the London College of Music in 1983.

McCormack, John (Count) (1884-1945) Irish tenor who studied under **Sabatini**. He made his début at Covent Garden in 1907 as Turiddù in Mascagni's *Cavalleria rusticana* and confirmed his success later in the same season as Don Ottavio in *Don Giovanni* and as the Duke in *Rigoletto*. He spent some time in the United States, where he sang with the Boston Opera Company (1910-11) and with the Chicago Opera Company (1912-13). He returned to Ireland in 1924, and spent most of the rest of his career singing a more popular repertory and making recordings of ballads. He was made a Papal count in 1928.

MacDowell, Edward (1861-1908) American composer, pianist and teacher, who studied at the Paris Conservatoire, then at Wiesbaden, and finally under **Raff** at the Hoch Conservatoire, Frankfurt. After spending a year (1881-2) as the chief piano teacher at the conservatoire at Darmstadt, he was given the opportunity to perform his first piano concerto before Liszt, who was highly impressed. Subsequently he was invited to take part in the Allgemeiner Deutscher Musikverein in Zurich. In 1887 he returned to the United States and settled in Boston, making his first American appearance in 1888. Between 1896 and 1904 he was professor of music at Columbia University. He continued to teach while giving concerts and producing his two piano concertos. His other piano works include the *First Modern Suite* (1880-1), *Forest Idylls* (1884) and *Woodland Sketches* (1896).

McEwan, Sir John Blackwood (1868-1948) Scottish composer and educationist. From 1893 he studied in London at the Royal Academy of Music. He became a teacher at the Athenaeum School of Music in Glasgow but returned to the Royal Academy in 1898. He was principal of the Royal Academy of Music from 1924 to 1936. He wrote several valuable books on musical structure and phrasing. His compositions include *Grey Galloway* (1908), one of three 'border' ballads for orchestra, and a symphony, *Solway* (1911).

Macfarren, Sir George (1813-1887) Composer and teacher who entered the Royal Academy in 1829. Composition was his principal study, and in 1837 he was appointed a professor at the Academy, where he taught for ten years. In 1875 he became professor of music at Cambridge, and Principal of the Royal Academy of Music. He was a prolific composer, producing many sacred works, operas, nine symphonies and a piano concerto.

Machaut, Guillaume de (1300-1377) French poet and composer. At an early age Machaut took holy orders and studied theology, probably in Paris. He served as secretary to John of Luxembourg, King of Bohemia (1323-46), and later to King Charles V of France and John, Duke of Berry. Machaut is most famous for his ballades, rondeaux for two, three or four voices, his *lais* and *virelais* (mostly for one voice), his motets and his Notre Dame Mass. He was one of the chief composers of the **ars nova** style.

machine head Mechanism used for securing and adjusting the tension of strings for instruments such as the double-bass, guitar and mandolin. The strings are attached to spindles that pass through the pegbox parallel to the frets on the fingerboard. Worm gears are attached to the ends of the spindles, and these are rotated by matching worm gears at the end of the pegs. By turning the pegs, the strings can be tensioned.

McIntyre, Donald (1934-) New Zealand operatic bass-baritone who studied at the Guildhall School of Music and made his début with the Welsh National Opera in 1959. The following year he joined Sadler's Wells; in 1967 he appeared at Covent Garden as Pizarro in Beethoven's *Fidelio*, and thereafter sang a wide variety of roles such as Jochanaan in *Salome* and Orestes in *Elektra* (Strauss), Golaud in Debussy's *Pelléas et Mélisande*, Scarpia in Puccini's *Tosca*, Kaspar in Weber's *Der Freischütz* and many Wagnerian roles: Klingsor and Amfortas in *Parsifal*, the title-role in *Der fliegende Holländer* and, the part with which he is most associated, Wotan in the *Ring* cycle.

Mackenzie, Sir Alexander (1847-1935) Scottish composer and violinist who at the age of ten was sent to study music in Germany. He returned to England in 1862 and won the King's Scholarship for a place at the Royal Academy of Music. In 1885-6 Mackenzie conducted the Novello Oratorio concerts. In 1888 he succeeded Sir George **Macfarren** as Principal of the Academy. His works include operas, concertos for piano and violin, chamber music and songs.

Mackerras, Sir Charles (1925-) Australian conductor and oboist who studied at the New South Wales Conservatoire. He held the position of principal oboist for the Sydney Symphony Orchestra (1943-6) and studied in Prague with Vaclav Talich (1947-8). From 1966 to 1970 he conducted at the Hamburg State Opera, and from 1970 to 1978 he was musical director of Sadler's Wells Opera/ English National Opera. He joined the Welsh National Opera in 1987. He has taken a specialist interest in Czech music, particularly the operas of Janáček, which he has conducted and recorded with great success. His ballets *Pineapple Poll* (1951) and *The Lady and the Fool* (1954) were arrangements for the Sadler's Wells company based on the music of Sullivan and Verdi respectively. He received a CBE in 1974 and was knighted in 1979.

Maconchy, Elizabeth (1907-) English composer of Irish parentage, who studied at the Royal College of Music. Although a talented piano soloist, she is better known as a composer. Her 14 string quartets (1933-84) are seen as the central strength of her work. She has also written several stage works (*The Birds*, 1968; *The King of the Golden River*, 1975) and a symphony and has composed works for chorus (*Heloise and Abelard*), orchestra, and solo instruments (*Romanza* for viola and piano, 1979). She was made a CBE in 1977.

McPhee, Colin (1901-1964) American composer whose best-known work is the symphony *Tabuh-Tabuhan* (1936), strongly influenced by the **gamelan** percussion orchestras of Bali, where McPhee lived during the 1930s. His other well-known composition is *Sea Shanty Suite* (1929), for a chorus of male voices. Apart from being a composer and pianist, McPhee also wrote on a variety of subjects, including modern music, jazz and various aspects of Indonesian life.

Maderna, Bruno (1920-1973) Italian composer and conductor. He studied with **Malipiero** in Venice, and in Milan, Rome and Vienna. His début as a conductor was in 1950. He moved to Darmstadt in 1954, where he taught and conducted. He was admired as a conductor of contemporary music; he gave the premières of **Nono**'s *Intolleranza* (1960) and **Berio**'s *Passagio* (1963), as well as fine accounts of an older repertory ranging from Monteverdi to Mozart. In 1954 he and Berio founded the Milan Radio Electronic Studio. He taught at Milan, Dartington, Salzburg and Rotterdam, and was director of the Tanglewood Festival (1971-2). His early works reflect the influence of **serialism**, but by about the 1950s he had begun to find a more accessible and more Italianate musical language. His numerous works for tape include *Musica su due dimensioni* (1952), the first composition to combine live instruments with tape; *Continuo* (1958); and *Ages* (1972). He has also composed operas and incidental music for the stage (*Satyricon*, 1973, based on Petronius); orchestral pieces (a piano concerto, 1959; a violin concerto, 1969; three oboe concertos; *Quadrivium* for percussion and four instrumental groups, 1969); vocal, chamber and solo instrumental pieces. He has edited or arranged works by **Vivaldi**, **Monteverdi**, **Josquin**, **Gabrieli** and other early composers.

madrigal Form of poetry and music which originated in Italy during the 14th century. During the 16th century the use of the term broadened, largely because of the impact of Franco-Flemish **polyphony** and composers such as Jacques **Arcadelt**, Costanzo **Festa** and Philippe **Verdelot**.

In 1588 a collection of Italian madrigals was published with translated texts in London, and this paved the way for the English form of madrigal. It usually employed a five-voice texture set to texts on pastoral and amorous subjects. The most notable composers of English madrigals were Thomas **Morley**, Thomas **Weelkes** and John **Wilbye**.

There are three major forms of madrigal: the madrigal proper, the canzonet and the ballett. The true madrigal is **through-composed** and contrapuntal in texture. It differs from the **ayre** in that the latter repeats the tune for each verse and is less contrapuntal. The ballett is also in strophic form, but has a fa-la-la refrain, and may be used as an accompaniment to dancing. The canzonet is sectional and includes repeats.

An important collection of madrigals – *The Triumphs of Oriana* (1601) – was edited by Thomas Morley, and includes 29 English madrigals by various composers addressed to Queen Elizabeth I.

Maelzel, Johann Nepomuk (1772-1838) German inventor who is best known for perfecting and patenting the **metronome**. He also constructed an automatic instrument that manipulated trumpets, flutes, drums, cymbals, strings and a triangle. At one time he was a close associate of **Beethoven**, but they later disagreed over the rights of a battle-piece composed by Beethoven for Maelzel's panharmonicon, a similar instrument but with clarinets, violins and cellos added.

maestoso (It.) Majestically. Indication that the music is to be played in a stately manner.

maestro (It.) Master. Title given by Italians to a distinguished musician, whether a composer, performer or teacher. It is now sometimes used, especially in the United States, by musicians addressing a conductor.

maggiore (It.) In a major key. The word is sometimes stated at a point in a composition where the major key returns after a prolonged section in a minor key, especially in **variations**, to prevent the performer from overlooking the change of key.

Magnard, Albéric (1865-1914) French composer who studied law before entering the Paris Conservatoire and later becoming a pupil of **d'Indy**. The influence of **Franck** and d'Indy on him was at first considerable. His early works, however, were not successful; after the failure of his opera *Yolande* in 1892 he concentrated on formality and austerity in his music. His remaining works reveal the influences of Wagner on the one hand and Gluck on the other. He produced two further operas, *Guercoeur* and *Bérénice* (1909, based on Racine), four symphonies, a number of chamber pieces that are classical in form, and numerous songs.

Magnificat The hymn of the Virgin Mary, regularly sung as a Vesper canticle in the Roman Catholic Church and as part of the evening service in the Anglican Church. The title is from the Latin version of the opening words: *Magnificat anima mea Dominum* (My soul doth magnify the Lord).

Choral settings have been produced by such composers as Purcell, J.S. Bach, **Stanford**, **Howells**, Vaughan Williams and **Tippett**.

Mahler, Gustav (1860-1911) Austrian conductor and composer who studied at the conservatoire in Vienna from 1875 to 1878. His first appointment as a conductor was in 1880 at a little summer theatre in Bad Hall, where his duties included putting out the stands and wheeling the prima donna's baby round in the intervals. It was the first step in a sensational career as a conductor that in ten years took him to the peak of his profession as chief conductor in Budapest. Born to a Jewish

Gustav Mahler

family, he was received into the Catholic Church in 1897, perhaps with an eye to the coveted direction of the Vienna Opera, where over the next ten years he battled to create a legendary ensemble. In 1902 he married Alma Schindler, a musician, daughter of a well-known Austrian painter, by whom he had two daughters, one of whom died in 1907. That same year he resigned and in January 1908 he joined the Metropolitan Opera, New York, and later gave concerts with the New York Symphony Orchestra, before moving to the New York Philharmonic as chief conductor. By 1911 his health was failing, and he returned to Vienna where he died on 18 May.

Despite Mahler's fame as a conductor, it is less than certain that he would satisfy modern taste; he made many modifications to classical scores, and conducted with great freedom of tempo.

The earliest work to survive is the cantata *Das klagende Lied* (1880-98), to an original text. An unhappy love affair inspired the *Lieder eines fahrenden Gesellen* (Songs of a Wayfarer) based on a collection of German folk-poetry called *Des Knaben Wunderhorn* (The Youth's Magic Horn). This music pervades his first four symphonies, offering a curious contrast in scale. The five movements of Symphony No.2 (1884) require solo voices and chorus and a huge orchestra. The Symphony No.3 (1896) extends to six movements, and explores the mysteries of nature and the dilemma of human existence. Symphony No.4 (1900), once conceived as part of the third, is on a smaller scale, and concludes with a child's vision of heaven. No.5 (1902) and No.6 (1904) are purely instrumental symphonies, but even without a text they convey Mahler's struggles with his fear of death. Fate added to his misery, for having composed to poems by Rückert the cycle *Kindertotenlieder* (Songs on the Death of Children), he had to endure the loss in 1907 of his four-year-old daughter. No.7 is again purely instrumental, but No.8, 'the symphony of a thousand', demands many soloists, a huge mixed chorus and a boys' choir, and a gigantic orchestra. Mahler completed a ninth symphony (1909) and the six-movement setting for two soloists and orchestra of Chinese poetry, *Das Lied von der Erde* (1908), but died without hearing them in performance. Mahler's music made little headway during his lifetime; its huge scale presented practical difficulties which few would undertake – the exceptions being Bruno **Walter**, and especially Willem **Mengelberg** with the Amsterdam Concertgebouw Orchestra. With the coming of the Nazis, it disappeared from programmes in continental Europe, but enjoyed a remarkable revival in the 1950s. Some saw in Mahler the forerunner of Schoenberg and his school; long-playing records simplified listening, while conductors revelled in the challenge of his huge scores; but most of all audiences, often of the younger generation, responded to the emotional power of Mahler's music. His time had come.

makam See **maqam**

malagueña (Sp.) Andalusian song and dance (similar to the **fandango**) in triple time, which originated in Málaga. The form is also sometimes used for instrumental music.

Malcolm, George (1917-) English organist, harpsichord-player and conductor. He studied at the Royal College of Music and at Oxford. From 1947 to 1959 he was in charge of the choir at Westminster Cathedral, and under his aegis its reputation was enhanced. He has conducted many famous orchestras and smaller ensembles, but it is as a harpsichordist that he has become best known. His recordings of the Scarlatti sonatas, Bach and Handel suites and earlier music reveal his dazzling technique and polished style.

Małcuzyński, Witold (1914-1977) Argentinian pianist of Polish origin who studied in Warsaw and with **Paderewski**.

After winning a prize in the Chopin Competition in 1937 he moved to France and made his Paris début in 1940. His repertory was mostly drawn from the great Romantic masters, and he was a supreme exponent of Chopin's music.

Malibran, Maria (1808-1836) Spanish mezzo-soprano, daughter of Manuel **García**. She sang in public as a child, but her adult début was in London in 1825 as Rosina in *Il barbiere di Siviglia*. She performed often with her father's company, travelling with it to New York where she sang many Rossini roles. Her Paris début in 1828 in *Semiramide* was the first of many triumphant appearances there, in Italy and again in London. She created the title-role in Donizetti's *Maria Stuarda* (1835) in Milan; her other great roles included Leonore in *Fidelio*, Amina in *La sonnambula* and the title-role in *Norma*. She died in Manchester as the result of a riding accident.

Malipiero, Gian Francesco (1882-1973) Italian composer and violinist. He studied in Vienna, Venice and Paris. In 1921 he was appointed professor of composition at the Parma Conservatoire. He was later appointed to posts in Padua and Venice. He composed operas, including *Venere prigioniera* (1955), 11 sinfonias and three sets of *Impressioni dal vero* (1910-22). He also composed ballet music, other choral and orchestral works, chamber music, pieces for piano, violin and piano works and songs.

Malipiero, Riccardo (1914-) Italian composer and critic, nephew of Gian Francesco **Malipiero**. A strict adherent of the **twelve-note** technique, his works in this mode include the opera *Minnie la Candida* (1942), *Cantata sacra* (1947) for solo voices, chorus and orchestra, a symphony (1949) and other works for string quartet, piano and chorus.

mandola Small stringed instrument of the lute family which is now obsolete. It originated during the Middle Ages in Italy, and in the 18th century was replaced by the **mandolin**. An alternative term is mandora.

Mandola

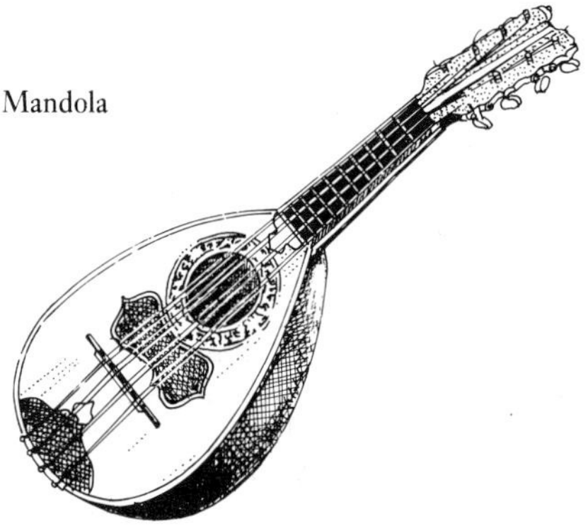

Mandolin

mandolin Stringed instrument related to the **lute** which evolved from the **mandola** in Italy during the 18th century. It has a more rounded back than a lute, and has four pairs of wire strings tuned like the violin and played with a plectrum. The fingerboard is fretted to facilitate fingering and **intonation**. Beethoven, Mozart and Mahler composed music for the instrument. An alternative spelling is mandoline.

mandora Alternative term for **mandola**.

Manfredini, Francesco Maria (1684-1762) Italian violinist and composer who studied under **Torelli** and **Perti**. In 1711 he became *maestro di cappella* in Monaco, and in 1727 at the cathedral in Pistoia. His most celebrated works are the six oratorios, but he also composed sinfonias, concertos, concerti grossi and chamber music.

Manfredini, Vincenzo (1737-1799) Italian composer, son of Francesco. He studied under **Perti** in Bologna and Fioroni in Milan. He became court composer in Russia, where he taught Tsar Paul I. His works include several operas, cantatas, a Requiem, ballets and harpsichord sonatas.

Manns, Sir August (1825-1907) German bandmaster and conductor. In 1855 he was engaged as a clarinettist in the orchestra of the newly erected Crystal Palace. When the conductor advertised one of Manns's compositions as his own, he was sacked and George Grove, who managed affairs at the Palace, appointed Manns in his place. The orchestra was for a while the only permanent orchestra in the country, and over the next 50 years Manns and Grove made the Crystal Palace Saturday afternoon concerts the most important regular orchestral activity in the London area. Manns reached a standard that allowed performance of the most difficult music of the day. As well as introducing new British works, he kept in touch with the latest works from abroad. Leading composers such as Gounod, Saint-Saëns and Dvořák came to conduct their music, and soloists of the calibre of Clara **Schumann** were glad to appear. Manns also conducted the mammoth Handel Festivals, though he was reckoned to be less successful with choirs. He was knighted in 1903.

manual Keyboard played with the hands; it refers especially to the keyboards of organs and harpsichords as distinct from the pedals.

maqam/makam (pl. **maqamat**) Technical term used throughout the Near and Middle East to mean mode or melody type. Its precise definition depends on the particular performing tradition concerned. In Iran it refers to the scale type, or mode, in which particular tunes or *gusheh* are cast, according to the Persian **dastgah** system. In Iraq, *maqamat* are modes defined more precisely, constituting a melodic entity subject to vocal or instrumental improvisation. Among Arab peoples, *maqam* in common usage refers also to performances of such forms.

maracas Percussion instrument used mainly in jazz and swing bands. It is a double rattle made of dried gourds containing beads or seeds, although the modern variety is often made of plastic and contains lead shot.

Marais, Marin (1656-1728) French composer and viol player. He studied the viola da **gamba** under Sainte-Colombe and was employed as a musician in the Royal chamber from 1679. He also studied composition under **Lully** and wrote four operas, including *Alcione* (1706), chamber music and compositions for the bass viol.

Marcello, Alessandro (1684-1750) Italian philosopher, mathematician, singer and composer. His published works include 12 solo cantatas, 12 sonatas for violin and continuo, six concertos for two flutes or violins and other concertos.

Marcello, Benedetto (1686-1739) Italian composer and theorist, brother of Alessandro **Marcello**. A former lawyer who studied music under **Lotti** and **Gasparini**, he began learning the violin but soon devoted his time to vocal music and composition. In 1712 he joined the *Accademia filarmonica* in Bologna. Apart from his best-known work, *Estro poetico-armonico* (settings for two parts of 25 psalms paraphrased by Giustiniani), he also composed more than 400 cantatas, several oratorios, concertos and sonatas.

march Piece of music with a regular rhythm in 4/4, 2/4 or 6/8, primarily intended to accompany groups in procession or on the march. Some of the most notable composers, from Purcell to Stravinsky, have written splendid marches: sometimes for theatrical use, as in Mozart's *Die Zauberflöte*, Beethoven's *Fidelio*, Verdi's *Aïda*, and Stravinsky's *The Soldier's Tale*;

sometimes for military purposes, such as those by Haydn, Beethoven, Wagner, **Roussel** and **Sousa**; others have treated the march as an evocative musical form – Beethoven in piano sonatas and symphonies, Schubert and Schumann in piano music, and Elgar in his five splendid concert pieces with the title *Pomp and Circumstance.*

Marchand, Louis (1669-1732) French organist, harpsichordist and composer. At the age of 14 he was appointed organist at Nevers Cathedral and in 1693 at Auxerre Cathedral. He settled in Paris in 1698 and by 1702 he was organist in three Parisian churches; in 1708 he became court organist. Apart from his works for organ, including the *Grand dialogue* and *Livre d'orgue*, he wrote harpsichord music, a collection of airs and a cantata.

Marenzio, Luca (1553-1599) Italian composer. It is uncertain where he studied, but it is likely that he was a member of the cathedral choir in Brescia. In 1574 he moved to Rome, where his most notable patrons were Cardinal Luigi d'Este and Virginio Orsini. Between 1596 and 1598 he was *maestro di cappella* to the King of Poland. Marenzio is noted mainly for his five- and six-voice madrigals, which number well over 200 and were published in Venice between 1580 and 1599. He published further books of madrigals for three and four voices, a book of twelve-part motets, and a complete series of motets for all church festivals.

marimba A tuned percussion instrument similar to the **xylophone**, but with shallower wooden bars. The compass is usually three to three and a half octaves, though larger models have been made, with an extended compass, which are then known as xylorimba or marimba-xylophone. It is usually played with softer beaters than the xylophone to produce the characteristic mellow tone. Most models have a damping or sustaining pedal. The marimba has often been used by modern

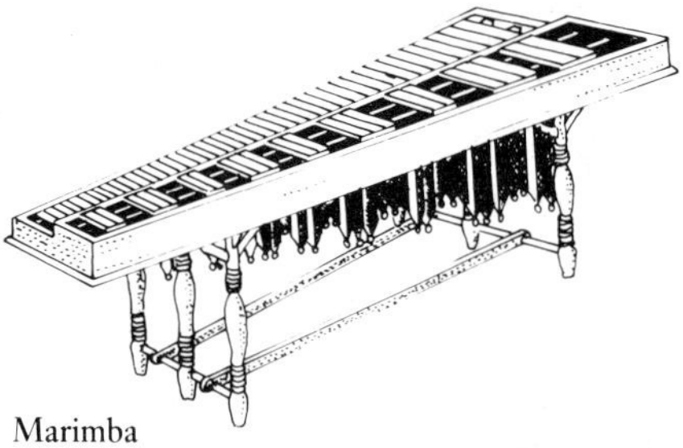
Marimba

composers: there is a concerto for marimba and vibraphone by **Milhaud**, and it is found in scores by Berg, Stravinsky and **Dallapiccola**. It is also used with great effect in popular music, especially in Latin-American bands. There is even a marimba band in the United States.

Markevich, Igor (1912-1983) Soviet conductor and composer. In 1927 he settled in Paris and studied under Nadia **Boulanger**. His compositions were at first greatly influenced by Stravinsky but later he found a more personal style. Markevich's works comprise a sinfonietta, a concerto for piano and orchestra, a cantata for soprano and male-voice choir, a serenade, a psalm and a partita. He has also written two ballets, *Rébus* (1931) and *L'envoi d'Icare* (1932). After 1945 he concentrated more on conducting, and as well as several major American orchestras he has conducted the Lamoureux Orchestra, Paris (1957-61), and the Monte Carlo Opera (1968-73).

Marpurg, Friedrich Wilhelm (1718-1795) German musical theorist and critic. He is noted for his unbounded admiration for **J.S. Bach**, whom he met in Leipzig shortly before the latter's death in 1750. Marpurg wrote a preface to an edition of *The Art of Fugue*, which appeared in 1752, and recommended Bach's contrapuntal techniques in his famous treatise on the fugue, *Abhandlung von der Fuge* (1753-4). He also introduced the musical theories of the French composer **Rameau** to Germany.

Sir Neville Marriner

Marriner, Sir Neville (1924-) British conductor and violinist. He studied at the Royal College of Music, and played with the Philharmonia and London Symphony Orchestras. In 1959 he founded the **Academy of St Martin-in-the-Fields** and remained its director until 1978, when he became conductor of the Minnesota Orchestra (until 1986). In 1969 he took up the position of conductor to the Los Angeles Chamber Orchestra. With the Academy he made numerous fine recordings of Bach, Handel, Haydn, Schubert (all the symphonies) and Mozart (all the symphonies and piano concertos); he has also recorded with other orchestras in Europe and the United States.

Marschner, Heinrich August (1795-1861) German composer and conductor, who studied under Schicht in Leipzig. In 1823, after a successful production of his opera *Heinrich IV und Aubigné*, produced by Weber three years earlier, he was appointed joint *Kapellmeister* of the Italian and German Opera in Dresden, and a year later he advanced to *Musikdirektor*. However, by 1827 he had settled in Leipzig as *Kapellmeister* of the theatre. From 1831 to 1859 he was conductor of the Hanover Hoftheater. He wrote a total of 13 operas, including *Der Vampyr*, *Der Templer und die Jüdin* and *Hans Heiling* (1832). He also wrote a ballet and incidental music, two symphonies, chamber music, piano music, more than 120 choral pieces for male voices and over 420 songs.

martenot Electrophonic device (an early form of **synthesizer**) invented by Maurice Martenot in 1929. It is more commonly known as *ondes martenot* and is operated by a piano-type keyboard; it is an electronic device using thermionic-valve oscillators to produce sound through loudspeakers. The instrument was used by **Honegger** in *Jeanne d'Arc au bûcher* (1938). It has also been incorporated into works by **Boulez** and **Messiaen**.

Martin, Frank (1890-1974) Swiss composer. He studied in Geneva under Joseph Lauber, and later in Rome, Zurich and Paris. In 1911, at the Swiss Music Festival, Martin made his first appearance as a composer with a performance of his *Trois poèmes payens*. His early compositions show a strong French influence, but he later developed his own brand of **serialism** with a tonal flavour in the harmony. He was first brought to general notice by his remarkable concert drama *Le vin herbé* (1938-41), a treatment of the Tristan legend for 12 solo voices, seven strings and piano. His settings of six monologues from *Jedermann* for baritone and piano, later orchestrated, placed him in the forefront of contemporary composers. Other works which have won international recognition include *Petite symphonie concertante* for harp, harpsichord, piano and strings, the *Concerto* for seven wind instruments and strings, settings of the poetry of Rilke in *Der Cornet*, an opera based on Shakespeare's *The Tempest*, and the oratorios *In terra pax* and *Golgotha*. He was the leading Swiss composer of his time.

Martini, Giovanni Battista (1706-1784) Italian composer, theorist and teacher, called Padre Martini. Although an important composer in his own right, his reputation as a teacher was such that J.C. Bach, Mozart, **Sarti**, Ottani and many others came to study under him. Martini learned singing and harpsichord under Predieri and counterpoint from Riccieri and **Perti**. In 1725 he became *maestro di cappella* of the church of San Francesco, Bologna, where he was also a priest. Apart from his contrapuntal sacred works, he also composed ensemble works, sinfonias, concertos, keyboard music and *intermezzi*.

Martini il Tedesco (1741-1816) Nickname of Johann Paul Aegidius Schwarzendorf, a German composer, organist and teacher. He moved to France in the mid-18th century and settled in Paris in 1764. In 1798 he became an inspector of the Conservatoire and in 1814 director of the court orchestra. His works include military music, symphonies, operas, cantatas, Masses and the song *Plaisir d'amour*.

Martinon, Jean (1910-1976) French conductor, composer and violinist. He studied at the conservatoires in Lyons and Paris. From 1951 to 1957 he conducted the Lamoureux Orchestra, and from 1963 to 1969 the Chicago Symphony Orchestra. His compositions include four symphonies and four concertos.

Martinů, Bohuslav (1890-1959) Czech violinist and composer. He studied at the Prague Conservatoire with **Suk**; he was a member of the Czech Philharmonic Orchestra from 1916 to 1923, when he moved to Paris to study with **Roussel**. There the influence of Stravinsky and Les **Six** transformed him from a gifted provincial rooted in folk-music to a cosmopolitan composer with an unmistakable individual personality. He first reflected the brittle jazzy fashions of the time with such works as *Half-time* (1925), *La bagarre* (1927), and *Revue de cuisine* (1927). He then turned to neo-classical forms and developed a dynamic rhythmic idiom in his *Concerto Grosso* (1938) and in one of his finest works, the powerful *Concerto for Double String Orchestra* (1938). In 1941 Martinů moved to America, and embarked on a series of six symphonies and other major orchestral works that have since taken their place in the repertory. In 1953 he finally returned to Europe. Martinů was prolific in every field: he composed seven string quartets, six piano concertos, and many other smaller orchestral and chamber works. Of his seven operas, *Julietta* (1938) and *The Greek Passion* (1959) have merited most attention, while the oratorio *The Epic of Gilgamesh* and the unusual *Field Mass* are frequently heard. It has, however, been suggested that if Martinů had been more self-critical he might have produced fewer works, but more consistently at the level of the best.

Martin y Soler, Vicente (1754-1806) Spanish composer. He began his career as an organist in Alicante, but soon turned to the composition of operas. By 1785, when he went to Vienna, he was well established and worked with Da Ponte, producing three operas including *Una cosa rara* (1786). In 1788 Martin travelled to St Petersburg; there he was later to become court conductor to Catherine II. In 1798, after a brief visit to London where he produced two more operas with Da Ponte, he returned to Russia; Tsar Paul I nominated him Privy Councillor. His works include operas, ballets, songs and cantatas.

Martucci, Giuseppe (1856-1909) Italian conductor, pianist and composer. He was born in Capua and studied at the Naples Conservatoire, later becoming professor of piano and director (1886). He conducted the first performance in Italy of Wagner's *Tristan und Isolde* (1888) and introduced symphonic works to the narrow Italian concert repertory. His compositions include two symphonies, a piano concerto and much chamber and piano music. He was labelled 'the Italian Brahms' for the high quality of his symphonic output and its evident debt to German models. His music was greatly admired by **Toscanini**, who retained it in his programmes throughout his American career.

mārvā/mārwā (India) One of the ten parent scales (**thāt**) in Hindustani music, corresponding to C, D♭, E, F♯, G, A, B, C′.

Marx, Joseph (1882-1964) Austrian composer, critic and teacher. In 1914 he was awarded a professorship in musical theory at the Imperial Music Academy in Vienna. From 1924 to 1927 he was principal of the Vienna Hochschule. Marx is best known for his 120 songs, many of high quality.

marziale (It.) In a martial or warlike fashion.

Mascagni, Pietro (1863-1945) Italian composer and conductor who studied at the Milan Conservatoire with **Ponchielli** until after two years he was dismissed for indolence. He earned his living as a double-bass player and conductor; then in 1890 his wife submitted his opera *Cavalleria rusticana* to a competition organized by the publisher Sonzogno. It won a prize and with its violent emotional story of Sicilian feuds found a permanent place in the repertory of every opera house, with its indissoluble twin, **Leoncavallo**'s *I Pagliacci*. Other Mascagni operas in the **verismo** style are still occasionally remembered, chiefly for attractive arias: *L'amico Fritz* (1891), *Iris* (1898), *Isabeau* (1911) and *Nerone* (1935). Mascagni never recovered from the success of *Cavalleria rusticana* and the unfulfilled expectations it aroused. He became official composer to Mussolini and drifted into disgrace and oblivion.

mask, maske Alternative spellings of **masque**.

Mason, Lowell (1792-1872) American composer, educationist and conductor. He composed, with the help of F. L. Abel, a collection of hymns based on Gardiner's *Sacred Melodies*, which subsequently became popular throughout the United States. In 1832 he established the Boston Academy of Music, and by 1838 he had obtained the mandate to teach in every school in Boston, leading to the introduction of music as part of the school curriculum. He published a large number of educational manuals and travelled widely in the United States and Europe, lecturing on educational methods. He also composed glees, children's songs and musical exercises.

Mason, Luther Whiting (1818-1896) American musician, entirely self-taught, who became superintendent of music in schools in Cincinnati, and later Boston. After Commodore Perry forced the opening of Japan in 1854, Mason was invited to introduce Western music into Japanese schools. Through his efforts Western music was eagerly taken up, especially songs – foreign visitors are still surprised to hear children singing Japanese words to such familiar tunes as *Sur le pont d'Avignon*, *Auld lang syne* and *Home, Sweet Home*, which are still known as 'Mason-songs'.

masque Stage entertainment cultivated for court occasions in England during the 17th century, but which originated in the Italian *intermedio* and the French ballet. The masque may be said to be the English form closest to Italian opera at this time. It involved the recital of poetry, singing, dancing and spectacle. The subject matter upon which the masque was based was mainly mythological, heroic or allegorical.

One of the most famous masques of the era is *Comus*, with words by John Milton and music by Henry **Lawes**. A second, Thomas **Arne**'s *Alfred* (1740), includes *Rule, Britannia!* Other writers of music for masque include **Campion** and Lanier.

In the 20th century, the term has been applied to pieces such as *The Crown of India* by **Elgar** (1912) and *Job, A Masque for Dancing* by **Vaughan Williams** (1931). Alternative spellings of the term are mask and maske.

Mass The most important part of the Roman Catholic liturgy, with the celebration of the Eucharist. The form of the Mass was established in the 6th century under Gregory the Great; although in Latin, it retains in the *Kyrie* a Greek section derived from the Eastern rite. The Mass is formed from two elements, interwoven in its celebration: the Proper, which varies according to the day, consists of the *Introit, Gradual, Offertory* and *Communion* and is sung, by rule, to **plainchant**; the Ordinary, or common of the Mass, for the congregation, unchanged throughout the year, consists of *Kyrie* (Lord have mercy), *Gloria* (Glory be to God), *Credo* (I believe), *Sanctus* (Holy, Holy, Holy), *Benedictus* (Blessed is he who cometh in the name of the Lord) and *Agnus Dei* (Lamb of God). Both parts were originally sung to the purely melodic Gregorian Chant. In the 12th and 13th centuries, Western Europe took the first steps towards the combination of melodies and musical form in settings of the Ordinary of the Mass, which led to the great **polyphonic** schools of composition, led by **Machaut** (1300-77) in France. From then until recently the priest sought to constrain the exuberance of the composer within a spiritual dimension; when **Dufay**, and later **Taverner**, **Fayrfax**, **Sheppard**, **Tye**, **Lassus** and others introduced secular tunes to their Masses, the Council of Trent in 1572 forbade their use. The polyphonic period reached its peak in the work of **Palestrina** (94 Masses), and other great Italian and Flemish composers. Unfortunately this also coincided with the Reformation, which in England disturbed the masterly school of composition led by William **Byrd**, whose three Masses are a glory of English music.

With the development of opera and instrumental music in the 17th century, settings of the Mass soon took on a secular flavour, musically often magnificent, but without the devotional spirit of polyphony. **J.S. Bach**'s Masses were settings of the Lutheran Mass cantatas, and unacceptable in the Roman rite. In the 18th and early 19th centuries the great Viennese school headed by **Haydn**, **Mozart** and **Beethoven** wrote music that could equally well have been performed in the theatre, with florid solos and a large orchestra. **Schubert**, who had been a choirboy in the Court Chapel, perpetuated this style, though curiously he always omitted from the text of the *Credo* the words 'I believe in the Holy Catholic Church' – which, strictly speaking, rendered his Masses liturgically unacceptable. The Viennese masters at least produced great music, but their successors, second-rate Romantics, turned the Mass into an empty secular concert.

The first steps of reform came in the 1860s with the formation in Germany of the *Cäcilienverein*, with the aim of introducing more suitable music. Masses by Palestrina and Lassus were published, albeit in poor editions; in 1869 a guide to plainchant was issued from Ratisbon (Regensburg), though it too incorporated many errors of notation and rhythm, later corrected in the authoritative Solesme editions. Bruckner matched this spirit with his fine settings of the Mass, although he still retained the instrumental accompaniment.

In England until 1829 it was illegal to sing the Mass in public, and thereafter the Viennese style held sway. The great music of the English polyphonic schools was virtually forgotten until revived by Sir Richard **Terry**, first at Downside Abbey and later at Westminster Cathedral. In 1899 he directed the first performance of Byrd's five-part Mass since the Reformation, and revealed the neglected glories of English church music. In 1903, Pope Pius X issued the encyclical *Motu proprio*, which reaffirmed the Church's insistence that its music should express and serve the spirit of the liturgy, excluding the Viennese style with its meaningless verbal repetitions and elaborate orchestral accompaniment. The reform was slow to work in continental Europe, but under Terry's guidance many English composers produced settings of the Mass suitable for the new dispensation – notably **Stanford**, **Vaughan Williams**, Herbert **Howells** and Charles **Wood**. Other notable settings in this century have been by **Stravinsky**, Frank **Martin**, **Britten** (for boys' voices), **Berkeley**, and **Messiaen** (for eight sopranos and four violins).

Massenet, Jules (1842-1912) French composer and teacher who entered the Paris Conservatoire at the age of 11 and studied under Laurent, Reber and Ambroise **Thomas**. In 1863 he won the Prix de Rome with a cantata, *David Rizzio*. His first opera, *La grand' tante*, was produced in 1867 at the Opéra-Comique, and in the same year his first orchestral suite was performed. In 1878 he was appointed professor of advanced composition at the Conservatoire, where **Bruneau**, Leroux, Pierne and **Charpentier** were among his pupils. Massenet had his first major success in 1877 with *Le roi de Lahore*, and thereafter dominated French opera with a series of charming works. He had a gift for melody, a masterly orchestral style, and an unerring eye for stories such as *Manon* (1884), *Thaïs* (1894) and *Sapho* (1897), exhibiting female characters of dubious morals and revealing costume, whose charms attracted the men and whose downfall reassured the women in his audience. In a more serious vein, *Werther* (1892), *Le jongleur de Notre-Dame*, with an all-male cast (1902), and especially *Thérèse* (1907) reveal a composer of considerable dramatic depth. If Massenet had been less concerned with success (he often visited the box-office to check the takings), and had developed his undoubted theatrical instinct, he might have won a place in the repertory for others of his 24 operas than the sole survivors, *Manon* and *Werther*. His effective *Scènes* for orchestra are attractive and often figure in programmes of light music.

Master of the King's (Queen's) Music(k) Office first created in 1626 under King Charles I. The Master was in charge of the entire royal musical establishment, both the choral and instrumental personnel. The first man to hold the post was Nicholas Lanier. The Master's main function to begin with was to direct the musicians on ceremonial occasions; from about 1700 he was required to compose odes to mark particular events such as royal birthdays. Between the late 18th century and the reign of George V the number of musicians was fixed at 24; there have been none since the accession of George VI in 1937. The duties of the Master are now more or less nominal, and the title is given as an honour to a leading musician of the day. Eminent holders have included **Boyce**, **Stanley**, **Elgar**, **Bax**, **Bliss** and (from 1975) Malcolm **Williamson**.

Masterson, Valerie (1937-) English soprano. She studied in Liverpool, at the Royal College of Music and in Milan and made her début in Salzburg as Nannetta in Verdi's *Falstaff*. In 1966 she joined the D'Oyly Carte company. She became a member of the English National Opera (then Sadler's Wells) in 1970, where her high, clear tone and charming manner established her as a great favourite in such roles as Pamina (*Die Zauberflöte*), Violetta (*La traviata*) and Constanze (*Die Entführung aus dem Serail*). She has been particularly successful in the French repertory (the title-role in Massenet's *Manon*; Marguerite in Gounod's *Faust*) and in Handel (Cleopatra in *Julius Caesar*; the title-role in *Semele*, which she sang at Covent Garden in 1982).

Masur, Kurt (1928-) German conductor who studied in Breslau and at the Leipzig Conservatoire. He held posts in Halle, Erfurt and Leipzig before being appointed conductor of the Dresden Philharmonic Orchestra in 1955. Two years at the theatre in Schwerin were followed by the post of musical director at the Berlin Komische Oper (1960-4). During a further five years in Dresden (1967-72) he became music director of the Leipzig Gewandhaus Orchestra (1970), where he was distinguished for his dynamic, carefully prepared readings of Beethoven, Schumann, Bruckner and Mendelssohn. In 1990 he was appointed music director of the New York Philharmonic Orchestra with effect from 1992.

Mather, Bruce (1939-) Canadian composer and pianist who studied under **Beckwith** at the Toronto Royal Conservatoire and under **Messiaen** and **Milhaud** in Paris. In 1966 he became a teacher of composition at McGill University in Montreal. His works include *Cycle Rilke* (1960) for tenor and guitar, *Ombres* (1967) for orchestra, a sonata for two pianos (1970), a wind quintet (1975) and *Au château de Pompairain* for mezzo and orchestra (1977).

Mathias, William (1934-) Welsh composer and pianist who trained in Aberystwyth and then at the Royal Academy of Music, where he studied composition under Lennox **Berkeley**. From 1959 he was a lecturer and professor of music at Bangor University. His works include pieces for orchestra, concertos, chamber music (two string quartets, 1968 and 1982), choral and church music, and the opera *The Servants* (1980).

mātrā (India) Smallest metrical unit in Indian music, grouped in **tālās** or rhythmic cycles.

Matsudaira, Yoritsune (1907-) Japanese composer who studied under **Tcherepnin**. His style combines **serial** procedures with Japanese traditional music. His works include two piano concertos (1946), *Ancient Japanese Dance* (1953), *Portrait B* (1968) and *Circulating Movements* (1972).

Mattheson, Johann (1681-1764) German singer, theorist and composer. He studied music in Hamburg and made his first appearance in 1696 with the Hamburg Opera. In 1699 his first opera, *Die Plejades*, was produced soon after he met **Handel**, who arrived in Hamburg in 1703, and they worked together on several operas. In 1719 the Duke of Holstein appointed Mattheson as court *Kapellmeister*. His works include many oratorios and cantatas, eight operas, sonatas for flute and violin and suites for clavier. He also wrote several books, including some on the subject of the state of music in Hamburg, a collection of biographies of contemporary musicians and theoretical works, including *Das neu-eröffnete Orchester* (1713), *Exemplarische Organisten-Probe* (1719) and *Der vollkommene Kapellmeister* (1739).

Matthews, Colin (1946-) English composer who studied at Nottingham under Whittall and **Maw**; brother of David **Matthews**. In 1960 he helped Deryck Cooke to prepare a performing version of Mahler's Symphony No.10 which, while it cannot be regarded as definitive, was well received and was published in 1976. Matthews assisted **Britten** in his later years. His works for orchestra, some in an **atonal** style, include sonatas (*Fourth Sonata*, 1975), *Night Music* (1977) and a cello concerto (1984). He has also written two string quartets (1979, 1982), a wind quintet, a partita for violin (1975), piano studies and a musical narrative, *The Great Journey* (1988). He was the featured composer at the 1990 **Bath Festival**, at which his new work *Five Concertinos* was performed; commissioned by the Ensemble InterContemporain, it was dedicated to Henri **Dutilleux**.

Matthews, David (1943-) English composer, brother of Colin **Matthews**; he studied at Nottingham and, like his brother, was an assistant to **Britten** in the late 1960s and also collaborated with Cooke on the Mahler Symphony No.10. His music, some of which is in a **serial** manner, has been influenced by Schoenberg and the style of the Second Viennese School; he has also learnt much from Britten and **Tippett**. His orchestral works include three symphonies; he has also written chamber music such as *Variations for Strings* (1986) and several string quartets. His orchestral piece *In the Darktime* (1985) was commissioned by the BBC. With his brother he has also helped to orchestrate much of the music of Carl **Davis**.

Matthews, Denis (1919-1989) English pianist. In 1935 he entered the Royal Academy of Music and studied under Craxton and **Alwyn**. He held the Thalberg Scholarship for two years and the Blumenthal Scholarship for three. He first appeared in London in 1939. He played in the RAF orchestra during World War II and in 1945 with the Royal Philharmonic Society. Although he had a wide repertory, he specialized in the classics, particularly Mozart and Beethoven. He became a professor of music at Newcastle University in 1971.

Maw, Nicholas (1935-) English composer who entered the Royal Academy of Music in 1955, where he studied with **Berkeley**. From 1958 to 1959 he studied in Paris under Nadia **Boulanger** and Deutsch, and has also taught, both in Britain and in the United States. His music combines contemporary **serial** procedures with traditional forms and outlook. His works include two operas, *One-Man Show* (1964) and *The Rising of the Moon* (1969), orchestral pieces including *Sinfonia* (1966), *Sonata* (1967) and *Odyssey* (1987), chamber music and songs. He has been influenced by the English school, including Britten and Tippett, as well as by Strauss and Bartók, and his music is vigorously tonal.

Maxwell Davies, Peter See **Davies, Peter Maxwell**

Mayr, (Johannes) Simon (1763-1845) German opera and church-music composer who worked in northern Italy. Born in Mendorf, Bavaria, he went to study in Bergamo and Venice, where his oratorios proved popular. *Saffo*, the first of his 67 operas, was staged in 1794. In 1802 he became *maestro di cappella* at the church of S. Maria Maggiore in Bergamo. He turned the choir school there into a proper music school, the ancestor of the city's conservatoire, and taught counterpoint, one of his pupils being **Donizetti**. In his later years, faced with the dazzling talent of **Rossini**, he gave up composing opera in favour of church music. Many of his operas use classical themes, such as *Il ritorno di Ulisse* and *Medea in Corinto*. His *Amor congiugale*, however, uses the same story-line as Beethoven's *Fidelio*.

Mayuzumi, Toshiro (1929-) Japanese composer who studied in Tokyo and at the Paris Conservatoire. His works combine Japanese sources with avant-garde Western methods. He was the first Japanese composer to produce *musique concrète* and electronic music (1955). His best-known pieces are the symphonies *Bacchanale* (1953) and *Mandala* (1960). He has also written an opera (*Kinkakuji*, 1976), several ballets, orchestral music (*Aria on a G-string* for violin and orchestra, 1978), choral, chamber and tape works, incidental music for the theatre and for films.

mazurka Polish national dance dating back to the 17th century and originating in the Mazovia region around Warsaw. The dance-figures are complicated and subject to much variation. They are performed to improvised music. Groups of four, eight or twelve couples perform the mazurka, and the music is in moderately fast 3/4 time. **Chopin** composed 55 mazurkas for piano, which not only illustrate his pianistic virtuosity, but also reflect the many possible moods and speeds of the dance.

mbira (Africa) African keyboard instrument – a tuned idiophone consisting of a sounding-board supporting wooden or metal keys over a resonator. The keys are plucked in syncopated stratified rhythms, typical of African musical systems.

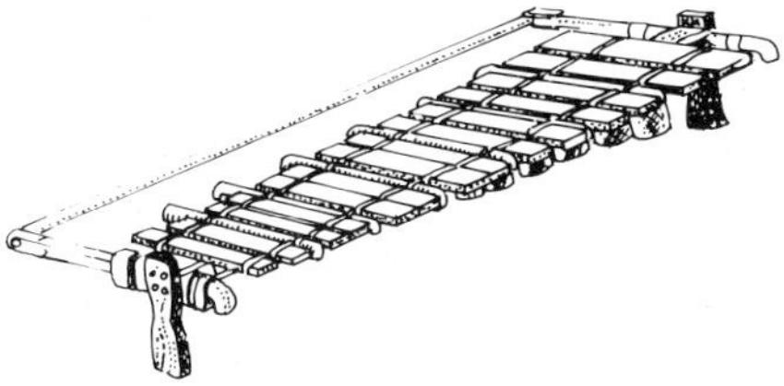

Mbira

Meale, Richard (1932-) Australian composer who studied piano at the New South Wales Conservatorium but is self-taught in composition. He worked as a planner for Australian radio concerts and was a lecturer at Adelaide University, becoming involved in the promotion of modern music. His works reveal the influence of **Messiaen** and **Boulez** (*Orenda* for piano, 1963), Spanish culture (*Homage to Lorca*, 1963), and Oriental music (*Images/Nagauta*, 1965; *Soon It Will Die*, 1969). He has written incidental music for the theatre, an opera (*Juliet's Memoirs*, 1975), a string quartet and various other works for small ensemble.

mean-tone temperament Method of 'tuning' an organ so that the major third intervals are as accurate as possible, making the **temperament** of six major keys and three minor keys reasonable. All other intervals are adapted to the major third intervals.

measure 1. In US terminology, what the British call the bar, that is, the space and time between one bar-line and the next. Also applied to the bar-line, which the Americans call the bar.
2. In earlier usage, a stately dance.

mediant Third degree of the major or minor **scale**, so called because it stands half-way between **tonic** and **dominant**.

Medtner, Nikolay (1880-1951) Russian composer and pianist. In 1892 he joined the Moscow Conservatoire and studied the piano under Pabst, Sapellnikov and Safonov and theory under **Arensky** and **Taneyev**. His career took him to Germany, the United States, France, Canada and finally England. He was greatly helped by the patronage of the Maharajah of Mysore, who paid for a substantial programme of recording.

Medtner is known mainly for his compositions for piano, particularly the sonatas; however, he also wrote three piano concertos, some chamber music and a large number of works for voice and piano.

Zubin Mehta

Mehta, Zubin (1936-) Indian-born conductor and double-bass player, son of Mehli Mehta, formerly a violinist in the **Halle** Orchestra and founder of the Bombay Symphony Orchestra. He studied in Vienna with Hans Swarowsky (1954-60), and won the Liverpool Conducting Competition in 1958. He has since enjoyed an international career: at the Montreal Symphony Orchestra (1961-7); the Los Angeles Philharmonic Orchestra (1961-76); as music director of the New York Philharmonic (1977-90) and of the Israel Philharmonic from 1977. He often appears as guest conductor at leading opera houses, including Covent Garden, and conducts and records with major symphony orchestras, especially the Vienna Philharmonic.

Méhul, Etienne Nicolas (1763-1817) French composer. After gaining some musical instruction from Hauser at the monastery of Val Dieu, Méhul moved to Paris in 1788, where he studied piano and composition under Edelmann. He was greatly influenced by **Gluck**, from whom he received valuable advice and encouragement to write operas. In 1790 Méhul's comic opera *Euphrosine* was produced and became popular throughout France. In 1793 he became an inspector of the newly founded Paris Conservatoire. He wrote more than 30 operas, including *Cora* (1789), *Le jeune sage et le vieux fou* (1793), *Uthal* (1806) and *Joseph* (1807). He also wrote four ballets, cantatas, patriotic songs, in particular *Chant du départ* (1794), symphonies and piano sonatas.

Meistersinger Member of a guild of poets and musicians who cultivated poetry and singing during the 14th to 16th centuries. The members passed through various stages from apprenticeship to mastery. They were middle-class burghers, tradesmen and artisans and not aristocrats such as the earlier *Minnesinger*. Wagner composed his opera *Die Meistersinger von Nürnberg* after careful research into the practices of the medieval guilds, and used some of their themes and structures.

Melba, Dame Nellie (Helen Mitchell) (1861-1931) Australian soprano who went to Europe in 1886 and studied in Paris under Marchesi. In 1887 she made her début as Gilda in *Rigoletto* in Brussels. She went the next summer to Covent Garden before singing at St Petersburg and touring Italy. Her appearances in London were regular until the outbreak of World War I, and she was fêted above all for her Juliette in Gounod's *Roméo et Juliette*. She also sang the title-role in *Lucia di Lammermoor*, Violetta in *La traviata* and Marguerite in Gounod's *Faust* with great success. She triumphed at the Metropolitan Opera, New York, and in Chicago. She created the title-role of Saint-Saëns's *Hélène* at Monte Carlo in 1904. Her extraordinary technique was allied to a voice of great purity. Melba became DBE in 1918.

Dame Nellie Melba

Melchior, Lauritz (1890-1973) Danish tenor. He studied at the Royal Opera School in Copenhagen and made his début there as a baritone in 1913, and as a tenor in 1918. He was soon recognized as one of the most distinguished Wagnerian tenors of his time. He sang at Bayreuth from 1924 to 1931 and at the Metropolitan Opera, New York, from 1926 to 1950. His recordings of Wagner with the soprano Frida **Leider** and the conductor Albert **Coates** have often been reissued and are classics in their field.

melisma Group of notes sung to a single syllable. The term sometimes applies to any florid vocal passage in the nature of a **cadenza**. The device came into use in **plainsong**, but became most popular in the 18th century in the works of such composers as **Handel**, being inserted either to emphasize emotion or to give an opportunity to display the technique of a virtuoso singer. The plural of the word, *Melismata*, is also the title of a collection of English vocal pieces by **Ravenscroft** (1611).

Mellers, Wilfrid (1914-) English critic and composer. After studying English and music at Cambridge (1933-8) he studied composition with **Rubbra** and **Wellesz** at Oxford. He held a variety of teaching posts, including Dartington Hall, Cambridge, Birmingham and Pittsburgh, before becoming professor of music at York University (1964-82). His reputation as a writer on music grew quickly, and from 1940 he was music editor of *Scrutiny*. His list of published books includes *Music and Society* (1946), *Studies in Contemporary Music* (1948) and *François Couperin and the French Classical Tradition* (1950).

mellophone Brass instrument of circular shape that is a simplified version of the orchestral **horn** and is used in marching bands. It is similar to a tenor horn, pitched in E♭ or F.

melodeon Type of **accordion** that is played with both hands. The right hand plays the melody by depressing

Melodeon

buttons arranged to play **diatonic scales** in one or two keys. The left hand has a set of accompanying chords and notes, produced by buttons for each key. Different notes are produced by each button, according to whether the bellows are being closed or opened.

melodic minor Variation of a minor **scale** in which the third and fourth notes of the upper **tetrachord** are sharpened when the scale is moving upwards. When the scale is moving downwards, these notes are flattened. The melodic minor is more lyrical in its effect than the harmonic minor scale.

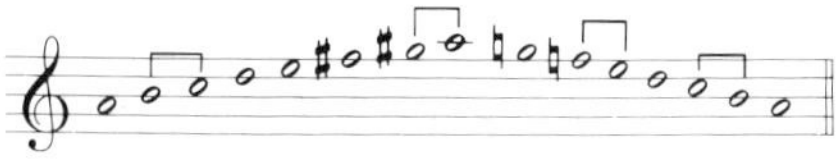

Scale of A melodic minor

mélodie (Fr.) Melody. Term used since the 19th century for accompanied art song. It is the French equivalent of the German *Lied*.

melodrama In music the term describes the speaking of a text to musical accompaniment. Notable examples are to be found in **Benda**'s *Ariadne auf Naxos* (1775); Mozart's *Zaïde* (1780); Schumann's *Manfred* (1849); Richard Strauss's *Enoch Arden* (1898); and Schoenberg's *Ode to Napoleon* (1942) and *A Survivor from Warsaw* (1947).

melody Succession of notes, usually of varied pitch, which present a shape recognized as expressive by the listener. The actual form is infinitely variable, from rhythmically free **plainchant** to the regular structures of a hymn-tune or the simple repetitions of a pop-tune. The rhythmic element is of profound importance, and if drastically altered may make a familiar melody quite unrecognizable, a phenomenon which has often tempted the plagiarist.

Melody is also used as a title, for example *Melody in F*, by Anton **Rubinstein** (1853).

membranophone Instrument in which the sound is produced by the vibration of a stretched membrane of skin. All forms of drum are included in this classification. See also **chordophone**; **idiophone**.

Mendelssohn(-Bartholdy), Felix (1809-1847) German composer, pianist and organist. The name Bartholdy was added when the family was converted from Judaism to Protestantism in 1816. He was a child prodigy as a pianist, making his début when he was only nine. At ten his setting for Psalm 19 was performed by the Berlin Singakademie. He wrote his first symphony in 1824, the comic opera *Die Hochzeit des Camacho* coming a year later. At 17 he composed the overture *A Midsummer Night's Dream* (originally for piano duet); the same year he entered Berlin University and studied for three years before determining upon music as his profession. He led the revival of interest in the music of **J.S. Bach**, with the first performance after more than 80 years of the *St Matthew Passion*, which he presented in Berlin in March 1829. Later in the same year he visited England, where he was received with great enthusiasm. His overture *The Hebrides* (1830) was inspired by a tour he made of Scotland during this visit.

The following two years he spent touring Germany, Austria and Italy, composing two symphonies. He was director of the Lower Rhine Music Festival in Düsseldorf, 1833-6. Between 1835 and 1846 he was conductor of the Leipzig Gewandhaus

Orchestra. During this period he wrote *Lobgesang*, a symphonic cantata, the *Scottish Symphony* (No.3), the *Variations sérieuses* (for piano) and a violin concerto. By 1843 he had founded the Leipzig Conservatoire, teaching the piano and composition. In 1846 he made his ninth and penultimate visit to Britain, where he conducted the first performance of his oratorio *Elijah* at the Birmingham Festival. As well as his five symphonies, including the *Reformation* (1830) and the *Italian* (1833), Mendelssohn wrote the overture *Die schöne Melusine* (1833), several concertos, seven string quartets and a great deal of other chamber music, choral works and part-songs. With his reverence for the past and his mastery of the established techniques of composition, counterpoint and form, Mendelssohn retained his classical strength despite the assaults of Romanticism. The smoothness and placidity of much of his work is often deceptive, though one is sometimes more aware of the well-oiled technique than of a profound inner motivation. It has been said that his family wealth insulated him from the stimulus of poverty, suffering and discontent that so potently affected many of his contemporaries. However, while certain well-known works have enjoyed a permanent place in the repertory, many others, especially among his chamber music and church music, are unjustly neglected and deserve attention.

Mengelberg, Willem (1871-1951) Dutch conductor who studied in Utrecht and at the Conservatoire in Cologne under Wullner. In 1895 he was appointed conductor of the Concertgebouw Orchestra of Amsterdam, where he remained all his life, and was responsible for raising it to world rank. His particular interpretations of Strauss and Beethoven stand at the forefront of his career. He also championed the music of **Mahler**, of which he gave many outstanding performances. He was at home in most of the Romantic repertory, though his Bach was also fine. Because he had performed in Germany during World War II he was unable to return to the Concertgebouw and was forced to retire. Recordings give some idea of his quality.

Menotti, Gian Carlo (1911-) Italian composer and conductor, now resident in Scotland. After studying in Milan for four years, Menotti emigrated to the United States at the age of 16. There he studied at the Curtis Institute in Philadelphia under Scalero. His compositions are mainly operatic, and his first, *Amelia Goes to the Ball*, was produced in 1937. This opera, along with *The Medium* (1946), *The Telephone* (1947) and *The Consul* (1950), attained great popularity; they demonstrate Menotti's dramatic skill as librettist as well as composer. In addition to more than 12 operas, including at least two produced for television (*Amahl and the Night Visitors*, 1951, and *The Labyrinth*, 1963), Menotti has written ballets, a cantata and a piano and violin concerto. Among his recent works is an opera in celebration of the 1988 Seoul Olympics. In 1958 he founded the Spoleto Festival and more recently the Charleston Festival.

Menuhin, Sir Yehudi (1916-) American-born violinist and conductor, now British. A child prodigy, he gave his first public recital in San Francisco at the age of eight and played with an orchestra two years later. In Paris he studied with the Romanian composer **Enescu** and in 1929 played three concertos in one programme with the Berlin Philharmonic under Bruno **Walter**. In 1932 he recorded Elgar's concerto with the composer conducting, a performance that many regard as still unsurpassed. He continued to follow a virtuoso career, often with his sister Hephzibah as his accompanist, and was soon regarded as one of the world's leading violinists. After the war he settled in London and contributed in many ways to English musical life. In 1957 he took up conducting and formed his own orchestra. From 1959 to 1969 he was artistic

Sir Yehudi Menuhin

director of the **Bath Festival**, and in 1963 established in Surrey a school for gifted children which bears his name. He was made an honorary KBE in 1963.

Mercadante, Saverio (1795-1870) Italian composer. Mercadante entered the Naples Conservatoire in 1808, studying under **Zingarelli**. He visited Spain and Portugal (1826-7), composing for the Italian opera in Madrid. He went to Paris in 1835. There he came under the influence of **Meyerbeer**, whose style replaced Mercadante's previous Rossinian style of composition. From 1840 until his death he was director of the Naples Conservatoire.

In addition to some 60 operas, including *Elisa e Claudio* (1821), *I briganti* (1836) and *Orazi e Curiazi* (1846), he wrote 21 Masses, four ballets, songs, orchestral and chamber music.

Merulo, Claudio (1533-1604) Italian organist, publisher and composer. In 1556 he was appointed organist at Brescia and later he moved to St Mark's in Venice in the same capacity. In 1584 he became organist at the ducal chapel in Parma. He composed **motets**, **madrigals** and organ music (mostly **toccatas**, **ricercari** and **canzone**).

messa di voce (It.) Placing of the voice. Technique of increasing and decreasing of vocal volume during one long-held note.

Messager, André (1853-1929) French composer, organist and conductor. He studied in Paris under **Saint-Saëns**, becoming the organist at St Sulpice in 1874. From 1901 to 1906 he held the position of artistic director at Covent Garden. In 1907 he became chief conductor of the Paris Opéra, and a year later was also appointed director of the Paris Conservatoire. His 28 operas include *La béarnaise* (1885), *Véronique* (1898) and *Béatrice* (1914). He also wrote music for ten ballets, of which *Les deux pigeons* is still a favourite, a symphony, some piano pieces, songs and cantatas.

Messiaen, Olivier (1908-) French composer, organist and teacher whose innovative musical compositions and theories have been among the most influential and individualistic of the 20th century. He entered the Paris Conservatoire in 1919 and studied composition with Paul **Dukas**, Marcel **Dupré** and others. In his spare time he read of India and ancient Greece. He also wrote down in musical notation the songs of all native birds, categorizing them by region. All these preoccupations, along with his own deep Catholic faith, were to have far-reaching implications for his future musical development. In 1931 he became organist at L'Eglise de la Trinité, Paris. In 1936 he joined the teaching staff of the Ecole Normale de Musique and the Schola Cantorum and established with André **Jolivet**, Daniel Lesur and Yves Baudrier the group of young French musicians known as *Jeune France*. Called up by the French Army at the start of World War II, he was captured in 1940 and held in a German concentration camp for two years. Released in 1942, he was appointed a professor of harmony at the Paris Conservatoire. Five years later he was given the specially created professorship of analysis, aesthetics and rhythm, and in

1966 he also became professor of composition. His pupils have included **Boulez**, **Stockhausen** and **Xenakis**.

Messiaen's church commitments and teaching have gone hand in hand with a career as an organ recitalist. As a virtuoso of the instrument he has been in demand throughout the world. But it is as a composer and theorist that he has placed an indelible stamp upon the music of the 20th century. His warm and exotic harmonies resemble those of Debussy and often use modal techniques. In orchestral works such as the huge *Turangalîla-symphonie* (1946-8) he utilizes the otherworldly sound of the ondes **martenot**; elsewhere he employs tuned gongs to give his work an Oriental flavour.

Messiaen's major compositions include the orchestral works *L'Ascension* (1933), *Oiseaux exotiques* (1955-6) – both also transcribed for organ – *Chronochromie* (1960) and *Des canyons aux étoiles* (1970-4); the song-cycle *Poèmes pour Mi* (1936); *Rechant* (1949), for 12 unaccompanied voices; the choral piece *La Transfiguration de Notre Seigneur Jésus-Christ* (1965-9); the piano works *Vingt regards sur l'enfant Jésus* (1944), *Cantique d'oiseaux* (1956-8) and (for two pianos) *Visions de l'Amen* (1943); *Nativité du Seigneur* (1935) for organ; and the extraordinary *Quattuor pour la fin du temps* (1940). This last work was written while Messiaen was a prisoner of war; it was scored for the only instruments available in the camp – violin, piano and clarinet. Messiaen's crowning achievement to date has been his monumental opera *St François d'Assisi* (1983), using his own libretto.

mesto (It.) Sad, gloomy.

metamorphosis Method by which a composer transforms a theme or motif, especially by tempo and rhythm, to represent various moods or poetic ideas. Metamorphosis was first exploited by **Liszt**, who used it regularly in his tone poems. **Hindemith** wrote an orchestral piece called *Symphonic Metamorphoses on a Theme by Weber* (1943); Richard **Strauss**'s *Metamorphosen* for 23 solo strings (1945) is well known.

metre The basic structure of pulses or beats in music or poetry. It may be designated in music by a time signature, such as 2/4, and in poetry by a description, such as iambic pentameter, which means a line of five feet, each accented like the word 'above' – for example, 'the cur'few tolls' the knell' of par'ting day". Rhythm is the variation of note lengths or accents imposed on the basic metre. The concept of poetic metre and structural accentuation is of great importance in music. Early pieces, such as **plainchant** and **madrigals**, were often in an irregular metre, where the stresses were determined by the words. With the introduction of bar-lines, a more regular metrical structure became the norm; only at the end of the 19th century were composers ready to vary the time-signature within a piece. In modern usage complex metres have been used to considerable effect, particularly in the music of Daniel **Jones** and Boris **Blacher**.

metronome Device invented by D. Winkel and perfected by J.N. **Maelzel** in 1814, consisting of a clockwork-driven upside-down rigid pendulum that may be weighted in different positions along its length, to produce a 'tick' at different rates per minute. It is used to define the speed of a piece, by indicating the number of pulses per minute of a stated unit, sometimes with the letters MM, although these are now usually omitted.

Metropolitan Opera, New York One of the foremost opera houses and companies in the world, founded in 1883 by private subscription. The first building was on Broadway at 39th Street; the first production was Gounod's *Faust*. The following year Leopold **Damrosch** instituted seasons of German opera, which continued until 1891, when French and Italian works were given under the direction of Maurice Grau. **Caruso** sang there in 1903, **Shaliapin** in 1907; **Mahler** conducted there (1908-10), and **Toscanini** (1908-15). American operas began to be given from 1909. The general manager from 1908 to 1935 was the Italian Gatti-Casazza; from 1935 to 1950 Edward Johnson; from 1950 to 1972 Rudolf Bing, who oversaw the company's move to new premises in the Lincoln Center (1966). James **Levine** became music director in 1975.

The world's finest singers have appeared at the Met: **Gigli, Pinza, Traubel, Melchior** and **Flagstad** in the 1920s, 1930s and 1940s; **Callas, Tebaldi, Nilsson, Sutherland, Caballé, Price** and **Milnes** in the 1950s and 1960s. Since then almost all of the world's most famous singers and conductors have been invited to perform, and the standard of production and music-making is very often superlative.

Meyer, Kerstin (1928-) Swedish mezzo-soprano who studied in Stockholm under Sunnegard and Skoldorz. She made her début there in 1952 as Azucena in *Il trovatore*, then continued her studies in Salzburg and Italy. She has sung in Vienna, Venice, Hamburg and Berlin, making her Covent Garden début in 1960. Among the roles she has created are Agave in Henze's *The Bassarids* (1966) and Mrs Arden in Goehr's *Arden Must Die* (1967). She has also sung at Bayreuth and at the Metropolitan, New York, in both established and new works.

Meyerbeer, Giacomo (Jakob Liebmann Meyer Beer) (1791-1864) German composer and pianist. A child prodigy, Meyerbeer first performed in public at the age of seven. After studying in Darmstadt under **Vogler**, he concentrated on writing opera, and became court composer to the Duke of Hesse. He visited Italy in 1816, where he was strongly influenced by **Rossini**, and this initiated a switch from the German to the Italian style. While in Italy he wrote six operas, all successful, particularly *Il crociato in Egitto* (1824). He then set to work with the librettist Eugène Scribe; together they produced almost all his remaining operas (which were written for the Paris Opéra), including *Robert le Diable* (1831) and *Les Huguenots* (1836).

From 1842 to 1849 Meyerbeer was Generalmusikdirektor at Berlin; for the reopening of the Berlin opera-house he composed the Singspiel *Ein Feldlager in Schlesein*, with Jenny **Lind** taking the principal role. Other successful operas include *Le prophète* (1849), *L'étoile du nord* (1854) and *L'africaine* (1865). He also composed choral, orchestral and piano music and songs.

Meyerowitz, Jan (1913-) German-born composer who became an American citizen in 1951. He studied under **Zemlinsky** in Berlin (1930-3) and then in Rome under **Casella** and **Respighi** (1933-7). In 1946 he moved to the United States, teaching at Tanglewood and in New York. As well as seven operas, including *Esther* (1957), Meyerowitz has written many choral works, a symphony, a cello sonata and songs.

mezza voce (It.) Half voice. A method of producing the singing voice as if under the breath, resulting not only in a soft tone, but in a quality different from that of full voice.

mezzo, mezza (It.) Half, as in **mezzo-soprano**; **mezza voce**, half voice.

mezzo-soprano Female singing voice, lower in range than **soprano** and higher in range than **contralto**.

mi, me The third note in the **tonic sol-fa** scale, and the note E in the fixed **doh** system.

Miaskovsky, Nikolai Yakovlevich (1881-1950) Russian composer who studied under **Glière**, **Lyadov** and **Rimsky-Korsakov**. From 1921 he taught at the Moscow Conservatoire. His works include 27 symphonies, symphonic poems, a sinfonietta, nine string quartets, three piano sonatas and songs.

Michelangeli, Arturo Benedetti (1920-) Italian pianist who studied at the Milan Conservatoire. In 1939 he won the Geneva International Music Competition. He made his début in England in 1946. He has toured widely and established a worldwide reputation. His relatively rare performances and recordings are always eagerly awaited.

microtonality Method of composing music using a tonal scheme that involves intervals smaller than a semitone (**microtones**).

microtone Interval smaller than a **semitone**. The Mexican composer Julián **Carrillo** devised a scale using microtones and also invented special instruments for the purpose. Quarter-tones have been used by **Bloch** in some of his chamber music, and by **Bartók**, although the use of microtones has been discussed (and indeed, put into practice) since the 16th century by **Vincentino** and others.

middle C Note of C that appears roughly in the middle of the piano keyboard. It is usually tuned to a frequency of 261.6 hertz.

Middle C

Mighty Handful Group of Russian composers led by **Balakirev** and including **Borodin**, **Mussorgsky** and **Rimsky-Korsakov**, who during the latter part of the 19th century began to promote a national music based on themes and forms taken from Russian folk-music.

Mignone, Francisco (1897-1986) Brazilian composer and conductor who studied at the São Paulo and Milan Conservatoires. His early works, such as *Suite campestre* (1918), show the influence of his Italian training, whereas in his middle period he was attracted by musical nationalism and in pieces such as the ballet *Maracatu de chico rei* (1933) he drew heavily on Brazilian folk and popular traditions. From the late 1950s he turned away from this folk influence and began to use **polytonality**, tone clusters, **atonality** and **serialism**, in pieces such as *Variacoes em busca de um tema* (1972).

Migot, Georges (1891-1976) French composer who studied at the Paris Conservatoire under **Widor** and **d'Indy** and won three consecutive composition prizes (1918-20). His early works show the influence of **Fauré**. His later works, such as the *Requiem* (1953), have **diatonic** melodies, while avoiding tonality in the music. Throughout his life he insisted on the close link between text and music, and the larger part of his output was of sacred works, including six oratorios on the life of Christ and a church symphony for 85 wind instruments.

Mihalovici, Marcel (1898-1985) French composer of Romanian birth. He studied in Bucharest, and then in Paris with **d'Indy**; he settled there in 1919, marrying the pianist Monique Haas. His music was influenced by **Enescu**, whom he knew in Paris; he was also a member of the Ecole de Paris, a group of eastern European composers and artists. Besides operas (*Phèdre*, 1949, based on Racine; *Krapp*, 1960, based on Beckett) and ballets (*Thésée au labyrinthe*, 1956) he wrote five symphonies, a violin concerto, rhapsodies and variations, chamber and piano works, songs and larger vocal pieces (*Sinfonia cantata*, 1963).

mi-kagura (Japan) Shinto ceremonial. *Kagura* (good music) is the generic term for all Shinto music. *Mi-kagura* comprises two types of song: *torimono*, songs intended to praise or invoke the gods, and *saibari*, songs to entertain the gods. Both are accompanied by an oboe (*hichiriki*), zither (*wagon*), flute and wooden time-marking clappers. See also **sato-kagura**.

Miki, Minoru (1930-) Japanese composer who studied in Tokyo and developed a synthesis of Eastern and Western styles. His first success was the *Trinità sinfonica* (1953), which won a prize; he next wrote several choral works (*Chasing the Light*, 1961; *Old Songs from Indo-China*, 1961) while earning a living composing film music. In 1964 he co-founded the Ensemble Nipponica, and from this time he turned back to traditional Japanese genres, his first such piece being *Sonnet* for **shakuhachi**. With the Ensemble he toured widely; he has made a number of recordings with it and has also been closely associated with the Tokyo Liedertafel. His *Symphony from Life* (1980), commissioned by the city of Kyoto, combines Japanese and Western styles.

Milan, Francisco (*fl.* early 15th century) Spanish singer and composer of *villancicos*, musical compositions akin to choral cantatas. He was employed in the 'chapel' (private musical establishment) of Queen Isabella of Castile and was one of the most popular composer-musicians of his day.

Milan, Luis de (*c.*1500-*c.*1561) Spanish musician whose most important publication was the *Libro de musica de vihuela de mano intitulado El Maestro* (1536). This is the earliest collection of vihuela (guitar) music and is unusual because the pieces give indications of tempo. In addition to the instrumental pieces – including more than 40 fantasias, showing a blend of homophony and **polyphony** – *El Maestro* contains a rich repertory of songs in Castilian and Portuguese.

Milford, Robin (1903-1959) English composer who studied under **Holst** and **Vaughan Williams** at the Royal College of Music. He was a prolific composer, but although several of his large-scale works received successful first performances, such as the oratorio *A Prophet in the Land* (Three Choirs Festival, 1931), none of them has been published. He is better known as a composer of songs in a simple, diatonic style, influenced by English folk-song.

Milhaud, Darius (1892-1974) French composer. He studied at the Paris Conservatoire under **Dukas**, Gédalge and **Widor**. He was a close friend of many contemporary painters and writers, notably Paul Claudel, with whom he wrote his huge opera *Christopher Columbus*. He was a member of Les **Six**. He travelled widely, including two years in South America as Claudel's secretary, which influenced early works such as the ballet *L'homme et son désir* (1918) and the dance suite *Saudades do Brasil* (1920-1). He composed the ballet *La Création du monde* (1923) following a tour of the United States, where he heard black jazz in Harlem.

From his earliest works, Milhaud used the technique of **polytonality**. His enormous output included music for chamber groups, often in unusual combinations such as choir, cello and oboe in the sixth of his chamber symphonies, and he used folk material from many countries. He also wrote the operas *Bolivar* (1943), *David* (1952), and some Jewish liturgical music.

military band Band of brass, woodwind and percussion, originally attached to a military regiment. The range of instruments involved varies in type and number. In England the military band usually consists of flute, piccolo, oboe, clarinet, bassoons, saxophones, horns (orchestral), cornets or trumpets, trombones, euphoniums, tubas and percussion. A double-bass is often included when the band is not marching.

Milkina, Nina (1919-) British pianist of Russian origin who studied in Paris and London and made her début at the age of 11. She has become particularly associated with Mozart, playing all his solo piano works on radio, and with Chopin, recording all the **mazurkas**. She has also recorded many of Scarlatti's sonatas, to which her fresh vivacious style is particularly suited.

Milner, Anthony (1925-) English composer and teacher. He was educated at the Royal College of Music, and after teaching at Morley College was appointed lecturer at King's College, London, in 1965, and then senior lecturer in music at Goldsmith's College, London, in 1971. He is also a professor of composition at the Royal College of Music. His oeuvre includes the fine cantata *The City of Desolation*, and other choral and instrumental works, often influenced by his Roman Catholic beliefs, and using many varied contrapuntal devices.

Milnes, Sherrill (1935-) American baritone. His début with the New York City Opera was in 1964 as Valentin in *Faust*, and his Covent Garden début was in 1971 in *Renato*. He has appeared throughout North and South America and Europe, and has become one of the most prolific recording artists of his time. His voice has been noted for its brilliant top range and extraordinary command of legato. Recently he has also taken up conducting, with some success.

Milstein, Nathan (1904-) American violinist of Russian birth. He studied with Auer and **Ysaÿe**, and made his début in Odessa in 1920. Later that year he played **Glazunov**'s concerto under the composer. While on a recital tour of Europe with the pianist **Horowitz** he decided to emigrate to the United States, where he became an American citizen in 1942, and an internationally famous virtuoso. His brother was Lewis Milestone, the film director.

minim Note that is half the time value of a semibreve and twice that of a crotchet. In the United States it is referred to as a half note.

minimalism Music in which the elements of composition are reduced to the narrowest ranges of harmony and rhythm. A characteristic is the constant repetition of short phrases or motifs, usually with slight changes so that the music progresses very gradually. Often there is a strong pulse, which has a hypnotic effect on the listener. The chief exponents of minimalism are Philip **Glass**, Terry **Riley**, La Monte **Young**, Steve **Reich**, Michael Nyman and John Adams.

Minkus, Léon (1826-1917) Composer and violinist of Austrian origin. He worked in Russia as a concert soloist and teacher and was conductor of the Bolshoi Theatre, Moscow (1862-72). He collaborated with the choreographer Saint-Léon on several ballets, performed in Paris. He also collaborated with **Delibes** on the ballet *La source* (1866). His ballet *Don Quixote* (1869) was well received in Moscow. While holding the post of ballet composer to the Imperial theatre in St Petersburg (1872-91) he wrote many more ballets, which were popular in their day but have now been all but forgotten.

minstrel General term for a travelling entertainer who sang to his own accompaniment. Minstrels existed between the 12th and 17th centuries. See also **jongleur**; **troubadour**; **trouvère**.

Minton, Yvonne (1938-) Australian mezzo-soprano. She studied in Sydney and moved to Europe in 1960, winning a Kathleen Ferrier Prize in the following year. Minton joined the Royal Opera in 1965, where her first important role was as Marina in *Boris Godunov*. She has also regularly visited the Cologne Opera and sung at the Chicago Opera, the Metropolitan Opera and the Paris Opéra. Her first Bayreuth appearance was as Brangäne in 1974. Her roles include Dorabella in *Così fan tutte*, Cherubino in *Le nozze di Figaro* and, most notably, Octavian in *Der Rosenkavalier*, which she has recorded with Solti and the Vienna Philharmonic Orchestra. In addition to her opera work she has a wide concert repertory, much of which has been recorded.

minuet Dance in triple time of French courtly origin that became popular throughout Europe in the mid-17th century. An instrumental form of the minuet was used as one of the movements in a **suite** during the Baroque period, and during the late 18th and early 19th centuries was incorporated into sonatas, quartets and symphonies, especially by such composers as Haydn, Mozart and Beethoven.

mirliton Instrument consisting of a pipe covered at one end with parchment or tissue-paper, into which the player blows, producing a reedy tone similar to a primitive oboe. The simplest form is the toy kazoo, which consists of a comb and a piece of paper. Tchaikovsky included a *Danse des mirlitons* in his ballet *Casse-noisette.*

Miserere Title of a sacred composition derived from the opening words of Psalm 51, which begins *Miserere mei, Deus* (Have mercy on me, O God). Settings in **polyphonic** style have been made by **Josquin**, **Lassus**, **Tye**, **Gabrieli** and **Allegri**, and one was incorporated into Act IV of Verdi's *Il trovatore* (1853). Another text from Psalm 4, beginning with the words *Miserere mihi Domine*, has a **plainchant** melody that was used for innumerable canons and other instrumental settings by Elizabethan composers.

misura (It.) Measure. It is used to refer to the regular movement of a piece, contradicted by the phrase *senza misura* – with free rhythm.

Mitropoulos, Dimitri (1896-1960) American conductor, pianist and composer of Greek birth. He studied at the Athens Odeion Conservatoire and at Brussels. He was conducting the Berlin Philharmonic Orchestra in 1930 when the pianist failed to appear for a performance. Mitropoulos successfully led the orchestra from the piano in Prokofiev's Piano Concerto No.3 – a practice that he then repeated in Europe and the Soviet Union. His American début was with the Boston Symphony Orchestra in 1936. He was conductor of the Minneapolis Symphony Orchestra for 12 years from 1937, and of the New York Philharmonic Orchestra from 1949 to 1958. An international conductors' competition bearing his name was established in New York, 1961.

Mixolydian mode Seventh **mode** and one of the original Ambrosian modes, starting on the note G and proceeding for an octave.

mode Term describing the way a scale is ordered. The modern usage is found in the major and minor modes of **diatonic** music. The word is generally applied to the system of modes evolved in the Middle Ages and known as church or ecclesiastical modes, although they were not confined to church music. Although the names were borrowed from ancient Greek usage, the modes themselves have no such relationship. They are best understood in relation to the white notes of the piano, as follows:

No.	Name	Range	Final	Dominant
I	Dorian	A-D	D	A
II	Hypodorian	A-A	D	F
III	Phrygian	E-E	E	C
IV	Hypophrygian	B-B	E	A
V	Lydian	F-F	F	C
VI	Hypolydian	C-C	F	A
VII	Mixolydian	G-G	G	D
VIII	Hypomixolydian	D-D	G	C
IX	Aeolian	A-A	A	E
X	Hypoaeolian	E-E	A	C
XI	Ionian	C-C	C	G
XII	Hypoionian	G-G	C	E

The odd-numbered modes are called authentic, with the melody kept within the compass of the given octave and ending on the specified final. The even-numbered modes are called plagal, and are prefixed with the phrase hypo- (Greek for under); they have the same final as the mode above but a different compass for the melody. The modes were found in **plainchant** and certain folk-music, but were pushed aside by the diatonic system at the end of the 16th century. In the 20th century composers such as **Vaughan Williams** and **Bartók** have used modal harmony under the influence of folk-music. The Lydian mode with its sharpened 4th was used with great charm in the opening phrase of Fauré's song *Lydia*.

moderato (It.) Moderate. A direction used either singly or in combination with other terms to qualify tempo. For example, *allegro moderato*, at a moderately lively speed.

Mödl, Martha (1912-) German soprano who studied in Nuremberg. She began as a mezzo, making her début in 1942, and with the Düsseldorf opera singing such roles as Dorabella in *Così fan tutte*, Eboli in Verdi's *Don Carlos* and the title-role in *Carmen*. From 1949 she sang as a soprano in Hamburg. She made her first appearance at Bayreuth in 1951, and became established as one of the foremost Wagnerian sopranos, singing Isolde and Brünnhilde as well as Sieglinde, Gutrune and Kundry. She appeared in London in 1949 (as Carmen), returning often in Wagner operas, and at Vienna in 1955 as Leonore in *Fidelio*. In her later career she sang several Strauss roles.

modo (It.) Mode or manner. For example, *in modo di*, in the manner of.

modulation Changing from one key to another in the course of a composition.

modulator Diagram used for instruction purposes in **tonic sol-fa**, and also for practice in sight-reading and modulation. It is in addition an instrument used to modulate sound signals electronically.

Moeran, Ernest John (1894-1950) English composer of Anglo-Irish descent. He studied at the Royal College of Music, and privately under John **Ireland**. His music shows the influence of Ireland and **Delius**, and of the folk-music of his native East Anglia. His earlier works tended to be in small genres such as the piano trio and violin sonata, but later he produced a series of large-scale works, such as the Symphony in G minor, which began to show the influence of **Sibelius**. He also wrote songs and unaccompanied choral works of great charm. The *Sinfonietta* (1944) is the one work of his most often played today.

Moiseiwitsch, Benno (1890-1963) British pianist of Russian birth. He studied in Russia and at Vienna, and made his début in Reading in 1908 after his family had settled in England. His career took him throughout Europe, the United States, the Far East, Africa and South America. He admired **Rachmaninov** greatly and was best known for performances of his music.

mokugyo (Japan) Wooden fish-mouthed slit gong, also known as the Chinese temple block. It is tapped with a padded stick and is used in Buddhist temple worship as a meditative aid during the incantation of the name of Buddha.

Molinari, Bernardino (1880-1952) Italian conductor. Between 1912 and 1943 he was artistic director of the Augusteo Orchestra in Rome and initiated popular open-air summer concerts there from 1929. He conducted mainly in Italy, only occasionally appearing in the rest of Europe and the United States. He made many transcriptions for symphony orchestra, including Debussy's *L'isle joyeuse*.

moll (Ger.) Minor. For example, *A moll* = A minor.

Moll, Kurt (1938-) German bass who studied in Cologne. His début in 1961 was in Aachen; he performed with various German companies before joining the Hamburg opera in 1970. He has appeared in Vienna, Paris, Salzburg and Bayreuth, and made his London début at Covent

Garden in 1977, singing Kaspar in Weber's *Der Freischütz*. Other roles include the Wagner repertory (King Marke in *Tristan und Isolde*, Pogner in *Die Meistersinger von Nürnberg*), Osmin in Mozart's *Die Entführung aus dem Serail* and the title-role of Massenet's *Don Quichotte*. His warm, flexible voice is coupled with a fine dramatic sense.

Molter, Johann Melchior (1696-1765) German composer. He held posts as *Kapellmeister* at various German courts. He visited Italy on two occasions, having the opportunity to meet **Vivaldi**, **Albinoni**, **Scarlatti**, **Pergolesi** and **Sammartini**. His works reflect the many influences to which he was exposed and show a steady development from the late **Baroque** style to the **galant**. He worked with court musicians, many of whom could play several instruments, and this enabled him to experiment with unusual and new instruments, such as the clarinet and the **chalumeau**. He composed a total of 167 symphonies.

molto (It.) Much, very. For example, *molto allegro* = very quickly.

Moment Structural concept devised by **Stockhausen** as an attempt to help the listener to overcome some of the difficulties of listening to **serial** music. A 'Moment' is a brief segment of a composition with its own musical characteristic. Each Moment is equal in status and equally dispensable. As the composer does not move forwards from a fixed point in time, but moves in all directions within cyclic limits, the Moments may be arranged in any order to achieve an indeterminate open form. An example of this is Stockhausen's work *Moments* (1962-4) for soprano, four choirs and 13 instruments.

Mompou, Federico (1893-1987) Spanish composer who initially studied the piano in Paris, but devoted his later career to composition. He was much influenced by **Debussy**, **Satie** and the new French school. His work is almost entirely restricted to intimate piano miniatures or slow songs of very similar style.

Monckton, Lionel (1861-1924) British composer and music critic. He studied at Oxford and trained as a lawyer. While a critic on the *Daily Telegraph*, he wrote music for several successful Edwardian musical comedies, including *The Arcadians* and *The Quaker Girl*.

Moniuszko, Stanisław (1819-1872) Polish composer who first came to notice with the publication of his *Songbook for Home Use* (1842). He became a popular opera composer, his first great success being the final version of *Halka*, which was performed in 1858. In 1859 he was appointed as the opera conductor at the Grand Theatre in Warsaw, where he composed several more operas. He is the most representative opera composer of the Polish 19th-century national school.

Monk, William Henry (1823-1889) English church musician and composer. He held the post of organist and choir-master in several London churches. He was also professor of vocal music at King's College, London, the National Training School for Music and at Bedford College, London. He was the editor of *Hymns Ancient and Modern* (1861), for which he wrote *Eventide*, the famous tune for *Abide with Me*. He wrote many other popular hymn tunes, anthems and service music.

Monn, Georg Matthias (1717-1750) Austrian composer and organist. He was organist at St Charles's Church in Vienna, and was also a teacher. None of his music was published during his lifetime, but he had a substantial local reputation. His output included symphonies and concertos which are in the early classical style, and more conservative chamber music and keyboard sonatas. He was the first composer to write a four-movement symphony with a third-movement **minuet**

(1740), and his treatment of fast movements (with development sections and full recapitulations in the tonic) heralded the emergence of **sonata form** in the symphony.

monodrama Stage work for one character, such as **Schoenberg**'s *Erwartung* (1909) for soprano and orchestra.

monody Composition that comprises a single melodic part presented over a simple chordal accompaniment, which formed the basis of the first **operas**. The earliest use of this type of composition can be found in Giulio **Caccini**'s *Le nuove musiche* (1601).

monophonic Music in a single melodic part, without harmony, as distinct from **homophonic**, which is a form in which the music moves by step in all the parts, with no variation in rhythm between them. See also **monody, polyphonic**.

monothematic Describing a composition based on a single theme. The term may apply to one movement or to a larger composition having several movements. Monothematic movements occur in the finale of Haydn's Symphony No.103 in E♭ (1795), and in the first movement of his Symphony No.104 in D major (1795).

Monsigny, Pierre-Alexandre (1729-1817) French composer who began to study composition at the relatively late age of 30, under Gianotti. *Les aveux indiscrets*, his first complete *opéra-comique*, was performed in 1759. In 1761 he started a long collaboration with the librettist Sedaine. After several more works in the *opéra-comique* vein he had an immense success with *Félix ou l'enfant trouvé* (1777).

Monte, Philippe de (1521-1603) Flemish composer. He held various positions in Italy, and from 1568 became choirmaster to the Habsburg court, spending the rest of his life in the post at Vienna or Prague. He had a wide circle of friends, including **Lassus** and **Byrd**. He composed about 260 sacred works, including 40 Masses, but is best known for his even larger secular output, comprising more than 1,100 madrigals which span his entire career. He was one of the most renowned and prolific composers of the 16th century.

Montéclair, Michel Pinolet de (1667-1737) French composer, teacher and double-bass player. From 1699 he was employed as a double-bass player at the Paris Opéra. The Opéra put on two stage works by him, *Les festes d'été* (1716) and *David et Jonathan* (1732), unusual for the period because of its biblical content. His other surviving works include three fine orchestral *Sérénades* (suites) and a few *cantates* (chamber cantatas). He also wrote a number of books about the theory and teaching of music, including one of the first violin 'methods'. Both his music and his theoretical writings influenced **Rameau**.

Monteux, Pierre (1875-1964) American conductor of French birth. He studied at the Paris Conservatoire and played viola at the Opéra-Comique while still a student. He conducted for Diaghilev's Ballets Russes (1911-14), for which he directed the premières of Stravinsky's ballets; other posts were at the Metropolitan Opera (1917-19), the Boston Symphony Orchestra (1920-4), the Amsterdam Concertgebouw Orchestra (1924-34, as second conductor), the San Francisco Symphony Orchestra (1936-52), and finally the London Symphony Orchestra (1961-4). He made many successful recordings but much preferred live performance.

Monteverdi, Claudio (1567-1643) Italian composer, singer, organist and viol player. Like many great musicians he started his career as a choirboy, learning to play the organ and the viol. He began composing while still a youth, and while serving the Duke of Mantua turned his attention to opera, inspired by the work of the **Camerata** in Florence. His first opera, *La favola d'Orfeo*, was performed in Mantua in 1607, and although we cannot be certain what instruments were used, it was the first time that what we would call an orchestra was used as accompaniment. *Orfeo* was followed a year later by *Arianna*, but little of it has survived. It is astonishing to consider that our admiration for Monteverdi is based on a fraction of his work, for at least 12 of his operas were destroyed. In 1613 he left Mantua to become Master of Music at St Mark's in Venice, where he produced much of his finest church music. Monteverdi is now recognized as one of the giants of Renaissance music – for the variety and imagination of his many madrigals, for the freedom of expression of his church music such as the celebrated *Vespers* (1610), and above all in the vivid drama of those operas that have survived. Now that scholars, if not always in agreement, have succeeded in creating practical performing versions of such works as *Il ritorno d'Ulisse in patria* and *L'incoronazione di Poppaea*, their deft command of character and situation has made such a powerful appeal to modern audiences that they have taken their place in the standard repertory. Monteverdi was not only one of the first composers of opera, but certainly one of the greatest.

Montgomery, Kenneth (1943-) British conductor who studied at the Royal College of Music under **Boult** and later in Siena. He was director of the **Bournemouth** Sinfonietta (1973-5), but was already working mostly in the field of opera, with Glyndebourne, Sadler's Wells and the Netherlands Opera. He made his Covent Garden début in 1975 with *Le nozze di Figaro* and was appointed musical director of Glyndebourne Touring Opera in 1976. Later that year he moved to the Netherlands Radio Orchestra.

Moog, Robert Arthur (1934-) American inventor of the 'Moog synthesizer' and other instruments, in collaboration with many composers. He founded the R.A. Moog Company in New York in 1954 to manufacture **thérémins**, and started the manufacture of synthesizers in 1965. His instruments became very popular following the success of Walter Carlos's *Switched on Bach* recording (1969), and Moog is still active in the development of new instruments.

Moore, Douglas Stuart (1893-1969) American composer, teacher and writer. His first compositions, while still a student at Yale, were popular songs. He studied with **d'Indy** and Nadia **Boulanger** in Paris in 1919. He held a teaching post at Barnard College, Columbia University, from 1926 until his retirement in 1962. Moore composed several operas, of which *The Ballad of Baby Doe* and *The Devil and Daniel Webster* are the best known. He also composed choral, orchestral and chamber works.

Moore, Gerald (1899-1987) English pianist who started a career as a recording artist in 1921, and began to specialize in piano accompaniment from 1925. From that time until his retirement in 1967 he accompanied virtually every eminent solo singer and instrumentalist in England and abroad, and raised the art of accompaniment to one of the highest prestige. His recordings include more than 500 Schubert songs with artists such as **Fischer-Dieskau** and **Schwarzkopf**. He was awarded the Grand Prix du Disque four times and, among other honours, he was made a CBE in 1954.

Moore, Thomas (1779-1852) Irish poet and musician. He trained and practised as a lawyer, but even as a law student in London he wrote songs, and the libretto for Michael **Kelly**'s opera *The Gipsy Prince* (1801). He became very popular following the serial publication of *Irish Melodies* (1808-34), in which he added new texts to old tunes. Apart from other collections of poems and songs, he was best known for *Lalla Rookh* – a story with four interpolated poems (1817), on which Schumann based his *Paradise and the Peri*. He also published lives of Sheridan (1825), Byron (1830) and Fitzgerald (1831).

Morales, Cristóbal de (*c.*1500-1553) Spanish composer of church music. He was born in Seville and trained there as a choirboy. From 1526 to 1531 he held the post of chapel-master, first at the cathedral of Avila and then at Plasencia in western Spain. From 1535 to 1545 he sang in the Papal choir in Rome and wrote most of his finest church pieces for it. His two volumes of Masses (1544) and popular Magnificat cycles rank him with **Palestrina** and **Victoria** in terms of the quality of their construction. Returning to Spain in 1545, he successively held the posts of chapel-master in Toledo and Málaga. In all he wrote some 23 Masses and about 90 motets. He ranks as Spain's first internationally famous composer.

morbido (It.) Gentle or delicate, but not morbid.

morceau (Fr.) Piece. For example, *morceau symphonique* = symphonic piece.

mordent **Ornament** written over a note to indicate that three notes are to be played in the time-value of the principal note. The **upper mordent** consists of the principal note, then the next note up, then the principal. The lower, or **inverted mordent**, is constructed in the same way, but using the note below the principal.

Upper mordent (above)
Inverted mordent (below)

Moreau, Jean-Baptiste (1656-1733) French composer and teacher. He served alongside Clérambault as *musicien ordinaire* at a school for young noblewomen established at St Cyr in 1686. While there he collaborated with Racine on several works, including a setting of his *Esther* (1689) which delighted the King, Louis XIV. Moreau was persuaded to write music of a popular nature by Lainez for his divertissement *Zaïre*, which brought him much success.

morendo (It.) Dying. It indicates that a phrase is to be allowed to die away. It may mean not only a decrease in volume and tone, but also in pace.

Morley, Thomas (1557-1602) English composer and music publisher, a master of the English **madrigal** tradition. He was probably born in Norwich. A student of William **Byrd**, he graduated from Oxford University in 1588 and travelled to London, where he became organist at St Paul's Cathedral and also a Gentleman of the Chapel Royal. In 1598 he won a 21-year monopoly on the printing of song-books and music paper and published *The Triumphs of Oriana*, a collection of madrigals dedicated to Queen Elizabeth I, to which he himself contributed. He also composed sacred music and lute songs, and wrote *A Plaine and Easie Introduction to Practicall Musicke*. Morley is best known for his balletts, of which *Now is the Month of Maying* and *It was a Lover and his Lass* are among the finest examples.

morris dance English folk-dance which derives from the *moresca*, a dance depicting a battle between Moorish and Christian soldiers, and was introduced into England in about the 15th century. It is danced in various kinds of symbolic fancy dress, with jingles tied to the dancers' legs, and is performed in two groups of six. Two of the dancers represent traditional characters, such as the Fool and the Queen of the May. The music is played by a pipe and tabor and sometimes a violin.

Moscheles, Ignaz (1794-1870) German pianist, conductor and composer of Czech birth. He was born in Prague, and studied there and in Vienna with **Albrechtsberger** and **Salieri**. After some success as a pianist he was asked by Beethoven to prepare the piano score of *Fidelio* (1814). He visited London in 1821 and 1823, and then moved to Berlin where he taught Mendelssohn the piano. He returned to London in 1826, and settled there as teacher and conductor until invited by Mendelssohn to join the staff of the new Leipzig Conservatoire, where he remained until his death. His compositions for the piano included many popular studies and eight concertos, but very few of them are heard today.

Mosolov, Alexandr Vasilyevich (1900-1973) Russian composer, born in Kiev. A hero of the 1917 Revolution, he early espoused the creed of Socialist Realism (then known as constructivism) with his 1927 ballet *Zavod* (The Factory), also performed as a concert piece under the English title *The Iron Foundry*. However, his avant-garde style incurred the displeasure of the Stalinist authorities and kept him out of favour for more than a decade. He regained official recognition during World War II, when he was commissioned to write patriotic songs, but he never attained musical eminence. His works include six symphonies, cello, violin and piano concertos, chamber music and songs. Some of his early songs use newspaper advertisements as texts.

mosso (It.) Animated. Usually preceded by *più* or *meno*.

Moszkowski, Moritz (1854-1925) German pianist and composer of Polish descent. He studied at Dresden and in Berlin, where he taught for many years while touring extensively as a pianist. He is best known for two books of piano duets, *Spanische Tanze*, and a piano concerto which has been revived and recorded with some success.

motet Short vocal composition for sacred use which evolved from 13th-century clausulae. Originally it appeared as an elaboration of a given **plainsong** melody with the contrapuntal addition of other melodies with a different text. The earliest motets were often written for three voices: *triplum*, *motetus*, and tenor, which was the lowest part.

In the 14th century the motet became **isorhythmic**, especially in the works of such composers as **Dufay**, **Machaut** and **Dunstable**. Dufay also introduced secular melodies into the motet form as a **cantus firmus**.

During the 15th century the motet form became more independent, and gradually developed into an elaborate form of **polyphonic** sacred composition set to Latin words not in the Mass. By the end of the 16th century this style reached its peak in the motets of **Palestrina, Lassus, Victoria, Tallis** and **Byrd**. At times during the 18th century it was difficult to distinguish the motet from the **cantata**, but between 1723 and 1729 the motet proper reached its climax with the composition by **J.S. Bach** of motets for a five-part chorus and two eight-part choruses. Among the 19th-century composers whose works included motets were **Brahms, Bruckner, Liszt** and **Gounod**, followed in the 20th century by **Franck, Poulenc, Vaughan Williams** and **Stanford**.

motif Alternative spelling of **motive**.

motion Movement upwards or downwards of a line of music. There are six forms of motion.

In a single part, a conjunct motion moves by steps of adjoining notes. Conversely, a disjunct motion occurs when the part moves by larger steps.

If two or more parts move together in the same direction they are said to be in similar motion, and if they move in opposite directions they are in contrary motion.

In oblique motion, one part moves while the other stands still. Parallel motion is similar motion in which the parts preserve a constant interval between them.

motive Brief melodic or rhythmic figure, too short to be called a theme. Some composers have used a motive in **programme music** or in opera in association with a character, object or idea. In such cases it becomes the leading motive or **leitmotiv** associated with, for example, **Wagner**.

moto (It.) Movement, pace.

Mottl, Felix Josef (1856-1911) Austrian conductor, composer and editor. He was appointed conductor at the court opera and the Philharmonic Society, Karlsruhe, in 1881. His conducting début at Bayreuth was in 1886 with *Tristan und Isolde* and *Parsifal*, and he was a regular guest conductor there. He conducted Wagner's *Ring* cycle at Covent Garden in 1890 and 1898, and prepared the first performances of *Parsifal* for New York in 1903. In the same year he took charge of the Munich opera-house. He also edited vocal scores of Wagner's operas, made orchestral arrangements of songs by many composers, arranged ballet suites and composed some pieces of his own.

motto Musical theme or figure that usually occurs at the opening of a composition and again during its course (in its original form or altered), in the manner of a quotation or allusion to some definite idea. The opening themes in Tchaikovsky's Symphonies No.4 (1877) and No.5 (1888) are examples of this. The motto may also be called a motto theme.

Moussorgsky, Modest Petrovich Alternative transliteration of **Mussorgsky, Modest Petrovich**.

mouth music (Scotland) Highland term for vocal music that is used to accompany dance when instrumental accompaniment is not available or permitted. Words are often personal, derogatory or humorous in nature. Also known as *port à beul*. See also **diddling**.

mouth organ Alternative term for **harmonica**.

mouthpiece Part of a woodwind or brass instrument that a player takes into the mouth or to which he or she applies the lips in order to produce a sound. An **oboe**'s mouthpiece consists of a double reed of cane, the tip of which the player takes between the teeth. In a **clarinet** the single cane reed is clamped over a slot on the underside of a plastic or ebonite mouthpiece by means of a ligature. The reed is placed on the player's bottom lip, with the top teeth resting on top of the mouthpiece. A **recorder** mouthpiece has a slot with a sharp edge cut in it at an angle so that the breath can be directed downwards but actually flows over the top of the tube as in a flute. A **flute**'s mouthpiece is a hole near one end of the instrument, and the player blows across it as someone might blow across the open top of a bottle. In a brass instrument a cup- or funnel-shaped metal mouthpiece made from a single casting fits into the top of the air column. It is pressed against the player's lips. The deeper and larger the cup, the more suitable the mouthpiece is for the mellow tones of the larger instruments, such as the **tuba** or **horn**. A shallow cup is ideal for the brilliant penetrating tones of the **trumpet**.

Mouton, Jean (1459-1522) French composer, one of the most important writers of **motets** of the early 16th century. He spent the earlier part of his life in various church positions and studied under **Josquin des Prés**. He joined the French court in 1502, serving Louis XII and François I. More than 100 motets, about 15 Masses and 20 chansons by Mouton survive. He is also important as the teacher of Adrian **Willaert**.

movable doh In the **tonic sol-fa** system, the concept that the scale, beginning with the tonic (doh), may start on any note.

movement Independent section of a large composition, such as a symphony, concerto or sonata. The French word *mouvement* is also used for **tempo** or speed.

Mozart, Leopold (1719-1787) Austrian composer and violinist, father of Wolfgang Amadeus **Mozart**. A violinist in the court orchestra, he became *Kapellmeister* to the Archbishop of Salzburg (1743-87). He recognized his son's genius, taking him on concert tours at a very early age, but has often been criticized for exploiting the boy's talents. He composed sacred music, symphonies and keyboard sonatas. His best-known compositions are the *Peasant Wedding Divertimento* and *Sinfonia da Caccia* (Toy Symphony), in which he included such 'instruments' as whistles and pistols. He also wrote a textbook on violin technique (1756) which was widely used.

Mozart, Wolfgang Amadeus (1756-1791) Austrian violinist, keyboard player, conductor and composer, son of Leopold **Mozart**. Realizing his son's prodigious gifts, Leopold took the six-year-old boy and his sister round the courts of Europe, showing off their talents at the keyboard. They were received at Versailles and spent two years in London, where Wolfgang composed his first symphonies under the tutelage of J.C. **Bach**. Later a triumphant visit to Italy confirmed the 14-year-old's feeling for the theatre with the opera *Mitridate, re di Ponto*, produced at Milan in December 1770. Few child prodigies retain their gifts into adulthood, but Mozart's genius blossomed in every field of music. When he was 12, his father drew up a catalogue of all that he had composed in the previous five years – it included operas, oratorios, six symphonies, three church trios, six divertimentos, an offertory, a *Stabat Mater* and many solos for violin, harpsichord and organ. The boy had a wicked sense of humour and entered happily into the musical circus acts favoured at the time – playing from sight, improvising, composing an aria on the spot and singing it to his own accompaniment. By the time he was 16, the catalogue of works that have survived reached 200, including many pieces that we count among his masterpieces, for example the motet *Exsultate, jubilate* (K165) and the delightful Symphony No.29 in A (K201). He poured out concertos for keyboard or violin, a new opera, *La finta giardiniera*, for Munich, a Mass for the cathedral, and divertimentos to entertain his patrons.

In these early years Mozart lived the life of the travelling musician, fêted by the nobility, yet remaining their servant. When he was concert-master in Salzburg he suffered, like his father, at the hands of his master the Archbishop. In 1780 he was commissioned to write an opera for Munich; the result was his first mature operatic masterpiece, *Idomeneo* (K366). But still he suffered from his master, and in 1781, when he resigned once more, he was literally kicked out. He now settled in Vienna, where he again met the Weber family – he had previously fallen in love with Aloysia, but now fell for her younger sister Constanze, whom he married, against his father's wishes, in 1782. Meanwhile in response to a commission from the Emperor Joseph II Mozart produced *Die Entführung aus dem Serail* (The Abduction from the Seraglio) to considerable acclaim. He was now recognized as a great musician, although his domestic happiness was continually plagued by money worries. In these years he produced masterpieces in every form, that today fill our concerts and recitals. In 1785 Haydn declared to Leopold that his son was the greatest composer he knew.

In 1786, when the taste of the court reverted to the Italian style, Mozart overcame official misgivings about the revolutionary tone of Da Ponte's libretto and produced *Le nozze di Figaro* (The Marriage of Figaro), regarded by many as his finest opera. It was so successful that in the following year he was invited to compose *Don Giovanni* for Prague, where he conducted the first performance to wild applause on 29 November 1787. Despite these successes, Mozart's somewhat

Wolfgang Amadeus Mozart

extravagant lifestyle and uncertain income created constant financial problems, for he was often in debt, although at the very height of his powers – in 1788 he completed his last three great symphonies, but it seems likely that he never heard them performed. After the success of his opera *Così fan tutte* (All Women are Like That) in 1790, he hoped that he might be appointed *Kapellmeister* in succession to **Salieri**, but Joseph **Weigl** was preferred. Mozart was even refused the post of second *Kapellmeister*. He was now troubled with illness, but hopeful that he might be able to accept an invitation to England. At this crisis in his life he composed music for a mechanical organ, sets of dances for court balls, two sublime string quintets, and what was to be his last piano concerto, in B ♭ (K595).

Then came two curious commissions: one from a well-known low comedian to write a sort of pantomime, which Mozart's genius converted into the masterly opera *Die Zauberflöte* (The Magic Flute); the other, which seemed ominous, was from a mysterious stranger to compose a *Requiem* – which, unknown to him, was to be passed off as another's work. Amidst these labours another commission turned up, which he could not afford to refuse – an opera for coronation festivities in Prague. Wearily he took up an old libretto by Metastasio, *La clemenza di Tito*, and completed the music in the inns on his way to Prague. By now in poor health, he returned to Vienna exhausted, but found strength to complete another sublime masterpiece, the Clarinet Concerto (K622). Feverishly he worked on the *Requiem*, but died on 4 December before he could complete it. Why this famous man was then buried like a pauper in a common grave, long since lost and forgotten, remains a mystery. His music, however, offers an incomparable monument to his genius, which transformed everything he touched, whether an inconsequential piece for mechanical organ or the musical glasses, or a sublime string quartet or symphony – it is, to quote from *Die Entführung*: '*Ein Vorgeschmack der Seligkeit*' – a foretaste of blessedness.

Mudge, Richard (1718-1763) English composer about whom very little is known. He studied at Oxford and became a vicar in Birmingham. In 1756 he moved to Bedworth, a living in the patronage of the Earl of Aylesford. He wrote a set of six **concerti grossi** for solo violins, string ensemble and various solo instruments, and a *Medley Concerto* with French horns.

Muffat, Georg (1653-1704) German composer and organist of French birth. He studied with **Lully** and others in Paris and later with **Pasquini** in Rome. He spent much of his life in Salzburg, and the last 15 years as *Kapellmeister* at the court of Johann Philipp, Bishop of Passau. He composed several orchestral suites, *concerti grossi*, violin sonatas and organ music. He is best known, however, for bringing the French style of **Lully** and the Italian style of **Corelli** to German performers.

Muffat, Gottlieb (1690-1770) German composer and organist. He entered the musical establishment at the Viennese court early in his career and remained there for more than half a century. He wrote exclusively for the keyboard, and these works are all in traditional Baroque forms such as the **toccata**, **prelude**, **capriccio**, **canzona**, **fugue**, dance **suite** and **ciaccona**.

muffle Means of reducing the volume of sound made by a **drum**, either by covering the membrane with a piece of cloth or by using sponge-head drumsticks.

Muldowney, Dominic (1952-) English composer who studied with **Harvey**, **Birtwistle**, Rands and **Blake**. He was composer-in-residence for the Southern Arts Association (1974-6) and was appointed resident composer to the National Theatre, London, 1976, where he worked on the very successful production of Gay's *The Beggar's Opera* (1982). He has written film and television scores. In 1990 the première of his song-cycle *Lonely Hearts* was given by the **London Sinfonietta**; based on the small advertisements in such magazines as *Time Out*, this work is scored for two groups, with two conductors, and a mezzo soloist.

multimedia Performance of a composition that includes music, poetry, drama, dancing and other events, but excludes opera and ballet. It was a form of music practised in the 1960s, particularly by Luciano **Berio**, who sometimes used electronics in his compositions.

Mumma, Gordon (1935-) American composer, performer of electronic music and horn-player. He studied at the University of Michigan. Mumma collaborated with Ashley and Milton Cohen to create mixed-media 'Space Theater' productions, involving light projections, dance, sculpture and electronic sound, and was co-founder with Ashley of the Co-operative Studio for Electronic

Music in Ann Arbor. In 1966 he joined Merce Cunningham's Dance Company as a composer and performer.

Munch, Charles (1891-1968) Violinist and conductor of Franco-German origin. He studied at the Strasbourg Conservatoire, with Flesch in Berlin and with Capet in Paris. He became professor of violin at Strasbourg and then at Leipzig, where he led the Gewandhaus Orchestra under **Furtwängler** (1926-33). His conducting début was made in 1933 in Paris, where he was based for many years and where he made a name conducting many first performances by French composers. He was chief conductor of the Boston Symphony Orchestra from 1948 to 1962, introducing much French music to the American public and conducting first performances of many American works. In 1967 he was invited to establish the new Orchestre de Paris, which the government had set up to challenge the great international orchestras of other countries.

Mundy, John (1555-1630) English composer and organist, son of William **Mundy**. He studied at Oxford, and was the organist at St George's Chapel, Windsor, for more than 40 years. He was a versatile composer; his output includes sacred and secular choral works, and keyboard pieces, to be found in the *Fitzwilliam Virginal Book*.

Mundy, William (1529-1591) English composer, father of John **Mundy**. After holding posts at several London churches, he was made a Gentleman of the Chapel Royal in 1564. He was highly regarded by his contemporaries and composed many sacred works. However, most manuscripts are marked simply 'Mundy', and it is impossible to know whether much of this music was by father or son.

Munrow, David (1942-1976) English player of early wind instruments. He studied at Cambridge and Birmingham Universities and lectured at Leicester University and the Royal Academy. In 1967 he formed the Early Music Consort of London, and the group brought polished performances of medieval and Renaissance music to wide audiences. He was much in demand as a recorder player, and was very influential in the growth of **authentic** performances.

Murray, Ann (1949-) Irish mezzo-soprano who studied in Manchester and at the London Opera Centre. Her début was in 1974 with **Scottish Opera**, when she sang the title-role in Gluck's *Alceste*. Since then she has sung with the English National Opera and in Hamburg, Zurich, La Scala, Salzburg and New York. Her Covent Garden début was in 1976 as Cherubino in *Le nozze di Figaro*. Her stylish presence and clear, firm voice are well suited to such parts as the Composer in Strauss's *Ariadne auf Naxos*, Rosina in *Il barbiere di Siviglia*, the title-role in *La Cenerentola* (both Rossini) and Dorabella in *Così fan tutte*. She has scored particular success in the title-role of Handel's *Xerxes* and the roles of Sextus and Annius in Mozart's *La clemenza di Tito*. She is married to the tenor Philip **Langridge**.

Murrill, Herbert (1909-1952) English composer and administrator, who studied at the Royal Academy (1925-8) and at Oxford (1928-31). He was music director for the Group Theatre, London. Murrill served in Intelligence during World War II. He was appointed to the BBC music staff and was Head of Music from 1950 until his death. He married the cellist Vera Canning.

Musgrave, Thea (1928-) Scottish composer who studied at Edinburgh University and in Paris with Nadia **Boulanger** (1950-4). Her earliest pieces were predominantly **diatonic** in style, but her style changed gradually through **chromaticism** into an orthodox **serial** technique by 1960. Her style changed again during the 1960s, becoming less conservative, more atonal and rhythmic.

Her output covers a wide range, from full-length stage works such as operas (*The Decision*, 1965; *Mary Queen of Scots*, 1977; *Harriet, the Woman Called Moses*, 1985) to *a cappella* choral motets, music for brass band and piano duets. She has also written a viola concerto for her husband, Peter Mark, commissioned by the BBC.

musica ficta Practice in medieval and Renaissance music of treating certain notes in a performance as though they were marked with **flat** or **sharp** signs. In order to make harmonic sense between the parts or to avoid awkward intervals such as the **tritone** between F and B, the leading note of the scale was often sharpened and the B often flattened, the latter especially in the **Dorian mode**.

musica figurata **Plainsong** decorated by auxiliary notes, or the addition of a **descant** sung against a fundamental melody.

musical bow One of the most basic and primitive of string instruments which consisted of a single string attached to a flexible stick. By flexing the bow, the tension of the string was altered and this allowed a change of note. The string was normally plucked, although in some cases it was bowed with a smaller bow. The musical bow was the predecessor of the lute and harp, and is still used in some parts of Asia and Africa.

musical glasses Alternative term for **glass harmonica**.

musica reservata 16th-century term for music intended for connoisseurs and private occasions, especially vocal music which faithfully interpreted the words. It was a term used in the 1550s to describe the music of **Lassus**.

music drama Alternative term for opera used by composers, especially **Wagner**, who thought that the older term implied obsolete methods and forms. His view of opera was that it should be a fusion of stagecraft, literature and music. Wagner exploited the **leitmotiv**, a device to enhance the drama and unify the music. He expressed his ideas on music and drama in *The Artwork of the Future* and *Opera and Drama* (1851).

musicology 20th-century word that applies to the scientific and scholarly study of music in all its aspects. The branches of musicology include acoustics, aesthetics, bibliography, history, biography, instruments, harmony and notation.

music theatre Term loosely applied to musico-dramatic works on a smaller scale than opera, sometimes performed on the concert platform.

musique concrète Term coined by a group of French composers (including Pierre **Schaeffer** and Pierre **Henry**) in the late 1940s to describe their electronic compositions, created in a studio, in which natural or 'concrete' sounds are recorded on tape and either used unembellished or mixed with more conventional musical resources.

Mussorgsky, Modest (1839-1881) Russian composer, one of the **Mighty Handful**. As a youth he was a foppish army officer, who delighted guests at parties with his fluent playing of popular operatic excerpts. At 19 he decided to devote himself to music and took lessons with **Balakirev**. His aim was realism, truth to life and free musical expression. He made his melodies fit the natural contours and rhythms of the texts of his songs and his operas; he used abrupt changes of key, new pungent harmonies and irregular rhythmic patterns, deliberately avoiding the conventions of smooth academic composition. Sadly, this vivid imagination was blunted by his addiction to drink, which made concentrated work so difficult that many pieces were left unfinished. Yet he left some splendid works: the superb collection *Songs and Dances of Death* (1875-7); the wit,

Modest Mussorgsky

charm and power of *Pictures at an Exhibition* (1874) for piano, now more familiar in **Ravel**'s orchestration; and the operas, of which only one was completed – his masterpiece *Boris Godunov* (1868-72). Few operas have suffered so many rejections, revisions and adaptations – its sympathetic treatment of the suffering Russian peasantry alarmed officials, just as the raw intensity of the music shocked the critics and many of his fellow musicians. His other operas, *Khovanshchina* (1873) and *Sorochintsy Fair*, were completed after his death by other composers. *Boris Godunov* was also completely rearranged by **Rimsky-Korsakov**, who set out 'to correct the technical impotence of Mussorgsky'. This 'purified' version held the stage for many years; it certainly brought the composer's name before the public, and strongly influenced Debussy and Ravel. Only when the original version was restored to the stage after World War II was Mussorgsky revealed as the composer of the greatest of Russian operas, and one of the most important composers of the 19th century.

Mustel organ Reed organ similar to the American organ. It was invented by Victor Mustel (1815-90) in Paris. The Mustel organ has a special device by which the top and bottom halves of the keyboard may be separately controlled for dynamic expression.

muta (It.) Change. Indication that a performer has to make a change between instruments. For example, A and B♭ clarinet, or in tunings of kettledrums or strings of the violin family temporarily tuned to abnormal notes.

mute Any of various devices that serve to reduce the volume of sound (and with it the tone) produced by an instrument. On bowed string instruments the mute is in the shape of a fork or clip whose prongs are made to grip the bridge and reduce its vibration, and with it the vibration of the strings. In brass wind instruments the mute consists of a cone-shaped piece of wood, metal or plastic inserted into the bell, although other forms of mute are also used, especially in jazz music. Other ways to apply a mute are to depress the soft pedal of a piano or to muffle a drum.

Muti, Riccardo (1941-) Italian conductor who studied in Naples and Milan. He made his début in Florence in 1966 and at Covent Garden in 1977 (*Aïda*). He was principal conductor of the Philharmonia Orchestra (1973-82) and music director of the Philadelphia Orchestra (from 1981). He was appointed musical director of La Scala, Milan, in 1986. He has made many outstanding recordings, including *Aïda* and other Verdi operas. His recording of Rossini's *William Tell*, made live at La Scala, Milan, was released in 1990.

Mutter, Anne-Sophie (1963-) German violinist. She studied with Erna Hönigberger and at the Winterthur Conservatoire with Aida Stucki. She became a member of the Berlin Philharmonic Orchestra and came to the attention of Herbert von **Karajan**. As his protégée she has had an astonishingly successful career, and with him she has recorded many of the great concertos: those of Beethoven, Bruch, Mendelssohn, Brahms, Mozart and (with the Vienna Philharmonic) Tchaikovsky. She has toured widely (London, 1990) and has had several works written for her, including *Rêve* for violin and orchestra by Moret.

Myslivec̆ek, Josef (1737-1781) Bohemian composer. He studied in Prague, and went to Venice in 1763 to learn opera composition. His first work, *Medea*, was produced in 1764 in Parma; its success led to an invitation to Naples, where *Bellerophon* was given in 1767, again to much acclaim. He settled in Italy and wrote operas for the theatres in Rome, Milan, Florence and elsewhere. He was admired throughout Italy, where he was known as 'il divino Boemo'. His reputation was such that he was asked to write an opera for Munich in 1773, and a few years later he made the acquaintance of Mozart, who expressed admiration for him. Besides nearly 30 works in the *opera seria* mould, he wrote oratorios, cantatas, four symphonies, concertos for keyboard, violin, cello and flute and many chamber pieces.

N

Nabokov, Nicolas (1903-1978) Russian-born composer, author and administrator who became an American citizen in 1939. He worked with **Diaghilev**'s Ballets Russes in the 1920s, and his own ballet-oratorio *Ode* (1928) was performed by the company in Paris, London and Berlin. In 1947 he became chief of the first broadcast unit of the Voice of America, was secretary-general of the Congress for Cultural Freedom, and director of the (West) Berlin Festival. He composed ballets, operas (*The Death of Rasputin*), orchestral and choral works, a piano concerto, a flute concerto, a string quartet and two piano sonatas. His publications include *Old Friends and New Music* (1951) and *Igor Stravinsky* (1964). He was the cousin of the writer Vladimir Nabokov.

Nachschlag (Ger.) After-stroke, referring to the two extra notes that conventionally form the end of some kinds of **trill**. The term also refers to a note or notes (shown in smaller print) added after a given note.

Nachtanz (Ger.) After-dance. For example, a quicker dance following a slower one, such as a **galliard** following the **pavane**.

Nachtmusik (Ger.) Night music, a composition played in the open air during the evening as a serenade to a loved one. A well-known example of this type of composition is **Mozart's** *Eine kleine Nachtmusik* for strings (1787).

nagauta (Japan) 'Long song', used to accompany **kabuki** dances, usually with **shamisen** (lute), flute and three drums: *ō-tsuzumi*, *ko-tsuzumi* and *taiko*. *Nagauta* was influenced by the *jōruri* song form, and evolved alongside *kabuki* dancing. It is now also performed in concerts and as domestic music. See also **tsuzumi**.

nai (Romania) Panpipes consisting of 20 or more bamboo tubes, open at the upper end and set in a concave row in order of size. They are glued together and fixed to a curved stick, the lower end plugged with beeswax in order to tune them to a **diatonic** scale. The instrument has a distinctive sound, with characteristic *portamenti* in slow solo melodies. It was made popular by the Romanian virtuoso Gheorghe Zamfir in film and television theme music, such as *Picnic at Hanging Rock* and *The Light of Experience*.

Nápravník, Eduard (1839-1916) Czech conductor and composer, who studied in Prague but moved to St Petersburg and was considered a Russian conductor. In 1869 he became principal conductor at the Imperial Russian Opera in succession to **Lyadov**. His opera *Dubrovsky* (1895) was successful in his time, but he was best known as a conductor, particularly of Russian opera. He was very influential in raising the standard of performance at the Maryinsky Theatre.

Nash, Heddle (1896-1961) The leading British lyric tenor of his generation, admired as much for his work in oratorio and recital as for his outstanding operatic performances. He studied in London at the Blackheath Conservatoire, and later in

Milan, where he made his début in 1924 as Almaviva in Rossini's *Il barbiere di Siviglia*. He combined an appealing timbre and a remarkable fluency of technique with a rare sensitivity to the text. His delivery, for example, of the lengthy expositions required of David in Wagner's *Die Meistersinger* prompted Ernest Newman to describe Nash as the finest exponent of the part he had ever witnessed. He was also a stylish exponent of the music of Mozart, and his recordings of songs and of Elgar's *The Dream of Gerontius* are regarded as among the finest of the century.

Nash Ensemble Chamber ensemble founded by Amelia Freedman in 1964. It has a core of 12 members (wind, strings, harp and piano), with additional players as necessary. Its repertory covers a wide spectrum from the Viennese classics to contemporary music; it has commissioned over a hundred works, including pieces by **Knussen**, Colin **Matthews**, David **Matthews**, **Maw** and **Payne**, among others. The ensemble has toured extensively all over the world, including the United States, the Soviet Union and Japan, and appears at many festivals; it also gives acclaimed series of concerts on the South Bank and at the Wigmore Hall, London. It has made numerous recordings, including one of **Poulenc**'s chamber works which won the 1987 Grand Prix International du Disque.

Nathan, Isaac (1790-1864) Australian composer of Polish-Jewish descent and English birth. He collaborated with Lord Byron on *Hebrew Melodies* (1815-19) by adapting ancient Jewish chants to Byron's poems. He was the royal music librarian until 1841, when he was forced to emigrate to Australia because of financial difficulties. In Sydney he opened a singing academy and wrote patriotic music: *Australia the Wide and Free* (1842) and *Song to Freedom* (1863). He wrote the first European operas in Australia, *Merry Freaks in Troublous Times* (1843) and *Don John of Australia* (1846), and was a teacher and conductor. He also made precise observations of Aboriginal musical practice, and transcribed it into such works as *Koorinda Braia* (1842).

National Youth Orchestra of Great Britain Few events revealed so powerfully the renaissance of music-making in Great Britain as the début of the National Youth Orchestra in 1947 under the baton of Reginald Jacques. The orchestra was founded and driven with single-minded enthusiasm by Dame Ruth Railton (1916-), the wife of Cecil King, the newspaper publisher. Her plan was to choose by audition the finest young players in the country, bring them together in the vacations for concentrated work under expert coaches, and give concerts under the leading conductors of the day. The secret of her success was discipline, in every aspect of the young people's activities. To hear them play Stravinsky's *Le sacre du printemps* under Simon **Rattle** or some of the most challenging works of the contemporary repertory under **Boulez** is to experience music-making of the highest order. The present director is the composer Derek **Bourgeois**.

Natra, Sergiu (1924-) Israeli composer, Romanian by birth. He studied at the Bucharest Academy of Music under Leo Klepper. His early music was influenced by Stravinsky, Prokofiev and Hindemith, although all these composers were banned in Romania. After World War II Natra and his contemporaries tried to compose music based on folk-song, but it was not well received by the 'proletariat' – those they were trying to reach. He settled in Tel Aviv in 1961 and was made professor at Tel Aviv University in 1976. His Israeli compositions are **atonal**.

natural Accidental (♮) that indicates that a note raised by a sharp or lowered by a flat (either in the key signature or previously in the written music) should be restored to its original position.

naturale (It.) Natural, indicating that a voice or instrument, after performing a passage in some unusual way (for example, falsetto or muted), is to return to the normal style of singing or playing.

Naumann, Johann Gottlieb (1741-1801) German composer who lived and travelled extensively in Italy, where he studied under **Tartini** and **Hasse**. In 1764 he became court composer of church music at Dresden, and *Kapellmeister* in 1776. In 1777 he was asked by Gustav III to develop the National Opera in Stockholm, and in 1782 the New Royal Opera House opened under his direction. His compositions include 26 operas, the best known being *Orpheus and Eurydice* (1786) influenced by Gluck, sacred music, and several works for the **glass harmonica**. He was aware of the *Sturm und Drang* movement of the early Romantics, and was one of the most esteemed composers of Europe in the late 18th century.

Navarra, André-Nicholas (1911-) French cellist who studied at the Paris Conservatoire with J. Loeb and **Tournemire**, and played with the Krettley String Quartet (1929-35), formed while he was still a student. In 1931 he made his solo début, with **Pierné** conducting, at the Colonne Concerts in Paris. He has been associated with Elgar's Cello Concerto, having performed this work with great success for his British début (1950) at the Cheltenham Festival.

Naylor, Bernard (1907-1986) English composer, the son of the organist and composer Edward Naylor (1867-1934). He studied at the Royal College of Music with **Holst**, **Vaughan Williams** and **Ireland**. He spent much time in Canada as a teacher and conductor, settling there in 1959. His own music had its origins in the English choral tradition (*Nine Motets*, 1952; *Three Sacred Pieces* for chorus and orchestra, 1971) but included a setting of Elizabeth Barrett Browning's *Sonnets from the Portuguese* for voice and string quartet.

NBC Symphony Orchestra See **Toscanini, Arturo**

Neapolitan sixth Chord comprising the notes F, A♭ and D♭, and correspondingly in other keys. The origin of the term is obscure, but it appears as early as the time of **Purcell** (1658-95).

Neel, Boyd (1905-1981) English conductor who was also a qualified doctor. He founded the Boyd Neel Orchestra (1932), which was later renamed Philomusica of London. The orchestra was noted for its revival of **Baroque** string music, little known at this time. **Britten** composed *Variations on a Theme of Frank Bridge* for the orchestra, which performed it at the Salzburg Festival (1937). This established the international reputations of Britten and the orchestra. Neel conducted the Sadler's Wells Opera (1945-6) and the D'Oyly Carte Opera (1948-9). He was made a CBE in 1953. He was appointed dean of the Toronto Royal Conservatory (1953-71).

negro spiritual Afro-American religious song whose lyrics are adapted from passages of the Bible. Many stanzas consist of repetitions of lines with short, recurrent, interjected refrains or responses for communal involvement. Frequent use is made of extemporization in the song's verses. Although patterned on white American models, negro spirituals nevertheless conform to African musical practice and are characterized by rhythms associated with the swinging of the head and upper body.

Neidlinger, Gustav (1912-) German bass-baritone who studied in Frankfurt and made his début in Mainz in 1931. He joined the Hamburg Opera in 1936, where he remained until 1950, singing such roles as Dr Bartolo in *Le nozze di Figaro*. He moved to Stuttgart, and in 1952 first appeared at Bayreuth, returning frequently until 1975. His début in London was in 1955 and at the Metropolitan, New York, in 1972. He has also appeared at the major European opera houses, including Vienna. His most notable roles are Wagnerian: Kurwenal, Klingsor, Telramund and especially a menacing Alberich in the *Ring* cycle, which he performed on the famous recording with **Solti**.

neo-classicism Movement in musical style that was current in the 1920s and 1930s. Generally, it implies a return to pre-Romantic ideals of objectivity and clarity of texture, although not only those of 18th-century classicism. It includes the revival of contrapuntal textures and forms (**fugue, passacaglia, toccata** and **madrigal**) from the Renaissance and Baroque while employing modern harmony, rhythm, tonality, melody and timbres. The principal neo-classical composers are **Stravinsky** (from the ballet *Pulchinella*, 1920, to the opera *The Rake's Progress*, 1948-51), **Prokofiev** (Symphony No.1, *Classical*, 1916), and **Hindemith** (*Ludus Tonalis*, for piano, 1943).

Neri, St Philip (San Filippo) (1515-1595) Italian saint and religious leader. He introduced the singing of the *Lauda Spirituale* which he developed from informal spiritual exercises. **Palestrina** and **Victoria** probably participated in his services. In 1575 his gatherings were recognized by Pope Gregory XIII as an official community – *Congregazione dell' oratorio* – and his spiritual exercises became an important aspect of the Catholic reform movement in Rome.

Nestorenko, Evgeny (1938-) Russian bass who studied in Leningrad and made his début there in 1963. He sang with the Maly and Kirov companies until 1971, when he moved to the Bolshoi Opera in Moscow. There he has become admired for his Russian roles – Dosifei in Mussorgsky's *Kovanshchina*, Khan Konchak in Borodin's *Prince Igor*, and the title-role in *Boris Godunov*, which he has sung at La Scala, Vienna and the Metropolitan. He is also successful as King Philip in Verdi's *Don Carlos*. His début at Covent Garden was in 1978. He has a wide concert repertory.

netori (Japan) Serene musical prelude to a performance of **gagaku** court music and dance. It is used to establish the mode of the composition and might be regarded as a formalized tuning of the orchestra, with instruments entering one by one in a fixed sequence, beginning with the **shō** mouth organ, followed by the **hichiriki** oboe, a flute and the **kakko** drum.

neum(e) (adj. **neumatic**) Sign used originally in the 7th century, indicating the single notes or groups of notes to which each syllable was to be sung. Neums were marked above the words of the text to serve merely as reminders of the general upward or downward direction of a melody already known to the singer.

Neumann, Václav (1920-) Czech conductor who studied with Pavel Dedecek and Metod Dolezil at the Prague Conservatoire. He also formed the Smetana Quartet, in which he played first violin, and later viola, giving concerts from 1945. In 1956 at the invitation of Felstein he conducted **Janáček**'s *The Cunning Little Vixen*, which was very successful; he gave more than 200 performances. He became chief conductor of the Czech Philharmonic Orchestra in 1968. He was music director of the Stuttgart Opera from 1969 to 1972. His repertory includes much Czech music, especially Janáček's. He is also a fine interpreter of Mahler. He became a Czech National Artist in 1977.

Neveu, Ginette (1919-1949) French violinist who made her début in Paris in 1926, aged seven, and later studied at the Paris Conservatoire under Carl Flesch. Neveu was best known for her performances of the concerto of Sibelius. She was killed in an air crash.

new music 1. A 'new' form of expressive music, a style first used by **Giulio Caccini**

in the 17th century, published in his work *Nuove musiche* (new music) and containing madrigals and arias for voice and thorough-bass.

2. It refers to the style of the music of **Liszt** and **Wagner** and their followers during the period 1850-1900, as opposed to the more traditional music of **Brahms**.

3. It refers to the various new techniques adopted in the early 20th century, such as **serialism** and **atonality**.

New Orleans style Original style of jazz that originated in the 1890s when black musicians played lively marches in processions leaving cemeteries after funerals, or for dancing and entertainment in Storeyville, the red-light district of New Orleans. The bands usually consisted of a cornet, trombone, clarinet, banjo and drums. As the majority of the players could not read musical scores, they improvised on a given tune such as *When the Saints Come Marchin' In* and *Oh Didn't He Ramble*. After the Storeyville district was closed in 1917, the centre of jazz activity moved from New Orleans to Chicago.

New Philharmonia Orchestra See **Philharmonia Orchestra**

New York Philharmonic Orchestra American orchestra founded in 1842, one of the oldest orchestras in the world. It incorporated the New York Symphony Orchestra in 1928, and for a while was known as the Philharmonic Symphony Orchestra. The first conductor and prime mover was the American Ureli Corelli Hill. Other conductors of note were Theodore Thomas (1877-91), **Mahler** (1909-11), **Mengelberg** (1921-30), **Toscanini** (1930-6), **Barbirolli** (1936-41), **Mitropoulos** (1950-8), **Bernstein** (1958-69) and **Boulez** (1971-8).

Nicolai, Otto (1810-1849) German composer and conductor. He studied in Berlin and Rome, where he was an organist for a while, and then conducted in Trieste and Turin. His most famous work, *Die lustigen Weiber von Windsor* (The Merry Wives of Windsor, 1849), is an example of early Romantic German comic opera. He was the first *Kapellmeister* of the Court Opera in Vienna (1841-7) and in 1847 became director of the Court Opera, Berlin. He founded the Vienna Philharmonic Orchestra in 1842. Apart from operas his work includes church music, part-songs and choral music.

Nielsen, Carl (1865-1931) Danish composer, the greatest of his nation, who studied at Copenhagen Conservatoire under Niels **Gade** and joined the Danish court orchestra as a violinist (1889-1905). His first important compositions were a string quartet, the *Little Suite* for string orchestra (both 1888) and his Symphony No.1 (1892), in a style somewhat reminiscent of Brahms. By the time of his

Carl Nielsen

second symphony, *The Four Temperaments* (1902), based on the medieval notion of character types, his style had progressed into a more formal, classically structured one which also revealed his awareness of current developments. During this period he wrote the first of his two operas, *Saul and David* (1902); his second, a comic opera, *Maskarade*, was completed in 1906. He became a conductor at the Royal Theatre in 1908, and began to achieve widespread recognition, travelling abroad to conduct his own compositions. His Symphony No.3, called the *Sinfonia espansiva*, and the Violin Concerto were written in 1911. He was conductor of the Copenhagen Musical Society, 1915-27; he taught at the Conservatoire from 1916 and became its director in 1930. The important works of his later years are the three symphonies – No.4, *Inestinguibile* (The Inextinguishable, 1916), No.5 (1922) and No.6, *Sinfonia semplice* (1925); the tone poem *Pan and Syrinx* (1918); concertos for flute (1926) and for clarinet (1928); and *Commotio* for organ (1931). Among his other works are a wind quintet (1922); choral works, including the well-known *Springtime in Funen* (1921); many songs, in a continuation and revitalization of the Danish song tradition; and chamber works. Nielsen was for long neglected outside Denmark, but is now recognized as a composer of the greatest importance, largely as the result of a campaign by the British composer Robert **Simpson**, who in his book *Carl Nielsen, Symphonist* (London, 1952) drew attention to his progressive tonality – starting in one key and finishing in another. Nielsen, along with **Sibelius** and **Stenhammar**, made a major contribution to the symphonic tradition in Scandinavia.

Nigg, Serge (1924-) French composer. He studied at the Paris Conservatoire with **Messiaen** and later studied **twelve-note** serial technique with **Leibowitz**. He was one of the first French composers to master this technique, as seen in his *Variations* (1947). With Désormière he founded the French Association of Progressivist Musicians, making journeys to Eastern Europe. His own music, with its combination of gentleness and fierceness as in *Visages d'Axel* (1967), shows an affinity with that of Ravel. Other works include two piano concertos, a violin concerto, several symphonic poems, vocal, chamber and instrumental music (*Scènes concertantes* for piano and strings, 1975).

Nikisch, Arthur (1855-1922) Hungarian conductor who played the piano in public as a child, then went on to study the violin at the Vienna Conservatoire. As a violinist in the Vienna Court orchestra (1874-7) he played under Brahms, Bruckner, Liszt, Verdi and Wagner. He then turned to conducting and was engaged first in Leipzig (1877-89) and subsequently appointed director of the Budapest opera. From 1895 he was simultaneously conductor of the Berlin Philharmonic and the Leipzig Gewandhaus orchestras. His international career took him often to England, where he conducted opera at Covent Garden – including a cycle of the *Ring* in 1913 – and the London Symphony Orchestra, which he took to America on its first tour. His masterly stick technique was unobtrusive, but produced passionate interpretations, particularly of the Romantic repertory.

Nilsson, Birgit (1918-) Swedish soprano. She studied at the Royal Academy in Stockholm and made her operatic début in 1946 as Agathe in Weber's *Der Freischütz*. She then gradually established herself as the leading Wagner soprano of her day. In 1954-5 she appeared as Brünnhilde in the *Ring* at Munich, became associated with this role and recorded it with Sir Georg **Solti**. In 1959 she made her début at the Metropolitan Opera, New York, as Isolde in *Tristan und Isolde*. Her British début was as Electra in Mozart's *Idomeneo* at Glyndebourne in 1952. She is noted also for the title-roles in Strauss's *Salome* and *Elektra* and Puccini's *Turandot*. She retired in 1982.

Nilsson, Bo (1937-) Swedish composer who was largely self-taught. There are influences of **Boulez** and **Stockhausen** in his music but he has his own distinctive combination of percussive and melodious sounds of voice or instrument, often using the alto flute. He became well known when his *Frequenzen* for eight instrumentalists was performed in Darmstadt (1956). His *Nazm* (1973) combines free form with specified formulae based on Turkish folk-music and jazz. It is scored for solo voices, chorus and orchestra, all amplified. Other pieces are *Déjà connu, déjà entendu* for wind quintet; *Madonna* for mezzo and ensemble, and film and television music.

Nin (y Castellanos), Joaquín (1879-1949) Cuban pianist and composer. He studied piano under Carlos Vidiella in Barcelona and **Moszkowski** and **d'Indy** in Paris. He was famous for his performances of Bach and early Spanish works, and his opposition to the performance of these on the harpsichord resulted in a celebrated exchange with **Landowska**. His compositions, including works for violin, piano, a ballet and songs for voice and orchestra, show his enthusiasm for Spanish Baroque music.

ninth Interval encompassed by nine notes of the scale, for example C to D inclusive.

no See **noh**

nobile, nobilmente (It.) Noble, nobly.

nocturne Night piece or instrumental serenade. It is generally a one-movement piece of a quiet, lyrical character, usually written for the piano. During the 18th century the term applied to short works such as Mozart's *Serenata notturna*. John **Field** is believed to have been the first composer of nocturnes and composed more than 20 for the piano, although it was **Chopin** who expanded the scope of the nocturne with 21 examples expressing a wide range of moods. Other notable composers of nocturnes were **Debussy** (*Nocturnes*, 1900) and **Britten** (*Serenade*, a song-cycle for tenor, horn and strings, 1943).

node Point in a vibrating string or air-column that is stationary and about which the vibrating string or column divides itself into separately vibrating segments.

noh/no (Japan) Theatre form originating from song-dances and folk theatre of the 14th century. *Noh* performances embody the essence of Buddhism – simplicity, serenity, meditation and mental control – the central focus being the symbolic dance imbued with mystical power. There are usually two actors, the *shite* (principal) and the *waki* (secondary), who wear masks and elaborate, symbolic costumes. A performance consists of alternate recitation and singing between the main actors, interspersed with dance and chorus. The vocal parts, showing the influence of Buddhist liturgical chant, comprise recurring melodic patterns shaped by a rigid metrical scheme in which 12 syllables, divided into groups of seven and five, are contained within a rhythmic period of eight beats. The instruments of the *noh* drama, the **hayashi** ensemble, are *noh* flute (*nohkan*) and three drums (two **tsuzumi** and one *taiko*). A full *noh* programme consists of five plays separated by comic interludes (*kyōgen*) and can last all day.

nonet Composition for nine instruments or voices. A group performing this type of composition often includes a mixture of stringed, wind and brass instruments. An example is **Spohr's** *Nonet* for string quartet, flute, oboe, clarinet, bassoon and horn.

non-harmonic note Note that is not harmonically associated with the chord which it precedes or follows. See also **auxiliary note**; **passing note**.

Nono, Luigi (1924-1990) Italian composer. He started his studies in law and then began to compose under the influence of

Malipiero. **Maderna** and Scherchen introduced him to **serial** methods and he won attention outside Italy with his *Orchestral Variations on a Note Series by Schoenberg*, Op.41, performed at Darmstadt in 1950. His other notable works are *Epitaph for Federico García Lorca* (1951-3) for speakers, singers and orchestra, *Incontri* (1955) for chamber ensemble, *Intolleranza* (1960), an opera combining live and recorded performances and using actors and film sequences, and *Sul Ponte di Hiroshima* (1962) for soprano, tenor and orchestra. His music became increasingly dry and didactic as he tried to use it to portray left-wing political views, such as *Non Consumiamo Marx* (1969), scored for voices and tape.

Nordheim, Arne (1931-) Norwegian composer who was concerned with novel sound combinations and a free **atonal** style. *Katharsis* (1962), commissioned by the Norwegian State Opera, was his first composition using electronics in combination with a live orchestra. His major work *Colorazione* (1968) combined instruments (Hammond organ and percussion) and equipment including a ring modulator and a tape delay. In 1975 he collaborated with Arnold Haukeland in the creation of *Sound Sculpture* – sounds are produced on 13 points of the sculpture, which begins to sing when daylight hits its photosensitive cells.

Nørgård, Per (1932-) Danish composer who was a pupil of Vagn **Holmboe** and Nadia **Boulanger**. His *Fragment VI* for six orchestra groups won the international first prize at the Dutch music week, Gaudeamus (1961). His music is influenced by **Sibelius**, **Ligeti** and the American **minimalists**. He was head of the Danish section of the International Society for Contemporary Music (ISCM) between 1965 and 1967. He has written operas, a ballet, vocal and chamber music and four symphonies (the fourth in 1981).

Norman, Jessye (1945-) American soprano who studied in the United States and made her operatic début in Berlin as Elisabeth in *Tannhäuser* (1969). Opera appearances followed in Rome, Florence and Covent Garden. Her roles include Aïda, Cassandra in *Les troyens* and, in 1985, Ariadne in Strauss's *Ariadne auf Naxos*. She has made many outstanding recordings including Wagner's *Wesendonk-Lieder* and the Liebestod from *Tristan und Isolde*, Strauss's *Four Last Songs* and Mahler's *Das Lied von der Erde*. A greatly popular artist, she frequently makes television appearances, and was chosen to sing *La Marseillaise* at the bicentennial celebrations of the French Revolution in 1989. She also sings programmes of black gospel music. Her tone is opulent and particularly vibrant in the lower registers.

Norrington, Roger (1934-) English conductor who studied at Cambridge and at the Royal College of Music under **Boult**. He sang as a tenor for several years and founded the Schütz Choir in 1962. From 1969 to 1985 he was music director of Kent Opera, a company which achieved great distinction under him before its demise in 1989. He founded the London Baroque and the London Classical Players, ensembles dedicated to giving **authentic** performances on period instruments. He was principal conductor of the **Bournemouth** Sinfonietta, 1985-9, and has been a guest conductor of orchestras around the world. In London he has appeared with the English National Opera and at Covent Garden, where he conducted Britten's *Peter Grimes* and *Albert Herring* in 1989. He was awarded the OBE in 1979.

Northern Sinfonia Orchestra founded in Newcastle upon Tyne by Michael Hall in 1958, the first permanent chamber orchestra in Britain, with about 30 members. It not only serves the whole of northern England but has toured frequently in Britain and abroad – notably to the United States, the Netherlands, Spain and Italy – and appears at many festivals. Among its numerous recordings is the first ever of Beethoven's Symphony No.9 on DAT (**digital** audio tape). It gave the première of the reconstructed score of Eisenstein's film *October* in 1989, and has commissioned several new works. Its principal conductors have included Rudolf **Schwarz** (1964-73), Christopher **Seaman** (1973-9), Tamás **Vásáry** and Ivan Fischer (1979-82) and, as artistic director, Richard Hickox (1982-9). From 1990 Heinrich **Schiff** was artistic director, with Hickox as principal guest conductor.

nota cambiata (It.) Changed note. A device in counterpoint, whereby an extra non-essential note is used on an accented beat.

notation The writing down of music by means of: 1. symbols, such as letters in Ancient Greek music; 2. by neums or signs, as in the Middle Ages; 3. in tablature for lute and organ music; 4. in notes according to the present system; 5. in syllabic form in movable **doh** systems such as the **Curwen** method.

In every age composers have sought a notation which would enable others to read and perform the music they have devised, but always assumed the unwritten conventions of the period. It is rarely sufficient to read notation like a blue-print: even in the elaborate scores of Mahler and Schoenberg, the performer has to use his musicianship and interpretative imagination to bring the written text to life. In modern times composers such as **Boulez** have sought through their notation to impose the last degree of control, while at the other extreme, **Stockhausen** and others have used graphical notation, where the musical interpretation is left to the free invention of the performer.

note 1. A single sound of a given **pitch** and precise duration.

2. A written sign for such a sound.

3. An alternative term for the key of a **keyboard**.

note-row The sequence of the 12 notes of the chromatic scale chosen as the basis for a **serial** composition.

notturno (It.) Equivalent of **nocturne**.

Novák, Vítězslav (1870-1949) Czech composer and teacher who studied under **Dvořák** at Prague Conservatoire; he was appointed professor there in 1909. He made a study of Slovakian and Moravian folk-melody and in his own composition was concerned with exploring the metamorphosis of a single theme, as in *Pan* (1910). His other important works include the opera *Karlstejn* (1915), the symphonic poem *In the Tatras* (1902) and the triptych *St Wenceslas* (1941). Debussy and Strauss as well as Dvořák were important influences on his style.

Novello, Clara (1818-1908) The daughter of Vincent **Novello**, she became one of the most famous sopranos of her day, earning the praise of **Mendelssohn** and Schumann. In 1838 Mendelssohn arranged for her to sing at the Gewandhaus concerts in Leipzig, which launched her career in Germany. She was a friend of **Rossini**'s and sang the title-role of his *Semiramide* (1841) and in the first performances of the *Stabat Mater* (1841). In 1851 she returned to England and established herself as an oratorio singer.

Novello, Ivor (David Ifor Davies) (1893-1951) British composer, the son of

Ivor Novello

Madame Novello Davies, well known in Wales and London as a teacher of singing. He began composing songs at the age of 15, and his greatest success was in 1914 with *Keep the Home Fires Burning*. He wrote many operettas in an anglicized Viennese style; the most popular, *The Dancing Years* (1939), ran almost continuously in London and on tour for ten years.

Novello, Vincent (1781-1861) London publisher, editor, organist and composer. He was organist at the chapel of the Portuguese Embassy (1797-1822). In 1811 he founded the music-publishing firm of Novello & Co., whose first publications were two volumes of *Sacred Music* (1811) and *Twelve Early Masses* (including three of his own and others by Haydn and Mozart). These were issued in vocal score with fully written-out piano and organ accompaniment rather than figured bass. His concern was to make music more accessible to less skilful musicians. He enriched music-making by making scores available and affordable.

number Self-contained musical piece in an **opera** or musical, so-called because originally each piece was separately numbered in the written score.

Nunc Dimittis Text from St Luke's Gospel ('Lord, now lettest Thou Thy servant depart in peace') which is sung in the Roman Catholic Church and in the Anglican Church at Evensong. It is often set by composers as a second part following the **Magnificat**.

nut Ridge at the end of the fingerboard of a stringed instrument just below the pegs, serving to raise the strings clear of the board. It is also the head of a screw attached to the heel of a violin bow to enable the hairs to be tightened.

Nyström, Gösta (1890-1966) Swedish composer who went to Paris in 1920, became a pupil of **d'Indy** and remained in the company of Scandinavian and French artists. He was also a talented painter. His early music such as *Ishavet* (1924-5) was influenced by **Debussy**, **Ravel** and **Stravinsky**'s *The Rite of Spring*. His *Sinfonia breve* (1929-31) combined polyrhythms and harsh dissonance, a style found shocking at the time. His music later became more harmonic and lyrical in conception, often referring to nature and the sea. An example of this is *The Tempest* (1934). His late works included two string quartets as well as concertos, songs, and symphonies (*Sinfonia seria*, 1963; *Sinfonia di lontano*, 1963; *Sinfonia tramontana*, 1965).

O

obbligato (It.) Term which originally meant that a part so marked was essential, but later came to mean that it was a subsidiary solo part, accompanying the main, usually vocal, solo.

oblique motion In harmony, movement in one of the parts while the other parts remain stationary. See also **contrary motion; similar motion.**

oboe Double-reed woodwind instrument, formerly called the **hautboy**, developed in France during the 17th century from the **shawm**. An oboe dating from about 1690 was equipped with six finger-holes and three keys. The bore was much wider at the top and expanded more gradually than in modern instruments. During the 19th century a complicated system of keys was added. Today the regular oboe has a range of two and a half octaves from B♭ below middle C.

Other members of the oboe family include the *oboe d'amore*, a **transposing** instrument sounding a minor third below the regular oboe; the **cor anglais**, which sounds a fifth below and is much bigger than the oboe, and was sometimes known as an English horn; and, less often used, the heckelphone or bass oboe, used in, for example, **Holst**'s *Planets* suite. Concertos for the instrument have been written by Vivaldi, Mozart, Richard Strauss, **Martinů** and **Vaughan Williams**, among others.

The oboe is a standard instrument in an orchestra, and it is often used as a solo instrument. Because it is one of the most difficult instruments to tune, it is used as the norm against which all the other orchestral instruments are tuned.

Oboe

Obrecht, Jacob (*c*.1450-1505) Flemish composer who spent some time in Italy and eventually died in Ferrara. He held important church-music positions in Bruges, Cambrai and Antwerp, succeeding Barbireau at Notre Dame, Antwerp, in 1492. He wrote **Masses, motets** and **chansons** to Dutch, French and Italian words. His music revealed a later style than **Ockeghem**'s, with imitation between the parts and definite cadences.

ocarina Pear-shaped wind instrument with finger-holes and a protruding mouthpiece, usually made of terracotta. It was invented by Giuseppe Donati in about 1860. It is mainly used as a toy and was featured in the musical *Call Me Madam* by Irving **Berlin** (1950).

Ockeghem, Johannes (*c.*1410-1495) Flemish composer, recognized during his lifetime as a master, the teacher of **Josquin des Prés** and **Busnois**. In the mid-1440s he entered the service of Charles I, Duke of Bourbon, and became *maître de chapelle* to the King of France in 1465. He composed **Masses**, **motets** and **chansons** which explored new sonorities and have a distinctive flowing style. His polyphonic *Requiem* is of importance as the earliest existing setting. Along with Josquin and **Dufay** he is one of the most important composers of the second half of the 15th century.

octave Interval of eight notes on the **diatonic scale**, the uppermost note having exactly twice the frequency (number of vibrations) of the lowermost note. Notes separated by an octave are denoted by the same letter.

octet Composition for eight voices, instruments or a combination of both. In Mendelssohn's String Octet in E♭ major (1825) it was limited to strings, whereas Beethoven's Octet in E♭ (1834) was for two oboes, two clarinets, two horns and two bassoons. Schubert's Octet (1824) was for string quartet, double bass, clarinet, bassoon and horn.

octobass Three-stringed **double-bass** measuring 12ft (4m) high, invented by Jean-Baptiste Vuillaume of Paris in 1849. It was very unwieldy and the strings were so thick and heavy that they had to be stopped by levers and pedals. The octobass was not considered a practical instrument.

octuor (Fr.) French equivalent of the English **octet**.

ō-daiko (Japan) Large, convex drum with two tacked skin heads. It is struck with sticks, but these differ according to the situation in which it is being used. In the **geza** percussion of the **kabuki** theatre, it is struck with two long, tapered sticks on both heads, generally as a representation of wind and rain. It is also struck one hour before the curtain rises (a ceremony known as *ichiban-daiko*) to indicate that a performance is due to take place.

In the Buddhist temple, only one head is struck with a single stick, and it is used as an accompaniment to the singing towards the end of a ceremony.

Finally, a crude version is used in the folk **hayashi** ensemble: it is placed on a crate with one head tipped towards the player and hit on the skin or rim with two blunt sticks.

ode Musical setting of a poem with alternating solos and choruses which is often dedicated to a monarch or deity. During the 17th and 18th centuries there were several English settings of odes in the form of **cantatas**, such as those by Purcell (*Come Ye Sons of Art*, composed for Queen Mary's birthday, 1694) and Handel (*Ode for St Cecilia's Day*, 1739). A 19th-century example is **Parry**'s setting of Milton's *Ode at a Solemn Music* (1887). The word is also used as a title for instrumental or orchestral works, such as Stravinsky's *Ode* or Copland's *Symphonic Ode*.

Offenbach, Jacques (1819-1880) French composer of German-Jewish origin and uncertain name who came from Offenbach am Main. He studied the cello and composition at the Paris Conservatoire, and subsequently played in orchestras and conducted. He was largely responsible for the development and popularity of the operetta, which became an established international genre. Most of his career was spent working in theatres such as the Théâtre Français, Bouffes Parisiens and Théâtre de la Gaîté, which he managed. His best-known works are *Orphée aux enfers* (1858), *La belle Hélène* (1864), *La vie parisienne* (1866), *La Grande-Duchesse de Gérolstein* and *La Périchole* (1868). His final and most serious work, though still an *opéra-comique*, was *Les contes d'Hoffmann*. This was unfinished at the time of his death, but was completed by **Guiraud** and produced in 1881.

offertorium (offertory) Part of the Proper of the Mass following the gospel or the Credo. It was originally an **antiphonal** chant, sung with a complete psalm, and accompanied the offering of bread and wine. In the 10th century the chants became more elaborate, with **melismas** in the responsorial style.

Ogdon, John (1937-1989) English pianist and composer. His compositions include a piano concerto, a sonata, and preludes for piano, but it was as a performer that he was best known. In 1962 he was a joint winner (with Vladimir **Ashkenazy**) of the International Tchaikovsky Competition in Moscow. His technique was powerful and agile, and his repertory vast, encompassing the Viennese classics, Romantics, Slavonic nationalists and, particularly, 20th-century works.

Ohana, Maurice (1914-) French composer of British and Spanish descent who studied in Paris and Barcelona. He began a career as a concert pianist before again studying in Paris, this time composition at the Schola Cantorum, and in Rome at the Accademia S. Cecilia. He returned to Paris, where in 1947 he became involved with **Dutilleux**'s and **Schaeffer**'s avant-garde studio work. He taught for many years and was a member of the Conservatoire's committee. The influences on his music are widely divergent, from **flamenco**, **Falla** and North African music to **Debussy** and **Boulez**; he has often experimented with micro-intervals. His works include operas (*Autodafé*, 1972), ballets, incidental music, film and radio scores; an oratorio, *Llanto por Ignacio Sanchez Mejias* (1950, based on Lorca), *Le tombeau de Claude Debussy* for soprano, zither, piano and orchestra (1962) and solo works for guitar, piano and oboe.

David Oistrakh

Oistrakh, David (1908-1974) Russian violinist who did not travel extensively in the West until the 1950s, even though he had won the Ysaÿe Prize in Brussels in 1937. His performances were characterized by his extraordinarily sweet tone, and many Soviet composers wrote works for him, including **Khachaturian** and **Shostakovich**. In 1945 he performed Bach's double violin concerto in Moscow with **Menuhin** – the first foreign artist to visit the Soviet Union after the war. His students included his son Igor and Valery Klimov. In 1954 he was named 'People's Artist of the USSR' and received the Lenin Prize in 1960.

Oistrakh, Igor (1931-) Soviet violinist somewhat overshadowed by his father and teacher David **Oistrakh**, but with a distinctive, less emotional and more modern style than his father's. In 1958 he was appointed to the staff of the Moscow Conservatoire and became a lecturer there in 1965. There are many recordings of father and son duos and double concertos, as well as performances with Igor as soloist and David as conductor.

Oldham, Arthur (1926-) English composer who studied at the Royal College of Music with **Howells**, and later with **Britten**. He has written several ballets (*Mr*

Punch, 1946; *Bonne bouche*, 1952), operas (*The Land of Green Ginger*, 1965) and many choral works, including sacred pieces (a *Mass for the Virgin Mary*, 1960; other Masses). His works for children include *Hymns for the Amusement of Children* (1962). He has also composed and arranged songs. He has had a distinguished career as a chorus-master, with the Scottish Opera Chorus, the London Symphony Orchestra Chorus and the choir of the French Orchestre Nationale.

oliphant Medieval horn made from an elephant's tusk or of gold. The oliphant was considered a symbol of high dignity by African kings during the 10th to 12th centuries.

Oliver, Stephen (1950-) British composer. He was a pupil of **Leighton** and Sherlaw **Johnson** and studied electronic music at Oxford. He has written the operas *Duchess of Malfi* (1971), *Ricercare* (1974), *Tom Jones* (1976), *Exchange* (1978) and a symphony. He also wrote the music for the Royal Shakespeare Company's *Nicholas Nickleby*, and for a number of radio and television productions, notably Tolkien's *The Lord of the Rings* for BBC Radio 4.

ondes martenot More common name for **martenot**.

Onslow, Georges (1784-1853) French composer of English descent who wrote operas, symphonies and chamber music, including more than 30 string quintets. He studied composition under Reicha in Paris. In 1842 he was elected to the Institut de France in succession to **Cherubini**. His compositions are now rarely heard, although he is known for his *Bullet Quintet* Op.38, in which he expresses the phases of illness and recovery, consequent upon being hit by a stray bullet during a boar-hunt.

Op. Abbreviation of **Opus**.

open Organ pipes whose upper ends are left open and which, unlike the stopped pipes, produce notes corresponding to their full length.

open form Compositions that can begin or end at any point in the score, at the performer's discretion. An example is **Stockhausen**'s *Zyklus* (1959) for solo percussionist, where the percussion instruments are arranged in a circle and the score is on spiral-bound pages, so that the player has freedom of choice to begin at any point and continue in a circular fashion until he or she reaches that point again.

Oper (Ger.) **Opera**, opera house or opera company.

opera Although the word covers any theatrical entertainment where the performers sing, and might include, for example, Chinese opera, it is usually taken to apply to the form developed in western Europe since its origin in Italy in the 17th century. The earliest examples were produced in Florence by a group around Giovanni de'Bardi known as the **Camerata**, with the intention of recreating ancient Greek drama; the text was declaimed in a form of **recitative**, interspersed with choruses. It is generally agreed that the first true opera was *Dafne*, text by Rinuccini, set to music by Corsi and Peri, and produced in 1594. **Monteverdi**'s *Orfeo* (1607) and *L'Arianna* (1608) introduced more sophisticated musical structures, with an elaborate orchestral accompaniment. From the first, Italianate music dominated the development of opera throughout Europe. Many of the court composers in Germany and Austria were Italian, or like **Hasse** and **Graun** composed in the Italian style, with largely Italian singers. Jean-Baptiste **Lully**, born Lulli in Florence, established the form of the French opera with a prologue and five acts, combining ballet-comedy, court airs, popular airs, recitative, pantomimes, dances and orchestral interludes. His successors, **Rameau, Delalande** and Campra, laid more emphasis on the ballet in a very formal court style.

In England, despite such successful efforts as *The Siege of Rhodes* (1656) by Nicholas Lanier, and above all **Purcell**'s *Dido and Aeneas* (1689), opera rapidly succumbed to the Italian taste, with the male **castrato** soprano as the star, although two of the most successful composers, **Handel** and J.C. **Bach**, were German.

From display to drama During the early years of the 18th century *opera seria*, by Italians and others, spread across Europe; the stars were male castrato sopranos; simple recitative linked a series of **arias**, the emphasis being on vocal display with mechanical repetitions rather than dramatic effect. Many of the librettos were by the prolific Italian dramatist Pietro Metastasio, who for some years was court poet in Vienna. His texts were set over and over again by many different composers, until the cultivated opera-goer almost knew them by heart. Although there were moves towards a more dramatic style, the major reform was effected by **Gluck** and his librettist Calzabigi – in Vienna with his operas *Orfeo* (1762) and *Alceste* (1767) and later in Paris with *Iphigénie en Tauride* (1779). Simple recitative gave way to **arioso**, and **scena**, arias and choruses were made part of the drama. In Gluck's words 'there should be one aim – and that is expressiveness'.

Comedy Although Italian style dominated Europe, new schools of opera in the local language grew up – notably in German, in Hamburg by composers such as **Keiser** and **Telemann**, and in Vienna's Karntnertor Theatre by the Hanswurst company. *Singspiel* was a popular form of opera, with stories about everyday life, often satirical, usually with a simple love-story; short songs and ensembles were linked by spoken dialogue. In 1778 the Emperor Joseph II instituted in Vienna what he called the German National *Singspiel*, with the intention of encouraging native poets and composers to produce works that could be understood by the local people. This natural style was also reflected in the development of operatic comedy in the early 18th century: Italian composers such as **Pergolesi**, **Paisiello**, **Cimarosa** and **Galuppi** created **opera buffa**, drawing on the Italian comedy tradition, especially the texts of Goldoni, often with a cast of familiar stock characters; the arias were short, with much less emphasis on vocal display, and each act ended with an elaborate ensemble.

In France **Rousseau**, **Philidor**, **Monsigny** and **Grétry** created **opéra-comique**, a charming, natural, somewhat romantic evocation of ordinary mortals, rather than gods and heroes. This was mirrored in England by the ballad opera, with simple familiar songs and spoken dialogue, typified by *The Beggar's Opera* (1728), **Arne**'s *Love in a Village* (1762), and **Dibdin**'s *Lionel and Clarissa* (1768). The potential of these forms was realized magnificently in the works of **Mozart**. He started by composing chiefly *opera seria*, but with *Idomeneo* (Munich, 1781) he produced a masterpiece which far transcended the current style with a rich orchestral accompaniment, complex ensembles, and a powerfully expressive chorus. With his comic operas, *Le nozze di Figaro* (Vienna, 1786) and *Così fan tutte* (1790), to librettos by Lorenzo da Ponte, he brought *opera buffa* to unparalleled levels of sophistication, enriched by subtle characterization and extended ensembles of variety. In *Don Giovanni* (1787) he fused many of the elements, producing a work of tragic power, enlivened by moments of near farce and enriched by music of rare depth and expression. In response to Joseph II's reforms he produced the most popular *Singspiel* of the day in *Die Entführung aus dem Serail* (1782), and later *Die Zauberflöte* (1791), where comedy alternates with passages of profound sublimity.

The 19th century Mozart's revelation of its potential foreshadowed the explosion of opera in the 19th century, matching the great expansion of prosperous middle-class audiences. Before the development of performing rights, opera was the only field where composers could make big money. Huge theatres were built in major cities like Milan, Paris, Vienna and London, while the rulers of the minor courts of Europe, notably in Germany, used opera for bolstering personal prestige.

In Italy the major force in the early years of the century was **Rossini**, who achieved success at the age of 19 with *Pietra del paragone* (Milan, 1812) and confirmed his genius with his comic masterpiece *Il barbiere di Siviglia* (Rome, 1816). When he moved to Paris in 1832, his florid style was displaced by the Romantic music of **Bellini** and **Donizetti**, who turned to a more dramatic idiom. **Verdi** strongly developed this aspect, and dominated Italian opera to the end of the century with his powerful music and vivid characterization. At the end of the century a more melodramatic, even violent idiom known as **verismo** was initiated by **Mascagni**'s *Cavalleria rusticana* (1890) and **Leoncavallo**'s *Pagliacci*.

In the early years of the century opera in Paris was dominated by foreign-born composers. **Cherubini**'s operas, such as *Les deux journées* (1800), had a powerful influence, especially on **Beethoven**'s only opera, *Fidelio* (1805), on the same theme. The Berlin-born **Meyerbeer** dominated French grand opera, in works with heroic themes and grandiose spectacle such as *Robert le diable* (1831) and *Les Huguenots* (1836). Rossini also influenced the lighter idiom of the *opéra-comique*, which, although not necessarily comedy, combined spoken dialogue with a more popular music style in works by **Hérold, Auber** and **Adam**. **Berlioz**'s style fitted neither of these categories: although he had little success in his lifetime, his three operas *Benvenuto Cellini*, *Béatrice et Bénédict* and especially *Les troyens* are now recognized as among the finest of their day. Later in the century the charming, melodious operas of **Gounod, Massenet, Bizet** and **Saint-Saëns** held the boards, along with imports from Italy and Germany.

Vienna, like many other European centres, succumbed to the Rossini craze, and made no significant contribution in the early years of the century. In Germany **Weber** created a new genre of Romantic opera in *Der Freischütz* and *Oberon*, with fantastic stories heightened by the imaginative use of the orchestra. **Wagner** at first retained the division into 'numbers', building on the romantic spirit of Weber allied to the heroic grandeur of Meyerbeer in his early operas *Rienzi* (1840) and *Der fliegende Holländer* (1841). Later he adopted a through-composed style for more realistic dramatic effect, exploring the world of German mythology in *Tannhäuser* (1845) and *Lohengrin* (1848). With *Tristan und Isolde* (1859) he began to explore the psychological power of music, bringing an entirely new dimension to opera that reached climax in *Der Ring des Nibelungen* and *Parsifal* (1882). Wagner transformed opera, wanting to create the complete artistic work, combining music, drama and spectacle. He was the first to have the house lights lowered during a performance; he wanted convincing acting, and he insisted on realistic costumes and scenery, with elaborate stage effects. He attained his ideal in the **Bayreuth** Festival Theatre, with superb acoustics, the conductor and orchestra completely hidden from the audience.

The rise of national feeling that marked the early years of the 19th century was evident in the development of national opera styles in Bohemia in the music of **Smetana**, in Poland in operas by **Moniuszko**, in Hungary in works by **Erkel** and Hubay, and above all in Russia, where **Glinka**, **Mussorgsky**, and **Borodin** explored the exotic brilliance of their native music.

The 20th century Until the end of the 19th century the public wanted new works and fine singers, not new productions or conductors. In the 20th, apart from the music of **Puccini**, whose highly dramatic but melodious operas were immensely successful, and to a lesser extent in Germany with the sensational operas of

Richard **Strauss**, audiences disliked 'modern' music, and preferred constant repetition of the established repertory. **Berg**'s *Wozzeck* (1925) and *Lulu* pleased the connoisseur with their vivid expressionism, but failed to command a wide audience. The only German composer to achieve an international reputation in recent years has been Hans Werner **Henze**.

In France **Debussy**'s atmospheric treatment of Maeterlinck's *Pelléas et Mélisande* took a new road, but remains a unique experiment. Attempts at showing contemporary life in such works as **Charpentier**'s *Louise* (Paris, 1900) and **Bruneau**'s setting of Zola's stories had a brief success. In Russia **Rimsky-Korsakov** developed the national style with colourful works such as *Le coq d'or* (1907), followed by the uneven but powerful operas of **Prokofiev** and **Shostakovich**. Opera in England during the early part of the century offered standard works with star singers in routine productions in London, or enthusiastic but underfunded companies performing in English. No composer of quality was revealed until the production at Sadler's Wells in 1945 of Benjamin **Britten**'s *Peter Grimes*. This heralded a notable renaissance of British opera, not only in quality of singing and production at our major theatres, but in the work of composers such as **Tippett** and **Walton**.

In America the high fees paid by opera companies, notably in Chicago and at the Metropolitan in New York, attracted the finest artists, and achieved high levels with singers such as **Caruso** under the direction of **Mahler** and **Toscanini**. But no native composer achieved any success before **Gershwin** produced his opera *Porgy and Bess* (1935); in recent years only Samuel **Barber**'s *Vanessa* (1958) has laid claim to international status, although Philip **Glass**'s operas *Einstein on the Beach* (1976) and *Akhnaten* (1985) have achieved great popularity. The American genius was for its own form of *Singspiel*, known as the musical.

Opera today commands ever greater enthusiasm, but remains largely a museum culture, in which great works of the past are revived with a constant search for new, often radical styles of production, sometimes in modern dress, overlaid with overt social and political messages. In many respects the standard of singing is higher than it has ever been in the past, with a welcome respect for accuracy and style. Television has played a major role in this expansion of interest, creating a new audience that no longer tolerates poor acting and staging. The only deterrent is the astronomic rise in costs, with huge fees for the stars, which could send opera in the theatre back to being an indulgence for the wealthy.

opera-ballet Combination of opera and ballet that originated in France during the 17th and 18th centuries, examples of which may be found in the work of such composers as **Lully** and **Rameau**.

opéra bouffe (Fr.) French comic opera of the 19th century, largely derived from the Italian **opera buffa**, such as **Offenbach's** operettas *Orphée aux enfers* (1858) and *La belle Hélène* (1864).

opera buffa (It.) Italian comic opera of the 18th and 19th centuries, which originated from the **intermezzo**. It is characterized by the use of recitative and the appearance of a chorus finale. The most famous operas of this type are **Pergolesi**'s *La serva padrona* (1733), **Rossini**'s *Il barbiere di Siviglia* and **Mozart**'s *Le nozze di Figaro*. The French rough equivalent is **opéra bouffe**, which is closer to musical farce than *opera buffa*.

opéra-comique (Fr.) French opera of the 18th century that was not necessarily humorous, but always involved spoken dialogue. One of the most notable exponents of this type of opera was François André **Philidor** (1726-95), whose works included *Le sorcier* (1764) and *Tom Jones* (1765). Other examples are

Gounod's *Faust* (1859) and **Bizet's** *Carmen* (1875).

Opera North Company founded in Leeds, Yorkshire, in 1978, originally as the northern branch of the **English National Opera.** The musical director and chief conductor of its orchestra, the English Northern Philharmonia, was David Lloyd-Jones, who became artistic director in 1981 when the company gained its independence from the ENO and took its present name. The company has pursued a policy of balancing the standard Mozart and Verdi operas with a more adventurous repertory, notably several Russian and Eastern European works: Mussorgsky's *Boris Godunov* and Prokofiev's *The Love for Three Oranges* have been particularly successful, as have Smetana's *The Bartered Bride,* Borodin's *Prince Igor* and Janáček's *Jenůfa* and *Katya Kabanova.* In 1983 the company commissioned *Rebecca* from Wilfred **Josephs**. Opera North has a consistently high level of attendance – 93 per cent in 1989; its programme is always stimulating, with the first British productions of **Nielsen**'s *Masquerade* and Verdi's *Jerusalem* (both in 1990) to its credit. Lloyd-Jones left in 1990 and Paul Daniel then became musical director.

opera-oratorio Term used by **Stravinsky** to describe his *Oedipus Rex* (1927), in which the singers are placed in a static position on the stage so that the work is half-way between an opera and an oratorio.

opera semi-seria (It.) Italian opera that is neither wholly comic nor wholly tragic. An example of this is **Mozart**'s *Don Giovanni* (1787), in which the plot is serious, although there are also comic elements.

opera seria (It.) Opera of the 18th and early 19th centuries in which the plot is heroic, mythological or tragic. Apostolo Zeno (1668-1750), the librettist, is considered one of its founders; Pietro Metastasio (1698-1782) was the most influential librettist of the genre, and his texts were set by numerous composers. The elaborate formal *da capo* aria at the end of a scene was an outstanding feature. The leading part was generally written for **castrato**; a leading lady and a tenor (for the weighty roles – kings and so on – now more usually sung by a baritone) made up the primary group of singers, with secondary castrato and female performers as required. Examples of the genre include **Galuppi's** *Artaserse* and Mozart's *La clemenza di Tito.*

operetta Light opera or musical comedy, normally with spoken dialogue. See also **musical comedy**.

ophicleide Large 19th-century bass instrument similar to the key bugle, with a cup-shaped mouthpiece and holes in the side covered with keys. It was a baritone instrument made in C or B♭, and was superseded by the **tuba** in about 1850.

opus (Lat.) Work. Used for the enumeration of a composer's works. Its abbreviated form is Op. Originally it was used by music publishers (not composers) in the early 18th century and more often for instrumental works. It was used for the works of **Handel**, although not for those of **Mozart**; from the time of **Beethoven** it began to be used regularly. The number of the opus does not necessarily indicate the date of its composition. Because there was some confusion with the number system, the works of some composers have their own classifications. These include **J.S. Bach** (BWV), **Mozart** (K), **Haydn** (Hob.), **Schubert** (D), D. **Scarlatti** (Kk) and **Vivaldi** (RV).

oratorio Large-scale composition for solo voices, chorus and orchestra with a libretto based on sacred words from the Bible or paraphrased from it. The form took its name from the Oratory of St Philip **Neri** in Rome, where scenes from the Scripture were enacted with music in the 16th century. It was there in 1600 that

Cavalieri's *Rappresentazione di anima e di corpo*, an operatic morality play demanding acting and ballet, was produced. Acting and dancing were soon abandoned, so that the oratorios of **Carissimi**, such as *Jephtha* (1650), are dramatic works sung with massive choruses.

The culmination of **Baroque** oratorio was achieved by **Handel** with his mastery of choral technique. Altogether he composed more than 20 oratorios, including *Israel in Egypt* (1739), *Messiah* (1741), *Samson* (1743), *Belshazzar* (1745) and *Solomon* (1749). Later oratorios include **Haydn**'s *Seven Last Words* (1797) and *The Creation* (1797), **Mendelssohn**'s *St Paul* (1830), **Liszt**'s *Christus* (1866), **Parry**'s *Job* (1888), **Elgar**'s *The Apostles* (1903) and **Walton**'s *Belshazzar's Feast* (1931).

Orchésographie Title of a French treatise on dancing published in 1588 by Thoinot **Arbeau**. The treatise is an important source of information about contemporary dance music. The tunes used as examples of dances were taken by **Delibes** for his ballet *Le Roi s'amuse*, and by **Warlock** for his *Capriol Suite*, Capriol being the name given to one of the participants in the dialogue form of the treatise.

orchestra A group of instrumentalists of varied size. The original Greek word described the front of the theatre where the chorus danced and sang. By the 18th century the word was applied to the instrumentalists in the theatre. In Germany the word *Kapelle* (from *capella*, chapel) was and still is often preferred, and in Britain the word 'band', although in modern times this is confined to groups of wind instruments or to popular groups, as in jazz. The orchestras of the 17th century were usually varied groups of stringed instruments, with a wide variety of wind instruments added for solos and harmonic support from a **continuo** instrument, such as a harpsichord, harp, lute, theorbo or organ.

By the early years of the 18th century the four-part string orchestra was established, with flutes, oboes, bassoons and horns as the standard wind section. When trumpets were added, they were invariably accompanied by the **timpani**. From about the middle of the 18th century clarinets gradually entered the orchestra, first in France, and later in Germany and Italy. It is a mistake, encouraged by modern performance practice, to assume that orchestras in the late 18th century were small; a large opera house in France or Italy might have had as many as 40 or 50 strings, with doubled woodwind. Trombones were regularly used in choral words to double the lower choral parts, and by the end of the 18th century they were an accepted feature of French opera orchestras, and soon were to be found in major orchestras throughout Europe, although often imported from the town band or the local military. The harp and simple percussion were added for special theatrical effects, but were rare in concert music.

The harmonic support provided by the continuo was rendered superfluous by the expansion of the orchestra at the beginning of the 19th century, with someone, often the composer, directing from the keyboard. Otherwise matters were controlled by the principal first violin, waving his or her bow, who continued to do so even after conductors appeared brandishing a baton – Mendelssohn and Wagner were subjected to this irritating practice in London, with often dire effects on the performance. The importance accorded the leading violin in Britain is preserved by his or her separate entrance at the start of a concert, a practice not followed in many places abroad, and observed with general amusement by visiting orchestras.

In the middle of the 19th century Wagner enlarged the orchestra to heighten its dramatic power, with, at first, triple and later quadruple woodwind, as many as eight horns, sometimes doubling as tenor tubas, and many trumpets, including a bass trumpet. The strings had to be enlarged to match this mass of tone, until the total approached a hundred players – with, optimistically, as many as 12 harps in one passage in the *Ring*. The French, led by Berlioz, expanded the percussion section with ever more exotic sounds, until in the music of Ravel as many as nine or ten players were needed. The mammoth orchestra of Wagner was even further expanded by Richard Strauss and Mahler, until the sheer cost began to make performances impractical without considerable subsidy. One consequence in the 20th century has been the development of the chamber orchestra, with as few as 20 or 30 players, sometimes strings alone; this is appropriate for many 18th-century works as well as the growing repertory provided by such composers as **Webern, Stravinsky, Milhaud, Martinů, Tippett** and **Britten**. When this development was followed by the chamber ensemble of solo instruments, suited to the spare linear style of **serialists** such as **Boulez, Maderna** and **Dallapiccola**, many avant-garde critics were ready to write the epitaph of the large romantic orchestra. Audiences, however, continue to revel in its rich palette of colour, although its repertory consists almost exclusively of music of the past.

As the orchestra developed in the 18th and early 19th centuries the layout of the players was often haphazard. Sir Michael Costa (1808-84) is credited with pioneering a more rational layout, grouping the wind together in the middle. It became standard practice to place the two violin sections on opposite sides, which encouraged composers from Beethoven to Elgar to write antiphonal effects. Although this layout was kept by such conductors as **Boult** and **Toscanini**, the modern practice is to have both sections on the conductor's left, to achieve better ensemble and greater brilliance. Another older feature was the line of double-basses along the back of the orchestra, to give a rich foundation to the tone. This was an aspect of one of several layouts favoured by **Stokowski**, who was continually experimenting to enhance the rich sonority he aimed to draw from an orchestra.

orchestration Art of blending and contrasting the tonal qualities of the various orchestral instruments. Some composers work out their first ideas in a **short score** by indicating the most important colouring of the instruments and their combinations. Upon completion in this form, they apply it to the final score.

Orchestre de Paris French symphony orchestra founded in 1967 following pressure from General de Gaulle to provide France with a world-class orchestra. Its conductors have included Charles **Münch**, Herbert von **Karajan**, Georg **Solti** and Daniel **Barenboim**.

Ord, Boris (1897-1961) English organist and conductor. He founded the Cambridge University Madrigal Society, and was responsible for making the choir of King's College internationally famous through its Christmas Eve broadcasts. He was made a CBE in 1958.

ordre (Fr.) 17th- and 18th-century French equivalent of **suite**.

Orff, Carl (1895-1982) German teacher, editor and composer, born in Munich. As a composer he is best known for *Carmina Burana* (1938), a section of the tripartite *Trionfi* which also includes *Il trionfo di Afrodite* and *Catulli Carmina*: it is a setting of poetry, often erotic, by medieval monks, preserved in a manuscript in the German monastery of Beuren. He strove for the creation of 'total theatre' with music, words and dance united as in Greek tragedy. In 1924 he formed the Günterschule for Gymnastics, Music and Dance in Munich. He wanted to explore and teach new relationships between dance and music, and was influenced in this by Mary Wigman, a pupil of Emile **Jacques-Dalcroze**.

organ Keyboard instrument of great antiquity, the earliest of which originated with the mouth-blown **panpipes**. The first mechanically-blown organ was the ancient

Greek **hydraulis**, invented in the 3rd century BC by Ctesibios of Alexandria. The organ can be the simplest and the most complex of musical wind instruments. It is simple because every pipe produces only a single note when a mechanical valve admits compressed air to it. It is complex because, in its fully developed form, it is a vast agglomeration of mechanisms controlling a huge number of tonal combinations.

With the introduction of bellows, air was blown into the **pipes**. These were opened and closed by an action of keys, and a keyboard of pedals, operated by the feet, was added to control the largest bass pipes. The number of pipes, measuring from 32ft down to less than an inch, was increased. They were made in a variety of shapes, with different speaking-mechanisms, each range being controlled by stops which could be brought into action or shut off at the performer's discretion. The number of **manuals** (hand keyboards) increased to three or more, which meant that a greater number of stops drawn before the performance could be controlled and varied.

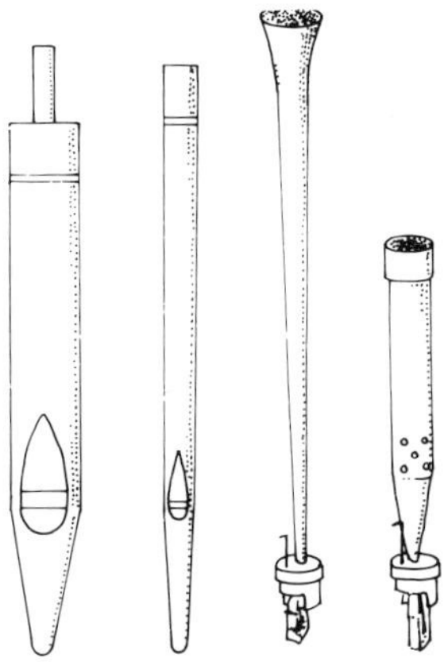

Four types of organ pipe

During the late 19th century, the bellows – previously blown by hand – were generally operated mechanically and devices by which whole ranges of stops could be activated in various combinations were invented. By using **couplers** which interlock the mechanisms of the keyboards, it was possible to play two or more sections at once from a single manual, and so bring into use the immense resources of the whole instrument, or to link certain stops on different manuals in new tonal combinations. Expression was added by **swell pedals** which produced crescendo and diminuendo, but beyond that the player's hands and feet have no power to vary the tone either in strength or in quality.

The organ was introduced into the English Church by the 8th century, and up to the 19th century it was still primarily associated with the Church. It is used as a **continuo** instrument; it also appears with the orchestra in such works as **Saint-Saëns**'s Symphony No.3, **Elgar**'s *Cockaigne* overture and at the beginning of Verdi's *Otello*. Its orchestral use is quite frequent in Britain because some large concert-halls, such as the Royal Albert Hall, have an organ built in (the Saint-Saëns symphony was written for performance there). There are organ concertos by Handel and **Poulenc**, among others.

The organ was popular in the cinema and theatre during the 1920s and 1930s. The electronic organ, with synthesized or sampled sounds, has an important place in serious as well as popular music. See also **electronic organ**.

organistrum Alternative term for **hurdy-gurdy**.

organ point Keys (pedals) of an organ that are played with the feet.

organum Earliest type of medieval polyphony, from the 9th to the 13th century, which appeared in sacred music and was based on **plainsong**. There are three basic types of organum.

In parallel organum the added voice moves wholly or mainly in parallel fourths or fifths with the chant, note for note.

In the 11th century, strict parallel organum was replaced by free organum, in which the added voice moves in a free succession of intervals, still moving note against note.

A new type of organum emerged in the early 12th century, called melismatic organum. A plainsong, or part of one, was assigned to one voice in long sustained notes to which was added a higher voice in faster-moving note-values.

Orgel (Ger.) **Organ**.

Ormandy, Eugene (1899-1985) Hungarian-born conductor and violinist who settled in the United States and became an American citizen in 1927. His first job there was playing in the Radio City orchestra, where he later had the chance to conduct. He became principal conductor of the Minneapolis Symphony Orchestra in 1931, and in 1938 succeeded **Stokowski** as conductor of the Philadelphia Symphony Orchestra. His repertory is concentrated on late Romantic and early 20th-century composers, and his recordings include Mahler's 10th Symphony. In 1948 he conducted the first symphony concert shown on American television – beating **Toscanini** on a rival network by 1½ hours. He was made an honorary KBE in 1976.

Eugene Ormandy

ornament Notated or improvised decorative notes or phrases added to the basic melodic line in vocal or instrumental music. The most common musical ornaments are **appoggiatura**, **acciaccatura**, **upper** and **lower mordents**, the **turn**, **slide** and **trill**.

Orozco, Rafael (1946-) Spanish pianist who studied with Alexis **Weissenberg** at the Academia Chigiana in Siena and gained the diploma of merit in 1964. In 1966 he won the Leeds Piano Competition and is particularly well known for his interpretation of **Rachmaninov**'s concertos.

Orr, Robin (1909-) Scottish composer. He was a pupil of **Casella** in Siena and Nadia **Boulanger** in Paris. He was a professor at Glasgow University until 1965 and thereafter at Cambridge. His compositions include two operas, *Full Circle* (1968) and *Weir of Hermiston* (1975), orchestral and chamber works, song-cycles and church music.

Orrego-Salas, Juan Antonio (1919-) Chilean composer and musicologist. He was a student of Thompson and **Copland** and was appointed professor of composition at the University of Chile in 1947. He was the founder and director of the Latin American Music Centre (1961), promoting Latin American music through festivals and broadcasts, setting up the largest existing library of scores and recordings of 20th-century music from this area. His own music involves a free style incorporating formal procedures taken from all periods after the Middle Ages.

ossia (It.) Or, maybe. Indication used by either the composer or an editor to introduce an alternative musical passage to the main text, which is normally easier to play than the original theme.

ostinato (It.) Persistent. A figure that is repeated throughout a composition. For example, if it is in the bass, it is called *basso ostinato* (ground bass). An ostinato occurs in the final section of Stravinsky's *Symphony of Psalms* (1930). Ostinato was greatly used by Holst, and more recently by **minimalist** composers such as **Glass** and **Reich**.

Ostrčil, Otakar (1879-1935) Czech composer, conductor and administrator who was concerned with encouraging modern music; in 1924 he founded The Society for Modern Music in Prague. He was responsible for introducing audiences to national composers such as **Janáček** and **Fibich**, and to international composers including Stravinsky and Schoenberg. In this way he was influential in moving Czech music away from the purely nationalistic towards a more international avant-garde. His own compositions include operas – *Legenda z Erinin* (The Legend of Erin, 1921) – but were largely orchestral, and, like his conducting, were analytical rather than romantic in style.

ottoni (It.) Brass instruments.

Ouseley, Sir Frederick Arthur Gore (1825-1889) English church musician, scholar and composer. As a child he was very precocious, composing from the age of three and developing an accurate musical ear – at the age of five he could recognize the key in which his father blew his nose. Educated at Oxford, he then went into the Church, returning to Oxford in 1855 as a professor. He was keen to purge religious music of all contemporary secular influences and modelled his own style on those of Mozart and Handel. In 1854 he founded the Church of St Michael and All Saints, Tenbury, which now houses his very valuable collection of manuscripts, books and scores.

Ousset, Cécile (1936-) French pianist who studied at the Paris Conservatoire with Ciampi. She won numerous competitions and commenced an international career, performing not only in Europe and the United States but also in Japan, Australia and New Zealand. Her British début was in 1980 at the Edinburgh Festival; since then she has often appeared on television and has been the subject of a BBC profile. Her recording of Brahms's Piano Concerto No.2 with **Masur** and the Leipzig Gewandhaus Orchestra won the Grand Prix du Disque; she has also made fine recordings of works by Ravel, Debussy, Mendelssohn, Liszt, Rachmaninov and Chopin. She has performed with many of the world's leading conductors and orchestras, and also gives master-classes.

overblowing Playing of a wind instrument in such a way that the upper harmonics are produced instead of the fundamental notes. Unwanted overblowing may occur in organ pipes if the wind pressure is excessive, but safety valves have been invented to prevent this.

overstrung Positioning of piano strings such that they are made in two ranges, crossing each other diagonally to save space and to secure greater length in the strings.

overtone Any note of the harmonic series except the first harmonic (fundamental). Sometimes also known as a partial. See also **acoustics**.

overture Instrumental composition that introduces an **opera**, **oratorio** or play. Some operas of the early 17th century incorporated the overture, but usually it was to alert the audience that the opera proper was about to begin.

Later in the same century the French overture was introduced by **Lully**, and the Italian overture by Alessandro **Scarlatti**. Lully's French overture had a slow introduction, with a predominance of dotted rhythms, followed by a quick movement of a somewhat lightly and freely treated contrapuntal style. The overture to Handel's *Messiah* is a typical example of the French style. The Italian type of overture was often called **sinfonia**. It had three sections, quick-slow-quick.

During the 18th century the French type of overture became a simple movement in

sonata-like form, such as **Haydn**'s *Creation* (1798) and **Mozart**'s *Die Zauberflöte* (1791). With **Gluck**'s opera *Iphigénie en Tauride* (1779), the overture anticipated the mood of the first scene in which a storm is represented. The same process of integrating the overture into the opera as a whole was followed in the 19th century by **Weber** (*Der Freischütz*, 1821) and in the preludes to the **music dramas** of **Wagner**'s.

The concert overture is an independent orchestral composition. Examples of these are **Berlioz**'s *Le carnaval romain* (1844) and **Brahms**'s *Academic Festival Overture* (1880). **Beethoven**'s operatic or dramatic overtures, the three *Leonora* overtures and *Coriolanus* (1807), are played as concert overtures. The term was also used by **J.S. Bach** to name four **suites** for orchestra.

Ozawa, Seiji (1935-) Japanese conductor who went to Europe in 1959. He was noticed by **Bernstein** while working with von **Karajan** in Berlin, and was invited to be assistant conductor of the New York Philharmonic Orchestra (1961-2). He has been music director of the Chicago Symphony Orchestra's Ravinia Festival, of the Toronto Symphony Orchestra, of the San Francisco Symphony Orchestra, and in 1973 was appointed director of the Boston Symphony Orchestra. In 1974 he made his Covent Garden début with *Eugene Onegin*. He has appeared regularly at Salzburg since 1969. He has a flamboyant but clear style, focusing on large 19th-century and early 20th-century works.

Seiji Ozawa

P

Pachelbel, Johann (1653-1706) German organist and composer who, after studying under Heinrich Schwemmer, went on to hold several important posts including that of organist at St Sebaldus's church in Nuremberg. He was one of the most productive and progressive composers of the 17th century. His work has never been entirely forgotten, and has recently been re-evaluated. It includes 94 organ fugues on the Magnificat, 78 choral preludes, chamber music and numerous suites and variations for the keyboard, of which his 11 concertato settings of the Magnificat and the *Hexachordum Apollinis* (1699) are perhaps best known. His keyboard compositions are of particular importance in their influence on **J.S. Bach**.

Pachman, Vladimir (1848-1933) Ukrainian pianist, who studied first under his father, a celebrated amateur violinist, and later at the Vienna Conservatoire. After a highly successful début in Odessa in 1896, he became dissatisfied with his performances and retired, only to resume his career ten years later, playing in all the principal cities of Europe and the United States. A particularly fine exponent of the work of **Chopin**, he was well known for his eccentricities in performance, often making remarks to his audience while playing.

Pacini, Giovanni (1796-1867) Italian composer, whose first performed opera (*Annetta e Lucindo*, 1813) was written at the age of 17. He wrote music with extraordinary speed. He composed 90 operas, mostly in the comic Rossini manner, and was also a prolific composer of sacred music. In 1834 he settled at Viareggio in Italy, and there he opened a music school which later transferred to Lucca. His best known and most successful opera was *Sappho*, first performed in Naples in 1840, but he is also remembered for his lively memoirs, a valuable source of information on opera of the period.

Paderewski, Ignacy (1860-1941) Polish pianist and composer who studied in Warsaw and Vienna, where he was once advised by his teacher Leschetizky to give up his career as a pianist; he went on to become a successful concert artist who played throughout the world and was a particular favourite with British audiences. His compositions include the romantic opera *Manru* (1901) and many works for the piano, including a piano concerto, the *Fantasie polonaise* and the *Minuet in G* (only the last has survived as part of the modern concert repertory). After the outbreak of World War I he collected large sums of money for the Polish relief fund and later became prime minister and minister of foreign affairs in Poland (1919), returning to his concert and teaching career in 1922. In 1936 he appeared in the British film *Moonlight Sonata*.

Paer, Ferdinando (1771-1839) Italian composer, originally a violinist, who became *maître de chapelle* to Napoleon, for whom he wrote the bridal march for his wedding to Marie Louise of Austria. Napoleon appointed him director of the

Opéra-Comique and later the Théâtre Italien in Paris, where Paer settled (1807). He wrote 53 operas, including *Leonora* (1804), based on the same plot **Beethoven** was to use in his opera *Fidelio* the following year, and also composed oratorios, Masses, motets and many instrumental works. In 1820 he numbered **Liszt** among his composition pupils.

Paganini, Niccolò (1782-1840) Italian violinist and composer whose virtuosity and personal magnetism brought him fame throughout Europe. He studied the violin with his father, Cervetto and Costa and composition with Ghiretti and **Paer**. At the age of 15 he was already playing his own compositions in order to display his virtuosity, pioneering the use of harmonics and retuning his instrument to obtain special effects. His career included a number of triumphant European tours (to Austria, France, Germany and England) during which he made a considerable personal fortune, at the cost of his health. His virtuosity encouraged other composers – such as Liszt, Schumann and Chopin – to expand the technical and expressive limits of their instruments, and his own compositions, in particular his bravura variations *Le streghe* (1813), are a considerable achievement. He wrote six concertos for violin and orchestra, another dozen or so sets of variations, sonatas, string quartets and 24 caprices for solo violin. **Rachmaninov**'s *Rhapsody on a Theme by Paganini* is based on the famous A minor Caprice, which has also been a favourite subject for variations by other composers: Schumann's piano studies, Brahms's piano variations, Lutosławski's variations for two pianos (later orchestrated), **Blacher**'s variations for orchestra, and **Lloyd Webber**'s for cello, used as the theme music for the television arts programme *The South Bank Show*.

Paisiello, Giovanni (1740-1816) Italian composer, most successfully of **opera buffa**. Between 1764 and 1784 he produced many works in Modena, Naples, Venice and at the Russian court of Catherine II at St Petersburg, and became musical director to Napoleon Bonaparte, who greatly admired his music. He was astonishingly prolific: his compositions include sacred music, 12 symphonies, six piano concertos and over 100 operas, the most famous of which are *Il barbiere di Siviglia* (later upstaged by Rossini's setting of the same story), *Il re Teodoro in Venezia*, and *Nina* (1789). From about 1790 his works became more serious in tone.

pakad (India) Short, melodic catch-phrase in a composition which is characteristic of, and therefore identifies, a particular **rāga** melody.

pakhāvaj/pakhāwaj (India) Double-headed barrel drum from northern India, played in a horizontal position with the hands. Used in **dhrupad** and to accompany the **bīn**.

Palestrina, Giovanni Pierluigi da (*c*.1525-1594) Italian composer, organist and choirmaster who was one of the most important figures in 16th-century music. He studied in Rome, and spent his musical life in the service of the Church. From 1544 he was organist in his home town of Palestrina, and moved to Rome again when its bishop became Pope Julius III. He was appointed *maestro di cappella* of the Julian Chapel at St Peter's, and also became a member of the Sistine Choir. He later held several other important appointments, including *maestro di cappella* of St John Lateran and S. Maria Maggiore, supervisor of musicians to Cardinal Ippolito d'Este, and a teaching post at the seminary. Much of his music was published during his lifetime, including four volumes of **motets** and six volumes of **Masses**. He composed 94 of these altogether, among them the *Missa Papae Marcelli*. He was a good businessman and his second marriage to a rich widow enabled him to publish 16 collections of his music during the last 13 years of his life. In his music, particularly that for the Church, the technique of

polyphony reached its peak.

Pallavicino, Benedetto (1551-1601) Italian composer, a monk who was a prolific and popular madrigalist. His work was esteemed by his contemporaries. He also wrote sacred music including psalms, motets, and four Masses which were published posthumously. He was appointed *maestro di cappella* in Mantua (1596-1601), preceding **Monteverdi**, and later retired to a monastery in Tuscany.

Pallavicino, Carlo (1630-1688) Italian composer, chiefly of opera, and one of the leading and most popular in Venice between 1675 and 1685, where all but one of his 20 operas were produced. He also wrote sacred music. Pallavicino divided his time between Venice and Dresden, where he was *Kapellmeister*, and where he died.

Palmgren, Selim (1878-1951) Finnish pianist, conductor and composer, who studied at Helsinki Conservatoire and then in Germany and Italy under **Busoni**. He toured and taught in the United States and Europe, where he was accompanied by his first wife, the singer Maikki Järnefelt. His works include many short piano pieces, two operas, choral works, five piano concertos and songs. His music is characterized by its technical mastery and pictorial quality, sometimes with a strong national flavour.

pan calypso See **calypso**; **steel band**

pandora 16th-century English stringed instrument similar to the **cittern**, with six or seven metal strings that were plucked with the fingers. It was often used as a **continuo** instrument.

panpipes Set of simple flutes of different lengths fixed side by side to give a scale when blown. Panpipes date back to antiquity, and are nowadays heard in the folk-music of many areas, especially Romania and Peru. Mozart used them for Papageno's signature-tune in *Die Zauberflöte*.

p'ansori (Korea) Dramatic narrative form, performed by a narrator who sings, speaks and gesticulates, accompanied by a drummer. It probably developed from an archaic form of shamanistic folk drama which may have included theatrical performance, but since the 18th century has been refined for courtly use. Musical resources include a variety of modes and rhythmic patterns which denote particular characters or moods. A full open-air performance, lasting up to eight hours, makes heavy demands on the narrator, who maintains a forced vocal delivery throughout.

pantomime Derived from the Greek 'all-imitating', it was probably originally a play in dumb-show. Since the 18th century, pantomime has been a popular form of stage entertainment in England. It is still based mainly on fairy-tales, and was influenced by the characters and forms of the Italian *commedia dell'arte*, including Harlequin, Pantaloon and Clown.

pantonality Term coined in the 20th century for **atonality**, in which music is not written in any definite key. Pantonal harmony is a feature of the music of such composers as **Ligeti**, **Schoenberg**, **Stockhausen** and **Webern**.

Panufnik, Andrzej (1914-) Polish composer and conductor who studied with Sikorski at the Warsaw Conservatoire, and later became conductor of the Krakow and Warsaw Symphony Orchestras. He left Poland in protest against political regimentation, settling in England in 1954. He was conductor of the Birmingham Symphony Orchestra between 1957 and 1959, resigning to concentrate on composition. His works include six

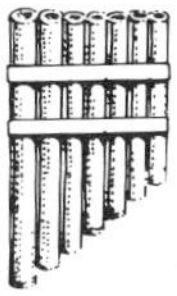

Panpipes

symphonies, of which the *Sinfonia Rustica* and *Sinfonia Sacra* are best known, film music, Polish folk-song settings, works for the piano, including a concerto, and instrumental works for small ensemble (*Metasinfonia* for organ, strings and timpani; *Concertino* for percussion and strings, 1980). Panufnik has also published an autobiography.

Papaïoannou, Yannis (1911-) Greek composer who studied with **Honegger** and at the Hellenic Conservatoire, where he later taught counterpoint and composition. He was almost solely responsible for encouraging Greek composers to adapt to avant-garde techniques, using **twelve-note** and total **serial** methods in his own compositions, which also reflect his interest in tribal music and Byzantine chants. His works include five symphonies, chamber music, songs and an orchestral tone poem after the poet Shelley, *Hellas*.

Papandopoulo, Boris (1906-) Yugoslav composer and conductor, born in Germany. He studied in Zagreb and Vienna, and became a noted conductor, working at various opera-houses in Yugoslavia. His compositions contain elements of folk-music, neo-classicism and the Baroque influence; they include six ballets, four operas, two symphonies and a *Sinfonietta* (1938). From about 1943 he produced many concertos, for violin, piano, trumpet and harpsichord, and the *Concerto for Four Timpani* (1969), an inventive and exhilarating piece; cantatas (*Legends of Tito*, 1960), oratorios (including a Passion), string quartets and other chamber music.

parallel motion The movement of two lines of music in the same direction by the same interval. Traditional harmony forbade parallel fifths, octaves and fourths with the bass, because they sounded poor and confused the tonality, although examples can be found in every great master from Bach downwards. Parallel motion of this sort, however, has become a feature in the 20th century, notably in the opening of Act 2 of Puccini's *La bohème* and in the music of **Vaughan Williams**. See also **conjunct motion**; **contrary motion**; **disjunct motion**; **oblique motion**; **similar motion**.

Paray, Paul (1886-1979) French conductor and composer who studied in Rouen and at the Paris Conservatoire. He won the Prix de Rome in 1911 and made his début in 1920, becoming principal conductor of the Concerts Lamoureux in 1923. His next appointment was with the Monte Carlo Orchestra; following this he returned to Paris to take up the post of principal conductor of the Concerts Colonne (1933) where, with a break during the war, he remained until 1952. Thereupon he moved to the United States as chief conductor of the Detroit Symphony Orchestra (until 1963). His compositions include the *Mass of Joan of Arc*, a ballet (*Artemis troublée*, 1922), two symphonies, piano and chamber music.

Parikian, Manoug (1920-1987) British violinist of Armenian descent, born in Turkey. He studied at Trinity College and made his début in Liverpool in 1947. He was leader of the Liverpool Philharmonic, and then of the Philharmonia Orchestra (1949-57) before embarking on a highly successful solo career. His fine technique and beauty of tone can be appreciated from his numerous recordings. Many composers wrote works for him, including **Goehr**, **Musgrave** and **Maconchy**.

Parker, Horatio (1863-1919) American organist and composer whose music is now largely neglected, despite its success during his lifetime. He studied in Boston and Munich where he was a pupil of **Rheinberger**. He held organ posts in New York and taught at the National Conservatoire when **Dvořák** was director, and later became professor of music at Yale. The oratorio *Hora Novissima* (1893) brought him to national prominence; his further works include cantatas, choral ballads, songs and anthems and other orchestral pieces. His second area of composition was theatre music, both incidental music for plays and two operas, *Mona* (1910) and *Fairyland* (1914).

parlando (It.) Speaking. In singing, it is used to give more emphasis to the natural articulation of the text than to sustaining the tone.

Parrott, Ian (1916-) English composer and teacher who identified himself closely with the language, culture and music of Wales. He studied at the Royal College of Music and later became professor of music at University College, Aberystwyth. His works include the opera *The Sergeant Major's Daughter*, a folk opera, *The Black Ram* (1952), a ballet, *The Maid in Birmingham*, three symphonies, choral works, songs and other instrumental pieces.

Parry, Sir Hubert (1848-1918) English composer, writer and teacher. He did not make his mark in public until his Piano Concerto was played in 1880 by Dannreuther, with whom he studied, and in the same year his choral scenes from Shelley's *Prometheus Unbound* appeared. His works include *Blest Pair of Sirens*, *Songs of Farewell* and *I was Glad* (1902). In 1916 he wrote the unison setting for Blake's *Jerusalem*, which has become a national song. He was the author of several books that helped to restore the place of music in academic life, including a study of Bach and a volume of the Oxford History of Music. From 1894 until his death he was director of the Royal College of Music and from 1900 to 1908 he was professor of music at Oxford University. An influential figure, he did much to infuse new vigour into the English musical scene. His church music is still often heard. He was knighted in 1898 and made a baronet in 1903.

Parsons, Geoffrey (1929-) Australian pianist, one of the outstanding accompanists of the day. He studied in Sydney and Munich and made his début in 1946 as a soloist; two years later he began a career as an accompanist. In 1950 he moved to England, where he established notable partnerships with several leading singers and instrumentalists, Elisabeth **Schwarzkopf**, Victoria de **los Angeles**, Paul **Tortelier** and Nicolai **Gedda** among them. He is an authoritative but subtle player, greatly admired for his sensitivity. He has made numerous recordings, and has also given televised master-classes.

part 1. The music written for a particular voice (e.g. the tenor part) or instrument (e.g. the flute part) in an ensemble, orchestra or choir.

2. A strand of melody in **polyphonic** music, e.g. fugue in four parts or four-part fugue.

3. A section of a cantata or oratorio which corresponds to an act in an opera.

Partch, Harry (1901-1974) American composer and instrument-maker who, having destroyed all his previous compositions at the age of 25, spent the Depression years wandering across the United States as a hobo and worked for some time as a lumberjack. His compositions include *Eight Hitchhiker Inscriptions from a California Highway Railing* and *US Highball, a Musical Account of a Transcontinental Hobo Trip*. Largely self-taught, he experimented with **microtonal** scales (using a system of intonation with 43 notes to the octave) and new experimental and often theatrical instruments, including the **marimba** eroica and **chromelodeon**.

partials Name given to the notes of the **harmonic series** produced when a string or column of air vibrates. The lowest note heard is known as the first partial, or fundamental tone, and the higher ones are upper partials or **overtones**.

partita Term used originally in the 18th century for a **suite** or set of variations. It also referred to a set of variations on a chorale tune, known as chorale partita.

Examples include **J. S. Bach**'s chorale partitas for organ. In addition, it is used as a name for modern works such as Walton's *Partita* for orchestra.

pas de deux (Fr.) In ballet, a dance for two, or music for such a dance.

paso doble Spanish dance in a martial 2/4 time, in which the movements of the dancer imitate the actions of a toreador and his cape.

Pasquini, Bernardo (1637-1710) Italian composer, harpsichordist and organist who was renowned in his day as a virtuoso keyboard player. He was also a considerable composer, mainly for the keyboard. He was the organist of S. Maria Maggiore, Rome, where he also played harpsichord continuo in the opera-house orchestra, with **Corelli** as his first violinist. Pasquini's output included 14 operas, suites for the harpsichord, oratorios, cantatas, sonatas, arias and motets, but despite his reputation little of his music was published.

passacaglia (It.) Originally a Spanish or Italian dance, similar to the **chaconne**. It is more commonly known as an instrumental piece consisting of continuous variations in slow triple time above a **ground** bass. One of the best-known examples is **Bach**'s Passacaglia in C minor for organ. The last movement of **Brahms**'s Symphony No.4, although not so entitled, is also in this form.

passage Any melodic or decorative section in a composition, e.g. a fortissimo or staccato passage.

passage work **Passage** in a composition that is designed to display the virtuosity of the soloist.

passing note Incidental note in a composition that moves between notes a third apart and creates a temporary **dissonance** with the prevailing harmony. See also **auxiliary note**.

Pasta, Giuditta (1798-1865) Italian soprano whose combination of lyric and dramatic genius brought her almost legendary fame in Europe. Her voice, though unequal, ranged from A to D''', and her sincerity of interpretation in performing roles such as Anna Bolena (which **Donizetti** wrote for her) and Desdemona (in Rossini's *Otello*) held audiences spellbound. Her special talents inspired several works by **Bellini**, including the operas *La sonnambula* and *Norma*. Her real success dates from the Paris season of 1821 and she appeared regularly in London, Paris and St Petersburg until 1837.

pastoral Light-hearted English madrigal with words of a rustic or pastoral character. The term also describes a flowing melodic piece for instruments or voices in 6/8 or 12/8 time that originated in rural Italy.

Patterson, Paul (1947-) English composer who studied at the Royal Academy of Music, where he later became a teacher. His earlier orchestral, ensemble and vocal works, some using electronic tapes and aleatory methods, include a *Requiem* in memory of President Kennedy. The performance of his Trumpet Concerto by Wilbraham first brought him to public notice in 1969. In the early 1980s his style moderated and became more accessible. Since then his *Mass of the Sea* (1984) has achieved wide public attention; he has also produced a *Missa Brevis* (1985, a commission from the Greenwich Festival) and a *Te Deum* for the Three Choirs Festival (1988). He has written other choral works, song cycles and instrumental music.

patter song Comic song in which the words are sung as fast as possible. Examples are the aria for Osmin in Mozart's *Die Entführung aus dem Serail*, for Figaro (the *Largo al factotum*) in Rossini's *Il barbiere di Siviglia*, for Dandini in *La Cenerentola*, and for Dr Bartolo in Mozart's *Le nozze di Figaro*. The style was brilliantly parodied by Sullivan in the Savoy operas, for instance 'The Chancellor's Nightmare Song' from *Iolanthe* (1891).

Patti, Adelina (1843-1919) Italian soprano who was the most famous member of the Patti family of singers. Taken to New York as a child, she made her début there in 1859 under the stage name Little Florinda. Essentially a coloratura soprano with a talent for dramatic interpretation, she sang in North and South America and the capital cities of Europe, making her London début as Amina in *La sonnambula* at Covent Garden (1861), where she sang 25 consecutive seasons. Her roles included the title-role in **Donizetti**'s *Lucia di Lammermoor*, Violetta in *La traviata*, Rosina in *Il barbiere di Siviglia*, and, later, Verdi's Aïda and Leonora in *Il trovatore.* She became legendary for the enormous sums paid to her, the jewels she wore and her refusal to attend rehearsals. She retired to a castle in Wales but was able to make a number of recordings at the age of 60, testifying to the tone and flexibility of her voice and the exemplary care she took of it.

patting juba American dance form that involves hitting the body in complex, syncopated patterns, typical of African rhythmic interplay, and suggests the rhythmic basis of **ragtime** and early jazz. It probably originated from the Afro-Caribbean juba dance, and may well be a rhythmic hand-and-body version of the **calinda** stick dance. It was often seen in 19th-century religious meetings in Louisiana.

Patzak, Julius (1898-1974) Austrian tenor who began by studying conducting in Vienna but turned to singing in 1926, making his début at Reichenberg Opera as Radamès in *Aïda.* His greatest roles were considered to be Florestan in *Fidelio* and the title role of **Pfitzner**'s *Palestrina*, and although his voice was never considered to be outstanding, his intelligence, musicianship and style made him one of the great singers of *Lieder* and oratorio.

pausa (It.) Rest.

pause Sign indicating that the note, chord or rest over which it is placed is to be held longer than its written value. The length of time for which it is held is normally left to the conductor's or performer's discretion.

pavane Slow courtly dance of the 16th and 17th centuries, normally in quadruple or duple time, that originated in the Padua region of Italy. It was serious and stately in character and was often followed by a **galliard** based on the same thematic material. **Ravel** revived the form in his *Pavane pour une infante défunte* for piano in 1899, which was later orchestrated and is now sometimes played on guitar.

Pavarotti, Luciano (1935-) Italian tenor who is noted for his vocal technique and a bright, vibrant voice of considerable beauty. He studied with Pola and Campogalliani, making his début at Reggio Emilia in 1961, where he won the international competition. He made his first London appearance at Covent Garden in 1963 as Rodolfo in *La bohème*, and the next year toured Australia with Joan **Sutherland**, with whom he has frequently sung. His début at the Metropolitan Opera, New York, was in 1968 (again as Rodolfo). Pavarotti specializes in *bel canto* repertory and has recorded extensively, his finest performances on disc being his Rodolfo for **Karajan**, and Arturo in *I Puritani* with Sutherland. He has also recorded most of the major Verdi operas, many with Sutherland. He has now reached a position of immense popularity and is considered one of the finest tenors in the Italian repertory today.

pavillon Bell of a horn, trumpet or trombone, named from its pavilion-like shape. In musical scores the direction *pavillon en l'air* occurs where the composer wishes the bell to be raised to increase the power of the tone.

Payne, Anthony (1936-) English composer who studied at Durham and became a music critic, working for the *Daily Telegraph* and the *Independent*. He began to compose seriously in the late 1960s in an **atonal** style. His works include a *Concerto for Orchestra* (1974); various pieces for unusual combinations of instruments (*The Song of the Clouds* for oboe, horns, strings and piano,1980); a series of short cantatas; a Mass for chorus and brass (1972) and other works for brass; *The World's Winter* (1976), based on poems by Tennyson, for soprano and small ensemble; chamber and piano works. He has written studies of Schoenberg and (with L. Foreman) Frank **Bridge**.

Pears, Sir Peter (1910-1986) English tenor and organist, who studied at the Royal College of Music and took lessons from Elena Gerhardt. He sang with the BBC Chorus and later with the Glyndebourne Chorus, making his stage début in 1942 as Hoffmann in *Les contes d'Hoffmann* at the Strand Theatre, London. He is closely associated with the music of Benjamin **Britten**, his lifelong companion, who wrote all his major tenor roles and many of his solo vocal works for Pears's very individual voice. Parts he created in Britten operas include the title-roles in *Peter Grimes* and *Albert Herring*, Captain Vere in *Billy Budd*, and Aschenbach in *Death in Venice*. He was also a notable singer of Schubert and Bach; with Britten as accompanist he recorded many arrangements of folk-songs and *Lieder*. In 1977 he was instrumental in setting up the Britten-Pears school of Advanced Musical Studies at Aldeburgh. He was knighted in 1978.

Sir Peter Pears

Pearsall, Robert Lucas de (1795-1856) English composer, whose main interest was in the revival of Renaissance music. He studied as a lawyer, but turned to music when living in Germany, eventually settling in the castle of Wartensee on Lake Constance. He wrote mostly vocal music, part-songs, including the well-known *In Dulci Jubilo*, and Anglican and Roman Catholic church music. His madrigals are perhaps the nearest musical equivalent to Gothic Revival and the Pre-Raphaelite school of painting in England.

ped. Abbreviation of **pedal point**.

pedalboard Keyboard of an organ that is played with the feet.

pedal clarinet Alternative term for double-bass **clarinet**.

pedal drum Kettledrum that is tuned by use of a pedal.

pedal point (Fr. *point d'orgue*) Device in composition whereby a bass note is sustained through a passage regardless of the harmonic movement above – the rule is that the harmony should be correct at the beginning and end of the pedal point.

The term also occurs in piano music (often abbreviated to ped.), where it indicates that the sustaining pedal is to be depressed until a point when its release is shown. It also occurs as an instruction in organ music to indicate which notes or passages are to be played on the pedals.

Peerson, Martin (1571-1651) English composer, virginalist and organist, who wrote mostly sacred and vocal music, but also works for viols and keyboard. He was organist at St Paul's Cathedral, London, from about 1624.

Peeters, Flor (1903-1986) Belgian organist, composer, musical editor and a renowned teacher who toured worldwide as an organ recitalist. He wrote piano works, songs and sacred choral music, but his most characteristic compositions are for the organ, for which instrument he wrote a three-volume book on organ method.

peg Device by which a string instrument is tuned. The strings are wound around the pegs, which rest in the pegbox at the end of the instrument's neck. The strings are tuned by a turn of the peg. A **machine head** is fitted to the **double-bass** and modern **guitar** in place of a pegbox.

Peking opera (China) Traditional Chinese theatre which incorporates aspects of regional entertainment forms from the environs of Beijing (Peking). It now involves both male and female actors, and consists of four main dramatic elements: singing, recitation, acting and acrobatics. Costumes are intricate and colourful, certain colours having associative and symbolic meaning. Two basic groups of instruments are used in Peking opera. The first is employed for military and battle scenes and comprises the double-reed **sona** and a variety of drums, gongs and cymbals, the last two of which are used to punctuate recitatives. The second ensemble generally accompanies arias and varies enormously according to the nature of the scenario. However, its most common instruments are bowed and plucked lutes, time-beating clappers and wood-blocks, and occasionally the **ti** flute.

pélog (Indonesia) One of two tonal systems, consisting of seven unequal intervals within an octave. In Java, there are three hemitonic **pentatonic** modes or *patet* drawn from the *pélog* scale: *barang*, *nem* and *lima*, each corresponding to specific times of the day. See also **slèndro**.

Penderecki, Krzysztof (1933-) Polish composer who was one of the first avant-garde composers to experiment with sounds such as hissing, screeching, sawing of wood, typewriters and rustling paper. He studied at Krakow Conservatoire, where he later taught. His earliest success came in 1959, and he quickly became known abroad for such works as *Anaklasis* and *Threnody for Hiroshima* (both 1960). Another important composition of this period is *Polymorphia* (1961), an expressive and beautifully constructed piece for 48 strings. Around 1964 his style changed and became more approachable, incorporating the idioms of more traditional music and increasing in dramatic expression: his *St Luke Passion* (1965) reflects this development, as does *Utrenia* (1971), another important sacred work. He has also composed three operas: *The Devils of Loudun* (1969), *Paradise Lost* (1978) and *Die schwarze Maske* (1986); film scores, incidental music, choral and vocal works, two symphonies (1973 and 1980) and other orchestral pieces with and without tape. He became a teacher at the Yale school of music in 1975.

penillion Ancient Welsh form of singing, usually performed to a harp accompaniment. The words and music are often improvised and sung as counterpoint or descant to the harp. The form is still practised, although the modern tendency is to rely on traditional tunes rather than improvisation.

penny whistle Alternative term for **tin whistle**.

pentatonic Scale of five notes within the octave; the black notes of the piano give such a scale. Pentatonic scales are frequently associated with Oriental music,

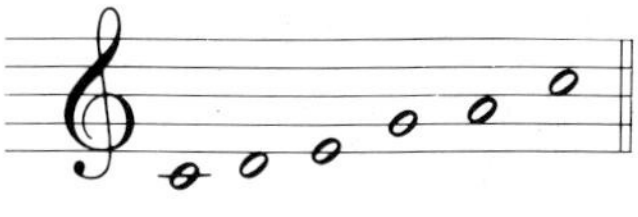

Pentatonic scale

but are also widespread throughout European folk-music, particularly in the anhemitonic mode, corresponding to C-D-E-G-A. See also **Japanese scales**.

Pentland, Barbara (1912-) Canadian composer and university teacher who was a pupil of **Copland**. She began composing at the age of nine, and her works include four symphonies, three string quartets, a piano concerto, a violin sonata and several piano works for children.

Pepin, Clermont (1926-) Canadian composer and educationist who studied with **Honegger**, **Jolivet** and **Messiaen**. Many of his compositions reflect his interest in physics and mathematics; they include the symphonic poems *Guernica* (1952) and *Le rite du soleil noir* (1955), and the ballets *At the Gates of Hell* (1953) and *The Phoenix* (1956). From 1967 to 1972 he was director of the Montreal Conservatoire and was also president of Jeunesses Musicales du Canada.

Pepping, Ernst (1901-1981) German composer who devoted himself to the cultivation of Protestant church music. He studied at the Berlin Conservatoire, and later became professor at the Kirchenmusikschule, Spandau. He wrote for organ, piano and orchestra, and composed a large number of choral works including a *St Matthew Passion*.

Pepusch, Johann Christoph (1667-1752) German-born composer, who settled in London in 1704. Largely self-taught, he wrote music for operas and masques at Drury Lane and Lincoln's Inn theatres and arranged music for the original production of Gay's *The Beggar's Opera* and its sequel *Polly*. An expert in music theory and history, he wrote a treatise on harmony and other theoretical books, and was a founder of the Academy of Ancient Music.

Perahia, Murray (1947-) American pianist, born in New York, where he also studied at Mannes College. He won the Leeds Piano Competition in 1972, making his London début as a recitalist in the following year. Since then he has appeared with many of the world's leading orchestras. He is particularly noted as an exponent of Mozart's piano concertos, all of which he has recorded; he frequently directs from the keyboard. Perahia was also involved in the artistic direction of the Aldeburgh Festival throughout the 1980s.

percussion instruments Musical instruments that produce sound when struck. They include instruments that may be tuned to a definite pitch, such as **kettledrums**, **glockenspiel**, **vibraphone**, **xylophone** and **tubular bells**, and instruments that produce sounds of indefinite pitch, such as the **side drum**, **bass drum**, **triangle** and **cymbals**. Within the percussion section of an orchestra, special effects are obtained by use of such instruments as **castanets**, **anvil**, **thundersheets**, motor-horn, whip and chains.

perdendosi (It.) Losing itself, an indication that the sound of a note or a passage is to become gradually weaker until it fades away.

perfect cadence **Cadence** in which the progression of chords is V-I, giving the impression that the phrase is complete.

perfect interval **Interval** of a fourth, a fifth or an octave.

perfect time Alternative term for triple time. Perfect time was represented by a full circle, and imperfect time by a half-circle. See also **time signature**.

Pergolesi, Giovanni Battista (1710-1736) Italian composer who wrote comic operas and is remembered for his intermezzo *La serva padrona* from the opera *Il prigioner superbo* (1733) and his *Stabat Mater* (1736), written shortly before his early death from tuberculosis. His other operas include *Lo frate 'nnamorato*, *La contadina astuta* and

L'Olimpiade; he also wrote many Masses and other sacred works. Some of his themes were used by **Stravinsky** in his ballet *Pulcinella* (1920).

Peri, Jacopo (1561-1633) Italian composer, who was one of the founding fathers of opera. A prominent member of the group of poets and musicians known as the **Camerata**, whose interest was in reviving Greek drama, he wrote what is considered the first opera, *Dafne* (1597), and later *Euridice* (1600). He was a musician at the Medici court and won considerable fame as a singer. He wrote several other operas, madrigals and ballets, of which few survive.

Perlman, Itzhak (1945-) Israeli violinist who by the age of 10, in spite of having suffered from polio, had already given several broadcasts with the Israel Broadcasting Orchestra and a recital on American radio. He studied at the Juilliard School and made his professional début at Carnegie Hall in 1963 and his London début in 1968. He has played with the London Symphony Orchestra, with the New York Philharmonic Orchestra and with other major American orchestras, and has recorded the concertos of such composers as Stravinsky, **Berg**, **Elgar**, Mozart and **Saint-Saëns**. His recitals with **Barenboim** and **Zukerman** are notable. He also plays the viola.

Itzhak Perlman

Persichetti, Vincent (1915-1987) American composer, conductor and teacher, who studied at the Philadelphia Conservatoire and Curtis Institute, and was a pupil of Roy **Harris**. He later became a teacher at Philadelphia and at the Juilliard School. Composing in a wide range of styles, he produced an important body of keyboard works as well as a ballet, *King Lear*, and sinfonias, cantatas and songs.

Perti, Giacomo Antonio (1661-1756) Italian composer who wrote 26 operas, later devoting himself to religious works, through which he achieved fame as both composer and teacher; he wrote over 300. He was *maestro di cappella* at San Pietro at Bologna for 60 years.

pesindhèn (Java) Female singer of the **gamelan** ensemble. She is the only woman in this all-male domain, and is often found in the 'soft style' of Javanese *gamelan* playing, singing sustained melodic lines, with **suling** (flute), **rebab** (spiked fiddle) and with a counter-melody by the male chorus.

Petrassi, Goffredo (1904-) Italian composer who was educated at choir school but did not undertake systematic studies until the age of 21. He studied at the Accademia di S. Cecilia, Rome (1928-32), where he became professor of composition in 1939. Influences included the music of Stravinsky and **Hindemith**. His compositions are neo-classical in style, but he also made individual use of **twelve-note** methods. His works include the operas *The Spanish Scream* and *Death in the Air*, the ballets *Portrait of Don Quixote* and *Orlando's Madness*, a piano concerto and choral works (including *Nonsense*, based on poems by Edward Lear). A favourite form of composition, a kind of substitute for the symphony, is the series of eight concertos for orchestra which he composed between 1934 and 1972. He is recognized as one of the most important Italian composers of his time.

Petrucci, Ottaviano dei (1466-1539) Italian music printer who issued many famous collections, which represent the most important body of music published at the beginning of the 16th century. He was the first to print music from movable type, and his successful method began the widespread circulation of the **polyphonic** style.

Pettersson, Gustaf Allan (1911-1980) Swedish composer and violist who studied at Stockholm Conservatoire (1930-9) and also with **Honegger** and **Leibowitz**. He was violist with the Stockholm Philharmonic Orchestra from 1940 to 1950, his career ending with the onset of rheumatoid arthritis. His music came to public notice with the first performance in 1968 of his Symphony No. 7 and the *Barefoot Songs*, written 25 years earlier. His 15 symphonies have recently attracted new interest, and many have been recorded.

Pfitzner, Hans (1869-1949) German composer and conductor born in Moscow. He studied theory and piano in Frankfurt, and later often performed as an accompanist. Among his earliest works were several operas, *Der arme Heinrich* (1893), *Die Rose vom Liebesgarten* (1900) and *Das Christ-Elflein* (1906). He settled in Strasbourg, where he held the posts of director of the Conservatory, conductor of the orchestra and director of the Opera, meanwhile composing his most important work, the opera *Palestrina*, first performed in Munich in 1917. This achieved considerable success and was greatly admired, by Thomas Mann among others.

During the 1920s Pfitzner received many honours, and published a number of essays and lectures. In 1929 came the choral fantasy *Das dunkle Reich*, to words by several poets including Michelangelo and Goethe. His last opera, *Das Herz*, was written in 1931. Shortly after this the Nazi régime came to power; Pfitzner was dismissed from his posts and spent his last active years conducting and accompanying. His music is romantic and traditionalist, often inspired by his deep love of literature, particularly the poetry of Eichendorff. His compositions include several choral works (*Von deutscher Seele*, 1921), many *Lieder*, concertos for piano and for violin, and two symphonies.

Philadelphia Orchestra American symphony orchestra founded in 1900. It was established by Fritz Scheel who was also its first conductor; he was followed by Karl Pohlig. The orchestra became one of the finest in the world under Leopold **Stokowski** (1912-38), when it broadcast regularly, made numerous recordings and toured widely, performing many important works new to the United States (Mahler's Symphony No.8 and works by **Scriabin**, **Schoenberg** and **Busoni** among them). This tradition was continued during 1938-78 when Eugene **Ormandy** was conductor. In 1981 Riccardo **Muti** was appointed musical director. The orchestra gives outdoor summer seasons annually and appears at many American festivals; it continues its tradition of fine recordings.

Philharmonia Chorus Founded in 1957 by Walter Legge, the chorus was an adjunct to the Philharmonia Orchestra; the first chorus-master was Wilhelm Pitz. It made its début with Beethoven's Ninth Symphony in a performance conducted by **Klemperer**. In 1964 it became an independent body. Since its inception it has been warmly regarded for its richness of tone and precision of attack, and has made numerous acclaimed recordings. It has toured widely both in Britain and abroad.

Philharmonia Orchestra Founded by Walter Legge of the Gramophone Company in 1945, primarily for recording. It was built into one of the finest ensembles London has known, chiefly under the baton of Herbert von **Karajan**, when he was forbidden public performance because of his involvement with the Nazis. The string sections included many outstanding players who subsequently followed careers as soloists – Manoug **Parikian**, Alan Loveday – or conductors – Neville **Marriner**, Arthur Davison. **Klemperer** was principal conductor and president, 1959-73. Other outstanding conductors who were associated with the orchestra in concerts and recordings were **Toscanini**, **Cantelli** and **Giulini**. In 1964 Walter Legge announced that he would disband the orchestra because conditions in London no longer permitted him to maintain the standard achieved by such orchestras as the Cleveland or the Berlin Philharmonic. The title was sold, but the orchestra reformed itself as a self-governing body under the name of the New Philharmonia, and maintained its reputation with fine concerts and recordings under a variety of conductors including **Maazel** and **Mehta**. It was able to revert to its original name in 1977. Riccardo **Muti** became principal conductor in 1974, Giuseppe **Sinopoli** in 1983.

philharmonic From the Greek 'friendly to harmony', a term used as a title of some orchestras and other musical organizations.

Philidor, François André Danican (1726-1795) French composer, the most famous member of a large family of musicians. Better known to his contemporaries as a chess-player, he was nevertheless a gifted composer of *opéra-comique* and had success with *Tom Jones* (1765) and *L'amant désguisé* (1769). His major choral work *Carmen seculare* (1779) was greatly admired in London and Paris.

Philips, Peter (*c.*1560-1628) English organist and composer, who left England to live in the Low Countries because he was Roman Catholic, yet always described himself as Inglese or Anglo. His best works are his madrigals and motets. Apart from **Byrd**, he was the most published English composer of his time. He was appointed organist at the Chapel Royal, Brussels, and was famous as an organist throughout the Netherlands.

Philomusica of London London chamber orchestra which evolved in part from the Boyd **Neel** String Orchestra in the late 1950s under the direction of Thurston Dart.

phrase Group of notes or chords that constitutes a definite melodic or thematic feature in a composition. Phrases are a form of punctuation in music because they allow a performer to apply correctly the stresses as indicated by a composer's phrase-marks.

Phrygian mode One of the authentic **modes**.

piangendo (It.) Weeping or plaintive.

pianissimo (It.) Instruction to play very quietly. See also **piano**.

piano Commonly used abbreviation for pianoforte, a keyboard instrument in which the strings are struck by felt hammers, rather than plucked as in the harpsichord, and so allow both soft (*piano*) and loud (*forte*) tones to be produced. The first instrument appears to have been made by Bartolomeo Cristofori in Florence at the beginning of the 18th century. It was later developed by the German organ-builder Gottfried Silbermann and his apprentice Johannes Zumpe, who designed the square piano in which the strings are parallel to the keyboard. Further refinements were made by Stein in Vienna, whose instrument Mozart liked; and by Broadwood in London, who gave one of his instruments to Beethoven. The invention of the iron frame allowed greater tension with thicker strings, giving a much more powerful tone, which was also enhanced by having one section of the strings placed over the other (overstrung). Many modifications were made to the piano during the 19th century to meet the fast-growing domestic market and the demands of the great piano virtuosos. Notable firms were the German Steinweg (later Steinway in the United

States), Bechstein, Blüthner, the Austrian Bösendorfer, and the French Pleyel. The grand piano was constructed in several sizes, the largest being for concert use and the smallest, the so-called baby grand, for the home. The upright piano was first developed by Robert Wornum in London (1829), and is now the instrument most often found in domestic use. The strings gradually diminish in thickness from the bottom to the top range. There are single strings in the bass, usually covered with copper wire; in the middle range there are usually two strings to a note, and in the upper range three. The left pedal sustains the sound by raising the dampers. The right, the so-called soft pedal, works in different ways: in the grand it moves the whole action sideways so that the hammers strike only one or two strings – hence the instruction *una corda* (one string) seen in early piano music; in the upright, the soft pedal moves the hammers closer to the strings, so diminishing their force. A few models have a third pedal in the middle, which enables the player to sustain selected notes.

The piano played a dominant role in the 19th century, as a solo instrument, in chamber music, and as an accompaniment to other instruments or the voice, in some of the greatest music by such composers as Beethoven, Schubert, Schumann, Chopin, Brahms, Debussy, and Ravel. Its great power allowed it to be matched against the full orchestra in concertos of heroic mould such as those by Brahms, Tchaikovsky and **Rachmaninov**. Although synthesized piano tone is produced by the electronic keyboards in common use among pop musicians, the true instrument remains the most widely used workhorse of the profession. However, despite outstanding compositions by **Shostakovich**, **Prokofiev** and **Bartók**, its role as a solo instrument has diminished in the 20th century to such an extent that it would be difficult to quote music of the first rank composed for it since 1950. Nevertheless the wealth of masterpieces of the past has undiminished appeal for amateur pianists, as well as for audiences when played by performers of the stature of **Barenboim, Ashkenazy** and **Perahia**.

piano accordion See **accordion**

pianoforte Alternative term for **piano**.

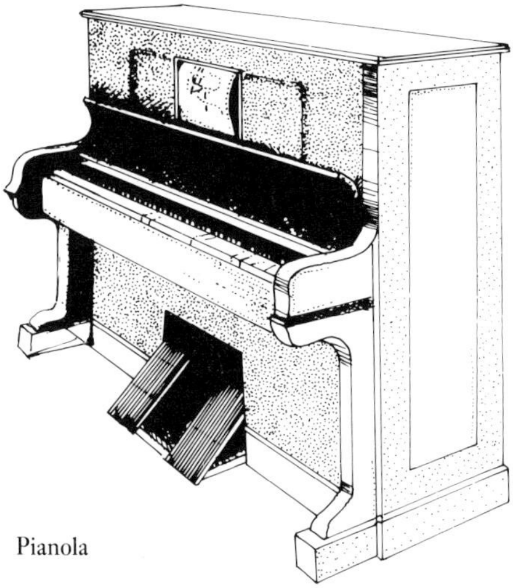

Pianola

pianola Trade name for a mechanical device (patented in 1897) attached to an ordinary **piano** whereby the hammers are made to strike the strings not by action of the hands on the **keyboard**, but by air pressure. A piece of music is represented by a roll of perforated paper, and the holes in it correspond to different notes. When the instrument is played, air passes through the holes in the paper and along tubes, and this makes the piano's hammers strike the strings. The mechanism and the air pump are set in motion by foot pedals or by an electric motor. With the introduction of the gramophone, pianolas lost their popularity. Also known as player pianos.

piano score **Score** that reduces orchestral parts to a version that is playable on the piano.

Piatigorsky, Gregor (1903-1976) Russian cellist, who studied at the Moscow Conservatoire and became principal cellist for the Moscow Opera Orchestra. In 1921 he left Russia to become first cellist with the Berlin Philharmonic Orchestra. He made his American début in 1929 and later settled in the United States, being naturalized in 1942. He was internationally known as both a soloist and a chamber music player, and was dedicatee and first performer of **Walton**'s Cello Concerto (1957).

pibroch (Scotland) Type of bagpipe music falling into the **ceòl mor** or 'big music' category. It includes laments, salutes and compositions in honour of important historical events. The form is basically a theme with specific variations and ornamentation. The term is derived from the Gaelic *piobaireachd*.

Picardy third English equivalent of **tierce de Picardie**.

Piccinni, Niccolò (1728-1800) Italian composer who studied in Naples and quickly became known there for his operas. At first these were in the comic vein, but his serious work *Zenobia* was well received in 1756. After this he was invited to produce operas for Rome; *La buona figliuola* (1760) established his reputation, and he wrote very many more over a period of some 15 years. A dramatic decline in his popularity led him to move to Paris in 1776; there he became a great rival of **Gluck**, and factions of 'Gluckists' and 'Piccinnists' developed. His *Didon* (1783) was acclaimed, but thereafter he had few successes. His operas number at least 130; the style of both the Italian and the French works, while not innovative, is elegant and charming.

piccolo Small **flute** pitched one octave above the normal instrument.

Pick-Mangiagalli, Riccardo (1882-1949) Italian composer and pianist, born in Bohemia. He studied in Milan, and began his career as a pianist. He is best known for his numerous works for the stage: *Il salice d'oro* (1912); *Il carillon magico* (1915); *Basi e bote* (opera, 1920); *Casanova a Venezia* (ballet, 1929). Other compositions include *Notturno e rondo fantastico* for orchestra (1914), a piano concerto, a string quartet, music for piano and choral works. He also taught, and was director of the Milan Conservatoire from 1936 to 1949.

pien (China) Extra auxiliary tones in a Chinese **pentatonic** scale. Often referred to as 'changing' tones, they are used as passing notes or to facilitate a change of mode.

Pierné, Gabriel (1863-1937) French conductor and composer who studied at the Paris Conservatoire from the age of eight. He won the Prix de Rome (1882) and succeeded **Franck** as organist of St Clotilde (1890). He became second conductor of Colonne's Orchestra (1903), becoming principal conductor in 1910. Debussy particularly praised Pierné for his sensitive interpretations of his music. He is best known for his oratorio *The Children's Crusade* and the ballet *Cydalise and the Satyr*, from which comes the *Entry of the Little Fauns*.

Pierson, Henry Hugo (1815-1873) English composer who studied with **Attwood** and Corfe, interrupting his musical career to continue his musical studies in Leipzig. There he met **Schumann** and **Mendelssohn** among others, settling in Germany in 1844. His reputation in Germany was considerable and his music continued to be performed after his death, but was not well received in England. A composer of opera, oratorio, songs and part-songs, his most successful works were the *Music for Goethe's Faust* and his symphonic poem *Macbeth* (1859).

piffero (It.) Rustic Italian flute-like instrument of the **shawm** family. It was often played in Italian cities such as Rome and Naples by pipers from the hills; they played tunes similar to those of the pastoral symphony in Handel's *Messiah*.

Pijper, Willem (1894-1947) Dutch composer, who was the most prominent composer of his country in the first half of the 20th century. Having studied with **Wagenaar**, he became professor at the Amsterdam Conservatoire in 1925, and director of the Rotterdam Conservatoire in 1930. Works such as his *Septet* (1920) and the Symphony No. 2 caused a sensation when first performed, and the Symphony No. 3, Piano Concerto and *Zes Symfonische Epigrammen* are major contributions to the Dutch orchestral repertory of the period. His method of composition was to build from what he called 'germ cells' – motifs or chords – and this had a great influence on later composers in the Netherlands. He wrote an opera (*Halewijn,* 1933), four string quartets and various concertos as well.

Pilkington, Francis (1562-1638) English composer, who described himself as a lutenist, and whose songs with lute are of particular quality. He was also a writer of madrigals, contributing one to *The Triumphs of Oriana*. He was chorister at Chester Cathedral and later a minor canon, remaining there until his death.

Pinkham, Daniel (1923-) American composer who studied at Harvard, Tanglewood and with Nadia **Boulanger**; he also learned the organ and the harpsichord. His distinguished teachers include **Copland**, **Honegger**, **Barber**, **Landowska** and **Biggs**. At first his works were neo-classical in style, but he developed a **serial** approach after the early 1950s. From about 1970 he incorporated electronic effects into his work. His compositions include much choral music – a series of cantatas (for Christmas, Easter, Ascension and a Wedding Cantata); a Requiem; a Passion; settings of Gerard Manley Hopkins, Emily Dickinson and parts of the Bible; two symphonies; an organ concerto; stage works, film scores and chamber music.

Pinnock, Trevor (1946-) English harpsichord-player and conductor. He studied in Canterbury, and made his début in 1971. In 1973 he founded the **English Concert**, an ensemble formed specifically for the **authentic** performance of Renaissance and Baroque music; since then its range has increased. Pinnock has made numerous recordings, often on early instruments; he is particularly admired for his Bach, Handel and **Scarlatti** performances, where his brilliant technique underpins his polished and authoritative style.

Pinza, Ezio (1892-1957) Italian bass known for his noble voice and fine looks as well as his considerable dramatic ability. He had a repertory of nearly 100 roles, singing at La Scala, Milan (1921-4), the Metropolitan, New York (1926-48) and Covent Garden (1930-9), and was a particularly fine Don Giovanni. After his operatic career finished he appeared in television, films and musicals, including *South Pacific* on Broadway (1949).

p'ip'a (China) Four-stringed lute, the body of which is made of hardwood and the top of tung wood. The modern version has 24 chromatically divided frets, six upper and 18 lower. Originally the *p'ip'a* was plucked with a plectrum, but now fingers and fingernails are used.

pipe Hollow tube used to produce a musical sound when air is vibrated through it, such as in an organ or a blown wind instrument. It is also a one-handed whistle flute played in some folk-music with a **tabor**.

pi'phat (Thailand) Percussive Thai orchestra of six to 14 players, which includes pairs of wooden-keyed **xylophones** and **metallophones**, circles of **gongs**, a hanging gong, a hand-hit, laced-head drum and a tacked-head drum hit with sticks. The only non-percussive instrument is the *pi pai*, a bulging oboe with a quadruple reed. It is an urban ensemble, often used to accompany theatre performances.

p'iri (Korea) Double-reed bamboo aerophone, with eight finger-holes and a wide dynamic and expressive range, played with a distinctively wide vibrato. Used in the **hyangak** and **tangak** orchestras and the **kagok** and **sijo** ensembles.

piston Valve on a brass wind instrument which when depressed increases the effective length of the tube and thus alters the range of notes available to the player. It is also the abbreviation for the *cornet à pistons*, the French name for **cornet**.

Piston, Walter (1894-1976) American composer and writer who studied at Harvard University and in Paris with **Dukas** and Nadia **Boulanger**. He was professor of music at Harvard from 1944 to 1960. In 1926 he began a fruitful relationship with **Koussevitzky** and the Boston Symphony Orchestra, which resulted in 11 of his works being given their premières by that orchestra (between 1927 and 1971). He was influenced by Stravinsky, **Fauré** and **Roussel**, and by Baroque style and genre. His considerable orchestral output included eight symphonies, concertos for violin, viola, clarinet, flute and two pianos, and his most popular work, the ballet suite *The Incredible Flutist* (1938). He also wrote five string quartets and other chamber music. He was author of three important books, on harmony (1941), counterpoint (1947) and orchestration (1955).

pitch The position of a note, according to the number of vibrations that produce it. The standard pitch of the A above middle C (from which all other notes are now reckoned and tuned in Western music) is at a frequency of 440 vibrations per second (hertz), which was fixed by international agreement in 1939. Prior to that time the accepted standard pitch varied to such an extent that until the middle of the 18th century there were at times three or four various pitches in use for different types of musical performance.

pizz. Abbreviation of **pizzicato**.

Pizzetti, Ildebrando (1880-1968) Italian composer and conductor, a noted critic and teacher who was the most respected conservative Italian musician of his day. He studied in Parma under Righi, having developed an interest in the theatre from an early age. He then taught there and in Florence; later he was director of the Milan Conservatoire and president of the Accademia di S. Cecilia in Rome. His works include the operas *Ifigenia* (1950), *Phaedra* (1909-12, one of several works with libretto by D'Annunzio) and *Murder in the Cathedral* (1958), and he was also a composer of incidental music for plays, instrumental and choral works.

pizzicato (It.) Plucked, indicating that the strings of an instrument should be plucked with a finger of the right hand, or occasionally with fingers of the left hand between bowed notes.

plagal cadence **Cadence** in which the progression of chords is IV-I, giving the impression of an Amen.

plagal mode Any of the series of modes in which the compass of the melody cast in that mode extends from dominant to dominant, rather than from final to final as it does in the authentic modes. Each plagal mode is linked to a corresponding **authentic** mode in that the same notes are used in each but the span of the notes involved in the plagal mode lies a fifth above the corresponding authentic mode when the modes are conceived of as equivalent to scales played on the white keys of the piano. (It should be noted that modes are orderings of pitch intervals and can be transposed from one key to another.) Plagal modes have the final in the middle, with a new dominant established three notes below where the dominant in the authentic mode is. Plagal modes are distinguished by the use of the prefix *hypo-*. For example, the Lydian mode is an authentic mode extending from F to F, with the final on F and the dominant of C. The Hypolydian mode is a plagal mode running from C to C with the final at F and a new dominant at A. See also **modes**.

plainsong Also known as plainchant or Gregorian chant. These are unaccompanied settings of the Christian liturgy, probably evolved from Greek and Jewish chants in the early Christian era, and codified in the Roman rite by Gregory the Great in the 6th century. The melodies were in the ecclesiastical **modes** with the rhythm determined by the text. This remained the music of the Church for the next 600 years, until in the 12th century the first steps were taken towards the combination of melodies in polyphony and consequently the development of harmony. Plainsong survived beside the flood of polyphonic composition, but was often corrupted with florid decoration, and usually accompanied by the organ, a pale shadow of its pristine glory. With the decline of Catholic church music in the 19th century, plainsong had been pushed out by music more suited to the concert-hall in the elaborate but unliturgical Masses of the Viennese masters and their inferior imitators. At the end of the 19th century, with the publication of the scholarly editions from Solesmes Abbey, a new interest was fostered in the performance of plainsong in the appropriate *a cappella* style. This reform was immediately accelerated by the issue in 1903 by Pope Leo X of the encyclical *Motu proprio*, which forbade the use of concert-style settings that distorted the liturgical texts, and encouraged instead the use of plainsong and the works of the polyphonic masters of the 16th century such as Palestrina. Largely through the pioneering efforts of Sir Richard Terry at Westminster Cathedral, this led to a great revival in Britain of plainsong in both the Roman and Anglican Churches.

player piano Alternative term for **pianola**.

plectrum Device made of wood, metal or plastic used to pluck the strings of some stringed instruments, including the lute, mandolin, electric guitar, zither and banjo. It is also attached to the jack of a harpsichord.

Pleeth, William (1916-) English cellist and teacher who studied in Leipzig with Klengel and made his début there in 1932. His London début came a year later. He has been a member of several chamber ensembles, including the Blech Quartet (1936-41) and the Allegri String Quartet (1952-67), and has been a notable teacher at the Guildhall School. His outstanding qualities are a warmth and colour of tone which he has succeeded in transmitting to his pupils, who included Jacqueline **du Pré** and Robert Cohen.

Pleyel, Ignaz Joseph (1757-1831) Austrian pianist, piano-maker and composer, who was enormously popular in his day and whose music was much published. A pupil of **Haydn**, he also studied in Rome, later becoming *Kapellmeister* in Strasbourg (1789). He settled in Paris (1795), where he founded a piano factory. His prolific output of music included two operas, 29 symphonies, 45 string quartets and other chamber music. Although his early works display inventiveness, his later compositions often re-used earlier works and were aimed largely at pleasing his audience.

Plowright, Rosalind (1949-) English soprano who studied in Manchester and at the London Opera Centre. Her début in 1979 was in Britten's *The Turn of the Screw* at the English National Opera. She has concentrated on the Italian repertory, where she has been particularly successful as Desdemona in Verdi's *Otello* and Queen Elizabeth in **Donizetti**'s *Maria Stuarda*, in which she made an exciting foil for Janet **Baker** in the title-role. Her recordings include Verdi's *Il trovatore*, with **Domingo**, and *La forza del destino*, with **Carreras**.

pneuma Vocal ornament sung to a single vowel in **plainsong**. An example is the word *Alleluia* when the final 'a' provided a vowel over which a melody was embellished.

pochette (Fr.) Small pocket-sized violin formerly used by dancing-masters in the 17th and 18th centuries.

poem Term introduced by various romantic composers, especially the symphonic poems written by **Liszt** and **Chausson** (*Poème* for violin and orchestra, 1896).

point End of the bow of a stringed instrument opposite that held by the hand (the heel).

point d'orgue (Fr.) Organ point. 1. **Pedal point**.
2. A sign over a note or rest indicating that it is unmeasured.
3. The same sign, usually over a 6/4 chord, also indicates the place for a **cadenza**.

pointillism Style of musical composition in which the notes appear to be disposed as isolated dots rather than in flowing melodic lines. It is a term derived from the school of painting in which dots of colour are applied to the canvas. Certain music by **Stockhausen** and **Webern** is described as pointillist.

pointing Distribution of the syllables of the psalms in **Anglican chant** according to the rhythm of the words as spoken.

pokok (Bali) Principal melody upon which the instruments of the Balinese **gamelan** orchestra elaborate, somewhat similar in concept to the Western **cantus firmus**.

polka Dance originating in Bohemia in the early 19th century, written in 2/4 time with vigorous rhythms.

Pollini, Maurizio (1942-) Italian pianist and conductor, who is known for the modern as well as the classical repertory. He made his début at the age of nine and studied at the Milan Conservatoire until 1959. He won the 1960 Chopin Competition in Warsaw. He has worked in the United States and Europe, and is particularly associated with Claudio **Abbado**. He often conducts from the keyboard and made his début as a conductor with Rossini's *La donna del lago* (1981). His recordings range from Beethoven, Mozart and Schubert sonatas and concertos to the works of **Schoenberg**, **Webern**, **Boulez** and **Nono**.

polonaise Polish dance of stately character that originated in the 16th century. The music is in 3/4 time and is characterized by **feminine cadences** at the end of each section, and also by dotted rhythms. Beethoven, Schubert and Liszt have used these features in their polonaises for piano. Between 1817 and 1846, **Chopin** composed 16 polonaises which expressed his strong patriotic sentiments.

polymodality Music that is based on more than one **mode**. An illustration of this is **Vaughan Williams**'s *Pastoral Symphony* (1921).

polyphonic Music that combines two or more independent melodic lines. Following the polyphonic period (13th to 16th centuries), when harmonic progressions were controlled by the independent melodies, the later polyphony of **Bach** was governed by the harmonic structure of the composition.

polyrhythm The simultaneous combination of different rhythms. A famous example is at the end of the first act of Mozart's *Don Giovanni*, where three stage bands each play in a different dance rhythm. Polyrhythm is frequently found in the music of the 20th century, especially in the music of Stravinsky, **Copland** and **Messiaen**.

polytonality System of composing music in which more than one key is used simultaneously. It was a system used by **Holst** and **Milhaud**. See also **atonality**.

Ponce, Manuel (1882-1948) Mexican composer, who studied in Italy, Germany and in Paris under **Dukas**. At the age of 14 he composed the gavotte made famous by the dancer Argentina. His other compositions include the well-known song *Estrellita* and classical works for guitar, which have been made part of the standard repertory by **Segovia**.

Ponchielli, Amilcare (1834-1886) Italian composer and organist, who despite the accepted importance of his work was never popular. Of the operas he wrote, only *La Gioconda* (1876) has survived into the modern repertory; from it comes the well-known *Dance of the Hours*. He was choirmaster at Bergamo Cathedral (1881) and taught composition at Milan Conservatoire from 1880.

Pons, Lily (1898-1976) American soprano of French origin who studied in Cannes and at the Paris Conservatoire, first learning the piano. From 1928 she sang at various French opera-houses, until in 1931 she was engaged by the Metropolitan, New York. There she made a sensational début in the title-role of Donizetti's *Lucia di Lammermoor*, a role which she sang often and to which her very high coloratura was ideally suited. She remained with the Metropolitan until 1961, touring occasionally and establishing herself as a great favourite in roles such as Gilda (Verdi's *Rigoletto*), Amina (**Bellini**'s *La sonnambula*), and the title-role in **Delibes**'s *Lakmé*.

Ponselle, Rosa (1897-1981) American soprano of Italian origin. She studied in New York, and made a remarkable début at the Metropolitan in 1918 as Leonora in Verdi's *La forza del destino*, with **Caruso**. She remained there until 1937, where her beautiful, rich, even tone and attractive stage presence scored triumphs in the title-roles of *Norma* (**Bellini**), *La Gioconda* (**Ponchielli**), *La vestale* (**Spontini**) and *L'africaine* (**Meyerbeer**). Other outstanding successes were as Donna Anna *in Don* Giovanni, Violetta in *La traviata* and Madeleine in **Giordano**'s *Andrea Chenier*. She made numerous recordings, from which the glorious qualities of her voice can be judged.

ponticello Bridge of a stringed instrument over which the strings are stretched so that they are kept clear of the belly of the instrument. *Sul ponticello* indicates that the player should play the instrument as close as possible to the bridge.

Poot, Marcel (1901-) Belgian composer and critic, who was one of the pupils of **Gilson**; in 1925 they founded *Les Synthétistes*, dedicated to new ideas in music. Also a pupil of **Dukas**, he wrote music for silent film, radio, plays and discovered the possibilities of using jazz in his first ballet *Paris in Verlegenheid* (1925). He also composed operas, five symphonies and a symphonic poem, *Charlot* (1926).

pop music Common name given to any form of popular music, probably coined in the 1950s to describe such performers as Elvis Presley and the Everly Brothers. Music is generally in a fast 2/4 or 4/4 time with syncopated rhythms. The structure of a pop song is often verse and refrain, with an eight-bar bridge. The regular formation was a group of four: a drummer, bass guitarist and second and lead guitarist. One or all of the band members provided the vocals. More recently, however, bands have tended to use more people and a greater variety of combinations of instruments, including large brass sections. Because of the rise of the recording industry (which for the greater part determines the quality and content of the music released), pop music has become a dominant and all-pervasive form in many countries of the world. The term is now also used to describe collections or concerts of the most popular classical music. See also **jazz**; **punk rock**; **reggae**; **rock**.

Popp, Lucia (1939-) Austrian soprano born in Czechoslovakia who studied at the

Bratislava Music Academy. She made her début as the Queen of the Night in Mozart's *Die Zauberflöte* (1963) and was principal soprano with the Vienna State Opera. She has made a number of recordings and has sung throughout Europe and the United States as a recitalist and in opera.

portamento (It.) Direction in vocal music or music for a bowed instrument to carry the sound from note to note without a break. It is also possible to achieve this effect with other instruments: the clarinet, for example, at the start of **Gershwin**'s *Rhapsody in Blue*, a trombone as in Kastchei's dance in Stravinsky's *The Firebird*, or the timpani as in **Bartók**'s *Concerto for Orchestra*.

portative organ Small **organ** with a single keyboard and flue pipes which could be suspended from the shoulder by a strap so that it could be carried in a procession.

Portative organ

Porter, Cole (1891-1964) American composer of popular songs, noted for the wit of his lyrics in songs such as *Let's Do It*, *Night and Day* and *I Get a Kick Out of You*. One of the most well-trained song-writers of the 20th century, he studied harmony and counterpoint at Harvard (1915-16). His first Broadway show (1916) made no

Cole Porter

impact, and he settled in Paris the following year before joining the French Foreign Legion; after three years with it he studied with **d'Indy** at the Schola Cantorum (1919). Some of his songs were performed in revues; his first major success was a musical, *Wake Up and Dream* (1929), followed by *Gay Divorce* (1932), starring Fred Astaire, and *Anything Goes* (1934), starring Ethel Merman. An accident led to an unproductive period which, however, was brought to an end with the triumph of *Kiss Me, Kate* (1948), based on Shakespeare's *The Taming of the Shrew*. Another success was *Can-can* in 1953. He also wrote songs for many Hollywood films, outstanding among them *High Society* (1956) with Bing Crosby, Grace Kelly, Frank Sinatra and Louis Armstrong. After the death of his wife in 1954 he spent the last ten years of his life in New York where he became a semi-recluse. His shows and songs have often been revived.

Porter, Quincy (1897-1966) American composer, violinist and educationist who was a pupil of **d'Indy** in Paris and **Bloch** in New York. He later became dean of the faculty of the New England Conservatoire (1938) and then professor at Yale (1946-65). His works include incidental music for Shakespeare's *Antony and Cleopatra* and

T.S. Eliot's *Sweeney Agonistes*, two symphonies, two piano concertos, ten string quartets and other chamber music.

Porter, Walter (1595-1659) English composer who wrote madrigals, motets and other sacred music. Possibly a pupil of **Monteverdi**, he was choirmaster of Westminster Abbey until choral service was suppressed in 1649, when he came under the patronage of Sir Edward Spencer.

position 1. In string-playing, the settings of the left hand on the fingerboard, successively numbered as the first finger moves up in tones.
2. The seven settings of the slide in trombone-playing, each producing the fundamental and its harmonics on seven successive notes of the scale of the basic key of the instrument – usually B♭ or F.
3. The layout of the notes of a chord – in root position the generating note is in the bass; as the notes are inverted, the generating note may move to the top, in the first **inversion**, or to second from the top in the second inversion.

positive organ Small organ used from the 10th to the 17th century that could be placed on a floor or a table, but unlike the **portative organ** could not be carried.

post-horn Brass instrument (similar to the **bugle** rather than the **horn**) which was able to produce only its fundamental note and the relative **harmonic series**. Post-horns were used by guards of the early mail coaches to announce their arrival when approaching towns or villages. Mozart incorporated it in his *Serenade in D*.

postlude Piece of music played at the end, perhaps of a church service, or to conclude a longer composition, for example at the end of Strauss's *Four Last Songs*.

Poston, Elizabeth (1905-1987) English composer and pianist who studied at the Royal College of Music and with Harold Samuel. Her first songs were published in 1925; shortly afterwards her violin sonata was broadcast by the BBC. She worked in a wide field of musical activities and was director of music in the Foreign Service of the BBC (1940-5). She wrote music for radio programmes, including dramatic works by Dylan Thomas and C.S. Lewis; she also composed choral music, songs and film music, notably for *Howards End* (1970). She was president of the Society of Women Musicians (1955-61). One of her most outstanding contributions is her work in the field of folk-song, and she edited collections of this music, which she gathered during her sojourns abroad in the 1930s, as well as collections of carols and hymns.

post-Romanticism Music of a style (represented by **Brahms**, **Liszt** and **Wagner**) written immediately after that of the Romantic period of the late 18th and early 19th century. The term has also been applied to the music of early 20th-century composers such as **Elgar**, **Mahler**, and **Sibelius**.

Poulenc, Francis (1899-1963) French composer and pianist who studied the piano first with his mother and later with Ricardo Viñes, and composition with

Francis Poulenc

Koechlin. He was greatly influenced in his early years by Jean Cocteau and Erik **Satie**, who advocated a link with Parisian folklore – the street songs, the music-halls and circuses. Poulenc first made an impression with his *Rhapsodie nègre*; this marked him as one of the new school of French composers, labelled Les **Six**, who expressed in their music the brittle, jazzy life of the Twenties in Paris. He set Cocteau's *Cocardes* for the bizarre combination of violin, trombone, bass-drum and triangle. In 1924 he was commissioned by **Diaghilev** to write the music for the ballet *Les biches*, a brilliant and charming score that in its revised form has held a popular place in the orchestral repertory. Poulenc's feeling for the poetry of his contemporaries is shown in his many attractive settings of Apollinaire, Eluard and Louise de Vilmorin, which were largely the result of his collaboration from 1935 with the distinguished French baritone Pierre **Bernac**. During the war Poulenc expressed in music the feelings of the resistance to German occupation, through the touching song simply entitled *C*, and especially in the unaccompanied choral setting of a poem by Paul Eluard, *Figure humaine* (1943), which ends with a hymn to liberty. Poulenc's music reveals a striking dual personality – on the one hand there is the cheeky charmer, with a rare gift for melody and piquant harmony, to be found in the *Concert champêtre* for harpsichord, the piano music, the flute and oboe sonatas, the songs and the comic opera *Les mamelles de Tirésias*; on the other there is the composer of deep religious feeling and serious purpose, in the opera *Dialogues des Carmélites*, the Mass in G, the motets, and especially the mystic *Litanies à la Vierge noire*. Fashions change, and a few years ago Poulenc's output was almost written off as little more than light music; but the inherent quality of his invention is above fashion, and continues to offer a fascinating range of musical experience.

Pousseur, Henri (1929-) Belgian composer who, having studied at the Brussels Conservatoire, wrote electronic music, influenced by the methods of **Webern**, **Stockhausen** and **Boulez**. He also studied with Boulez. He has written operas, symphonies, chamber music, a quintet in memory of Webern and music for tape, such as *Trois visages de Liège* (1961). In 1958 he founded a studio for electronic music in Brussels.

praeludium Alternative term for **prelude**.

Praetorius, Michael (*c.*1571-1621) German composer, born of a Lutheran family. He studied in Torgau and Frankfurt an der Oder and joined the musical establishment of the Duke of Brunswick-Wolfenbüttel in 1595 as an organist. In 1604 he became *Kapellmeister*, and entered his most productive phase of composition. In 1613 the duke died, and Praetorius moved to Dresden, then on to Magdeburg and various other German cities. He created altogether well over 1,000 sacred works – motets, psalms and hymns – of which one of the best-known is an arrangement of a Christmas carol, *Es ist ein Ros' entsprungen*. His strong Lutheran faith was the driving force behind his vast output, although he also composed some secular pieces, most of which are lost (except a set of dances, *Terpsichore*, of 1612). He wrote a treatise, *Syntagma musicum*, which is of inestimable value to musicologists.

Pralltriller (Ger.) German equivalent of **upper mordent**.

precentor Ecclesiastical dignitary in an Anglican church who is in charge of the vocal church music. He is superior to the organist.

pre-classical Style of composition that followed the Baroque music of the first half of the 18th century and preceded the classical music of the later century. Composers such as C.P.E. **Bach** and J.C. **Bach** were active during the pre-classical period.

prelude Instrumental piece played as an introduction to a church service, preceding a **fugue**, or forming the first part of a **suite**. In addition, it sometimes forms the introduction to an act of an opera.

preparation In harmony, the process of sounding a note first in a chord with which it is **consonant** and then again in a chord against which it is **dissonant**. The dissonance is then said to be prepared, or if it has not been treated in this way, it is said to be an unprepared dissonance.

prepared piano Piano that has been altered by placing various objects on the strings to produce special effects. John **Cage** is especially noted for his music produced by prepared pianos. One example is his work *A Book of Music* (1944) for two prepared pianos.

Prés, Josquin des See **Josquin des Prés**

prestissimo (It.) Very fast indeed. See also **presto**.

presto (It.) Fast. Indication that the music should be played very fast. *Presto* indicates a speed faster than **allegro**.

Preston, Simon (1938-) English organist and harpsichordist who is noted for his perfectionism and virtuosity. He has held a number of important organ posts and was appointed organist of Westminster Abbey in 1981. A particularly fine interpreter of **Liszt** and **Messiaen**, he has made a number of recordings including a much admired version of Handel's organ concertos.

Prêtre, Georges (1924-) French conductor who studied at the Paris Conservatoire and with Clatyens. He made his début in 1946 at the Opéra-Comique and has since worked throughout Europe and the United States, most successfully in opera. He often worked with **Callas**, recording *Tosca* and *Carmen* with her. A conductor of both classical and modern music, he is particularly dedicated to **Poulenc**'s music, conducting the first performances of the *Voix humaine* and *Gloria*, and he has recorded most of Poulenc's orchestral music. He is currently the conductor for the Vienna Symphony Orchestra.

Previn, André (1929-) German-born American pianist, conductor and composer who emigrated with his family to the United States in 1939. After studying in Berlin and Paris he became a successful jazz pianist, making a number of recordings, and worked as a composer and arranger of film music in Hollywood. He later settled in England, where he has won fame as a presenter of music on television, and he is a noted champion of English music, in particular **Walton** and **Vaughan Williams**. His compositions include a symphony, concertos, chamber music and piano works, and he has also written scores

André Previn

for the musicals *Coco* (1969) and *Good Companions* (1974). He was conductor in chief of the Houston Symphony Orchestra (1967), principal conductor of the London Symphony Orchestra (1969-79), of the Pittsburgh Orchestra (1976-86) and, in 1986, music director of the Los Angeles Philharmonic.

Prey, Hermann (1929-) German baritone, who studied at the Berlin Music Academy, making his début at the Wiesbaden State Theatre in 1952. He is internationally known as an opera singer, his more notable roles being Figaro in both *Le nozze di Figaro* and *Il barbiere di Siviglia*, and Papageno in *Die Zauberflöte*, but he is also a particularly fine *Lieder* singer who has made a number of recordings. He founded the Schubertiade Festival at Hohenems in 1976.

Price, Leontyne (1927-) American soprano, who studied at the Juilliard School, New York. She began her career as a concert performer, but after her television appearance in *Tosca* (1955) she became a highly successful opera singer, one of the finest Verdi sopranos of the day. She has sung in Europe and the United States, making her début at Covent Garden in 1958 and at the Metropolitan, New York, in 1961. She created the role of Cleopatra in Barber's *Antony and Cleopatra* (1966). She has recorded *Aïda* with **Solti** and *Tosca* with **Karajan**, among other works. Her repertory also includes Bess in *Porgy and Bess*.

Price, Margaret (1941-) Welsh soprano, who studied at Trinity College and made her début with the Welsh National Opera in 1962 as Cherubino. She is a noted *Lieder* singer and has been a guest at many European opera houses, especially in Mozart roles: she is considered one of the finest current interpreters of Fiordiligi in *Così fan tutte*, Donna Anna in *Don Giovanni* and Pamina in *Die Zauberflöte*. She also excels in Verdi, as Amelia in *Simon Boccanegra* and Nannetta in *Falstaff*. Her recordings include a recital of Verdi songs and *Tristan und Isolde* with Carlos **Kleiber**. She is particularly admired in Germany, where she has performed often. She has appeared on television as Salud (*La vida breve*) and as Tatyana in Tchaikovsky's *Eugene Onegin*. She was awarded a CBE in 1982.

prick song 15th- to 18th-century term for written ('pricked') rather than improvised music.

prima donna (It.) First lady. The chief female singer in an opera.

Primrose, William (1904-1982) Scottish violist, who began his career as a violinist, but changed to viola on advice from his teacher, **Ysaÿe**, becoming one of the world's leading solo violists. He has appeared as a soloist in Europe and the United States. He settled in the United States in 1937 and was principal viola with the NBC Symphony Orchestra from 1938 to 1942. In 1944 he commissioned a viola concerto from **Bartók** and inspired other composers such as **Rubbra**, **Fricker** and **Hamilton** to write for him. He was made a CBE in 1953.

principal 1. The leading player of a section in an orchestra, who usually takes solo parts when necessary.

2. One of the singers who take the leading parts in an opera, as opposed to members of the chorus. However, a principal **tenor** is someone who takes principal roles, but is not necessarily the leading tenor of the opera company.

3. An organ stop of the open **diapason** type, but sounding an octave higher.

Pritchard, Sir John (1921-1989) English conductor, whose career was divided between opera and concerts. He was *répétiteur* at Glyndebourne and later its musical director (1969-77); he was also a guest conductor at other leading European opera houses. His other appointments include those of conductor of the Royal Liverpool Philharmonic Orchestra and

Sir John Pritchard

principal conductor of the Cologne Opera. In 1983 he was appointed chief conductor of the BBC Symphony Orchestra. His last appointment was at the Théâtre de la Monnaie in Brussels. He was always a champion of new music, conducting premières of **Britten**'s *Gloriana*, **Tippett**'s *The Midsummer Marriage* and *King Priam*, and **Henze**'s *Elegy for Young Lovers*. He was knighted in 1983.

Prix de Rome Prestigious prize for composition, awarded annually by the Académie des Beaux-Arts in Paris. It was established in 1803, and discontinued in 1968. The winner was obliged to spend several years in Rome, studying and composing works to be sent to Paris for evaluation. Among the most famous winners were Berlioz (who hated Rome and came back early), **Gounod, Bizet** and Debussy.

programme music Music that represents a story, picture or other extra-musical elements. The earliest examples of this type of music are the 14th-century **caccias**, which often depicted hunting scenes in a colourful manner. The **chansons** of **Janequin** attempted to convey extra-musical sounds such as birdsongs. Beethoven's *Pastoral Symphony* (1808) expresses his feelings on going to the countryside, which was a new approach to programme music. Other composers who have used this form include Richard Strauss (tone poems), Debussy (*La mer*, 1903-5) and **Honegger** in his steam-locomotive epic (*Pacific 231*, 1923).

progression Movement from one **note** or **chord** to its successor. See also **harmony**.

progressist Group of French Communist composers, such as **Durey** and **Nigg**, who after 1945 became active in composing music in accordance with the Communist doctrine of mass appeal. One of Durey's works was entitled *La longue marche*, to words by Mao Tse-tung.

progressive jazz Alternative term for cool **jazz**.

progressive tonality Type of music in which the work or movement opens in one key and, progressing through other keys, ends in another. It was a system used by **Mahler** and Carl **Nielsen**.

Prokofiev, Sergei (1891-1953) Russian composer, who was taught by his mother from the age of three and had already tried his hand at an opera by the age of nine. He entered St Petersburg Conservatoire (1904), and was a pupil of **Rimsky-Korsakov**, composing and publishing several works while still a student, including the Piano Sonata No.2 and the Piano Concerto No.1. He made his début as a pianist in 1908. From 1914 he lived abroad, first in London, where he heard Stravinsky and met **Diaghilev**; the latter asked him to write a ballet score, although it was not performed until 1921. During this period he wrote his first opera, *The Gambler* (based on Dostoevsky), followed in 1919 by *The Love for Three Oranges*, composed in Chicago; he also wrote his first symphony, the *Classical* (1917). He then moved to Paris, where he produced the opera *The Fiery Angel* (1923) and the ballets *Le pas d'acier* (1927) and *L'enfant*

Sergei Prokofiev

prodigue (1929). Never fully at home in the West, he returned to the Soviet Union in 1934 where he suffered under Stalin's doctrine of social realism, condemned with others as a formalist, which led to a tendency to popularize his style in works such as *Peter and the Wolf*. He found outlets for his music in film scores such as those for *Lieutenant Kijé*, *Ivan the Terrible* and *Alexander Nevsky*, and in ballets such as *Romeo and Juliet* and *Cinderella*. His opera *War and Peace* was performed in its complete version (1957) only after his death, despite his numerous revisions in an attempt to secure a performance. Although regarded as avant-garde in his youth, he was fundamentally a romantic melodist and was successful in a wide range of works which are crucial to the 20th-century repertory. His output also included seven symphonies, five piano concertos, two violin concertos, piano sonatas and chamber music.

prolation Division of the **semibreve** into **minims** in old notation, where according to the **time-signature** a semibreve could be equal to two minims (minor prolation) or three mimims (major prolation).

promenade concert Originally an orchestral concert at which the audience walked about during the programme, first held in London in 1838. Modern promenade concerts now usually entail a large part of the audience standing or sitting on the floor of the main body of the auditorium (having bought lower-priced tickets). The most famous of this type of promenade is the summer series at the Royal Albert Hall, London, started by Sir Henry **Wood** in 1895 and run by the BBC since 1928. Originally held at the London Queen's Hall, they continued there until the building was destroyed in 1941. They are now held almost exclusively at the Royal Albert Hall. The programme is very varied, sometimes arranged around a theme, and often including specially commissioned works. Performers include many famous orchestras and soloists. The opening and last nights of the Proms are special occasions where the mainly young audience shows much enthusiasm.

psalm Text taken from the Book of Psalms in the Old Testament, usually sung as part of the offices of the Roman Catholic Church and of the Anglican morning and evening services. Paraphrases in verse are known as metrical psalms. Psalms have also been set as **anthems** or **cantatas** by composers such as Bach, Mendelssohn, **Roussel**, **Bruckner** and **Vaughan Williams**. There are also some instrumental works entitled Psalms, such as **Reubke**'s organ sonata *The 94th Psalm*.

psalter Book that contains the psalms as used in the Christian Church as part of the liturgy. The earliest surviving psalters are those by Miles Coverdale, *Goostly Psalmes and Spirituall Songes* (*c.*1538), and *The Psalter of David Newely Translated into Englyshe Metre* (1549), by Robert Crowley. The psalter often indicates the chant to which the psalm is to be sung.

Puccini, Giacomo (1858-1924) Italian composer, born in Lucca to a musical family – his father was a church composer.

At first he was going to follow family tradition, but, fired by seeing a performance of Verdi's *Aïda*, he decided on an operatic career instead. He studied at the Milan Conservatoire under **Bazzini** and **Ponchielli**, who encouraged his ambitions. His first opera, *Le villi*, on the same theme as **Adam**'s famous ballet *Giselle*, was produced in 1884 and was fairly successful; it initiated a lifelong association with the publisher Giulio Ricordi, who recognized a bankable composer when he heard one. His next opera, *Edgar*, was not well received, but *Manon Lescaut* (1893), somewhat influenced by the **verismo** vein then becoming current, was a triumph and established Puccini's reputation both at home and abroad. *La bohème* followed in 1896. This touching, sentimental love-story, with its fragile heroine and its scenes of joyous revelry in spite of dire poverty, has become one of the most popular operas of all time; it was not, however, hugely successful on its first showing. *Tosca* (1900) is, in contrast, a work of high drama, offering a wonderful opportunity for the lyric-dramatic soprano; the confrontation between Tosca and the villainous Scarpia is one of the most intense moments in opera. The third of Puccini's most appealing works is *Madama Butterfly* (1904), in which the Oriental setting gave him scope for unusual melody.

A domestic tragedy held back the composer's creativity until *La fanciulla del West* (The Girl of the Golden West) was given at the Metropolitan, New York, in 1910. *La rondine* (1917) has never achieved great popularity, although the three operas of the *Trittico – Il tabarro*, *Suor Angelica*, *Gianni Schicchi* – are performed quite often, particularly the last with its famous soprano aria *O mio babbino caro*. However, the final masterpiece from Puccini's pen was to achieve outstanding and lasting success – this was *Turandot*, the tale of a heartless Chinese princess, which again offers an immense challenge to the dramatic soprano. It was unfinished at his death, and an ending was constructed by Franco **Alfano**. At its first performance, conducted by **Toscanini**, the music stopped at the point where 'the maestro laid down his pen'. All Italy mourned him; his house at Torre del Lago became a museum, and the venue for an annual music festival.

The power of his characterizations, his instinctive theatrical skill, his original harmonies and his masterly handling of the orchestra, have ensured that Puccini's operas have retained a prominent place in the regular repertory of the world's opera-houses.

Pugnani, Gaetano (1731-1798) Italian violinist and composer, who travelled widely and spent long periods in London and Paris, otherwise working for most of his life at the Turin court where he became leader and teacher from 1770. His compositions include violin sonatas, operas, ballets and cantatas. His playing was known for its power and eloquence, and he was probably partly responsible for the development of the modern bow.

punk rock Style of music that became popular during the 1970s, characterized by harsh sounds, very loud shouting and discords. Punk rock spoke to the young people of the decade of violence and frustration, and made its own protest against urbanization and the economic recession of the time. The music of punk cannot be extricated from the costume of its adherents, being very intimidating in style, with grotesque make-up (for boys as well as girls), black leather, ragged jeans, chains and junk jewellery. Some punk songs were banned by radio and television, because they were considered offensive.

Purcell, Henry (1659-1695) One of the greatest English composers, whose music was largely ignored for more than 200 years, and whose reputation was finally restored by **Vaughan Williams**, **Britten** and **Holst**. He was first a choirboy in the Chapel Royal, the musical establishment revived on the restoration of King Charles II to the throne in 1660. He remained closely connected to the court and the royal family throughout his short life. Among his teachers were Pelham **Humfrey** and John **Blow**. In 1674 he took up the post of organ-tuner at Westminster Abbey, and a few years later became composer to the royal musicians; he had already published some songs. In 1679 he became the organist at Westminster Abbey in succession to Blow, and three years after that the Chapel Royal organist.

His earliest important compositions were a set of *Fantasias* for strings, published in 1680; derived from the Renaissance polyphonic tradition, their strongly contrasting sections and striking harmonies place them firmly in the Baroque age. At this period he started to compose incidental music for the stage, writing a great deal of it over the next years – songs, dances and instrumental sections for plays by Congreve, Fletcher and Dryden, among others. His music for the play *Abdelazer* by Aphra Behn provided the theme for Britten's *Young Person's Guide to the Orchestra* 250 years later. His set of 12 trio sonatas was published around this time (1683).

While looking after the royal orchestra (he was appointed Master of the King's Instruments in 1683) and supplying music for the theatre, Purcell was also turning out many fine sacred works. He composed around 70 full and verse anthems altogether, services, psalms and hymns. The anthem *My Heart is Inditing* was written for the coronation of King James II in 1685; the very fine *Te Deum* and *Jubilate in D* in 1694. In addition, Purcell's official court appointments meant that he was called upon to produce odes and welcome songs to mark ceremonial occasions. One of the most famous of the odes is that for Queen Mary II's birthday in 1694 – *Come, Ye Sons of Art, Away*; he composed six for her altogether, as well as her Funeral March. The welcome song *Sound the Trumpet* for James II (1687) and *Hail, Bright Cecilia* for the saint's day in 1692 are other well-known pieces.

Purcell's greatest achievement was his only true opera, *Dido and Aeneas* (1689), on Virgil's story of the Carthaginian queen and the Trojan prince who left her to fulfil his destiny by founding Rome. Dido's lament, *When I am Laid in Earth*, is a deeply moving expression of despair and has become rightly celebrated. His other works in the genre were 'semi-operas', plays with extensive musical sections; among them are the masques *The Fairy Queen* (1692) and *The Indian Queen* (1695). Purcell wrote an immense number of cheerful secular songs and catches, many of which are very attractive, but it is perhaps in the expression of deeper emotions that this great composer reached a pinnacle of achievement, with his subtle rhythms and harmonies.

pūrvi (India) One of the ten parent scales (**thāt**) in Hindustani music, corresponding to C, D♭, E, F♯, G, A♭, B, C′.

Puyana, Rafael (1931-) Colombian harpsichordist who was a pupil of Wanda **Landowska**, studying at the New England Conservatoire. He made his first European tour in 1955, making his New York début in 1957 and his London début in 1966. His wide repertory includes music from the 16th to the 18th centuries as well as modern works. He has made many recordings and has had several works written for him by composers such as Evett, **McCabe**, Houpon and Orbon.

p'yōngjo (Korea) One of the most common **pentatonic** modes, corresponding to C, D, F, G, A.

Q

qawalī (India) Muslim devotional song of northern India and Pakistan.

qin (China) See **ch'in**

quadrille Square dance originating from military horse displays which was introduced to French ballet during the 18th century. It was taken to England at the beginning of the 19th century, where it became a ballroom dance with five different sections. Each section has its own music, mainly drawn from popular songs and fashionable operatic tunes. The Lancers is a type of quadrille.

quadruple counterpoint Four-part **invertible counterpoint**.

quadruplet Four notes played in the time of three.

Quantz, Johann Joachim (1697-1773) German composer of about 500 concertos and other works for the flute. He also taught King Frederick the Great of Prussia to play the flute, made technical improvements to it and wrote a treatise on the subject.

quarter note Alternative term for **crotchet**.

quarter tone Note whose pitch is half-way between two adjacent semitones. Quarter tones were not used in Western music until the 20th century, when they have been used by such composers as **Haba, Bartók** and **Bloch**. See also **microtone**.

quartet Any composition written for four vocalists or instrumentalists, or the group that performs such a piece. For example, a string quartet normally consists of two violins, viola and cello. Strictly speaking, a string quartet is normally in the form of a **sonata** for four stringed instruments. In a piano quartet the piano usually replaces one violin. A vocal quartet normally consists of soprano, alto, tenor and bass.

Quartetto Italiano String quartet founded in 1945 by Paolo Borciani (1922-); the other members were Elisa Pegreffi (1922-), Franco Rossi (1921-) and (from 1946) Piero Farulli (1920-). It has toured extensively and has a very wide repertory ranging from Mozart to **Webern**. It has also made notable recordings of the Beethoven and Brahms quartets, and has been very successful in the Romantic French repertory and contemporary Italian works. Preparation is meticulous, technique faultless; the intensity of interpretation is memorable.

quaver Note that has half the time value of a **crotchet** or an eighth that of a **semibreve**. In the United States it is known as an eighth note.

Quaver

Quilter, Roger (1877-1953) English composer who studied in Frankfurt. He is admired for his charming songs, mainly settings of Shakespeare and other English poets, and his attractive *A Children's Overture* for orchestra based on traditional nursery rhyme tunes.

quintet Any composition written in five vocal or instrumental parts, or the group that performs such a piece. For example, a string quintet is the same as a string **quartet**, with an extra viola or cello. A piano or clarinet quintet consists of a piano or clarinet and a string quartet.

quintuplet Group of five notes of equal time value played in the time of three or four notes.

Quintuplet

quodlibet Composition in which tunes are combined simultaneously. A notable example is found at the end of the prelude to Wagner's *Die Meistersinger*.

R

Rabaud, Henri (1873-1949) French composer who was a pupil of **Massenet**, among others, at the Paris Conservatoire, where he later became professor of harmony, succeeding **Fauré** as director in 1920. He was known for his catch phrase 'modernism is the enemy', and his cantata *Daphne* won him the Prix de Rome (1894). After travelling in Europe he became gradually reconciled to the modern movement and enjoyed an immense success with the oratorio *Job* (1900). He also conducted frequently at both the Opéra and the Opéra-Comique in Paris, and himself composed eight operas, including *L'appel de la mer*, based on Synge's *Riders to the Sea*.

Rachmaninov, Sergei Vassilievich (1873-1943) Russian composer and pianist who studied initially at the St Petersburg Conservatoire (1882) and later the Moscow Conservatoire (1885-92). During this time he showed himself to be an outstanding pianist, and wrote the well-known *Prelude* in C♯ minor and his first piano concerto (1891), but he also scored success with his first opera, *Aleko* (1893), which was composed as his graduation work and which earned him a gold medal won by only two previous students. His Symphony No.1 was written in 1895; its first performance two years later was very poorly received, and his creativity shrivelled as a result. Rescued from despair by psychiatric treatment and by the offer of a conducting post with a Moscow opera company, he was able to establish himself in this new field, appearing in London in 1899, and his confidence returned with the success of his Piano Concerto No.2 (1901), a work which remains a great concert favourite. His conducting career continued at the Bolshoi Theatre, Moscow, for which he composed two operas (*Francesca da Rimini*; *The Miserly Knight*). By 1906 he was becoming increasingly uneasy about the political situation in Russia, and the following year took a house in Dresden, where his Symphony No.2 (1907) and the symphonic poem *The Isle of the Dead* (1909) were written. His first visit to the United States was at this time, when he toured as a concert pianist and performed his third

Sergei Rachmaninov

piano concerto. His career in Russia was interspersed with periods of composing: the *Preludes* Op.32 (1910), a liturgical work, songs and a piano sonata. The choral symphony *The Bells* was completed in 1913; it is one of his finest works.

On the outbreak of revolution in 1917 Rachmaninov was able to take his family out of Russia; they journeyed to Sweden and then on to the United States, where they settled. Here he decided to concentrate on his career as a pianist, realizing that it was more likely to earn him a living than his compositions could – he had had to leave most of his worldly goods behind in Moscow. He was soon established as one of the leading pianists of the day, noted for the combination of a precise technique and a flowing, lyrical style; he made a number of recordings. Being so busy a performer left him little time to compose; however, his Piano Concerto No.4 appeared in 1926, followed by the enduringly popular *Rhapsody on a Theme of Paganini* (1934), his Symphony No.3 (1936) and the *Symphonic Dances* (1940). Rachmaninov composed many beautiful songs throughout his life – outstanding is the wordless *Vocalise*, one of the Opus 34 group composed in 1912. His compositions remain an indispensable component of the Romantic repertory.

racket Double-reed woodwind instrument that was in use between the 16th and 18th centuries. Its long tube was folded many times, so that the actual size of the instrument seemed small. Alternative names for the racket are ranket and sausage bassoon.

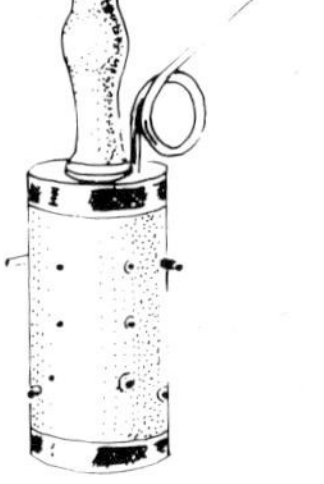

Racket

Raff, Joachim (1822-1882) German composer, born in Switzerland. He studied in Schwyz and afterwards taught for several years; an early set of piano works was published in 1844. He embarked on a further period of study in Zurich before going to Germany under the aegis of Liszt, whose assistant he became in Weimar in 1850, an influence he returned by helping his master with his orchestration. After six years he moved to Wiesbaden, where he married and began his most prolific period of composition. He was also a fine teacher, and in 1877 became director of the Hoch Conservatoire in Frankfurt. He produced a great quantity of compositions: piano music – fantasies, caprices, impromptus, serenades, dances and suites; 11 symphonies; concertos for piano, violin and cello; choral music; songs; chamber works; and several operas, of which only two were performed (*King Alfred*, 1853; *Dame Kobold*, 1870). In his day he was almost as famous as Wagner and Brahms.

rāga (India) Melodic material that forms the basis for composition and improvisation. The term means colour.

A rāga is designated by a name that often includes reference to its scale or mode. Its melodic substance is defined by characteristic ascending and descending tone patterns, ornamentation and embellishment, particular tonal emphases, mood or **rasa**, and an associated time of day.

The term also applies to a performance, generally an improvisation, of a *rāga* as defined above. Most *rāgas* comprise two principal movements, an unmeasured introductory section (**ālāp**), followed by a fixed composition (**gat**), with improvisation, in a fixed temporal cycle (**tāla**).

ragtime Style of piano music that probably originated in the **minstrel** shows of the late 19th century. It was popular until the 1920s and was then replaced by **jazz**. Ragtime has a syncopated melodic line usually accompanied by a 2/4 march-type bass. Classic examples are Scott **Joplin**'s

Maple Leaf Rag and Zez Confrey's *Kitten on the Keys*.

Raimondi, Pietro (1786-1853) Italian composer and opera director who, having studied in Naples, wandered Italy in great poverty, finally producing a successful opera in Genoa (1807). He had further successes as an opera director in Rome, Naples and Milan, and was appointed professor of composition at Palermo Conservatoire (1832). His compositions include sacred music, ballet, some 60 operas and oratorios, including *Giuseppe*.

Raimondi, Ruggero (1941-) Italian bass, who is considered to be one of the finest interpreters of the 19th-century repertory. He studied in Rome, making his opera début at Spoleto in 1964, and has since sung at Glyndebourne (1969) and the New York Metropolitan (1970). He has been a member of La Scala, Milan, since 1970 and has won great praise, particularly in the role of Mozart's Don Giovanni, which he has sung many times all over the world and which he interpreted memorably in Joseph Losey's film of the opera (1978). His other roles include Scarpia in *Tosca*, Amonasro in *Aïda*, Fiesco in *Simon Boccanegra*, and the title-role in Mussorgsky's *Boris Godunov*. He has made numerous recordings, including a recent *Aïda* with **Abbado**.

Rainier, Priaulx (1903-1986) South African composer and violinist, whose compositions reflect the language and music of the Zulus, as well as the influence of Bartók and Stravinsky. Having studied at the South African College of Music, in 1920 she won a violin scholarship to London, where she settled, concentrating on composition from 1935. Her works include *Barbaric Dance Suite* (1949) and *Requiem* (1955-6). She was professor of music at the Royal Academy of Music (1943-61).

rallentando (It.) Indication that the music is to decrease in tempo. Often abbreviated to rall.

Rameau, Jean-Philippe (1683-1764) French composer and theorist who worked as an organist in France (1702-22), when he came under the patronage of the wealthy financier La Pouplinière. His first book, *Traité de l'harmonie* (1722), caused considerable controversy, with its theory of the derivation of harmony from a mathematical and physical basis; it was of major importance, and was followed by other theoretical writings throughout his life, which were also the subject of lively debate. By 1733 he had written numerous keyboard pieces, published in three books (1706, 1724, 1728 – the last including the well-known portrait of a hen, *La poule*), some cantatas and some church music. At the age of 50 he was anxious to turn to opera, and following the success of *Hippolyte et Aricie* he quickly established himself as the leading French composer for the stage, writing more than 20 operas and opera-ballets, such as *Les Indes galantes* (1735), *Castor et Pollux* (1737), *Dardanus* (1739), *La princesse de Navarre* (1745), *Platée* (1745), *Pygmalion* (1748) and *Naïs* (1749). His fourth and last book of keyboard pieces was published in 1741. He was the champion of French music against the Italian party led by **Pergolesi** in the so-called *Guerre des Bouffons*.

Rameau, Jean-Pierre (1922-) French flautist, who is well known as a soloist specializing in 18th-century chamber music, and for whom composers such as **Poulenc** and **Jolivet** have written. He was founder of the French Wind Quintet (1945) and the Paris Wind Ensemble (1953), and is author of *Ancient Music for the Flute*. He was appointed professor of flute at the Paris Conservatoire.

Randegger, Alberto (1832-1911) Italian conductor, singing teacher and composer who studied in Trieste with **Ricci**, becoming known locally as a composer of sacred music and operas such as *Il lazzarone*. He settled in London, where he became professor of singing at the Royal Academy of Music (1860) and wrote further operas (*The Rival Beauties*). He was also conductor at Drury Lane and Covent Garden (1887-98).

Rands, Bernard (1935-) English composer of avant-garde music who studied in Wales at University College, Bangor, and in Italy with **Dallapiccola**, **Boulez** and **Maderna**, among others. He spent two years in the United States as visiting Fellow at Princeton and Illinois universities. He has also held the position of lecturer at Bangor (1961-70) and professor at York University (1970). His compositions have involved work in electronic music studios in many cities, and they include the orchestral piece *Wildtrack One*, *Refractions* for 24 performers and *Expressione IV* for two pianos. In 1984 he was awarded the Pulitzer Prize for *Canti del Sole*.

Rangström, Ture (1884-1947) Swedish conductor, critic and composer who was largely self-taught. A number of his works are associated with August Strindberg, including the Symphony No.1, *In Memoriam Strindberg*, and incidental music written to Strindberg's *Till Damaskus*. He was also one of the most important Swedish song-writers, writing more than 50 songs with orchestral accompaniments. In 1907 he settled in Stockholm as a critic and was conductor of the Göteborg Symphony Orchestra (1922-5). He was founder of the Society of Swedish Composers (1918).

rank Set of organ pipes of the same quality arranged in an ascending scale, one pipe for each note of the organ keyboard. An alternative term is stop.

ranket Alternative term for **racket**.

Rankl, Karl (1898-1968) Austrian-born conductor and composer, who was a pupil of **Schoenberg** and **Webern**. He worked in Germany and Austria as a conductor of opera from 1925 to 1938, becoming resident in Britain from 1939; he was musical director at Covent Garden from 1946 to 1951. His works include eight symphonies and the opera *Deirdre of the Sorrows*, based on the play by Synge, which won a prize in the 1951 Festival of Britain.

rant 17th-century term that was applied loosely to many different English dances. The term may have been a corruption of **courante**.

ranz des vaches Swiss cowherds' song or alphorn signal used in mountainous districts to call cattle. There are many different tunes, varying according to each locality. A *ranz des vaches* has been used by some composers, such as Rossini in the overture to *William Tell* (1829), Beethoven in the *Pastoral Symphony* (1809) and Berlioz in the third movement of the *Symphonie fantastique*.

rasa (India) Aesthetic concept in the Indian arts. In music there is said to be a direct connection between musical expression in a particular **rāga** and the evocation of one or more of the nine *rasas* (love, humour, sadness, anger, heroism, fear, horror, surprise, peace). While music is particularly suited to the expression of the more profound *rasas*, good musicians often demonstrate their skill and personality by portraying a variety of *rasas*.

Rathaus, Karol (1895-1954) Polish composer, later American, who studied in Vienna with **Schreker** and began his career as a pianist in 1919. He moved to Berlin the following year, where he produced two symphonies, a concert overture, a suite, a ballet (*Der letzte Pierrot*, 1927) and an opera (*Fremde Erde*, 1930). Between 1932 and 1938 he lived in Paris and London, moving to the United States and taking up a teaching post at Queen's College, New York, in 1939. His other compositions include many film scores, a third symphony, songs, chamber and piano pieces.

rattle Noise-producing toy occasionally used as an orchestral percussion instrument.

Rattle, Simon (1955-) English conductor who studied at the Royal Academy of Music (1971-5) and founded and conducted the Liverpool Sinfonia (1970-2). In 1974 he won the John Player International Conducting award and has since worked at Glyndebourne and with the London Sinfonietta. From 1979 he has been principal conductor of the City of Birmingham Symphony Orchestra, which he has brought to the front rank through his careful preparation and the close relationship he has developed with the players. His accounts of **Sibelius**, **Janáček**, Stravinsky and especially Mahler are outstanding, and he has made some fine recordings of Sibelius and Mahler symphonies. In 1990 he made his début at Covent Garden, conducting Janáček's *The Cunning Little Vixen*. He has also worked closely with the Los Angeles Philharmonic Orchestra, conducting *Wozzeck* in 1989.

Ravel, Maurice (1875-1937) French composer whose works are remarkable for their impressionist style and mastery of orchestration. He studied piano and composition at the Paris Conservatoire, where among his teachers were **Fauré** and Gédalge; his originality failed to impress the authorities, however, and he never won the Prix de Rome. He was friendly with **Chabrier** and **Satie**, both of whom contributed something to his style. His early piano works were influenced by the brilliant virtuosity of Liszt, which can be traced in *Jeux d'eau* (1901) and *Miroirs* (1905). A String Quartet (1903) was dedicated to Fauré. He responded to the prevailing current of exoticism in both music and art by composing the delicately sensuous song-cycle *Shéhérazade* for soprano and orchestra (1903), and by turning repeatedly to Spanish rhythms and motifs. These colour the *Rhapsodie espagnole* (1908), the opera *L'heure espagnole* (Spanish Time, 1911), and above all the familiar *Boléro* (1928), a work in which the monotony of the single theme is transmuted by the sense of excitement engendered through the very gradual crescendo. In total contrast to this Spanishness, although still on a Spanish theme, is the gravely charming *Pavane pour une infante défunte* (Pavane for a Dead Infanta, 1899), a piano work which Ravel later orchestrated; a 16th-century slow dance form, it is not really a mourning piece but evokes the Spanish princess of the title solemnly dancing at a Renaissance court.

Maurice Ravel

Ravel had various disputes over a long period with the musical establishment of the day, but they did not affect his creativity, which flowed freely during the years before World War I. His piano cycles *Gaspard de la nuit* (1908) and *Valses nobles et sentimentales* (1911), groups of songs (*Histoires naturelles*, 1906, depicting various birds; *Chants populaires*, 1910) and *L'heure espagnole* were followed in 1912 by two ballets: the fairytale *Ma mère l'oye* (Mother Goose) and *Daphnis et Chloé* – the latter for **Diaghilev**'s Ballets Russes. Another song-cycle set the poems of Mallarmé (1913).

By now his music had earned him

widespread admiration, and his reputation was secure; but he was deeply upset by the outbreak of war and by his mother's death in 1916, and his rate of composition slowed. In 1917, however, the piano suite *Le tombeau de Couperin* was completed, a tribute in Baroque dance form not only to the composer of the title, but to friends who were killed in the war. *La valse* (1920) was composed for Diaghilev; it is a compelling *danse macabre*. A delightful opera, *L'enfant et les sortilèges* (The Child and the Spells, 1925), again reveals Ravel's ability to enter the world of childhood; the characterization of the animals and objects is both apt and inventive.

In 1930 Ravel rose to the challenge of composing a piano concerto for the left hand, for the one-armed pianist Paul **Wittgenstein**. A year later a more appealing piano concerto was written; this was his last major work before the onset of the incapacitating illness which finally killed him.

Ravenscroft, Thomas (*c.*1590-1633) English composer and publisher who wrote sacred music, madrigals and part-songs, but is best known as a collector and editor of popular songs, published in the books *Pammelia*, *Deuteromelia* (in which the round *Three Blind Mice* is to be found) and *Melismata*. Some of the songs included were his own compositions. He was also editor of the London edition of the psalter *The Whole Booke of Psalmes* (1621), in which 55 of the 105 settings were his own.

Rawsthorne, Alan (1905-1971) English composer, who began by studying dentistry and architecture before turning to music at the age of 20. He studied in Manchester and with Petri, following this with a teaching post. His first important work was the *Theme and Variations* for two violins (1938); a year later his *Symphonic Studies* was given in Warsaw. This and his first piano concerto (also 1939, reworked for orchestra 1942) established him as a composer with a strongly individual style and a firm grasp of his material.

After serving in the forces during World War II he concentrated on major compositions, producing his first symphony (1950), various concertos (for oboe, 1947; for violin, 1948; for string orchestra, 1949; for piano, 1951), some chamber music and a variety of theatre and film music. He turned to choral music with *A Canticle of Man* (1952). A ballet, *Madame Chrysanthème*, was produced in 1955, with choreography by Frederick Ashton; a second violin concerto was written in 1956 and a second symphony, the Pastoral, in 1959. His Symphony No.3 (1964) and a cello concerto are works of great imaginative power disciplined by masterly use of resources. Other important works are *Medieval Diptych* (1962), *Carmen vitale* (1963) and a *Ballade* for piano (1967); his last years were mainly devoted to writing chamber works.

ray Second note of the **tonic sol-fa** scale.

re The old name for the note D in **solmization**, which is still used in Latin countries.

Read, Gardner (1913-) American composer who studied with **Pizzetti** and **Copland**. He has taught at several American universities and has worked as a radio commentator and writer on music. His compositions include four symphonies, piano and organ music and the operas *Villon* and *The Golden Journey to Samarkand*.

realism 1. The use of real sounds in music, such as birdsong calls, bells, anvils and cannon-fire. In some instances recordings of these sounds are played, while in others musical instruments are used to imitate them.

2. An alternative term for the Italian **verismo**.

realization Act of writing out a full version of a piece of music that was left incomplete by the composer. This might, for example, involve completing the harmony of a 17th-century piece from the basso **continuo** line. Realization involves more than editing, but less than arranging.

rebab Spiked fiddle, with one or more strings, widespread throughout Asia and the Far East. It is held vertically and balanced on a long spike.

rebec Obsolete stringed instrument, similar to the violin, which was of Arab origin and an ancestor of the violin family. It was a pear-shaped instrument with three gut strings played with a bow. The rebec survived in France until the 18th century, but its use was mainly limited to the accompaniment of singing and dancing by **troubadours**.

recapitulation Section of a composition in which the original subjects are restated after their development. See **sonata form**

recit. Abbreviation of recitative.

recital Musical performance given by a solo instrumentalist, a singer with piano accompaniment or duettists. Other musical performances without action are known as concerts, although in popular music the term concert is now used even for performances by solo singers.

recitative Form of singing used in **opera** and **oratorio**, described by **Caccini** at the beginning of the 17th century as speaking in music. The text is sung to notes written out usually in 4/4 time, with a rhythm related to natural speech rather than the written values. There are two kinds of recitative: *recitativo secco* and *recitativo accompagnato* (often also known as *recitativo stromentato*). The recitative was used to advance the action of the piece.

Recitativo secco consists of the rapid declamation of words, punctuated by chords on the keyboard and possibly another instrument such as the *viola da gamba*. The accompaniment is often only at the **cadence** points.

Recitativo accompagnato has an orchestral accompaniment and not only moves the action of the plot forward, but often precedes an **aria** with a dramatic declaration setting out the character's emotions.

Handel's *Messiah* is an example of an oratorio in which recitative is used extensively. The work tells of the life of Christ, and the words to the recitative sections are drawn directly from the Bible. These lead to arias which, by contrast, are used to comment upon the action.

recorder Whistle-headed flute that was used throughout Europe between the 16th and 18th centuries. It was formerly known as the English flute. The recorder is held vertically and blown through a mouthpiece in which the air is diverted by a block of wood (the fipple). This produces a milder tone than the flute. The most widely used recorders are the treble, tenor, descant, soprano and bass. In the 20th century the instrument was revived by Arnold **Dolmetsch** as a relatively inexpensive and easy way to teach children the basics of music.

Recorder

recte et retro (Lat.) Form of **canon** in which the imitating voice plays or sings the first theme backwards.

reed instruments Musical instruments in which the sound is produced by the vibration of the reed (a tongue of thin cane or metal). In beating-reed instruments, such as the **clarinet**, the reed vibrates against an air slot; in free-reed instruments (**harmonica**, **accordion** and **concertina**), it vibrates through a slot, and in the double-reed instruments (**oboe** and **bassoon**) two reeds vibrate against each other. With the exception of the **flute**, all the woodwind instruments of an orchestra are reed instruments.

reed organ Type of keyboard instrument that uses free-beating reeds to produce individual notes. As there are no pipes, the reeds are activated by air blown across them. Among the instruments in this group are the harmonium and the American organ, in which the air pressure is produced by pedal-operated bellows or an electric motor. The air pressure to an accordion is produced by pumping bellows with the arms, and with the mouth organ the player blows air directly over the reeds. See also **reed instruments**.

reed pipe Organ pipe in which sound is produced by causing a reed to beat regularly against an opening into the pipe. The reeds are all of the single-beating type, similar to that of the clarinet. The actual tone quality produced by reeds ranges from the **diapason** tone of the basic flute-work to brilliant and powerful reeds of marked individual character. See also **reed instruments.**

reel Irish or Scottish dance, also found in North Yorkshire as part of the Long Sword dance, the influence of which can be traced in dances as far afield as the Caribbean and United States. It is a rapid dance performed by two or more couples, the music flowing smoothly in quadruple metre. The Irish version is generally faster than the Scottish.

refrain In verse songs and anthems, a strain that returns with the same words at the beginning, middle or end of each verse.

regal Small portable reed organ that was in use from the 15th to the 17th centuries. It was used in churches to accompany singing. Some models could be folded like a book, and were named Bible-regal. The regal was said to have been invented by Heinrich Traxdorff of Nuremberg in about 1460.

Reger, Max (1873-1916) German composer and organist who studied in Munich and Wiesbaden after becoming organist at the church of Weiben in Bavaria at the age of 13. He toured Europe as a pianist and conductor, and became professor of composition at Leipzig University in 1907. He also held posts in Meiningen and Jena. His prodigious output in a working life of only 26 years includes important works for organ (chorale fantasias, preludes and fugues), orchestral works (*Variations and Fugue on a Theme of Mozart*, 1914), choral music (*Die Nonnen*, 1909), piano and chamber pieces and over 250 songs.

reggae (Caribbean) Highly rhythmic Jamaican song form popular from the late 1960s onwards. It is a synthesis of Afro-American popular music and Afro-Jamaican traditional music, containing traces of African religious music and Christian revivalist songs. The lyrics are often concerned with political and social comment, and frequently imbued with Rastafarian values.

The form originated in the urban lower-class music of the 'rudie boys' and is associated with its forerunners **ska** and rock-steady.

register Part of the compass of an instrument or the human voice that is said to have its own particular tone-quality. Examples are the human head and chest registers.

Reich, Steve (1936-) American composer of the **minimalist** school, whose work deals with very gradual changes in time and the possibilities of using multiples of the same instrument, making use of minimal material (such as a single chord in *Four Organs*) to construct his music. In 1966 he founded the group Steve Reich and Musicians and he has established his own electronic studio in New York. Other works include *Pitch Charts* (1963), *Piano Phrase* (1967), *Music for 18 Instruments* (1975), *The Desert Music* (1983), and *Different Trains* (1990).

Reichardt, Johann Friedrich (1752-1814) German composer, the author of several books on composition and criticism, who also published collections of music. He was musical director at the Prussian court of **Frederick the Great** and Frederick William II until his dismissal in 1793 for his sympathy with the French Revolution. A forerunner of Schubert in song composition, he wrote some 100 songs and 12 operas, including *Hänschen und Gretchen* and a setting of Milton's *Morning Hymn*.

Reimann, Aribert (1936-) German composer, who is also well known as an accompanist to singers, and in particular to **Fischer-Dieskau**. He studied with **Blacher** and Rausch in Berlin and his works include the opera *A Dream Play* (after Strindberg), songs and choral pieces. He has also set texts by Shakespeare and Shelley.

Reincken, Johann Adam (1623-1722) German organist and composer. It is said that **Bach** often walked from Lüneburg and later Cöthen to Hamburg to hear him play at St Catherine's, where he was organist from 1663. He was a pupil of Heinrich **Scheidemann** and a masterful technician; his best-known compositions are his keyboard arrangements from *Hortus Musicus*.

Reiner, Fritz (1888-1963) Hungarian-born conductor who was a particularly famed interpreter of Richard Strauss, Wagner and **Bartók**. He was principal conductor at Dresden Staatsoper, where he conducted the German première of Strauss's *Die Frau ohne Schatten* in 1919. Later he settled in the United States where he was principal conductor with the Cincinnati Symphony Orchestra (1922-31), the Pittsburgh Symphony Orchestra and the Metropolitan Opera, New York. In 1953 he took over as chief conductor of the Chicago Symphony Orchestra (1953), which under his direction became in Stravinsky's opinion the most precise and flexible orchestra in the world. He also taught at the Curtis Institute, Philadelphia, where Leonard **Bernstein** was among his pupils. He worked at Covent Garden (1936, *Tristan und Isolde*) and Vienna (1955, *Der Rosenkavalier*). He was celebrated for the tiny movements of his baton and also for the ruthless management of his orchestras. He made many superb recordings, especially with the Chicago orchestra.

Reizenstein, Franz (1911-1968) British composer and pianist of German birth who studied in Berlin with **Hindemith**, settling in England in 1934 in order to escape the Nazi regime; there he studied with **Vaughan Williams**. From 1958 he taught piano at the Royal Academy of Music. His compositions include the oratorio *Genesis*, the cantata *Voices of Night* and two Hoffnung concert pastiches, *Let's Fake an Opera* and *Concerto Popolare*.

related keys Keys that are harmonically close so that **modulation** between them is relatively simple and concordant. For example, major and minor keys that share the same key signature (e.g. C major and A minor) are said to be related.

relative pitch Ability to identify or sing intervals from a known note. See also **absolute pitch**.

reminiscence-motive Recurring theme in the composition of an **opera**, linked to a specific character or an emotion.

repeat Restatement of a section of a composition, not written out a second time, but indicated by signs or marks used in conjunction with a **double bar**. In classical music the expositions of movements in **sonata form** are nearly always marked for a repeat.

Two methods of indicating a repeat

répétiteur 1. Member of an opera company who coaches the singers or chorus, teaches them their parts, and guides them in the interpretation.
2. Inside player at the front desk of the string section of an orchestra who helps the principal.

reprise 1. A repeated section of a composition.
2. The reappearance of the first subject in a **sonata-form** movement at the point where the **recapitulation** begins.
3. The reappearance of a song or dance number in a musical or operetta.

Requiem Mass for the dead, in the Roman Catholic rite. The name is taken from the opening words of the Introit, *Requiem aeternam dona eis, Domine* (Grant them eternal rest, Lord). The form differs slightly from that of the plainsong Mass developed since the early Middle Ages: it has an Introit, Kyrie, Gradual, Tract, Sequence, Offertory, Sanctus and Benedictus, Agnus Dei and Communion; the usual Gloria and Credo are omitted. The early **plainsong** Requiem is still used. Polyphonic versions were composed in the 15th and 16th centuries by **Ockeghem**, **Lassus** and **Palestrina**. Many more were written for Church use in the 17th and 18th centuries. From the time of Mozart's Requiem (1791, unfinished), they have been composed on too large a scale for an actual service, and are generally given at concerts; sometimes only parts of the liturgy have been set. Fine Requiems have been written by Berlioz (1837), Bruckner (1845), Verdi (1874), Dvořák (1891), **Fauré** (1900), **Duruflé** (1947) and **Britten** (*War Requiem*, 1961, combining the liturgical text with settings of Wilfred Owen's poems). Brahms's *German Requiem* is not a Mass, but a setting of Biblical excerpts.

Resnik, Regina (1922-) American mezzo-soprano who formerly sang soprano and has sung at the New York Metropolitan and at Covent Garden in both voices. She made her début in New York (1942) in *Macbeth* and has since been a notable interpreter of the roles of Amneris in Verdi's *Aïda*, Klytemnestra in Strauss's *Elektra* and **Bizet**'s Carmen, in which opera she also made her début as director in Hamburg (1971).

resolution Process by which a **discord** is made into a **concord** by resolving the dissonant note, usually downwards, to a harmony note.

resonance Characteristic of an object whereby it vibrates to a note of a certain pitch. A resonator may be the cavities in the human skull, the hollow in a musical instrument such as a guitar, or a concert hall.

Respighi, Ottorino (1879-1936) Italian composer, conductor, string-player and pianist, who was probably the most internationally successful Italian composer of his generation. He studied in Bologna, with **Rimsky-Korsakov** in St Petersburg and later in Berlin with **Bruch**. From 1903 to 1908 he pursued a career as a violinist and violist, and later became professor of composition at the Liceo di S. Cecilia, Rome (1913). He taught to the end of his life, and conducted his own works in both Europe and the United States. His first important work was the song *Aretusa* (1911); it was followed by a vast work, the *Sinfonia drammatica*, which is now seldom heard. His most popular and admired work is *Le fontane di Roma* (The Fountains of Rome, 1916), a vivid orchestral picture of the city; *I pini di Roma* (The Pines of Rome, 1924), in which the composer made innovatory use of a nightingale's song on a gramophone record, although similarly filled with colourful orchestral effects, is not quite as successful. In his later compositions Respighi began to make use of elements from early music, notable in *Lauda per la natività del Signore* (1930). He also made arrangements of such music, as in the suites *Ancient Airs and Dances* and *The Birds*; and of later composers, for example Rossini in the ballet *La boutique fantasque*.

response In Catholic and Anglican church music the choral and congregational cadences answering the versicles read or chanted by the priest, such as 'Amen', or 'Have mercy upon us...' in the Litany.

rest Period of silence on the part of a performer corresponding to a given number of beats or bars. If the performer is to rest for an entire movement, the word *tacet* (silent) appears in the music.

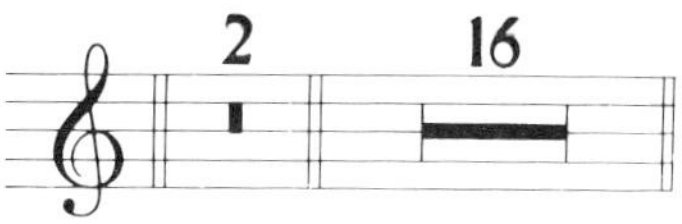

Two bars and 16 bars rest

resultant tone Alternative term for **combination tone**.

retenu (Fr.) Retained, a direction indicating that the tempo should be held back.

Reubke, Julius (1834-1858) German pianist and composer, whose early death cut short a promising career. The son of Adolf Reubke, the organ-builder, he was a pupil of **Liszt**. The works published before his death include the organ sonata *The 94th Psalm*, piano works and songs.

Reutter, Hermann (1900-1985) German composer and pianist, who was a highly successful accompanist to singers such as Sigrid Onegin, **Schwarzkopf**, **Hotter** and **Fischer-Dieskau**. He held a number of appointments at the German music schools including that of director of the Stuttgart Academy (1956-66). A composer in many genres, Reutter is particularly admired for his stage works, such as the opera *Saul* (1928), and songs, and is considered to be one of the foremost proponents of the *Lied* tradition in the 20th century.

Revueltas, Silvestre (1899-1940) Mexican violinist, conductor and composer whose compositions were greatly influenced by Mexican folk-songs, although he did not directly quote from them. He studied and worked in both Mexico and the United States, and from 1929 to 1935 was assistant conductor of the Mexican Symphony Orchestra. His compositions include the much-played symphonic poem *Sensemayá* (1938).

Reyer, Ernest (1823-1909) French composer and critic who championed composers such as Wagner, Berlioz and **Bizet**. He began his musical career in Paris in 1848, and over the next 14 years composed a substantial body of music, including the successful *Oriental Symphony* (1850) and *Le Sélam*. His activities as a critic account for his very small output over the next 46 years of his life, but he had successes with the operas *Sigurd* (1884) and *Salammbô* (1890), based on the novel by Flaubert.

rfz. Abbreviation of **rinforzando**.

rgya-gling (Tibet) Oboe used in Buddhist ritual, with a conical wooden body about 60 cm (23 in) in length, seven finger-holes and a single thumb-hole. The mouthpiece, which grips the double reed, has a disc against which the player rests his lips. It resembles the more ubiquitous **zurna**, with the exception of the large, flared silver or copper bell, which gives it a sweeter yet still powerful sound. In rituals pairs of *rgya-gling* play short pieces, which are usually themes subject to much variation.

rh Abbreviation for right hand. The letters are written above or below the bass staff in piano music, to indicate that the section is to be played by the right instead of the left hand.

rhapsody Musical form that came to prominence in the 19th century. Usually free in form, the rhapsody often made use of elements derived from folk-music. Typical examples include **Liszt**'s *Hungarian Rhapsodies* (1852) and **Dvořák**'s *Slavonic Rhapsodies* (1878). Among more recent rhapsodies are **Gershwin**'s *Rhapsody in Blue* (1924) and **Rachmaninov**'s *Rhapsody on a Theme of Paganini* (1934).

Rheinberger, Joseph (1839-1901) German organist, composer and conductor who held his first organ post at the age of seven. He studied and taught at Munich Conservatoire, composing a number of operas, symphonies and chamber music, but is remembered for his elaborate and challenging organ compositions, in particular the 20 organ sonatas. Rheinberger achieved lasting fame as a teacher of the organ.

Rhodes, Helen See **Hardelot, Guy d'**

rhythm One of the three basic elements that go to make up Western music, rhythm is the creative manipulation of events, such as accent and note-lengths, which define the passing of time. In early music and many other cultures rhythm alone holds sway, often dependent on the fluctuating patterns of speech; when the metrical framework is firmly set by the use of time-signatures and barlines, rhythm brings the contents to life, and creates a sense of movement.

rhythm and blues Style of popular music that developed from traditional **blues**, with the more emphatically rhythmic elements of modern rock music. The popularity of rhythm and blues grew with the acceptance by young whites of the music of black American singers such as Bo Diddley and Chuck Berry. In the 1960s their music also influenced many leading British pop groups.

ribible Alternative term for **rebec**.

Ricci, Ruggiero (1918-) American violinist, who made his début at the age of ten in New York, making his first tour of Europe in 1932 and going on to have a brilliant international career. He is a notable interpreter of the works of **Paganini** and reintroduced the recently discovered Concerto No.4 in 1971. He has had a number of works written for him by **Ginastera** and von **Einem**. He has been a teacher at the Juilliard School since 1975.

Ricciarelli, Katia (1946-) Italian soprano who studied at the Venice Conservatoire and made her début in 1969 in Mantua as Mimì in *La bohème*. She won the Verdi Award in 1970 and the Italian Radio award the following year, since when her warm, dramatic soprano and attractive stage manner have been in demand for Verdi roles. She is an outstanding Leonora (*Il trovatore*) and Elisabeth (*Don Carlos*), but the role for which she has won most recognition is Desdemona (*Otello*), which she sang in the 1986 Zeffirelli film with **Domingo**. Her recordings include *Aïda*, *Ballo in maschera*, *Don Carlos* and *Falstaff*. She has appeared at the Metropolitan, New York; Covent Garden; San Francisco; and all over Europe, in a wide range of Puccini, **Bellini**, and **Donizetti** roles as well as Verdi.

ricercare (It.) To search out. A 16th–18th-century instrumental piece in the style of a fugue, using all forms of variation technique available to ornament the principal theme.

Richter, Franz (1709-1789) Bohemian composer, who entered the service of the Mannheim court (1747) first as a singer and violinist and then as court composer. He was later appointed choirmaster at Strasbourg Cathedral (1769-89). He was one of the leaders of the Mannheim School of symphonists, and also wrote some 30 Masses, two Requiems and two Passions.

Richter, Hans (1843-1916) Hungarian horn-player and conductor who was particularly associated with **Wagner**, beginning with his preparation of the fair copy of the *Meistersinger* score (1867). He also helped Wagner to complete the score of the *Ring* cycle, and was chosen to conduct the first performance of the whole cycle at **Bayreuth** (1876). He returned frequently to Bayreuth throughout his career. He held a number of important conducting appointments and in 1877 travelled to London with Wagner, where from 1879 to 1897 he gave an annual series of what came to be known as the Richter concerts. He was the permanent conductor of the Hallé Orchestra, Manchester (1900-11) and of the London Symphony Orchestra; he also conducted at Covent Garden. He championed several English composers, including **Elgar**, who dedicated his first symphony to him.

Richter, Karl (1926-1981) German organist, harpsichordist and conductor who was a specialist in the choral works of Bach and Handel. He joined the staff of the Munich Academy in 1951 and was appointed professor in 1956.

Richter, Sviatoslav (1915-) Soviet pianist and conductor who is among the outstanding pianists of the 20th century. Largely self-taught, he was *répétiteur* at Odessa Opera at the age of 15 and assistant conductor by the age of 18. A specialist in the works of **Prokofiev**, he has toured throughout Europe and the United States and has appeared at the Aldeburgh Festival a number of times in association with **Britten** and **Rostropovich**.

ricochet In string-playing, **staccato** effect produced by letting the bow bounce on the strings.

Ridout, Alan (1934-) English composer who studied at the Royal College of Music and went on to become lecturer at Cambridge University (1963), and then professor at the Royal College of Music (1969). In this didactic capacity he has made numerous radio broadcasts, and many of his compositions are for children or amateur choirs. His work as a composer is closely linked with his residence in Canterbury and includes the opera *The Pardoner's Tale*, based on Chaucer. His work reflects his eclectic musical interests, from **polyphony** to **serialism**. He has written a number of other operas; cantatas; song-cycles; six symphonies; concertos for various instruments; and organ works (*Stations of the Cross*, 1978).

Riegger, Wallingford (1885-1961) American composer and conductor who worked and studied in Germany, eventually settling in the United States, where he established his reputation with his first major work, a piano trio (1920). He wrote for Martha Graham's dance company and a number of scores for other American choreographers. Other works such as the *Study in Sonority* and *Music for Brass Choir* demonstrate the originality and importance of his compositions, which made a significant impression on his contemporaries although he achieved no real fame.

Ries, Ferdinand (1784-1838) German pianist, conductor and composer. He was the son of Franz Anton **Ries** and a pupil of Beethoven in Vienna (1801-5), collaborating with Wegeler on one of the most important early biographies of Beethoven (1838). He toured Europe and Scandinavia as a pianist, and worked in London (1813-24), retiring to Germany where he conducted eight Lower Rhine Fests (1825-37). His compositions include three operas, 18 symphonies, nine piano concertos and other instrumental works.

Ries, Franz Anton (1755-1846) Violinist who was a member of the German family of musicians of the same name. He was able to take his father Johann's place in the orchestra at the age of 11 and went on to become leader of the electoral court orchestra. He was a friend and teacher of **Beethoven**.

Rieti, Vittorio (1898-) American composer of Italian origin, who studied with **Casella** and **Respighi** among others. He lived in Paris from 1925, where he formed close ties with Les **Six** and was founder-director of the group La

Sérénade, dedicated to modern chamber music (1931-40). He wrote a number of ballets for **Diaghilev**, later choreographed by Balanchine, the most successful of which was *Barabau*. He settled in the United States in 1939, where he taught at a number of American colleges. Later works include operas (*Maryam the Harlot*, 1966) and more ballets (*Scenes Seen*, 1975); there are seven symphonies altogether, two violin concertos and a considerable volume of chamber and instrumental pieces.

riff Jazz term for a short written phrase or figure that is constantly repeated.

Rifkin, Joshua (1944-) American musicologist, pianist, conductor and composer whose principal areas of research are Renaissance and Baroque music. As a pianist and conductor he has made several recordings, including most of the rags of Scott **Joplin**, and his compositions include chamber music and songs. He has also worked with **Stockhausen**.

rigaudon 17th-century French dance in duple time, probably originating in Provence or Languedoc.

Riley, Terry (1935-) American **minimalist** composer and performer whose interest is in the quality of sound rather than thematic development. He uses repetition of short phrases, sometimes freely combined by the performer with other repeated motifs, creating constantly changing relationships between the parts. He has frequently toured Europe performing his own works, such as *Mescalin Mix* and *Dorian Reeds*, and his most important work of the 1960s, *In C* (1964). Since 1970 Riley has devoted much of his time to the study and performance of Indian music, which has been one of the influences on his most recent work, *Salome Dances for Peace*, a two-hour-long piece for string quartet (1990) with elements of folk and jazz as well. Riley taught at Mills College between 1971 and 1980.

Joshua Rifkin

Rimsky-Korsakov, Nikolai (1844-1908) Russian composer and conductor who in early life was consumed by his ambition to be a naval officer, but after meeting **Balakirev**, **Cui** and **Mussorgsky** in 1861 was persuaded to pursue a career as a composer. He received great encouragement from Balakirev, who guided him in the composition of his Symphony No.1 in E♭ minor, the first of real importance by a Russian composer, while he was as yet ignorant of the basic rules of harmony and counterpoint. His talent for orchestration was already clear, and he was asked by **Dargomizhsky** to complete the scoring of his opera *The Stone Guest*. He also produced the opera *The Maid of Pskov* (1868-72). On the strength of this work, he was appointed professor of the St Petersburg Conservatoire, and continued to teach himself in secret.

He was then appointed Inspector of Naval Bands (1873), a post created entirely for him, allowing him time to undertake his own education, producing a number of academic compositions including *Six Piano Fugues* (1875), although little serious work came of these years. His compilation of two collections of Russian folk-songs led him to a new and successful phase in composition, blending fantasy and the

Nikolai Rimsky-Korsakov

comic in the operas *May Night* (1870) and *Snow Maiden* (1882).

After the death of his friend **Mussorgsky** in 1881, he devoted himself to setting the composer's works in order, including revisions to the operas *Khovanshchina* and later *Boris Godunov*, only interrupting this work to write two of his most colourful compositions, the *Capriccio espagnol* (1887) and *Schéhérazade* (1888). In 1887 another friend, **Borodin**, died, and he felt obliged to complete work on his unfinished opera *Prince Igor*. After hearing Wagner's *Ring* in 1889, Rimsky-Korsakov devoted himself to opera for practically the rest of his active life: he composed *Christmas Eve* (1895), *Sadko* (1896), *Kitezh* (1905) and several others, including the opera-ballet *Mlada* (1892). In 1905, he came into conflict with the authorities because of his sympathy with revolutionary students, and he reflected these conflicts in his last satirical opera, *The Golden Cockerel*.

Rimsky-Korsakov's compositions, which include three symphonies as well as chamber music and songs, are distinguished by their rich orchestration and literary references. Many of them have become very popular, and have influenced such composers as his best-known pupil, **Stravinsky**. His book *Principles of Orchestration* (1891) has also been very influential.

rinforzando (It.) Reinforcing. Indication that a particular note or phrase is to be emphasized. It can also mean a quick **crescendo** from *piano*. It is often abbreviated to rinf. or rfz.

ring shout Afro-American call-and-response religious song and dance. A circle of people move in single file singing and stamping their feet in a repetitive fashion, the tempo gradually building up until participants are seemingly entranced or 'possessed by spirits'. The ring shout represented an attempt to provide an acceptable form of dance, an integral part of African worship, within a Christian context. It was prevalent in the United States from the 1860s.

ripieno (It.) Full. 1. In *concerti grossi*, the group of instrumentalists apart from the soloists (the *concertino*). An alternative term is *tutti*.

2. A part that fills in or supplements another.

ritardando (It.) Slowing. Indication that the music is to decrease in tempo, often abbreviated to rit.

ritornello (It.) A refrain, usually instrumental; a passage which recurs between other episodes, such as verses in a song or solo passages with other themes in a concerto.

ritsu (Japan) One of the two basic **pentatonic** scales in Buddhist music theory and **gagaku** court music. See **Japanese scales**

Rivier, Jean (1896-) French composer. He studied at the Paris Conservatoire

(1922-6), having been invalided in World War I, and quickly took a leading position among the avant-garde with his String Quartet (1924). Other works from between the wars include several settings of songs by Apollinaire; an opera, *Vénitienne* (1936); piano music, and orchestral pieces such as a *Burlesque* for violin and orchestra (1929). Rivier composed many scores for radio, seven symphonies, concertos for various forces (flute and strings, 1955; clarinet and strings, 1958; brass, timpani and strings, 1963; trumpet and strings, 1971); choral music, including a Requiem; and songs. He taught at the Paris Conservatoire from 1962 to 1966.

Roberts, Bernard (1933-) British pianist who studied at the Royal College of Music. He has an extensive repertory ranging from the 18th century to contemporary music, but it is as a Beethoven specialist that he is particularly admired; he has made fine recordings of the Beethoven sonatas. He broadcasts regularly on Radio 3, and has performed at all the major British festivals. He gives annual master-classes at the Dartington International Summer School.

Rochberg, George (1918-) American composer and critic, who studied at the Mannes School and Curtis Institute where he later taught. Influenced by **Schoenberg** and **Mahler**, he developed an individual form of **serialism** in works such as the String Quartet No.2, later broadening his range to include tonal idioms, for instance in his *Contra Mortem et Tempus*. Several of his works contain Jewish references, including his choral psalm settings in Hebrew.

rock music Type of popular music that originated in the **rock 'n' roll** of the American 1950s. Rock covers many varieties and forms of vocal and sometimes purely instrumental music, usually played by bands of anything from two to twelve or more players. The minimum configuration usually consists of guitars and drums, but many bands also use brass, woodwind, piano and other instruments. Rock is normally divided into types, such as jazz-rock, funk-rock, heavy rock, etc.

rock 'n' roll Style of music that first appeared in the 1950s, probably originating in the twelve-bar blues of New Orleans jazz, and forming the beginning of pop music. Rock 'n' roll involved a vocalist and guitar (often electric guitar) and originally the term covered all styles of pop music. Early examples are Bill Haley's *Rock Around the Clock* (1955) and Elvis Presley's *Blue Suede Shoes* (1956). The term is now used to mean a specific form of popular music, with characteristic rhythms and sequences. Rock 'n' roll eventually gave birth to **rock music**, with all its sub-types.

rococo music Style of music of the early and mid-18th century that was characterized by a light and delicate elegance in the **homophonic** style. It is said to relate to a style of visual art that evolved in France at that time. Some of the music by **Couperin**, **Telemann**, J.C. **Bach** and Mozart was associated with this form.

Rodgers, Richard (1902-1979) American composer whose partnership with the lyric-writers Lorenz Hart and Oscar **Hammerstein II** led to a series of stage musicals and songs which enjoyed

Richard Rodgers

unprecedented success. With Hart he had a number of Broadway hits including *Babes in Arms* (1937) and *Pal Joey* (1940), with songs such as *My Funny Valentine*, *The Lady is a Tramp* and *Bewitched, Bothered and Bewildered*, and by the time of Hart's death (1943), their collaboration had produced 30 stage musicals and a number of films and film versions of their stage shows. Rodgers continued his success with Hammerstein, with whom he wrote the 'first American vernacular opera' *Oklahoma!* and had further success with *South Pacific*, *The King and I* and *The Sound of Music*. He was made a member of the National Institute of Arts and Letters and was presented with numerous doctorates by American universities.

Rodrigo, Joaquín (1901-) Spanish composer who, blind from the age of three, studied with **Dukas** and was much encouraged by **Falla**. He also studied in Paris for a while. He was appointed professor of music history at Madrid University in 1947. He toured Europe and the United States over the next few years to prepare performances of his works. Many Spanish and French honours have been awarded him, including the Gran Cruz del Mérito Civil. Rodrigo is best known for his works for guitar and orchestra, *Concierto de Aranjuez* (1939) and *Fantasía para un gentilhombre* (1954). His other works include concertos for piano, violin, cello and harp; solo guitar and piano music; a ballet (*Pavana real*, 1955) and an opera (*La azuzena de Quito*, 1965); and a variety of vocal music. Although sometimes regarded as a retrogressive figure, his compositions, which combine agreeable tunes with picturesque Spanish ambience and folklore, are immensely influential among contemporary Spanish composers.

Roger, Florimond French composer who wrote under the pen-name of **Hervé**.

Roger-Ducasse, Jean (1873-1954) French composer who was a pupil of **Fauré**. He studied at the Paris Conservatoire, where he was later appointed professor of composition (1935-40). His compositions include the mime drama *Orpheus* (1913) and a comic opera, *Cantegril* (1931), and he completed and orchestrated Debussy's *Rhapsody for Saxophone and Orchestra*.

Rogers, Bernard (1893-1968) American composer who studied at the New York Institute of Musical Art and was a pupil of **Bloch**. He was chief critic of *Musical America* (1913-24) and professor of composition at the Eastman School (1929-67). His compositions include the opera *The Warrior* (1944). His treatise *The Art of Orchestration* is a standard work.

Rogg, Lionel (1936-) Swiss organist who is best known for his recordings of Bach's complete organ works on 18 records, laying the foundation for a career as an international recitalist who specializes in Bach. He was appointed professor at the Geneva Conservatoire in 1960.

Roldán, Amadeo (1900-1939) Cuban composer and conductor who was much influenced by African music, making liberal use of Afro-Cuban rhythms and themes. His works include the ballet *Rebamberamba*, the orchestration of which includes indigenous Cuban instruments, and *Overture on Cuban Themes*. He was conductor of the Havana Philharmonic Orchestra and professor at the Havana Conservatoire (1935).

Rolfe Johnson, Anthony (1940-) English tenor who studied at the Guildhall School of Music and made his début at Glyndebourne. He has made a notable career in opera, oratorio and recital, specializing in Baroque music. His opera roles include Orfeo (Monteverdi), Jupiter (Handel's *Semele*), Lensky (Tchaikovsky's *Eugene Onegin*) and the Mozart repertory. He has recorded Handel's *Acis and Galatea*, *Hercules* and *Ode for St Cecilia's Day*, Monteverdi's *Orfeo* and Bach's *Christmas Oratorio*.

roll Technique in percussion-playing whereby an instrument (drums or cymbals) is struck by two drumsticks in very rapid succession, to produce a virtually continuous sound. The technique is used in many ceremonial works, for example (usually) at the start of *God Save The Queen* and in Haydn's *Drum Roll Symphony*.

rol-mo (Tibet) Music, especially instrumental music, associated with Buddhist ritual. More specifically, it refers to the loud, large-bossed cymbals, also known as *sbub-chal*. With the frame drum (*rnga*), these punctuate the syllables of sung texts, whether measured or not. In measured hymns, the cymbals and drum function as time-beaters, whereas in unmeasured **dbyangs**, they merely mark time. In instrumental interludes, the cymbals also provide various rhythmic patterns, either solo or as part of the ensemble (which may include **rgya-gling**, **dung-chen**, trumpets made from shell or bone, bells and drums).

Roman, Johan Helmich (1694-1758) Swedish composer who acted as leader of the court orchestra in Stockholm, studying in London under **Pepusch** and **Ariosti** from 1714 until his return to Stockholm in 1720, where he became *Kapellmeister* (1729). His works include a Swedish setting of the Mass and his most performed composition, *Drottningholmsmusiquen*.

romance Term with only a vague meaning in music. It normally implies a short piece of an emotional and quiet nature. The French equivalent sometimes means a short song for solo voice, and the term has also been used for the slow movement of some concertos. The Italian and German forms are *romanza* and *Romanze* respectively.

Romantic music Artistic style that evolved in the late 18th and 19th centuries, matching the social upheavals implied by the French Revolution, where the formal structures of classical practice were gradually broken down in the search for more personal, individual expression. This could already be detected in the later works of **Mozart**, for example the Symphony No.40 and the D minor Piano Concerto, and developed rapidly in the music of **Beethoven, Schubert** and **Schumann**. Literary works had a powerful influence, especially the poetry of Byron and the novels of Sir Walter Scott, which inspired many musical compositions such as Schumann's *Manfred*, **Berlioz**'s *Waverley* overture and **Donizetti**'s *Lucia di Lammermoor*. Then there was music inspired by the reaction of the composer to natural vistas, such as **Liszt**'s *Années de Pèlerinage*, or to paintings, such as **Mussorgsky**'s *Pictures at an Exhibition*. Romantic music was rhapsodic in style, improvisatory, impassioned, free in melody, harmony and structure. Inevitably, when freedom tended towards anarchy and incoherence, there was a reaction at the start of the 20th century, which led to the discipline of **Schoenberg**'s serial method, and to neo-classicism, though some commentators have described these movements as the dying gasps of Romanticism.

Romberg, Sigmund (1887-1951) Hungarian-born American composer, who was best known as a writer of popular operettas such as *Maytime* (1917), *The Student Prince* (1924) and *The Desert Song* (1926). Having studied in Vienna with Heuberger, he settled in the United States (1909), becoming an American citizen. In the 1930s he moved to Hollywood, where he wrote film scores. In 1942 he formed his own orchestra and toured the United States with it.

Ronald, Sir Landon (1873-1938) English composer and conductor who studied at the Royal College of Music. His first post was at Covent Garden; in 1892 he became conductor of a touring opera company, and accompanied Melba on her United States tour in 1894. He returned to Covent Garden to conduct Gounod's *Faust* in

1896. His next important appointment was as guest conductor of the London Symphony Orchestra. He was a friend of Elgar, and conducted the première of his Symphony No.1 in Rome in 1909. He appeared with most of the main orchestras in Britain, including the Royal Albert Hall Orchestra (1909-14). In 1910 he became principal of the Guildhall School. He composed many songs – among them *Down in the Forest* – operettas and overtures. He was a noted critic.

rondeau (Fr.) 1. A 13th-century poetic and musical structure derived from the monophonic trouvé form which had a recurrent **refrain** with the same words and music. In the 14th century **polyphonic** settings were made by **Machaut** in three parts for voice and two instruments.
2. An alternative term for **rondo**.

rondo (It.) Composition in which one theme (known as the rondo theme) recurs intermittently. A rondo normally appears in the form ABACADA, and sometimes makes up the final movement of a sonata or concerto. The other sections (B,C,D, known as episodes) are usually written to contrast with the theme, which may be varied each time it appears.
A simple rondo form combined with **sonata form** (known as sonata-rondo form) has a structure that can be expressed as ABACABA, where A and B represent the exposition and recapitulation, and the episode C, the development. An outstanding example of the rondo form is the **adagio** from Beethoven's Piano Sonata No.8, *Pathétique* (1799). Other works in rondo form include Mendelssohn's *Rondo capriccioso in E* for piano (1837), and the tone poem *Till Eulenspiegel* (1895) by Richard Strauss.

root Lowest note of a triad or four-note chord in root position. When the chord is inverted, the note that was originally the root is still considered as such, although it is no longer at the bottom of the chord. See also **inversion**; **triad**.

Ropartz, Guy (1864-1955) French composer who studied at the Paris Conservatoire with **Massenet** and also with **Franck**. He was director of the Nancy Conservatoire from 1894 to 1919, and then conductor of the Strasbourg orchestra until 1929. He is best known for his symphonies *La cloche des morts* (1887) and *La chasse du Prince Arthur* (1912), and the opera *Le pays* (1910).

Rore, Cipriano de (1516-1565) Flemish composer, who is best known as a writer of Italian madrigals. A pupil of **Willaert** in Venice, he lived in Italy and held several church and court posts, succeeding Willaert as choir master of St Mark's, Venice (1563). His compositions also include sacred music, such as the *St John Passion* (1557).

Rorem, Ned (1923-) American composer who is best known as a writer of many songs, such as the song cycles *Poems of Love and the Rain* (1963) and *Sun* (1967). He studied under such teachers as **Wagenaar** and **Honegner**, and was particularly influenced by **Poulenc** during his years in Paris (1952-8). He wrote seven operas (including *Miss Julie*, 1965, and *Fables – Five Very Short Operas*, 1970, after La Fontaine), three symphonies and a great deal of choral and chamber music, as well as other frequently performed orchestral pieces such as *Air Music* (1974). He has also written the books *The Paris Diary of Ned Rorem* (1966) and *Critical Affairs, a Composer's Journal*.

Rosbaud, Hans (1895-1862) Austrian conductor and pianist who was a renowned interpreter and champion of 20th-century music, conducting first performances of **Bartók**'s Piano Concerto No.2 and **Schoenberg**'s *Moses und Aron*. He held numerous conducting posts, including those at the Strasbourg Opera (1941-4), the Munich Philharmonic Orchestra (1945-8), and that of chief conductor at the Aix-en-Provence Festival (1947-59). He toured widely as a guest conductor in Europe, South America and Africa.

Roseingrave, Thomas (1688-1766) Irish composer, son of the organist Daniel Roseingrave. He studied in Dublin and later in Italy, where he learnt the harpsichord and became friendly with Domenico **Scarlatti**. In about 1715 he settled in London, composing, editing some of Scarlatti's sonatas – he was largely responsible for the latter's popularity in England – and playing the organ at St George's, Hanover Square. He also taught, and it was his disappointment over a love-affair with a pupil which caused a breakdown in about 1737. He returned to Ireland in 1753, where his only opera, *Phaedra and Hippolitus*, was produced. He wrote a set of cantatas (1735) and several anthems, songs, *Lessons* for harpsichord and various fugues for organ.

Rosen, Charles (1927-) American pianist who studied at the Juilliard School between the ages of seven and 11 and has become a noted performer of the works of Debussy, Beethoven and, in particular, of Bach's Goldberg Variations. He was professor of music at the State University of New York from 1971 and has written two books, *Classical Style* (1971), one of the most important books on this difficult subject, and *Schoenberg* (1975).

Rosenberg, Hilding (1892-1985) Swedish composer, pianist and conductor who is held by many to be a leading figure in 20th-century Swedish music. He spent a number of years writing incidental music for the theatre, the scores of which gave rise to several large-scale works, including the opera *The House with Two Doors* (1969). His other works include the opera *Journey to America* (1932) in which the celebrated *Railway Fugue* is to be found, the ballet *Orpheus in Town* and a tetralogy of stage oratorios after Thomas Mann's *Joseph and His Brethren*. He taught theory and piano in Stockholm (1916-30) and was conductor of the Royal Swedish Opera (1932-4).

Rosenmüller, Johann (1619-1684) German composer who taught in Venice for nearly 20 years. He wrote Masses, other sacred music and suites of instrumental dances. Rosenmüller's music, much respected in Germany, was of particular importance in transmitting the Italian style of composition to the north.

Rosetti, Francesco Antonio (Franz Anton Rösler) (1746-1792) Prolific Bohemian composer who wrote mostly orchestral and chamber music. He held posts as conductor of the orchestra of Prince Öttingen-Wallerstein and later at the court of Ludwigslust. His contemporaries compared him with Mozart and Haydn, although his work is now largely forgotten.

rosin Sticky preparation made of oil of turpentine rubbed onto the hair of the bows of stringed instruments to produce the required friction on the strings. It is also used by ballet-dancers on their shoes to give grip.

Rossellini, Renzo (1908-1982) Italian composer and critic, who composed in the 19th-century Italian tradition and was a noted opponent of innovation. He wrote several film scores for his brother, the director Roberto Rossellini, and others, including *Rome, Open City* (1945). He also composed operas, such as *Uno sguardo dal ponte* (1961) based on Arthur Miller's *A View From the Bridge*, and he was director of Monte Carlo Opera from 1973.

Rosseter, Philip (1568-1623) English lutenist, composer and theatrical manager who was appointed to the court of James I. He was a composer of airs with lute and other accompaniment, published in the *Booke of Ayres* (1601), the first half of which is devoted to works by Thomas **Campion**. He also published *Lessons for Consort* (1609). He was the manager of a company of boy actors called Children of the Revels.

Rossi, Luigi (1598-1653) Italian singer, organist and composer, who was recognized as one of the leading musicians of his time. His fame was largely due to his chamber cantatas, his major achievement. He also played a role in the development of opera, in that his opera *Orpheus* was the first Italian opera to be heard in Paris (1647).

Rossi, Salomone (1570-1630) Italian composer, who was important in the history of music for his pioneering of the trio-sonata and chamber duet. He was a colleague of **Monteverdi** at the court of Mantua, where he spent most of his working life (1587-1628). Among other works he wrote seven books of madrigals and Hebrew psalms.

Rossi-Lemeni, Nicola (1920-) Italian bass singer, of mixed Italian and Russian parentage. He made his début in Venice in *Boris Godunov* (1946) and has since sung regularly at La Scala, Milan, and in New York and London, specializing in Russian and modern opera. Rossi-Lemeni sang in the first performance of **Pizzetti**'s *L'Assassino nella cathedrale* (1958). He has also worked as an operatic stage director.

Rossini, Gioachino (1792-1868) Italian composer, one of the greatest composers of comic opera in the **buffo** style, although he is also important as a composer of **opera seria**. Apprenticed as a child to a blacksmith, he sang in church choirs and learnt to play the horn; by the age of 15 he was playing the harpsichord in theatres. He entered Bologna Academy in 1806. He was first commissioned in 1810 to write the comic opera *La cambiale di matrimonio* for Venice. On the strength of that he was asked to compose *La pietra del paragone* (1812) for La Scala, Milan, and in 1813 he consolidated his reputation with two further operas, *Tancredi*, a serious work, and *L'italiana in Algeri* (The Italian Girl in Algiers), a comedy. He turned out many other works, nearly all comic, during this period, not all of them meeting with success. In 1815 he was appointed music director of the Teatro S. Carlo in Naples, and also of the Teatro del Fondo, also in Naples, by the impresario Barbaia, whose mistress, the singer Isabella Colbran, he married.

He was able to carry on with commissions from other houses, and in 1816 produced two comic masterpieces. *Il barbiere di Siviglia* (The Barber of Seville, based on the first of the trilogy of plays by Beaumarchais) at first had a disastrous reception. It is one of the most popular comic operas written, full of joyous melody, deftly handled ensembles and inspired characterization. *La Cenerentola* (Cinderella) is a delightful, witty version of the fairy-tale. In these works Rossini gave full rein to his penchant for amusing patter-songs and for the crescendo finale – he was even referred to as 'Signor Crescendo'. For the Teatro S. Carlo he composed *Otello* (1816), which represents a real development in his dramatic music. It was followed by *La gazza ladra* (1817), *Mosè in Egitto* (1818), *La donna del lago* (1819) and *Maometto II* (1820); his last opera to be composed in Italy was *Semiramide* (1823). Rossini settled in Paris as director of the Théâtre-Italien, where he wrote further operas: *Il viaggio a Reims* (1825), *Le siège de Corinthe* (1826), *Moïse et Pharaon* (1827), *Le comte Ory* (1828) and, his masterpiece in the serious vein, *Guillaume Tell* (1829), a lengthy work full of grandeur and opulent music, spectacle and dance. Some of these works were adaptations of earlier operas.

Tell marked the end of his career as a writer of opera. For the next 25 years he composed little, suffering from ill-health and battling to obtain his pension from the French authorities. A few attractive short pieces were published as *Soirées musicales* in 1835, but not until he returned to Paris in 1855 did his spirits revive, thanks largely to his second wife, Olympe, and her careful nursing. He settled there and became the centre of artistic and intellectual life until his death; during this period he again began to compose, writing a number of piano works, the *Petite messe solonnelle* (1863) and ensembles which he described as *Péchés de Vieillesse* (Sins of Old Age, 1857-68).

Rostal, Max (1905-) Austrian violinist, teacher and composer, who is a noted exponent of contemporary music and is much sought after as a teacher. Among his teaching posts he has been professor at Berlin State Academy (1927-30), professor at Guildhall School of Music (1944-58) and professor at Cologne State Academy and Berne Conservatoire from 1957. He settled in England in 1934, and was recognized as one of the leading violinists of his day. He was awarded the CBE in 1977.

Rostropovich, Mstislav (1927-) Soviet cellist, who is recognized as one of the greatest of the 20th century, achieving international success, and for whom **Shostakovich**, **Britten** and **Prokofiev** have all written. Rostropovich completed Prokofiev's cello concerto after the composer's death; he also formed a close friendship with Britten and has often played at the Aldeburgh Festival. He has worked as a pianist, accompanying his wife, the soprano Galina **Vishnevskaya**, and also held posts as a conductor, at the Moscow Bolshoi (1968) and the Washington National Symphony Orchestra (1977). He left the Soviet Union in 1974 and was deprived of Soviet citizenship in 1978;

Mstislav Rostropovich

however, in 1990 he was able to return for a concert tour. His compositions include piano concertos and a string quartet.

rota Occasional alternative for **round**.

Rothenberger, Anneliese (1924-) German soprano who studied in Mannheim. After ten years with the Hamburg Opera in 1946-56 she appeared at Glyndebourne in 1959 as Sophie in Strauss's *Der Rosenkavalier*, in Salzburg as Zdenka in *Arabella*, and frequently in Vienna and Munich. She was Sophie in the film of the opera made in 1960, and sang Zdenka for her début at the Metropolitan, New York, also in 1960. She has created several parts, including the title-role of **Sutermeister**'s *Madame Bovary* (1967), and has been successful in the title-role of **Berg**'s *Lulu*. She has also been a delightful Adele in Johann Strauss's *Die Fledermaus*.

Rothwell, Evelyn (1911-) English oboist and teacher, who studied at the Royal College of Music. She has worked with a number of orchestras including the Scottish Orchestra (1937) and the London Symphony Orchestra (1935-9), and has since performed as a soloist and recitalist. She married Sir John **Barbirolli** in 1939. Several works by composers such as **Rubbra** and Arthur **Benjamin** have been dedicated to her, and in 1948 she gave the first performance in modern times of Mozart's Oboe Concerto. She is author of several books, including *Oboe Technique* (1953), and from 1971 has been professor of oboe at the Royal Academy. She was awarded the OBE in 1984.

round Short canon for unaccompanied voices, in which the voices, entering in turn, all sing the same melody at the same **pitch** or an octave apart. *London's Burning*, a popular round dating from the 16th century, is an example.

Rousseau, Jean-Jacques (1712-1778) Swiss philosopher, composer and writer on music, who was important for two of his poetical-musical creations, *Le devin du village* (1752), which anticipated French *opéra-comique*, and *Pygmalion* (1770), which inaugurated the genre of spoken drama with instrumental interjections known as melodrama. He also devised a new system of musical notation, published in *Dissertation sur la musique moderne*, which, however, was not adopted. His extreme hostility to French music was demonstrated in his controversial *Lettre sur la musique française* (1753), taking the Italian side in the *Querelle des Bouffons*. In 1768 he published the *Dictionnaire de musique*.

Roussel, Albert (1869-1937) French composer who started his professional career as a naval officer, but resigned his commission in 1894 to study music with **d'Indy** at the Schola Cantorum in Paris, where he joined the staff in 1902. His compositions were marked with a pungent harmonic idiom and a rigorous intellectual grasp that marked him out from the more impressionist of his contemporaries, and led him to write four fine symphonies, a rare accomplishment for a French composer. His voyages to the East left him with a lifelong interest in Oriental mythology and art, reflected in his opera-ballet *Padmavati* and the choral and orchestral *Evocations*. His orchestral music has a lean, clear sonority emphasized by the motor rhythm that invigorates so much of his work. Of the symphonies, No.3 has a compelling unity of theme, and No.4 a relentless power; there is something of neo-classical clarity about the *Suite in F* and the *Sinfonietta* for strings. There is a piano concerto, some smaller orchestral pieces and several chamber works. He was a fruitful composer for the ballet, though his *Bacchus et Ariane* is now heard usually in the concert-hall. His setting of *Psalm 80*, for which he preferred an English text, is a powerful work, unaccountably neglected in Britain.

Royal Academy of Music College of music founded in London in 1822 by John Fane, Lord Burghersh, later 11th Earl of Westmorland. Its first principal was William **Crotch**. The academy was granted a royal charter in 1830. It provides a wide range of courses for performers, composers, teachers and students and boasts many highly-respected past pupils and teachers.

Royal Albert Hall Concert hall built in London in 1871 on the site of part of the Great Exhibition. It is now used for many types of entertainment, from rock concerts and beauty contests to the BBC Henry Wood Promenade Concerts that continue each night throughout the summer season. The hall is round in shape and has a capacity of 6,500. An acoustical problem of an intrusive echo was finally solved in 1968 with the suspension of saucer-shaped absorbers from the roof (see **acoustics**). Seats and boxes were sold in perpetuity at the time of its construction, and still change hands for considerable sums.

Royal College of Music British school of music established in 1873 as the National Training School of Music and reorganized under its present name in 1883 (the date at which it received its Royal charter). The Royal College's directors have included Grove (1883-4) and **Parry** (1895-1918), and it is renowned for its fine library and collections.

Royal Festival Hall Concert hall built in London in 1951 at the time of the Festival of Britain. Although the interior won praise for its appearance and comfort, the acoustics were initially criticized for being hard and unsympathetic. This was partly as a result of a deliberate plan to even out the reverberation periods of different frequencies, and partly, it is alleged, because the roof was lowered to save money. This fault has been corrected with electronic reverberation provided by a large number of loudspeakers hidden in the walls round the platform. Nearby on the south bank of the Thames are the Queen Elizabeth Hall, used for smaller orchestral

Royal Festival Hall

and choral concerts and recitals, and the smaller Purcell Room, for recitals.

Royal Liverpool Philharmonic Orchestra British symphony orchestra which developed in association with the Liverpool Philharmonic Society, founded in 1840 to promote choral and orchestral concerts. Its first conductor was J.Z. Hermann. Other conductors have included Alfred Mellon, Max **Bruch**, **Charles Hallé**, Henry **Wood**, Thomas **Beecham**, Malcolm **Sargent**, Hugo Rignold, John **Pritchard**, Charles **Groves**, Walter **Weller** and David **Atherton**. The present conductor (since 1987) is Libor Pešek.

Royal Opera House, Covent Garden Britain's premier opera house is the third theatre to be erected on the site in Bow Street, backing on to what was until a few years ago the main fruit and vegetable market for London. The first theatre, used mainly for plays, was erected in what was originally a convent garden in 1732; with Drury Lane Theatre nearby, the area soon became one of the most fashionable parts of town. The first Covent Garden theatre

Royal Opera House

was burnt down in 1808, but quickly replaced by another, which in 1847 was named the Royal Italian Opera. This too was destroyed by fire in 1856, but parts of the edifice were retained for the construction of the present building in 1858. At that time opera-giving was a private enterprise, confined mainly to the few summer months of the London season under such famous impresarios as Frederick Gye and Augustus Harris. Operas were given in Italian regardless of their provenance, and although the leading singers of the day were attracted by the rich fees to be earned in London, the staging was primitive, and orchestral playing and conducting of a modest standard. Towards the end of the century, operas began to be given in the original language, sometimes by visiting companies such as that from Hamburg, conducted by Mahler, and later by the house company. In recognition of this, the theatre was renamed the Royal Opera House in 1892. In the first half of the 20th century, seasons of opera and ballet, notably from Russia, were mounted by private syndicates, often associated with Sir Thomas **Beecham** who was artistic director in the years preceding World War II. During this period the world's greatest singers were heard in a repertory chiefly devoted to a narrow range of Italian and German opera. For the duration of the war the theatre was turned into a dance-hall, but in 1946 reopened for the first time as a publicly subsidized theatre with resident opera and ballet companies, and a policy of encouraging British artists and composers. The first general administrator was Sir David Webster; he was succeeded by Sir John Tooley and the present General Director, Jeremy Isaacs. The music directors have been Karl **Rankl** (1946-51), Raphael **Kubelik** (1955-8), Sir Georg **Solti** (1961-71), Sir Colin **Davis** (1971-86) and Bernard **Haitink** (from 1987). The ballet (Royal Ballet, 1956) has been under the artistic direction of Dame Ninette de Valois, Sir Frederick Ashton (1963-70), Sir Kenneth MacMillan (1970-7), Norman Morrice (1977-86), and Anthony Dowell (from 1986). Covent Garden seats just under 2,000, and is one of the most beautiful opera houses in the world, with excellent acoustics.

Royal Philharmonic Orchestra Founded in 1946 by Sir Thomas **Beecham** to perform at the Royal Philharmonic Society's annual subscription concerts. Financial support came from a holding company set up by Beecham and from lucrative recording contracts. After Beecham's death in 1961 the orchestra became independent (1963), its 'royal' status confirmed by statute in 1966. It was the resident orchestra for Glyndebourne (1943-63) and at the Edinburgh Festival. In 1950 it became the first British orchestra to tour the United States since 1912, giving over 50 performances in a nine-week schedule. On Beecham's death Rudolf **Kempe** became principal conductor (1961-75); Sir Charles **Groves** was associate conductor from 1968, Walter **Weller** principal conductor from 1979. The orchestra has toured widely, and has made many recordings, some with pop musicians.

Royal Philharmonic Society Association formed in London in 1813 by J.B. Cramer, P.A. Corri and W. Dance, as the Philharmonic Society, for the cultivation of good orchestral music. The inaugural concert was given at the Argyll Rooms, conducted by Muzio **Clementi**. A royal charter was granted in 1912. Throughout its history the RPS has continued to promote concerts, engaging a variety of orchestras and conductors, and presenting new works to London audiences. The society has always been proud of its connection with Beethoven (on his deathbed the RPS sent him a cheque for £100). To commemorate his centenary they performed all his symphonies and had a special Gold Medal made. Among some of the recipients of the medal were **Brahms**, **Sibelius**, **Rachmaninov**, **Stravinsky** and **Shostakovich**.

Rozhdestvensky, Gennadi (1931-) Soviet conductor, son of the conductor Nicolai Anosov; he took his mother's maiden name to avoid confusion. He studied at the Moscow Conservatoire, and started his career at the Bolshoi Theatre in 1951. Other appointments include chief conductor of the USSR Radio Symphony Orchestra, 1960-5, and principal conductor of the Bolshoi Theatre, 1965-70. He toured the United States as conductor of the Leningrad Philharmonic in 1973. He became music director of the Stockholm Philharmonic, 1975; chief conductor of the BBC Symphony Orchestra, 1978-81; and chief conductor of the Vienna Symphony Orchestra in 1981. An exciting and colourful performer, he is reputed to be less interested in rehearsal, and therefore has tended to be more successful as a guest than as a permanent conductor.

Rózsa, Miklós (1907-) Hungarian-born American composer, best known for his scores for films such as *The Thief of Baghdad* (1940), *The Jungle Book* (1942), *Spellbound* (1945), *Double Indemnity* (1944) and *Ben Hur* (1959). He studied at Leipzig Conservatoire (1925-9) and Trinity College, London (1930-4), emigrating to the United States, 1940, where he was composer for MGM (1948-62). His other works include a violin concerto, a piano sonata and a concerto for strings, all revealing the influence of Hungarian folk-music.

rubato (It.) Robbed. Indication that the tempo of the music may be 'robbed' in order to add expression to a bar, or more likely, a phrase. There are two manners of applying *rubato*: according to Mozart and Chopin, the left hand keeps a regular tempo while the right plays the melodies somewhat freely; the modern approach tends to have both hands moving together in free treatment of rhythm. A subtle *rubato* is the secret of expressive performance, and characteristic of all great artists; it has been neglected in modern times in the search for an 'objective' reading of the notes, often against the original expectations of the composer.

Rubbra, Edmund (1901-1986) English composer and pianist who studied with **Holst**, **Vaughan Williams** and Morris, among others, and became a leading English exponent of the symphony, writing 11 in all. He worked as a teacher and music critic and wrote music for a travelling theatre company before recognition came with the performance of his first symphony (1937). Two more symphonies followed (1937, 1939), establishing him firmly in the front rank of English composers. During World War II he formed a piano trio. He was lecturer in music at Oxford University (1947-68) and professor of composition at the Guildhall School of Music from 1961. His prolific output as a composer reflects some influence from **Ireland**, **Bax** and **Holst**; he was also interested in the **polyphonic** music of the Renaissance. The Symphony No.5 has an almost 'chamber' feel to it, while the next three are fuller in scoring, warm and lyrical in tone. No.9, *Sinfonia Sacra*, is a choral work, and is a fine example of Rubbra's preoccupation with vocal forces and church music. There are other orchestral pieces – overtures, concertos for viola, piano, and violin; several Masses; sacred pieces such as *Song of the Soul* (1953) and *Veni Creator Spiritus* (1966); four string quartets and much other chamber music; and songs, including the cycle of Chinese poems *The Jade Mountain* (1962).

Rubinstein, Anton (1829-1894) Russian pianist and composer, who was one of the greatest pianists of the 19th century. He was also a prolific composer whose works are now largely forgotten, but who is remembered for the *Melody in F* for piano and the opera *The Demon* (1871). He studied under **Liszt** among others and toured as a soloist throughout Europe and the United States. He held the position of court pianist at St Petersburg and conductor of the Vienna Philharmonic

Orchestra (1871-2). He was founder of the St Petersburg Conservatoire (1862).

Rubinstein, Artur (1887-1982) Polish pianist, who made his first appearance in Łódź at the age of seven, and is now recognized as one of the great players of the century. He studied in Berlin, making his début in 1897. His international career was well established by the outbreak of World War I, during which he remained in London (he had made his début there in 1912), and with his gift for languages acted as an interpreter. During the 1920s he neglected his playing somewhat while enjoying great success socially, but by 1937 he applied himself again to serious study, undertook an American tour and regained his international reputation.

He settled in Hollywood in 1939 and became an American citizen in 1946. He continued to play, seemingly with undiminished power, until his 90th birthday, also making many outstanding recordings of a wide repertory (his Chopin being particularly admired). The numerous honours bestowed on him include the KBE (1977) and the United States Medal of Freedom. He also wrote two volumes of highly entertaining memoirs.

Ruckers Family Flemish family of harpsichord- and virginal-makers, whose instruments influenced the manufacture of stringed keyboard instruments throughout Western Europe. Over 100 Ruckers instruments still exist, their sound being much emulated by 20th-century harpsichord-makers. The firm was founded in 1579 by Hans Ruckers (1550-98), who was succeeded by his sons, Joannes (1578-1642) and Andries (1579-1645), production continuing until 1667.

Ruggles, Carl (1867-1971) American composer and painter who as a youth earned his living playing in Boston theatre orchestras, going on to study at Harvard University with J.K. Paine among others (1903-7). He wrote few works, which he constantly revised, including *Angels* for six trumpets (1938); *Men and Mountains*; *Sun-Treader* (1931); *Evocations* for piano; and an *Organum* for orchestra. In the last years of his life he devoted his creative energies to painting. He was an important but neglected composer of great originality.

Ruhrtrommel (Ger.) German equivalent of **tenor drum**.

rumba Cuban dance of African origin in quick 2/4 time. It became popular in European and American ballrooms in the 1930s.

Russolo, Luigi (1885-1947) Italian composer who used a variety of sounds and materials in his compositions, and who in his Futurist manifesto (1913) *L'arte dei rumori* included in the orchestra explosions, shrieks, screams and groans. He developed a number of instruments, including the Russolophone, for which he also invented **graphic notation**. His compositions include *Meeting of the Automobiles and Aeroplanes* and *Awakening of a City*.

RV Abbreviation for *Ryom Verzeichnis*, used as a prefix by Peter Ryom when compiling a catalogue (1974) of **Vivaldi's** works.

ryo (Japan) One of the two basic **pentatonic** scales in Buddhist musical theory and **gagaku** court music. See **Japanese scales**

Rysanek, Leonie (1926-) Austrian soprano, who is noted as a singer of Richard Strauss roles. She made her début in Innsbruck (1949) and has since sung at Covent Garden (1953) and at the New York Metropolitan (1959). She has appeared regularly at the Bayreuth Festival since her début there as Sieglinde in *Die Walküre* in 1951.

Rzewski, Frederik (1938-) American composer and pianist who studied at Harvard University, working as a professional pianist from 1960. He has taught courses in new music at Cologne and is co-founder of the music studio Musica Elettronica Viva in Rome. Influenced by **Cage** and **Stockhausen**, with whom he has worked, he has written compositions involving dancers, film and tape and has also explored collective improvisation.

S

Sabata, Victor de (1892-1967) Italian conductor and composer who studied in Milan with Saladino and Orefice. Between 1929 and 1953 he was at La Scala, first as conductor and then as musical and artistic director. He made appearances in the United States (1938), Bayreuth (1939) and London (1946). Sabata is especially associated with the operas of Verdi and Wagner, his interpretations of which have been compared to **Toscanini**'s. His own compositions include operas, symphonic poems and incidental music.

sacbut Alternative spelling of **sackbut**.

Sacchini, Antonio (1730-1786) Italian composer who, after early successes in Italy, went to London (1773-82), where he produced 17 operas. In 1782 he settled in Paris, where his work was influenced by **Gluck**, and he became a rival to **Piccinni** with his comic and serious operas. His most notable success was the opera *Oedipe à Colonne* (1785). Altogether he wrote about 60 operas. His other works included church music, symphonic poems, violin sonatas and songs, as well as string quartet pieces.

Sacher, Paul (1906-) Swiss conductor who founded the Basle Chamber Orchestra in 1926, for which he commissioned works from many composers such as **Bartók**, Richard **Strauss, Hindemith, Stravinsky**, **Martinů**, **Honegger** and **Tippett**. Sacher also founded the distinguished chamber ensemble Schola Cantorum Basiliensis (1933).

sackbut Forerunner of the **trombone**. The sackbut differed from the modern trombone mainly in the fact that the bell of the latter has a slightly wider flare. The instrument was often associated with the **cornett**, being used in ceremonies such as those at St Mark's, Venice, and on royal occasions in England. Alternative spellings are sacbut, sagbut and sacquebot.

Sadie, Stanley (1930-) British musicologist, editor and critic who, after teaching at Trinity College of Music, London (1957-65), became music critic to *The Times* (1964) and editor of *The Musical Times* (1967-87). Later he became editor of *The New Grove Dictionary of Music and Musicians* (published in 1980). Among his books are studies of Mozart and Handel. He was appointed CBE in 1982.

Sadler's Wells English theatre and opera house, situated in north London. The present theatre was opened in 1931, and was built by Lilian Baylis to present opera, ballet and drama in conjunction with the Old Vic. It stands on the site of the theatre built in 1765 to replace gardens and a building (called the 'musicke house') erected in the 17th century by a Mr Sadler. The opera and ballet companies became Sadler's Wells Opera (renamed **English National Opera** in 1974) and Sadler's Wells Ballet (renamed the Royal Ballet in 1956), but they are no longer resident in the theatre.

Saeverud, Harald (1897-) Norwegian conductor and composer who studied at

Bergen and Berlin. He wrote nine symphonies, including the *Minnesota Symphony*, concertos for piano, violin, oboe and cello, variations for chamber orchestra, and incidental music for Shakespeare's *Rape of Lucrece* and Ibsen's *Peer Gynt.*

sagbut Alternative spelling of **sackbut**.

saibara (Japan) Folk-song form adapted for use as court music and accompanied by the **gagaku** ensemble.

Saint-Saëns, Camille (1835-1921) French composer, conductor, organist and pianist. At the age of ten he made his début as a pianist; in 1848 he went to the Paris Conservatoire and entered **Halévy**'s composition class in 1851. He was also a pupil of **Gounod**. In 1855 Saint-Saëns's first symphony was performed, and from 1857 until 1877 he was organist at the Madeleine, Paris. Between 1861 and 1865 he taught at the Ecole Niedermeyer, where his pupils included **Fauré** and **Messager**. Together with Romain Bussine he founded the Société Nationale de Musique in 1871. Saint-Saëns often performed in England, and in 1892 he received an honorary doctorate at Cambridge.

He was a prolific composer, and among his works were 12 operas, including the biblical opera *Samson and Delilah* (which was prohibited on the French stage on account of its subject, but was produced at Weimar in 1877 and has remained in the repertory) and *Henry the Eighth* (1883). He was the first French composer to make use of the form of the tone poem, following his friendship with **Liszt**. Works in this form include *Le rouet d'Omphale* (1871), *Phaëton* (1873), *Danse macabre* (1874) and *La jeunesse d'Hercule* (1877). His other compositions include five symphonies (No.3 is with organ and two pianos and was dedicated to Liszt), five piano concertos, three violin concertos, two cello concertos, chamber, church and choral music. Although it was not performed during his lifetime, *Le Carnaval des animaux* (1886) has become very popular.

Salieri, Antonio (1750-1825) Italian composer, conductor and teacher who lived mainly in Vienna. There he was a pupil of **Gassmann** (1766), and later became court composer and conductor of the Italian opera (1774) and court *Kapellmeister* (1788). It was said that he intrigued against **Mozart,** but the suggestion that he poisoned him is almost certainly false.

Salieri was conductor of the Tonkünstler Society until 1818, and played the continuo in the first performance of Haydn's *Creation* in 1798. Among his pupils were Beethoven, **Hummel**, Liszt and Schubert. He composed about 40 operas, including *Armida, Tarare, Falstaff* (after Shakespeare) and *Angiolina.* His other works include three symphonies, concertos, chamber music, sinfonias, Masses, a Requiem, litanies and other church music.

Sallinen, Aulis (1935-) Finnish composer who studied at the Sibelius Academy, Helsinki (1955), and later (1965) became a member of the staff, when he divided his time between teaching and composing. At one stage he was also manager of the Finnish Radio Symphony Orchestra. His works include four symphonies, two operas (*The Red Line*, 1978, and *The King Goes Forth to France*, 1984), four string quartets, a violin concerto (1968), a cello concerto (1976) and four choral pieces.

Salomon, Johann Peter (1745-1815) German composer, violinist, conductor and impresario. After studying at Bonn he joined the Electoral orchestra (1758), and in 1765 he became court musician at Rheinsberg to Prince Henry of Prussia. Having settled in London (1781), where he became a concert violinist and conductor, he organized concerts at the Hanover Square Rooms during the two visits made by **Haydn** (1791-2 and 1794-5). As a result of these visits, Haydn dedicated the 12 London symphonies (Nos.93-104) to him. He also wrote four French operas and an English one (*Windsor Castle*, for the marriage of the Prince of Wales, 1795), symphonies, canzonets and chamber music.

In 1813 he became a founder member and leader of the Philharmonic Society.

saltando (It.) Bowing technique whereby the bow rebounds on and off the string.

saltarello (It.) Italian dance of the 16th century that involves a series of jumps. It is similar to the Neapolitan tarantella, and is usually in compound duple time. Mendelssohn used the form for the last movement of his *Italian Symphony*.

Salzburg Festival Annual summer festival of music and drama founded in 1920 in Salzburg, Austria, the birthplace of **Mozart**. The Festival presents operas, concerts and recitals, with the works of Mozart and Richard Strauss filling most of the repertory. In 1949 the old riding school (*Felsenreitschule*) was used for opera for the first time, and in 1960 the new *Festspielhaus*, adjoining the old one, was opened with a performance of *Der Rosenkavalier*. Among the many famous conductors who have appeared at the summer Festival are **Bohm**, **Furtwängler**, **Krauss**, Strauss and **Toscanini**.
An Easter Festival, under the direction of Herbert von **Karajan**, was inaugurated in 1967.

Salzedo, Carlos (1885-1961) French-born American composer and harpist who studied at the Paris Conservatoire. He moved to the United States in 1909 at the invitation of **Toscanini** to become first harp at the Metropolitan Opera, New York. His interest in modern music is reflected in his compositions for the harp, which emphasize the instrument's potential in contemporary music. In collaboration with Edgard **Varèse**, he founded the International Composers' Guild in 1921. Salzedo's works include concertos, solos, duets, chamber music, sonatas, and songs with harp accompaniment.

Salzedo, Leonard (1921-) English composer and former pupil of Herbert **Howells**. He is best known for his ballet music, such as *The Fugitive* (1944) and *Witch Boy* (1956), although his other works include seven string quartets, two symphonies, a concerto for percussion (four players without orchestra) and film music.

Salzman, Eric (1933-) American writer and composer who was a pupil of **Sessions** and **Stockhausen**, among others. He is particularly known for the use of electronic music and his interest in multimedia theatrical works and environmental music. His works include *Verses and Cantos* (1967), *The Nude Paper Sermon* (1968-9), *The Conjuror* (1975), *Noah* (1978) and *Toward a New American Opera* (1985).

sam (India) Principal beat (**mātrā**) of the rhythmic cycle (**tāla**); the point in time at which the rhythmic and melodic phrases coincide, indicated by a hand-clap on count one when beating time.

Saminsky, Lazare (1882-1959) Russian-born American composer and conductor. He was a pupil of **Lyadov** and **Rimsky-Korsakov** at St Petersburg Conservatoire, and later became a director of the People's Conservatoire at Tiflis. Following a period in London, he went to the United States and later became naturalized. In 1924 he was one of the founder-members of the League of Composers, and was also appointed director of the Jewish Temple of Emanu-El. Saminsky's works include the opera-ballets *The Vision of Ariel*, *Lament of Rachel* and *The Daughter of Jephtha*, the chamber opera *Gagliarda of the Merry Plague*, five symphonies, symphonic poems, and music for Jewish worship.

samisen See **shamisen**

Sammartini, Giovanni Battista (*c.*1700-1775) Italian composer who spent his whole life in Milan as a church musician where, from 1730, he became *maestro di cappella* at Milan Cathedral and one of the founders of the Philharmonic Society (1728). Gluck was one of his pupils (1737-

41). During his musical career, he was Italy's most important symphonist and made a major contribution towards the founding of a modern style of instrumental music. He was much admired by Mozart, J.C. **Bach**, **Boccherini** and **Haydn**, who later took up the style created by Sammartini. He was a prolific composer whose output consisted of 77 symphonies (the earliest are similar in form to trio sonatas, with only three parts written out); two operas; two oratorios; three Masses and other church music; six string quintets; 20 string quartets and almost 200 trios.

Sammartini, Giuseppe (1695-1750) Italian oboist and composer, brother of Giovanni. Before leaving Italy in 1728 for London, where he spent the rest of his life, he was an oboist of the Teatro Regio Ducale, Milan. He played in London with **Handel** and **Bononcini** from 1728, and between 1732 and 1744 was director of the Hickford's Room concerts with Arrigoni. He was also appointed director of chamber music to the Prince of Wales (1736).

Among his works were a setting of Congreve's masque *The Judgement of Paris*, 112 *concerti grossi* (1728-47), the four *Giuseppe St Martinis Concertos* (1754), concertos for harpsichord and for violin, many sonatas for various instruments, and nine cantatas and other vocal pieces.

samvādī (India) Consonant tone of a **rāga** which acts as the complement of the sonant (**vādi**) and usually lies at an interval of a fourth or fifth above it.

Sándor, György (1912-) Hungarian-born pianist who settled in the USA in 1939. He studied at the Budapest Conservatoire with Bartók and **Kodály**, and he is particularly noted for his performances and recordings of the works of both of these composers. In 1945 Sandor gave the first performance of Bartók's Piano Concerto No.3. He has recorded the complete solo piano compositions of Prokofiev.

san-hsien (China) Plucked stringed instrument with a hollow cylindrical body, both sides of which are covered with snakeskin. It has a long flat neck, no frets and three strings. It is played either with the fingernails or with a plectrum. The *san-hsien*'s Japanese relative is the **shamisen**.

sanjo (Korea) Solo instrumental genre of 19th-century origin, consisting of 3–6 movements based on folk-tunes, which the soloist (usually a **kayagŭm** player) uses as a basis for improvisation. The accompanying **changgo** drum provides the rhythmic patterns which change between movements, becoming gradually faster and more complex. Various instrumental *sanjo* styles are maintained in traditional schools of playing.

sankyoku (Japan) Chamber music ensemble, literally 'music for three'. It consists of **koto**, **shamisen** and **shakuhachi**, the last having replaced a bowed lute.

santoor (India) See **santur**

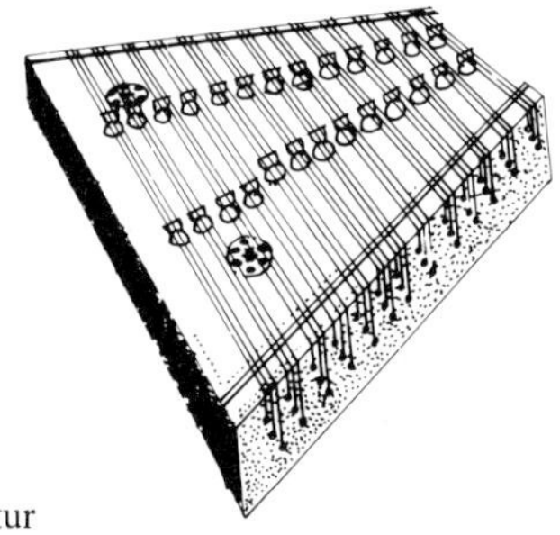

Santur

santur/santoor (India) Trapezoid board zither from Kashmir which has 25 quadruple courses of strings, played with two light wooden hammers. Used throughout northern India.

sarabande 16th-century Spanish dance in a slow 3/2 time which became popular throughout Europe in the 17th and 18th centuries. There is a characteristic stop of rhythmic flow on the second beat of alternate bars.

sārangī (India) Bowed, fretless lute with a parchment belly and sympathetic strings, probably of central Asian origin. Its distinct vocal quality makes it ideal as an accompaniment to the voice in the classical genres of northern Indian music.

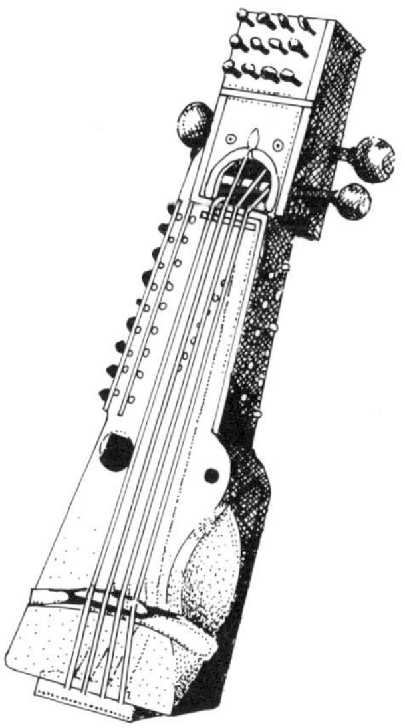

Sārangī

Sarasate, Pablo (1844-1908) Spanish violinist and composer who was among the most famous virtuosi of his time. He gave his first public concert when he was eight years old, and in 1856 went to Paris to study at the Conservatoire as a pupil of Alard. For the rest of his life he gave concert tours throughout Europe and the United States. He first appeared in London in 1861. Sarasate's compositions included *Zigeunerweisen*, an orchestral fantasy, four books of Spanish dances and many other pieces for violin.

sargam (India) System of **solfège** used to memorize or notate melodies. The name is taken from the first four mnemonics of the native scale, represented by the syllables Sa Re Ga Ma Pa Dha Ni. *Sargams* are also set compositions sung to these syllables, either as independent exercises or as passages in vocal improvisations. See also **khyāl**.

Sir Malcolm Sargent

Sargent, Sir Malcolm (1895-1967) British conductor and organist. Following his studies at the Royal College of Organists, where he was awarded the Sawyer Prize (1910), he became assistant organist at Peterborough Cathedral. He made his début at a Promenade Concert in 1921, where he conducted his own work *Impressions of a Windy Day*; this attracted the attention of Sir Henry **Wood**, who advised him to take up conducting as a career. He subsequently conducted the Royal Choral Society (from 1928), the Hallé Orchestra (1939-42), the Liverpool Philharmonic Orchestra (1942-7) and the BBC Symphony Orchestra (1950-7). Sargent's impeccable appearance and his extraordinarily effective control of an orchestra attracted a wide and enthusiastic following, especially at children's concerts and at the Henry Wood Promenade Concerts, at which he was chief conductor from 1948 until shortly before his death.

sarod (India) Plucked, fretless lute with a parchment belly and sympathetic strings, used throughout northern India, but probably of central Asian origin.

saron (Java) One-octave, bronze metallophone of the **gamelan** ensemble, with keys resting over a sound box. It is struck with a wooden or bone mallet and is found in three sizes, *panerus*, *barung* and *demung*. Together they play versions of the basic melody line.

sarrusophone Brass wind instrument with a double reed mouthpiece (a member of the **oboe** family), invented in 1856 by the Frenchman Sarrus. Various sizes have been used by some continental military bands, but the double-bass sarrusophone was the only instrument of this type that had any success. Compositions that demand the use of the sarrusophone include **Delius**'s *Dance Rhapsody No.1* (1908) and **Saint-Saëns**'s *Requiem* (1878).

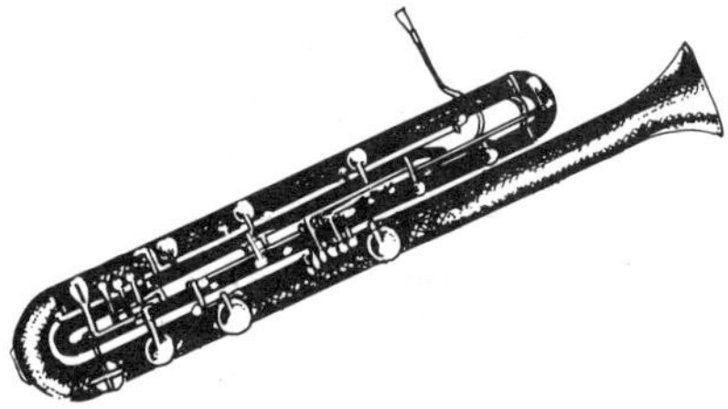

Sarrusophone

Sarti, Giuseppe (1729-1802) Italian conductor and composer who studied at Padua and Bologna. He became organist at Faenza Cathedral, Bologna (1748-52). In 1753 he went to Copenhagen as director of the Mingotti opera company, and in 1755 was appointed court *Kapellmeister*, a position he held (apart from three years in Italy) until 1775. He acted as *maestro di cappella* at Milan Cathedral (1779), and in 1784 was made musical director to the Russian court in St Petersburg. While in Russia he collaborated with Empress Catherine II in one of the country's earliest operas, *The First Government of Oleg* (1790). Although Sarti wrote more than 70 operas, most of them are now forgotten, apart from a single air (*Fra due litiganti*) which Mozart used as part of the hero's supper-music in *Don Giovanni*. He also wrote church music and harpsichord sonatas.

Satie, Erik (1866-1925) French composer whose parents were both musicians, although his rebellious approach to his musical education meant that he spent only a year at the Paris Conservatoire (to the surprise of his contemporaries). At the age of 40 he returned to study at the Schola Cantorum under **d'Indy** and **Roussel** (1905-8). In the 1890s he made a precarious living playing at cafés and composing music for the Rosicrucian Society.

Satie had considerable influence upon Les **Six**, a group of French composers who were endeavouring to avoid elements of **Romanticism** and **Impressionism** in French music. Jean Cocteau was also associated with the same group, and it was through him that Satie's works were performed more widely. This association also led to his collaboration with **Diaghilev** and Picasso in the ballet *Parade* (1917).

He was an eccentric composer who often dispensed with bar lines altogether, adopted a mocking satirical air and gave his compositions strange titles such as *Deux pièces froides* (1897), *Trois morceaux en forme de poire* (1903) and *Choses vues à droite et à gauche (sans lunette)* (1912). Some of Satie's other works include a symphonic drama, *Socrate* (1918), for four sopranos and

Erik Satie

orchestra, many piano pieces and two further ballets, *Mercure* and *Relâche* (1924). Possibly his most famous work is the collection of *Trois Gymnopédies* (1888) for piano.

sato-kagura (Japan) Shinto folk and festival music. *Kagura*, literally 'good music', is the generic term for all Shinto music. The repertory embraces both song and dance music and it is played by the folk **hayashi** ensemble, comprising three drums and flute. See also **mi-kagura**.

Satsuma-biwa (Japan) Type of **biwa** or lute.

Satz (Ger.) Movement. *Tonsatz* is a musical setting or composition; *Hauptsatz* is a main theme; *Nebensatz* is a secondary theme.

Sauguet, Henri (1901-) French composer and critic who studied the piano and organ at Bordeaux and was a pupil of **Canteloube** and **Koechlin**. His introduction by **Milhaud** to **Satie** led to the formation of the school at Arcueil in 1923. In 1936 he succeeded Milhaud as music critic to *Le Jour-Echo de Paris*. His works were mainly in a lighter vein and included the opera *Les caprices de Marianne* (1954), the ballets *Les forains* and *La chatte* (1927), the song-cycle *La voyante*, three symphonies and two string quartets.

saùng-gauk (Burma) Arched harp with 13, 14 or 16 strings stretched between a curved acacia root and a decorated bowl resonator. Of ancient origin, it may have been brought from Buddhist India by the Mon hill-tribe, who still play a five- to seven-stringed harp. This royal harp formed the basis of Burmese music theory, and is associated with an extensive repertory of court songs. It is held in the player's lap, the right hand plucking the strings from the outside, leaving the left hand to add any embellishments by pulling on the strings at the arch. It is usually accompanied by hand cymbals and clappers.

Sauret, Emile (1852-1920) French violinist and composer who was a pupil of **Bériot**. His career began at the age of ten, when he visited London. He played in the United States from 1872 as well as in Scandinavian and other European capitals. Sauret taught at the Royal Academy of Music in London (1891), when he succeeded Sainton as violin professor, and in 1903 he took up a similar post at Chicago. His works include two concertos, *Ballade* and *Légende*, and many pieces for the violin.

sausage bassoon Alternative term for **racket**.

sautillé (Fr.) Alternative term for **saltando**.

Savoy Operas Name for the operettas composed by **Sullivan** with librettos by W.S. Gilbert, and produced by Richard D'Oyly Carte at the Savoy Theatre, London, from 1881. These operettas included *Iolanthe* (1882), *Princess Ida* (1884), *The Mikado* (1885), *Ruddigore* (1887), *The Yeomen of the Guard* (1888) and *The Gondoliers* (1889).

Sawallisch, Wolfgang (1923-) German conductor who studied at the Munich Hochschule für Musik with Joseph Haas. He made his début in Augsburg (1947), where he remained until 1953, when he became musical director at the opera in Aachen. From 1957 to 1959 he conducted at the Wiesbaden opera; from 1959 to 1963 in Cologne, and between 1957 and 1962 at the **Bayreuth** Festival. Since 1971 he has been music director of the Bavarian State Opera, Munich.

Sax, Adolphe (1814-1894) Belgian instrument-maker who continued the business started by his father. He studied the flute and the clarinet at the Brussels Conservatoire before establishing himself in Paris (1842), where he made several improvements to wind instruments. His chief inventions were the **saxhorn** and the **saxophone**.

saxhorn Group of instruments of the brass family, invented by Adolphe **Sax** who patented them in 1845. They are made in seven different pitches, covering between them a range of some five octaves. They are: the soprano in E♭, alto in B♭ (both also called **flugelhorns**), tenor in E♭, baritone in B♭ (both also called althorns), bass in B♭, bass **tuba** in E♭ (bombardon) and contrabass in B♭.

saxophone Brass wind instrument with woodwind characteristics, invented by Adolphe **Sax** in the 1840s. It is a cross between the **clarinet** and the **oboe**, having a single reed clarinet-type mouthpiece and a conical bore like the oboe.

There were originally 14 instruments in the family, but today they are limited to the following: soprano in E♭ (occasionally used in military bands); soprano in B♭ (sometimes used in jazz bands); alto in E♭; tenor in B♭; baritone in E♭ and contrabass in B♭, which is rarely used.

Saxton, Robert (1953-) English composer who studied with Elisabeth **Lutyens** and at Cambridge under **Holloway**. His work reflects something of the **serial** tendencies of **Berio**, as well as being in some cases richly romantic. His orchestral works include *Ring of Eternity* (1983) and *Circles of Light* (1985). He has also composed a Viola Concerto (1986) and a Violin Concerto, which was commissioned by Michael Vyner for the 1990 Leeds Festival and which explores new ways of interacting between violin and orchestra.

saz (Persia) General term for a stringed instrument, covering various types of plucked lute in Iran, Turkey, Armenia, Azerbaijan, Albania, Greece and Yugoslavia. The *saz* appears in different sizes and tuning, but all have a pear-shaped, wooden resonator and usually

Saxophone

eight to ten strings (including drones) in two or three courses.

scale In Western music, the division of the octave into a series of steps: in the chromatic scale into 12 semitones. Diatonic scales are major or minor – in the major scale the combination of tones and semitones as shown in the key of C major is essentially defined by the third note being a whole tone above the second:

The minor scale is defined by the third note being a semitone above the second; the rest of the minor scale varies according to the context. The theoretical forms of C minor are as follows.

Natural minor:

The melodic minor varies in ascending and descending:

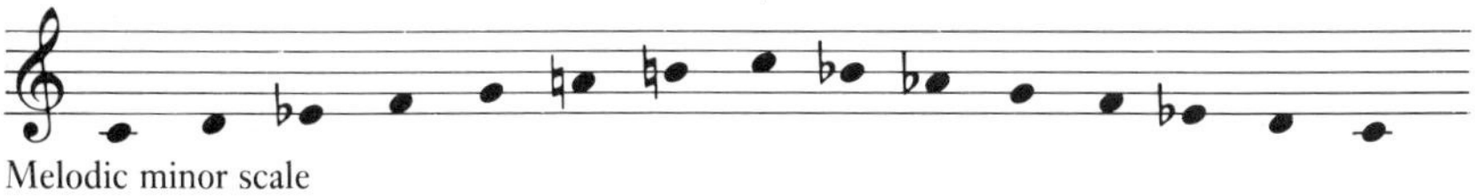

Melodic minor scale

Harmonic minor:

The intervals so shown apply to all other keys.

In the whole-tone scale, the octave is divided into seven equal tones:

Composers have sometimes invented an arbitrary scale for expressive effect – Verdi, for example, used what he called *scala enigmatica* for his *Ave Maria* for unaccompanied women's voices.

Scarlatti, Alessandro (1660-1725) Italian composer who, upon the success of his first opera, *Gli equivoci ne sembiante* (1679), was appointed *maestro di cappella* to Queen Christina of Sweden in Rome. He moved to Naples as conductor of the San Bartolomeo opera (1683-4), and *maestro di cappella* to the court (1684), where he remained for nearly 20 years, although in 1702 he went to Florence with his son Domenico to enjoy the patronage of the Medicis. For two years he was *maestro di cappella* at S. Maria Maggiore, Rome, before finally returning to his old position in Naples in 1709.

Alessandro Scarlatti is considered to be one of the founders of the Neapolitan school of opera, and formulated some of its notable characteristics, such as the **da capo** aria which was to dominate opera for two centuries. Probably his greatest work was the opera *Mitridate Eupatore* (1707). Altogether Scarlatti wrote over 40 operas, about 600 chamber cantatas for solo voice and continuo, ten Masses and 35 oratorios.

Scarlatti, Domenico (1685-1757) Italian composer, harpsichordist and organist. After studying with his father Alessandro, he was appointed organist and composer to the court in Naples (1701) where he composed his first two operas, *Ottavia ristituita al trono* and *Giustina* (1703). He travelled widely, visiting Florence, Venice (1708) and Rome, where it is said that he engaged with Handel in a contest in harpsichord and organ playing. While in Rome (1709-14) he became *maestro di cappella* to the exiled Queen of Poland, and of the Cappella Giulia (1714-19). In about 1720 he became *maestro* to the royal court in Lisbon, where he taught Princess Maria Barbara; when she married into the Spanish royal family in 1729 he followed her, and spent his remaining years in Madrid in her service, composing many of his sonatas for her.

Domenico Scarlatti was the greatest Italian composer for harpsichord of his age. He wrote more than 550 sonatas, mostly in one movement in binary form, of which the first pieces to be published were in the *Essercizi per gravicembalo* (1738). They have been catalogued by Ralph **Kirkpatrick** (with Kk numbers). Scarlatti's other works include 12 operas, cantatas and church music, including a *Stabat Mater*. His sonatas were important influences on **sonata form** and considerably expanded the virtuosity of the keyboard instrument, using cross-handed techniques and **acciaccatura**.

scat singing Vocal style adopted by jazz singers in which syllabic sounds are used instead of words.

scena Extract from an opera used in a concert performance during the 18th century. In the 19th century it developed into a concert work for solo voices on a large scale, usually a **recitative** followed by **arias** with orchestral accompaniment.

Schaeffer, Pierre (1910-) French composer and writer who trained as a radio technician, and in 1948 became associated with Pierre **Henry**. Together they pioneered the concept of *musique concrète*, in which 'natural' or non-musical sounds were incorporated. Their first major work in this medium was *Symphonie pour un homme seul* (1950), and in 1951 they founded the *Groupe de Musique Concrète* studio. The experimental opera *Orphée* was produced by Schaeffer in 1953.

Schafer, R. Murray (1933-) Canadian composer who was a pupil of **Weinzweig**, Guemerov and **Fricker**, and resident composer at the Simon Fraser University, Vancouver. He is an active promoter of modern music, and his interest in mixed media and ecology led him to initiate the World Soundscape Project to fight noise pollution. Among his works are *Loving/Toi* (1965), *Requiem for a Party Girl* (1972), *East* (1973), *North/White* (1973), *Waves* (1976), and *Apocalypsis* (1976, for 500 performers).

Scheidemann, Heinrich (*c.*1595-1663) German composer, organist and teacher who was a pupil of his father and later of **Sweelinck**. He succeeded his father as organist at St Catherine's Church, Hamburg, in 1625, and was there until his death from the plague when he was succeeded by **Reincken**, one of his pupils. Scheidemann, the leading composer of the north German school of organists, produced many fine works, especially his chorale arrangements, and he also contributed to Part V of Rist's hymn-book *Neue himmlische Lieder* (1651). Some of his other works are Magnificat settings, chorale fantasias and the Toccata in G.

Scheidt, Samuel (1587-1654) German organist and composer who studied with **Sweelinck** in Amsterdam. In 1609 he became court organist at Halle to the Margrave of Brandenburg, and *Kapellmeister* in 1619, a position he lost in 1625 as a result of the progress of the Thirty Years' War, but which he was able to resume in 1638. Scheidt was a prolific composer whose works included madrigals, motets and organ music. His most notable work was the collection *Tabulatura Nova* (1624).

Schein, Johann Hermann (1586-1630) German composer who became a choirboy in the court chapel at Dresden (1599), and later studied at Leipzig University (1607). In 1615 he was appointed *Kapellmeister* at the court of Weimar and in 1616 became cantor at St Thomas's School, Leipzig, where he remained until his death.

He composed mainly vocal music such as *Fontana d'Israel* (1623), which contains biblical words set for four or five voices and instruments, *Cantional* (1627), an important collection of Lutheran hymns with a figured bass part, instrumental dances and wedding and funeral cantatas.

Schenker, Heinrich (1868-1935) Austrian musical theorist and writer who studied with Bruckner at the Vienna Conservatoire. His books, such as *Neue musikalische Theorien und Phantasien*, *Das Meisterwerk in der Musik* and *Der freie Satz*, have had an important influence on the development of analytical theory. His intention was primarily to improve the understanding and interpretation of the German classics from Bach to Brahms, but few performers, apart from **Furtwängler**, seem to have accepted his guidance. One barrier was the fact that they were available only in German, but now in translation they have opened up a new school of analysis, which has come to dominate contemporary critical thinking, especially in the United States. Schenker's approach owes something to *Gestalt* psychology, and propounds the distinction between 'background', the current vocabulary of a musical language, and 'foreground', the individual original contribution of the composer. He also propounded the theory that musical form can be reduced to one cadential progression, and devised a form of graphic notation for demonstrating this basic structure free of decorative and transitional elements.

Scherchen, Hermann (1891-1966) German conductor and viola player. He was a member of the Berlin Philharmonic Orchestra (1907-10), studied with

Schoenberg and took particular interest in the performance of new music by founding a society for that purpose in Berlin in 1918. After holding a series of conducting posts he emigrated to Switzerland, where he held master classes in the study and performance of contemporary music. He conducted the first performance of works by many leading composers. He has left a valuable book on the technique of conducting, and a volume of essays entitled *The Nature of Music*.

scherzando (It.) In a light-hearted, playful manner.

scherzo (It.) Joke. A title given to a piece or movement, generally of a light-hearted or witty character, though sometimes with an ironic or bitter flavour. It was used by **Monteverdi** in his *Scherzi musicali*. It was first applied in the classical symphony by Beethoven, who recognized that the traditional minuet and trio had been transformed by Haydn and himself into a fast, brilliant movement which required a different description. It usually, though not invariably, was third in a four-movement work, and because of its origin was mostly in 3/4 time. Later, the usage was less restricted, and the name returned to its original connotation of a witty piece of no set form or metre.

Schibler, Armin (1920-1986) Swiss composer who studied at Zurich Conservatoire, and in 1942 became a pupil of **Burkhard**. Among his compositions are three operas (*The Spanish Rose-tree, The Devil in the Winter Palace* and *The Feet in the Fire*); an oratorio (*Media in Vita*); three symphonies; violin, piano, trombone and horn concertos; and string quartets.

Schiff, Heinrich (1951-) Austrian cellist and conductor who studied in Vienna with Kuhne and Navarra. His repertory extends from Bach to **Lutosławski**, and in the course of his career he has played with the Vienna, Berlin, Israel and Los Angeles Philharmonic Orchestras and the Amsterdam Concertgebouw; he appears regularly in Britain. He has recorded all the major cello concertos – those of **Dvořák, Elgar**, Haydn, Schumann, Lutosławski, **Vivaldi** and **Shostakovich**, for which he won the Grand Prix du Disque – and the Bach solo suites. His conducting career began in 1984, and in 1990 he became artistic director of the **Northern Sinfonia**.

Schikaneder, Emanuel (1751-1812) German actor, singer, playwright and theatre manager. He wrote the libretto for **Mozart**'s *Die Zauberflöte* (1791), which he also produced and performed in as Papageno; he wrote another 50 or so libretti.

Schillings, Max von (1868-1933) German composer and conductor who studied in Bonn and Munich, where he came to know Strauss. In 1892 he went to Bayreuth as an assistant, and became chorus-master in 1902. His first three operas, *Ingwelde* (1894), *Der Pfeifertag* (1899) and *Moloch* (1906), were quite well received, although they were considered a little too close to Wagner in both style and content. His fourth, *Mona Lisa*, was produced at Stuttgart in 1915; it was a considerable success and was given at the Metropolitan, New York, in 1922. He was conductor and later music director of the Stuttgart opera (1908-18) and administrator of the Berlin opera (1918-25). Later he toured extensively as a conductor and made numerous recordings.

Schipa, Tito (1888-1965) Italian tenor who began his career as a composer of piano pieces and songs, but later studied singing with Piccoli in Milan. He made his début as a tenor in Vercelli (1912). Between 1920 and 1932 he was a member of the Chicago Civic Opera, and for several seasons he sang at the New York Metropolitan. Returning to Italy, he continued to appear at La Scala and in Rome until 1950 and later in the Italian provinces, but he never appeared at Covent Garden, although he did make concert appearances in London.

Schippers, Thomas (1930-1977) American conductor who first appeared in public playing the piano at the age of six, and became a church organist when only 14. He studied at the Curtis Institute, Philadelphia, and with Olga Samaroff. In 1948 he made his début with the Lemonade Opera Company, and after appearances with the New York City Opera Company and the New York Philharmonic Orchestra he appeared at the New York Metropolitan and La Scala in 1955.

At the opening of the new Metropolitan at the Lincoln Center in 1966, Schippers conducted the première of **Barber**'s *Antony and Cleopatra*. Other appearances were at La Scala, Milan (1967), Bayreuth (1963) and Covent Garden, London (1968). Between 1970 and 1977 he was conductor of the Cincinnati Symphony Orchestra.

schleppend (Ger.) Dragging. *Nicht schleppend* is a direction that the pace of the music should not be allowed to drag.

Schlick, Arnolt (*c.*1460-*c.*1521) German organist, composer and theorist. Having travelled widely, he went to Frankfurt in 1486 where he was organist for the coronation of Maximilian I. Further travels took him to Holland, Strasbourg and Worms and in 1511 he became a member of the Heidelberg court chapel. During this time he gained a reputation for testing new organs, and in 1511 he published a treatise on organ-building and playing entitled *Spiegel der Orgelmacher und Organisten*. Schlick's works include sacred organ music and pieces for lute. He also wrote the music for the coronation of Charles V in Aachen (1520).

Schmidt, Franz (1874-1939) Austrian cellist, pianist and composer. As a boy he learnt the piano and played at dancing-schools to eke out the family finances. He studied with Leschetizky and then at the Vienna Conservatoire, and in 1896 became cellist in the Court Opera orchestra. His distinguished teaching career began when he taught the cello at the Conservatoire from 1901 to 1908. In 1922 he was appointed professor at the Vienna Staatsakademie, a director from 1925 to 1927, and director of the Musikhochschule from 1927 to 1931. His works are romantic in style, with rich orchestration reminiscent of Mahler and Bruckner, and with elements of Slav and Magyar music. They include four symphonies, two operas (*Notre Dame*, 1902-4, and *Fredigundis*, 1916-21), chamber and organ music, several sets of variations (*Variations on a Hussar Song*, 1931) and his most important and admired work, the oratorio *The Book of the Seven Seals* (1937).

Schmidt-Isserstedt, Hans (1900-1973) German conductor who studied with **Schreker** and at the University of Cologne, where he graduated in 1923. He began his career at the Wuppertal opera, and from 1928 to 1931 conducted at Rostock. He appeared as principal conductor at the Hamburg State Opera (1935-42) and then director of the German Opera in Berlin (1942-5). Schmidt-Isserstedt also founded and directed the Northern German Radio Symphony Orchestra (1945-71). He made many guest appearances all over the world, and fine recordings of Mozart and Beethoven (including a complete cycle of the latter's symphonies).

Schmitt, Florent (1870-1958) French composer who began his studies in Nancy before going to the Paris Conservatoire, where he was a pupil of **Dubois**, Lavignac, **Massenet** and **Fauré**. At his fifth attempt he won the Prix de Rome (1900). He became director of the Lyons Conservatoire (1922-4) and music critic of *Le Temps* (1929-39). Among his early works are piano duets inspired by his European travels (*Feuillets de voyage*; *Reflets d'Allemagne*); a psalm setting (*Psalm 47*, 1904); a piano quintet (1908) and a ballet, *La tragédie de Salomé* (1907), later recast as a symphonic poem. The works of his mature years include two symphonies, a considerable output of piano music, chamber works, incidental and film music (*Salammbô*, 1925, a film of Flaubert's novel).

Schnabel, Artur (1882-1951) American pianist and composer of Austrian origin who studied with Essipova and Leschetizky, and with Mandyczewski in Vienna. He appeared in many solo recitals and also accompanied artists such as **Casals, Szigeti** and **Primrose**. He was considered a thoughtful interpreter, especially in his playing of Beethoven, Schubert and Brahms, and his recordings of the Beethoven sonatas are outstanding for their expressive qualities. His compositions include orchestral and chamber music, one piano concerto and other piano pieces.

Schnebel, Dieter (1930-) German composer whose compositions reflect his tendency to experiment with new choral techniques, variable form and **aleatory** music. Examples of his methods include *Nostalgia*, which is for conductor alone, *Drei Klang* (1977), for three simultaneously broadcast ensembles, and his symphonic improvisations, *Thanatos-Eros* (1979).

Schnittke, Alfred See **Shnitke, Alfred**

Schobert, Johann (*c.*1735-1767) German composer and harpsichordist who lived in Paris, where he was in the service of the Prince of Conti from about 1720. As a result of his development of keyboard technique, he greatly influenced some of **Mozart**'s early piano sonatas and concertos, and Mozart also used one of Schobert's sonata movements as the second movement of his Piano Concerto (K39, 1767). Apart from keyboard music, Schobert also composed chamber works, concertos, sinfonias and comic operas.

Schoeck, Othmar (1886-1957) Swiss composer and conductor who studied in Zurich and in Leipzig with **Reger**. By the time he left school he had composed several songs, and at the age of 20 he wrote a *Serenade* which was widely admired. From about 1908 he was conductor of several Zurich choirs; from 1917 he also conducted concerts at St Gall. He became one of the leading Swiss composers of his time, with almost 400 songs to his credit, settings of the great German Romantic poets (principally Goethe, Mörike and Eichendorff). He wrote settings of Eichendorff and others for voice and orchestra or chamber ensemble, of which *Elegie* (1923) is one of the most beautiful. Also outstanding are the cycles *Das Wandsbecker Liederbuch* (1936) and *Das holde Beschieden* (1950). Apart from some orchestral pieces – concertos for violin, cello and horn – Schoeck's other major achievements were operatic: *Venus* (1922), *Penthesilea* (1927), *Vom Fischer und syner Fru* (1930), *Massimilla Doni* (1937) and *Das Schloss Dürande* (1943).

Schoenberg (Schönberg), Arnold (1874-1951) Austrian composer who started his working life in a bank before becoming a chorus-master in 1895. The only formal music training he received was from his friend **Zemlinsky**, who introduced him to the music of Wagner. This had a profound effect upon the young Schoenberg. Towards the end of the 1890s he earned his living by conducting theatre orchestras. He taught for a brief period at Stern's Conservatoire, Berlin, and in 1903 went to Vienna where two of his many pupils were **Webern** and **Berg**. His first Chamber Symphony (1906) and the String Quartet No.2 illustrate his transition from tonal to **atonal** composition. The monodrama *Erwartung* (Expectation, 1909), the opera *Die glückliche Hand* (The Favoured Hand) and the song-cycle *Pierrot lunaire* (1912) are all fully atonal. In 1911 he returned to Berlin and, after serving in World War I, continued to teach at the Prussian Academy of Arts until 1933. His works from this period include the operas *Von Heute auf Morgen* (From One Day to the Next, 1930) and *Moses und Aron* (1932) and the oratorio *Die Jakobsleiter* (Jacob's

Ladder), which remained unfinished. By 1933 he found life under the Nazi regime intolerable and moved to the United States, where he became an American citizen in 1940.

Following his progress into atonality, Schoenberg formulated what became known as **twelve-note** composition, which was basically a return to **polyphony** and was described by him as a 'higher and better order'. His works from 1921 to 1933 especially exemplified this style, although some of his later works written in the United States show a tendency to return to a more traditional handling of form and tonality. Among these later works are *Kol nidre* (1938), on a sacred Jewish theme; *Ode to Napoleon* for speaker, strings and piano (1943); *A Survivor from Warsaw* (1947); a violin concerto, a piano concerto and a number of chamber works.

He also wrote several influential theoretical works, including *Counterpoint* (1911) and *Structural Functions of Harmony* (1948). Schoenberg's influence has been seminal for many 20th-century composers, such as **Boulez**, although audiences have not warmed to his compositions.

Schönbach, Dieter (1931-) German composer whose music often includes visual aspects, such as film and dance. Apart from the conventional orchestral and chamber music, his output also includes numerous multimedia works.

Schönherr, Max (1903-1984) Austrian composer and conductor who studied in Marburg and Graz. His conducting career, which had begun in Graz, developed at various theatres in Vienna. From 1931 he was a conductor on Vienna Radio, where he gave stylish renderings of operettas by the Strauss family and others and became recognized as an expert in the genre. His own compositions were also in this lighter vein, and have become popular in their turn (*Austrian Dances*, 1937). In 1968 he turned to the study of Viennese composers and published several books and many articles.

Schottische Ballroom dance in 2/4 time, fashionable during the 19th century, similar to but slower than the **polka**. It is not to be confused with the *écossaise*.

Schreier, Peter (1935-) German tenor and conductor who studied with Polster in Leipzig and with Winkler in Dresden. He made his début in Dresden (1959) as the First Prisoner in Beethoven's *Fidelio*. Since then he has appeared in Berlin, New York, Vienna, Salzburg, London and Hamburg. Apart from being a gifted actor, he is also considered an outstanding Mozart singer and has been compared with **Tauber** and **Wunderlich**.

Schreker, Franz (1878-1934) Austrian composer and conductor who studied with Fuchs and **Gardiner** in Vienna, where he founded the Philharmonic Choir (1911). One of his earliest successes was the ballet *The Birthday of the Infanta* (1908), after a story by Oscar Wilde. He was director of the Berlin Hochschule für Musik (1920-32) until the Nazis dismissed him from his position. His first serious opera, *Der ferne Klang* (1901-10), made a powerful impression on his contemporaries, although two subsequent operas, *Die Gezeichneten* (1918) and *Der Schatzgräber* (1920), received wider acclaim. Later operas include *Irrelohe* (1924), *Der singende Teufel* (1928) and *Der Schmied von Gent* (1932). Among his other works were a ballet, *Rokoko* (1908), *Chamber Symphony* (1916) and songs.

Schröder-Devrient, Wilhelmine (1804-1860) German soprano who studied in Vienna and made her début in 1821 as Pamina in *Die Zauberflöte*. She sang Agathe in **Weber's** *Der Freischütz* and then Leonore in Beethoven's *Fidelio*, which became her most famous role and established her as one of the earliest great operatic actresses – her performance aroused the admiration of Wagner, who heard her in Dresden. She sang Donna Anna (*Don Giovanni*), Desdemona (Rossini's *Otello*) and the title-role in

Bellini's *Norma*, creating the Wagner roles of Senta (*Der fliegende Holländer*) and Venus (*Tannhäuser*). She appeared in Paris and London during the 1830s. From the late 1830s her voice deteriorated somewhat and she retired from the stage in 1847.

Schubert, Franz (1797-1828) Austrian composer who was taught the violin by his father and the piano by his eldest brother. He had a few lessons in counterpoint from his choir-master Michael Holzer, and when aged 11 he was admitted to the Imperial Choristers' School, Vienna, where he attracted the attention of **Salieri**. He was already composing: songs, string quartets and (in 1813) his Symphony No.1. Leaving there in 1814, Schubert joined his father's school as an assistant master, but he had no enthusiasm for teaching and left his post after four years at the suggestion of his friend Michael Vogl, the singer. Apart from two visits to Hungary in 1818 and 1824, where he acted as a domestic musician to the Esterházy family, Schubert spent all his life in Vienna.

In 1814 he wrote a Mass, a string quartet and his first great song, *Gretchen am Spinnrade* (after Goethe), and completed his first opera, *Des Teufels Lustschloss*. It was always his ambition to compose a successful opera, and he continued to tackle this form throughout his life, but the nine operas he wrote (including *Alfonso und Estrella* and *Fierabras*) were not popular and some were not even performed.

By 1815 Schubert was composing prolifically: two symphonies, much piano music and about 150 songs, including a setting of Goethe's *Der Erlkönig* (The Erl-King) which graphically depicts the terror of the supernatural. It was at about this time that the 'Schubertiads' began – evenings when he played his compositions to an ever-widening circle of appreciative friends. From about 1817 date two songs on which he later based more extensive works: *Der Wanderer* (Fantasia, 1822) and *Die Forelle* (The Trout) (Quintet, 1819). The years 1822 and 1823 saw some great achievements, including the *Unfinished Symphony*, the song-cycle *Die schöne Müllerin* (The Fair Maid of the Mill) and the incidental music for *Rosamunde*. The great string quartets in A minor and D minor (*Death and the Maiden*) followed. The latter is filled with foreboding: it may have been a reflection of the composer's own frame of mind, for by this time he was seriously ill. His illness did not prevent the composition of his Symphony No.9, the *Great C Major* as it is known (1825), or that of the sad, yearning song-cycle *Winterreise* (Winter Journey, 1827). One of his last and greatest chamber compositions was the String Quintet (1828). In addition there were more songs, some grouped together and published as *Schwanengesang* (Swansong). He wrote a great deal of music for solo piano, as well as piano duets. Impromptus and *moments musicaux* feature among the shorter pieces but there are also sonatas. In particular his last sonata, No.21 in B♭, is considered his greatest, although No.18 in G major and No. 20 in A major are also outstanding pieces.

Schubert gained no financial success in his lifetime from the nine symphonies, chamber music, numerous piano sonatas and duets, and the songs (nearly 600) that he composed: he made one public concert appearance (1828) which was sufficiently successful for him to buy his own piano. Yet his genius speaks to everyone: there is no emotion that is not expressed in his sublimely beautiful music, whether the bleak sorrow and despair of *Winterreise* or the sheer infectious *joie de vivre* of the *Trout Quintet*.

Schuller, Gunther (1925-) American composer, horn-player and conductor who studied at St Thomas's Choir School (1938-42), and taught at the Manhattan School of Music (1950-62), Yale School of Music (1964-7) and the New England Conservatoire, of which he was president from 1967 to 1977. In the 1950s he played with Miles Davis and in 1957 he coined the phrase 'third stream', a form of music that incorporates the virtues of both jazz and classical styles. His works include a Horn Concerto (1944), *Symphonic Tribute to Duke Ellington* (1955), the opera *The Visitation* (1966), a double-bass concerto (1968), *The Five Senses*, a television ballet (1967), a violin concerto (1976), various orchestral pieces, and film music.

Schuman, William (1910-) American composer who studied at Columbia University and at the Mozarteum, Salzburg. He was director of the Juilliard School of Music, New York (1945-61), and holds honorary doctorates from 20 American colleges and universities. He was president of the Lincoln Center from 1962 to 1969. Schuman's interest in early American music and themes is reflected in his romantic, rhapsodic style, which sometimes employs groups of instruments performing at different tempi. His works include ten symphonies (composed 1936-76), concertos, four string quartets, a ballet, *Undertow* (1945), an opera, *Mighty Casey* (1953), a fantasy entitled *Song of Orpheus* (1962), and *To Thy Love*, a choral fantasy (1973).

Schumann (Wieck), Clara (1819-1896) German pianist and composer who was taught by her father, Friedrich Wieck. She made her first public appearance at the age of nine, and gave her first concert just before her 11th birthday at the Leipzig Gewandhaus. Her marriage in 1840 to Robert **Schumann** was violently opposed by her father. After her husband's death (1856) she lived in Berlin and Baden-Baden until her appointment (1878) as chief piano professor at the Hoch Conservatoire, Frankfurt. Her works include a Piano Concerto in A minor, a Piano Trio in G minor, Variations on a Theme by Robert Schumann, other piano pieces, and several sets of songs. She was internationally noted as a performer and made many visits to England.

Schumann, Elisabeth (1888-1952) German soprano who studied in Berlin, Dresden and Hamburg where she made her stage début in 1909, remaining with

Elisabeth Schumann

the opera there until she joined the Vienna Opera (1919-37). She made her first appearance in the United States in 1921 and at Covent Garden in 1924. In 1938 she settled in the United States, where she taught at the Curtis Institute, Philadelphia, and became an American citizen in 1944.

She possessed a voice of superb clarity and her performances of works by Mozart and Strauss were considered incomparable.

Schumann, Robert (1810-1856) German composer, born in Zwickau, a small town not far from Leipzig. He thought for a while of being a writer, but was forced to study law. He was soon bored, and amused himself with wine and women, but was so profoundly affected by hearing **Paganini** that he resolved that music must be his life. In 1830 he moved into the house of the famous teacher Friedrich Wieck and began serious study of the piano. He tried to improve his technique with a mechanical device, but succeeded only in damaging the tendons of his right hand. With a career as a virtuoso now out of the question, he turned to composition and journalism. In 1834 he founded the *Neue Zeitschrift für Musik*, often basing his articles on the doings of an imaginary club, the Davidsbund, whose members fought, like David, against the Philistines. At the same time a torrent of music flowed from his pen, for example *Papillons*, Op.2, a set of witty and charming miniatures of striking originality. He became engaged to a young lady from Asch, and used the letters in their German connotations (A♭,C, B; or A, E♭, B) in various orders as the thematic basis for one of his finest piano works, *Carnaval*; he wrote his splendid *Symphonic Variations* on a theme by her guardian. By now he and young Clara Wieck, a highly gifted pianist, were clearly attracted to each other, but Wieck was outraged that his brilliant 16-year-old daughter should be mixed up with a dissipated, unstable young man who had no prospects, composed wild music, and upset everyone with his journalism. It was the start of a long battle that was resolved only after legal action: Robert and Clara were married on 12 September 1840.

Schumann was now in the full flood of creation. In 1840 he composed no fewer than 138 songs of the highest quality, including the cycles *Dichterliebe*, *Liederkreis*, and *Frauenliebe und Leben*; in 1841, having composed virtually nothing for orchestra, he produced two Symphonies (No.1 in B♭ and what was later to be revised as No.4 in D minor), a sinfonietta he called *Overture, Scherzo and Finale*, and the *Fantasie* for piano and orchestra, later expanded into the Piano Concerto. The following year he threw himself into the study of chamber music; in five weeks he composed three string quartets, Op.41, and added the superb Piano Quintet Op.44, the Piano Quartet Op.47, and the Piano Trio Op.88, known as *Fantasiestücke*. But this manic explosion of work took its toll and he had a breakdown: the first shadows were falling across his life. The Schumanns moved to Dresden in December 1844, where Robert completed the Piano Concerto in A minor, and at Christmas 1845 presented Clara with a new Symphony in C (his third, although it is called No.2). His intense creativity came in manic bursts, interspersed with bouts of illness and depression. In 1848, despite revolutionary upheavals in Dresden, he completed his opera *Genoveva*, and his fine incidental music for Byron's *Manfred*, then rounded off the year with one of his most charming works for the piano, his *Album for the Young*, Op.68. In 1850 he was offered the post of music director in Düsseldorf, and was inspired to write a five-movement symphony (No.3, known as the *Rhenish*), the Cello Concerto, and a series of concert overtures on literary themes. But he was unable to control the orchestra, and in October 1853 was forced to resign. His mental condition deteriorated badly – it was possibly syphilitic in origin, a legacy of his wild youth – and on 27 February 1854 he tried to commit suicide by throwing himself into the Rhine. A few days later he was committed to an asylum, where he spent the rest of his life.

Although it had a profound influence on later composers, such as Brahms, Tchaikovsky and Debussy, Schumann's music at first was regarded by many as outrageous and ugly. Even his wife, a constant advocate of his music, never played *Carnaval* in full in public because she felt that the audience could not take it. When she played the Piano Concerto in London it was dismissed as unlovely and turgid. Only in the last years of the 19th century was Schumann recognized as one of the truly great composers for the piano, in the beautiful concerto, the sonatas, and especially in those inimitable sets of short pieces such as *Davidsbündlertänze*, *Kreisleriana*, or *Faschingsschwank aus Wien*, that delight yet torment so many pianists with their technical demands. The songs are in the front rank of *Lieder*: vocal lines of wayward passion and charm blend with piano parts of astonishing variety and power. Now, as the result of eloquent performances by such conductors as **Furtwängler** and **Szell**, the symphonies too are accepted as outstanding examples of their form, and confirm Schumann's place as one of the greatest figures of the Romantic movement.

Schurmann, Gerard (1928-) Dutch composer, born in Indonesia and now resident in England. He was a pupil of **Rawsthorne**. His works include the song-cycle *Chuench 1* (1966), *Variants* (1970), a piano concerto (1973), a violin concerto (1978), the cantata *Double Heart* (1977) and the opera-cantata *Piers Plowman* (1980).

Schütz, Heinrich (1585-1672) German composer who started his career studying law at Marburg University, but then went to Venice (1609-12), where he studied music under Giovanni **Gabrieli**. Returning to Kassel as court organist, he left for Dresden in 1614, where he was appointed *Kapellmeister* to the Elector of Saxony. Apart from further visits to Venice and also a period in Copenhagen (1633-41), he spent the rest of his life in Dresden.

It is said that Schütz was the greatest German composer before **J.S. Bach**. Influenced by the works of Gabrieli, and to a certain extent by those of **Monteverdi**, he was able with his later compositions to strike the perfect balance between Italian and German styles. Such an achievement made a very significant contribution to the development of the **oratorio**. His Four Passions (*Matthew*, *Mark*, *Luke* and *John* – 1665-6), reveal very little use of chorale melodies. His only opera, *Dafne* (1627), is lost but it is held to have been the first German opera ever written. His other works include *Psalmen Davids* for two, three or four choirs of voices and instruments (1619), *Resurrection Oratorio* (1623), *Symphoniae sacrae* (Parts I, II and III, 1629, 1647, 1650), a ballet, *Orpheus and Eurydice* (1638), *The Seven Words from the Cross*, a choral piece (1660), *The Christmas History* (1664) and *Deutsches Magnificat* (1671).

Schwarz, Rudolf (1905-) Austrian-born British conductor who studied the violin and piano, playing the viola in the Vienna Philharmonic Orchestra. In 1923 he became an assistant conductor at the Düsseldorf Opera, and later (1927-33) conductor at the Karlsruhe Opera. He then became musical director of the Jewish Cultural Union in Berlin until 1941, when he was sent to Belsen concentration camp. After the war he moved to England by way of Sweden and in 1947 became musical director of the Bournemouth Symphony Orchestra. He later directed the City of Birmingham Symphony Orchestra (1951-7), the BBC Symphony Orchestra (1957-62) and the Northern Sinfonia (1967-74).

Schwarzkopf, Elisabeth (1915-) German soprano who studied with Lula Mysz-Gmeiner and Maria Ivogun. She made her début at the Berlin City Opera (1938), where she soon established herself as a brilliant soprano in the opera *Ariadne auf Naxos* by Richard Strauss. In 1943 she joined the Vienna State Opera and moved from there in 1950 to La Scala in Milan. She also appeared at Covent Garden for several seasons beginning in 1947, where she confirmed her position as one of the leading sopranos of her generation, singing an extensive repertory of both German and Italian roles. She appeared regularly at the Salzburg Festival (1949-64), where she shone in Mozart and Strauss. Her greatest roles were as the Countess in *Le nozze di Figaro*, Fiordiligi in *Così fan tutte*, Donna

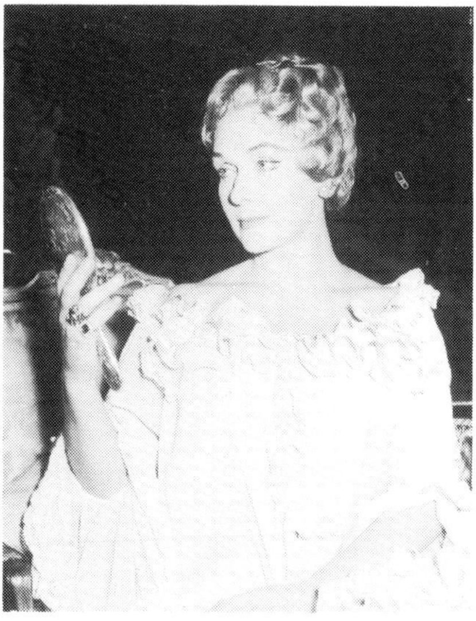

Elisabeth Schwarzkopf

Elvira in *Don Giovanni* and the Marschallin in *Der Rosenkavalier*. In 1951 she created the role of Anne Truelove in Stravinsky's *The Rake's Progress*. A matchless singer of *Lieder*, above all those of Schubert and Wolf, she made many outstanding recordings in conjunction with her husband, Walter Legge, not only of these and of her operatic roles but also of operetta. Her account of Strauss's *Four Last Songs* is an unforgettable example of her rich, lustrous soprano.

Schweitzer, Albert (1875-1965) Alsatian theologian, medical missionary, organist and musical scholar. He studied the organ at Strasbourg and with **Widor** in Paris. He became an authority on Bach, writing a biography which was published in France (1905) with an enlarged version in Germany (1908). Most of his life after leaving his post as principal of the theological college in Strasbourg was spent in Africa as a medical missionary. He visited Europe periodically to give organ recitals of Bach's works, and in 1952 was awarded the Nobel Peace Prize.

Sciutti, Graziella (1927-) Italian soprano who studied in Rome and made her début at Aix-en-Provence in 1951 in **Menotti**'s *The Telephone*. She was particularly successful in the Mozart soubrette roles of Susanna (*Le nozze di Figaro*), Zerlina (*Don Giovanni*) and Despina (*Così fan tutte*). She sang at Glyndebourne (1954-9), in San Francisco, Salzburg and Vienna. Her clear, light voice and vivacious stage presence have been well suited to the roles of Norina (**Donizetti's** *Don Pasquale*) and Rosina (*Il barbiere di Siviglia*). She has also produced some operas.

scoop Fault in singing in which a note is approached from below its true pitch instead of being attacked cleanly.

scordatura Altering the customary tuning of the strings of an instrument, e.g. the violin solo in the second movement of Mahler's Symphony No.4, or the cellos for the final chord of Stravinsky's *Rite of Spring*.

score Copy of any musical composition written in several parts on separate staves, with the coincident notes appearing vertically over each other. Players in orchestras or other ensembles normally read from music giving only their own parts, whereas the conductor has a full score showing all the parts combined. The usual layout of orchestral scores is to show the woodwind at the top, brass in the middle, and strings at the bottom. Harps and percussion are placed between brass and strings.

On a vocal score, the voice parts for operas and operettas are usually given with piano accompaniment.

On a piano score, the orchestral and vocal parts are reduced to a simple piano transcription.

Short scores are composers' sketches reduced to a few staves, to be elaborated and fully written out later.

Scotch snap Technical name for rhythmic figures inverting the order of dotted notes, the short note coming first instead of last. It is found in many Scottish songs, such as *Comin' through the Rye*, and in the **strathspey**. During the 17th and 18th centuries the Scotch snap was a device popular in Italy, and it was called by German and French writers the 'Lombardic rhythm'.

Scott, Cyril Meir (1879-1970) English composer and poet who went to the Hoch Conservatoire, Frankfurt, at the age of 12 for a period of 18 months. Returning there in 1895, he became a member of the Frankfurt Group with **Grainger**, **Gardiner**, O'Neill and **Quilter**. In many respects his works had a greater following abroad than in England, possibly explained by the fact that his work did not lie in the stream of traditional English music. He was basically a melodist and lyricist with a very individual taste in harmony that had its roots in French Impressionism. His works include an opera, *The Alchemist* (1917), three symphonies (1900, 1903 and 1939), concertos for violin, piano and horn, chamber music and songs. He also wrote books on occultism, naturopathy, osteopathy and homeopathy, and several volumes of poetry.

Scottish Chamber Orchestra Ensemble founded in 1974 and based in Edinburgh. It has an extensive touring programme, appearing frequently in Glasgow (where it has an office) and giving an annual season in the Highlands of Scotland; it has toured widely, in Europe, Israel, Japan and the United States. The principal conductor is Jukka-Pekka Saraste and Sir Peter Maxwell **Davies** is Associate Composer/Conductor. The repertory, which is broad and encompasses Mozart, Dvořák and Mendelssohn, includes much of Davies's music. For the 1990 Glasgow Year of Culture it has commissioned two concertos (*Strathclyde Concertos* Nos.3 and 4) from him, as well as works from Nigel Osborne and Peter Nelson. The orchestra has made numerous recordings and broadcasts.

Scottish National Orchestra Symphony orchestra founded in 1891 and established in Glasgow in 1893 under Sir George **Henschel** as the Scottish Orchestra, and renamed in 1951. It is a permanent orchestra that operates all the year round, giving concerts in Edinburgh, Glasgow and other Scottish towns. Its conductors have included Sir Frederick **Cowen**, Sir John **Barbirolli**, Walter **Susskind**, Karl **Rankl**, Sir Alexander **Gibson** (1959-84) and Neeme Järvi (from 1984).

Scottish Opera Company founded in Glasgow in 1962 by Sir Alexander **Gibson**, conductor of the **Scottish National Orchestra**. Under Gibson, who remained artistic director until 1987, the company has built up a considerable reputation. It tours not only in Scotland and the north of England but in Europe, as well as giving an almost continual season in Glasgow at the Theatre Royal, its permanent home since 1975. Among the company's most notable successes have been Wagner's *Ring* cycle (1971), Berlioz's *Les troyens*, Mussorgsky's *Boris Godunov*, Verdi's *Otello* and *Falstaff* and several **Britten** works. It makes regular appearances at the Edinburgh Festival. Operas commissioned for it from Scottish composers include Robin **Orr**'s *Full Circle* and Thea **Musgrave**'s *Mary Queen of Scots*. The present music director is John Mauceri.

Scotto, Renata (1934-) Italian soprano who studied in Milan with Ghiriardini and Llopart. She made her début as Violetta in Verdi's *La traviata* (1953) at the Teatro Nuovo, Milan, and joined the company at La Scala, singing Amina in **Bellini's** *La sonnambula*, Adina in **Donizetti's** *L'elisir d'amore* and the title-roles in *Madama Butterfly* and *Lucia di Lammermoor*. Her début in London was in 1957, at Covent Garden in 1962 (in *Butterfly*) and at the New York Metropolitan Opera in 1965. Since about 1973 she has undertaken heavier roles such as the title-role in *Norma*, Amelia in *Simon Boccanegra* and Lady Macbeth in *Macbeth*.

Scriabin, Alexander (1877-1915) Russian pianist and composer who gave up a military career to study music at the Moscow Conservatoire under Safonov and **Taneyev**. He began a career as a pianist, and became professor of piano (1898-1903) at the Conservatoire following a brilliant series of concert tours in Europe. Later in life he devoted himself entirely to composition and occasional appearances as a pianist. He invented a new system of harmony based on the 8th to the 14th notes of the **harmonic series** but missing out the 12th, and usually arranged in fourths. The influence of Chopin can be seen in his early piano works, and in his orchestral works that of Wagner is evident.

Scriabin's early works include a piano concerto (1894), three symphonies (1895, 1901 and 1903), two piano sonatas, studies and preludes. From about 1902 he was influenced by his philosophical and theosophical interests, notably his study of Nietzsche and the teachings of Madame Blavatsky, and his style progressed. The

main work of this period is *Le poème de l'extase* (1908) for orchestra, which established his reputation. It was followed by *Prometheus* (1911) and sketches for *Mysterium*, a work conceived as a fusion of several arts, which remained unfinished. Most of his later work was for solo piano.
His name is sometimes transliterated as Skryabin.

Sculthorpe, Peter (1929-) Australian composer who studied at Melbourne University Conservatoire, and was a pupil of **Rubbra** and **Wellesz** at Oxford. His rejection of European music techniques in search of an Australian non-tonal style led him to study Eastern music, especially that of Bali and Tibet. The influence of this music is reflected in some of his works.
Among his compositions are nine string quartets, *Music for Japan* (1970), the opera *Rites of Passage* (1973) and *Lament for Strings* (1976). He has also written much film and stage music.

Seaman, Christopher (1942-) British conductor who was formerly a percussionist. He was principal conductor of the BBC Scottish Symphony Orchestra (1971-7), and the Northern Sinfonia (1974-9). He has gained a wide following as a conductor of the National Youth Orchestra and the Robert Mayer Concerts for Children.

sean-nós (Ireland) Literally the 'old style', a slow, lyrical song or air sung in Gaelic. Generally it is unaccompanied, with improvised variations and melismatic embellishments. It survives today mainly in the Connemara region.

Searle, Humphrey (1915-1982) British composer and writer on music. He studied music with **Ireland** in London and in Vienna under **Webern**, from whom he learnt **twelve-tone** serialism. He later worked at the BBC and with the Sadler's Wells Ballet company, and taught at the Royal College of Music. His works include five symphonies, chamber music, such as *Intermezzo for Eleven Instruments* (1947), ballets (*Noctambules*, 1956) and a piano concerto. He also wrote operas, the first of which was a one-act setting of a Gogol story, *The Diary of a Madman* (1958), which made use of electronic music as well as a traditional orchestra. The others are *The Photo of the Colonel* (1964) and *Hamlet* (1968). Three powerful cantatas are among his finest works: *Gold Coast Customs*, *The Riverrun* and *The Shadow of Cain*.

sebell Alternative spelling of **cebell**.

secco (It.) Dry. Used either as a direction to players or to mean a form of **recitative** (*recitativo secco*).

second Interval of one tone between two notes (major second) or one semitone (minor second).

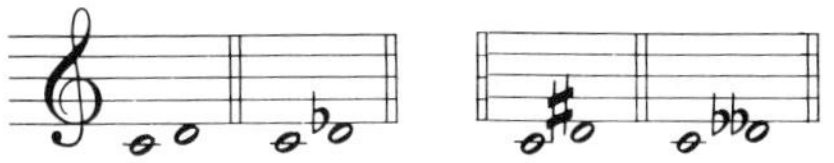

Major 2nd	Minor 2nd	Aug 2nd	Diminished 2nd

secondary dominant The **dominant** in the key of the dominant; that is, if the composition is in C major, the dominant is G, and the dominant of the key of G major is the chord of D (termed the secondary dominant of C major).

secondo (It.) Second, usually referring to the lower of the two parts in a duet.

sedenka song (Bulgaria) Song performed on an evening occasion when women gather together for communal sewing, knitting and embroidering.

Seefried, Irmgard (1919-) German soprano who studied at the Augsburg Conservatoire and joined the Aachen Opera under **Karajan** (1939), where she made her début (1940) as a priestess in Verdi's *Aïda*. She joined the Vienna State

Opera in 1943 and was chosen by **Strauss** to sing the Composer in *Ariadne auf Naxos* during his 80th birthday celebrations. Seefried is especially well known as a Mozart singer and has performed throughout the world. She has also made a name as a *Lieder* singer.

Segovia, Andrés (1893-1987) Spanish guitarist who was self-taught and first appeared in public at the age of 14. From his first concert appearance in Paris (1924), he was received with international acclaim and regarded as foremost among modern guitarists. His influence on the younger generation was considerable. Composers such as **Falla**, **Casella**, **Villa-Lobos** and **Castelnuovo-Tedesco** have written works especially for him. He himself arranged for the guitar many pieces by J.S. Bach and others originally written for the lute.

Andrés Segovia

segue (It.) Direction to the performer to proceed with the next section without a break.

seguidilla (Sp.) Dance in triple time dating back to at least the 16th century. The original form, *seguidilla manchega*, came from La Mancha, although it is possible that it was of Moorish origin. The *seguidilla* is played on guitars, often accompanied with castanets, and sometimes with violin and flute. The vocal accompaniment usually consists of four-line verses followed by three-line **refrains**.

Seiber, Mátyás (1905-1960) Hungarian cellist, composer and conductor who studied with **Kodály** at the Budapest Academy of Music (1919-24). He joined the staff of the Hoch Conservatoire, Frankfurt (1928-33), and then settled in London (1935), where he spent the rest of his life. In 1943 he founded, with **Chagrin**, the Society for the Promotion of New Music, and taught at Morley College (1942-57). His style of music developed from a Hungarian mode to incorporate elements of Oriental music and jazz. Seiber's works include the opera *Eva spielt mit Puppen* (1934), *La Blanchisseuse*, ballet music (1942), the cantata *Ulysses* (1947), three string quartets, *Improvisation for Jazz Band and Symphony Orchestra* (with John **Dankworth**, 1959), piano and film music.

Seixas, Carlos de (1704-1742) Portuguese organist and composer who was taught by his father, whom he succeeded as organist at Coimbra Cathedral (1718). From 1720 until his death he was organist to the court in Lisbon, at first serving under Domenico **Scarlatti**. He is mainly remembered for his keyboard sonatas and choral works.

semibreve Note having half the length in time of a breve and double the length of a minim.

semichorus Group of singers detached from a chorus for the purpose of obtaining **antiphonal** effects or changes of **tone colour**. It does not necessarily comprise half of the chorus, but perhaps represents only a segment of it.

semi-opera Modern term for certain 17th- and 18th-century operas in which music (rather than the spoken word) plays a less dominant part than in the full opera form.

An example is Purcell's opera *King Arthur* (1691). See also **masque**.

semiquaver Note having half the value of a **quaver** and a sixteenth that of a **semibreve**. In American terminology, it is also known as a sixteenth note.

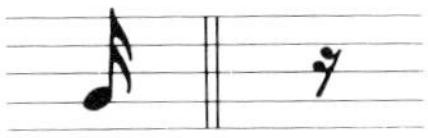

Semiquaver

semitone Smallest interval commonly used in Western music. It is the interval between one key and the next on the piano, whether a black or white note. Also known as a minor second.

semplice (It.) Simple. Direction indicating that a passage or whole composition is to be performed in an unaffected manner.

sempre (It.) Always – as in *sempre più mosso*, always getting faster.

Senesino (*c.*1680-*c.*1750) Italian castrato who studied in Bologna and sang in Genoa, Naples and Venice before going to Dresden in 1719. There Handel heard him and invited him to sing in London in his recently formed company; he created many Handel roles, in *Giulio Cesare*, *Tamerlano*, *Rodelina*, *Flavio* and *Orlando* among others. He quarrelled with Handel and joined a rival company in 1733. After five years he returned to Naples. His voice was a powerful and flexible **alto** of great beauty.

Senfl, Ludwig (*c.*1486-*c.*1543) Swiss composer who was a pupil of Heinrich Isaac, whom he succeeded as *Kapellmeister* to Maximilian I (1496-1519). When the emperor died, Senfl joined the Bavarian court in Munich. His works included Masses, magnificats, motets and about 150 German songs.

senza (It.) Without, as in *senza sordini*, without mutes.

septet Composition for seven voices or instruments, or the group that performs such a work.

septuplet Group of seven notes to be fitted into the time of four or six.

Septuplet

Serafin, Tullio (1878-1968) Italian conductor who studied at the Milan Conservatoire and played the violin at La Scala before making his conducting début in 1898 at Ferrara. He became assistant to **Toscanini** at La Scala in 1903 and principal conductor there from 1909 to 1914. He first appeared at Covent Garden in 1907, returning many times throughout his career. In 1924 he went to New York and conducted at the Metropolitan for ten years, giving the first American performances of several important operas (*Simon Boccanegra*, *Turandot*). He returned to Rome as artistic director of the Teatro Reale (1934-43), with periods at La Scala and Chicago. He was closely associated with the careers of Maria **Callas**, with whom he made many recordings, Joan **Sutherland**, and other famous singers of the *bel canto* repertory.

serenade Song or operatic air sung in the evening, by a lover at the window of his mistress; the accompaniment often imitates that of a guitar. In the 18th century the instrumental serenade evolved into a form which usually began and ended with a march, and included an extended movement with a violin solo. In later years the name was applied very loosely to many forms of vocal and instrumental composition.

serenata 18th-century term for a type of **cantata** approaching operatic form, such as Handel's *Acis and Galatea* (*c.*1720).

serialism Music constructed on the basis of a recurrent series of notes. This compositional technique developed in the 1920s from **Schoenberg**'s **twelve-note** system (itself derived from his experiments with **atonality**). The system worked in the following way: all twelve notes on the staff were used in an order laid down by the composer. No note could be repeated until each of the other 11 had sounded (with certain exceptions). Composers such as **Berg** and **Webern** used this form and slightly modified the technique, until **Messiaen** greatly enlarged its scope by adding other musical components (for example, rhythmic figures) as material to be serialized. This enlarged form has come to be known as total serialism; **Boulez**, **Nono** and **Stockhausen** are among its chief exponents. The rise of **electronic** music (with its ability to create new sounds and to programme-in motifs and repetitions) and **aleatory** music has now shed doubts on the future of serialism, but it remains as the first real break from traditional methods of composition that has radically altered the range of techniques open to the present-day composer.

Serialism is also known as the serial technique or serial music.

Serkin, Rudolf (1903-) American pianist of Austrian parentage who studied in Vienna with **Schoenberg** and others. He excels particularly in his interpretations of Bach, Mozart, Beethoven and Schubert. Serkin appeared frequently with the violinist Adolf Busch, whose daughter he married. From 1939 he taught at the Curtis Institute, Philadelphia. After settling in the United States he played in many chamber recitals. He has additionally been director of the Marlboro Festival in Vermont. His son Peter is also a fine pianist.

Serly, Tibor (1901-1978) American composer of Hungarian birth. He studied in Budapest with Kodály, whose influence was considerable. On settling in the United States in 1924 he played violin and viola with various orchestras. In the 1940s he worked out his own chromatic scale system, which he called the *modus lascivus*, and wrote several compositions in this mode: a concerto for trombone (1953), the *Piano Concertino 3 x 3* (1967) and a ballet (*Cast Out*, 1973). His most famous work outside this group was his Viola Concerto (1929). He completed the Viola Concerto and the Piano Concerto No. 3 of **Bartók**.

Serocki, Kazimierz (1922-1981) Polish pianist and composer who was a pupil of Sikorski and Nadia **Boulanger** (1947-8), and was active in promoting modern music, with a special interest in instrumental sounds, spatial composition and **aleatory** techniques. During the early 1950s he toured Europe as a pianist, but then devoted himself to composition. His works include *Musica Concertante* (1958), *Segmenti* for chamber ensemble and percussion (1961), *Swinging Music* (1970), *Ad Libitum* (1974) and *Pianophonie* (1978).

Serov, Alexander Nikolaievich (1820-1871) Russian composer and critic who was originally in the civil service and studied music by taking a correspondence course. He later became a music critic, and following a visit to Germany (1858) became an ardent admirer of Wagner. A series of articles by Serov paved the way for Wagner's 1865 visit to Russia, in which he organized the country's first performance of *Tannhäuser*. Serov achieved considerable success with his first opera, *Judith* (1863), and he followed it with the still more successful *Rogneda* (1865); some influence from these is discernible in certain works by Tchaikovsky, **Mussorgsky** and **Borodin**.

serpent Brass instrument of the cornet family, often made of *papier-mâché*, introduced in the 16th century. It is eight feet long and bent in a series of curves to form a snake-like shape. The lowest note the serpent is capable of is the B♭ below the bass staff, and its compass is three octaves. The serpent fell out of use in the 19th century.

service Musically unified setting of the Anglican **canticles** and responses from the Book of Common Prayer. These include English translations of the *Venite*, *Te Deum*, *Benedictus*, *Benedicite* or *Jubilate* at Matins, and of the *Magnificat*, *Nunc Dimittis*, *Cantate Domino* or *Deus Misereatur* at Evensong. For the service of Holy Communion the settings are of the *Kyrie*, *Credo*, *Sanctus*, *Benedictus*, *Agnus Dei* and *Gloria*. During the 16th and 17th centuries the terms short service and great service were used to distinguish between less and more elaborate settings of the service.

sesquialtera Mixture stop on an organ containing ranks sounding a twelfth (one octave and a fifth) and a seventeenth (two octaves and a third) above written pitch.

Sessions, Roger (1896-1985) American composer who studied with **Bloch** and then went to Europe (1925-33). Returning to the United States, he held several important teaching posts at Princeton, Berkeley and Harvard, and was considered the outstanding teacher of the day; he received numerous honours, including the Pulitzer Prize. His early compositions became progressively more chromatic and expressionistic, although in the 1950s he adopted **serial** procedures. With his later works he showed greater brevity. His compositions include the operas *Montezuma* (1941-63) and *The Trial of Lucullus* (1947), nine symphonies and a cantata, *When Lilacs Last in the Dooryard Bloom'd* (1970). He also wrote a violin concerto, a piano concerto, other orchestral pieces such as the *Rhapsody* of 1970, two string quartets and a quintet, three sonatas for piano and one for violin, and other pieces in various genres. His writings include the important textbook *Harmonic Practice*, other books and numerous articles.

Serpent

seventh **Interval** of seven notes (counting the lowest and highest notes), or eleven semitones for a major seventh (say, C-B) and ten semitones for a minor seventh (say, C-B♭). A diminished seventh is equivalent to a major sixth (C-A).

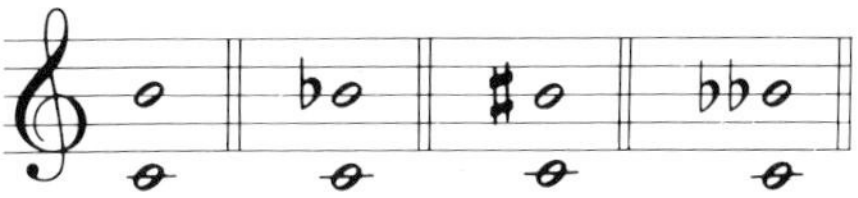

Major 7th	Minor 7th	Aug 7th	Diminished 7th

sextet Composition for six voices or instruments, or a group that performs such a work.

sextuplet Group of six notes of equal time value played in the time of four. Also known as a sextolet.

sforzando (It.) Direction indicating that a note or chord is to be strongly emphasized by adding an accent. An alternative version is sforzato, and the term is often abbreviated to Sf.

Sgambati, Giovanni (1841-1914) Italian composer, pianist and conductor who studied in Trevi and Rome. He began his career as a pianist and established himself on the international circuit, playing in many different countries including Britain. In 1862 he became a friend and pupil of Liszt, whose music he popularized in Italy, conducting the first Italian performance of the *Dante Symphony* (1866). Through Liszt he also met Wagner, who admired his music and helped to get some of it published. His compositions include two fine piano quintets (1866, 1876), a string quartet, some songs, a Requiem and a variety of orchestral works – an overture, a piano concerto, symphonies, a *Te Deum*. The majority of his output, however, was for the keyboard: nocturnes, a prelude and fugue, suites and other collections. Sgambati was one of the founders of the S. Cecilia Liceo Musicale in Rome (1877), and taught there until his death.

shake Alternative English term for **trill**.

shakuhachi (Japan) Long flute of Chinese origin. It is made from a piece of bamboo that tapers from the bell towards the mouthpiece and is also slightly bowed so that the bell curves gently upwards. The *shakuhachi* has four finger-holes on top and one below, and is blown across the end. It has a mouthpiece which is cut obliquely outwards, with a piece of bone or ivory inserted into the playing edge. Holes can be half covered to produce microtonal inflections known as *meri-kari*. The *shakuhachi*, as a solo instrument, was played by both Buddhist priests and itinerant *samurai*, and eventually found its place in the chamber **sankyoku** trio and in the **kabuki** ensemble. It was included by **Takemitsu**, along with the **biwa**, in his orchestral work *November Steps*.

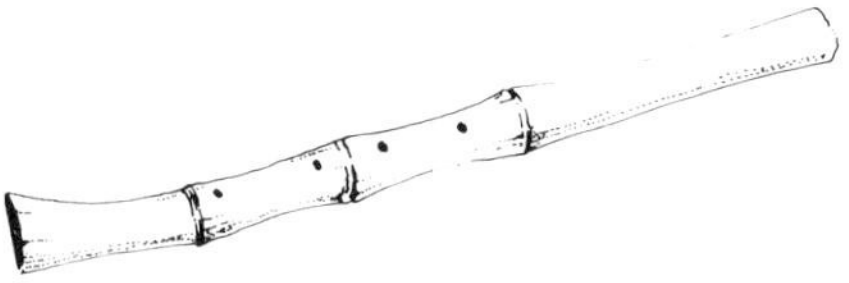

Shakuhachi

Shaliapin, Feodor Ivanovich (1873-1938) Russian bass singer who, after a childhood spent in poverty, joined a provincial opera company and then studied briefly with Dmitri Usatov in Tiflis (1893). In 1894 he made his first appearance at St Petersburg, and in 1896 joined Mamontov's Company in Moscow, which was the beginning of his future fame. His first appearance abroad was at La Scala, Milan (1901), and later (1913) he was engaged by **Diaghilev** to sing in Paris and London. Shaliapin left the Soviet Union in 1920, and from 1921 to 1925 sang at the New York Metropolitan Opera. His last stage appearance was at Monte Carlo in 1937. In his day he was considered unrivalled as a singing actor. His greatest role was the title-role in **Mussorgsky**'s *Boris Godunov*, but he also excelled in French, Italian and other Russian bass parts, as well as in baritone roles, for which his voice was sufficiently flexible.

Feodor Shaliapin

An alternative transliteration of his surname is Chaliapin.

shamisen/samisen (Japan) Plucked stringed instrument with a long neck and a body made of four pieces of wood. The square sound-box is covered with catskin. An additional piece of skin is attached to provide reinforcement against the percussive blows of the large, fan-shaped, ivory plectrum (*bachi*). It has three strings of twisted silk which pass over an ivory bridge to a rope tailpiece. The upper two strings pass over a metal bridge at the top of the neck, where they are then attached to tuning pegs, but the lowest string passes through a notch in which it vibrates, providing the characteristic buzzing sound.

There are three basic tunings. The *shamisen* may be found in the **sankyoku** trio, the **bunraku** puppet theatre, the **kabuki** theatre and in the **nagauta** ensemble.

Shankar, Ravi (1920-) Indian sitarist and composer who has had a highly successful international career spanning more than 50 years, and is widely acclaimed as one of the greatest living sitarists. He received his early musical training from Ustad Allauddin Khan, subsequently becoming very active as a composer, performer and producer in India. Since his first major European tour in 1956-7 he has captured a worldwide audience, delighting them with his virtuosic technique. He has appeared with Western artists (including Yehudi **Menuhin** and George Harrison), and has made educational films; he has done much to popularize Indian music and to foster the appreciation of it in the West. His book *My Music, My Life* was published in 1969.

shanty Sailors' work-song with a strong rhythmical element, sung in the days of sailing ships to aid the rhythmic movements required when pumping, hauling ropes, hoisting sails and so on. The probable derivation is from the French word *chantez*, sing. An alternative spelling is chanty.

shape note Notation system in white spiritual singing, common in the United States during the 18th century. In order to facilitate the learning of part-singing, each syllable in the system known as **fasola** was given a distinctively shaped note-head. Two systems were in widespread use: the Little and Smith system, and the Law system, which could be used without staff notation. Also known as buckwheat notation.

Shapero, Harold (1920-) American composer who studied initially at Malkin Conservatoire, Boston, and then under **Piston, Krenek, Hindemith** and **Boulanger**. From 1970 to 1971 he was

Ravi Shankar

composer-in-residence at the American Academy in Rome. His works include *Symphony for Classical Orchestra* (1947), a cantata, *Poems of Halevi* (1954), *On Green Mountain*, for jazz combo (1958), two ballets and several piano pieces, two of which involve the use of a synthesizer.

Shaporin, Yury (1887-1966) Russian composer who graduated in law at St Petersburg University, and in 1913 entered the Conservatoire there to study under Sokolov, **Steinberg** and **Tcherepnin**. On leaving he became interested in stage music and founded the Great Dramatic Theatre with Gorky and Blok. Among his works are a symphony (1911), chamber music, incidental music for films and the stage, and one opera, *The Decembrists* (1953), based on a revolutionary incident in 1825.

sharp 1. A sign (♯) that raises a note by a semitone.

2. A note that, through either fault or design, sounds of higher pitch than written. Thus, a singer may be said to be singing sharp.

Sharp, Cecil (1859-1924) British folklorist and composer who, after a period in Australia (1889-92), returned to London where he became principal of the Hampstead Conservatoire (1896-1905). In

1899 he began collecting folk-songs and dances, which eventually totalled nearly 5,000. He founded the English Folk-Dance and Song Society (1911) and visited the United States (1916-18), collecting songs in the Appalachian Mountains, where many English songs were still preserved in their original form by descendants of 17th-century emigrants.

sharp keys Keys that have sharps in their **key-signatures**. The key of G major has one sharp, D major has two sharps, A major has three sharps, E major has four sharps, B major has five sharps, F♯ major has six sharps and C♯ major has seven sharps. In each case the relative minor keys have the same signatures as the major keys given.

Shaw, Geoffrey (1879-1943) English composer and administrator. He studied at Cambridge and became a music teacher. In 1928 he became the Board of Education's music inspector, and did much to encourage musical activity in schools and educational establishments. He was an adjudicator at numerous festivals and competitions. In 1920 he became organist at St Mary's Church, Primrose Hill, North London, succeeding his brother Martin **Shaw**. His compositions were mainly church music, although he wrote an opera, *All at Sea* (1952).

Shaw, Martin (1875-1958) British organist and composer who studied at the Royal College of Music, London, and became organist at several London churches. In association with **Vaughan Williams** he edited the hymn book *Songs of Praise*, and in 1935 became musical director to the diocese of Chelmsford. His works include the opera *Mr Pepys* (1926), a choral piece, *The Seaport*, motets, string quartets, and about 100 songs.

shawm Primitive woodwind instrument originating in the Middle East, with a double-reed mouthpiece and a wide bell. The largest types had bent tubes and were therefore similar to the **bassoon**. By the 13th century shawms were in use in Europe, and during the 17th century, with the addition of keys, they evolved into the modern **oboe**. The shawm in its original form is still used in folk-music in such countries as Tibet.

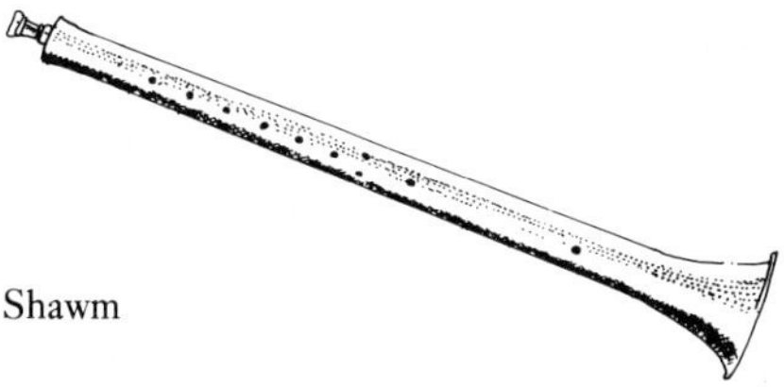

Shawm

Shchedrin, Rodion (1932-) Soviet composer who attended the Moscow Choral School (1948), where he began to compose; in 1951 he went to the Moscow Conservatoire to study with Shaporin. He is one of the most prominent Soviet composers, although his works are rarely heard in the West. His output includes the ballet *The Little Humpbacked Horse* (1956), an opera, *Not Love Alone* (1961), two symphonies, two piano concertos, three string quartets, incidental music and film scores. He is married to the ballerina Maya Plisetskaya, for whom he composed his version of Bizet's *Carmen* for strings and percussion.

sheng (China) Wind instrument, belonging to the mouth-organ family, which consists of a gourd wind-box and 17 tubes with brass reeds. It is used both in Chinese folk-music and in the classical Chinese orchestra. It is believed to have originated from the **khaen** of Laos, but predates its other relative, the Japanese **shō**. Variations are: in southern music – the wind chest is made of red wood, there are 17 pipes but only 13 have reeds; in northern music – the wind chest is copper and 14 out of the 17 pipes are reeded. The inclusion of the silent pipes is said to maintain an aesthetic visual balance.

Sheppard, John (*c*.1515-*c*.1560) English composer who learned his music as a choirboy at St Paul's Cathedral, London, under Thomas Mulliner. In 1542 he became organist and choirmaster at Magdalen College, Oxford, and later was a member of Queen Mary's Chapel Royal. His five Masses include *The Western Wynde, The French Masse* and *Playn Song Mass for a Mene*. He also composed other Latin and English church music.

Shield, William (1748-1829) British violinist and composer who studied music with **Avison** in Newcastle, where he appeared as a solo violinist from 1763. In 1772 he came to London as second violinist of the opera orchestra. Following the success of his first opera, *The Flitch of Bacon* (1778), he was appointed composer to the Covent Garden Theatre, and in 1817 he was appointed Master of the King's Music. Apart from his operas and other dramatic works, Shield also wrote string quartets, trios, songs and two treatises on harmony and thorough-bass (1800 and 1817).

Shifrin, Seymour (1926-1979) American composer who studied at the Juilliard School and at Columbia University, New York. In 1951 he went to Paris as a Fulbright Scholar to study with **Milhaud**. He taught at the University of California

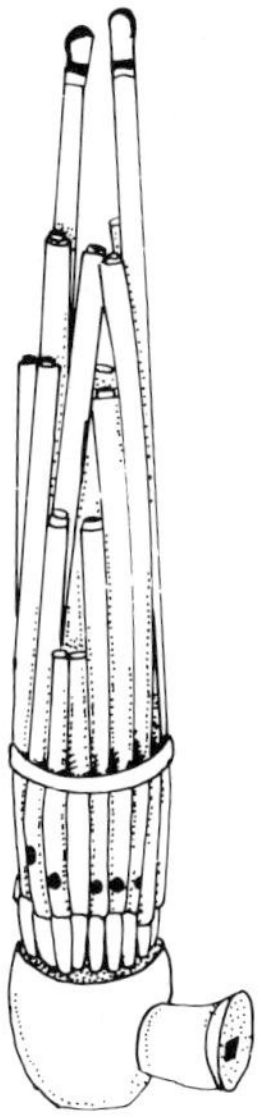

Sheng

(Los Angeles) and Brandeis. His work has neo-classical clarity; there are also influences of **Schoenberg** and his school. Apart from *Music for Orchestra* (1948) many of his works are for chamber ensemble, piano or solo singer; they include *Satires of Circumstance* (1964) for mezzo and small ensemble.

shimmy American ballroom dance that became popular after World War I. It was accompanied by jazz music and involved shaking the hips and shoulders.

Shirley-Quirk, John (1931-) British baritone who studied with Roy Henderson, and sang in St Paul's Cathedral choir (1961-2). He made his début at Glyndebourne (1962) in Debussy's *Pelléas et Mélisande*, and has since created various roles in **Britten's** operas such as *Death in Venice* (1973). His repertory is vast and includes *Lieder*; he is considered a thoughtful and sensitive artist.

Shnitke, Alfred (1934-) Soviet composer and teacher. He attended the Moscow Conservatoire from 1953 to 1958. He taught counterpoint and composition there from 1961 to 1972, working also at the Moscow Experimental Studio of Electronic Music. He has been influenced by writers of **serial** music as well as by such composers as **Stockhausen**, **Ligeti** and **Cage**. His works include the opera *The 11th Commandment* (1962); the ballets *The Labyrinth* (1971) and *Yellow Sound* (1974); a number of orchestral works including two symphonies and four violin concertos; several choral works, including the oratorio *Nagasaki* (1958), *Requiem* (1974) and *Seit Nüchtern und Wachet* (1982); several chamber works; and *The Stream* (1969) for tape.

shō (Japan) Close relative of the Chinese **sheng**, this mouth-organ has 17 reed pipes joined to a cup-shaped wind-chest. It is said to be modelled after the wings of a phoenix; the pipes are divided into two symmetrical sets in balancing pairs, two being silent to give an aesthetic balance to the instrument. The player blows through a mouthpiece set into the wind-chest and covers selected holes in the pipes to produce a variety of chords. The result is an ethereal sound in the **gagaku** orchestra. Its pipes are susceptible to moisture so the *shō* is regularly rotated over a charcoal burner during breaks in a performance to dry the reeds.

shōko (Japan) Bronze gong that is suspended in a standing frame, and appears in three sizes. It is played on the inside (back) with two hard-tipped sticks in the **gagaku** court orchestra, where it is used to subdivide the musical phrase by single beats.

shōmyō (Japan) Buddhist chant imported from China, based on sacred texts (*sutras*) and hymns. It is recorded in **neumatic** script and consists of stereotyped melodic patterns which vary between sects.

short score **Score** that is one of the composer's first drafts, in which he or she roughs out ideas for arrangement, etc.

Shostakovich, Dmitri (1906-1975) Russian composer who studied at the Conservatoire in Petrograd (Leningrad) and was encouraged by **Glazunov**. As well as composition he learnt the piano, and helped to support his family by accompanying silent films. His Symphony No.1 achieved international recognition for him at the age of 18. His second and third symphonies were less well received, but he now turned to stage music and produced his first opera, a satirical work, *The Nose* (1928). His second opera was *Lady Macbeth of the Mtsensk District* (1934); at first an outstanding success, acclaimed as a great, ideologically sound Soviet achievement, it suddenly came under bitter attack from the authorities, in an onslaught which was seen as strong disapproval of modernism. It was suppressed until 1963, when it was revised

Dmitri Shostakovich

and presented under the title of *Katerina Ismailova*. Meanwhile Shostakovich's Symphony No.5 (1937), which was subtitled *A Soviet Artist's Reply to Just Criticism*, was well received by the authorities and the public alike; he was accepted into the fold once more.

During World War II he was in Leningrad while the city was under siege, and composed his Symphony No.7, which he dedicated to the city and which earned him heroic status. It was given in most Western countries and became a symbol of resistance to the Nazis. However, in 1948 a purge of progressive artists was manifested in a resolution severely criticizing Shostakovich (and Prokofiev), and until the death of Stalin five years later he kept his more unorthodox music (including his Violin Concerto No.1) under wraps, in the meantime producing works that would not offend the retrogressive temper of the times. The Symphony No.10 appeared in 1953 and its masterly quality was recognized everywhere. The composer now produced two further symphonies, No.11 (*The Year 1905*) and No.12 (*The Year 1917*), which appeared to maintain the conservative outlook under which he had suffered; at the same time his first Cello Concerto (1959) and the String Quartets Nos.7 and 8 are music of the highest order. Symphonies No.13 (*Babi Yar*, 1962) and No.14 (1969) were both settings of poems, the one for chorus and the other for soloists; they were critically acclaimed. His last symphony, No.15, returned to the purely orchestral form.

A prolific composer, Shostakovich produced 15 string quartets, sonatas for violin, viola and cello, much piano music and several scores for ballets, films and theatre. He is, however, best remembered as the leading symphonist of the 20th century.

shruti/sruti (India) Smallest pitch interval thought to be perceivable in Indian musical theory. There are said to be 22 *shrutis* to one octave, but in practice they are never used to form a scale in this way. Particular *shrutis* are selected in a **rāga** to produce the correct intonation or 'colour' peculiar to the latter.

Shuard, Amy (1924-1975) English soprano who studied at Trinity College and was also coached by Eva **Turner**. Her operatic début was in 1949 in Johannesburg, as Aïda. On her return to London she joined the Sadler's Wells Opera, singing a wide variety of roles including the title-role of the first English *Katya Kabanova* (**Janáček**). At Covent Garden in 1958 she scored a triumph in the title-role of Puccini's *Turandot*, and was the first English Brünnhilde in the *Ring* cycle there (1964). She sang in North and South America, Vienna and Milan.

Sibelius, Jean (1865-1957) Finnish composer, the greatest of his nation, whose nationalist feeling is manifest in many of his works. He was born into a Swedish-speaking family, but learnt Finnish at school. He studied in Helsinki, then with the help of a government grant was able to study counterpoint with Becker in Berlin and, later, orchestration with Fuchs in Vienna. Returning to Finland in 1891, Sibelius became passionately nationalist; his first major work, *Kullervo* (1892), a choral symphony on episodes from the Finnish national epic *Kalevala*, scored a great success and placed him at the forefront of Finnish musical life. The tone-poem *En Saga* of the same year also called on the *Kalevala*; the orchestral suite *Karelia* and the four *Lemminkäinen Legends* of 1895 (which incorporate the elegiac *Swan of Tuonela*) likewise illustrate the national legends and are widely performed. The tone poem *Finlandia* (1899) was strongly patriotic, at a time when Finland was trying to struggle free of the Russian empire, and retains its symbolic status as a quasi-national anthem.

At this juncture Sibelius essayed his first symphony (1899); a great success, it still owed something to the style of Tchaikovsky, whose influence was very marked during Sibelius's formative years as

Jean Sibelius

a composer. The second symphony (1902) was also somewhat Tchaikovskian. It was followed by the Violin Concerto (1903), one of the most important works in the modern repertory, romantic in tone. After this a change of style became apparent, when the next symphony showed a move to a more classical mode. Symphony No.4 (1911) makes much use of the tritone interval and is sombre in mood; No.5 needed a long period of gestation before its first performance in 1915 and was much revised. The sixth (1923) and seventh (1924) symphonies round off his magnificent symphonic oeuvre, the seventh being one long unbroken movement. Sibelius made a number of trips abroad, to England, France, Austria and, in 1914, the United States. After World War I he composed little of importance except for the tone-poem *Tapiola* (1926), and the incidental music for a Shakespeare play, *The Tempest*; he retired to his country villa, where he lived on for nearly 30 years.

siciliana (It.) Sicilian dance-form in slow 6/8 or 12/8 time, usually in a minor key. Arias in *siciliana* rhythm were common in the 18th century.

side drum (snare drum) (Ger. *kleine Trommel*; It. *tamburo*; Fr. *tambour petit* or *caisse clair*) Small drum of indefinite pitch with two heads of skin or plastic stretched over a diameter of about 15 ins (40 cm) and a depth which may vary from 5 to 8 ins (12 to 20 cm). The upper is known as the 'batter head' and the lower as the 'snare head' with eight or more snares of gut, nylon or wire, which give the characteristic sound. The snares may be loosened by a lever to give a clear sound, about an octave lower in pitch and not unlike that of the deeper military drum. It is usually played with wooden sticks, according to the player's taste and the musical requirement. It needs considerable skill, especially in playing the sustained roll produced by

Side drum

recurring double beats known as Daddy-Mammy. Other patterns have self-explanatory names: diddle, paradiddle, flamacue, and single, double, and triple ratamacue. The lead into a single stroke may be a flam (an **acciaccatura**), a drag (a two-note lead) or a ruff (a three-note lead). Jazz has introduced the rim shot, and other beaters, notably the wire brush. Contemporary composers have vastly extended the range of side-drum effects, and the consequent demands on the player's skill.

Siepi, Cesare (1923-) Italian bass singer who studied at Milan Conservatoire. He made his début in Verdi's *Rigoletto* in Schio, near Venice (1941), but his career was interrupted by World War II, during which he sought refuge in Switzerland because of his anti-Fascist activities. After the war he resumed his career, appearing in Venice, Covent Garden and Milan. Between 1950 and 1974 he was a member of the New York Metropolitan Opera, where he sang in most of its repertory.

sight reading Art of playing or singing music at the first reading.

signature Directions placed on a score to indicate time (**time-signature**) or key (**key-signature**).

sijo (Korea) Short lyric song-form, which is similar in style to **kagok** (except for a distinctive use of falsetto), but with a more simple structure. The verse form of three-line stanzas dates from early dynastic times (7th-8th centuries), but the tunes in the current repertory are of much more recent origin. The *sijo* was traditionally accompanied by the **changgo** drum, but is now often complemented by a small instrumental ensemble, such as **p'iri**, **taegŭm** and **haegŭm**.

Silja, Anja (1940-) German soprano who studied with her grandfather Egon von Rijn, and made her début at the age of ten in Berlin. She was greatly influenced by Wieland **Wagner**, and closely associated with the Bayreuth Festival from 1960, where she appeared in *Wozzeck*, *Lulu*, *Otello*, *Salome* and *Elektra*, as well as in the operas of Richard Wagner. Her début at Covent Garden was in 1963 as Leonore in *Fidelio*; she sang the same role at her Metropolitan début in 1972. Silja is a vivid and compelling actress.

Sills, Beverly (1929-) American soprano who studied in New York with Estelle Liebling, and made her début in Philadelphia (1947). She joined the New York City Opera in 1955, Covent Garden in 1970 and the New York Metropolitan in 1975. She became director of the New York City Opera in 1979. Sills has a repertory of more than 60 roles, including Cleopatra in Handel's *Julius Caesar*, Elizabeth in **Donizetti**'s *Roberto Devereux*, Violetta in *La traviata* and the title-roles in **Massenet's** *Manon* and Donizetti's *Lucia di Lammermoor*, and has been successful in contemporary American operas.

silver band Band similar to the **brass band**, but in which the instruments are coated with a lacquer that makes them look as if they are made of silver.

Silvestri, Constantin (1913-1969) Romanian composer, conductor and pianist, born in Bucharest, where he studied at the Conservatoire. He worked as a pianist for some years, until in 1935 he was appointed to the music staff of the Bucharest Opera, where he was later conductor and music director (1955-60). After a highly successful engagement as a guest conductor with the London Philharmonic Orchestra he settled in England in 1960, and was the acclaimed conductor of the Bournemouth Symphony Orchestra from 1961 until his death. His many fine recordings preserve his strikingly individual interpretations.

similar motion In harmony, the movement of two parts in the same direction. The opposite is **contrary motion**. See also **parallel motion**; **oblique motion**.

simile (It.) Direction indicating that the manner of performance should continue as already indicated.

simple interval **Interval** between two notes of an **octave** or less. See also **compound interval**.

simple time Any **metre** in which the beats can be subdivided into two. Simple duple time is the name given to the signatures 2/2, 2/4, 2/8. Simple triple time applies to the signatures 3/2, 3/4, 3/8. Simple quadruple time applies to 4/2, 4/4, or 4/8. See also **compound time**.

Simpson, Robert (1921-) British composer and musicologist who originally intended to become a doctor of medicine, but after two years began to study music under **Howells** (1942-6). He joined the BBC as a member of the music staff and was a producer for many years (1951-80). He has also written studies of the works of **Nielsen**, Bruckner, **Sibelius** and Beethoven, whose influence on his own music has been considerable. Early in his composing career he made use of **serial** techniques, but all those works have been destroyed and his output since then has been firmly tonal.

In 1951 he produced what is now called his Symphony No.1, and this was the beginning of a considerable symphonic oeuvre: nine works in all. Some of these are depictions of certain moods or states of mind; all show originality in their instrumentation. He has also written eight string quartets, a concerto for violin and one for piano, a clarinet quintet, a horn quartet, the motet *Media morte in vita sumus* (1975) and music for brass band.

Sinding, Christian (1856-1941) Norwegian pianist and composer who trained as a violinist, but in 1874 abandoned the violin and went to Leipzig University to study composition. He spent 40 years in Germany and a brief time in the United States (1920-1), where he taught theory and composition at the Eastman School, New York.

His works include an opera, *Der heilige Berg* (1912), orchestral, chamber and piano music and about 250 songs. Probably his best-known work is the piano piece *Rustle of Spring* (1896).

sinfonia 1. An alternative term for **symphony**.

2. Used by Bach for many of his three-part compositions.

3. Used during the early Baroque period to refer to an instrumental piece played at the beginning of an opera – what we now call the **overture**.

4. A small symphony orchestra.

sinfonia concertante (It.) Used by Haydn and Mozart to refer to an orchestral piece that featured one or more solo instruments.

sinfonietta (It.) 1. A small-scale **symphony**. It has been used as a title for orchestral pieces by such 20th-century composers as **Roussel**, **Prokofiev**, **Janáček** and **Moeran**.

2. A small symphony orchestra.

Singspiel (Ger.) Form of popular **opera** in Germany and Austria during the 18th century, in which the dialogue was spoken rather than sung. The French equivalent of the *Singspiel* was the **opéra-comique**.

The principal composer of the *Singspiel* was Johann Adam **Hiller** (1728-1804), whose work *Die Jagd* (1770) had a comic plot. In **Mozart**'s operas *Die Entführung aus dem Serail* (1782) and *Die Zauberflöte* (1791) the score often included features of both *Singspiel* and **opera seria**.

Sinopoli, Giuseppe (1946-) Italian conductor and composer who after attending the Venice Conservatoire studied composition with **Maderna** and **Stockhausen**. He went to Vienna in 1972, where he studied conducting. He founded the Maderna Ensemble in 1975 and made his operatic début conducting *Aïda* in Venice in 1978. He has also appeared at Covent Garden and at the Metropolitan,

New York. His compositions include a piano concerto, vocal music and some tape works. He has been principal conductor of the Philharmonia Orchestra since 1984, and has made numerous recordings of the Romantic and 20th-century repertories.

sitār (India) Stringed instrument predominant in northern India, related to the **bīn**, which it has almost superseded. It is a long-necked, plucked lute and occasionally has a small gourd fastened to its upper end. It has movable frets, with additional **drone** and sympathetic strings.

Sitār

Six, Les Group of six French composers who, in 1917, formed an anti-Impressionist movement of a **neo-classical** nature. The Six were Darius **Milhaud**, Arthur **Honegger**, Francis **Poulenc**, Germaine **Tailleferre**, Georges **Auric** and Louis **Durey**. Erik **Satie** and Jean Cocteau were associated with the group.

sixth Interval of six notes (counting the lowest and highest notes). A major sixth consists of nine semitones (say, C-A), and a minor sixth consists of eight semitones (say, C-G♯). See also **augmented sixth**; **Neapolitan sixth**.

sixty-fourth note Alternative term for **hemidemisemiquaver**.

ska (Caribbean) Jamaican popular dance music, which originated in the late 1950s, with rhythms characterized by a persistent off-beat emphasis adapted from American **boogie-woogie** and **rhythm and blues** styles, particularly those of black musicians from the southern states. From the mid-1960s it was replaced by a slower, modified form known as rock-steady, which soon was to develop into **reggae**.

Skalkottas, Nikos (1904-1949) Greek composer who began studying the violin at the age of five and entered the Athens Conservatoire at ten, graduating in 1920. In 1921 he won a scholarship to the Hochschule für Musik in Berlin, where he studied with **Schoenberg, Weill** and Jarnach.

Although he had a promising career as a violinist, he concentrated on composition. Returning to Athens in 1933, poor and ill, he played the violin in an orchestra and composed in his spare time. Some of his works show the influence of Schoenberg, whereas others have been influenced by his collection of Greek folk-music.

Skalkottas's works include three piano concertos, the ballet *The Maiden and Death* (1938), *36 Greek Dances* (1931-6), an overture entitled *The Return of Ulysses* (1942-3), chamber works, and piano pieces.

sketch 1. A short instrumental piece, usually for the piano, which describes some scene in musical terms.

2. Used to refer to the first draft of a composition.

Slatkin, Leonard (1944-) American conductor who studied at the Juilliard School. He was associate conductor of the St Louis Symphony Orchestra, becoming music director in 1979. He has also worked with the New Orleans Philharmonic and has appeared many times in Britain and Europe. His wide repertory includes modern and Romantic music.

slatt Norwegian folk-tune played on a **Hardänger fiddle**. Originally it was in the form of a march. **Grieg** and fellow

Norwegian composers have transcribed the *slatt* for other instruments.

slèndro (Indonesia) One of two tonal systems, consisting of five nearly equal tones within an octave. In Java, there are three *patet* (modes) in slèndro tuning: *manyura*, *sanga* and *nem*, corresponding to specific times of the day. See also **pélog**.

slentem (Java) One-octave, bronze metallophone of the **gamelan** ensemble, with thin keys resting over bamboo resonating chambers. It is struck with a padded disc attached to the end of a stick. In the 'soft style' of Javanese *gamelan* playing, the *slentem* carries the basic melodic line, while other instruments elaborate upon it.

slide 1. The technique of passing from one note to another on stringed instruments by moving the finger along the string instead of lifting it; a **glissando**.

2. A device on a **trombone** for changing the length of the tube in order to make available different ranges of **harmonics**.

3. An **ornament** consisting of two notes leading up to a principal note.

Slobodskaya, Oda (1888-1970) Russian soprano who studied in St Petersburg (Leningrad) and made her début there as Lisa in *The Queen of Spades* (Tchaikovsky) in 1919, singing many other Russian roles as well. She sang Parasha in Stravinsky's *Mavra* in Paris (1922); this was the first of many tours which she made to the West, and she eventually settled in London. Her first London appearance was in *Rusalka* (**Dargomizhsky**); she also sang Venus in *Tannhäuser* and in the first production of **Delius**'s *Koanga*. She made many broadcasts and recitals, especially of Russian songs, and later taught at the Guildhall School.

Slonimsky, Nicolas (1894-) Russian author and composer who studied at St Petersburg Conservatoire, and in 1923 settled in the United States where he became a naturalized citizen in 1931. He was conductor of the Boston Chamber Orchestra (1927-34), and conducted his own work *Fragment from Orestes* in 1933. Another of his works was *Suite in Black and White* for piano. He was particularly well-known as editor of the *International Cyclopedia of Music and Musicians*, a position he first held in 1946.

slur Arching stroke written over two or more notes indicating that they are to be played **legato**, or with one stroke of the bow. It is also used in vocal music where two or more notes are to be sung in the same syllable.

Slur

Smalley, Roger (1943-) British composer and pianist who studied with **Fricker** at the Royal College of Music and attended **Stockhausen**'s courses in Cologne. His repertory as a pianist included many of Stockhausen's works, and he also helped to make known the latter's electronic compositions in Britain. In 1967 he was artist-in-residence at King's College, Cambridge, and in 1970 he founded Intermodulation, a modern-music ensemble. Since 1976 he has lived mainly in Australia.

For a period Smalley experimented with Renaissance material and procedures, but later followed Stockhausen by adopting moment-form, improvisatory elements and electronic music. His works include *Missa brevis* for 16 solo voices (1967) and its companion pieces, *Gloria tibi Trinitas I*, *Missa parodia I* and *II*; *Pulses* (1969), *Beat Music* for 55 players (1971), *Strata* (1973), *Zeitebenen* for tape (1973), *Accord* (1975) and *Echo I-III* (1978). He has also written a string quartet, a piano concerto (1985) and an 'entertainment', *William Derrincourt*, on an Australian subject.

Smetana, Bedřich (1824-1884) Czech (Bohemian) composer, pianist and conductor. The son of a master brewer, he started lessons on the piano and the violin at the age of five and played in public when he was seven. By the age of 16 he could list 14 compositions for string quartet or piano, being particularly proud of some polkas. When he was 19 he wrote: 'By the grace of God and with his help I shall one day be a Liszt in technique, in composition a Mozart.' A post as piano teacher to a family in Prague helped him with much-needed money to continue his studies, but in desperate straits he sent some compositions to Liszt, asking for a loan to set up a music school; Liszt arranged for some of the music to be published, but Smetana received neither loan nor fee, though Liszt remained a friend and adviser throughout his life. In 1849 he married his childhood sweetheart, Katerina Kolar, and was able to set up his music school; in 1855 he put on a concert in Prague, conducting his own music and playing solos, but having made little impression took up a position in Göteborg, Sweden, as conductor and teacher.

Despite being a poor Czech speaker he resolved to learn the language and create a Czech national style. On their way home in 1859, his wife became ill and died. In the following year, having remarried, he turned to the theatre and with his historical opera *The Brandenburgers in Bohemia* (1863) and the comic opera *The Bartered Bride* (1864) opened a new era in Czech national music, although the latter opera was not an immediate success. Having been appointed conductor in 1866, in 1868 amid scenes of great celebration Smetana laid the foundation stone of the new national theatre, and conducted the first performance of his dramatic opera *Dalibor*. With this, *Libuše* (1871), and *The Kiss* (1875) Smetana revealed himself a dramatic composer of a high order. With his hearing severely impaired as a result of syphilis, he was forced in 1874 to give up conducting, but began the composition of the six tone-poems which he called *Ma Vlast* (My Homeland). They include *Vltava*, the picture of the river that flows through Prague, and *From Bohemia's Woods and Fields*. He also composed the fine autobiographical string quartet *From my Life* (1876), where he recalls the tinnitus that signalled the onset of his deafness by giving the violin a high sustained note at the start of the finale. In his last years he was accorded great honours, but became insane and died in an asylum.

Smith Brindle, Reginald (1917-) English composer who studied in Bangor, North Wales, and with Dallapiccola in Italy, where he worked for Italian radio. At first his music inclined to the **serial**; the Symphony of 1954 was followed by *Variations on a Theme of Dallapiccola* (1955) and *Via Crucis* (1960). Later he tended to electronic music (*Apocalypse*, 1970) which was sometimes combined with conventional forces (*The Walls of Jericho* for tuba and tape, 1975). He has also composed **aleatory** works, and much music for guitar.

Smyth, Dame Ethel (1858-1944) British composer who entered Leipzig Conservatoire in 1877, where she also studied privately with Herzogenberg. Her earlier operas (*Fantastic*, 1898, and *The Forest*, 1903) were produced in Germany, but her best were probably *The Wreckers* (1906) and *The Boatswain's Mate* (1916). Smyth's works were full of strong rhythms and well orchestrated, and in spite of her firm belief in English musical nationalism, the influence of earlier training in Germany is evident. Her Mass in D (1891), for instance, has a somewhat Beethovenian flavour.

On her return to England in 1910 she became active in the movement for women's suffrage, and in that cause she spent two months in prison (1911). She composed *The March of Women* (1911) as the battle-song of the militant suffragettes. A choral symphony, *The Prison*, was written in 1930; other works include orchestral pieces, chamber music and songs. She was created a DBE in 1922.

snare drum Alternative term for **side drum**.

soave (It.) Sweet, gentle.

Söderström, Elisabeth (1927-) Swedish soprano who studied in Stockholm, where she made her début in 1947. Since joining the Royal Swedish Opera, Stockholm (1950), her highly successful career has taken her to Glyndebourne, Salzburg, Covent Garden and the Metropolitan Opera, New York. She was one of the finest singing actresses of the 1960s and 1970s, and is especially well-known for her roles in the operas of Mozart, Strauss, **Janáček** and Tchaikovsky. Her Leonore in Beethoven's *Fidelio* is also outstanding. She has made fine recordings of Janáček's operas *Jenůfa* and *Katya Kabanova*.

Elisabeth Söderström

soh, so Name given to the fifth note of the scale in the **tonic sol-fa** system and the note G in continental practice.

Sohal, Naresh (1939-) Indian composer who studied in England with Jeremy Dale Roberts and Alexander **Goehr**. His works include a harmonica concerto, a piece for unaccompanied soprano saxophone, a piece for unaccompanied flute and vocal pieces.

Soler, Antonio (1729-1783) Spanish friar, organist and composer who was a pupil of Domenico **Scarlatti** (1752-7). He was a chorister at Montserrat and in 1750 was appointed *maestro de capilla* at Lérida Cathedral. In 1752 he entered the Escorial monastery, becoming organist and choirmaster there the following year. Soler's works include Masses, motets and other sacred music, quintets and concertos for organ. His best-known works are the 120 sonatas for harpsichord, many of them based on Spanish dance-forms.

sol-fa See **tonic sol-fa**

solfège (Fr.), **solfeggio** (It.) 1. The system of instruction in sight-singing and ear-training, in which the student names the notes. The scale of C is *do re mi fa so la si do*; these names are unchanged by chromatic alteration. The system is also categorized as the fixed do or **doh** system, as opposed to the movable do system, **tonic sol-fa**, invented by **Curwen**, in which the tonic note of a key is the do. Solfège is regarded in many countries as the essential foundation of musical skill; at the Paris Conservatoire a student, however gifted, would not be eligible for the highest awards without qualifying in solfège.

2. Singing exercises to develop various aspects of vocalization, in which the notes are named as above.

solmization Designation of the musical **scales** by means of syllables. The notes of the Greek **tetrachords** were already designated by syllables, but in the 11th century **Guido d'Arezzo** replaced them by the **hexachords** and used the Latin syllables Ut, Re, Mi, Fa, Sol, La for their six notes, Si being added later for the seventh and Ut being replaced by Do (except in France). The syllables were derived from the hymn for the festival of John the Baptist (770), the first syllable beginning on successive notes of the hexachord: *Ut* queant laxis; *Re*sonare fibris; *Mi*ra gestorum; *Fa*muli tuorum; *Sol*ve polluti; *La*bii reatum; *S*ancte *I*oannes. The seventh syllable, Si, was derived from the initial letters of the last line. The **tonic sol-fa** is a modern derivative of this system.

solo Composition or part of a composition played by a single performer with or without accompaniment.

Solomon (Solomon Cutner) (1902-1988) English pianist of great distinction, who first appeared as a child prodigy at the age of eight playing Tchaikovsky's Piano Concerto No.1, having been taught with unrelenting severity by Mathilde Verne, a period he later recalled with great bitterness. A severe stroke at the age of 53 left him paralysed, but his recordings reveal a player of wide sympathies and deep musical understanding. He was made a CBE in 1946.

Solti, Sir Georg (1912-) Hungarian-born conductor and pianist who studied piano with **Dohnányi** and composition with **Kodály** and **Bartók** at Budapest Conservatoire. He was a *répétiteur* at the Budapest Opera, then worked with **Toscanini** at the Salzburg Festival in 1936 and 1937, moving to Switzerland in 1939, where he came to notice by winning an important piano competition. In 1946, despite his lack of musical experience, he was appointed music director of the Munich Opera; in 1952 he moved to Frankfurt, and raised the opera company there to a high standard. This success led to his being appointed music director at Covent Garden in 1961, a position he held with distinction for ten years. During this time he often conducted the world's leading orchestras in concerts and recordings, and in 1971 was appointed music director of the Chicago Symphony Orchestra, from which he retired in 1989. His award-winning records have covered a very wide range. Most outstanding were the first complete studio recording of Wagner's *Ring*, made with the Vienna

Sir Georg Solti

Philharmonic, operas by Mozart, Verdi and Puccini, and a series of Beethoven's symphonies. He was made an honorary KBE in 1971, and became a British citizen in 1972.

Somers, Harry (1925-) Canadian composer who was a pupil of **Milhaud** in Paris. His opera *Louis Riel* (1967) is considered to be the finest by a Canadian. It was commissioned by the Canadian Opera Company in Toronto, and has since been broadcast on both radio and television. Somers wrote two other operas, *The Fool* (1953) and *The Homeless Ones* (1955). He has also written three string quartets, orchestral and vocal pieces.

Somervell, Sir Arthur (1863-1937) British composer and educationist who was a pupil of **Stanford** and **Parry**. In 1894 he became a professor at the Royal College of Music, and in 1901 an inspector of music in schools, for which work he was knighted in 1929. His works include choral music, songs and piano pieces.

sona (China) Wind instrument, literally 'brass-mounted horn', because of its wide, open brass mouth. It is a folk instrument with a small, double-reed mouthpiece, fixed to a wooden pipe, with six upper finger-holes and one behind.

sonata In Italian it means literally a piece 'sounded' as opposed to *toccata*, touched, in keyboard music, and *cantata*, sung. Originally therefore it was applied to a piece of instrumental music other than for keyboard, and had no specific formal connotation. In the 18th century it came to be applied to instrumental works for a solo keyboard, or for other solo instruments with keyboard accompaniment. These consisted sometimes of one movement, for example the harpsichord sonatas of Domenico **Scarlatti**, but later of three or four, which displayed an organic relationship and the use of **sonata form** in the first and sometimes in the last movement. This form of the sonata reached its peak of development in the classical period in the works of Haydn, Mozart, Beethoven and Schubert, but it would be misleading to suggest that it was rigidly adhered to – indeed, in the late piano sonatas of Beethoven it is difficult to find any consistent pattern. This tendency was further extended later in the 19th century – Liszt's piano sonata, for example, is in one movement. In the 20th century the name has been freely applied not only to solo works, but to works for instrumental ensembles, though composers have been much less inclined to use the term, because of its traditional formal connotations.

sonata form Also called *first movement form*, it describes an extended movement, usually the first of classical and many later sonatas, symphonies or chamber works. It is in three parts, sometimes preceded by an introduction: in the first part, or **exposition**, the main ideas are presented, usually consisting of a first group of theme or themes in the tonic key, followed by the contrasting second group in a related key, usually the dominant or the relative minor, and ending in that key; in the second part, or **development**, the composer plays around with the themes, developing them by repetition or fragmentation, or by ingenious combinations, always using key contrast to heighten the progress of the movement; in the third part, or **recapitulation**, the composer repeats the first part, usually with some freedom, but ends in the tonic key. This is sometimes followed by a coda or tail-piece, which may introduce new thematic material.

The form so described exists only in the eye of the analyst, for there are as many variants as there are compositions. According to the theorist **Schenker** it should be considered as the expansion of three chords, of which the first and third are of the tonic or home key, and the middle one the dominant or relative minor. Its power, however, lies in the contrast of themes and keys, struggle and resolution – a power which was at the heart of Western symphonic music.

song A term loosely used to describe any short vocal composition, whether solo or accompanied, although it is also applied to the sounds produced by birds and whales. One may assume that primitive man's earliest attempts at music were with the voice, and in a sense this natural expression survived in folk-songs, which seem always to have existed beside the more elaborate music of ancient Egyptian ceremonies, Greek tragedy, or manifold religious activities. Our earliest certain knowledge of 'song' comes from its sly intrusion as a **cantus firmus** into medieval church music. The first art-songs were the ballads and lays of the **troubadour**, the minstrel or the court jester, probably performed with an improvised accompaniment on a plucked string instrument. The development of the modern form of song depended largely on the forms of lyric poetry, with its repeated stanza and simple metres; this was remarkably demonstrated in the **madrigals** and lute songs of the 16th and 17th centuries, which have preserved poetry, often by unknown hands, which otherwise would have been lost. Outstanding exponents of this form were Luis de **Milan** (1500-61) in Spain and John **Dowland** (1563-1626) in England. Such music was intended for intimate performance, at best for a rich patron, but often in the home. Many Italian songs now performed under the title *Arie antiche*, for example by **Caccini** or Benedetto **Marcello**, are arrangements of what are usually called arias, part of an extended secular or sacred work.

The next important development of the solo song was in the 18th century in German-speaking countries; in English-speaking countries they are now universally given the generic title of *Lieder*, though to the German the word simply means songs, and would be applied to the works of the Beatles as well as to Brahms. The influence of folk-song is evident in the melodies of Mozart's *Das Veilchen*, Schubert's *Heidenröslein*, Brahms's *Kinderlieder*, and especially Mahler's settings of the folk-poetry of *Des Knaben Wunderhorn*, but the essence of the *Lied* was the continually varied melodic line, with the closely integrated accompaniment underlining and elaborating the emotional expression of many fine examples of German Romantic lyric poetry, set by Schubert, Schumann, Brahms and **Wolf**.

Comparable French poetry developed later, in the second half of the 19th century, and stimulated the composition of songs by such composers as **Massenet**, **Fauré**, **Debussy** and **Duparc**, who produced the French equivalent of the *Lied*, called *mélodie*, as opposed to the folk-like, strophic *chanson*, which would be used for the works of Edith Piaf or Cole Porter. The *mélodie* was developed in the 20th century in the fine songs by **Ravel**, **Poulenc** and **Messiaen**. While Britain could not boast composers comparable with the German genius, the wealth of English poetry in the 19th century provided material for many songs of a sentimental or patriotic character, favourites at Victorian ballad concerts, as well as round the parlour piano on a Sunday evening. The 20th century ushered in a glorious period of English song, comparable with the great achievements of the Tudor period. Once again it was stimulated by the wealth of lyric poetry that appeared at this time, beautifully set by **Vaughan Williams**, **Warlock**, Armstrong **Gibbs**, **Delius**, **Moeran**, or **Gurney**. Similar schools of song were found in Russia, notably in the fine examples by **Mussorgsky**, Tchaikovsky and **Rachmaninov**. In recent years composers have turned aside from the established form with piano accompaniment, preferring to compose for the solo voice with chamber ensemble in settings which few would care to describe as songs. There is, however, unflagging appeal in the popular forms produced with such charm by **Gershwin**, Cole **Porter**, Paul McCartney or Stephen Sondheim, dealing, as songs have always done, with love, the changing seasons, life and death.

song-cycle Group of songs set to a number of poems with a connecting narrative or other unifying feature. Examples include Schubert's *Die schöne Müllerin* (1823), Beethoven's *An die ferne Geliebte* (1816), **Debussy's** *Chansons de Bilitis* (1897) and **Vaughan Williams's** *On Wenlock Edge* (1909).

sopila (Yugoslavia) Conical oboe with six finger-holes. On the island of Krk, where they are most commonly used, two different sizes are paired, playing in a narrow interval style. See also **diaphonic song**.

soprano Highest female voice, with an effective range of more than two octaves, the lowest note being around middle C. The soprano voice has three categories and they are classified as dramatic, lyric or coloratura. Boy sopranos are known as trebles. Soprano also refers to instruments that sound in that range, for example the soprano saxophone.

Sor, Fernando (1778-1839) Spanish guitarist and composer who was educated at the choir school of the monastery at Montserrat. He went to London (1815), to Russia to see the performance of his ballet *Cendrillon* (1822), and finally to Paris (1826).

Sor became a celebrated guitarist and teacher who composed mainly for his instrument. His other works include the operas *Telemaco* (1797) and *Don Trastillo* (1797, now lost), and seven ballets (three of which have been lost), two symphonies and three string quartets.

Sorabji, Kaikhosru Shapurji (Leon Dudley Sorabji) (1892-) British-born composer and pianist, son of a Parsee father and Spanish mother, who was mainly self-taught. He has appeared in London, Paris and Vienna as a pianist in performances of his own works. His compositions include many works for piano such as a two-hour *Opus clavicembalisticum* (1929-30), orchestral and organ pieces. In 1940 he banned public performances of his compositions, with the exception of works involving two performers; this ban was relaxed in 1976.

sordino Italian term for **mute**.

sostenuto (It.) Sustained, a direction to indicate either style or tempo of performance.

Sotin, Hans (1939-) German bass who studied in Dortmund and in 1964 joined the Hamburg opera. There he quickly took on many important roles in the German repertory, including Wotan in the *Ring* cycle. He appeared at Glyndebourne as Sarastro in *Die Zauberflöte* in 1970, and has sung in Chicago, at the Metropolitan, New York, at Bayreuth, Vienna, and Milan. His roles include Hunding (*Die Walküre*), Fafner (*Siegfried*), King Marke (*Tristan und Isolde*), Hans Sachs (*Die Meistersinger von Nürnberg*) and Baron Ochs (*Der Rosenkavalier*). He has a considerable recital and concert repertory and has made many recordings.

sotto voce (It.) Indication that a passage is to be performed in an undertone. Originally applied to vocal music, it also came to be applied to instrumental music.

soubrette (Fr.) In opera and operetta, a stock but usually secondary role, such as a maid or serving girl, played by a singer with a light soprano voice. An example is Despina in Mozart's *Così fan tutte* (1790). Occasionally a *soubrette* may assume a principal role, such as Serpina in **Pergolesi**'s *La serva padrona* (1733).

soul music Form of African-American popular music, derived from gospel music blended with **rhythm and blues**. Its popularity since the 1960s has given international fame to such artists as Ray Charles, James Brown, Otis Redding and Aretha Franklin.

Sousa, John Philip (1854-1932) American bandmaster and composer whose early career was as an orchestral violinist. In

1880 he became master of the US Marine Corps Band and in 1892 formed his own band, which achieved international fame and popularity. He composed several operettas, including *El Capitan* (1895), but he is mainly known for his marches such as *The Thunderer* (1889), *The Washington Post* (1899), *King Cotton* (1895), *The Stars and Stripes Forever* (1897) and *Hands Across the Sea* (1899).

sousaphone Instrument of the **tuba** family, mainly in use in the United States. It sounds in the bass register and has an enormous bell turned upwards and through two right angles. It was invented for use in the band of John **Sousa** in 1899.

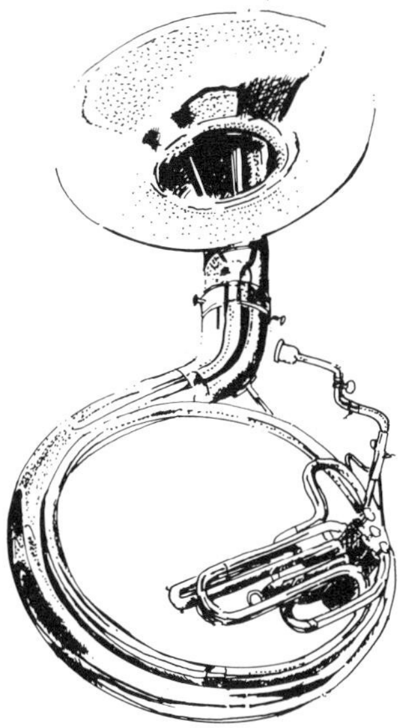

Sousaphone

Souster, Tim (1943-) British composer who was a pupil of **Stockhausen, Berio** and Richard Rodney **Bennett**, and formerly a BBC producer. His works were very much influenced by rock music and group improvisation techniques. Together with **Smalley** he founded the ensemble Intermodulation (1970). His works include *Chinese Whispers*, for percussion and three synthesizers (1970); *Triple Music*, for three orchestras (1970); *Spectral* (1972); *Arcane Artefact* (1976); and *Arboreal Antecedents* (1978).

soutenu (Fr.) Sustained. Alternative term for the Italian **sostenuto**.

Souzay, Gerard (1920-) French baritone who studied with Pierre **Bernac** and made his début in Paris in 1945. He sang in London the same year and in New York in 1950. He is notable for his mastery of the 17th- and 19th-century French repertory: **Lully** and **Rameau**; **Berlioz**, **Fauré** and **Debussy**. He is also an outstanding interpreter of German *Lieder*: Schubert, Schumann and **Wolf**. He has had several operatic roles, beginning with the title-role in Monteverdi's *Orfeo* in New York (1960). He has made numerous fine recordings of his song repertory, often accompanied by Dalton Baldwin.

species counterpoint Counterpoint is taught in five progressive stages, known as the five species. In each, the student adds one or more lines above, or below, a **cantus** *firmus*, of one note to the bar, and works within a limiting set of grammatical rules.

In the first species, one note is written against each note of the *cantus firmus*. The second species consists of two notes against each note of the *cantus firmus*; the third species, four against one. The fourth species is concerned with **suspensions**, and the fifth species allows a combination of any of the preceding species.

speech song (Ger. *Sprechgesang*) Form of singing midway between speech and song. It is used especially by **Schoenberg** in his *Pierrot lunaire* (1912), a song-cycle of 21 poems.

Speer, Daniel (1636-1707) German composer, theorist and writer who composed mainly church music and **quodlibets**. He is probably best known for his theoretical writings, such as *Grund-richtiger Unterricht* (1687), which deals with performance practice.

spiccato Light **staccato** produced on stringed instruments by the bow bouncing on the string with alternating up and down bowing; there is also thrown *spiccato* with several notes in one bow.

spinet Instrument of the **harpsichord** family, in use between the late 17th century and the end of the 18th century. It was wing-shaped, with strings running diagonally to the keyboard (as opposed to parallel to it, as was the case with the **virginals**).

An alternative name for the spinet was the couched harp. The term spinet is also incorrectly used to mean a square piano.

Spinet

spinto (It.) Pushed. Operatic style in which the voice (especially one with highly lyrical qualities) is used in a more forceful manner.

spirito (It.) Indication that a movement or passage is to be performed briskly and energetically (*con spirito*).

spiritual Type of religious folk-song developed by African slaves in America, originally during the religious revival there, which began in the 1740s. Many follow a structure in which lines sung by a soloist alternate with choral refrains, as in *Swing Low, Sweet Chariot*. Spirituals such as *Go Down Moses* reflect the sense of identity that blacks have felt with the Israelites in bondage in Egypt. Sir Michael **Tippett** used five very popular spirituals as chorales in his oratorio *A Child of Our Time*. They included *Steal Away*, *Nobody Knows the Trouble I Seen*, *Go Down Moses*, *By and By* and the intensely devotional *Deep River*.

Spohr, Louis (Ludwig) (1784-1859) German composer, violinist and conductor who first learned music from his parents. He was employed as a violinist at the court of the Duke of Brunswick, who paid for his private tuition and arranged for him to go on a concert tour with Franz Eck. Returning to Brunswick (1803) as a celebrated violin virtuoso, he became leader in the Duke of Gotha's orchestra (1805-12), and then musical director of the Theater an der Wien, Vienna (1812-15). He was also conductor of the Frankfurt Opera (1817-19) and from 1822 musical director at the court of Kassel. In 1842 Spohr became the first musician of importance to support Wagner when he helped him to produce *Der fliegende Holländer* (1843) at Kassel. It is said that Spohr was one of the first orchestral conductors to use a **baton**.

Spohr's output was extremely varied and he is considered a leading early Romantic. He wrote 11 operas including *Faust* (1816), the première of which was conducted by **Weber**, *Zemire und Azor* (1819) and *Jessonda* (1823), his greatest operatic success. Spohr also wrote 15 violin concertos, nine symphonies, four clarinet concertos, chamber music, 34 string quartets, seven string quintets and more than 90 songs.

Spontini, Gaspare (1774-1851) Italian composer and conductor who studied at Naples Conservatoire (1793-5). His first opera (*Li puntigli delle donne*, 1796) was produced in Rome and was an immediate success. In 1798 he went to Palermo with the Neapolitan court as musical director, and in 1802 to Paris where his opera *La vestale* (1807) led to his recognition as one of the leading opera composers of the day. He also came under the patronage of the Empress Josephine, and was appointed director of the Théâtre-Italien in 1810. Spontini became musical director to the court of Frederick William III in Berlin (1820), and although he introduced excellent reforms at the court opera, his success was overshadowed by the acclaim given to **Weber**'s *Der Freischütz* (1821), and the acceptance of German opera in general. In addition, because of his autocratic and difficult nature he continued to clash with court officials, and conceived an intense dislike for **Meyerbeer**, whose works were outgrowing his in popularity. Finally he was pensioned off in 1842 and went to live in Paris. He became deaf in 1848 and returned to his birthplace, founding a music school in Jesi. His other operas include *Milton* (1804), *Julie* (1805), *Ferdinand Cortez* (1809), *Olympie* (1819) and *Agnes von Hohenstaufen* (1829).

Sprechgesang See **speech song**

springer An **ornament** in which an extra note is inserted between two other notes. It is the opposite of an **appoggiatura,** because it robs the preceding note of part of its time value.

Springer

square piano Form of **piano** that is rectangular in shape with strings running parallel to the keyboard.

sruti (India) See **shruti**

stabile (It.) Orchestra that is permanent, regular or resident.

staccato (It.) Indication that notes marked with dots above them should be slightly shorter than their normal time value and distinctly separated. The shortness of the notes and the degree of separation is a matter of style and individual judgement, determined by the tempo and character of the movement.

Stade, Frederica von (1945-) American mezzo-soprano who studied in New York and joined the Metropolitan Opera in 1969. Her début a year later was in *Die Zauberflöte.* She has often sung Cherubino (*Le nozze di Figaro*), a part in which she excels; she is also an admired Octavian (*Der Rosenkavalier*), Dorabella (*Così fan tutte*) and Rosina (*Il barbiere di Siviglia*). She made her Glyndebourne début in 1973 (as Cherubino) and has sung at Covent Garden, Paris and various American houses. She has a wide concert and recital repertory and has made a number of recordings.

Stadler, Anton (1753-1812) Austrian clarinettist and basset-horn player who was a member of the Vienna Court Orchestra. He was a close friend of **Mozart,** who wrote for him the Trio, K498, for piano, clarinet and viola (the 'Kegelstadt', 1786), the Clarinet Quintet, K581 (1789) and the Clarinet Concerto in A Major, K622 (1791). He wrote some works for the clarinet and the basset-horn. He also prepared a plan for a music-school education (1800).

Square piano

Städtische Oper (Ger.) Municipal Opera, either a house or a company.

staff Set of five horizontal lines on which music is commonly notated. The position of a note on or between the lines (along with the key signature) denotes its pitch. The system of time signature and bar lines indicates the rhythmic component. An alternative form is stave. See also **score**.

Stainer, Sir John (1840-1901) English composer, organist and scholar who became a chorister in 1848 at St Paul's Cathedral, and in 1854 an organist, first in London, then in Tenbury. He studied at Christ Church, Oxford (1859-66), and founded the Oxford Philharmonic Society. He was organist at St Paul's Cathedral (1872-88), but because of failing eyesight had to resign. He assisted Sir Frederick **Ouseley** in founding the Musical Association. He was knighted in 1888 and the following year was appointed professor of music at Oxford. From 1881 he was principal of the National Training School for Music.

His compositions are mainly of sacred music, including services, hymns and anthems; the oratorios *Gideon* (1865) and *The Crucifixion* (1887), and the cantata *The Story of the Cross* (1893), all of which remain popular to the present day. He was a scholar of early music, being president of the Plainsong and Medieval Music Society and editing (with his son and daughter) an important collection. He edited other collections, notably *Christmas Carols New and Old* (1871).

Stamitz, Anton (1754-*c.*1809) Bohemian violinist and composer and brother of Carl **Stamitz**, a pupil of his father and **Cannabich**. Together with his brother he went to Paris (1770), where he settled as a violinist in the court orchestra. His works included 12 symphonies, and concertos for violin, viola, flute and oboe.

Stamitz, Carl (1745-1801) Bohemian violinist and composer, son of Johann Wenzel **Stamitz**. He entered the Mannheim orchestra as second violinist (1762), and in 1770 he went to Paris where he achieved great success as both violinist and composer. From 1777 he travelled widely until in 1794 he settled in Jena as musical director at the university. He wrote more than 50 symphonies, 38 *symphonies concertantes* and a great deal of chamber music.

Stamitz, Johann Wenzel (1717-1757) Bohemian violinist and composer who received his early teaching from his father. He was appointed to the Mannheim court in 1741 as violin virtuoso and later (1750) as music director. Under him the Mannheim orchestra became the most famous in Europe: he was responsible for training the players in precision of attack, and this style was the foundation of the 'Mannheim School'. His works included 74 symphonies and concertos for violin, harpsichord, flute, oboe and clarinet.

Standford, Patric (1939-) English composer who was a pupil of **Rubbra, Malipiero** and **Lutosławski**. Some of his compositions occasionally use **aleatory** techniques. His works include *Christus-Requiem*, for narrator, child and adult voices and orchestra, two symphonies, two string quartets and a sonata for unaccompanied violin.

Stanford, Sir Charles Villiers (1852-1924) English composer, teacher, conductor and organist who studied at Queen's College, Cambridge (1870-3) and in Germany, and was appointed organist of Trinity College (1873-82). For the Cambridge University Musical Society he composed *The Resurrection* (1875) and other works. His reputation was further advanced when Tennyson asked him to write the incidental music for *Queen Mary* (1876). When the Royal College of Music opened in 1883 he was made professor of composition, and from 1885 to 1902 he was conductor of the London Bach Choir. In 1887 he was elected professor of music at Cambridge, and in 1902 knighted. He was a prolific composer of sacred music: services, anthems and motets. Some of his finest oratorios and cantatas include *The Three Holy Children* (1885), *The Revenge* (1886), *Songs of the Sea* (1904) and the *Stabat Mater* (1907). He also composed ten operas, including *Shamus O'Brien* (1896), *Much Ado About Nothing* (1908) and *The Travelling Companion*, which was performed posthumously. His instrumental music included seven symphonies, three piano concertos, two violin concertos, string and piano quartets and two cello sonatas.

Stanley, John (1712-1786) English composer and organist who was blind from the age of two, but became a pupil of **Greene** and held various organ posts in London. In 1779 he succeeded **Boyce** as Master of the King's Musick. He became famous for his organ voluntaries, and in addition he wrote 12 cantatas, six concertos for strings, the dramatic pastoral *Arcadia* (1761) and keyboard and chamber works.

Starker, Janos (1924-) Hungarian cellist who studied at the Budapest Academy of Music, becoming first cello in the Budapest Opera orchestra. In 1948 he settled in the United States where he rapidly achieved fame playing for the Dallas Symphony Orchestra, the orchestra of the New York Metropolitan, and the Chicago Symphony Orchestra. He has toured widely in Europe and the United States as a soloist.

steel band (Caribbean) Trinidadian ensemble, associated with Carnival, whose music is often referred to as pan calypso. Tempered steel drums are made from oil-drums and are tuned by beating the top into a concave shape and hammering segments to the appropriate pitch. Adjacent sections are generally at an interval of a 3rd, 4th, 5th or 6th. In each band there are bass pans, rhythm pans (including double second pans, double guitar pans, treble guitar pans and cello pans), and tenor pans. See also **calypso**.

Stefano, Giuseppe di (1921-) Italian tenor who became prominent at La Scala, Milan, from 1947 and has since appeared elsewhere in Europe and the United States, making his New York début at the Metropolitan in 1948 as the Duke of Mantua in Verdi's *Rigoletto*. He first appeared at Covent Garden in 1961, singing Cavaradossi in Puccini's *Tosca*. In his later career he sang somewhat heavier roles such as Don José in *Carmen* and Radamès in *Aïda*. He was **Callas**'s last partner.

Steffani, Agostino (1654-1728) Italian composer, clergyman and diplomat who learned music as a choirboy at Padua and later in Munich, where he studied under Kerl. Following further studies in Rome (1673-4), he returned to Munich and became court organist in 1675. After studying theology he was ordained a priest (1680), and then served the Duke of Hanover (1688) and the Elector Palatine (1703) as musical director and diplomat. He was appointed ambassador to Brussels (1698). In 1706 he was elected Bishop of Spiga and Apostolic Vicar in 1709.

Steffani's works include operas, some of which were much admired in their day, vocal duets, madrigals, chamber sonatas for two violins, viola and double-bass, and motets.

Steinberg, Maximilian (1883-1946) Russian composer who studied at the Moscow Conservatoire as a pupil of **Rimsky-Korsakov**, and also of **Lyadov** and **Glazunov**. Steinberg later (1934) became director of the Leningrad Conservatoire. He wrote five symphonies, the ballets *Midas* and *Till Eulenspiegel*, a dramatic fantasy on Ibsen's *Brand*, two string quartets and a violin concerto. He also edited for publication Rimsky-Korsakov's *Principles of Orchestration* (1912).

Steinberg, William (1899-1978) German-born conductor who later settled in the United States. He studied in Cologne and in 1920 became **Klemperer**'s assistant at the Cologne Opera. In 1929 he became the musical director of the Frankfurt Opera, where he conducted the première of **Schoenberg's** *Von Heute auf Morgen* (1930). In 1933 he was removed from his post by the Nazis. He became associated with the Jewish Culture League, and from 1936 to 1938 conducted the Palestine Symphony Orchestra. After his move to the United States, he conducted the NBC Symphony Orchestra (1938), the Buffalo Philharmonic Orchestra (from 1945) and from 1952 the Pittsburgh Symphony Orchestra. His performances of Verdi, Wagner and Strauss were widely praised.

Steinspiel (Ger.) Original term for **stone chimes**.

Steinway & Sons Firm of piano-makers, founded by Heinrich Steinweg (later Henry Steinway, 1797-1871) in Brunswick (1836). He emigrated to the United States with his five sons in 1850, and by 1853 had established his firm, which in time expanded to include branches in London (1875) and Hamburg (1880).

Stenhammar, Wilhelm (1871-1927) Swedish composer, conductor and pianist who was a pupil of his father and also studied the piano in Berlin (1892-3) with Barth. He had a successful career as a conductor with the Stockholm Philharmonic Society (1897-1900), the New Philharmonic Society (1904-6) and the Göteborgs Orkesterförening (1906-22). His works were influenced by Wagner's music, but he also drew on Swedish folk-tunes. He wrote two operas (*The Feast of Solhaug* and *Tirfing*), two symphonies, two piano concertos and many songs.

Stern, Isaac (1920-) American violinist of Russian origin who studied in San Francisco, where he made his début in 1935. He has travelled widely, performing not only as a soloist but also in a successful trio with Istomin and **Rose**. Stern has a

Isaac Stern

wide repertory, ranging from Bach to Bartók, and is considered among the most expressive and vibrant of modern violin virtuosi. He has recorded many of the standard concertos; he has also given the first performances of works by **Bernstein** and Maxwell **Davies**, among others, and has played for various film sound-tracks.

Stevenson, Ronald (1928-) Scottish composer and pianist whose work makes use of Scottish literary and musical sources. He studied in Manchester and at the Accademia di S. Cecilia in Rome, then taught in Cape Town for two years (1963-5). Since settling in Scotland he has performed all over Europe and in Britain, where his piano-playing is admired for its eloquence and grandeur. He has written numerous compositions for the piano, including the *Passacaglia on DSCH* (the initials representing **Shostakovich**), a *Fantasy on Themes from Busoni's Faust* (1959), which indicates his keen interest in this composer, and two concertos. His orchestral works reflect his study of Scottish pipe music and of a wide variety of musical cultures. He has also written for numerous critical journals.

sthāyī/astāī (India) First section of a vocal composition which is set in a particular mode (**rāga**) and rhythm (**tāla**), and used as the basis for subsequent improvisation. Its main theme often recurs during improvised passages as a refrain, or framing device. See also **antarā**.

Stich-Randall, Teresa (1927-) American soprano who studied in Hartford and New York. Her career began when she created the part of Gertrude Stein in Virgil **Thomson**'s *The Mother of Us All* (1947). She sang Nannetta in Verdi's *Falstaff* (1950), with **Toscanini**; the following year she won a singing competition in Lausanne and spent several seasons in Europe, singing at Basle, Salzburg and Vienna. Her roles have included Fiordiligi (*Così fan tutte*), the Countess (*Le nozze di Figaro*), Donna Anna (*Don Giovanni*), Gilda (*Rigoletto*) and the title-role in Strauss's *Ariadne auf Naxos*. She has also been admired in concert performances, notably of Bach and Handel.

Still, William Grant (1895-1978) American composer who was educated at Wilberforce University and studied music at Oberlin Conservatoire and later at Boston with **Chadwick** and **Varèse**. He was the first black American to compose a successful symphony (*Afro-American Symphony*, 1931) and to conduct a major symphony orchestra. His other works include an opera, *Blue Steel*, the ballets *La Guiablesse* and *Sahdji*, songs and chamber music.

stochastic music Theory of music evolved by Yannis **Xenakis**, based on mathematical laws of chance and computer indeterminacy. His compositions are given the prefix ST, followed by a number indicating how many performers are required. His string quartet ST4 (1956-62) is an example.

Stockhausen, Karlheinz (1928-) German composer who studied at the Cologne Conservatoire (1947-51) and in Paris with **Messiaen** and **Milhaud**. Since 1953 Stockhausen has worked at the electronic music studio of West German Radio, Cologne, and at the same time has studied phonetics at Bonn, which has influenced his composition. Much of his music combines live performers with pre-recorded sound, but he has also written music for the traditional media. Since 1958 he has travelled widely as a performer, conductor and lecturer, when on occasions he can be seen sitting at a console in the middle of an auditorium, manipulating a mixing desk to control and transform live musical performance into a new electronic-sound product. His electronic music includes *Gesang der Jünglinge* (1955-6), *Kontakte* (1959-60), *Telemusik* (1966) and *Hymnen* (1966). In addition, Stockhausen elaborated group compositions such as *Kontrapunkte* (1953), *Zeitmasse* (1956) and

Gruppen (1957), the last work consisting of three orchestras and three conductors. Another example of his music is the composition *Zyklus* (1959) for one percussionist, where the performer begins at a point of his own choosing and then goes through the score, finishing at the same point. Since 1977 he has been working on an opera cycle, *Licht*, intended to include a different work for every night of the week; of these, three are completed (*Donnerstag*, 1980; *Samstag*, 1984; *Montag*, 1988 – Thursday, Saturday and Monday).

Stokowski, Leopold (1882-1977) American conductor, born in London to a Polish father and Irish mother. After studies at the Royal College of Music and at Oxford he was appointed organist at St James's, Piccadilly, and then at St Bartholomew's Church in New York. With very little experience, he was invited to take over the Cincinnati Symphony Orchestra in 1909. From 1912 to 1938 he was music director of the Philadelphia Orchestra, and soon made it one of the great orchestras of the world, with a tone quality which was known as the Philadelphia sound. Stokowski was one of the first conductors to take recording seriously, with a series of records which testify to the quality of the orchestra under his command and to his highly individual interpretations. He included an enormous amount of contemporary music in his programmes, and ranged over a wide repertory, chiefly of Romantic music; his arrangements of Bach's organ music also became enormously popular. His international fame was greatly enhanced by his collaboration with Walt Disney on the film *Fantasia*. He was later conductor of the All-American Youth Orchestra, the NBC Orchestra, New York City Orchestra, and Houston Symphony Orchestra.

Leopold Stokowski

Stolz, Robert (1880-1975) Austrian composer and conductor who was a pupil of **Humperdinck**. He lived in the United States (1940-6), and is chiefly known for his operettas, such as *Wild Violets* and *White Horse Inn*. Stolz also wrote a large number of songs and film music.

stone chimes Ancient Chinese percussion instrument which consisted of sixteen stone slabs of different thicknesses. Modern stone chimes have been used by **Orff** in his operas. In Germany the instrument is known as *Steinspiel*.

stop Device by which the registration of the organ can be regulated and altered.

stopping Act of placing the (usually left-hand) fingers on the strings of stringed instruments in order to change the pitch.

Storace, Stephen (1762-1796) British composer of Italian parentage who studied at the Conservatoire of S. Onofrio in Naples, and later went to Vienna, where he became friendly with Mozart. Returning to London in 1787, he conducted Italian operas at Drury Lane (1792-3). His works included several operas, such as *The Haunted Tower* (1789) and *The Pirates* (1792), and also a ballet, *Venus and Adonis*.

Stradella, Alessandro (1644-1682) Italian singer, violinist and composer. He composed operas and oratorios and in 1658 became composer to Queen Christina of Sweden, in whose service in Rome he remained for several years. He also composed much sacred music. He was forced to leave Rome in 1677 and travelled to Genoa. There he produced a comic opera, *Il Trespolo tutore*; he led a disreputable existence and was eventually murdered.

Stradivari (Stradivarius), Antonio (*c.*1644-1737) Italian violin-maker based in Cremona who was a pupil of Nicolò **Amati**. He is acknowledged as the finest maker of violins in the world, especially during the period 1700-25. His two sons Francesco and Omobono continued the business after their father's death.

Stratas, Teresa (1938-) Canadian soprano of Greek descent who studied in Toronto and made her début there in 1958 as Mimì in *La bohème*. A year later she joined the Metropolitan, New York. Her wide repertory includes Micaëla (*Carmen*), Cherubino and Susanna (*Le nozze di Figaro*), Desdemona (*Otello*), Mélisande (**Debussy**'s *Pelléas et Mélisande*) and the title-roles in **Smetana**'s *The Bartered Bride* and **Berg**'s *Lulu*. In 1982 she sang Violetta in Zeffirelli's film of *La traviata*, with **Domingo**.

strathspey Scottish folk-dance in quadruple time whose name was derived from the strath (valley) of the River Spey in the 18th century. It is characterized by the use of a dotted quaver-semiquaver and its retrograde (commonly known as the 'Scotch snap').

Straus, Oscar (1870-1954) Austrian composer and conductor who studied in Berlin and worked in a number of provincial theatres at the start of his career (1893-9). He became a pianist at a cabaret in Berlin, and there he composed a number of songs which achieved rapid popularity. He returned to Vienna and began composing operettas. *Ein Walzertraum* (1907) and *Der tapfere Soldat* (1908), better known under its English title *The Chocolate Soldier*, scored great success, the latter particularly appealing to United States audiences. He lived in New York and Hollywood during the war, returning to Austria in 1948. He composed the music for the film *La ronde* (1950). The total of his operettas was more than 40, and he wrote about 500 songs as well as film scores and ballets.

Strauss, Eduard (1835-1916) Austrian composer and conductor, youngest son of Johann **Strauss** the Elder. He was drawn to composing through the busy career of his brother Johann **Strauss** the Younger. He studied composition, violin and harp, and worked in his brother's orchestra. He conducted his own and his brother's waltzes, and was director of the Strauss orchestra with his second brother, Josef. He toured Europe, appearing in London in 1885, and went to the United States in 1890. His compositions number about 300 and include waltzes, polkas and galops.

Strauss, Johann (the Elder, 1804-1849) Austrian violinist, conductor and composer. The son of an innkeeper, he was apprenticed to a bookbinder, although he learned the violin and the viola and was allowed to study with Seyfried. He joined **Lanner**'s band, of which he became deputy conductor, but in 1825 he formed his own orchestra for which he composed 150 waltzes, 28 galops, 19 marches and 14 polkas. With the increasing popularity of dances – especially the waltz – Strauss travelled widely in Europe, and while in Paris added the **quadrille** to the music of the Viennese ballrooms. His best-known composition is the *Radetzky March* (1848).

Strauss, Johann (the Younger, 1825-1899) Son of Johann **Strauss** the Elder, who was discouraged from following his father's profession, but studied the violin secretly with Drechsler. At the age of 19 he formed his own orchestra, playing his own and his father's waltzes. The first performance of this ensemble in 1844 was so successful that one number had to be repeated 19

Johann Strauss

times, and the younger Strauss's fame came to rival that of his father. When Strauss the Elder died, the two orchestras amalgamated.

Following a meeting with **Offenbach** in 1863, Strauss was encouraged to write operettas, and in the same year he was appointed director of the Imperial Court Balls in Vienna. He was kept frenetically busy with this post, especially at Carnival time each year; he was also expected to tour Europe, following the footsteps of his father, and visited Russia and (in 1867) England. He also made a trip to the United States during which he conducted an extraordinary concert with many thousands of musicians.

His operettas include *Die Fledermaus* (1874), *Eine Nacht in Venedig* (1883) and *Zigeunerbaron* (1885). Among his many famous waltzes are *The Blue Danube* (1867) and *Tales from the Vienna Woods* (1868). He also wrote the ballet *Aschenbrödel* and many marches and polkas.

Strauss, Richard (1864-1949) German composer and conductor whose father was principal horn-player at the Munich opera house. He himself began piano lessons at the age of four, and when he was 12 had his first composition (*Festmarsch*, for orchestra, Op.1) published. He studied philosophy and aesthetics at the University of Munich (1882), and in 1884 was made assistant musical director of the Meiningen Court Orchestra. His conducting career continued with posts in Weimar and Bayreuth; he returned to Munich as chief conductor of the Opera. In 1908 he went to Berlin to conduct both the court and the Opera orchestras, and from 1919 to 1924 was director of the State Opera in Vienna. During the 1920s he travelled widely in Europe and the United States. Strauss's reputation as a conductor in German opera was supreme, both in his own music and in that of other composers, especially Mozart.

His career as a composer – ultimately the most celebrated of his generation in Germany – falls into two distinct periods. With his early orchestral piece *Aus Italien* (1887), the result of a visit to Italy in 1885, he began a series of **tone poems**: *Macbeth* (1890), *Don Juan* (1888), *Tod und Verklärung* (Death and Transfiguration, 1889), *Till Eulenspiegel* (1895). *Also sprach*

Richard Strauss

Zarathustra (Thus spake Zarathustra, 1896) gained popular currency when it was used for the soundtrack of Stanley Kubrick's film *2001* in 1968. *Don Quixote*, a graphic depiction not only of windmills and sheep but also of the Don's clouded mind (he is represented by the solo cello), and *Ein Heldenleben* (A Hero's Life, 1898) round off a group of works which were Strauss's inimitable contribution to the genre.

In the 1890s he turned to opera, and although his earliest, *Guntram*, was a failure he went on to create works ranging over a vast spectrum, from the Wagnerian intensity and drama of *Salome* (1905) and *Elektra* (1908) to the romantic fairy-tale of *Die Frau ohne Schatten* (The Woman without a Shadow, 1919) and the delights of *Ariadne auf Naxos* (1912), *Arabella* (1933), *Capriccio* (his last opera, 1942) and one of his most enduringly popular operas, *Der Rosenkavalier* (1911).

At the rise of the Nazi regime Strauss continued to work in Germany, conducting at Bayreuth in 1933 when **Toscanini** withdrew. By now an old man, he wished only to be allowed to get on with his composition undisturbed. However, his librettist, Stefan Zweig, was Jewish, as was Strauss's daughter-in-law, and eventually he was forced to resign his post as president of the Reichsmusikkammer. *Metamorphosen* (1945) is his response to the war and his deep distress at what he perceived was the destruction of his country's cultural heritage.

Among his other works were the *Symphonia domestica* (1903) and the *Alpine Symphony* (1915); a violin concerto (1882), two horn concertos (1883 and 1942), an oboe concerto, and many songs from all stages of his career. His final work, the *Four Last Songs* for soprano and orchestra (1948), is a glorious outpouring of the human spirit which forms a fitting end to his career.

Stravinsky, Igor (1882-1971) Russian-born composer whose father was a singer at the Imperial Opera. His parents refused to allow him to pursue a musical career, so he studied law at St Petersburg University. In 1907 he became a pupil of **Rimsky-Korsakov**, who showed some of his work to **Diaghilev**. As a result, Diaghilev commissioned *The Firebird* (1910), a short ballet based on a Russian fairy-tale, for his Ballets Russes; the success of this led to further ballets, written for Diaghilev in Paris, *Petrushka* (1911), about a puppet with human instincts, and *Le sacre du printemps* (The Rite of Spring, 1913), which caused a riot on the opening night – the audience found it unmusical, and the dancers had to count its odd, driving rhythms aloud to be able to perform – but it changed the course of musical history. An opera-ballet followed, *The Nightingale* (1914), a Chinese fairy-story as attractive in its way as *The Firebird*. At this point World War I broke out; Stravinsky left for Switzerland, where he remained until 1920, and then returned to France until 1939. During this period the influences of Russian folk-music remained strong, in *The Soldier's Tale* (1918), a play with music, and *Les noces* (The Wedding, 1923), a ballet with chorus, evoking a Russian peasant ceremony.

At the same time Stravinsky's music was developing in a different direction. This was first manifest in *Pulcinella* (1920), another ballet for Diaghilev, this time in a **neo-classical** idiom, based on themes of **Pergolesi**. Another work in the same style was the Piano Concerto with wind instruments (1924). A starkly dramatic opera-oratorio, *Oedipus Rex* (1927), was followed by the last of his ballets for Diaghilev, *Apollon musagète* (1928), a coolly beautiful neo-classical work for strings, and *Le baiser de la fée* (The Fairy's Kiss, 1928), another ballet, this time in a more Russian style, based on themes of Tchaikovsky. The *Symphony of Psalms* (1930) was the first major work for voices; it followed his embrace of the Orthodox faith again after a long break. Other important works of the 1930s include the Violin Concerto (1931), the ballet *Perséphone*, and the concerto *Dumbarton Oaks* (1938), commissioned by the wealthy American patron Robert

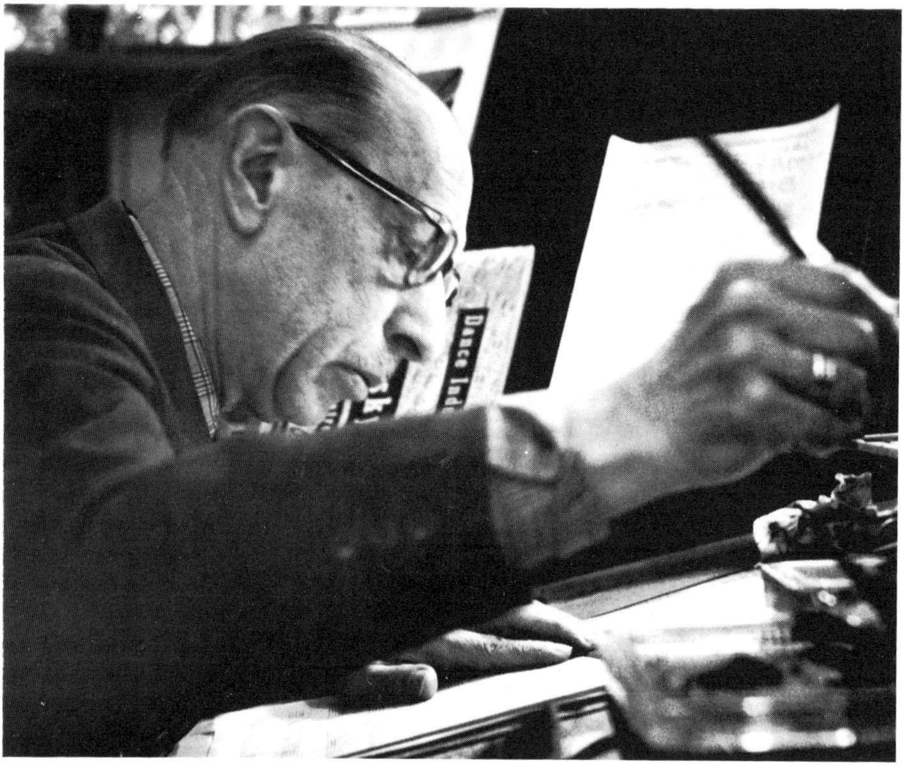

Igor Stravinsky

Woods Bliss and his wife. The *Symphony in C* was partly composed in the United States, where Stravinsky moved in 1940 with his second wife Vera; he became an American citizen in 1945. Although he was unsuccessful in his attempts at film music, he developed a fruitful collaboration with another leading figure in the ballet world, George Balanchine, who had choreographed *Apollon* and for whom he produced several fine works including *Scènes de ballet* (1944), *Orpheus* (1948) and *Agon* (1957). A substantial opera project, *The Rake's Progress*, was produced in 1951 to a libretto by W.H. Auden and Chester Kallman; after this, possibly through his association with Robert **Craft**, who was an enthusiast for the work of **Schoenberg** and **Webern**, Stravinsky developed a **serial** technique, in which most of the works of the 1950s and 1960s were composed. One of his last works, the cantata *Requiem Canticles* of 1966, forms a fitting apotheosis to the extraordinarily diverse works of this man, one of the seminal figures of the 20th-century musical scene.

street piano Alternative term for **barrel organ**.

Streich, Rita (1920-1987) German soprano who studied in Augsburg and Berlin. Her début was in 1943 at Aussig (now Usti nad Labem in Czechoslovakia), as Zerbinetta in Strauss's *Ariadne auf Naxos*. She sang in Berlin and Vienna, and her pure high voice was ideal for the roles of Gilda (*Rigoletto*), Olympia (**Offenbach**'s *Les contes d'Hoffmann*), the Queen of the Night (*Die Zauberflöte*) and Sophie (*Der Rosenkavalier*). She went to the United States in 1957, singing Sophie in San Francisco. She was a noted recitalist towards the end of her career.

stretto (It.) Overlapping of entries of a **fugue** subject. It is also a direction that a passage should accelerate or become intensified.

strict counterpoint Traditional name for **counterpoint** written according to the rules of the **species**.

Striggio, Alessandro (*c.*1540-1592) Italian organist, lutenist, violinist and composer who was in the service of Cosimo de' Medici at Florence during the 1560s. He subsequently visited several European courts and became a virtuoso performer on the **lira da gamba**. His works included a 40-part setting of *Ecce beatam lucem* (1568) for 10 four-part choirs, and many madrigals.

stringed instruments Instruments in which the sound is produced by the vibration of stretched strings. Such instruments may be bowed or plucked. Although the sound produced by the harp and piano is made by their vibrating strings, they are not normally considered to be stringed instruments.

Stringed instruments may be fretted (lute, cittern, mandolin, guitar, ukulele and banjo), or unfretted (violin, viola, cello and double-bass).

stringendo (It.) Indication that a passage is to be performed with increasing speed and intensification.

strophic Song in which each verse is sung to the same tune, rather than being **through-composed**.

Stuart, Leslie (1864-1928) British composer whose real name was Thomas A. Barrett. He composed several musical comedies such as *Floradora*, and the song *Lily of Laguna*.

student's counterpoint Alternative term for **strict counterpoint**.

study Instrumental piece, usually for a single instrument, written for the purpose of technical exercise and display. Some pieces have an artistic value too, such as the 27 studies for piano written by Chopin which are often performed as concert works. The French equivalent is *étude*.

subdominant Fourth **degree** of the major or minor scale. For example, F is the subdominant in the key of C major or minor.

subito (It.) At once, immediately.

subject Musical theme which is of primary structural importance. See also **fugue**.

submediant Sixth **degree** of the major or minor scale above the **tonic**. For example, A is the submediant in the key of C major or C minor.

Subotnick, Morton (1933-) American composer who was a pupil of **Milhaud** and **Kirchner** and who has become very active in electronic music. He has produced some pure **tape** works, multimedia and theatre pieces, and also 'sound-environments' for shops and offices. His composition *Silver Apples of the Moon* (1967) is thought to be the first electronic work composed for issue as a gramophone record. Some of his other works include *Electric Christmas* (1967), *Before the Butterfly* (1976) and *A Sky of Cloudless Sulphur* (1980).

suite Instrumental composition consisting of a sequence of stylized dances. In the late 17th century a tradition was established of including four regular dance movements: the **allemande**, **courante**, **sarabande** and gigue. They were written in the same **key**, probably because suites were often written for lutes, which had to be newly tuned for each key. Other dances such as the gavotte, bourrée, minuet, loure, polonaise, rigaudon and passepied were included between the sarabande and the gigue, and they could all be preceded by a prelude.

J.S. Bach was a prolific composer of suites, especially his English and French suites and **partitas** (suites in groups of six).

The suite declined in the second half of

the 18th century, although at the end of the 19th century it re-emerged in a freer form in such compositions as **Rimsky-Korsakov**'s *Schéhérazade* (1888), Tchaikovsky's *Nutcracker Suite* (1892, after the ballet) and **Grieg**'s *Peer Gynt Suite* (1875).

Suk, Josef (1874-1935) Czech composer and violinist who entered Prague Conservatoire in 1885, graduated in 1891 but stayed on for a further year to study with **Dvořák**, whose daughter he married. He was a prominent member of the Czech String Quartet, and in 1922 was appointed professor of composition at the Prague Conservatoire.

Some of Suk's works contain elements of Bohemian folk-music. Among his compositions are two symphonies (1899 and 1906, the latter, the *Asrael*, a vast work written after the tragic early death of his wife), the Piano Quintet in B Minor (1893), the symphonic poems *A Summer Tale* (1907) and *Harvest-tide* (1917), and a Mass in B♭ major (1931).

Suk, Josef (1929-) Czech violinist, grandson of the above. He studied in Prague and made his début at the age of 11. He became leader of the theatre orchestra in Prague, and formed chamber ensembles – the Prague Quartet (1951) and the Suk Trio (1952); the latter has toured extensively and earned widespread admiration. He has played with the Czech Philharmonic for many years (from 1959) and has made solo appearances all over the world. His technical mastery is at the service of a lyrical, expressive style. He has made many recordings, including an award-winning account of the Bach unaccompanied partitas and sonatas.

suling (Indonesia) Bamboo, end-blown vertical flute in several sizes, with four to six finger-holes and a rattan band which helps to direct the air. It is used in a wide variety of ensembles including the 'soft style' of Javanese **gamelan** playing. The *suling gambuh* is the largest version and is found in the **gambuh** theatre ensemble of Bali.

Sullivan, Sir Arthur (1842-1900) British composer and conductor who studied at the Royal Academy of Music under Sterndale **Bennett** and Goss. He also made further studies at Leipzig Conservatoire (1858-61).

In 1869 he was introduced to W.S. Gilbert, who in 1875 commissioned him to set *Trial By Jury*. This was the beginning of a very successful partnership between the two, especially when Richard D'Oyly Carte leased the Opéra-Comique Theatre, London, in which to put on their operettas. There performances of such works as *The Sorcerer* (1877), *HMS Pinafore* (1878) and *The Pirates of Penzance* (1879) took place, and during the production of *Patience* (1881) they moved to the newly-built Savoy Theatre.

In 1883 Sullivan was knighted, and from 1885 to 1887 he was conductor of the Philharmonic Society concerts. The relationship between Gilbert and Sullivan was professional rather than social, and at times it was rather strained. Their highly successful Savoy operas include *Iolanthe* (1882), *Princess Ida* (1884), *The Mikado* (1885), *Ruddigore* (1887), *The Yeomen of the Guard* (1888), *The Gondoliers* (1889), *Utopia Limited* (1893) and *The Grand Duke* (1896). Sullivan's other works included the opera *Ivanhoe* (1891), anthems, chamber music and hymns, such as the ever-popular *Onward Christian Soldiers*.

summation tone In acoustics, one of two **resultant tones** heard when two notes are sounded loudly together. The summation tone is the higher of these two notes, and represents the sum of the frequencies of the two original notes. The lower of the resultant tones is known as the **difference tone**.

supertonic Second **degree** of the major or minor scale above the **tonic**. For example, D is the supertonic in the key of C major or minor.

Supervia, Conchita (1895-1936) Spanish mezzo-soprano who studied in Barcelona and made her début in Buenos Aires in 1910. The following year – still only 16 – she sang Octavian in the first Rome performance of *Der Rosenkavalier*. She sang the title-role in *Carmen* and Charlotte in **Massenet**'s *Werther* in Chicago (1915) and then a number of roles in Milan; at this point she undertook the Rossini coloratura mezzo repertory, scoring triumphs in the title-roles of *La Cenerentola*, *L'italiana in Algeri* and Rosina in *Il barbiere di Siviglia* and singing them at Covent Garden (1935). She had an outstandingly attractive stage presence coupled with a thrillingly rich voice which can be appreciated from her many recordings.

Suppé, Franz von (1819-1895) Austrian composer who studied law at the University of Padua, going on to Vienna to study music with Sechter and Seyfried. In 1840 he became third conductor of the Theater in der Josefstadt. Other appointments in Vienna were *Kapellmeister* of the Theater an der Wien (1862-5), the Kaitheater (1862-5) and the Carltheater (1865-82).
Suppé's main compositions were operas, operettas and incidental music. Some of his greatest successes in Viennese operetta were *Die schöne Galatea* (1865), which was influenced by **Offenbach**'s parodies, and *Die leichte Kavallerie* (Light Cavalry, 1866). Probably his masterpiece was *Boccaccio* (1879). He also wrote the overture *Poet and Peasant* (1846) as well as choral and orchestral works.

surbahār (India) Large, plucked lute-type instrument from northern India, effectively a bass **sitār**, tuned a fourth or fifth lower than the *sitār*, invented in the early 19th century for playing the older **rāga** style. It is constructed in virtually the same way as the *sitār*, and is played with a similar technique. It is chiefly used with *sitār* players alongside, or in place of the normal *sitār*. There are a few great masters of the instrument, notably Imrat Khan.

Surinach, Carlos (1915-) Spanish-born composer and conductor who became an American citizen in 1959. His works include three symphonies, *Symphonic Variations* for orchestra, *Songs of the Soul* for chorus, *Flamenco Meditations* for voices and piano, and ballet scores.

Susato, Tielman (*c.*1500-*c.*1561) Dutch music publisher, editor and composer who worked in Antwerp and was the most outstanding Dutch music publisher of his time. He published Dutch songs and dances, and volumes of Masses, motets and chansons by the leading composers of the day, including some of his own works.

suspension Device in harmony whereby a note is sounded as part of a **chord** and held over while a second chord is sounded, and resolved downwards by step on to a note of the second chord. The suspension is prepared on a weak beat, held over a strong beat, and resolved on the next weak beat. In a retardation the resolution is obtained by rising one note on the scale.

Susskind, Walter (1918-1980) British conductor of Czech origin who made his début at the German Opera House, Prague, in 1932. From 1942 to 1945 he conducted with the Carl Rosa Opera Company, and then at Sadler's Wells in 1946. He was also conductor with the Scottish National Orchestra (1946-52), the Toronto Symphony Orchestra (1956-64) and the St Louis Symphony Orchestra (1968-75).

Sutermeister, Heinrich (1910-) Swiss composer who entered the Basle Conservatoire and later studied with Courvoisier and **Pfitzner**. In 1934 he settled in Berne as operatic coach at the local municipal theatre. He became professor of composition in 1963 at the Hochschule für Musik in Hanover. Sutermeister's works include the opera *Romeo und Julia* (based on Shakespeare), the ballet *Das Dorf unter dem Gletscher*, orchestral works and chamber music.

Dame Joan Sutherland

Sutherland, Dame Joan (1926-) Australian soprano who initially studied in Australia and then at the Royal College of Music with Clive Carey. She began her career as a dramatic soprano, then, under the guidance of her husband, the conductor Richard **Bonynge**, and especially also of Tullio **Serafin**, she revealed a **coloratura** technique of rare quality. She made her London début in 1952 at Covent Garden, but it was not until 1959 that she made a sensation with her appearance in the title-role of **Donizetti**'s *Lucia di Lammermoor*, the role in which she made her début at the Metropolitan, New York. One of the great sopranos of the century, known as La Stupenda in Italy, she has appeared all over the world in the *bel canto* repertory: her greatest roles, apart from Lucia, are Violetta in *La traviata* and the title-role in **Bellini**'s *Norma*, but she has also sung Handel, various French roles and operetta with great success. Most of her performances since the 1960s have been conducted by Bonynge. She has made numerous recordings, including *La traviata* with **Pavarotti**, and recently **Cilea**'s *Adriana Lecouvreur* with **Bergonzi**. She was made a DBE in 1979.

Suzuki method System of teaching young children to play the violin, developed in Japan in the 1930s by Shinichi Suzuki (1898-). His institute was founded in 1950. The method involves learning by listening and repetition and requires the involvement of the child's parents. It has had astonishingly successful results, although not always meeting with approval from other teachers.

Svendsen, Johan (1840-1911) Norwegian composer, violinist and conductor who studied with Hauptmann, **David**, **Richter** and **Reinecke** at Leipzig Conservatoire. He formed friendships with Liszt and Wagner, and in 1872 he played at Bayreuth at the inauguration of the Festival Theatre. As the most prominent Norwegian conductor of his day, Svendsen toured Europe, and in 1883 was appointed conductor of the Royal Opera, Copenhagen. His compositions include two symphonies, *Carnival in Paris* (1872), violin and cello concertos, *Norwegian Rhapsodies*, chamber and piano music.

Svetlanov, Evgeny (1928-) Russian conductor who studied in Moscow and worked in radio before joining the Bolshoi, where he was principal conductor from 1962 to 1964. He was principal conductor of the USSR State Symphony Orchestra from 1965, and has made a speciality of Russian symphonic music – Tchaikovsky above all, **Miaskovsky**, **Shostakovich**, **Prokofiev** and **Khachaturian**; he has also promoted the music of **Shchedrin** and other contemporary Russian composers. He has made numerous recordings, including all the Tchaikovsky symphonies, and has made frequent appearances outside the Soviet Union.

Swayne, Giles (1946-) English composer who studied at Cambridge, the Royal Academy of Music and with **Messiaen**. His orchestral works include *Orlando's Music* (1974) and *Pentecost Music* (1977); a work for 28 unaccompanied voices, *Cry* (1978) and an opera, *Le nozze di Cherubino* (1984).

Sweelinck, Jan Pieterszoon (1562-1621) Dutch composer, organist and teacher who studied under his father, the organist at the Oude Kerk, Amsterdam, and whom he succeeded in the post. He taught many pupils, including Samuel **Scheidt** and Heinrich **Scheidemann**. Sweelinck was a celebrated organist and a highly skilled harpsichordist. His fame rests on his keyboard pieces, of which he composed about 70: over 20 sets of variations; **toccatas**, **fantasias** and other pieces. In them he developed further the forms and style of the English school, such as **Bull** and **Philips**, and derived some influence also from Italian and Spanish keyboard composers. He wrote prolifically for voices: over 250 psalms, **motets**, **chansons**, **madrigals** and other sacred and secular pieces.

swell Device on an organ for increasing and diminishing the volume of sound. It is also found on certain 18th-century harpsichords.

swell organ One of the manuals of an organ, the pipes being enclosed in the swell box.

swing **Jazz** style, popular in the 1930s and 1940s. Swing bands consisted of independent sections of trumpets, trombones, saxophones and percussion. Swing bands played carefully orchestrated melodies with little or no improvisation, except in the solo sections. Prominent swing bands were led by such names as Duke **Ellington**, Benny Goodman, Tommy Dorsey, Harry James, Count Basie, Woody Herman and Glenn Miller. Each band had its own distinctive style of playing.

Swingle Singers French vocal group founded by Ward Lemar Swingle in 1962. It gave a distinctive rendering of vocal arrangements of Baroque and classical instrumental music, especially that of Bach, and achieved wide popularity. Swingle II, a British vocal group founded in 1973 by Swingle after the Swingle Singers was disbanded, has followed the same style, but with a wider repertory.

sympathetic strings Set of strings in certain types of bowed instruments which vibrate and sound in accord with those actually touched by the bow.

symphonia In some contexts, the same as **symphony**. Richard **Strauss** in his work *Symphonia domestica* (1904) used it to describe his domestic life in musical terms. See also **sinfonia**.

symphonic band Alternative term for **concert band**.

symphonic poem Alternative term for **tone poem**.

symphonic study A term not in standard use, but which has been applied to an orchestral work similar to a **tone poem**. It is said that the term was invented by **Elgar** for his *Falstaff* (1913).

symphony The word derives from the Greek and literally means 'sounding together'. It was used very loosely for many years to describe a short instrumental piece at the beginning or in the middle of a theatrical or vocal work. The Italian *sinfonia* indicated an overture to an opera, often in three sections. In the early 18th century composers such as J.C. **Bach** and **Wagenseil** produced concert symphonies in three or four slow movements, of which the first was usually in **sonata form**, the second a slow movement followed by a minuet and trio, and a rondo finale. Josef **Haydn** brought the form to a high peak of development and freedom of expression in his 104 catalogued symphonies, notable for their variety and range of invention, with the orchestra expanded to about 60 players for his famous London series. **Mozart**'s 41 symphonies reveal a deepening of emotion and intensity, profoundly influencing those of **Beethoven**, whose nine great symphonies, culminating in the choral Ninth, brought the form to its peak in the classical period. This depth and power of expression, with a certain severity of style, avoiding exotic colours such as the percussion or harp, thereafter stamped the symphony as a serious undertaking, the highest form to which a composer could aspire. The classical pattern perfected by Beethoven was followed by **Schubert** (with nine), **Mendelssohn** (with five) and **Schumann** (with four), whose works showed a ripening Romantic expression that found its fullest flowering in the ten symphonies of the Bohemian **Dvořák**, with their echoes of folk idiom. **Brahms**'s four superb symphonies and **Bruckner**'s more expansive ten look back to more classical methods, although strongly flavoured with a rich melodic style.

Although the symphony was the speciality of the German school, composers of other nations at this period contributed valuable examples to the canon – notably **Méhul** and **Cherubini** in France, **Berwald** in Sweden, and **Fodor** in the Netherlands.

In 1830 **Berlioz** completed his *Symphonie fantastique* in five movements, a remarkable expansion of the symphonic idea, based on a programme prompted by his initially unsuccessful wooing of Harriet Smithson. This was followed in 1839 by his dramatic symphony *Roméo et Juliette* for soloists, chorus and orchestra. Berlioz's handling of the orchestra and his free form were to have a profound influence on the Russian romantic symphonists such as **Tchaikovsky** (with seven), **Rimsky-Korsakov** (three), **Borodin** (three) and **Glazunov** (eight). Berlioz also influenced **Mahler**, whose ten mammoth works expanded the form to its ultimate dimensions – his No.8 (1907) in two parts, popularly known as the Symphony of a Thousand, requires seven soloists, a mixed choir, a boys' choir and a huge orchestra. The Finnish **Sibelius** in his first symphony (1899) seemed to be following the romantic pattern of Tchaikovsky, but in his six later symphonies evolved a much sparer idiom which owed more to synthesis than antithesis. In the 20th century, despite the weakening of tonality and sonata form, the symphony has survived premature announcement of its demise, and neglect by such composers as Debussy, Ravel, Schoenberg, Berg and Bartók.

Its continued vitality is to be found in the expressive riches of **Elgar**'s two outpourings of personal emotion; in the brilliance, variety and intensity of **Prokofiev**'s seven; in **Shostakovich**'s superb cycle, from the dazzling youthful genius of his first, completed at the age of 19 in 1925, to the bitter personal document of his No.15 (1971); in the four dynamic examples from **Roussel**, untypical of the French tradition; in **Vaughan Williams**'s nine, somewhat uneven documents of his changing style, and **Walton**'s two characteristically brilliant works. Only in Italy did the obsession with opera exclude interest in the symphony. **Stravinsky**'s experiments with a neo-classical style naturally led him to try its most demanding form in the *Symphony in C* and the *Symphony in Three Movements*. In the United States the 20th century produced several prolific composers of symphonies – the romantic Howard **Hanson**, the intellectual Roger **Sessions**, the eclectic William **Schuman**, and the warm-hearted Roy **Harris**. In recent years, works by radical composers such as **Tippett**, **Lutosławski** and Maxwell **Davies** confirm that the symphony is still regarded as the supreme vehicle of musical expression.

syncopation Deliberate changing of the normal accent from the strong beat of a bar to one that usually carries a weak beat. This can be achieved by placing a stress on the weak beats, by putting rests on the strong beats, or by holding over a note that first occurs on a weak beat to an accented position. It is a device widely used, especially in **jazz** music.

synthesizer Electronic device (often with keyboard, but sometimes in the form of an electronic guitar) that creates musical sounds through a complex of oscillators, circuits, filters and magnetic tape-recorders. Through a complicated process of modification, mixing, amplification, envelope variations and serialization, the final result is a series of composite sounds which are recorded directly

on multiple-track magnetic tape.
The first synthesizer was produced in 1955, and in 1969 a more complex machine was invented by Robert **Moog** and is known as the Moog synthesizer, which is controlled by a piano-type keyboard.

Szell, George (1897-1970) Hungarian-born American conductor who turned the Cleveland Orchestra into an outstanding body of musicians of internationally acclaimed excellence. Born in Budapest, Szell first showed himself to be a child prodigy as a pianist, studying with Max **Reger** and appearing with the Vienna Symphony Orchestra at the age of 10. Later turning to conducting, he directed the Berlin Philharmonic Orchestra in one of his own pieces when he was only 17. He impressed Richard Strauss, who in 1915 appointed him to the staff of the Berlin Staatsoper. He later held conducting posts in Strasbourg, Prague, Darmstadt, Berlin and Prague again. In 1936 he became conductor of the **Scottish Orchestra**, retaining the job until 1939.
In 1931 he had already made his US début with the St Louis Symphony Orchestra. With the outbreak of World War II, he moved to the United States permanently and in 1946 took American citizenship. During the war he conducted at New York's Metropolitan Opera.
From 1946 until his death Szell conducted the Cleveland Orchestra. A man with a prodigious memory for musical detail as well as a mordant wit, he was noted for his attention to sound balance and for the chamber-like clarity of his orchestra in performance. He was a well-known interpreter of Wagner, Strauss and Mahler, as well as Mozart and Beethoven, and has left many fine recordings in all areas of his repertory.

Szeryng, Henrik (1918-1988) Polish-born violinist who studied with Flesch in Berlin and later with Nadia **Boulanger** before settling in Mexico, where he became naturalized in 1946. He toured internationally from the mid-1950s and was active in the performance of contemporary Mexican music. His recordings include the complete works of Mozart for violin and orchestra; he also made many recordings with Artur **Rubinstein**.

Szigeti, Joseph (1892-1973) Hungarian-born violinist who settled in the United States in 1926. He studied in Budapest with Hubay and was also helped by **Busoni** and **Joachim**. He made his début in 1902, following which he made extensive European tours. He also gave the first performances of the violin concertos by **Busoni** and **Bloch**.

Szokolay, Sandor (1931-) Hungarian composer who was a pupil of Farkas. Most of his music is vocal and choral, and shows the influence of primitive and folk-music. His works include concertos for violin (1956), piano (1958) and trumpet (1968), and the oratorios *The Power of Music* (1969), *Blood Wedding* (1964) and *Samson* (1973).

Szymanowski, Karol (1882-1937) Polish composer who studied with his father, in Warsaw and in Berlin. His first composition, produced when he was eight years old, was a set of piano preludes; at the age of 13 he heard Wagner's music for the first time and was deeply impressed. His earliest important compositions – two symphonies, a piano sonata and an opera, *Hegith* (1913) – show the influence of Wagner and Strauss; their forms are somewhat akin to those of **Reger**. Before the outbreak of World War I he was able to travel extensively, and this enabled him to absorb the influences of Stravinsky, Debussy and **Scriabin**. The result was a certain Orientalism in some works, notably his masterpiece, the opera *King Roger* (1926), which after a long period of neglect has recently been revived in London as part of a Szymanowski season (1989). After the war he also composed his third symphony (1916), his Violin Concerto No.1 (1916) and various piano cycles and sonatas. In 1919 he became professor of composition and director of the Conservatoire in Warsaw. He composed works in a nationalist vein, including song-cycles and the ballet *Harnasie* (1931), mazurkas for piano and a *Stabat Mater* (1926) which draws on Polish themes as well as early music. The choral *Veni Creator* (1930), a fourth symphony and a second violin concerto concluded his main output.

T

tablā (India) Pair of single-headed drums used extensively throughout northern India. It more specifically refers to the right-hand drum used with the **bāyān**, and is tuned to the tonic (Sa) of the **rāga** by hammering small wooden chocks (which are wedged between the body of the drum and goathide laces, connected to the upper and lower rims) to tighten or relax the skin-head.

tablature System of writing down music not in notes, but by means of letters or numbers. Originally it was used for the **lute**, but the only modern instruments for which tablature notation is now normally in use are the **ukulele** and **guitar**.

table piano Alternative term for **square piano**.

tabor Small hand-held **drum** with two heads made of animal skin, often used in Britain to play folk-music.

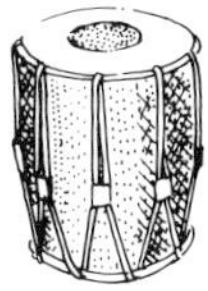

Tabor

Taburot, Jehan Anagrammatic pen-name of Thoinot **Arbeau**.

tacet Direction indicating that an instrument or performer is to be silent for a time; for example, for the duration of a movement.

taegŭm/taekum (Korea) Transverse flute, used in both court and folk-music. It has six finger-holes and an additional hole covered with a membrane which produces its characteristic nasal tone. The largest of the Korean flute family.

Tailleferre, Germaine (1892-1983) French composer, a pupil of **Ravel** and a member of Les **Six**. Her work was generally lightweight in style with only occasional excursions into the **serial** and **polytonal** modes of composition. Concertos for piano and harp are among her compositions, together with many operas and ballets. The best known of these are *Marchand d'oiseaux* (1923) and *Parisiana* (1955).

tailpiece Fan-shaped piece at the opposite end to the **peg box** where the strings of instruments such as a **fiddle, viol** or **violin** are attached.

Takemitsu, Toru (1930-) Japanese composer, largely self-taught, although he did undertake sporadic periods of study with Kiyose. Although his style is highly original, the most important influence on him was **Debussy**, from whose *Jeux* he quotes at the end of his orchestral piece *Green* (1967). He was also influenced by the expressionism and **serial** techniques of **Schoenberg** and his school, by *musique concrète*, and other experimental work.

Takemitsu is Japan's foremost composer,

and has evolved an impressionistic idiom that nevertheless retains a Japanese flavour. This is evident in his most important large-scale work, *November Steps*, composed for the New York Philharmonic Orchestra in 1967, which has solo parts for two Japanese instruments, the **shakuhachi**, a bamboo flute, and the **biwa**, a Japanese lute. Other works of importance include *Coral Island* (1962), for coloratura soprano and chamber orchestra, which uses **aleatory** techniques; *Ai* (1956), a taped interpretation of the sound of the Japanese word for 'love'; *Requiem* for strings (1957); *Ring* (1961), for flute, guitar and lute, the four movements of which may be performed in any order; *Quatrain* (1975); and *A Flock Descends into the Pentagonal Garden* (1977, for full orchestra). Takemitsu has organized experimental workshops and was art director of the Space Theatre, Osaka, for EXPO 70. He has also composed several tape works, much chamber music, and numerous film scores (including *Seppuku*). Recent outstanding compositions are *From Far Beyond Chrysanthemums and November Fog* (1983) for violin and piano, *Tree Line* (1988) for chamber orchestra and *My Way of Life* (1990) for chorus, baritone and orchestra.

tāla (India) System of rhythmic cycles, characterized by a repeating pattern of four to 16 or more beats (**mātras**) subdivided into groups. In addition to a stress on the first beat (or **sam**) of the cycle, the first *mātra* of each group is also emphasized. As an example, the most popular *tāla*, called *tīntāl*, comprises 16 beats grouped 4 + 4 + 4 + 4.

Talich, Václav (1883-1961) Czech conductor, violinist and artistic director of the Prague National Opera from 1935 to 1945. Talich studied the violin under Sevcik and conducting under **Nikisch**, before going on to conduct various minor European orchestras. His later fame derives from his work with the Czech Philharmonic Orchestra (1919-41). After the takeover of Czechoslovakia by the Communists in 1948 he was frequently dismissed for his dissent and just as frequently reinstated for his talent. Talich retired in 1956; his superb recordings, principally of the Czech repertory, have recently been reissued on compact disc.

Tallis, Thomas (*c*.1505-1585) English composer and organist at Waltham Abbey until its dissolution in 1540. Tallis's early compositions were influenced by composers such as **Fayrfax**, whose work he surpassed in both scale and complexity. He was able to compose sacred works for both the Roman Catholic Church and the new Anglican liturgy (after 1547). His works include Masses, motets, anthems, many works for the keyboard and two of the earliest known **plainsong** settings. His achievements were recognized by Elizabeth I when she granted Tallis and his pupil **Byrd** the lucrative music-printing monopoly in 1575.

His best-known works are the 40-voice motet *Spem in Alium* and his second *Lamentation*, with its innovative use of **modulation**. His five-voice *Magnificat* and *Nunc Dimittis* are also justly famous. Tallis was one of the finest English composers of his day – indeed, one of the finest in Europe. One of his themes formed the basis for a work by **Vaughan Williams**, and several other later English composers have drawn from him.

Talma, Louise (1906-) American composer, born in France. Talma studied in Paris under Nadia **Boulanger** and in New York with Howard Brockway, before taking a teaching post at Hunter College, New York, where she has lived since 1928. Her various works include an opera, *The Alcestiad* (performed in Frankfurt, 1962), as well as an oratorio, *The Divine Flame* (1948), and many smaller pieces. She was made Professor of Music at Hunter College in 1952, and has collected many awards and prizes.

talon (Fr.) Heel of the **bow** of a stringed instrument.

Talvela, Martti (1935-1989) Finnish bass. Talvela's powerful voice and stage presence made him ideally suited for the grand roles in the operas of Verdi and Wagner as well as the title-role in **Mussorgsky**'s *Boris Godunov*. He studied in Stockholm and performed in many of the major European operatic centres including Bayreuth, Salzburg, Berlin and Milan. He was art director of the Savonlinna Opera Festival from 1972 to 1980.

tambour (Fr.) Alternative term for **drum**.

tambourine Small **drum** with a single skin stretched over the edge of one side of its rim, into which jingles are set to add to the sound when the skin is struck or rubbed by the hand. The drum can also be shaken to obtain the jingling sound. The tambourine is of Arab origin.

tāmbūra (India) Vertically held, plucked tube-zither with a gourd-bowl as its base, often mistakenly referred to as a member of the lute family. It has four open metal strings, usually tuned in the order of a fifth, a pair of upper tonics and a lower tonic. These are gently plucked throughout most genres of Indian music to provide the **drone**, emphasizing the relationship between the tonic of the **rāga** and the solo melody.

tamtam Alternative term for **gong**. Sometimes also spelled tam-tam.

tān (India) Rapid melodic patterns used in both vocal and instrumental improvisations. They are used to brilliant effect in **khyāl**, usually sung to an open vowel 'a'.

Taneyev, Alexander Sergeyevich (1850-1918) Russian composer and uncle of the more famous Sergey Ivanovich **Taneyev**. Alexander Sergeyevich graduated from St Petersburg University and subsequently pursued a successful career in the civil service alongside his activities as a composer. He studied with **Rimsky-Korsakov** and Petrov. One of his best-known works, the Symphony No.2, was an attempt to write a specifically Russian composition and was not a great success. His talents were more evident in his lighter pieces, which included bagatelles, serenades and mazurkas.

Taneyev, Sergey Ivanovich (1856-1915) Russian composer, pianist and teacher. Taneyev was educated at the Moscow Conservatoire, studying composition under Tchaikovsky. The two were later to become close friends.

The 1880s saw Taneyev increasingly involved in the Conservatoire, reluctantly accepting a series of posts until he was made director in 1885. **Scriabin** and **Rachmaninov** were among his pupils at this time. Taneyev's own music was at first a closely-guarded secret between Tchaikovsky and himself, but successful performances of his cantata *John of Damascus* (1884) and his symphony in D minor (1885) made him less reticent. His most ambitious work was his opera *The Oresteia* (performed in 1895), while his most successful instrumental work was his Symphony in C minor (1898).

tangak (Korea) Literally 'Tang music', a term used to distinguish secular court music of Chinese origin from native music or **hyangak**. Although the repertory constitutes a rare survival of medieval Chinese music, the only two remaining examples (excluding some additional dances) are actually instrumental versions of love-songs dating from the Song era (960-1279). Originally sung with instruments, they are now played by an orchestra which includes **taegŭm**, **haegŭm**, **p'iri**, bell-chimes, stone chimes, barrel drum, bowed **zither** and wooden clapper.

tangent One of a series of small pieces of metal used to strike the strings of a **clavichord**.

tango Dance of Argentinian origin, closely resembling the Cuban **habanera**. It is a fairly slow dance in 2/4 time with a syncopated rhythm. The tango became popular during and immediately after World War I.

Tansman, Alexandre (1897-1986) French composer, conductor and pianist. Born in Poland and educated at Łódź Conservatoire, Tansman moved to Paris in 1919, where he settled. He toured with the Boston Symphony Orchestra as pianist in 1927 and later began to conduct his own works. Early influences included Chopin, Ravel and Stravinsky; the latter was a close friend whose death inspired Tansman's best-known work, the elegiac *Stele* (1972). Tansman wrote many large and smaller-scale works, and was as at home with **serial** and **polytonal** methods of composition as with more conventional techniques.

tanto (It.) So much, too much. For example, *allegro ma non tanto*, fast but not too fast.

tape Magnetic tape that is used to record sound. It is now used in a variety of ways. The most widespread use is in the recording of musicians either in the studio or at a concert, for mass production by the record industry. More innovative uses include the production and recording of electronically generated sounds to be used as backing for a live performance or, indeed, to constitute a performance in itself.

tarogato Hungarian single-reed **woodwind instrument** now fitted with a **saxophone** mouthpiece. It is sometimes used for the shepherd's call in Wagner's *Tristan und Isolde*.

Tárrega, Francisco (1852-1909) Spanish guitarist and composer. Trained in both guitar and piano, Tárrega played a prominent role in revitalizing the guitar as a serious musical instrument.

He studied at the Madrid Conservatoire in the 1870s and during the 1880s was giving recitals throughout the capitals of Europe. As well as composing, he arranged for the guitar many works by Chopin, Mendelssohn and **Thalberg**. Through his teaching he has had an enormous influence on the 20th-century guitar revival, his pupils including Pujol and Robledo.

Tartini, Giuseppe (1692-1770) Italian composer, violinist and teacher. Tartini studied law in Padua before fleeing the city and taking refuge in a monastery at Assisi because of disapproval of his marriage. Returning in 1715, he played in the orchestra there and, after an interval of several years spent in Prague, founded a school of violin-playing in 1728. He described **resultant tones** (only fully understood by Helmholtz much later) and a new type of violin bow. His compositions include various religious vocal works, many *canzone* and sonatas, the most famous of these being the *Devil's Trill* sonata, probably composed after 1745.

tasto (It.) The **key** of an instrument. For example, *tasto solo* is a direction to a keyboard **continuo** player to play only the **bass** notes. It also means the **fingerboard** of a stringed instrument.

Tate, Jeffrey (1943-) English conductor who studied at Cambridge. He intended to go into medicine, but joined the music staff at Covent Garden in 1971; he also worked at Bayreuth and Cologne. He made his conducting début in 1978 with *Carmen* at Göteborg; he first conducted at the Metropolitan, New York, with a performance of **Berg**'s *Lulu* (1980), and at Covent Garden in 1982 (*La clemenza di Tito*). He has been principal conductor at Covent Garden since 1986, where he has given a range of operas including Strauss's *Arabella* (which he has recorded). He is principal conductor of the English Chamber Orchestra and principal guest conductor with the Orchestre Nationale de France and the Geneva Opera.

Tate, Phyllis (1911-1987) English composer of operatic, choral and children's music. Tate studied at the Royal Academy of Music but discarded all her work from this period. Her best-known works are the *Sonata for Clarinet and Cello* (first performed in 1947), the *Serenade* for solo voices and ensemble, and, more spectacularly, her opera *The Lodger*, which was produced in 1960. Tate was not a prolific composer and was generally more at home with smaller-scale compositions.

Tauber, Richard (1891-1948) Tenor, composer and conductor, born in Austria, later a naturalized Briton. Tauber came from an operatic family and studied with Carl Beines at Freiburg. His début, in 1913 in *Die Zauberflöte*, was an immediate success and he sang most of the great tenor parts during the next five years. However, it was in lighter operas and operettas that he found greatest fame, especially in **Lehár**'s *Das Land des Lächelns* (The Land of Smiles), which played in Drury Lane in 1931. His Don Ottavio in *Don Giovanni* with the Vienna State Opera at Covent Garden in 1947 was a great success. Archive recordings give a good idea of his distinctive voice.

Tausig, Carl (1841-1871) Polish pianist and composer, a favourite pupil of Liszt, whom he accompanied on many of his tours (and who later described his technique as infallible). Tausig gave wild, virtuoso performances which were only partly understood by contemporary critics. His playing was passionate, strident and extravagant. His compositions are negligible for the most part, although a piano exercise, *Tägliche Studien*, is still used today.

Tavener, John (1944-) English composer educated at the Royal Academy of Music. While still a student, taught by **Berkeley** and **Lumsdaine**, Tavener composed two religious cantatas of which one, *The Whale* (1965), was later recorded by the Beatles' company, Apple Records. Much of his work is related to his devotion to the Greek Orthodox Church: it includes three Requiems, works based on the writings of St John of the Cross (*Nomine Jesu*, *Coplas* and *Ultimos Ritos*), the *Canticle of the Mother of God* and other pieces such as *Lamentation, Last Prayer and Exaltation*. His strongest affinity is with the late Stravinsky of *A Narrative and a Prayer*. His most ambitious work is his multi-layered *Celtic Requiem* (1969), which draws on children's games, poetry and church music. He has also written an opera, *Thérèse* (1976), songs and incidental music.

Taverner, John (*c*.1490-1545) Foremost English composer of the early 16th century. Taverner's early life remains a mystery, but by 1525 he was first instructor of the choir at Cardinal College, Oxford, and in 1530 held a similar position in Boston, Lincolnshire. It is likely that most of his works were composed in the 1520s and 1530s, at the time Wolsey was fostering the development of English music. Most of Taverner's music was composed for the Church and he excelled in the composition of ambitious, large-scale Masses (including the *Gloria tibi Trinitas*) and Magnificats (of which he wrote three), as well as motets and antiphons. He adapted certain of his own Latin works for English translation. He also composed some secular partsongs and instrumental pieces. His works draw on the best elements of the florid style of the era and prepared the way for **Tallis**, **Tye** and **Sheppard** in the 1540s and after.

Taylor, Deems (1885-1966) American composer and critic who studied in New York. He composed while at university, but his first musical job was as a critic, and he worked for several journals until 1932. His first opera, *The King's Henchman* (1927), was produced at the Metropolitan, where it was highly successful; so was his next, *Peter Ibbetson* (1931), also seen at the Metropolitan. He described broadcast operas and concerts for CBS radio (1931-43), and wrote several lively books. His other operas are *Ramuntcho* (1942) and *The Dragon* (1958); he also wrote symphonic poems, and other works for orchestra (*A Christmas Overture*, 1943; *Restoration Suite*, 1950), choral music and a string quartet.

Tchaikovsky, Piotr Ilyich (1840-1893) Russian composer, the foremost Russian musical figure of his generation. He learnt the piano at a very early age, but first worked at the Ministry of Justice; he became more and more involved in the world of music, and in 1863 enrolled at the St Petersburg Conservatoire, studying composition with Anton **Rubinstein**. He was invited to become professor of harmony at the Moscow Conservatoire in 1866, and at the same time composed his first symphony, *Winter Daydreams*. The following year he met Berlioz, and also became involved with **Balakirev** and the **Mighty Handful**, whose nationalistic and romantic inclinations were directly opposed to Rubinstein's conservatism. Tchaikovsky would have seemed a natural choice as the sixth member of the group, but the association was never consolidated – possibly because of the difficulties of communication between Moscow and St Petersburg. However, Balakirev provided the impetus for Tchaikovsky to compose the fantasy-overture *Romeo and Juliet* (1870), his first major work. He had already written an unsuccessful opera, *The Voyevoda* (1869), material from which was incorporated in his next, *The Oprichnik* (1874); his nationalist sympathies are evident in his use of Russian folk-songs in this work, and in his second symphony, the *Little Russian* (1872). His third symphony, the *Polish*, and the Piano Concerto No.1 date from 1875; the overture *Francesca da Rimini* and *Variations on a Rococo Theme* from 1876; the ballet *Swan Lake* from 1877. The ballet did not achieve unqualified success until it was produced in 1895 in St Petersburg; since then it has been unfailingly popular and is in the repertory of every major ballet company in the world.

By now Tchaikovsky was deeply troubled by the homosexuality which he had striven to suppress for years. Believing that marriage was the answer, he took as his wife a girl whom he barely knew; the result was catastrophic and he had a breakdown. He was helped through this period by the moral support of his brother Modest and of his patron Nadezhda von Meck (with whom he corresponded; they never met). The story of his greatest opera, *Eugene Onegin* (1879), has clear parallels with his own situation. His Symphony No.4 (1878), with its highly original and charming motifs, and his Violin Concerto of the same year also show his genius flowing freely, undimmed by his troubles. The *1812 Overture* and the *Serenade for Strings*, two very different works from about 1880, are again among his most popular.

After this he spent some time abroad, trying to recover his equilibrium, and composed little until 1885 when his *Manfred* symphony (after Byron) was completed. Another splendid symphony, No.5, and the fantasy-overture *Hamlet* (1888) followed a couple of fairly unsuccessful operas, but in 1890 he produced two masterpieces, the opera *The Queen of Spades* and the ballet *The Sleeping Beauty*. Tchaikovsky's reputation stood high, and he visited the United States in 1891; his best ballet score, *The Nutcracker*, was composed in 1892; but the problems of his private life were pressing on him, and his mood of despair was powerfully expressed in the gloomy finale of his sixth symphony, named *Pathétique* at the suggestion of his brother Modest. Soon after its first performance, despite warnings, he drank contaminated water, possibly as a form of suicide, contracted cholera and died a few days later.

The rich melodic invention and masterly, colourful orchestration have won his music a special place in the affections of a wide range of listeners and a prominent place in all concert programmes.

Tcherepnin, Alexander (1899-1977) Composer, pianist, conductor and the son of Nikolay **Tcherepnin**. He was a precocious composer and pianist. He studied at the St Petersburg Conservatoire but fled the Soviet Union with his family in 1921 as the political climate turned against them, and settled in Paris, where he came to know **Martinů** and **Beck**. He toured the Far East, where he met his wife, and later settled in the United States. His music, composed in Paris, London and the United States, is traditional with some evident influence from **Prokofiev**. His works include ballets, operas and many smaller pieces, but his best works are probably his Symphony No.2 (1951) and Symphony No.4 (1957). Other works are his six piano concertos, vocal and chamber music.

Tcherepnin, Nikolay (1873-1945) Russian conductor and composer. A pupil of **Rimsky-Korsakov** at the St Petersburg Conservatoire, Tcherepnin concentrated his energies on music for ballet, collaborating with **Diaghilev** for the first season of the Ballets Russes in Paris in 1909. He moved permanently to Paris in 1921 (after a successful career in his homeland) and there produced works combining his Russian idiom with the latest French style. Two later works, the operas *Swat* (1930) and *Vanka* (1932), mark a return to the Russian style and perhaps reflect his personal sense of exile.

te Seventh note of a major scale when using the **tonic sol-fa** system. In French and Italian, spelled as si.

Tear, Robert (1939-) Welsh tenor and conductor. Tear was a choral scholar at King's College, Cambridge. He joined the St Paul's Cathedral Choir in 1961, and in 1963 the English National Opera. His voice is suited to operatic and choral roles such as the Evangelist in Bach's Passions, various Handel heroes (Jupiter in *Semele*), Lensky in Tchaikovsky's *Eugene Onegin*, Britten roles and a memorably cynical Loge in *Das Rheingold*. He has a very wide operatic repertory and has made several recordings of English songs, as well as of music by **Rachmaninov** and **Weber**. He was appointed CBE in 1984.

Tebaldi, Renata (1922-) Italian soprano and former pupil of Carmen Melis. Chosen by **Toscanini** to sing at the reopening of La Scala in 1946, Tebaldi has since gone on to sing in England, North and South America and throughout her native Italy. Her voice was judged ideal for the roles of Violetta in *La traviata* and the title-role in *Tosca*, and the improvement of her dramatic technique in her later career has established her as one of the world's greatest sopranos. Her fine recordings include Verdi's *Otello* and *Don Carlos*.

Te Deum Laudamus 'We praise thee, O God.' Latin hymn of thanksgiving used by many Christian churches. It may be sung either to a traditional **plainsong** setting or to settings with orchestral accompaniment, such as those by Haydn and Berlioz.

tegotomono (Japan) Important type of **koto** music of the **jiuta** genre, so called because of its use of *tegoto* (instrumental interludes). Its basic form is *maeti* (fore-song), *tegoto* and *atouta* (after-song), and it may be extended to include further alternating songs and instrumental interludes.

Te Kanawa, Dame Kiri See **Kanawa, Dame Kiri Te**

Telemann, Georg Philipp (1681-1767) Hugely prolific German composer, theoretician and writer. Without any formal training, Telemann had composed arias, motets and an opera by the age of 12. He studied law at Leipzig but was soon spending more time, and gaining more success, at his music. He subsequently held posts at Soren, Eisenach (where he probably met **J.S. Bach**), Frankfurt, where he was *Kapellmeister* and city music director, and Hamburg. There his duties included the composition of two cantatas every Sunday and larger works annually. In the age supposedly dominated by Bach, Telemann's output was greater and he was probably far better known. He produced both secular and religious music: of the former, his three sets of *Tafelmusik* (1733) stand out, as well as his concertos and keyboard suites. Of the religious works his oratorios and Passions are notable; he composed about 1,700 cantatas. Other works include several operas (of which the best known is *Pimpinone*, 1725).

temperament System of tuning whereby compromises are made in order to produce a series of notes which, although mostly a fraction out of perfect tuning, are nonetheless acceptable to the ear, avoid awkward gaps between tones, and allow modulation to any **key** without difficulty.
Equal temperament is the division of the **octave** into twelve equal **semitones**. In this system the amount that each note gives and takes from its perfect tuning is slight enough to deceive the ear, which will accept, for example, C♯ and D♭ as identical, although when perfectly in tune they are different notes. **J.S. Bach**'s collection of preludes and fugues, *The Well-Tempered Clavier* (Book I – 1722, Book II – 1744), demonstrates this system.

tempered timing See **just intonation**, **temperament**

temple block Percussion instrument in the shape of a hollow wooden box that produces a dry, rapping sound when tapped. It can be in various sizes, giving different pitches, although not tuned to any one clear note.

Templeton, Alec (1909-1963) Welsh composer and pianist, born blind. After a period as a radio entertainer in London, Templeton left to work in the United States. He has written many pieces for orchestra and solo piano, but his most famous work is probably his pastiche of Bach, *Bach goes to Town*.

tempo Speed at which music is played. Some indication is usually given at the head of the music, such as **allegro**, **adagio** or **andante**, or in the appropriate vernacular. A more accurate indication of speed is given by using a **metronome** mark, annotated in terms of beats per minute.
The word tempo is also used with other words to give more precise speed markings. For example, *tempo giusto* (in strict time), *tempo ordinario* (common time, moderate speed) and *tempo primo* (at the original pace).

Tennstedt, Klaus (1926-) German conductor who studied in Leipzig. He worked in Halle and Dresden before becoming conductor of the Schwerin Orchestra (1962-71) and music director of Kiel Opera (1972). Appearances in Toronto and Boston were followed by his début in London in 1976, where he became music director of the London Philharmonic Orchestra in 1983. He became chief conductor of the North German Radio Orchestra in Hamburg and principal guest conductor of the Minnesota Orchestra in 1979. Tennstedt's repertory is extensive; it covers opera and particularly the symphonies of Beethoven and Mahler, for which he is much admired.

tenor Highest adult male voice. Until about the middle of the 19th century the upper register was sung with falsetto tone, but since then the whole range has usually been sung in full chest voice, a development which greatly distressed Rossini and other musicians of the time. It is now classified according to the weight of tone and the style of singing: light tenor, Almaviva in Rossini's *Il barbiere di Siviglia*; lyric tenor, Rodolfo in Puccini's *La bohème*; *tenore spinto*, Manrico in Verdi's *Il trovatore*; heroic tenor (*Heldentenor*), the title-role in Wagner's *Siegfried*. It is also used to describe instruments with a range comparable to that of the tenor voice, for example tenor **saxophone** and **tenor drum**.

tenor clef **Clef** in which the note C is positioned on the second line down. Instruments that play from the tenor clef include the tenor trombone, double-bass, cello and bassoon.

tenor drum Drum of indefinite pitch that is half-way between the **snare drum** and

bass drum in size. It has no snares. In a marching band, the instrument is held at the side of the player's body.

tenor tuba Alternative term for **euphonium**.

tenuto Direction indicating that a note is to be fully sustained, up to and sometimes slightly longer than its strict time value.

ternary form Vocal or instrumental piece in three distinct sections, the third of which is a repetition of the first. The three sections are commonly designated as ABA. The middle section is usually a contrast, sometimes based on similar but more often on different thematic material, but always relevant in style if not in mood. Examples of ternary form may be found in the da **capo aria**, and in minuets or scherzos with trios.

Terry, Sir Richard (1865-1938) English organist. He was music-master of several schools, including Downside (1896), and in the course of his work began researching English music of the 16th century. He became organist of Westminster Cathedral on its foundation in 1901, and laid down a standard form for the sung Roman Catholic liturgy in England. His scholarship was demonstrated in his editing and revival of much important English 16th-century music: works by **Byrd**, **Tallis**, **Philips**, **Morley** and many other composers were performed under his aegis for the first time in centuries. He also published the *Westminster Hymnal*. He was knighted in 1922.

Tertis, Lionel (1876-1975) English viola-player and pioneer soloist on that instrument. Tertis studied violin at Leipzig and the Royal Academy of Music in London, where he was urged to take up the viola. He toured Europe and the United States giving recitals, much of his music being specially commissioned by him from composers such as **McEwen**, **Bax** and **Bridge**. Tertis used a larger than normal viola designed for him by Arthur Richardson. From 1936 he spent his time promoting interest in and encouraging students of the viola, and made many transcriptions for the instrument.

tessitura (It.) Prevailing range of a composition or voice part. It may be high, low or normal for the voice or instrument concerned.

tetrachord 1. The sequence of notes within a perfect fourth, consisting of two tones and a **semitone**, but not necessarily in that order.

2. An ancient Greek four-stringed instrument also called a tetrachordon.

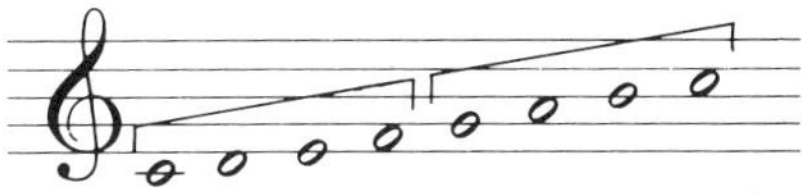

Tetrachord

Tetrazzini, Luisa (1871-1940) Italian soprano who made her début in her native Florence as Inés in *L'africaine* in 1890, and quickly established herself as the greatest **coloratura** soprano of her time. Her reputation abroad was as high as in her native Italy, with her triumphs extending from St Petersburg to Buenos Aires. From 1908 she sang mostly in the United States, appearing at **Hammerstein**'s Manhattan Opera House.

Tetrazzini's technical skills were astonishing and her voice strong, even in the higher registers. In later years she taught in Milan, her pupils including Lina Pagliughi.

Teyte, Dame Maggie (1888-1976) English soprano who studied in Paris with Jean de Reszke. In 1906 she made her début in Paris in a little Mozart Festival organized by Reynaldo **Hahn**, and the following year appeared in opera for the first time in Monte Carlo. She then returned to Paris with a contract at the Opéra-Comique. She was chosen in 1908 to be the second interpreter of Mélisande in Debussy's *Pelléas et Mélisande*, and her great success in this role – which she studied at length with the composer – opened many doors. She sang in opera in London and in the United States, and also very successfully in musical plays, but she was particularly admired for her interpretations of the songs of Debussy and **Fauré**, happily preserved in many fine recordings. She was made DBE in 1958.

Thalben-Ball, Sir George (1896-1987) British organist and international recitalist who studied at the Royal College of Music, becoming a fellow of the Royal College of Organists at the age of 16. He performed at the Henry Wood Promenade Concerts for many years, and more recently advised the BBC Music Department.

Thalberg, Sigismond (1812-1871) Austrian pianist and composer. Thalberg was perhaps the greatest virtuoso pianist in an age of virtuosi. Studying under Sechter and **Hummel**, then later with Pixis and Kalkbrenner, he evolved a technical command of his instrument rivalled only by Liszt, with whom he conducted a good-natured contest throughout the 1830s. He toured Europe and the United States, finally retiring to Naples in 1863. His compositions are mostly negligible, written more as showcases for his ability than as works in their own right.

thāt (India) Mode type or parent scale in Indian musical theory. In the classification system of Hindustani **rāgas** devised by Bhatkhande (1860-1936), there are ten *thāts*, grouping together those *rāgas* which share the same basic scale. The *thāt* of a *rāga* corresponds to the mode to which the instrument is tuned.

theatre organ Alternative term for **cinema organ**.

thekā (India) Set rhythmic pattern extending over a complete time cycle (**tāla**), played on the **tablā** drums. Such patterns, of which there are several for each *tāla*, are learned using the mnemonic system of **bols**. In performance, a *thēka* is repeated continuously as a time-keeper, while also serving as a point of departure for rhythmic interplay with the soloist.

theme Musical idea that forms an essential structural part of a composition. It is a passage that returns in one form or other throughout a piece of music. A theme is generally complete in itself, whereas a **motif** is a (usually shorter) figure which contributes something to a larger conception. In a **fugue** the theme is also known as the **subject**. See also **theme song**; **variations**.

theme song Song or some other musical theme that recurs in a musical play in association with a particular character. See also **leitmotiv**.

Theodorakis, Mikis (1925-) Greek composer. Theodorakis supplemented early influences from Byzantine and Cretan folk-music with a course at the Paris Conservatoire in the 1950s, where he began to compose in earnest. With the credential of having his first ballet, *Antigone*, produced at Covent Garden in 1959, Theodorakis returned to Greece to launch an impassioned attack on the conservative musical establishment there.

The 1960s saw an increase in his revolutionary activities and when a right-wing government gained power he was imprisoned, 1967-70. As well as ballets, he has composed song cycles, oratorios and film scores, including the highly successful *Zorba the Greek*, all of which touch on the issues of Greek history and national character.

theorbo One of the largest members of the **lute** family. The theorbo has a double peg-box with one set of strings passing over the fingerboard and stopped in the normal fashion. The second set of strings does not have a fingerboard and the strings are played open.

thérémin Electronic instrument invented by Lev Thérémin (1896-) in Russia in 1920 and originally known as the etherophone. It consists of an upright pole through which a high-frequency electric current is passed. The proximity of any object (such as a hand) changes the rate of oscillation of the current and thus is able to produce different tones. The first composition to be written for the instrument was the *First Airphonic Suite* by Joseph Schillinger.

Thibaud, Jacques (1880-1953) French violinist and child prodigy. Thibaud made his first public recital at the age of eight in Bordeaux. Engaged by Edward Colonne in 1889, his appearances in the Concerts Colonne launched his career. His partnership in a trio with **Cortot** and **Casals** in the 1920s and 1930s resulted in their famed recording of Schumann's Piano Trio in B♭, 1926. Thibaud maintained a highly polished tone in his playing and excelled in works by Mozart and the French Romantics.

Thiman, Eric (1900-1975) English composer and organist, largely self-taught. He was a professor at the Royal Academy of Music from 1932; Thiman's career was committed to music education for all. His compositions are appropriately simple and direct, finding great popularity among amateur musicians. His choral works have proved more successful than those for orchestra, and the former include *The Last Supper* (1930) and *The Temptations of Christ* (1952).

third **Interval** encompassing three notes of the scale, being four semitones for a major third (C-E) and three semitones for a minor third (C-E♭). A diminished third (C-E♭♭) is equivalent to a major second.

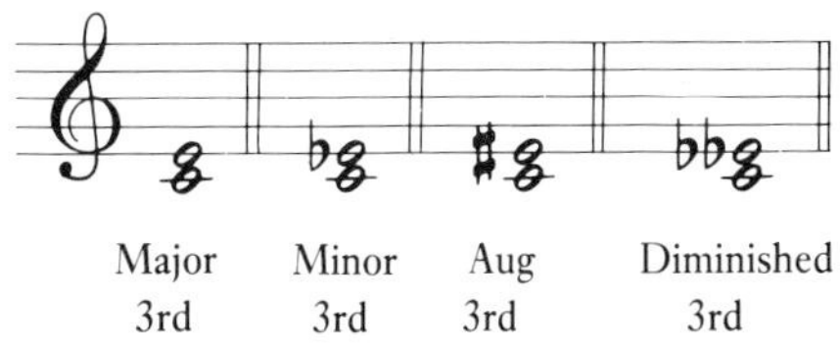

thirty-second note Alternative name for **demisemiquaver**.

Thomas, Ambroise (1811-1896) French composer of operas. His early education at the Paris Conservatoire under Bernd **Zimmermann** and Dourlen was completed privately under Kalkbrenner (for piano) and Barbereau (for harmony). After a stay in Rome, where he forged a friendship with Ingres, he returned to Paris and began producing the comic operas which were to ensure his fame. Chief among these are *Hamlet* (1868) and *Mignon* (1866), the latter receiving more than 1,000 performances at the Opéra-Comique during the following 30 years. His operas are now rarely performed, although arias from them are still sometimes heard.

Thomas, Arthur Goring (1850-1892) English composer. Trained as a civil servant, he took up music seriously only in 1873. He studied under Emile Durand in Paris, then **Sullivan** and Prout at the Royal Academy of Music before completing his first opera, *The Light of the Harem*, performed in 1879. He wrote several other operas and some choral works, but few are of popular interest now.

Thomson, Bryden (1928-) Scottish conductor. He studied at the Royal Scottish Academy of Music, in Hamburg and at the Mozarteum in Salzburg. He has been principal conductor of several major British orchestras including the BBC Philharmonic (1968-73), the music director of the **Ulster Orchestra** (1977-85) and, from 1988, of the **Scottish National Orchestra**. He has promoted the music of many 20th-century English composers, among them **Bax**, **Harty**, **Ireland** and **Vaughan Williams**, and is particularly highly regarded for his interpretations of **Elgar**. He is also noted for his association with Scandinavian music – having worked in Denmark and Sweden in the 1960s – and has recorded **Neilsen's** symphonies and orchestral works with the Scottish National Orchestra.

Thomson, Virgil (1896-1989) American composer, pianist and critic. At Harvard he specialized in choral training and studied composition with Edward Burlingame Hill. In 1921 he went to France to study organ and composition with Nadia **Boulanger** – a fellow student was Aaron **Copland** – and later settled there, as part of the group of painters, poets and musicians around Cocteau and Les **Six**. He met the writer Gertrude Stein in 1925; he asked her for an operatic libretto in 1927, and received a study of religious life in Spain which eventually took its title from her notes, *Four Saints in Three Acts*, although finally there were four acts and some 30 saints. He returned to New York in 1940 and was appointed music critic of the New York *Herald Tribune*, a position he filled with controversial distinction until 1954. Other works included the opera *Lord Byron* and another, often produced in American universities, *The Mother of Us All*. He also wrote three symphonies, a cello concerto and film scores. His chamber works, apart from three string quartets, are almost all *Portraits* of his friends. This colourful and entertaining personality has left a delightful autobiography, with vivid accounts of the French and American artistic worlds.

thorough-bass Alternative term for **continuo**.

Three Choirs Festival One of the oldest English festivals, dating back to 1724, when it was a means of raising funds for cathedral charities. It has been held annually since then at one of the cathedral cities of Gloucester, Hereford and Worcester, taken in rotation. It originally consisted of performances of liturgical music and anthems, and this practice still continues. The festival encouraged the performance of new English works, and in particular those by **Sullivan, Parry** and **Elgar**. Among the première performances played there were **Vaughan Williams**'s *Fantasia on a Theme of Thomas Tallis* (1910), **Bliss**'s *A Colour Symphony*, **Holst**'s *Choral Fantasia* (1931) and **Howells**'s *Hymnus Paradisi* (1950).

through-composed song Song in which each verse is set to different music. From the German *durchkomponiert*.

thumrī (India) Light, classical, vocal genre usually sung by women's voices. It is characteristically graceful with romantic lyrics. Developed during the 19th century, it is still popular and is one of the freest forms in northern Indian music. It may mix **rāgas**, folk-tunes and popular song, providing the emotional intensity is not lost.

thundersheet Sheet of flexible metal used to simulate thunder in certain compositions. It is suspended from a wooden pole and shaken or struck with a soft **drumstick**.

ti (China) Transverse bamboo **flute**, usually with six finger-holes, a blowing hole, and one further hole covered with a membrane which when caused to vibrate produces the distinctive tone of this popular instrument. It also has two decorative holes at the lower end holding silk string tassels.

tie Musical notation in the form of an arching stroke, used to connect two notes of the same **pitch**, or a group of such notes in chords, indicating that the second note of the pair is not to be sounded.

Tie

tierce de Picardie (Fr.) Picardy third. In a musical piece composed in a minor key, a device that ends the piece on a major chord.

Tilson-Thomas, Michael (1944-) American conductor and pianist. Tilson-Thomas studied at the University of California, then in Bayreuth and England before taking up a post with the Boston Symphony Orchestra in 1969. He worked as the music director of the Buffalo Philharmonic throughout the 1970s, and was principal guest conductor of the Los Angeles Philharmonic Orchestra (1981-5). He was made principal conductor of the **London Symphony Orchestra** in 1988.

timbale (Fr.) Alternative term for **kettledrum**.

timbre Alternative term for **tone colour**.

timbrel Ancient form of **tambourine**.

time The time of a piece of music is its division into units of two, three, four or more beats per bar. The speed at which the music moves does not affect its time, but only its **tempo**. The time remains constant (duple, triple, quadruple) until there is a change of **time-signature**.

time-signature The indication of the metrical structure of the bar, at the beginning of a piece, and wherever the metre changes. It is usually written with the unit of pulse at the bottom – 1 for a breve, 2 for a minim, 4 for a crotchet, 8 for a quaver and so on, and the defining number above – so that 3/4 means three crotchets to a bar. It is not uncommon, particularly among French composers, to use only the defining number, without the unit of pulse. 4/4 is sometimes denoted by C, and 2/2 by ₵. The C has nothing to do with 'common time'; these symbols are survivals from an earlier method of notation, where a circle indicated triple time (perfect) and a half-circle quadruple (imperfect) time. See also **compound time**; **simple time**.

timpani Alternative term for kettledrums.

Tinsley, Pauline (1940-) English soprano who studied in Manchester and at the London Opera Centre with Joan **Cross**. She made her début in 1961, and joined the Welsh National Opera, where she sang Elsa in Wagner's *Lohengrin*, Susanna in *Le nozze di Figaro*, Lady Macbeth in Verdi's *Macbeth* and the title-roles in *Aïda* and *Turandot*. In 1963 she joined the Sadler's Wells Opera, singing the Countess (*Le nozze di Figaro*), Fiordiligi (*Così fan tutte*), Donna Elvira (*Don Giovanni*), Leonore in Beethoven's *Fidelio* and Queen Elizabeth in Donizetti's *Maria Stuarda*. She has sung in Germany, the Netherlands and the United States, and was a memorable Lady Billows in Britten's *Albert Herring* at Covent Garden (1989).

tin whistle Simple, rudimentary pipe of the **fife** or **recorder** type, which has a small range of high notes controlled by six finger-holes. Also called a penny whistle or flageolet.

Tippett, Sir Michael (1905-) English composer, one of the greatest of the 20th century. He studied at the Royal College of Music and took a job as a school-teacher in Oxted, Surrey, to earn a living while he started to compose. He took charge of a

Sir Michael Tippett

choir there and was able to bring in a local dramatic society to produce operas. By 1930 he realized that a further period of study was necessary, and spent two years with the composer and teacher R.O. Morris. His first opera, *Robin Hood*, was written in 1934, a year after he had become conductor of the Morley College Orchestra in South London; he was appointed the college's director of music in 1940. His first important works were the *Concerto for Double String Orchestra* (1939), and the oratorio *A Child of Our Time* (1941), on the topical subject of Jewish persecution by the Nazis. His left-wing sympathies were by now clear, and he was a conscientious objector during World War II, spending a couple of months in prison in 1943.

His first symphony (1945) was followed by his first major opera, *The Midsummer Marriage* (first performed in 1955), an exploration of the psychological growth of the protagonists which encompasses many sources and themes. A work of soaring brilliance for strings, the *Fantasia on a Theme of Corelli* (1953), was followed by the second symphony and the Piano Concerto (1955). Tippett's next opera was *King Priam* (1962), which showed something of the influence of late Stravinsky and again deals with the individual's moral and psychological development. *The Knot Garden* (1970) is another opera in which the relationships between the characters are examined and resolved. Throughout all his vocal music Tippett has been concerned with the problems of comprehending the good and evil in the self and of contributing to the greater good of humanity through that comprehension: naturally it is in the operas that he has most scope to explore these themes, and he has continued the quest in *The Ice Break* (1977) and his most recent work, *New Year* (1990). His cantatas and oratorios often pursue similar ideas (*The Vision of St Augustine*, 1965; *The Mask of Time*, 1982). His Symphony No.3 reflects the predilection for the blues and other motifs from black American music that is apparent in his later works. Tippett has also composed fine string quartets and piano sonatas as well as a number of song-cycles (*Songs for Dov*, 1970). His originality and moral clarity have contributed greatly to English musical life in this century.

toccata Single-movement keyboard work of free or sectional form which usually lays stress on brilliance and rapid execution alone. Claudio **Merulo** (1533-1604) was responsible for organizing and developing the toccata in its sectional form, which usually consisted of five sections, alternately free and fugal, the former of a brilliant character. Modern toccatas are works in an essentially rhapsodic style.

Toch, Ernst (1887-1964) Austrian-born composer, teacher and pianist who became a naturalized American. Entirely self-taught, Toch was heavily influenced by Mozart's string quartets in his youth and remained primarily a composer of chamber music. Toch taught and composed in Berlin, London and then in the United States from 1934. During his stay in England he composed a set of orchestral variations on the chimes of Big Ben. His compositions are neo-classical in style (although some of his work verges on **atonality**) and include seven symphonies, four operas, choral works, two piano concertos, 13 string quartets, song cycles and film music. Toch's early work remains his most accomplished, from which his piano piece *Kleinstadtbilder* of 1929 might be singled out.

todī (India) One of the ten parent scales (**thāt**) in Hindustani music, corresponding to C, D♭, E♭, F♯, G, A♭, B, C′.

Toeschi, Carl Joseph (1731-1788) German composer and violinist. A member of the Mannheim Court Orchestra from 1752, he led it from 1759 and moved to Munich with the orchestra in 1778. Toeschi composed more than 60 symphonies and 30 ballets, many influenced by J.W. **Stamitz** and Filtz. He was regarded as a leading German composer of the time and some of Mozart's work (notably the *Paris Symphony*) bears traces of his influence. His chamber piece *Quatuors dialogués* (1766) was important in defining the different instrumental roles in that genre.

Tōgaku (Japan) 'Music of the left', or that of Chinese origin, in **gagaku** court music, as distinguished from 'music of the right' (**Komagaku**), being that of Korean and Manchurian influence. In addition to wind and percussion instruments, the orchestra employs two stringed instruments (lute and zither), except when accompanying **bugaku** dance.

Togni, Camillo (1922-) Italian composer and pianist, influenced by **serialism**. A pupil of Margola and **Casella**, Togni graduated in the piano, music aesthetics and philosophy. He worked as a pianist until 1953 but has concentrated chiefly on composition since then. Togni was one of the first Italian composers to abandon **neo-classicism** for the complexities of **twelve-note** serialism in 1940. Heavily influenced by **Schoenberg**'s work, Togni's most successful compositions are his *Piano Capriccios* (1954-7), which aim to widen the expressive scope of serial music.

Tomášek, Václav (1774-1850) Czech composer and teacher. An early post as tutor and composer to Count Buquoy (1806-22) eventually enabled Tomášek to establish his reputation as a composer and teacher in Prague. He also travelled widely, meeting Haydn and Beethoven. His work lies between the classical and Romantic traditions, and includes influences from the nationalist compositions favoured by his pupil, Jan **Voříšek**. Among his operas, symphonies and piano works are a great number of German and Czech songs, of which *Nähe des Geliebten* (1815) is probably the best known.

Tomasi, Henri (1901-1971) French composer and conductor. Tomasi studied the piano, counterpoint and composition at the Paris Conservatoire before making his reputation with the opera *L'Atlantide* in 1954 and consolidating it with *Miguel de Manara* in 1956. Influenced by Ravel, Tomasi's music is elaborate and intense in feeling. He also wrote many orchestral pieces which showed his considerable abilities as an orchestrator.

tombeau In 17th-century French music, a memorial work. An example is Ravel's *Le tombeau de Couperin* (1920), a suite for piano such as **Couperin** might have composed, but resembling him in spirit rather than in style.

Tomkins, Thomas (1572-1656) Welsh composer in the school of **Byrd**. An early appointment as instructor of the choir at Worcester Cathedral was succeeded by the post of organist at the Chapel Royal in 1621. Little is known of his life after 1628. Tomkins wrote a huge number of anthems and services, together with several **madrigals** and a large volume of instrumental works, chiefly for the keyboard. He was jointly responsible for the music at the coronation of Charles I, but is principally remembered now for his madrigals, *Songs of 3, 4, 5 and 6 parts* (1622).

Tommasini, Vincenzo (1878-1950) Italian composer whose personal fortune enabled him to compose free from financial constraints. After studying at Rome and under **Bruch** in Berlin, Tommasini travelled widely. Influenced by Debussy – about whom he wrote an important article – Tommasini's francophilia did not stop him associating himself with **Casella**'s *Società italiana di musica* during its existence from 1917 to 1919. Tommasini wrote operas, music for ballets (mostly unperformed), many orchestral pieces and piano sonatas. His music is praised for its impressionistic interpretations of Debussian techniques. He is best known for his ballet for **Diaghilev**, *The Good-Humoured Ladies*, a brilliantly orchestrated version of Domenico **Scarlatti**'s harpsichord sonatas.

Tomowa-Sintow, Anna (1941-) Bulgarian soprano. She studied in Sofia and made her début in 1967 in *Nabucco*. She first sang at Salzburg in 1973, and thereafter established a notable partnership with **Karajan**, singing frequently there and in Vienna. She made her Covent Garden début in 1975 as Fiordiligi in *Così fan tutte*. She has made many recordings with Karajan, including the Verdi and Mozart *Requiems*, Strauss's *Four Last Songs* and *Der Rosenkavalier* and Mozart's *Don Giovanni*.

tomtom High-pitched **drum**, an imitation of an African drum, used in dance bands and occasionally in the orchestra.

tonada (Sp.) Type of ballad that originated in the 16th century. The Chilean composer Pedro **Allende** (1885-) revived it by composing 12 tonadas for piano.

tonadilla (Sp.) Stage interlude for singers derived from the **tonada** and introduced into Spain during the 18th century. **Granados** wrote a piano piece called *Tonadillas*.

tonality Sense of **key**. It is often applied to a work or movement, which is said to have for example B♭ tonality; but it is also used more generally to describe the relationship between keys that may occur through modulation in the course of a work.

tone 1. The interval of a major second between two notes on the **diatonic** scale. See also **scales**; **temperament**.

2. One of the eight melodic formulae to which a **psalm** was sung in **plainsong**. Also known as a Gregorian tone.

3. The quality of musical sound produced by an instrument and a record-player.

4. A pure note from which **overtones** have been omitted.

5. The American term for note.

tone colour Quality or sound characteristic of a particular instrument or voice. The defining **frequency** of a note is the **fundamental** of a series of other notes which are simultaneously present. Such additional notes, known as **overtones,** are not distinctly audible but they determine the quality. Tone colour is also known as timbre.

tone poem Also known as symphonic poem, a large-scale orchestral work, usually in one movement, with a descriptive title and based on some literary work, legend or scene. The term was first introduced by **Liszt** in the mid-1850s with his *Prometheus* (1850). Altogether, Liszt wrote eight such compositions. Other tone poems include *Má Vlast* (1874) by **Smetana**, *Danse macabre* (1874) by **Saint-Saëns**, *The Sorcerer's Apprentice* by **Dukas** (1897) and *Till Eulenspiegel* by Richard Strauss (1895).

tonguing Articulation on a **wind instrument** by use of the tongue to produce notes that are separate from each other and well defined. This may be done by the forming of the sound 'T', 'T-K' (double tonguing) or 'T-K-T' (triple tonguing).

tonic First note (keynote) of a **scale**. For example, the tonic of the key of G major or G minor is G.

tonic sol-fa English system of notation introduced in the 1840s by John **Curwen**. The principle of the system is that each note of the scale is given a singing syllable. The eight notes of the scale become doh, ray, me, fah, soh, lah, te, doh. The system is now used with a movable doh so that, in the key of E♭ major, doh is E♭ and soh (the **dominant**) is B♭, whereas in the key of C, doh is C and soh is G. In minor keys the lah of the major key becomes the tonic and me the dominant.

tonus (Lat.) 1. An alternative term for **Gregorian tone**.

2. An alternative term for **mode**.

3. Shorthand for **tonus peregrinus**.

tonus peregrinus (Lat.) Medieval name for the **Aeolian mode**, now applied to an Anglican **chant** based on **plainsong** in that mode.

Torelli, Giuseppe (1658-1709) Veronese composer and violinist, remembered mostly as the developer of the instrumental **cantata**. Torelli worked in various small orchestras in Italy before moving to the court of the Margrave of Brandenburg in 1697. Within two years he was performing in Italy again and by the time of his death was among the best-known violinists of his age. He composed sonatas, sinfonias and concertos, but it is the last for which he is best known. Works such as his *Concerti grossi con una pastorale*, published in 1709, redefined the structure of the concerto (in particular the role of the **ritornello**) for subsequent composers.

Tortelier, Paul (1914-) French cellist, conductor and composer. Tortelier made his début at the Concerts Lamoureux and went on to play as soloist with the Boston Symphony Orchestra in 1937. His London début was in 1947; that in New York, in 1955. He has since become one of the world's best-known soloists and teachers,

Paul Tortelier

numbering Lamasse and Jacqueline **du Pré** among his pupils. In 1964 he began the first of his series of master-classes, of which many were televised. His compositions include *Israel Symphony* (1956) and *Offrande* (1971), based on the works of Bach. His recordings are many, notably the Bach cello suites. The warmth and poetry of his playing have ensured his deserved popularity. He has three children who are also musicians: Yan Pascal Tortelier (violin), Maria de la Pau (piano) and Pomona Tortelier (cello).

Toscanini, Arturo (1867-1957) Italian conductor, one of the most admired and influential of the century. Having revealed a remarkable memory and a musical gift, he was enrolled at the age of 11 at the Parma Conservatoire. He graduated in 1885 with the highest possible marks. The following spring he was engaged as principal cellist and assistant chorus-master in an opera company put together to play in Brazil. The conductor was incompetent, and the 19-year-old Toscanini offered to take over a performance of *Aïda*: he was a sensation, and conducted the rest of the tour – 19 performances of 11 operas – from memory. A few months later he made his Italian début. In 1895 he became chief conductor in Turin, with a new orchestra and a free hand: he opened his season with the first performance by an Italian company of Wagner's *Götterdämmerung*. A few months later he gave the première of *La bohème*, to Puccini's great delight. In 1899 he was appointed chief conductor at La Scala, Milan. In 1908 he was called to America to join Mahler as conductor at the Metropolitan. In 1920 he took the newly formed orchestra of La Scala on a 16-week tour of the United States and Canada, and made his first gramophone records. In 1926 he fell foul of the Fascist government, and was glad to receive an offer to become chief conductor of the New York Philharmonic Orchestra, a post he held until 1936. For the next few years he travelled between New York and Europe, appearing with the BBC Symphony Orchestra, the Vienna Philharmonic, the Salzburg and

Arturo Toscanini

Bayreuth Festivals. In 1937 the NBC of New York founded for him a symphony orchestra with which he worked until he retired in 1954 at the age of 87.

Toscanini brought an unparalleled intensity and concentration to his conducting; in his early years he set an unheard-of standard of orchestral playing, with attention to every detail of performance: intonation, balance, phrasing, articulation. In some respects he demanded utter faithfulness to the score, but was not above making radical changes to the orchestration to achieve the clarity he demanded. Many fine recordings, usually taken live from concerts, survive to reveal the legendary quality of this astonishing musician, and along with video-recordings of televised concerts have been reissued on compact disc.

Tosti, Sir Paolo (1846-1916) Italian composer of songs and singing teacher. Tosti studied violin under Pinto and composition under **Mercadante** before moving to Rome and composing the songs which made his reputation. Tosti was taken on as a singing teacher by Princess Margherita of Savoy, and his popularity enabled him to take a similar position with the British royal family when he settled in London in 1880. He was knighted in 1908.

total serialism See **serialism**

touch Manner in which a pianist strikes the keys of a piano. The impact of the fingers upon the piano can affect only the loudness or softness of a note, although different pianists are able to make differences to the sounds produced as a result of their touch.

touche (Fr.) **Fingerboard** of a stringed instrument.

Tourel, Jennie (1900-1973) American mezzo-soprano of Russian birth. She moved to Paris in 1918 and sang there for many years, as Cherubino (*Le nozze de Figaro*), Charlotte (Massenet's *Werther*) and in the title-role of *Carmen*. Her début at the Metropolitan, New York, was in 1937 as Mignon in **Thomas**'s opera of that title. She sang Rosina (*Il barbiere di Siviglia)* and Adalgisa (**Bellini**'s *Norma*) and created the role of Baba the Turk in Stravinsky's *The Rake's Progress*. She excelled in the French recital repertory and became a specialist in the music of **Bernstein**. She taught at the Juilliard School after her singing career was over.

Tournemire, Charles (1870-1939) French organist and composer. Organist at St Pierre in Bordeaux at the age of 11 and later at St Seurin, Tournemire studied under **Bériot** at the Paris Conservatoire. His mysticism ill-equipped Tournemire for the materialist age in which he lived and his works stand as records of his faith. His *L'orgue mystique* is an organ work of immense scale composed over five years (1927-32).

Tourte bow Designed by François Tourte (1747-1835), the Tourte bow is concave in shape – previous bows were convex. It is now in common use for the violin, viola and cello. Most English double-bass players also favour the Tourte bow. See also **bow**.

Tovey, Sir Donald (1875-1940) Musicologist, pianist, composer and conductor. After studying at Oxford University and with **Parry**, Tovey played as pianist with **Joachim**'s quartet before his appointment to the chair of music at Edinburgh University in 1914, where he was conductor of the Reid Orchestra. His early works were performed in the 1900s, but after 1914 his only major composition was an opera, *The Bride of Dionysus* (1929). Tovey's critical essays are still read, although his music has fallen into relative obscurity.

toy Old English term for a composition of a light, playful character. Also spelled toye.

toy symphony Symphony scored for strings, and sometimes a piano, and augmented with toy instruments imitating the cuckoo, quail and nightingale. An example was attributed to Haydn, but was probably composed by Leopold **Mozart**. Toy symphonies have also been written by Mendelssohn and Malcolm **Arnold**.

traditional jazz Form of **jazz** that was popular between the late 1940s and the early 1960s and includes the original **New Orleans style** and **Dixieland**. The craze spread from the United States to Britain, where Humphrey Lyttelton and Chris Barber were among its main exponents.

Traetta, Tommaso (1727-1779) Italian composer of operas. Traetta trained in Naples under Porpora and **Durante** before coming under the influence of **Jommelli** in 1753. With his appointment to the court at Parma in 1758 he began to write many full-scale operas, but dwindling funds drove him to Venice in 1765 where he completed his one acknowledged masterpiece, the opera *Antigone* (1772). He was popularly acclaimed almost everywhere in Europe, except London, many of his compositions anticipating works by Benda and Mozart (especially *Idomeneo*).

transcription 1. The act of arranging a composition for instruments different from those specified in the original.
2. The act of translating music from one notational form into another.

transposing instrument Musical instrument pitched in a **key** other than C major, for which music is written down as if its basic **scale** were C major. For example, a **clarinet** in B♭ automatically plays the scale of that key when the music is written in C major. If it is to play a piece in F major, the music must be written in G major. The most common transposing instruments in an orchestra are **French horns**, clarinets and **trumpets**.

transposition Performing music in a different key than written, or the subsequent written appearance of music in other than its original key.

transverse flute **Flute** that is blown from the side, as opposed to one which is blown from the end.

trascinando (It.) Dragging. Holding back the speed.

Traubel, Helen (1899-1972) American soprano. She studied with Vetta Karst and

Helen Traubel

made her début in St Louis in 1926. Traubel became America's greatest Wagnerian, rivalled only by Kirsten **Flagstad**, whom she replaced at the Metropolitan Opera, New York, in 1941. She retired from opera to write mystery novels after 1953, making occasional appearances in films and television shows.

Travis, Roy (1922-) American avant-garde composer. Travis studied at the Juilliard School from 1947 to 1950, later in Paris and at Columbia University. He has worked as a teacher at the University of California. His compositions are mostly of electronic music and include most notably an opera, *The Passion of Oedipus* (1965).

treble Highest voice in a vocal composition in several parts. The term is derived from the Latin word *triplum*, which was the top part in the earliest three-part **motets**. It is also the term for a boy's voice that has not yet 'broken'.

treble clef Highest-pitched **clef** in modern musical notation. It is a G clef, in that the flourish centres on the G line. Also known as the violin clef.

Treble clef

Tredici, David del See **Del Tredici, David**

Tremblay, George Amédée (1911-1982) Canadian composer and pianist. After his move to the United States in 1919 he gained a reputation as an important performer of avant-garde work. He studied with **Schoenberg** in 1936. In 1965 he founded a school to investigate **serial** composition techniques. He wrote various orchestral and chamber works, including three symphonies dating from 1949, 1952 and 1973.

tremolo Rapid repetition of a single note to produce a tremulous effect, especially associated with bowed instruments when very fast bowing is executed. A tremolo can also be produced on **kettledrums**, and on a wind instrument by control of the breath.

tremulant Mechanical device on an **organ**, operated by a draw-stop, that causes the sound to fluctuate in pitch and power to produce a **vibrato** effect.

trepak Russian dance of Cossack origin in animated 2/4 time. Perhaps the most engaging example is to be found in the ballet *Casse-noisette* (Nutcracker) by Tchaikovsky.

triad Three-note chord built in thirds in root position. The mode is determined by the bottom third – major or minor; the size of the interval between the bottom and the top note, a fifth, determines whether the triad is augmented or diminished. Triads may be **inverted**; in the first inversion the bottom note moves up an octave, in the second inversion the next note also moves up an octave. Diatonic harmony evolved in the 16th century, based on the relationship between triads on different notes of the scale.

triangle Cylindrical steel bar bent into a triangle shape. The sound is produced by striking it with a metal beater. The tinkling sound of the triangle is of indefinite pitch. It was first introduced into orchestras and military bands in the mid-18th century.

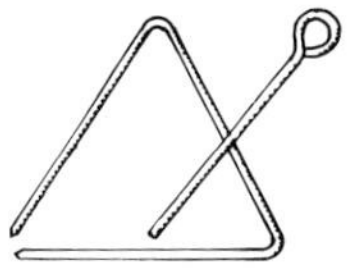

Triangle

trill An **ornament** consisting of the rapid alternation of the written note with a note above, the interval being determined by the place in the scale, or the wish of the composer. It may end with a turn or *Nachschlag* (as in the example), a

Trill

convention usually followed, whether written or not, well into the 19th century. Composers such as Mahler then began to indicate whether trills should so end, sometimes by expressly forbidding the concluding turn – *ohne Nachschlag*. Performance practice in earlier periods suggests that trills were often improvised, especially at cadences, and were probably played more slowly than the modern fast and brilliant version.

trio Chamber work for three voices or instruments, or a group that performs such a composition. For example, a piano trio is a piece for a piano, violin and cello; a string trio usually consists of a violin, viola and cello. Haydn achieved considerable fame with his piano trios and altogether composed 31. He also produced 20 string trios.

The middle section of a minuet or march was also known as the trio, because it was originally scored for three instruments. This name survived, although by the 18th century the music was composed for any number of performers, from one or two to a full orchestra.

trio sonata Type of composition played from the late 17th to the early 18th century by an ensemble consisting of two violins and one cello, or bass viol, with an accompaniment supplied by a harpsichord played from a **figured bass** part. See also **sonata**.

triple concerto **Concerto** for three solo instruments. The most famous example is Beethoven's Triple Concerto in C major for piano, violin, cello and orchestra (1804).

triple counterpoint Form of **invertible counterpoint** in which three voices may change positions without significantly affecting the integrity of the composition. See also **counterpoint**.

triplet Group of three notes played in the time of two of the same value. They are written tied together with a small figure 3 placed above or below the tie.

triple time Time-signature in which there are three beats in a bar. For example, 3/4 indicates three **crotchets** (known as **simple time**), and 9/8 indicates nine **quavers** in three groups of three (known as **compound time**). See also **duple time**.

tritone Alternative term for the interval of a diminished fifth.

tromba (It.) **Trumpet**

tromba marina (It.) Stringed instrument with a single string and played with a **bow**, measuring more than 2m (6ft) long. The instrument was used in Europe between the 12th and 18th centuries. It has acquired a variety of names, such as the German names *Nonnengeige* (nun's fiddle), *Trumscheit* (drum log) and *Brummscheit* (humming wood). Its nautical name is said to come from Italy, because of the instrument's resemblance to the speaking trumpets on Italian ships.

Tromboncino, Bartolomeo (*c.*1470-*c.*1535) Italian composer and developer of **frottole**. A native of Mantua, Tromboncino was a well-known composer in that town even before his murder of his wife and her lover made him a notorious one. He seems to have spent the years between 1502 and 1508 in the service of Lucrezia Borgia, and after that moved to Venice.

His most important work was in secular music, particularly the large number of *frottole* he composed. Together with Cara, he was the most significant innovator in this form.

trombone Brass instrument that evolved from the **sackbut** in the 16th century, in

which the length of the tubing is varied by a slide. This has seven positions, based on each note of the basic diatonic scale of the instrument, now usually in B♭. The first position has the slide fully in; the seventh has it fully out, producing a fundamental diminished fifth lower, that is E on the B♭ instrument; the player can produce the harmonic series on each of these fundamentals. This meant that until the invention of valves, the trombone was the only brass instrument that could produce a complete chromatic scale. In its early development the trombone was confined to church music, because of its solemn tone. Mozart used it in *Die Zauberflöte* to add solemnity to the Masonic ritual; the first use in symphonic music would appear to be by Beethoven in his Symphony No.5 but it was Berlioz who first realized its dramatic potential. There are several sizes of trombone: 1. Treble or soprano, also known as *tromba di tirarsi*, found in the music of Bach and others, now obsolete.
2. Alto, pitched in E♭, commonly found in early 19th-century scores, but now usually replaced by the tenor; the alto however is increasingly used in **authentic** performances of early music, and was requested by Britten in *The Burning Fiery Furnace*. The part has the alto clef.
3. Tenor, pitched in B♭, the commonest instrument today – it may be fitted with a valve ('the plug') which can put it into F. The part may have tenor or bass clef.
4. Bass: the G trombone, with a handle on the slide for the extended positions, was commonly used in Britain, but has long since given way to the bass in F.
5. Contrabass, pitched in B♭ an octave below the tenor; requested occasionally by Wagner and others but rare today. In brass bands, the tenor trombone part was commonly treated as a transposing instrument, with the part written in the treble clef, a 9th above the sounding pitch; this is now giving way to orchestral notation at pitch. The valve trombone was developed in the 19th century and was used in Russia and Italy – Verdi specifically wrote for it in *Falstaff*. The trombone is a favourite instrument in jazz groups, where some players using a special mouthpiece have cultivated a soft velvety tone to great effect. The tone in both straight and jazz playing may be altered by placing various types of mute in the bell. Trombone sonatas have been composed by **Hindemith**, and concertos by **Rimsky-Korsakov** (for the valved instrument), **Bloch** and **Milhaud**.

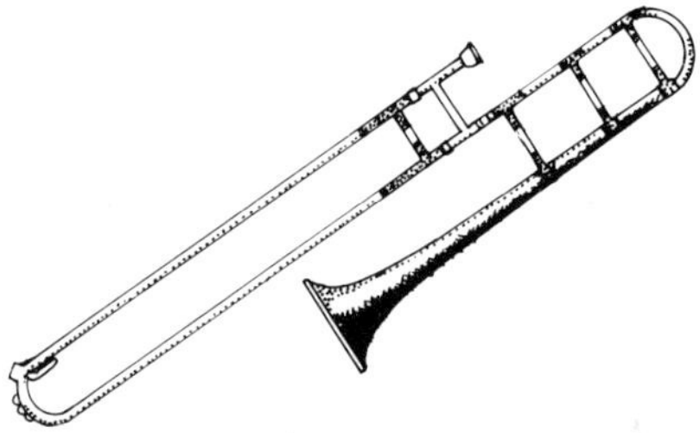

Trombone

trompong (Indonesia) Row of ten small, horizontally mounted, knobbed gongs with a range of two octaves. *Trompongs* are always played in pairs, the *trompong pengarep* being the larger leading version, while the *trompong barangan* is pitched an octave higher and follows.

tronco, tronca (It.) An instruction to cut a note off.

trope Interpolation into a liturgical chant, dating from the 8th or 9th century. At first tropes were vocalized as musical **ornaments** or sung (sometimes as **melismas**) on syllables of certain words. Later they became so important that special words were newly written for them.

troppo (It.) Too much, a musical direction that is often used in the negative, such as *non troppo*, not too much.

troubadour (Fr.) Poet-musician from Provence and south-west France. They were active from about the 12th century until the 14th. Some *troubadours* were of noble birth, and some of humble origins, but most were attached to courts or noble families and most were well educated. The *troubadours* (along with the **trouvères**) provided the majority of French secular music at this time. Many of their poems and melodies still survive, and these include love poems, satirical poems, laments, pastorals, ballads and chronicles. Among the musical forms used by the troubadours are the *ballade*, *rondeau* and *virelai*. Notable *troubadours* include Bertrand de Born and Marcabru of Gascony.

trouvère (Fr.) Poet-musician of northern France in the 12th and 13th centuries whose form of art was similar to that of the **troubadour**. Notable *trouvères* include Adam de **la Halle** and Quesnes de Béthune.

Troyanos, Tatiana (1938-) American mezzo-soprano who studied at the Juilliard School and made her début in 1963 as Hippolyta in **Britten**'s *A Midsummer Night's Dream*. She sang Cherubino (*Le nozze di Figaro*) and the title-role in *Carmen*. She joined the Hamburg Opera in 1965, and made her Covent Garden début in 1969 as Octavian in *Der Rosenkavalier*. She has sung the Composer in Strauss's *Ariadne auf Naxos* and Poppea in **Monteverdi**'s *L'incoronazione di Poppea*, and has appeared at many major festivals including Salzburg.

trumpet Metal instrument dating from ancient Egypt, used for signals in battle and ceremonies in peace. The early trumpet was a straight brass tube with a flared bell, like the posthorn, until craftsmen in the 15th century learned to fold the tube into a manageable size. **Monteverdi** used five in his *Orfeo* (1607), the highest of which he called the *clarino*. This name persisted for the high part, with the lower called *principale*. Since players could produce only the harmonic series, they could not achieve a complete scale and a true melodic line until they reached the higher harmonics; this style of playing persisted for about a century, with the instruments pitched usually in C or D, for example, in the music of Bach and Handel. From the middle of the 18th century trumpeters limited themselves to the few notes of the common chord in the middle and lower registers, and this meant that classical composers could rarely use them for melodic playing. In the early 19th century piston valves were introduced, so that the varied lengths of tubing could be brought into use with a simple movement of the fingers, although removable crooks remained in use for some time. This allowed much greater freedom to composers, but required larger orchestras to balance the greater sonority. The noble tone of the F trumpet was favoured by composers such as Dvořák, Brahms and Bruckner. More recently, in Britain and the United States, the smaller B♭ instrument became the standard, often with an extra valve to put it into A. In Germany the rotary-valved trumpet was in general use, while in France the piston-valved C trumpet was favoured for its bright tone. In recent times small (*piccolo*) trumpets have been designed in various keys for the playing of the Baroque *clarino* parts, and are sometimes also used for more modern music with extremely high passages.

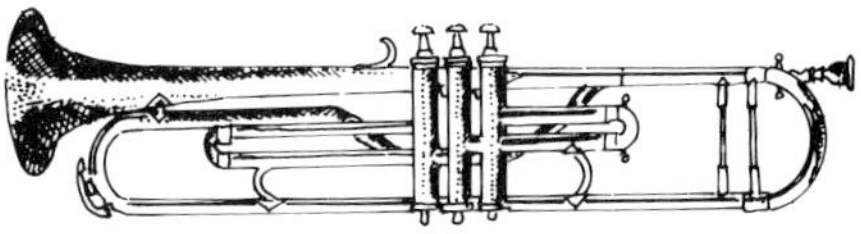

Bass trumpet

Professional players may also use several different instruments, depending on the character of the part. Wagner invented the bass trumpet to provide another line in the brass choir – the current instrument sounds an octave lower than written, and is usually played by a trombonist. There are parts for it in Stravinsky's *Le sacre du printemps* as well as Wagner's *Ring*. The trumpet has always been an important feature of jazz, often played in a very high register with great power. In both straight and jazz playing, a wide variety of mutes is used, as well as the hand or a hat to modify the tone. There are concertos for trumpet by **Vivaldi**, Bach (solo in Brandenburg No.2), **Telemann**, Haydn, **Hummel**, **Horovitz**, Arutunian, Capel **Bond**, and Iain Hamilton (jazz trumpet).

trumpet voluntary Composition for the **organ**, and not for the **trumpet** as the title would suggest. The tune is played on the **trumpet stop** of the organ. For many years the work known as *The Trumpet Voluntary*, made famous by Henry **Wood**'s arrangement, was wrongly attributed to **Purcell**. However, it was established as having been composed by Jeremiah Clarke (*c.*1673-1707) and originally entitled *The Prince of Denmark's March*.

tsuzumi (Japan) Hourglass-shaped drum with two lashed heads of skin, of which there are three main types. 1. The *Ko-tsuzumi* is the smallest of the three, and the most important in the **hayashi** ensemble of the **noh** drama. It has horsehide heads stretched over iron rings, with a smaller ring of lacquered deerskin on the back to dampen reverberation. It is held on the right shoulder and struck with the left hand.

2. The *Ō-tsuzumi* is the larger of the pair in the **noh** ensemble, with heads made of cowhide. It is held on the left hip and struck with one to three fingers of the right hand.

3. The *San-no-tsuzumi* is used in the **komagaku** court orchestra. It is played on its side.

tuba The generic name for a family of brass instruments whose common features are a deep tone, a semi-conical bore and the fact that they are all played held upwards. With the introduction of **trombones** into the orchestra it was soon clear that a deep-pitched brass instrument was required. At first composers wrote for the **ophicleide**, a bass keyed bugle, with holes varying the length of the vibrating air column. This was superseded by the orchestral tuba in F, invented about 1835. Since then a variety of instruments have been designed to give different effects for different purposes.

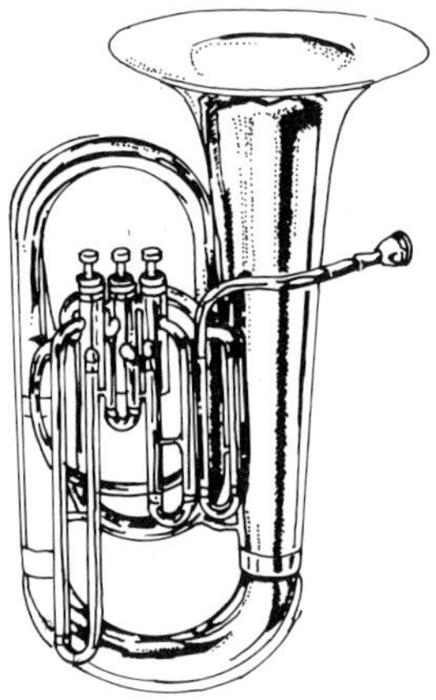

Tuba

There is the small B♭ tenor, known as the **euphonium**, which is used in brass bands, but was also scored for by **Holst** in *The Planets*, and is often used for the solo in **Ravel**'s orchestration of **Mussorgsky**'s *Pictures at an Exhibition*; next comes the E♭ bass a 5th lower; then there is the double B♭ a further 4th lower. There are tubas in C, and Wagner required a contrabass tuba in E♭. These are made usually with four to six valves. All orchestral tuba parts are notated at pitch. The brass band has four basses: two double E♭ and two double B♭ tubas, notated in the treble clef as transposing instruments of devastating distance. The tuba is occasionally required to be muted by inserting what looks like a small barrel into the bell. The so-called Wagner tubas are in fact a variety of horn – the *Ring* requires two tenors in B♭ and two basses in F. Other composers who have written for them include Bruckner, Stravinsky and Richard Strauss.

tubular bells Series of metal tubes hung on an upright frame and struck with a hammer to produce a bell-like sound. Tubular bells are tuned and are in sets usually covering an octave. The most common tuning is in the diatonic scale of E♭, but chromatic sets are also made. See also **bells**.

Tuckwell, Barry (1931-) Australian horn-player and conductor. Tuckwell played with the Melbourne and Sydney Symphony Orchestras before going to Britain in 1950. He was chairman of the London Symphony Orchestra from 1959 to 1968, since when he has played in the Tuckwell Wind Quintet and the London Sinfonietta. He is the foremost horn-player of his generation; his repertory is very wide and includes a large number of contemporary works. He has been engaged in research into the materials and design of the horn with the object of improving tone and performance. His many recordings include the Mozart concertos; he has had several works dedicated to him.

Tudor, David (1926-) American pianist, avant-garde composer and joint inventor of 'happenings' with John **Cage**. From the late 1940s, Tudor has been associated with Cage, **Feldman** and **Wolff**, his virtuoso piano-playing proving ideal for the performance of their work. He taught at the Black Mountain College with Cage in the 1950s and has been very active in the composition and performance of electronic and mixed-media works. Among these are *Cartridge* (1966, in collaboration with Cage), *Bandoneon!* (1966) and *Reunion* (1968), which accompanied a chess game played between Cage and Marcel Duchamp.

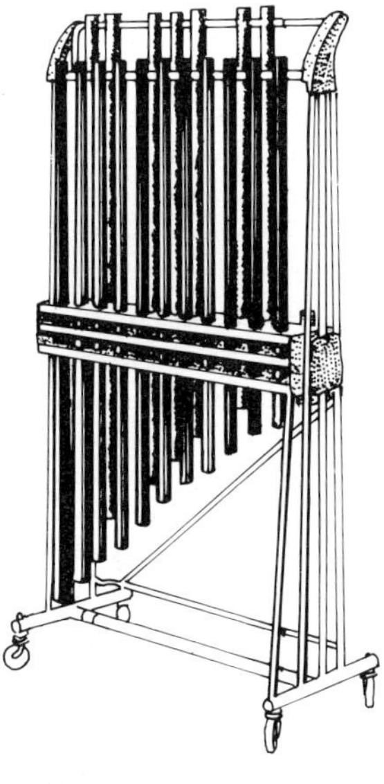

Tubular bells

Tunder, Franz (1614-1667) German composer of church music and organist. Born in Bannesdorf, Tunder was appointed court organist at Gottorf in 1632 and travelled to Florence some time after – the origin of an Italianate influence in his work. He later held a position in Lübeck from 1641 until his death.

Although little of Tunder's music has survived, his **preludes** and choral arrangements can be heard as influences in **Buxtehude**'s later development of them. His choral cantatas began another line of development which was to culminate in the work of **Bach**.

tune 1. Loosely applied to the melody of a piece.

2. Used to describe the pitch of a sound, in that it is said to be either in tune (correct) or out of tune (incorrect).

3. As a verb, it means to adjust the pitch of an instrument until it is correct.

tung-hsiao (China) Vertical bamboo flute (originally made of jade and occasionally found in copper or marble), with a blowing hole at the top and five finger-holes on top and one behind. It has two additional decorative holes at the lower end which hold silk string tassels.

tuning fork Two-pronged metal instrument which gives a fixed pitch, usually A = 440Hz, for tuning instruments or voices. It is said to have been invented by John Shore in 1711.

tupan Large double-headed drum used to accompany the dance music of Yugoslavia, Bulgaria, Greece and Turkey. It is suspended over the player's left shoulder and is struck by the left hand with a small drumstick and by the right hand with a large beater.

turca, alla (It.) In the Turkish style – like the sound of the percussion of the **Janissary** bands, which was imitated by Mozart and other Viennese composers at the end of the 18th century, and was often known as Turkish music. Compare the overture to Mozart's opera *Die Entführung aus dem Serail*, with its violent percussion rhythm, with his *Rondo alla turca*. Some early pianos had a device which produced a similar percussion sound.

Turchi, Guido (1916-) Italian composer, administrator and critic. Turchi studied at the Rome Conservatoire and later under **Pizzetti**, joining the staff at Rome in 1941. He was director of the Parma and Florence Conservatoires simultaneously from 1967 to 1972 and has written for several newspapers. His compositions figure prominently in the post-war renewal of Italian music and demonstrate a consistent rejection of the formal innovations of the European avant-garde. Although most of his music is purely instrumental, his greatest achievement is probably his opera *The Good Soldier Schweik* which, a decade in the making, was first performed in Milan in 1962.

Tureck, Rosalyn (1914-) American pianist who studied in Chicago and at the Juilliard School. Her début in New York came in 1936, and in Europe in 1947. She has toured extensively and has often appeared in Britain. Since the late 1930s she has made a speciality of Bach's keyboard works, which she performs either on the harpsichord or the piano. She has recorded much of this music, including the 48 Preludes and Fugues (*Das wohltemperirte Clavier*). She has also performed much modern American music. She has conducted, and has taught at several famous institutions.

Turina, Joaquín (1882-1949) Spanish composer. Born in Seville (to which his music frequently alludes), Turina travelled to Madrid; there he first met **Falla**, who became a close friend. He then went to Paris, where he studied with **d'Indy** at the Schola Cantorum and heard the music of Debussy. Turina's first major success came in Madrid with the performance of his symphonic poem *La Procesión del Rocio* in 1913. He wrote a great number of works for the piano and several for orchestra, including the acclaimed *Sinfonia sevillana* of 1920. His most frequently heard composition is *Oración del torero* for strings (1925). He also wrote two operas (*La sulamita*, 1900; *Jardín de oriente*, 1923), other stage works, chamber and guitar music, notably *Hommage à Tárrega* (1932).

turn **Ornament** that consists of four or five notes replacing the single note, above or below which the sign is placed. Its use is complex and varied according to period and context. The example shows common interpretations.

Turn

Turner, Dame Eva (1892-1990) English dramatic soprano celebrated for her portrayal of Puccini's Turandot. She studied in Bristol and at the Royal Academy of Music and made her début with the Carl Rosa company at Covent Garden in 1920 as Santuzza in **Mascagni**'s *Cavalleria rusticana*. Her other roles with the company included the title-roles in *Madama Butterfly*, *Tosca*, *Aïda* and Leonora in *Il trovatore*, and Wagner's Brünnhilde. In 1924 she was spotted by Panizza, **Toscanini**'s assistant at La Scala, Milan, and so began her international career. She toured Germany and South America before returning to Covent Garden in *Turandot* (1928), in which she was described as ideal by **Alfano**, the composer who finished the opera. She became equally admired for her Wagner roles, notably Isolde (*Tristan und Isolde*) and Sieglinde (*Die Walküre*), and was a splendid Agathe in **Weber**'s *Der Freischütz*. She retired after a farewell performance of *Turandot* in 1948, and thereafter taught many now famous singers. Her recordings are not extensive, but include her memorable rendering of the *Turandot* aria *In questa reggia*. She was created a DBE in 1962.

tutti Passage in which all performers play. It also applies where all passages of a concerto, for example, are played by the entire orchestra, and in a choral work it indicates the full participation by the chorus.

twelve-note serialism Method of composition devised by **Schoenberg** and first used by him between 1919 and 1921 in the *Five Piano Pieces* Op.23, the *Serenade* Op.24 and the *Piano Suite* Op.25, and promulgated in 1923 as 'A method of composing with 12 notes which are related only with one another. This means, of course, that no note is repeated within the series and that it uses all 12 notes of the chromatic scale, though in a different order. It is in no way identical with the chromatic scale.' Schoenberg intended that this material should be used with all the usual methods of composition – especially the traditional contrapuntal devices of **inversion**, **retrograde** and **retrograde inversion** form. All the formal elements of music, melodies, themes, phrases, motives, figures and chords in unlimited variety may be drawn from the basic note-row. Schoenberg's disciples, **Berg** and **Webern**, took up the method, and together they have become known as the Second Viennese School. Despite Schoenberg's original insistence on the strictness of his method, his followers, especially Berg, and even he himself treated it with freedom. Under pressure from the Nazis and lack of interest elsewhere, the method languished until the post-war period, when it was rediscovered and developed in many countries by a new generation of composers, although Schoenberg's prophecy that with the passing of time people would find his themes as easy to whistle as those of Mozart has not been fulfilled.

Tye, Christopher (*c*.1505-*c*.1572) English composer of whose life little is known. Tye first appears as a lay clerk in King's College, Cambridge, in 1537. He was introduced at court before 1550 and served as master of the choir at Ely Cathedral, later becoming a deacon. Little of his music has survived intact, but his compositions include a Mass, *Euge Bone*, and a choral work, *The Acts of the Apostles*, published in 1553.

Tyrwhitt-Wilson, Gerald See **Berners, Lord**

U

Uchida, Mitsuko (1948-) Japanese pianist who studied in Tokyo and Vienna. Her repertory includes Beethoven, Debussy and **Schoenberg**, but she is best known for her Mozart interpretations and has recorded the complete sonatas, for which she won the Record of the Year award in 1989, and the complete concertos with Jeffrey **Tate** and the **English Chamber Orchestra**. She has toured widely in Europe and the United States, and appeared at many festivals. She was acclaimed for her BBC television series on Mozart's piano music, and has also appeared on German television.

'ud Short-necked, plucked **lute** of the Arab world, forerunner of the Western lute. It was probably of Persian origin, but was adopted by the Arabs in the 7th century and became widespread throughout Muslim lands from Spain to India.

Although the *'ud* is no longer found in Iran, it is still common in parts of North Africa and the Near East. From early Arabic and Persian texts which demonstrate the importance of the *'ud* in Middle-Eastern musical theory, it is known that the instrument once had four strings and frets, but is now generally fretless with five, six or seven strings.

uillean pipes (Ireland) Literally 'elbow' pipes. The air bag of this form of **bagpipe** is filled by bellows held under the arm and pressed against the body by the elbow. The chanter has a range of two octaves, while two closed chanters may provide tonic and dominant chords when the keys are depressed with the wrist. There are three drones. Also (incorrectly) known as **union pipes**.

ukulele, ukelele Small four-stringed **guitar** developed in Hawaii by the Portuguese in the 19th century. It may be played from a notation resembling the old lute **tablature**. The word ukulele literally means 'the jumping flea'. A version with a skin-covered, metal-framed body is called the ukulele-banjo. See also **banjo**.

Ulster Orchestra It was founded originally as a chamber orchestra by the Arts Council of Northern Ireland in 1966 – with Maurice Miles as its music director – to give regular concert series in Belfast and other places in Northern Ireland. In May 1981 the orchestra was enlarged from 35 to 55 players, by an amalgamation with the Northern Ireland orchestra of the BBC which helps with the funding. Subsequent conductors were Sergiu Comissiona (1967-9); Edgar Cosma (1969-74); Alan Francis (1974-7); Bryden **Thomson** and Vernon **Handley**. The orchestra first made recordings in 1979 to mark the centenary of Hamilton **Harty**, and has since made many notable additions to the Chandos catalogue in music by **Elgar**, **Bax**, **Delius**, **Britten**, **Bridge** and **Grieg**.

una corda Direction in **piano** music to indicate the use of the **damping pedal**, which shifts the action so that only one string is struck by the hammers instead of two or three.

undulating stop Organ stop that controls a rank of pipes deliberately tuned marginally sharp or flat to produce a regular beating when used with another stop.

union pipes See **uillean pipes**

unison Two notes sounding together at the same **pitch**. It also applies to the singing of the same tune by men and women an **octave** apart.

unit organ Compact pipe organ in which the number of pipes required is reduced by a process of borrowing. For example, an eight-foot stop and a four-foot stop share pipes for the part of their range that overlaps, instead of having completely separate sets of pipes as in a normal organ. **Cinema organs** are built on this principle.

unprepared dissonance See **preparation**

upbeat Movement of a conductor's baton in an upward direction, and the pulse that this represents, preparing the downbeat on the first beat of the following bar. See also **downbeat**.

upbow Motion of a **bow** in the playing of stringed instruments in the direction from the **point** to the **heel**, that is, the player is pushing the bow. The opposite is known as the **downbow**.

upper mordent **Ornament** that indicates that three notes are to be played in the time-value of the principal note, consisting of the principal note, plus the note above it, then returning to the principal note again. See also **double mordent**; **inverted mordent**.

upper partial Alternative term for **overtone**.

upright piano Piano that is built in such a way that its strings are in a vertical position rather than a horizontal one as in a **grand piano**. See also **piano**.

V

va. Abbreviation of **viola**.

vādī (India) Principal tone (*sonant*), besides the tonic, in a **rāga**, and the note that occurs most frequently in the melody. Depending on its relation to the tonic (Sa), the *vādī* is said to evoke the characteristic mood (**rasa**) of the rāga. See also **samvādī**.

Valen, Fartein (1887-1952) Norwegian composer who studied at Oslo Conservatoire from 1906 to 1909 and then in Berlin with **Bruch** until 1913. He was the music librarian at Oslo University for many years. He evolved a **serial** method under the influence of **Schoenberg**'s theories, and produced a substantial number of important works, including four symphonies, concertos for piano and for violin, two string quartets and choral music.

valse (Fr.) Alternative term for **waltz**.

valve Keys added to brass wind instruments, invented in the early 19th century, which make it possible for **horns, trumpets** and **cornets** to produce the complete **chromatic scale** instead of only the natural harmonics. Valves are fitted to all members of the **saxhorn** family and have also been used for the **trombone** as a substitute for the **slide**. See also **acoustics**.

vamp To improvise an instrumental accompaniment or introduction, for example, to a song.

Van Allan, Richard (1935-) English bass who studied in Birmingham and first sang at Glyndebourne in 1964. His début at Covent Garden was in 1971 in *Turandot*. He is a regular performer with the English National Opera, where his intelligent acting and accurate, clear singing have served well in the title-role and Leporello in *Don Giovanni*, the title-role in *Boris Godunov*, King Philip in *Don Carlos* and Pooh-Bah in *The Mikado*. Also in his repertory are Figaro in *Le nozze di Figaro*, Don Alfonso in *Così fan tutte*, Mephistopheles in Gounod's *Faust*, Ochs in *Der Rosenkavalier* and Claggart in **Britten**'s *Billy Budd*. He is director of the National Opera Studio.

Vanhal, Johann Baptist (1739-1813) Bohemian composer and keyboard-player who studied with **Dittersdorf**. During a long and highly productive career he worked in Italy and Vienna. His music was held in high esteem by Haydn, who gave many performances of his symphonies (he wrote over 400) in Eszterhazá. He is regarded as an influential figure in the development of the symphony and the string quartet during the classical period in Austria.

Varady, Julia (1941-) Romanian soprano who studied in Bucharest. Her début was with the opera company in Cluj. She then sang in Italy for a while, and joined the Munich Opera in 1972. She made her début at the Metropolitan, New York, in 1978 as Donna Elvira in *Don Giovanni*. The warmth and intensity of her portrayals are well suited to the principal Mozart, Verdi and Puccini roles and Strauss's *Arabella*; she has also been a memorable Judith in **Bartók**'s *Duke Bluebeard's Castle*, which she has recorded. She is married to the baritone Dietrich **Fischer-Dieskau**.

Varèse, Edgard (1883-1965) French-born composer. He studied with **d'Indy** at the Schola Cantorum and with **Widor** at the Conservatoire. He settled in the United States in 1915, and before going there destroyed practically all his compositions. His creative life therefore can be judged only from this point on. His first major work was *Amériques* (1921), for large orchestra, including a police siren; other works from this period are *Hyperprism*, *Octandre*, *Intégrales* and *Arcana*. In 1921 he founded the first of several organizations for the promotion of new music: the International Composers' Guild. He spent five years in Paris once more, where he wrote *Ionisation* for percussion (1931) and *Density 21.5* for solo flute – the title referring to the specific gravity of platinum, of which most flutes are made. He was a pioneer in the creation of new and unusual instrumental sounds, and in the use of tapes and electronic devices: *Déserts* for wind, percussion and tape was one of his first such works (1954), followed by *Poème electronique* (1958). His last work, *Nocturnal* for voices and chamber orchestra, was unfinished.

variation In a sense all development in composition is variation, the elaboration of a perceived structure, usually melodic, sometimes harmonic or rhythmic. However, the word is narrowly applied to a form of composition in which a theme or melody, original or borrowed, is subjected to a number of variations, which may be separate or linked. One variation may vary the rhythm and decorate a theme; another may retain the harmonies with new thematic lines; another may use the intervals of the theme as basis for a completely different metrical structure. Each variation is usually in a contrasting tempo. This form of composition was already in use early in the 16th century, notably in **Byrd**'s *Variations on 'The Carman's Whistle'*. In the 17th century a favourite method was to use the **ground bass**, a single phrase repeated over and over again, while different themes and counterpoints were developed above. Later composers produced some monumental sets of variations – notably Bach's 30 *Goldberg Variations*, and Beethoven's 33 *Variations on a Waltz by Diabelli*. Beethoven often used the form without the name, for example in the finale of the *Eroica Symphony*, giving rise to the observation that for him composition was variation. Brahms was attracted by the form and left superb sets on themes by Handel, **Paganini**, and on Bach in the finale of his Symphony No.4. **Elgar**'s set on an original theme, *Enigma*, is unique in its use of the form to present a set of musical portraits of his friends.

Varnay, Astrid (1918-) Swedish-born soprano, resident in the United States for most of her life. She specialized in the operas of Wagner and Richard Strauss and performed regularly at the Metropolitan Opera, New York (where she made her début in 1941), Covent Garden (début, 1948) and at Bayreuth. After 1962 she took on mezzo roles such as Herodias and Klytemnestra in Strauss's *Salome* and *Elektra*. She has made some fine recordings of Wagner's *Ring*.

Varviso, Silvio (1924-) Swiss conductor, primarily of opera, appearing at the Metropolitan Opera, the Stockholm Opera, Covent Garden, Glyndebourne and Bayreuth. He was appointed musical director at the Paris Opéra in 1981.

Vásáry, Tamás (1933-) Hungarian pianist and conductor who made his piano début at eight years old, then studied with his compatriot **Kodály**. He made his London and New York débuts in 1961 and has since established himself as a specialist in the music of Liszt. He began conducting in 1971 and was musical director of the **Northern Sinfonia** from 1979 to 1982.

vaudeville Satirical French song which is thought to have originated in the valley of Vire in Normandy, the home of Oliver Basselin (*c.*1400-1450). Similar songs, always with verse and refrain, were used to conclude a play. Mozart used this device at the end of *Die Entführung aus dem Serail* (1782). The term also came to be used to mean a play with such songs interspersed.

Stage performances featuring songs and dances became known as vaudeville in France in the 19th century, and the term was also used for the same type of entertainment in the United States, which in England is commonly known as music hall.

Vaughan Williams, Ralph (1872-1958) English composer whose generally romantic but highly personal idiom is derived from his researches into English folk-song and dance and his love of Tudor music. He studied with **Parry**, **Wood** and **Stanford** at the Royal College of Music and in Cambridge; he was later taught by

Ralph Vaughan Williams

Bruch and **Ravel**. His life-long interest in folk-music began in earnest in 1903, and a vast number of his later works were adaptations or arrangements of the songs he collected. His first opera, *Hugh the Drover* (1914), incorporated folk-songs; his song-cycle with string quartet and piano, *On Wenlock Edge* (1909), is also an example of this pastoral side to his oeuvre, as is the piercingly beautiful *The Lark Ascending* for violin and orchestra (1914). In 1906 he became editor of the *English Hymnal*, which stimulated his interest in early music; one of the results of this preoccupation is the *Fantasia on a Theme by Thomas Tallis* (1910) for strings, a work of visionary quality. His cycle of nine symphonies began with *A Sea Symphony* (1909, with chorus); other notable ones are No.2, *A London Symphony*; No.3, *A Pastoral Symphony*, a lyrical example of this vein; No.6, a bleak work reflecting the horrors of war; and No.7, *Symphonia Antarctica*, based on his music for the film *Scott of the Antarctic*. The visionary aspect of his work was continued in the 'masque for dancing' *Job* (1931) and the opera *The Pilgrim's Progress* (1951), based on Bunyan's novel. In 1938 he composed the *Serenade to Music* for 16 solo voices and orchestra, a setting of excerpts from Shakespeare's *Merchant of Venice* which is one of his most appealing works. He wrote five operas altogether: the others are *Sir John in Love* (1929), like Verdi's *Falstaff* based on *The Merry Wives of Windsor*; *The Poisoned Kiss* (1929), and *Riders to the Sea* (1932), based on the play by J.M. Synge. His incidental music for the theatre, films and radio includes that for Aristophanes' *The Wasps*, of which the overture is best known. Apart from numerous songs, carols and hymns he composed concertos for piano, for oboe and for tuba; the suite *Flos campi* for viola, chorus and orchestra (1925); *Five Variants of 'Dives and Lazarus'* (the folk-song); a string quartet (1944) and the *Fantasia on Greensleeves*, as well as sacred choral works. He was active also as a teacher at the Royal College of Music and as a conductor. He was awarded the Order of Merit in 1935.

The particularly English quality of Vaughan Williams's work has a perennial appeal which is not debased even by its use in television advertising and as background music.

Vautor, Thomas (*c.*1580-*c.*1620) English composer and one of the last of the school of madrigalists. *Sweet Suffolk Owl* is his best-known piece.

Vecchi, Orazio (1550-1605) Italian composer, choirmaster and priest. He was *maestro di cappella* at various cathedrals, including Modena, and moved to Correggio in 1586, where he remained until 1593. During this time he composed numerous works, both sacred and secular: *Lamentations* for four voices, motets, madrigals and canzonets. He also wrote *L'Amfiparnaso*, a dramatic sequence of madrigals. This was not intended for the stage, but is generally considered to be a link to early opera. In 1598 he was appointed to the Este court in Modena, where he attained great popularity. His other main groups of works are the *Selva di varia ricreatione* (1590), *Il convito musicale* (1597) and *Le veglie di Siena* (1604).

vedic chant (India) Hymns of the four sacred Hindu scriptures (*Rig Veda, Sāma Veda, Yajur Veda, Athārvā Veda*) which are said to have been received by divine revelation in the first millennium BC. In Indian music history, the highly ornamented tunes of the *Sāma Veda*, as preserved by a few Brahmins, are thought to be the fount of the Sanskritic tradition of Indian music.

veenā (India) See **vīnā**

Végh, Sándor (1912-) Hungarian violinist, founder of the Végh String Quartet, famous for its interpretations of the **Bartók** quartets.

veloce (It.) Indicates uninterrupted smoothness of performance rather than increase in speed.

vent (Fr.) Wind. For example, *instruments à vent*, wind instruments.

Ventadorn, Bernart de (*c.*1135-1195) French **troubadour**, poet and composer, one of the circle attached to the court of Eleanor of Aquitaine. He may have visited England when she married Henry Plantagenet (later Henry II) in 1152. A few of his poems and melodies have survived.

Veracini, Francesco Maria (*c.*1690-1768) Italian violinist and composer of the High Baroque, noted for his violin sonatas and for operas, including *Rosalinda*, based on Shakespeare's play *As You Like It.*

verbunkos 18th-century Hungarian recruiting dance for soldiers, who performed it in full uniform with swords and spurs; the name is derived from the German *Werbung*, recruiting. It had a slow introductory section called a *lassu*, and a quick (*friss*) section. *Verbunkos* were included in some works such as Liszt's *Hungarian Rhapsody* No.2 (1852), **Bartók**'s *Rhapsodies for Violin and Orchestra* (1928), and the **intermezzo** from **Kodály**'s *Háry János* (1926).

Verdelot, Philippe (*c.*1475-1550) Flemish composer, also singer and choirmaster, who spent the greater part of his life in Italy, and is chiefly remembered for his madrigals.

Verdi, Giuseppe (1813-1901) Italian opera composer, the son of a village inn-keeper in Le Roncole, near Parma. The house, little more than a hovel, still stands, and confirms the composer's humble origins. When the father realized his son's great talent, he found the money for a little four-octave **spinet**, which Verdi kept for the rest of his life. In his early years he was helped by local patrons to obtain the necessary training, and in his teens responded by turning out hundreds of marches for the local band and various pieces of church music. But he left it too late by four years for admission to the

Milan Conservatoire, and was forced to study privately, relying on the generosity of his patron Antonio Barezzi, soon to be his father-in-law. Through the help of a friend in Milan his first opera, *Oberto*, was produced in November 1839 at La Scala, the first theatre in Italy. Its success was modest but enough to prompt the manager to commission three more. Of these *Un giorno di regno*, a comedy, failed miserably, perhaps because it was composed at a time of personal tragedy, for within a few months Verdi lost through illness his two children and his wife. With *Nabucco*, however, he found his touch and in the famous chorus of Hebrew slaves, *Va pensiero*, composed what soon became a hymn to freedom.

The theatres in Italy were run by impresarios who engaged not only singers and conductors but also composers. They had resident poets for providing the libretti, either new or some that might have been set already, perhaps more than once, and were therefore safe from interference by the all-powerful censor. Singers came first, and composers were expected to suit their individual vocal qualities, good and bad – the orchestra and the staging were of minor importance. These were the conditions in which Verdi worked for the next ten years, as he said, as a galley slave; a new opera every few months, forced to accept singers and texts he despised, trapped in a style of music that he struggled to change. By 1850 his fame and his financial worth were well enough established for him to be able to dictate his own terms, financial as well as artistic, and with his three middle-period masterpieces, *Rigoletto*, *Il trovatore* and *La traviata*, he raised opera in Italy to a new level of musical expression and dramatic truth. His music was heard in the leading theatres of Europe and he often travelled abroad to conduct. In London in 1847 he met Giuseppina Strepponi, a famous soprano, and soon settled down with her, a union that was to last for 50 years. Commissions came from abroad: he wrote *Les vêpres siciliennes* for Paris, *La forza del destino* for St Petersburg, and *Aïda* to inaugurate the new Cairo opera house in 1871 – *not* for the opening of the Suez canal. Meanwhile the movement for Italian unity under the King of Piedmont-Sardinia was gathering pace, and it was soon realized that Verdi's name provided a slogan, *Viva Verdi*, that could with impunity be painted on walls and shouted in the streets, for it signified *V*ittorio *E*mmanuele *R*e *d'I*talia.

In 1874, Verdi conducted the first performance of his *Requiem* in memory of the writer Manzoni; it was soon recognized as one of the great choral works of the century. After this there was a long period when it seemed that his composing career was over, until at the prompting of his publisher Ricordi, the composer and poet Arrigo **Boito** tempted him with a version of *Othello*. Verdi, a lifelong admirer of Shakespeare, hesitated but finally accepted, and *Otello* was produced in Milan on 5 February 1887. It was a triumph, although critics accused him, absurdly, of Wagnerism, chiefly because of the new importance of the orchestra. Two years later Boito brought him another Shakespeare libretto, this time a version of *The Merry Wives of Windsor*; again Verdi resisted – he remembered well his early failure with comedy, and protested that he was too old. But again he could not resist, and *Falstaff* was produced in Milan on 9 February 1893. Although this was Verdi's last involvement with the stage, in his last years he composed his four sacred pieces, perhaps a reconciliation of his own ambiguous attitude to religion. He died on 27 January 1901, after a stroke, and was accorded a funeral of proportions that matched a life of struggle and triumph. He had become a national hero, but a world artist.

Veress, Sándor (1907-) Hungarian composer and teacher and colleague of **Bartók** in the study of Hungarian and Romanian folk-music. His own compositions include *Homage to Paul Klee* for two pianos and strings, symphonies, concertos and chamber works.

Veretti, Antonio (1900-1978) Italian composer and teacher. He studied at the Bologna Conservatoire with **Alfano**, whose influence was apparent in his early works; later he adopted a more neo-classical style, and eventually turned to **twelve-tone** composition. He wrote several works for the stage (*I sette peccati*, 1956), oratorios (*Il figliuol prodigo*, 1942) and other vocal works, two symphonies, a piano concerto and film scores. He founded a conservatoire in Rome and was director of several other conservatoires in Italy.

verismo (It.) Reality – an operatic style with stories based on realistic contemporary life, often violent, frequently sordid, but always passionate, ushered in by the success in Rome in 1890 of **Mascagni**'s story of Sicilian feuds, *Cavalleria rusticana*, and developed by **Leoncavallo** (*Pagliacci*), **Giordano** (*Andrea Chenier*) and to a lesser extent by **Puccini** in *Fanciulla del West* and *Il tabarro*. *Verismo*, with its shrieks and shouts, its muttering and moaning, spelt the death of **bel canto**. It spread beyond Italy and influenced Alfred **Bruneau** (who brought Zola to the stage), **Massenet**, Strauss, and eventually **Berg**.

Verrett, Shirley (1931-) American mezzo-soprano who studied in Chicago, Los Angeles and at the Juilliard School. Her début was in 1957 in **Britten**'s *The Rape of Lucretia*, and she first sang in Europe in 1959. She made a great impression in the title-role of *Carmen* at the Spoleto Festival in 1962, and has sung the role many times since. Other roles in which her dramatic ability and wide vocal range are used to advantage are Azucena (*Il trovatore*), Eboli (*Don Carlos*), Amneris (*Aïda*), Selika (**Meyerbeer**'s *L'africaine*), Dalila (**Saint-Saëns**'s *Samson et Dalila*) and Dido (Berlioz's *Les troyens*); she has also been successful in the soprano roles of Norma (**Bellini**), Lady Macbeth (Verdi) and Tosca (Puccini).

verse In Anglican church music, a service or piece (such as an anthem) that makes use of a solo voice (as opposed to a full choir) for some passages. The verse **anthem** features such passages.

verset Short organ piece containing some reference to a given **plainsong** tune. The name is derived from an arrangement used in the Roman Catholic Church of replacing every other sung verse of **psalms** by interludes on the organ to relieve the supposed monotony of plainsong.

Viadana, Lodovico Grosso da (1560-1630) Italian composer and monk who adopted his name from his birthplace. He wrote **madrigals**, songs and a large collection of instrumental *concerti ecclesiastici*.

Viardot, Pauline (1821-1910) French mezzo-soprano, daughter of the Spanish tenor Manuel **García** and sister of Maria **Malibran**. She studied with her family and with Liszt, and made her stage début in 1839 as Desdemona in Rossini's *Otello*. She created the role of Fidès in **Meyerbeer**'s *Le prophète* (1849) and in 1859 sang Orfeo in **Gluck's** *Orfeo ed Euridice* in Berlioz's edition, in which she scored a tremendous success. She was the first singer of Brahms's *Alto Rhapsody*. She was instrumental in forwarding the careers of **Gounod**, **Massenet** and **Fauré**, and was at the centre of an intellectual circle which included Chopin, George Sand and Turgenev, whose mistress she was. She also promoted Russian music in the West.

vibraphone Percussion instrument, similar to the **marimba**, in which the resonating lids are made to vibrate by means of electric motors, and thus produce a bell-like sound. The vibraphone has been used in the modern orchestra by a number of composers including **Britten, Berg** (*Lulu*, 1934) and **Messiaen** (*Trois petites liturgies de la Présence Divine*, 1944).

vibrato (It.) Shaken – indicating a rapid but mute fluctuation in pitch which is used to improve tone. It is now almost universally used in string playing and is produced by a rapid movement of the left hand. In wind instruments the effect can be obtained by control of the breath and **embouchure**.

Vicentino, Nicolà (1511-1572) Italian Renaissance composer and scholar, interested in the revival of ancient Greek music. He also composed **madrigals**.

Vickers, Jon (1926-) Canadian tenor, noted for his versatility in major operatic roles by Wagner, Verdi, **Britten** and others. He has made many appearances at Covent Garden (where he made his début in 1957), the Metropolitan Opera, New York (début in 1960), Bayreuth and La Scala. His roles include Florestan in Beethoven's *Fidelio*, the title-roles in Verdi's *Otello* and *Don Carlos*, Tristan in Wagner's *Tristan und Isolde* and the title-role in Britten's *Peter Grimes*. He is a powerful actor with a ringing heroic tenor.

Victoria, Tomás Luis de (*c*.1548-1611) Spanish composer of the High Renaissance who spent many years as organist and choirmaster in Rome (hence the alternative spelling of his name as Vittoria). He was a priest in Rome and chaplain to the Dowager Empress in Madrid; it is likely that he studied with **Palestrina**, whose funeral he is known to have attended. He wrote a large body of choral church music – Masses (including a Requiem), magnificats, motets, hymns, psalms – in the polyphonic style of his time, but charged with a degree of drama and passion that distinguishes it from the music of Palestrina. All his work is Latin sacred music, and testifies to the position he is considered to hold as the greatest composer of Renaissance Spain, and one of the finest in the Europe of his time.

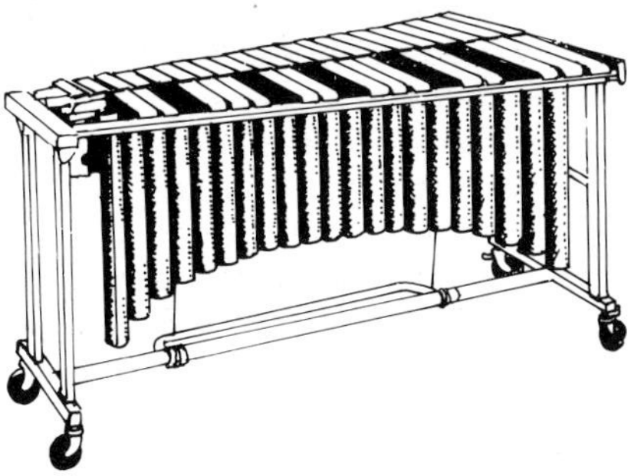

Vibraphone

Victory, Gerard (1921-) Assumed name of the Irish composer and conductor Alan Loraine. Among his works are several operas, in English or Gaelic. He has also acted as director of music for Radio Telefis Eireann.

vide (Fr.) Indication that a player should play on an open string.

video Since the 1970s the revolution in 'home entertainment' has meant that top-class opera and ballet with international casts have come within the reach of a huge audience. Thousands of people who are rarely or never able to go to an opera-house have benefited from the enterprise of many video production companies. The Royal Opera House, Covent Garden, and the English National Opera have created video films of their most popular productions, which are on sale by post and at their own shops. Some older films of great performances have also been preserved on videotape. Sometimes productions are specially filmed, so that the full range of possible effects can be utilized; in other cases the video is a straight record of the stage performance. There are also available many compilations of excerpts, as well as behind-the-scenes documentaries such as a portrait of von **Karajan** at work.

Vienna Boys' Choir Austrian choir founded in 1498 when it was part of the chapel of the former Austrian imperial court. It is internationally known for its secular performances. It tours widely and performs with the Vienna State Opera.

Vienna Philharmonic Orchestra Austrian orchestra founded in 1842 under the composer/conductor Otto **Nicolai**. Its activities were cut short by the 1848 Revolution and did not resume on a regular basis until 1860. The Vienna Philharmonic is one of the world's greatest orchestras. Its principal conductors have included many legendary musicians and interpreters of the classics, notably Hans **Richter**, Gustav **Mahler**, Felix **Weingartner**, Wilhelm **Furtwängler**, Bruno **Walter**, Karl **Böhm**, Herbert von **Karajan** and Claudio **Abbado**. The Vienna Philharmonic Orchestra is an autonomous organization formed from members of the Vienna State Opera. Its recordings of a huge repertory are too numerous to list, and are always of the highest quality.

Vierne, Louis (1870-1937) French organist who studied with **Franck** and **Widor**. He was organist at Notre Dame Cathedral, Paris, until his death and professor of that instrument at the Schola Cantorum. His works include five organ symphonies. Vierne was blind from birth.

Vieuxtemps, Henri (1820-1881) Belgian violinist and composer who made his début aged six and toured Europe and the United States as one of the greatest violin virtuosi of his time. He studied with **Bériot**, Sechter and **Reicha**, and was noticed by **Paganini**. Berlioz too had praise for him, not only as a performer but as a composer. He became violin professor in St Petersburg and Brussels, where he taught **Ysaÿe**. His seven concertos for the instrument are notable additions to the Romantic concerto repertory.

vif (Fr.) Lively. Sometimes appears as *vivement*, in a lively way.

Vignoles, Roger (1945-) English pianist, one of the leading accompanists of the day, notable for his great sensitivity to the requirements of his colleagues. He studied at Cambridge and at the Royal College of Music and began his career as a *répétiteur* at Covent Garden (1969-71). His partnerships with the singers Thomas **Allen**, Kiri Te **Kanawa**, Arleen **Auger** and especially Sarah **Walker** are outstanding; among his fine recordings are Schumann's *Dichterliebe* with Allen and the complete songs of **Duparc** with Allen and Walker. He has also collaborated with many instrumentalists, among them Ralph Kirshbaum (cello) and Nobuko Imai (viola), and has toured extensively in Europe, the United States and Japan.

vihuela (Sp.) Spanish **lute**, made in the shape of a **guitar**. It dates back to at least the 13th century, but became obsolete in about the 16th century.

Villa-Lobos, Heitor (1887-1959) Brazilian composer, the first Latin American one to enjoy international fame. He studied the cello and also learnt to play the guitar; at the age of 18 he set out on a journey through Brazil which provided him with thematic material for some of his later works. On his return he studied composition, but was not very disciplined and quickly went his own way. After various commissions including that for his Symphony No.3, a picture of World War I (1922), he went to Paris, where he was received with enthusiasm. He returned to Brazil in 1930 and settled into the musical establishment, teaching and advising. He founded the Academy of Music in Rio in 1945. He wrote operas, ballets, symphonies and many other orchestral, instrumental and vocal works. His best-known compositions are *Chôros*, a group of pieces inspired by South American native and popular music, and *Bachianas Brasileiras*, pieces combining the styles of J.S. Bach and Brazilian musical idioms (including the descriptive 'Little Train of the Caipira'). His preludes and studies for guitar are among his most popular and enduring works.

villancio (Sp.) 1. A 16th-century Spanish song made up of several verses with refrains between them.

2. A 17th-century Spanish term for an extended **cantata** with orchestra, often sung at Christmas.

villanella (It.) Part-song of the mid-16th century, set to rustic words and light in character.

villanelle (Fr.) Vocal setting of a poem which consists of stanzas of three lines, the first and third lines of the opening stanza being repeated alternately as the third line of the succeeding stanzas. It is similar to the Italian **villanella**, but not identical.

vīnā/veenā (India) Ancient name associated with several types of harp and lute in India. It now refers to the plucked lute of southern India which resembles the **bīn** of the north, having fixed frets and no sympathetic strings. There is, however, only one small gourd, attached to the upper end of the neck.

viol A type of bowed stringed instrument first developed in Italy in the 15th century, current until it was supplanted by the **violin** family at the end of the 17th. The viols had frets on the fingerboard like a guitar, and could all be called viola da **gamba**, because they were played resting on the knee, or in the case of the bass (commonly known as viola da gamba), held *between* the knees, rather like a **cello**. Both shape and number of strings depended on local practice. In England a consort of viols, for which **Purcell** and others wrote, consisted of two trebles, two tenors and two basses. There were also the division viol, a small bass viol used for elaborate figurations, and the lyra viol for special tonal effects. The viol has been revived in recent times for the **authentic** performance of early music, although the **double-bass** with its flat back and sloping shoulders has always proclaimed its viol ancestry.

Viol

viola Bowed four-stringed instrument that is the tenor member of the **violin** family. Its strings are tuned at intervals of a fifth, the lowest being C below middle C (C, G, D, A). The viola is the third member of the string section of the orchestra and the string quartet. For many years it was poorly played, and thought unsuitable for solos, although Berlioz wrote *Harold en Italie* for it as a commission from **Paganini**. Its emancipation may be attributed to the English player Lionel **Tertis**, who at the beginning of the 20th century astonished musicians by playing violin concertos because of a lack of solo music for his instrument. Composers responded and that want has been filled by concertos from **Hindemith**, **Walton**, and **Bartók**. Tertis was also the stimulus for a design of a larger viola, with a richer tone, but this has not been widely adopted.

Viola

viola da braccio In effect, the name given to the violin or viola in the 17th century, as these were played on the arm.

viola da gamba See **viol** or **gamba**

viola d'amore Bowed stringed instrument of the **viol** type, but not related to the viol family; it is played like a **violin**. The *viola d'amore* has seven bowed strings and seven to 14 sympathetic strings not touched by the bow, but vibrated with those actually played. It was a popular instrument of the 18th century. It was included by **Meyerbeer** (*Les Huguenots*) and **Janáček** (*Katya Kabanova*).

violin Smallest and highest of the current bowed stringed instruments, with four strings tuned G (below middle C), D, A, E. It has a range of four octaves.

Violins were first made in Italy during the middle of the 16th century. They evolved from the fiddle and the *lira da braccio*. The master violin-makers came from three families in Cremona, the most famous members of which were Nicolo **Amati** (1596-1684), Giuseppe **Guarneri** (1698-1744) and Antonio **Stradivari** (1644-1737).

With the increasing importance of strings in the orchestra, and the emergence of the string quartet as a medium for chamber music, came the virtual eclipse of the **viol** in the 18th century and its replacement by the violin and other members of its family. Since the time of Stradivari there have been subtle but important variations in design, especially in Germany and France, and early instruments have been modified. The finger-board has been lengthened and angled down; the bass bar stuck under the belly has been enlarged; the bridge has been reshaped to allow better separation of strings; the strings themselves, once of gut, are now usually synthetic or metal-covered gut.

In an orchestra the players are normally divided into the first and second violins, corresponding to higher- and lower-pitched parts. The leader of the first violins is also the leader of the orchestra, and dictates such things as bowing.

The brilliance of the violin encouraged the writing of solo concertos from the 18th century onwards by a vast number of composers both major and minor.

Violin

violoncello Full name of the lowest member of the violin family; usually shortened to **cello**.

violone Alternative term for the double-bass **viol**.

Viotti, Giovanni Battista (1755-1824) Italian violinist and composer who studied in Turin with **Pugnani** and at first played in the court orchestra there. He travelled with Pugnani to various European cities in 1780, in the course of which his Violin Concerto No.3 was published. He scored a great success as a performer in Paris, where he went in 1781. He joined Queen Marie Antoinette's musical establishment, and set up an opera-house which presented the works of **Cherubini** and many other Italian and French composers. Following the French Revolution he moved to London in 1792, where he was again very well received. However, in 1798 he was ordered out of England as a spy and lived in Germany for a while. He returned to England in 1801, but did not play in public again, although he continued to compose.

His last appointment was as director of the Paris Opéra (1819-21). His compositions include almost 30 violin concertos and sonatas, as well as several string quartets and trios.

virginal Earliest form of **harpsichord**.

virtuoso A musician who has achieved complete mastery over the instrument he or she plays. It is not an attribute that a musician is born with, but something that begins with a basic talent and is gradually developed by an obsessive dedication to practice.

Vishnevskaya, Galina (1926-) Russian soprano who studied in Leningrad and made her début there as an operetta singer in 1944. She joined the Bolshoi company in 1952, singing Tatiana in Tchaikovsky's *Eugene Onegin*, Natasha in **Prokofiev**'s *War and Peace* and many other roles in the Russian repertory. Her début at the Metropolitan, New York, was in 1961, and at Covent Garden the following year; on both occasions she sang the title-role in *Aïda*. Her other roles include Leonore (Beethoven's *Fidelio*) and the title-roles in *Madama Butterfly*, *Tosca* and *Katerina Ismailova*. She is married to the cellist Mstislav **Rostropovich**, and has often appeared with him at **Aldeburgh** and elsewhere, singing the music of **Britten** and **Shostakovich**.

Vitali, Giovanni Battista (*c.*1632-1692) Italian violinist and composer, both a church and court musician who is said to have been a pioneer of the Baroque trio sonata.

Vitali, Tommaso Antonio (1663-1745) Italian violinist and composer, son of Giovanni Battista **Vitali**. A famous chaconne for violin is attributed to him.

Vitry, Philippe de (1291-1361) French composer, priest and courtier. Little of his own music has survived, but he is important in musical history for his treatises on **ars nova**, which marked a link between the music of the Middle Ages and that of the Renaissance.

Vittoria, Tomás Luis de Alternative spelling of Tomás Luis de **Victoria**.

vivace (It.) Direction that a piece of music should be played in a lively, animated manner.

Vivaldi, Antonio (1678-1741) Italian composer, violinist and priest (known as *il prete rosso*, 'the red priest', on account of his hair). The son of a Venetian violinist, he took holy orders in 1703, but did not continue long with his priestly duties because of poor health. In the same year he became a teacher at one of the four girls' orphanages in Venice, the Ospedale della Pietà, and was eventually *maestro di cappella*; he was connected with the orphanage for much of his life. The high level of talent fostered there is apparent from the variety of instruments for which Vivaldi composed his numerous concertos, but it is for the violin that the majority were written. He also produced many fine sonatas for violin, flute and cello. In 1711 his collection of 12 violin concertos, *L'estro harmonico*, was published. This added to his growing fame, particularly in Germany, where his music was well received. Bach admired it and indeed transcribed some of the violin pieces for keyboard; the Dresden court commissioned works from him. From about 1713 Vivaldi started to write operas, and produced more than 45 altogether (*Orlando finto pazzo*, 1714; *Griselda*, 1735), the production and promotion of which necessitated long journeys around Europe. However, less than half of these works survive, and are little heard nowadays. In another vein, he wrote a number of sacred pieces which are vigorous and rhythmic in character; among them are three oratorios (*Juditha triumphans*, 1716, and two which are lost), Masses, motets and psalms.

It is the concertos, however, for which he is most renowned. Of the 500 or so in total that he produced, nearly half are for violin, and many of these are programmatic works. The set published in 1725 includes *Le quattro stagioni* (The Four Seasons), a vivid description of the phenomena typifying each stage of the year – the spring song of birds, the languorous heat and thunderstorms of summer, the rhythm of horses' hooves in the autumn hunt, the pleasure of being indoors by a fire when the ice is on the river in winter. These four concertos are not only Vivaldi's most famous work but are among the most popular 'serious' music today; several recordings of them appear consistently in the classical Top Twenty, and appeal particularly to young people whose musical knowledge may be limited – a reflection, perhaps, of the years Vivaldi spent composing for the girls of the orphanage.

vivo (It.) Lively, little used as an instruction. The more common term is **vivace**.

Vlad, Roman (1919-) Romanian composer, scholar and teacher, who has worked mainly in Italy. His works include the ballet *La dama delle camelie*, and *Variazione concertanti* for piano and orchestra, extracted from a theme in Mozart's *Don Giovanni.*

Vladigerov, Pancho (1899-1978) Bulgarian composer and pianist, whose works include the opera *Tsar Kaloyan*. His son Alexander (1933-) is also a composer and conductor.

vocalise (Fr.) Name given to vocal exercises, and to a popular wordless song-piece by **Rachmaninov**, originally with piano accompaniment but later arranged for orchestra alone.

vocalize To sing a piece without words, but on one single vowel; also to practise vocal exercises.

vocal score **Score** that gives the vocal parts in full, reducing the orchestral score to a piano part only. The alternative American term is piano-vocal score.

voce (It.) Voice. The direction *colla voce* (with the voice) indicates that the accompaniment should allow the vocal part some freedom and follow accordingly.

Vogel, Vladimir (1896-1984) Swiss composer of German and Russian parentage who was at first influenced by **Scriabin** and **Busoni**. In 1918 he went to Berlin to study, and was drawn to the work of the expressionists and **Schoenberg**. From 1925 his reputation began to spread abroad. His music made a particular feature of the use of speech alongside song (*Sprechlieder nach August Stramm*, 1922), a form developed to a high degree in *Thyl Claes*, a huge work in two parts written between 1938 and 1945. The words of the Swiss sculptor Hans Arp are the basis for *Arpiade* (1954), which used a speaking chorus in an ingenious way. Vogel's adoption of **twelve-tone** method is apparent from his Violin Concerto of 1937. His choral works include *Wagadu's Untergang durch die Eitelkeit* (1930), *Jona ging doch nach Ninive* (1958) and *Flucht* (1964); he also wrote orchestral pieces, chamber music and film scores.

Vogelweide, Walther von der (*c.*1170-1230) German *Minnesinger.* Only about eight of his melodies have survived, but he is an important figure in medieval music. He features in Wagner's *Tannhäuser* and *Die Meistersinger von Nürnberg.*

Vogler, Georg Joseph (1749-1814) German composer, pianist, organist and teacher. He held many teaching posts, numbering **Meyerbeer** and **Weber** among his pupils. He composed operas, sacred music and organ works.

voice No doubt the first music was uttered by the human voice, and it remains a supreme vehicle of musical expression. Experts are by no means unanimous in their analysis of the vocal functions, but it is generally agreed that the basic sound is produced by breath acting on the vocal cords in the larynx or voice-box (Adam's apple).

The main categories are as follows: **soprano, mezzo-soprano, alto** (or **contralto**); **counter-tenor** or male alto, **tenor, baritone** and **bass**. A boy's voice, usually called treble, is a clear soprano which with puberty normally breaks into the adult baritone. In the past this change was occasionally stopped by castration (see **castrato**).

A man and woman seem to have two voices, chest and head, separated by a break; men, apart from counter-tenors, usually sing with the lower voice, women with the upper, although training can produce what is called the mixed voice which seems to combine characteristics of both. Depending on fashion, dramatic necessity and sheer fatigue, tenors occasionally use the falsetto or head voice for their upper register, a practice which was universal until the middle of the 19th century, when the chest voice began to be taken throughout the range. On the other hand female singers may use the unmixed chest voice to great dramatic effect, a practice more followed in the past than today.

The term voice is also used to mean one melody or theme in a polyphonic composition.

voice leading (US) Part-writing, from the German *Stimmführung*.

voix celeste 2.4m (8ft) organ stop with two pipes to each note, one tuned slightly sharper than the other, so that they produce an ethereal wavering quality.

volante (It.) Flying. Fast and light.

Volkonsky, Andrei (1933-) Swiss-born composer who worked in the Soviet Union before emigrating to Israel in 1973. Compositions, influenced by **Schoenberg**, include the cantata *Dead Souls* and *Serenade to an Insect*, for small orchestra.

volles Werk (Ger.) Full organ.

volta (It.) Time. For example, *prima volta* – first time, *seconda volta* – second time and *ancora una volta* – once again.

volti subito (It.) Indication that a quick turn of the page of a score is necessary.

voluntary Organ music intended for use in the church, but not part of the service. It is played at the beginning of the service and especially at the end when the congregation leaves. See also **trumpet voluntary**.

von Stade, Frederica See **Stade, Frederica von**

Voříšek, Jan (1791-1825) Bohemian composer, pianist and organist, and friend of **Hummel** and **Moscheles**. He studied piano, violin and organ, as well as composition, and was a child prodigy. At ten he entered the Prague Gymnasium. Later he studied with **Tomášek**, who was a formative influence. He settled in Vienna, where he came to the attention of Beethoven and Schubert and was admired by them. He wrote symphonies, concertos, sonatas and a group of piano pieces entitled *Impromptus*. There were many other works for keyboard; his Piano Sonata Op.20 was dedicated to the wife of Beethoven's doctor, who attended him in his last illness.

Vorschlag (Ger.) The equivalent of **appoggiatura**.

Vorspiel (Ger.) Prelude or overture.

Vranický, Anton (1766-1820) Moravian composer and violinist who studied with Haydn and Mozart and served Prince Maximilian Lobkowitz (Beethoven's patron). His works include symphonies and violin concertos. The German spelling of his name is Wranitzky.

Vranický, Paul (1756-1808) Moravian composer and violinist, brother of Anton **Vranický**. He played in the Eszterházy Orchestra under Haydn. He composed operas, symphonies and string quartets. The German spelling of his name is Wranitzky.

vuota (It.) Direction to string-players to play a note or notes on an open string.

W

Waart, Edo de (1941-) Dutch conductor and oboist, musical director of the Netherlands Wind Ensemble, principal conductor of the Rotterdam Philharmonic Orchestra, and a frequent guest conductor elsewhere in Europe and the United States. He was music director of the San Francisco Symphony Orchestra, 1977-85, and of the Minnesota Orchestra from 1986. He has made recordings of an extensive repertory ranging from Bach to **Gershwin**.

Wagenaar, Bernard (1894-1971) American composer and violinist, born in the Netherlands, the son of Johan **Wagenaar**. He studied at Utrecht and was a teacher for some years before emigrating to the United States in 1920. He worked as a violinist with the New York Philharmonic Orchestra and taught at the Juilliard School. His compositions include four symphonies, a Sinfonietta, a Triple Concerto, a Violin Concerto and the *Song of Mourning* (1944), a piece in memory of Dutch patriots killed in the war; vocal music, string quartets and music for various solo instruments.

Wagenaar, Johan (1862-1941) Dutch composer and teacher who studied in Utrecht and Berlin. He taught in Utrecht, becoming director of the Conservatoire and cathedral organist as well as conducting two choirs. From 1919 to 1937 he was director of the Hague Conservatoire. His works are romantic in style and include two operas (*The Doge of Venice*, 1901; *The Cid*, 1915); an overture, *Cyrano de Bergerac* (1905); a symphonic poem (*Saul and David*, 1906); a cantata (*The Shipwreck*, 1889); a piece for mezzo and orchestra, *Aveux de Phèdre*; and several organ pieces.

Wagenseil, Georg Christoph (1715-1777) Austrian composer and music master to the Empress Maria Theresa. Wagenseil composed numerous operas, symphonies and instrumental pieces that mark a transition from the Baroque to the classical style.

Wagner, Richard (1813-1883) German composer, a giant of the 19th century, with a profound influence on music, the theatre, philosophy, aesthetics and politics. It is probable that he was the natural son of a Jewish actor, Ludwig Geyer, his step-father. He was educated at the Leipzig Gymnasium and for a while at the University, and in 1833 obtained a position as chorus-master of the opera in Würzburg. The following year he completed his opera *Die Feen* (The Fairies), which waited 50 years to be produced, followed by *Liebesverbot* (The Ban on Love, based on *Measure for Measure*, 1836). Wagner earned his living as a conductor of growing authority, until in 1839 he went with his wife, Minna, to Paris, to spend two poverty-stricken years trying to make his way as a composer, coming under the influence of French grand opera developed by **Spontini** and **Meyerbeer**. His first success came with the production of his opera *Rienzi* in Dresden in 1842, which led to his being appointed court conductor. But already the sheer length and difficulty of his music was meeting resistance from artists and critics alike; *Der fliegende Holländer* (The Flying Dutchman) fared badly in Dresden (1843), and worse in Berlin.

He had always written his own texts, and now began work on a series of what he later called music dramas, based on German mythology – he took first the story of *Tannhäuser*, produced with some success in 1845, and then completed *Lohengrin*. In May 1849, when revolution erupted in Dresden, he mounted the barricades and was forced to flee, first to **Liszt** in Weimar, then to Zurich, and to Paris, where he hoped to find fame. Meanwhile Liszt mounted *Lohengrin* with great success in Weimar. On his return to Zurich, Wagner began work on a new cycle of mythological operas that was to be *Der Ring des Nibelungen* (The Nibelung's Ring), and under the influence of a love affair with Mathilde Wesendonck, the wife of a rich businessman, was drawn to the story of Tristan and Isolt.

Although his operas were now beginning to be performed in other theatres, he was desperately short of money. When his exile from Germany was revoked he visited Vienna and hoped that *Tristan und Isolde* would be performed, but it was abandoned as impossible after 77 rehearsals. After this experience he started work on *Die Meistersinger von Nürnberg* (The Mastersingers of Nuremberg), intending to write an opera that could easily be produced in any theatre, but his debts forced him to continue his wanderings, short of money but always requiring luxury and the devotion of an attractive woman. In fact he was saved by King Ludwig II of Bavaria, who had become besotted with Wagner and his music, and now offered him, as it seemed, unlimited funds. In delight the composer hurried to Munich and at once made plans for the production of *Tristan und Isolde* (1865) and *Die Meistersinger* (1868), with the eminent musician Hans von **Bülow** to help him as conductor; Bülow's wife Cosima, Liszt's daughter, provided the devotion. When the court in Munich rebelled against his presence and the drain on the exchequer, Wagner was forced to leave. In 1870 he married Cosima, who had already borne him two daughters, his first wife Minna having died four years earlier. In 1871 the town council of Bayreuth agreed to build a special festival theatre, and in 1876 under the baton of Hans Richter *The Ring* was given there complete for the first time, followed, in 1882, by *Parsifal*, Wagner's last music drama. He died in Venice at the age of seventy.

A brief biography does scant justice to Wagner's artistic achievement. He revolutionized the approach to conducting; his performances of the classics set a style that held sway for nearly a century. He took chromatic harmony to its ultimate complexity; he transformed the nature of musical expression, by revealing its power to reach the emotions without the intervention of the conscious mind; his development of the **leitmotif**, to express a character's personality or an abstract concept such as redemption through love, allowed him to weave a seamless stream of music that gripped the audience's feelings as they witnessed cosmic dramas. He brought to the musical stage unheard-of dramatic style: he made singers see their roles as part of a drama, rather than as vehicles for vocal display; he insisted on the correct setting and costumes; he put the auditorium in darkness, and concealed the orchestra and conductor so that the audience's attention was concentrated on the stage. His writings alone would fill a large shelf. Like Caesar he bestrode the world, and his contemporaries surrendered or rebelled: there were no half-measures. Those who followed, such as Bruckner, Strauss and Mahler, proudly acknowledged their debt, but there was hardly a major figure who was not influenced in some way, even if it led to deliberate rejection of his musical personality. Many of his ideas, such as overt anti-semitism, have long since lost credence, but his music continues to obsess musicians and audiences alike.

Wagner, Siegfried (1869-1930) German composer and conductor, the son of Richard and Cosima **Wagner**. He studied with **Humperdinck** and became artistic director of the Bayreuth Festival. He also composed operas, symphonic poems and other works.

Wagner, Wieland (1917-1966) German opera producer and director, the son of Siegfried **Wagner**. He was active in the Bayreuth Festival before World War II; but his most important work was done after the war, when he became co-director of the Festival with his brother Wolfgang. Their revolutionary productions marked an exciting new chapter in the Festival's history, and helped to purge it of Nazi associations.

Wagner-Régeny, Rudolf (1903-1969) German composer and conductor, active mainly in Berlin before and after World War II. His works, primarily operas (*Der Günstling*, 1935; *Die Bürger von Calais*, 1939) and ballets, were influenced by the music of Kurt **Weill** and **Schoenberg**; they caused him to fall from favour with the Nazis. After the war he taught and composed in a **twelve-tone** manner. The works of his last period are sacred in character and include several cantatas.

Wagner tuba See **tuba**

wagon (Japan) Six-stringed **zither**, with the strings passing over inverted V-shaped bridges placed to provide its fixed open-string tuning. Its musical function is generally to play stereotyped patterns. The *wagon* is indigenous to Japan and is used in *kagura shinto* music and **gagaku** court music.

Walcha, Helmuth (1907-) German organist, blind since youth, who studied in Leipzig and has held important posts, as organist and teacher, throughout Germany. His début was in Leipzig in 1924; he has given numerous international recitals, and played in London in the late 1960s. He has recorded all the organ music of J.S. Bach, and is recognized as an outstanding interpreter, faithful to the composer's intentions and expressing them with absolute clarity. He is also a composer of organ works.

Waldhorn (Ger.) Forest horn or hunting horn. It is a natural horn, consisting of a single, coiled tube without valves.

Waldteufel, Emile (1837-1915) Alsatian-French pianist, who studied at the Paris Conservatoire, served at the court of the Empress Eugénie, and wrote many dances, including the well-known waltz *Les Patineurs* (Skaters' Waltz).

Walker, Ernest (1870-1949) English composer and musical scholar, who studied at Oxford University, then became music director at Balliol College. His compositions include a *Stabat Mater*. Walker also wrote, with Sir Jack **Westrup**, *A History of Music in England*.

Walker, Sarah English mezzo-soprano. She studied violin at the Royal College of Music and singing with Vera Rozsa. She made her début in 1970 at Glyndebourne in *La Calisto*. In recitals she has formed a notable partnership with Roger **Vignoles**, with whom she has made a number of recordings (including the complete songs of **Duparc**). She has also achieved great success as an opera-singer, in numerous roles ranging from Poppea in **Monteverdi**'s *L'incoronazione di Poppea* to Rose Parrow in Maxwell **Davies**'s *Taverner*. Other roles include Dido in Berlioz's *Les troyens*, the Countess in Tchaikovsky's *The Queen of Spades*, Baba the Turk in Stravinsky's *The Rake's Progress* and Dalila in **Saint-Saëns**'s *Samson et Dalila*.

Wallace, Vincent (1812-1865) Irish composer, who played the organ and violin as a boy, emigrated to Australia, then returned to London, where he composed *Maritana* and at least six other operas. Wallace's other works – songs and piano solos – also gained great popularity in Victorian England.

Wallace, William (1860-1940) Scottish composer and musical scholar, who practised medicine before embarking on a career in music. He wrote symphonic poems, probably the first by a British composer, was a professor at the Royal Academy of Music, and wrote a book, *A Study of Wagner.*

Walmisley, Thomas Attwood (1814-1856) English organist, principally at Cambridge University, where he was also professor of music and composer of church choral and organ music. He did much to revive interest in the music of J.S. Bach. He was also a noted mathematician.

Walter, Bruno (1876-1962) Jewish conductor born in Germany. His family name was Schlesinger, which he later changed. At the age of 17 he got a job as *répétiteur* in the Cologne opera, and moved to Hamburg a year later. Here he met **Mahler**, and was able to conduct in public for the first time. From there he moved through Breslau (Wrocław), Pressburg (Bratislava) and Riga. After a brief, unhappy period in Berlin, he joined Mahler in Vienna. But in the anti-semitic atmosphere there Walter passed 11 difficult years. He took engagements abroad and in 1909 made his début at Covent Garden, conducting Ethel **Smyth**'s *The Wreckers*. In 1913 he moved to his first important post, as music director in Munich; he conducted the première of Mahler's *Das Lied von der Erde* there in 1911, and Symphony No.9 in Vienna in 1912. Later he worked through a series of appointments and guest engagements in Europe and America. With the coming of Hitler he was forced out of his position with the Leipzig Gewandhaus Orchestra in 1933, and from Vienna in 1938; he became a citizen of France, and then sailed to the United States in October 1939. There he divided his time between Los Angeles and New York, conducting at the Metropolitan and the New York Philharmonic. He recorded much of his favourite repertory with an orchestra of indifferent quality, the Columbia Symphony. Walter had a particularly happy association with Britain – his mellow, even sentimental approach suited British taste. After the war his memorable concerts in Edinburgh with the **Vienna Philharmonic** and Kathleen **Ferrier** were landmarks in post-war music-making. His most valuable recordings are generally held to be those taken from Mahler concerts in Vienna in 1937, and the fascinating rehearsals of Mozart, Beethoven and Wagner taken in New York. He wrote an interesting study of Mahler, whom he knew intimately, and a revealing autobiography.

Walton, Sir William (1902-1983) English composer, who was largely self-taught and developed a distinctive style, noted for clear, bright orchestration and certain affinities with jazz music. He studied at Oxford and was an intimate of the Sitwell family for almost ten years after he left; he created an early sensation with *Façade* (1922), settings of satirical poems by Edith Sitwell (better known today in the form of two orchestral suites or as a ballet), and with his overture *Portsmouth Point* (1925). His Viola Concerto (1929) was also written during this period, and can be seen as his first mature production. A substantial work

Sir William Walton

of the next few years was the oratorio *Belshazzar's Feast* (1931), a contribution to the English tradition by a composer who was already viewed with admiration and, to some extent, suspicion for his somewhat 'Parisian' modernity. His Symphony No.1 (1935) and Violin Concerto reveal the influence of **Elgar**, although the symphony also owes certain elements to **Sibelius**. It was conducted at its première by Hamilton **Harty**, who became a close associate and gave Walton much encouragement. Other friends and associates included Lord **Berners**, Constant **Lambert** and the conductor Malcolm **Sargent**.

In 1934 Walton had begun composing film music; he was also commissioned to write a ceremonial march for the coronation of King George VI in 1937, *Crown Imperial*. Film and ballet music occupied him during the war years: the patriotic *The First of the Few* (1942), with its *Spitfire Prelude and Fugue*; *The Wise Virgins* (1940), – an arrangement of Bach pieces – and *The Quest* (1943), both for the Sadler's Wells Ballet; and three Shakespeare plays filmed with Laurence Olivier, of which *Henry V* became the most famous, the score being particularly evocative and admired.

After the war Walton married and settled in the Italian island of Ischia, from where he travelled to the United States, Britain, Russia and Australasia to conduct his own compositions. His later works include two operas, *Troilus and Cressida* (1954, premièred at Covent Garden) and *The Bear* (1967, for the Aldeburgh Festival); a Cello Concerto (1956), and another symphony (1960). He also composed a second coronation march, this time for Queen Elizabeth in 1953: *Orb and Sceptre*. Among his other works are a set of variations on a theme by **Hindemith**, whom he greatly admired, and another on an impromptu by **Britten**; some witty songs, and a number of sacred pieces including a *Missa brevis* (1966) and an unaccompanied motet, *Cantico del sole* (1974), which was among his last works. Knighted in 1951, Walton was awarded the Order of Merit in 1968.

waltz Dance in 3/4 time, which can be slow or fast. The origin of the waltz is said to have been the German *Ländler* in the late 18th century. The name is taken from the German *walzen* (modern *wälzen*), meaning to turn. An early form, consisting of two sections of eight bars, may be found in the works of Mozart and Beethoven, and it was developed by Schubert and **Weber**, the first composer to adopt the waltz as a purely instrumental form.

At the beginning of the 19th century the waltz spread to France and England where it became a popular ballroom dance. The compositions of the **Lanner** and **Strauss** families achieved immense popularity. Waltzes not intended for the ballroom have been written by many composers, other than those already mentioned, including **Chopin**'s fourteen piano waltzes.

Wanhal, Johann Alternative spelling of the name of **Johann Vanhal**.

Ward, John (1571-1638) English composer, representative of late Renaissance and Tudor music with his output of madrigals and many other pieces for viols and the virginal.

Warlock, Peter (1894-1930) Assumed name of Philip Heseltine, English composer and writer on music, a friend of **Delius**, **Moeran**, **Lambert** and other leading British musicians of his generation. He was self-taught, with no musical background. After his meeting with Delius in 1910 his interest in music was decisively stimulated. His friendship with van **Dieren** gave him the confidence to write a number of songs, which were published in 1919 and very well received. Meanwhile his studies of early music continued, and by the mid-1920s he was recognized as an authority. As a composer he is noted above all for his songs, including the song-cycle *The Curlew* for tenor with instrumental accompaniment; many love-songs; and witty, sometimes bawdy drinking-songs. Warlock also wrote the popular *Capriol Suite* for strings, based on French dances by **Arbeau**.

water organ Alternative term for **hydraulis**.

Watkins, Michael (1948-) English composer, who studied with Elisabeth **Lutyens** and Richard Rodney **Bennett**, and has made a special study of the guitar and lute, which feature in some of his works. His Double Concerto for oboe and guitar won the Menuhin Composition Prize in 1975.

Watts, Helen (1927-) Welsh contralto, who sang in the Glyndebourne chorus and took many operatic roles, but is noted primarily for her performances in **oratorio**, especially of Bach, Handel and **Elgar**. She was made CBE in 1978.

wayang kulit (Indonesia) Shadow play with leather puppets which are operated by a single puppeteer or *dalang* and used at temple festivals, cremation and purification ceremonies; it is generally performed late at night. The texts are based on the *Mahābhārata*. In Bali it is accompanied by the *gendèr wayang*, a quartet of two pairs of ten-keyed **gendèr**. For dramatic or battle scenes from the *Rāmāyana*, drums, gongs and cymbals are added.

Webbe, Samuel (1740-1816) English organist and composer of a wide range of church and vocal music, from Masses and motets to secular songs and choruses. His son Samuel also wrote vocal music and music textbooks.

Weber, Carl Maria von (1786-1826) German composer, conductor and pianist. When he was ten he started piano lessons and revealed such talent that he was put to study with Michael Haydn. While he was still 13, Weber composed his first opera (now lost) and several other pieces, and was apprenticed in Munich to Aloys Senefelder, a year after Senefelder had invented the process of lithographic printing. In Salzburg the 15-year-old boy completed his first important work, the opera *Peter Schmoll*, with an overture that still holds a place in the orchestral repertory, although performances of the opera itself are rare. He then set to work in Vienna under the stern tutelage of Abt Vogler. The hard work soon paid off, for at the age of 17 he was appointed *Kapellmeister* in Breslau, where he stayed for two difficult years, composing his opera *Rübezahl* and trying to impose much-needed reforms.

His next post, which he later called 'a golden dream', was in the service of the Duke who ruled Karlsruhe in upper Silesia, for whom he composed a fanfare for 20 trumpets, two symphonies, and a horn concerto. From there he moved to Stuttgart and produced another opera, *Silvana*, and the music for Schiller's drama *Turandot*, which in the 20th century provided one of the themes for Hindemith's *Metamorphoses*. Music now flowed from his pen – the opera *Abu Hassan* made good use of the fashion for the exotic and revealed his growing orchestral skill and his dramatic flair, while his mastery of the keyboard prompted several important and influential works for the piano.

He was appointed director of the Prague Opera in 1813, where he spent four rather unhappy years, apart from the pleasure of finding a wife, the charming young singer Caroline Brandt. He now explored a new realm of Romantic feeling, in his attractive and expressive songs, his brilliant music for the clarinet and in his imaginative piano sonatas. In 1817 he was called to Dresden as *Kapellmeister* to the King of Saxony, and there completed his operatic masterpiece, *Der Freischütz* (The Free-Shooter), a tale of a marksman who makes a pact with the devil to obtain magic bullets to give him victory in the shooting contest. In *Der Freischütz* Romantic opera was born – a new world of magic and spells, where the forests and mountains rang with the sound of the huntsmen's horns and young lovers swooned. A commission from Vienna followed for the opera *Euryanthe*; despite an incoherent libretto, he composed splendid music, which, with its rich

Romantic harmony, powerful characterization and brilliant use of the orchestra, was a strong influence on Wagner. Weber was now internationally known but was working himself to death, seriously ill with tuberculosis. The actor-manager Charles Kemble invited him to compose a new opera for Covent Garden. Faced with a libretto in English, he took 157 lessons and mastered the language in a matter of months. Unfortunately he lavished his genius on an impossible libretto put together by a successful writer of pantomimes, James Robinson Planché. He was plunged into exhausting work, conducting concerts and struggling to complete *Oberon* amid the chaotic conditions he found at Covent Garden – he completed the last song on the eve of the première on 11 April 1826. He managed to conduct 12 highly successful performances, but fatally drained his strength. On the morning of 5 June he was found dead in his room. His remains were not returned to Dresden until 1844, when they were interred to the accompaniment of the chorus *An Webers Grabe* composed by Wagner.

Webern, Anton von (1883-1945) Austrian composer and conductor, who attended the University of Vienna, where he studied musicology with Guido Adler and took the degree of Doctor of Philosophy in 1906. He pursued a career as a conductor in theatres in Bad Ischl, Teplitz, Danzig, Stettin and Prague. In 1918 he became conductor of the Vienna Workers' Symphony Concerts, and was associated with **Schoenberg**'s Society for Private Performance. From 1927 until 1938 he was adviser and conductor for Austrian radio, and often visited London to conduct for the BBC. Although he was not Jewish, his music was banned, and he drifted into obscurity and was forgotten. In 1945 he was killed by mistake by an American soldier.

Webern's early music, dating back to 1899, is a pale reflection of late Wagner and Richard Strauss, and it is not until he became a pupil of Schoenberg in 1904 that he revealed the individual personality which later was to become such an important feature of the Second Viennese School. From the rich complexity of the orchestral *Passacaglia* Op.1 (1908) he developed an obsession with purity of style and form, paring down his music almost to nothing – the six pieces for large orchestra Op.4 can be played in about nine minutes, the fourth consisting of only six bars, while the fourth of the *Six Bagatelles* for string quartet Op.9 (1913) is seven bars long. His music by now being freely atonal, he found in Schoenberg's **twelve-note** system the ideal framework for his ideas: 'We did not create the new law ourselves, it forced itself overwhelmingly upon us...adherence is strict, but it is salvation.' Drawing on his expert knowledge of medieval contrapuntal devices, he developed an intricate canonic procedure, culminating in the Symphony Op.21. He found texts a stimulus to his imagination, and some of his most significant music is to be found in his songs and choral music, despite their extreme technical difficulty.

Webern's music was rediscovered after his death by the post-war avant-garde in Germany, France and Italy and powerfully influenced the music of **Stockhausen**, **Dallapiccola**, **Nono**, **Boulez**, and **Stravinsky**. Webern's example prompted the development of total **serialism**, where every element – note-lengths, register and dynamics as well as pitch – was serially organized. Another powerful influence was in the development of the small chamber ensemble, which has come to play such a dominant role in contemporary composition. However, Webern's success with composers was not echoed by the general public, and time has not fulfilled his prophecy that 'in fifty years everyone will experience this music as natural, even children.'

Weckerlin, Jean-Baptiste Théodore (1821-1910) Alsatian-French composer of operas, oratorios and songs; also librarian at the Paris Conservatoire, and editor of collections of old French music.

Weelkes, Thomas (*c.*1575-1623) English composer of some of the finest **madrigals**, noted for their daring harmonies and expressiveness. His life is not well documented before 1597, when his first volume of madrigals was composed. He was appointed organist of Winchester Cathedral and stayed there until about 1602. During this period two further volumes of madrigals were published, and he also contributed to the collection honouring Queen Elizabeth, *The Triumphs of Oriana* (1601) – his madrigal was entitled *As Vesta was from Latmos Hill Descending.* He became organist at Chichester Cathedral in about 1602, and in 1608 his fourth and final book of madrigals appeared. He also composed numerous anthems, some services and other sacred pieces. After about 1613 he declined into drunkenness and disorderly behaviour.

weighted scale Basic analytical method used primarily for determining the pitch characteristics of a **monody**. Various criteria for investigation can be chosen, for example the frequency or the total duration of particular notes in a melody. Results are presented in the form of a written scale, generally that of the melody studied, with its tones being assigned relative duration values, e.g. crotchet, quaver, etc., according to the data obtained.

Weigl, Joseph (1766-1846) Austrian composer, a godson of Haydn, who studied with **Salieri** in Vienna. Weigl held several court appointments, and wrote operas in the prevailing German and Italian styles, which were very popular in his lifetime.

Weikl, Bernd (1942-) Austrian baritone who studied in Hanover and joined the Hanover Opera in 1968. His international career began in 1972. He has sung all the major Wagner roles at Bayreuth and has appeared at numerous festivals around the world. His début at Covent Garden in 1975 was as Figaro in *Il barbiere di Siviglia.* He has also sung Jokanaan in *Salome*, Mandryka in *Arabella* (both Strauss) and Gérard in Giordano's *Andrea Chenier.* Recently he has scored a success as Hans Sachs in *Die Meistersinger von Nürnberg* (1990). He has a wide recital and concert repertory and has made several recordings.

Weill, Kurt (1900-1950) German-born composer. Although his earliest success was with a bitter opera, *Der Protagonist*, he realized the need for a more approachable style with the comedy *Der Zar lässt sich photographieren* (1928). In that year he established a fruitful collaboration with Bertold Brecht in a remarkable version of *The Beggar's Opera*: *Die Dreigroschenoper*, combining the jazz idiom with Brecht's biting attack on capitalism. This was followed by *Aufstieg und Fall der Stadt Mahagonny* (1929), a satirical view of life in America; *Der Jasager*; and *Die Bürgschaft* (1930), works which ought to have been trapped in their period style, but in fact have commanded a universal allegiance denied to apparently more distinguished contemporaries. In 1933 Weill emigrated to America and started a new career as a composer of highly successful Broadway musicals, such as *Knickerbocker Holiday* (1938), *Lady in the Dark* (1940) and *One Touch of Venus* (1943). Weill has achieved the remarkable distinction of writing hit songs such as *September Song* and *Surabaya Johnny*, fine traditional operas, as well as his Brecht collaborations, and two outstanding symphonies.

Weinberger, Jaromír (1896-1967) Czech composer who lived and worked for many years in the United States. He studied in Prague and with **Reger** in Leipzig. He achieved fame with his folk-opera *Svanda the Bagpiper* (1927), a dance from which remains a popular concert piece. An important work of the pre-war years was *Valdštejn* (1937), based on Schiller's play. He moved to the United States when the Nazis took power. Other works include the orchestral variations and fugue on *Under the Spreading Chestnut Tree.*

Weiner, Leo (1885-1960) Hungarian composer and teacher who studied in

Budapest, Berlin, Vienna and Leipzig, and was professor of composition at Budapest State Academy. His compositions include two violin concertos, a Hungarian folk-dance suite for orchestra and three string quartets.

Weingartner, Felix (1863-1942) Austrian composer and conductor. One of the outstanding conductors of his generation, he studied philosophy and music in Leipzig, and with Liszt in Weimar, who arranged for a performance of his opera *Sakuntala* in 1884. After a number of posts as an operatic conductor, he was *Kapellmeister* in Berlin from 1891 to 1898. In 1907 he succeeded Mahler as director of the Vienna Opera; in 1912 he moved to Hamburg and subsequently worked in Darmstadt, at the Vienna Volksoper, and in Boston. From 1927 to 1935 he was director of the Basle Conservatoire. He often appeared as guest conductor in London, where his interpretations of Beethoven in concert and on record were greatly admired. He was a pioneer in recording and the first to record all the symphonies of Beethoven. His books include studies of symphonic composers, and in particular his highly influential guide to the interpretation of Beethoven symphonies. He was as prolific a composer as a husband – he composed, for example, seven symphonies, but with as little success as in his five marriages.

Weinzweig, John (1913-) Canadian composer of Polish parentage. He studied at Toronto University, where he founded an orchestra. A period of study at the Eastman School, Rochester, followed, during which he was influenced by the music of **Stravinsky** and **Schoenberg**. He returned to Toronto and there was commissioned to write much music for radio. After World War II his output became more chamber-like in scale. In 1951 he formed the Canadian League of Composers for the Propagation of Contemporary Music, and the Canadian Music Centre. Weinzweig's works include a ballet, *Red Ear of Corn*; a violin concerto (1954); six *Divertimentos* for orchestra; chamber music; and vocal works (*Wine of Peace*, 1957).

Weir, Gillian (1941-) New Zealand organist who studied at the Royal Academy of Music and made her début in 1965. She is internationally acclaimed for her performances, notably of the music of **Messiaen**. She also plays the harpsichord.

Weir, Judith (1954-) Scottish composer who studied with **Tavener**, at the Massachusetts Institute of Technology and at Cambridge with **Holloway**. She has written orchestral and instrumental pieces (*The Art of Touching the Keyboard*, 1983), but has come to prominence through the lively and well-characterized music of her operas. The humorous and ironic *A Night at the Chinese Opera* (1987) is the best known; *The Consolations of Scholarship*, *King Harald's Saga* and *Missa del Cid* have been recorded with Odaline de la Martinez conducting.

Weisgall, Hugo (1912-) Czech-born American composer and conductor who studied at the Curtis Institute and with Roger **Sessions**. He later taught at the Juilliard School, and has done much to promote American music. He has composed several operas, including *Six Characters in Search of an Author* (after the play by Pirandello).

Weiss, Sylvius Leopold (1686-1750) German composer and associate of J.S. Bach, **Fux** and **Quantz**, who held court appointments in Dresden, Prague and Rome. He was noted primarily as a lutenist, composing more than 600 pieces for the instrument.

Weissenberg, Alexis (1929-) Bulgarian-born pianist who studied at the Juilliard School and has since played with most of the world's leading orchestras. He is noted for his virtuoso style and his wide repertory.

Weldon, John (1676-1736) English composer and organist. He was a pupil of **Purcell**, organist at New College, Oxford, and the Chapel Royal, and composer of operas, masques and incidental music to Shakespeare's *The Tempest*, which was formerly attributed to Purcell.

Welitsch, Ljuba (1913-) Bulgarian soprano who studied in Sofia and Vienna, making her début in Sofia in 1936. She sang in Graz, Hamburg and Munich before joining the Vienna Opera in 1946, where she quickly came to attention. In 1944 she sang the title-role in *Salome* at a performance to honour Strauss on his 80th birthday, and thereafter her exciting voice and dramatic stage presence brought her great fame in this part; she sang it in London in 1947. Her roles included Donna Anna (*Don Giovanni*), Minnie (Puccini's *La fanciulla del West*), and the title-roles in *Tosca*, *Aïda* and **Janáček's** *Jenůfa*. Her voice declined in the early 1950s, but a few recordings made before this show her vocal powers at their peak.

Weller, Walter (1939-) Austrian violinist and conductor, leader of the Vienna Philharmonic Orchestra, 1961-9. He was the founder of the Weller String Quartet and principal conductor of the Royal Liverpool Philharmonic (1977), the Royal Philharmonic (1979) and other British orchestras.

Wellesz, Egon (1885-1974) Austrian-born British composer who was a pupil of **Schoenberg** and later taught in Vienna. He evolved a highly personal style, blending atonality with a richly chromatic idiom, a powerful tonal flavour and soaring melodies. He composed many works for the theatre, notably the ballet *Achilles auf Skyros* (1924), the chamber opera *Scherz, List und Rache* (1928), and perhaps his finest opera, *Die Bakchantinnen* (1931). In the 1930s he produced a number of important choral works, including four Masses, turning more and more to a tonal idiom. This was evident too in a number of orchestral works, culminating in perhaps his finest, *Prosperos Beschwörungen* (1936). In 1938 he settled in England, becoming a lecturer in Oxford, where he developed his special study of Byzantine music, and teaching young composers, such as Edmund **Rubbra.** He now began a series of nine symphonies which show their allegiance to Mahler, and a number of chamber works, including an Octet (1949) designed to be performed with Schubert's. He also produced the beautiful setting of Gerard Manley Hopkins's poems entitled *The Leaden Echo and the Golden Echo* (1944) for soprano, violin and cello. Wellesz successfully assimilated a remarkable range of influences into a highly personal and expressive idiom, that places him high in the post-Mahler tradition.

Well-tempered Clavier, The See **wohltemperirte Clavier, Das**

Welsh National Opera Company founded in 1946 and now one of the finest in Britain. Its base is the New Theatre in Cardiff but it tours widely for much of the year, around Wales as well as the south and west of England.

Menna by Arwel **Hughes**, one of the first operas in Welsh, was produced in 1956; the repertory at that time consisted largely of Verdi, Rossini and Mozart, under a succession of music directors including Vilem Tausky and Sir Charles **Groves**. In 1968/9 James **Lockhart** became music director and Michael Geliot artistic director, and the style of productions became more challenging. The first British production of **Berg**'s *Lulu* was given in 1971; various **Britten** works such as *Billy Budd* were also presented. In 1973 Richard Armstrong became music director and Brian McMaster general administrator; the repertory was extended to include **Janáček**'s *Jenůfa* and *The Cunning Little Vixen*, Strauss's *Elektra*, Wagner's *Tristan und Isolde* and an acclaimed *Ring* cycle (1986). The company has presented many works by Welsh composers (for example, **Hoddinott**'s *The Beach at Falesa*), and has promoted the careers of a number of internationally known Welsh singers (among them Gwyneth **Jones**, Margaret **Price** and Geraint **Evans**). It has an outstanding chorus (which was amateur until about 1968) and a fine orchestra, the Welsh Philharmonia, formed in 1970. Since 1986 the music director has been Sir Charles **Mackerras**.

Werle, Lars Johan (1926-) Swedish composer who studied at Uppsala University and joined the staff of Swedish Radio. His best-known work to date is the opera *Dreaming about Thérèse*, designed to be performed theatrically 'in the round', with the orchestra surrounding the audience.

Wert, Giaches de (1553-1596) Flemish composer who went to Italy as a boy and served at the court of Mantua, where he influenced **Monteverdi**, especially in the composition of madrigals.

Wesley, Samuel (1766-1837) English organist and composer, the son of Charles Wesley, the noted hymn-writer, and nephew of John Wesley, the founder of Methodism. He composed an oratorio, *Ruth,* at the age of eight, and at 16 mounted family concerts with his brother Charles. His compositions for orchestra at this time were very fine, and included symphonies and concertos which have been revived and published with success in modern times. His great promise was, however, blighted by the severe effects on his mind and personality of a fall that resulted in a head injury. The finest music of the later period was for the Roman Catholic Church, which he had entered at the age of 18, notably the motet *In exitu Israel.* An outstanding organist, he was overwhelmed by the revelation of the music of J.S. Bach, and worked hard to spread this gospel, by performance and by orchestral arrangements. In some ways a tragic figure, Wesley was nevertheless one of the most striking musicians of his time.

Wesley, Samuel Sebastian (1810-1876) English composer and organist, natural son of Samuel **Wesley,** the most influential figure in the development of Anglican music in the 19th century. He inherited his father's talent as an organist, but not his religion, and started his career at the age of 16 as organist in leading London churches. At 22 he was appointed to Hereford Cathedral, and later moved to Exeter, Leeds Parish Church, Winchester and Gloucester. In a famous pamphlet he proclaimed the need to reform not only the musical standards in the Anglican Church, but also the remuneration of organists and choirmen, at a level which would be welcome today. His compositions were chiefly for the Church, including the well-known anthem *Thou wilt keep him in perfect peace.*

Westrup, Sir Jack (1904-1975) English scholar, professor, writer and conductor. He studied at Oxford University, where he was instrumental in founding the University Opera Club. After working as a schoolmaster and a music critic, in 1933 he was appointed lecturer in music in Newcastle-on-Tyne, professor of music in Birmingham (1944-6), and in Oxford (1947-71). At Oxford he was unusually active for a professor in the practical music-making of the university, conducting the university orchestra and in particular the Opera Club in a number of memorable performances, exploring what were then the byways of the operatic repertory, including Berlioz's *Les troyens,* Verdi's *Macbeth* and **Marschner**'s *Hans Heiling.* His writings included studies of Purcell, Handel, and Liszt, and numerous contributions to works of reference and periodicals. He was knighted in 1960.

Whettam, Graham (1927-) English composer who is self-taught and became a music teacher. He conducted choirs and wrote film music in order to earn a living while pursuing his more serious composing career. Among his output, which reveals something of the influence of **Bartók**, are four symphonies, concertos for clarinet and for cello, a ballet, *The Masque of the Red Death* (1968), violin sonatas, string quartets, *Music for Brass* and much music for children.

White, Robert (*c.*1535-1574) English composer. As organist and choirmaster at Westminster Abbey he wrote mainly church choral music in the rich polyphonic style of the Tudor period. His name is also sometimes spelled Whyte.

whole note Alternative term for **semibreve**.

whole-tone scale **Scale** that progresses by steps of whole tones only. No more than two such scales are possible, one beginning on C and the other on C sharp (or its enharmonic D♭), but each can begin at any point because there is no keynote. The whole-tone scale has six different notes, the one beginning on C being C-D-E-F♯-G♯-A♯-C. The use of this scale is very much associated with the compositions of Debussy and Liszt.

Whyte, Robert Alternative spelling of the name of Robert **White**.

Whythorne, Thomas (*c.*1528-1595) English composer of many secular part-songs and pieces for viola and other instruments. He travelled widely in Italy and his rediscovered autobiography, written in a form of shorthand, was published in 1961. His name is also sometimes spelled Withorne.

Widor, Charles Marie (1844-1937) French composer and organist. He studied in Brussels with Fétis and Lemmens and in 1870 became organist at the parish church of St Sulpice, Paris, where he remained for more than 60 years. His first ballet, *La Korrigane,* was produced in 1880. At around this time he was writing music criticism, and he also became professor of organ and composition at the Paris Conservatoire, where his pupils included Louis **Vierne,** Albert **Schweitzer, Honegger** and **Milhaud.** He revered the music of J.S. Bach above all, and was renowned for his playing of it; with Schweitzer he produced a complete edition of Bach's organ works. He also published a treatise on orchestration, which was a revision and updating of Berlioz's treatise. Widor composed operas, symphonic poems and concertos, but his best-known works are the ten organ symphonies, a form which he originated, and two orchestral symphonies with organ; the toccata from the fifth organ symphony is very frequently heard.

Wieniawski, Henryk (1835-1880) Polish composer and one of the most famous violin virtuosi of the 19th century. He began his studies at the Paris Conservatoire aged eight, and later travelled all over Europe giving concerts with his brother Józef. In 1860 he settled in St Petersburg; he was appointed violinist to the Tsar of Russia and taught at the St Petersburg Conservatoire. He also made a concert tour of the United States with Anton **Rubinstein,** and spent two years as professor of violin at the Brussels Conservatoire. His compositions for violin are brilliant and demand a virtuoso technique: they include two sets of studies (*L'école moderne*; *Etudes-caprices*) and two concertos, the second of which, dedicated to his friend and rival **Sarasate,** is a richly expressive piece still frequently heard.

Wilbye, John (1574-1638) English composer of some of the finest **madrigals.** He was in the service of a minor noble family, the Kytsons, in Suffolk when his first volume of madrigals was published in 1598, and it is likely that he remained with them for almost 30 years. During that time he was probably in active communication with the musical scene at court in London. In 1601 he was one of the contributors to the collection *The Triumphs of Oriana,* published by **Morley** in honour of Queen Elizabeth. His second collection of madrigals was published in 1609: it contains *Draw on Sweet Night,* one of the finest achievements of the English madrigal school. From about 1613 he composed little that is worthwhile apart from a couple of anthems.

Wild, Earl (1915-) American pianist who studied with Egon Petri, performed with **Toscanini** and is celebrated for his interpretations of Liszt. He is also a fine exponent of **Gershwin**'s music. His own compositions include an oratorio and a ballet.

Wilde, David (1935-) English pianist who studied with Franz Reizenstein and Iso Elinson at the Royal Manchester College, and with Nadia **Boulanger**. He was a BBC staff accompanist in Glasgow, 1959-62. Wilde was winner of the Liszt-Bartók Prize in Budapest in 1961; Professor at the Royal Academy of Music, 1965-7, and in Manchester, 1967-9. An admired recitalist and concerto player, he is now professor in Hanover.

Wilkinson, Marc (1929-) French-born Australian composer and conductor who studied with **Messiaen** and **Varèse**. He has worked with the Royal Shakespeare Company and the National Theatre and written music for many plays (works by Osborne, Stoppard and Schaffer among them) and films.

Willaert, Adriaan (1490-1562) Flemish composer who first studied law, then abandoned this for music, travelling to Bohemia and Italy and becoming choirmaster at St Mark's, Venice. In that capacity he wrote much church music, but was also one of the finest composers of **madrigals**.

Willan, Healey (1880-1968) English organist and composer who settled in Canada, holding academic posts at Toronto University and composing an opera, orchestral and organ music and some choral pieces. He was also an authority on medieval **plainsong**.

Willcocks, Sir David (1919-) English organist and conductor who studied at the Royal College of Music, where he was later director (1974-84), and King's College, Cambridge, where he was organist for 17 years (1957-74). As a cathedral organist, teacher at Cambridge University and conductor of such groups as the London Bach Choir, he has been at the centre of English musical life for many years, specializing in choral English music, and composing some church and choral music of his own. He was knighted in 1977.

Williams, Grace (1906-1977) Welsh composer who studied with **Vaughan Williams** at the Royal College of Music and with Egon **Wellesz**. Her compositions include *Penillion* for orchestra, based on a traditional form of Welsh bardic singing, and other works with Welsh associations; a trumpet concerto (1963); *Sea Sketches* for strings (1944); an opera, *The Parlour* (1961); a symphony; and various choral works and songs.

Williams, John (1941-) Australian guitarist who studied at the Royal College of Music and with **Segovia**. He has made many tours, some with his fellow-guitarist Julian **Bream**, and has done much to bridge the gap between concert and popular music, especially by his association with the pop group Sky. Several works have also been written for him. He was awarded the OBE in 1980.

Williams, John Towner (1932-) American composer who studied with

John Towner Williams

Castelnuovo-Tedesco and at the Juilliard School, and began his career as a pianist in the Hollywood studios of 20th-Century Fox. He has since produced many scores for films and television (*Jane Eyre*; *Star Wars*; *Fiddler on the Roof*), and composed some concert works including *Sinfonietta* for wind, *Essay* for strings and a symphony.

Williamson, Malcolm (1931-) Australian composer who succeeded Sir Arthur **Bliss** as Master of the Queen's Music in 1975. He studied with Eugène **Goossens** in Sydney and with Elisabeth **Lutyens** and Erwin Stein in London; in addition to piano he learnt the horn, violin and organ. He settled in England in the 1950s and has since held posts at Westminster Choir School and Princeton University. His Piano Concerto No.1 (1958) was performed by him at its première. He composed his first symphony, his Organ Concerto and Organ Symphony at this time. His style owes something to **Messiaen, Britten** and jazz, and like Britten he has also written music for children (*Julius Caesar Jones*, 1966). His compositions include the operas *Our Man in Havana* (1963, based on the novel by Graham Greene) and *The Happy Prince* (based on the fairytale by Oscar Wilde), the *Mass of Christ the King* (1977), and other choral works. There are two further piano concertos (1960, 1962), a violin concerto (1965), a piano quintet (1968), and a second symphony (1969). Since about 1970 the stage works have become very brief and are often designed for the audience to join in. Williamson has also composed many songs, including the cycles *A Vision of Beasts and Gods* (1958), *From a Child's Garden* (1968) and *Hammarskjöld Portrait* (1974); cantatas (*The Death of Cuchulain*, after Yeats); hymns, carols and other church music. His more recent music has tended to be popular in style.

Wilson, John (1595-1674) English musician whose versatile gifts as singer, lutenist, viol player and composer earned him the posts of court musician to both Charles I and Charles II and a professorship at Oxford University. He may also have acted in Shakespeare's company of players, as well as setting many of Shakespeare's verses to music.

Wilson, Thomas (1927-) Scottish composer who studied in Glasgow and later taught at the university. He was drawn to the technique of **serial** composition and wrote a violin sonata in that style (1961). He has written orchestral pieces – two symphonies, *Touchstone* (1967), a sinfonietta and other works for brass band, much sacred choral music including two Masses and a Te Deum, songs, chamber and piano pieces. His two operas are *The Charcoal Burners* (1968) and, his most ambitious work, *The Confessions of a Justified Sinner*, based on the book by James Hogg.

wind band Band comprising mixed woodwind and brass instruments, usually with percussion. In England the term **military band** is preferred, as opposed to **brass band** (which is made up only of brass instruments).

Windgassen, Wolfgang (1914-1974) German operatic tenor, prominent at the Bayreuth Festival in such great Wagnerian roles as Siegfried, Tristan and Parsifal. He made his début in 1941, and at first sang roles from the Italian repertory. He sang at Covent Garden for many years from 1955, and at the Metropolitan, New York, from 1957. His Bayreuth career lasted for about 20 years (from 1951). He was also artistic director of the Stuttgart Opera.

wind instruments Musical instruments in which the sound is produced by the vibration of air in a tube. **Organs** and **accordions** do not come into this category, which usually refers to instruments blown by the player. Wind instruments in an orchestra are commonly divided into brass (horn, trumpet, trombone and tuba) and woodwind (flute, clarinet, oboe, bassoon, piccolo, cor anglais); the saxophone is also a wind instrument.

wire brush Drumstick with a head of several stiff wires used on side-drums and cymbals by drummers in dance and pop music. It produces a characteristic brushing sound.

Wirén, Dag (1905-1986) Swedish composer who studied at the Stockholm Conservatoire and in Paris. He was influenced by Stravinsky and **Prokofiev**, and his works were **neo-classical** in style; many of them are based on the idea of the evolution or development of a single musical motif or 'cell'. They include much stage and film music (the ballets *The Oscar Ball*, 1949; *The Evil Queen*, 1960; incidental music for several Shakespeare plays); five symphonies and the Sinfonietta; concertos for cello, violin and piano; choral music (*Doomsday*, 1930), songs and some fine string quartets, five in all. His most popular pieces are the *Little Suite* (1941) and the *Serenade for Strings* (1937). He was also a music critic and journalist.

Wise, Michael (1648-1687) English organist and choirmaster at Salisbury Cathedral, and composer of anthems and other church music and part-songs. He was also a Gentleman of the Chapel Royal, and Master of the Choristers at St Paul's Cathedral.

Wishart, Peter (1921-1984) English composer and teacher who studied with Nadia **Boulanger** and held teaching posts at the Guildhall School of Music and Drama, King's College, London, and elsewhere. He composed *Clytemnestra* (1973), *The Captive* (1960), *The Clandestine Marriage* (1971), and other operas, symphonies, concertos and choral pieces.

Withorne, Thomas Alternative spelling of the name of Thomas **Whythorne**.

Witt, Jeremias Friedrich (1771-1837) German composer and violinist, famous as the composer of the so-called 'Jena' Symphony, formerly attributed to Beethoven. He also composed operas and oratorios, as well as much instrumental music.

Wittgenstein, Paul (1887-1961) Austrian pianist brother of the famous philosopher; he was a pupil of Leschetizky, but lost his right arm in World War I. Subsequently he commissioned several major composers to write pieces especially for him, most notably **Ravel** (*Concerto for the Left Hand*), Richard **Strauss**, **Prokofiev** and **Britten**. He settled in the United States in 1939. In 1957 he published an autobiography detailing how he overcame his disability.

wohltemperirte Clavier, Das Two sets of **preludes** and **fugues** by **J.S. Bach** for keyboard (BWV 846-893). In this instance the word *Clavier* means any keyboard instrument, and not just the clavichord. The two sets in the collection each consist of 24 works, which were published in 1722 and 1744 respectively. The preludes and fugues are in major and minor keys in ascending order. The two sets are commonly known as The Forty-Eight. The English translation of the title is *The Well-tempered Clavier.*

Wolf, Hugo (1860-1903) Austrian composer, mainly of *Lieder*. During his brief sojourn at the Vienna Conservatoire he became friendly with Mahler. By 1877 he had already composed songs, piano music and part of a symphony, and was received sympathetically by Wagner, but coolly by Brahms, experiences which may have decided his life-long admiration for one and contempt for the other. His natural gift was for the composition of songs, and an early love-affair inspired him to his first great outpouring in 1880, chiefly settings of Eichendorff and Lenau. In 1884 he took a position as music critic of the Wiener Salonblatt, and attacked some of Vienna's most revered idols – particularly Brahms and his supporters. He paid the price for his outspoken views: in 1886 his tone poem *Penthesilea* was received with contemptuous laughter; his string quartet was returned by the Rose Quartet, and publishers treated him with reserve. In 1888 two of his songs were performed in public for the first time, and soon after he was able to get some published. This modest success seemed to unlock his genius. In the next three years nearly two hundred songs poured from him, in four great song-books which include many of his finest creations. In March 1888 he produced 20 settings of Mörike – *Gebet* and *Verborgenheit* were composed in a single day. He turned to Eichendorff with such masterpieces as *Der Musikant* and *Liebesglück*; and then over 50 settings of Goethe, with such wonderful songs as *Anakreons Grab* and *Der Schäfer*. He completed this extraordinary outpouring with settings from the Spanish and Italian *Song-books* of Heyse and Giebel, recreations of folk-poetry that called forth some of his most charming songs, like *Alle gingen, Herz, zur Ruh* and *Und willst du deinen Liebsten sterben sehen*. He turned aside for a moment from songs to complete his delightful *Italian Serenade* for string quartet, later arranged for orchestra. His opera *Der Corregidor* was completed in 1896, after which he suffered a complete breakdown.

Wolff, Christian (1934-) French-born American composer, a prominent scholar, but largely self-taught. His works, influenced by **Varèse** and **Cage** among others, make use of electronics and the 'prepared piano', and he has also evolved his own system of notation.

Wolf-Ferrari, Ermanno (1876-1948) Italian composer of German ancestry. He studied in Munich under Rheinberger and visited Milan, where he met the publisher Ricordi; his music was not, however, well received in Italy and he went back to Munich. He composed mainly operas, generally light and tuneful with bright, accomplished orchestration. With the success of his first opera, *Cenerentola,* he was able to return to Venice, where he was director of the Conservatoire for some years. Later he took up an appointment in Salzburg. His operas include *The School for Fathers* (after Goldoni), *Il segreto di Susanna* and *I gioelli della Madonna*. His *Idillio-concertino* (1933) is a charming work for small ensemble; he composed much other chamber music, some vocal works and several other operas which were less successful than those mentioned.

wolf note Jarring sound produced between certain intervals on keyboard instruments tuned in **meantone temperament**, or on string instruments by defective vibration on a certain note or notes.

Wolpe, Stefan (1902-1972) German-born composer who studied with **Busoni** and **Webern**, collaborated with the dramatist Bertold Brecht, and after a period of work in Palestine settled in the United States, becoming an American citizen. His compositions – operas, ballets, orchestral and instrumental works and songs – use his own special kind of **serialism** and are influenced also by traditional Jewish music.

Wood, Charles (1866-1926) Irish teacher and composer, who studied at the Royal College of Music, then taught there and at Cambridge University, **Vaughan Williams** being among his pupils. His compositions include the opera *The Pickwick Papers*, choral and instrumental pieces and much church music.

Wood, Haydn (1882-1959) English composer of orchestral and instrumental works, but chiefly remembered today for his songs, tinged with a gentle sentimentality, including *A Brown Bird Singing* and *Roses of Picardy*.

Wood, Sir Henry (1869-1944) English conductor and organist who studied at the Royal Academy of Music, began conducting opera, and in 1895 was engaged by the impresario Robert Newman to direct a new series of Promenade Concerts in London (originally so named because the audience could walk about). His career and his name were thenceforth

Sir Henry Wood

associated with these famous concerts. Wood also conducted at many other British music festivals, and was a champion of new music by, among others, Mahler, **Scriabin**, Debussy, **Sibelius** and **Schoenberg**. **Vaughan Williams**'s *Serenade to Music* was written in his honour. He also made several orchestral transcriptions and arrangements, including the *Fantasia on British Sea Songs*, still a popular feature on the Last Night of the Proms. He was knighted in 1911 and made a Companion of Honour in the year of his death.

Wood, Hugh (1932-) English composer who studied at Oxford University and with Mátyás **Seiber**, and has since held teaching posts at the Royal Academy of Music and Morley College, London, at Liverpool University and elsewhere. He has also broadcast frequently. His compositions include *Scenes from Comus* (1965) for soprano, tenor and orchestra; a violin and a cello concerto; three string quartets; and a number of song-cycles – to poems by Robert Graves, Pablo Neruda, Ted Hughes and Edwin Muir.

Wood, Thomas (*c.*1530-1592) Scottish churchman who compiled an interesting and valuable collection of mainly Scottish vocal and instrumental music, widely known as the *St Andrew Psalter* or *Thomas Wode's Part Books*. Additions to his collection were made by others in the following century.

Wood, Thomas (1892-1950) English composer who travelled to Australia and did much to popularize the song *Waltzing Matilda*. His own compositions include the cantatas *Chanticleer* and *The Rainbow*, and three cycles of sea-songs for chorus and orchestra.

woodland flute Organ stop controlling a 4ft or 8ft pipe with inverted mouths producing a sound similar to the claribel stop.

woodwind instruments Musical instruments generally made of wood, and so classified, although the wooden flute is now rarely seen. In these instruments a column of air is made to vibrate by one or two reeds, or through a blow-hole. Woodwind instruments are made to produce the notes of the scale by opening holes in the side wall of the tube; when this is done in succession it has the effect of temporarily shortening the air column and so raising the pitch of the **fundamental** obtained, by scalewise **degrees**. The woodwind instruments of the orchestra are the **flute**, **clarinet**, **oboe**, **bassoon**, **piccolo** and **cor anglais**.

Wordsworth, William (1908-1988) English composer, a descendant of the poet, who studied in Edinburgh and lived for many years in Scotland. His compositions, in a generally traditional style, include six symphonies, six string quartets and other chamber works and songs.

working out Alternative term for **development**.

Wq. Abbreviation of Wotquenne. Alfred Wotquenne (1867-1939), a Belgian musicologist and scholar, compiled a catalogue (1905) of **C.P.E. Bach**'s works, and used Wq. as a prefix to indicate the number of a piece in the catalogue. He also catalogued **Gluck**'s works.

Wranitzky Alternative spelling of the name of Anton and Paul **Vranický** .

Wunderlich, Fritz (1930-1966) German tenor who studied in Freiburg and joined the Stuttgart Opera in 1955, making his début as Tamino in *Die Zauberflöte*. He sang in Frankfurt, Munich and Vienna. His reputation grew as a fine Mozart singer (Don Ottavio in *Don Giovanni* was another part in which he excelled), and he was also successful as Henry in Strauss's *Die schweigsame Frau*, Lensky in Tchaikovsky's *Eugene Onegin* and Alfredo in Verdi's *La traviata*. He was one of the most outstanding lyric tenors of his day, his career cut tragically short.

Wuorinen, Charles (1938-) American composer, pianist and teacher. He studied at Columbia University, taught there in his turn and has also been active in the promotion of new music. His own works encompass a wide range of forms and styles, tonal, **serial** and electronic: they include *Time's Encomium* and *Contrafactum.*

Wurlitzer American firm of instrument-makers founded in 1858 by Franz Wurlitzer (1831-1914). It achieved fame through its production of electric and electronic pianos and organs. In addition, the firm became world-famous for its rare violin collection, and is the leading stringed-instrument dealer in the United States.

X

Xenakis, Iannis (1922-) Composer of Greek parentage who studied in Paris with **Honegger**, **Milhaud** and **Messiaen**, and adopted French citizenship. It was not until 1954 that he composed his first work, *Metastasis*. He is one of the most innovative composers of his time, employing among other things a method called *stochastic* whereby the mathematics of probability are applied to the form of a piece of music (not to be confused with **aleatory** music). In this connection he founded a School of Mathematical and Automated Music in Paris. His works are mostly for large or unusual instrumental ensembles, or for tapes and other electronic devices: they include *Atrées* (1962); *Nomos gamma* (1968); *Pour les baleines* (1982); *Thallein* (1985). His choral music (*Cendrées*, 1974; *Pour la paix*, 1982) and works for small chamber ensemble (*Tetras* for string quartet, 1983) are also an important part of his output, which in recent years has become more reminiscent of folk-music. His *Knephas* (1990) is a work for 40 voices *a cappella*. Xenakis has also been an engineer and architect, working with Le Corbusier.

xiao (China) See **hsiao**

xoomij/chöömij (Mongolia) Vocal form distinguished by its use of multiphonics. The male singer simultaneously produces two notes by forcing air through his vocal cords, emitting a low drone rich enough in harmonics so that, by tensing his cheek and tongue muscles, he can select high tones to form a whistle-like melody. Thus there are no words to these songs, but only vowel sounds produced by manipulation of the mouth cavity.

xylophone Percussion instrument usually constructed of fine rosewood bars, although proprietary synthetic materials such as Kelon and Klyperon have been introduced. Each bar is suspended by cords, or laid on felt over a matching tubular resonator. The standard ranges are four octaves from middle C, or three and a half octaves from F above middle C, laid out like the piano with the 'black' notes raised at the back. It is normally beaten with hard-headed sticks, or softer ones made of felt or rubber. The part may be written at pitch or more usually an octave lower than sounding. Saint-Saëns was the first composer to use it, in his *Danse macabre* (1874); it has since become a familiar member of the percussion section, and a vehicle for solo virtuosity in a lighter vein. Modern composers such as **Boulez**, **Tippett**, **Lutosławski** and **Takemitsu** have given the xylophone considerable prominence and make great demands on players, who can rarely look at the

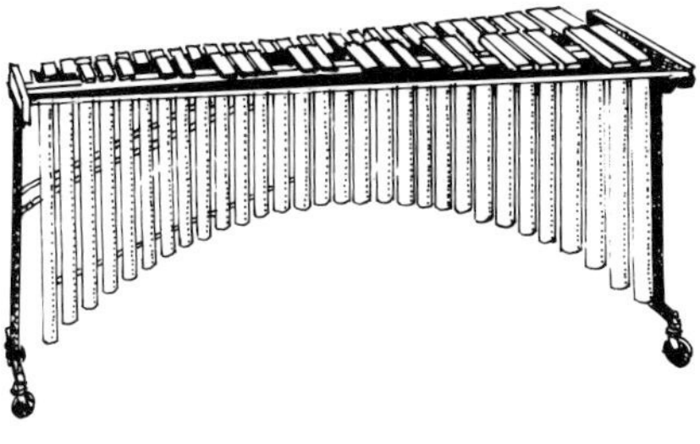

Xylophone

conductor, whatever the rhythmical complications, unless they know the part by heart.

xylorimba Percussion instrument (combining the names of **xylophone** and **marimba**) with a range of five octaves.

Y

Yamash'ta, Stomu (1947-) Japanese musician who studied at Kyoto Music Academy and in the United States, and has achieved world fame as a virtuoso percussionist, playing both jazz and concert music. Among his own compositions are *Prisms* for solo percussion, and some film scores. He also directs the Red Buddha theatre and dance company.

Yepes, Narciso (1927-) Spanish guitarist who has done much to revive the repertory of guitar music of his own country, but has also recorded all the lute music of J.S. Bach. He often plays a ten-string guitar of his own design. His recordings include works by **Rodrigo**, **Tárrega** and **Villa-Lobos**.

yo (Japan) One of the two principal scales of folk origin. See **Japanese scales**

yodel Type of singing without words that is practised in alpine countries. It is usually sung by men in falsetto, with rapid changes to **chest voice**, very free in rhythm and metre. Normally it uses the restricted scale of the natural **harmonics** of instruments such as the **Alpenhorn**.

Yonge, Nicholas (*c.*1550-1619) English chorister who is famous for editing and publishing *Musica Transalpina*, two volumes of Italian **madrigals** translated into English. He is thus credited with having introduced the madrigal to England and ushering in a golden age of English music.

Young, Alexander (1920-) English tenor who studied at the Royal College of Music; he has taught at the Royal Northern College and founded the Jubilate Choir. His début was in 1950 at the Edinburgh Festival, in Strauss's *Ariadne auf Naxos*. He has created numerous roles, such as Prince Philippe in *The Dinner Engagement* by **Berkeley** (1954), and was particularly associated with the role of Tom Rakewell in Stravinsky's *The Rake's Progress*. He has an exceptionally wide repertory, specializing in Handel's works, of which he has made many recordings.

Young, La Monte (1935-) American composer who studied with **Stockhausen**. His own work has something of the same novelty of thinking about it. He describes one of his pieces as 'building a fire in front of the audience', and another as 'draw a straight line and follow it'. *The Tortoise, his Dreams and Journeys* calls for voices and electronics.

Young, William (?-1671) English flautist, violinist and composer who travelled widely in Europe and was a pioneer in the development of the Baroque **trio sonata**. After the English Restoration he returned home and joined the King's Band.

Ysaÿe, Eugène (1858-1931) Belgian violinist and composer. He studied with **Wieniawski** in Brussels and **Vieuxtemps** in Paris, and became leader of the orchestra which was later the Berlin Philharmonic. He was professor of violin at the Brussels Conservatoire and founded the Ysaÿe Concert Society. As one of the greatest virtuosi of his time he toured

Europe and the United States, introducing many new works. He was closely associated with a circle which included **Franck**, **d'Indy**, **Fauré** and **Saint-Saëns**, among others; many of these composers created works for him. In the latter part of his life his bowing arm developed a tremor and he was forced to turn to conducting, at which he was also highly successful, particularly during his stint at the Cincinnati Symphony Orchestra (1918-22). As a composer he wrote violin concertos and sonatas, and an opera in Walloon; his works have considerable depth and originality.

yüeh-ch'in (China) Instrument known as the 'moon guitar' after the shape of its body. It has a short neck and ten frets and is plucked with a small plectrum. A single-stringed version is used in the Chinese opera, whereas in the Chinese orchestra a two- to four-stringed version is used, often in pairs to increase the volume.

Yun, Isang (1917-) Korean composer, who studied in his own country and Japan and then in Europe. He has also taught in Berlin. His works, combining Western **serialism** with traditional Korean musical idioms, include the operas *The Dream of Liu-Tung* (1965) and *The Butterfly's Widow* (1968), orchestral and instrumental works.

Z

Zabaleta, Nicanor (1907-) Spanish harpist who studied in Madrid and Paris. As well as retrieving much old music for the harp he has commissioned new works for the instrument from, among others, **Milhaud** and **Krenek**. He is responsible for the great revival of the harp as a solo instrument, and has made many recordings of his wide repertory.

Zachau, Friedrich Wilhelm (1663-1712) German composer and organist. As organist at the Liebfrauenkirche, Halle, he became **Handel**'s first important teacher, for which he is chiefly remembered today. He also wrote church cantatas and organ preludes and fugues.

Zacher, Gerd (1929-) German composer who studied with **Messiaen**, **Boulez** and **Stockhausen**. He is also a noted organist, giving the first performance of several new works for that instrument and featuring it in his own compositions (*Diferencias*, 1961; *Orumambel und Orpordulayglia*, 1972).

zampogna (It.) Bagpipe from the Calabrian region of Italy, consisting of an air-filled bag, a chanter and four drones, two of which have finger-holes to allow variation of the notes accompanying the melody.

Zandonai, Riccardo (1883-1944) Italian composer who studied with **Mascagni** and wrote operas, mainly in the prevailing **verismo** style, including *Francesca da Rimini*; he also wrote instrumental (*Concerto andaluso*), orchestral and choral works.

zapateado (Sp.) Dance for a single performer in 3/4 time and with the rhythmic accents marked by the stamping of the heels, rather than by **castanets**; from the Spanish *zapata*, shoe.

Zarlino, Gioseffo (1517-1590) Italian monk and musical theorist who studied with **Willaert** in Venice and succeeded him as choirmaster at St Mark's. In his musical treatises Zarlino proposed the system of tuning for keyboard instruments known as equal **temperament**, which has been of tremendous significance in the development of Western music.

zarzuela (Sp.) Light musical or comic opera, generally of a satirical nature. The libretto has spoken dialogue and allows for improvisation, in which even the audience joins.

Zelenka, Jan Dismas (1679-1745) Bohemian composer and double-bass player, active in the musical life of Dresden. He studied in Vienna and Venice, but most of his life was spent in Dresden in the royal orchestra. He composed a variety of sacred pieces, including 12 Masses and three oratorios. He wrote an opera which was performed in 1723 in Prague, and many instrumental works in the Baroque style of the time.

Zelter, Carl Friedrich (1758-1832) German composer who lived and worked for most of his life in Berlin, teaching mainly vocal and church music, and composing choral works and about 200 songs. One of his pupils was **Mendelssohn**, with whom he joined in reviving the music of J.S. Bach.

Zemlinsky, Alexander von (1872-1942) Austrian composer, born in Vienna of Polish parents. In 1906 he was appointed conductor at the Volksoper, and moved to similar positions in Mannheim (1908), Prague (1911), Berlin (1927) and Vienna (1932). He emigrated to the United States in 1938. Zemlinsky was an influential teacher and one of the group around **Schoenberg** in Vienna in the early years of the century. He numbered among his pupils Schoenberg himself, Erich **Korngold,** and Mahler's wife, Alma, whose lover he was alleged to have been before her marriage. Zemlinsky was for many years the forgotten man of the Vienna quartet, whose names were musically encoded by **Berg** in his Chamber Concerto. His rich romantic style, exhibiting extreme chromaticism, never became **atonal** or **serial**, and consequently was out of fashion in the post-war rediscovery of the Second Vienna School. But now that his fine *Lyric Symphony* (1897) with soprano and baritone soloists, his operas *Der Zwerg* (1922) and *Eine florentinische Tragödie* (1917), based on plays by Oscar Wilde, have been produced with considerable success, his work is seen to be an important post-Mahlerian development.

Zenatello, Giovanni (1876-1949) Italian tenor who studied in Verona and made his début in Naples in 1899. He sang at La Scala, Milan, from 1903, where he created the role of Pinkerton in Puccini's *Madama Butterfly* (1904). He visited London, where he sang Riccardo in Verdi's *Un ballo in maschera* (1905) and the title-role in Giordano's *Andrea Chenier*. In 1907 he first sang at the Metropolitan, New York, and remained in the United States for most of his career, visiting Chicago and Boston. His greatest roles were the title-part in Verdi's *Otello*, Radamès in *Aïda* and Don José in **Bizet**'s *Carmen*. After his

Efrem Zimbalist

retirement from the stage in 1933 he taught, and was instrumental in furthering Maria **Callas**'s career.

Zimbalist, Efrem (1889-1985) Russian-born violinist who studied at the St Petersburg Conservatoire with Leopold Auer and made concert tours of Europe before settling in the United States and taking American citizenship. There he became director of the Curtis Institute. He also composed a concerto and other works for the violin.

Zimmerman, Franklin (1923-) American musical scholar who has produced a full catalogue of the music of **Purcell**. He has taught at a number of universities and colleges, including Southern California and Pennsylvania.

Zimmermann, Bernd Alois (1918-1970) German composer. He studied in Cologne and Bonn, but had to do military service during World War II. Afterwards he was able to resume his studies in Cologne and Darmstadt; he later taught at Cologne. His compositions cover a wide range of styles and techniques, incorporating **serialism**, **jazz** and **electronic** music. They include the opera *Die Soldaten* (1960); a number of works intended as ballets as well as for the concert-hall; much incidental music for film and radio; symphonies, concertos, choral and instrumental pieces. He also wrote illuminatingly on the music of his time.

Zingarelli, Niccolò Antonio (1752-1837) Italian composer and violinist, also choirmaster at Milan Cathedral and St Peter's, Rome, and teacher of **Bellini**. He composed many operas (including *Giulietta e Romeo,* 1796) and sacred music.

zither Generic name for an ubiquitous instrument – a plucked chordophone, which has a box or tube resonator and strings over frets or bridges. The zither was developed during the 18th century from the **cittern**, from which it took its name. It consists of a shallow box with no neck but with either two curved sides or one curved and one straight side. There are usually five melody strings stretched over a fretted **keyboard**, with up to 40 accompanying strings in addition. It is played with the fingers, the bass strings alone being struck with a **plectrum** fixed to the thumb by a ring.

Other more primitive zithers exist, such as the trough zither, the Indian **vīnā** (a stick zither) and the long zithers of China and Japan (**koto** and **qin**). The Arabian *qanun* derives from these instruments.

The zither gained world-wide popularity when it was featured in the film *The Third Man* (1949), with music written and played by Anton Karas.

Zither

zoppa, alla (It.) Music played in a syncopated rhythm.

Zukerman, Pinchas (1948-) Israeli violinist and viola-player who studied in Israel and at the Juilliard School. He made his début in London and New York in the same year (1969). He is acclaimed both as a soloist and as a chamber musician, generally with Daniel **Barenboim** and Itzhak **Perlman**, and has had a close association with the English Chamber Orchestra. His recordings cover a wide range from Bach to **Berg**. Since 1971 he has also conducted, and was musical director of the St Paul Chamber Orchestra in Minnesota from 1980.

zurna General term for various kinds of oboe of ancient origin which occur throughout Asia and south-eastern Europe. The name is Persian ('festival flute'), although local names are commonly used: *ghayta* in North Africa (see **gaida**), *shehnai* in India and *sarunai* in Malaysia. The instrument consists of a conical wooden pipe flared at the lower end. A mouthpipe holds a double reed, at the base of which there is usually (but not in Iraq, Turkey or India) a surrounding metal disc, placed against the player's lips. It is normally played outdoors in ensembles with drums, for use in dances, games, processions and village festivals. Some members of the ensemble may play drones, often using circular breathing.

zydeco (US) Modern, black, Cajun music of the French-speaking bayou region of Louisiana. It is characterized by rhythmic accompaniment of accordion, fiddle and/or steel-stringed guitar. Contemporary groups add drums and amplification.

Picture Credits

The publishers would like to thank the following for permission to reproduce the illustrations on the pages indicated.
Clive Barda: 226, 282, 468. Mansell Collection: 45, 63, 88, 105, 110, 150, 178, 202, 218, 345, 482 top, 482 bottom. Popperfoto: 1, 19, 31, 39, 41, 44, 48, 50, 55, 58, 60, 71, 72, 79, 92, 100, 102, 113, 129, 130, 154, 155, 156, 162, 168, 191, 214, 228, 241, 244, 245, 257, 267, 276, 278, 281, 291, 299, 302, 310, 323, 326, 341, 351, 355, 359, 368, 370, 381, 392, 397, 403, 407, 417, 424, 435, 436, 446, 452, 456, 457, 460, 462, 469, 478, 480, 484, 488, 509, 510, 511, 540, 549, 553, 560, Redferns: 77, 145. Royal Festival Hall: 426 top. Royal Opera House: 426 bottom. Topham: 23, 57, 147, 247, 254, 286, 298, 315, 322, 378, 394, 396, 416, 448, 505, 525.